MW01051250

YUFA!

A Practical Guide to
Mandarin Chinese
Grammar

YUFA!

A Practical Guide to
Mandarin Chinese
Grammar

Wen-Hua Teng

Senior Lecturer,
Department of Asian Studies,
University of Texas at Austin, USA

HODDER
EDUCATION
PART OF HACHETTE LIVRE UK

Orders: please contact Bookpoint Ltd, 130 Milton Park, Abingdon, Oxon OX14 4SB.
Telephone: (44) 01235 827720. Fax: (44) 01235 400454. Lines are open from 9.00 – 5.00,
Monday to Saturday, with a 24-hour message answering service. You can also order
through our website www.hoddereducation.co.uk.

British Library Cataloguing in Publication Data
A catalogue record for this title is available from the British Library

ISBN: 978 1 444 10913 9

First Published 2011
Impression number   10 9 8 7 6 5 4 3 2 1
Year   2017 2016 2015 2014 2013 2012 2011

Copyright © 2011 Wen-Hua Teng

All rights reserved. No part of this publication may be reproduced or transmitted in
any form or by any means, electronic or mechanical, including photocopy, recording,
or any information storage and retrieval system, without permission in writing from
the publisher or under license from the Copyright Licensing Agency Limited.
Further details of such licenses (for reprographic reproduction) may be obtained
from the Copyright Licensing Agency Limited, Saffron House, 6-10 Kirby Street,
London EC1N 8TS.

Cover photo © Keren Su/China Span/Getty Images
Typeset in 10/12pt Minion by Graphicraft Limited, Hong Kong
Printed in Great Britain for Hodder Education, part of Hachette UK, 338 Euston Road,
London NW1 3BH.

Contents

Section 2

How to use this book

YUFA! aims to provide a practical guide to Mandarin Chinese grammar in a way that benefits both teachers and learners of Chinese as a foreign language. Also, *YUFA!* aims not only to present how Mandarin Chinese is structured, but also to show how the language is actually used in real life. In other words, equal emphases are placed upon forms and uses. In particular, there are three major components:

1. The first section focuses on the core structures of Chinese.
2. The second section emphasizes the importance of contexts in which Chinese is used.
3. Exercises to assess knowledge of each specific structure or usage.

The following special features are designed to make this book user-friendly:

- Simple and straightforward statements are used to give you a clear understanding of structures and usages, avoiding linguistic jargon wherever possible.
- Realistic situations are created to show you how grammar can be an effective tool for communication and not simply a set of rules to be learned and never used.
- Tables are provided when necessary to provide you with a clear view of grammar concepts or rules.
- A glossary of terms specifically relevant to Chinese grammar will help you to grasp the meaning of often complex concepts of grammar.
- Each grammar structure or usage is supported by examples given in simplified Chinese characters, pinyin and English translation so you can see at a glance what is needed in all three language systems.
- Mechanical drills are avoided within the exercises; instead, various types of exercise are provided to help you absorb grammar knowledge painlessly.
- Level indicators, both in grammar and usage explanations and in exercises, are adopted to indicate levels of difficulty to help you evaluate your own progress.
- Related grammar points are cross-referenced by using the icon ☞. Using these you will be able to acquire an in-depth understanding of the grammar points that are cross-referenced.
- Grammar points that may be of special difficulty for speakers of English are indicated by the icon 👁 so you may gauge your own progress.
- An index that helps you to locate grammar points quickly and to navigate the book easily.

Chinese language textbooks that focus on the development of learners' communicative skills often do not offer comprehensive and systematic explanations of grammar concepts. *YUFA!* is an ideal reference book that can complement any textbook. Its easy-to-understand explanations, user-friendly designs and realistic scenarios are created with the goal of making learning Mandarin Chinese grammar a painless experience. We hope that you will enjoy what this book offers and reach the proficiency level that is your own ultimate goal.

Glossary

Affirmative–negative question	A question that is seeking an answer of either *yes* or *no*.
Aspect	There are no tenses in Chinese; instead, there are aspects, which indicate the stages of an event, such as progression, continuation and completion.
Attributive	A constituent in a sentence that appears before the noun to modify it. For example, in the sentence 王先生有一个漂亮的女朋友 (*Wáng xiānsheng yǒu yí ge piàoliàng de nǚ péngyǒu*: 'Mr Wang has a pretty girlfriend'), 漂亮 is an adjective that is used attributively, and it is the attributive.
Auxiliary verb	An auxiliary verb is used to indicate desire, wishes, obligation, assumption, possibility, ability, permission, etc. It is followed by a verb. An auxiliary verb is also called a modal verb.
Comment	See **topic–comment structure**.
Complement	(In Chinese) A word that appears after a verb or an adjective to complete or expand the meaning of the verb or adjective.
Complex sentence	A complex sentence includes a subordinate (dependent) clause and the main (independent) clause. In Chinese, the subordinate clause appears before the main clause.
Definiteness	A noun or noun phrase that has been mentioned before or whose existence/identity is known to people engaged in the communication is considered to be 'definite'. See also **indefiniteness**.
Degree adverb	An adverb that specifies the intensity (or degree) of an adjective or another adverb; for example, 很 (*hěn*: 'very'), 非常 (*fēicháng*: 'extremely'), 相当 (*xiāngdāng*: 'quite').
Dependent clause	See **subordinate clause**.
Direct object	Certain verbs such as 给 (*gěi*: 'to give'), 告诉 (*gàosù*: 'to tell'), 教 (*jiāo*: 'to teach') can have two objects, a 'person' and a 'thing'. The 'thing' is the direct object and the 'person' is the indirect object. In Chinese, the indirect object follows the verb and the direct object follows the indirect object.
Disyllabic	A two-character word is disyllabic. See also **monosyllabic**.
Indefiniteness	A noun or noun phrase is 'indefinite' when no one engaged in the communication knows about its identity or when only the speaker knows about its identity. See also **definiteness**.

Independent clause	See **main clause**.
Indirect object	See **direct object**.
Interlocutor	A participant in a conversation or communication.
Interrogative pronoun	Interrogative pronouns in Chinese are similar to the *wh*-words in English. In Chinese, besides being used to ask questions, interrogative pronouns can be used to make statements as well.
Main clause or **main sentence**	The clause in a complex sentence that is complete in meaning. It can function independently without a subordinate clause. See also **subordinate clause**.
Measure word	A word that appears after a number, 这 (*zhè*: 'this'), 那 (*nà*: 'that'), 哪 (*nǎ*: 'which'), 几 (*jǐ*: 'how many') or 每 (*měi*: 'every') and before a noun. With rare exceptions, the use of the measure word is not optional.
Modal particle	A particle that is used at the end of a sentence to express certain moods. Also called a sentential particle since it appears at the end of a sentence.
Modal verb	See **auxiliary verb**.
Monosyllabic	In Chinese, each character has one syllable. A one-character word is monosyllabic.
Non-subject–predicate construction	A sentence that does not have either a subject or a predicate.
Object pre-position	When the object in a sentence is definite, it can be placed at the beginning of the sentence or before the verb. Such an object is called a pre-posed object.
Particle	A character with grammatical or pragmatic functions but without a clear definition; for example: 吗 (*ma*) is a modal particle; 了 (*le*) is both a perfective aspect particle and a modal particle.
Passive structure	A grammatical construction in which the subject is the recipient of the action indicated by the verb, not the performer of the action.
Placement verb	A verb that is not used to indicate an action but is used to indicate someone or something being in a state of rest as the result of that action. For example, 写 indicates an action in 他在纸上写了三个字 (*Tā zài zhǐ shàng xiě le sān ge zì*: 'He wrote three characters on the paper'), but is used as a placement verb in 纸上写着三个字 (*Zhǐ shàng xiě zhe sān ge zì*: 'Three characters were written on the paper').
Predicate	What is being said about the subject of the sentence. It should be noted that it is possible for a Chinese sentence not to have a subject or a predicate.
Pre-existent in the context	A noun or a situation whose existence is known by the people engaged in the conversation or communication is considered to be 'pre-existent in the context'.

Relative clause	A sentence or a phrase (containing a verb) that is used to modify a noun. In Chinese, a relative clause appears before the noun it modifies.
Sentential particle	See **modal particle**.
Sentential subject	The subject of a sentence that is itself a complete sentence.
Subject	What or whom a sentence is about.
Subject–predicate construction	A sentence that is composed of a subject and a predicate that follows the subject.
Subordinate clause	Also called a dependent clause. It is part of a complex sentence and is not complete in meaning. Therefore, it cannot function independently. In Chinese, a subordinate clause appears before the main clause.
Time phrase	A word or phrase that indicates when an action occurs.
Topic–comment structure	A sentence of which the predicate is one or more complete sentences. The subject in such a sentence is referred to as the topic, and the predicate is the comment.

Section 1

1 The basic formation of a Chinese sentence

A Chinese sentence can typically be classified as either a subject–predicate construction or a non-subject–predicate construction. Another structure generally referred to as the 'topic–comment' structure is also common in Chinese.

Level 1/2/3

1.1 The subject

The following are some of the key grammatical features of the subject in a Chinese sentence.

(a) Definite subjects

The subject of a sentence is generally of a definite nature; i.e. it is a specific entity that is known to both the speaker and the listener.

☞ See Chapter 3 for more information on the definiteness of nouns.

> 昨天**王老师**来我家。 (王老师 is definite.)
> *Zuótiān Wáng lǎoshī lái wǒ jiā.*
> Yesterday Teacher Wang came to my house.

> (Improper: 昨天一个客人来我家。 (一个客人 is indefinite.)
> Correct: 昨天我家来了一个客人。
>   *Zuótiān wǒ jiā lái le yí ge kèrén.*
>   Yesterday a guest came to my house.

☞ See 20.8 for word-order rules.

(b) Non-definite, generic subjects

An entity of non-definite nature that is generic in meaning can also serve as the subject.

> **菠菜**很有营养。 (菠菜 is generic.)
> *Bōcài hěn yǒu yíngyǎng.*
> Spinach is nutritious.

> **熊猫**真可爱。 (熊猫 is generic.)
> *Xióngmāo zhēn kě'ài.*
> Pandas are really cute.

(c) What can be a subject?

Words and phrases that function as nouns, pronouns, proper nouns, numerals, adjectives or verbs can serve as the subject.

王老师：**你的学生**真聪明。（你的学生 is a noun phrase.）
Wáng lǎoshī: Nǐde xuéshēng zhēn cōngmíng.
张老师：**聪明**没有用，**努力**最重要。（聪明 and 努力 are adjectives.）
Zhāng lǎoshī: Cōngmíng méiyǒu yòng, nǔlì zuì zhòngyào.
Teacher Wang: Your students are really smart.
Teacher Zhang: Being smart is of no use; being hard-working is most important.

(d) Sentential subjects

A complete sentence can serve as the subject without any particular marker. It should be noted that a comma can be used after a sentential subject, especially when the subject is long.

在中国，**丈夫做家务**，是一件很平常的事。（丈夫做家务 is the subject.）
Zài Zhōngguó, zhàngfū zuò jiāwù, shì yí jiàn hěn píngcháng de shì.
In China, husbands doing housework is a very common thing.

Expletive 'it' in English has no counterpart in Chinese. This means that a sentence with a sentential subject may have different word orders in English and Chinese.

儿子不听她的话，让她很难过。
Érzi bù tīng tāde huà, ràng tā hěn nánguò.
It saddens her (= makes her sad) that her son does not listen to her.

 In English, a sentential subject is frequently introduced by the phrase '(the fact) that . . .'. Note that such a phrase is not used in Chinese. The phrase 'the fact that' does not have a counterpart in Chinese.

王先生喜欢李小姐不表示李小姐也喜欢王先生。
Wáng xiānsheng xǐhuān Lǐ xiǎojiě bù biǎoshì Lǐ xiǎojiě yě xǐhuān Wáng xiānsheng.
The fact that Mr Wang likes Miss Li does not mean that Miss Li likes Mr Wang, too.

(e) Subjects in passive sentences

The subject is not always the performer of the action; it is sometimes the receiver of the action.

☞ See 22.3 for unmarked passive.

我的车修好了。（车 does not perform the action of 修。）
Wǒde chē xiū hǎo le.
My car has been fixed.

1.2 The predicate

`Level 1/2/3`

The predicate in a Chinese sentence can be any of the following:

(a) Simple verbs, compound verbs or verbal phrases

It should be noted that a sentence with a simple verb as its predicate rarely appears without at least one other element, such as a particle or a time phrase. When it does appear without another element, it is usually in context.

(Situation: Wang is throwing a party. Li and Zhang are talking about it.)

李：你们**去**吗？
Lǐ: Nǐmen qù ma?
张：我**去**；我女朋友**不去**。
Zhāng: Wǒ qù; wǒ nǚ péngyǒu bú qù.
Li: Are you (plural) going?
Zhang: I am going; my girlfriend is not.

妈妈：昨天的晚会，你跟妹妹表演了什么节目？
Māma: Zuótiān de wǎnhuì nǐ gēn mèimei biǎoyǎn le shénme jiémù?
儿子：我**唱歌**，她**跳舞**。（唱歌 and 跳舞 are both compound verbs.）
Érzi: Wǒ chànggē, tā tiàowǔ.
Mother: What did you and your younger sister perform at yesterday's evening party?
Son: I sang; she danced.

我喜欢李小姐；李小姐**不喜欢我**。（喜欢李小姐 and 不喜欢我 are verbal phrases.）
Wǒ xǐhuān Lǐ xiǎojiě; Lǐ xiǎojiě bù xǐhuān wǒ.
I like Miss Li; Miss Li does not like me.

(b) Adjectives

👁 It should be noted that 是 is not used in this case.

In a simple positive descriptive statement, a degree adverb or a complement of degree should be used. When the degree adverb 很 is used, it does not literally mean 'very', but is only used to fulfil this basic grammar requirement.

我爸爸在大使馆工作，他**很忙**。（Do not say 他忙 or 他是忙; 很 does not have a literal meaning of 'very' in this sentence.）
Wǒ bàba zài dàshǐguǎn gōngzuò, tā hěn máng.
My father works at the embassy. He is busy.

我累得**要命**。（要命 is a complement of degree; therefore, there is no degree adverb before 累.）
Wǒ lèi de yàomìng.
I am extremely tired. (= I am tired to death.)

When the adjective appears alone, a comparison is implied.

我有弟弟，也有妹妹。弟弟**大**，妹妹**小**。
Wǒ yǒu dìdi, yě yǒu mèimei. Dìdi dà, mèimei xiǎo.
I have a younger brother and I also have a younger sister. My younger brother is older (than my younger sister).

王：你们学校，男老师**多**还是女老师**多**？
Wáng: Nǐmen xuéxiào, nán lǎoshī duō háishì nǚ lǎoshī duō?
丁：女老师**多**。
Dīng: Nǚ lǎoshī duō.
Wang: At your school, are there more male teachers or more female teachers?
Ding: There are more female teachers.

Some adjectives are not associated with a matter of degree but are used to indicate a fact. The predicate in such a sentence is 是 + adjective + 的.

☞ See 19.11 for more information.

这件大衣**是蓝的**。
Zhè jiàn dàyī shì lán de.
This coat is blue. (This is to indicate a fact.)

这件大衣**很好看**。
Zhè jiàn dàyī hěn hǎokàn.
This coat is pretty. (This is to indicate an opinion.)

王老师**是男的**还是**女的**？（男 and 女 are adjectives, and it is improper to refer to individuals as 男人 or 女人.）

Wáng lǎoshī shì nán de háishì nǚ de?
Is Teacher Wang a man or a woman?

(c) Nouns

Such a predicate is frequently used to indicate age, time, day, date, year, amount of money, etc. It should be noted that such a sentence is usually a simple positive statement or a question with an interrogative pronoun.

王先生三十五岁，王太太三十 (岁)。
Wáng xiānsheng sānshí wǔ suì, Wáng tàitai sānshí (suì).
Mr Wang is 35 years old; Mrs Wang is 30.

现在几点？
Xiànzài jǐ diǎn?
What time is it now?

这本书多少钱？
Zhè běn shū duōshǎo qián?
How much is this book?

In a negative sentence or an affirmative–negative question, a noun alone cannot be the predicate. A verb must be used; thus the predicate would be a verbal phrase.

王：今天是不是星期三？
Wáng: Jīntiān shì bú shì xīngqī sān?
张：今天不是星期三，是星期四。
Zhāng: Jīntiān búshì xīngqī sān, shì xīngqī sì.
Wang: Is today Wednesday?
Zhang: Today isn't Wednesday; it's Thursday.

(d) Complete sentences

This is an example of the topic–comment structure, in which the subject is considered the topic, and the complete sentence is the comment. A topic can have more than one comment.

☞ See 1.4.

王先生	心脏不好，血压也很高。
Wáng xiānsheng	*xīnzàng bù hǎo, xuěyā yě hěn gāo.*
↓	↓
Subject	Predicate: 心脏不好 and 血压很高 are complete sentences.
(Topic)	(Two comments)

Mr Wang's heart is not good and his blood pressure is also high.

Level 2/3

1.3 Non-subject–predicate constructions

A non-subject–predicate construction is a sentence whose initial constituent is not the subject but is the predicate, or a sentence whose constituent is neither a clear-cut subject nor a predicate.

The following are typical non-subject–predicate constructions.

(a) Subjectless sentences

A subjectless sentence starts with a verbal phrase, although the verbal phrase can be preceded by a time phrase or a location.

☞ See Chapter 20 for more on subjectless sentences.

(b) Imperative sentences

An imperative sentence is used to give orders and commands or make strong suggestions and requests, etc. The subject 你 or 你们 is implied.

☞ See Chapter 7 for more on imperative sentences.

(c) Elliptical sentences

An elliptical sentence is typically used when the context is clear and the meaning can be understood without both the subject and the predicate being present.

The subject of a sentence is omitted when it is the same as the subject of the previous sentence.

> 丁：你的车是蓝色的还是绿色的？
> *Dīng: Nǐde chē shì lánsè de háishì lǜse de?*
> 李：蓝色的。(Both the subject 我的车 and the verb 是 are omitted.)
> *Lǐ: Lánsè de.*
> Ding: Is your car blue or green?
> Li: Blue.

The predicate of a sentence can be omitted if what is omitted is clear in meaning.

> 张：谁自愿来唱个歌？
> *Zhāng: Shéi zìyuàn lái chàng ge gē?*
> 王：我!
> *Wáng: Wǒ!*
> Zhang: Who wants to volunteer to sing a song?
> Wang: Me! (I volunteer.)

Level
3

1.4 The topic–comment structure

The Chinese language is viewed by many as topic prominent. The topic must be a noun or noun phrase that is definite and has been mentioned in the conversation or is pre-existent in the context.

(a) When the comment is a complete sentence

Usually the comment is a complete sentence used to elaborate on the topic.

> 这家饭馆，　　　服务很好。
> *Zhè jiā fànguǎn,　　fúwù hěn hǎo.*
> 　　↓　　　　　　　　↓
> Topic　　　　　　　Comment (服务很好 is a complete sentence.)
> Service at this restaurant is good.

(b) When the comment is another topic–comment structure

Sometimes, a comment itself can be a topic–comment structure. There is frequently a comma between the topic and the comment.

(Situation: Wang knew that Zhang had taken two tests yesterday, and Wang wanted to find out how Zhang had done in the tests.)

王： *Wáng:*	昨天的考试， *Zuótiān de kǎoshì,* Topic	你考得怎么样？ *nǐ kǎo de zěnmeyàng?* Comment (a complete sentence)	
张： *Zhāng:*	(那两个考试，) *(Nà liǎng ge kǎoshì,)* Topic	中文的，我考得不错， *Zhōngwén de,* *wǒ kǎo de bú cuò,* Comment #1 中文的，我考得不错， Topic　　Comment	英文的，我考得不好。 *Yīngwén de,* *wǒ kǎo de bù hǎo.* Comment #2 英文的，我考得不好。 Topic　　Comment

Wang: How did you do in yesterday's tests?
Zhang: Of the two tests, I did fine in the Chinese one, and I did poorly in the English one.

1.5 Basic Chinese word order

(a) Subject + verb + object

Subject + verb + object (S + V + O) is generally considered the basic word order in a Chinese sentence of the subject–predicate construction. However, many variations exist, most notably the 把 structure.

☞ See Chapter 21 for the 把 structure.

我	认识	王小姐。
Wǒ	*rènshì*	*Wáng xiǎojiě.*
S	V	O

I know Miss Wang.

(b) Object pre-position

When the object is definite, such an object is, more often than not, moved to the beginning of the sentence (O + S + V) or moved before the verb (S + O + V).

☞ See Chapter 3 for more on the definiteness of nouns.

O + S + V and S + O + V are regarded by some as topic–comment structures.

这本书，	我	看过了。	这本书，	我看过了。
Zhè běn shū,	*wǒ*	*kàn guo le.*		
O	S	V	↓	↓
↓				
Pre-posed object			Topic	Comment

I have read this book.

In the O + S + V sentence, a comma may be, and frequently is, used after the object.

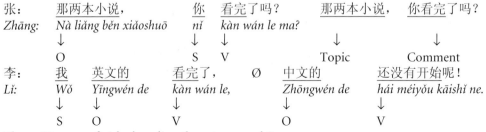

Zhang: Have you finished reading those two novels?
Li: I have finished reading the English one; I have not started the Chinese one yet.

Do not pre-pose a non-definite object.

> 我认识一个中国学生。 (一个中国学生 is non-definite; it cannot be pre-posed.)
> *Wǒ rènshì yí ge Zhōngguó xuéshēng.*
> I know a Chinese student.

(Situation: Zhang and Wang are looking at a photograph. Zhang points at two people in the photo and asks Wang a question. Wang points at each of them when answering.)

> 张：你认识这两个人吗？ (or 这两个人，你认识吗？)
> *Zhāng: Nǐ rènshì zhè liǎng ge rén ma?*
> 王：这个(,)我认识；这个(,)我不认识。
> *Wáng: Zhè ge(,) wǒ rènshì; zhè ge(,) wǒ bú rènshì.*
> Zhang: Do you know these two people?
> Wang: I know this one; I don't know this one.

Although an object may be definite, it is not usually pre-posed if it is not pre-existent in the context.

> 张：昨天你在小王的生日舞会上，看见了哪些人？
> *Zhāng: Zuótiān nǐ zài Xiǎo Wáng de shēngrì wǔhuì shàng, kànjiàn le nǎ xiē rén?*
> 李：我看见了小丁跟小陈。 (Improper: 小丁跟小陈，我看见了。)
> *Lǐ: Wǒ kànjiàn le Xiǎo Dīng gēn Xiǎo Chén.*
> Zhang: Whom did you see at Xiao Wang's birthday party yesterday?
> Li: I saw Xiao Ding and Xiao Chen. (Although Xiao Ding and Xiao Chen can be considered definite, they should not be pre-posed because they are not pre-existent in the context.)

> 张：昨天你看见小丁跟小陈没有？
> *Zhāng: Zuótiān nǐ kànjiàn Xiǎo Dīng gēn Xiǎo Chén méiyǒu?*
> 李：小丁，我看见了；小陈，我没有看见。
> *Lǐ: Xiǎo Dīng, wǒ kànjiàn le; Xiǎo Chén, wǒ méiyǒu kànjiàn.*
> Zhang: Did you see Xiao Ding or Xiao Chen yesterday?
> Li: I saw Xiao Ding; I didn't see Xiao Chen. (Ding and Chen have been mentioned by Zhang; therefore, they can be pre-posed by Li.)

When the adverb 都 is used with a verb (都 + V) to refer to the object, object pre-position is no longer an option but a must.

> 这两个人，我都不认识。 (Incorrect: 我都不认识这两个人。)
> *Zhè liǎng ge rén, wǒ dōu bú rènshì.*
> I don't know either of these two people.

> 李：你喜欢喝茶还是(**喜欢喝**)咖啡？
> *Lǐ: Nǐ xǐhuān hē chá háishì (xǐhuān hē) kāfēi?*
> 丁：(**茶跟咖啡，**)我都喜欢。 (Incorrect: 我都喜欢茶跟咖啡。)
> *Dīng: (Chá gēn kāfēi,) wǒ dōu xǐhuān.*
> Li: Do you like to drink tea or coffee?
> Ding: I like both (tea and coffee).

When 都 is used to refer to the subject, object pre-position becomes optional.

> 我和我妹妹都认识那个人。 (= 那个人，我和我妹妹都认识。)
> *Wǒ hé wǒ mèimei dōu rènshì nà ge rén.*
> Both my younger sister and I know that person.

(c) Placement of prepositional phrases

A prepositional phrase (preposition + object) usually appears before the verb. 'Prepositional phrase + verb' is the verbal phrase of the sentence.

☞ See Chapter 6 for more on prepositions.

◈ In English, a prepositional phrase typically appears after the verb.

张：你爸爸**在哪里**工作？（在哪里 is the prepositional phrase; 在哪里工作 is the verbal phrase.)
Zhāng: Nǐ bàba zài nǎlǐ gōngzuò?
李：他现在没有工作；他**在家**写书。（在家 is the prepositional phrase; 在家写书 is the verbal phrase.)
Lǐ: Tā xiànzài méiyǒu gōngzuò; tā zài jiā xiě shū.
Zhang: Where does your father work?
Li: He does not have a job now; he is writing a book at home.

我去花店**为我女朋友**买了一束花。
Wǒ qù huādiàn wèi wǒ nǚ péngyǒu mǎi le yí shù huā.
I went to the flower shop to buy a bunch of flowers for my girlfriend.

(d) Placement of time phrases

A time phrase (indicating when an action takes/took place) can appear at the beginning of the sentence or before the verbal phrase although the connotations might be slightly different. 几点 (*jǐ diǎn*: 'what time') is an exception; it is unusual for 几点 to appear at the beginning of the sentence.

昨天晚上小明在家写信。(= 小明**昨天晚上**在家写信。)
Zuótiān wǎnshàng Xiǎomíng zài jiā xiě xìn.
Xiaoming was writing letters at home yesterday evening.
(Incorrect: 小明在家昨天晚上写信。(在家写信 is the verbal phrase.))

你**几点**要去上课？(Unusual: 几点你要去上课？)
Nǐ jǐ diǎn yào qù shàng kè?
What time are you going to class?

(e) Placement of adverbs

Adverbs appear before the verbal phrase or the adjective.

When more than one adverb is used in a sentence, the order in which these adverbs appear is based on the general rule that the modifiers precede the word being modified.

我觉得这个电影**也**很好看。
Wǒ juéde zhè ge diànyǐng yě hěn hǎokàn.
I think that this movie was also good. (Possibility: One person, more than one movie.)

我**也**觉得这个电影很好看。
Wǒ yě juéde zhè ge diànyǐng hěn hǎokàn.
I also think that this movie was good. (Possibility: One movie, more than one person.)

In rare cases when several common adverbs appear in one sentence, the following is the most acceptable word order (although note that this is not the only acceptable order):

也 + 都 + 常 (常) + 只 + 一起 (常 and 只 can be switched depending on the actual situation.)

王老师：我的学生**都**很聪明。
Wáng lǎoshī: Wǒde xuéshēng dōu hěn cōngmíng.
李老师：我的学生**也都**很聪明。　(Improper: 我的学生都也很聪明。)
Lǐ lǎoshī: Wǒde xuéshēng yě dōu hěn cōngmíng.
Teacher Wang: All my students are smart.
Teacher Li: All my students are also smart.

小王**常常只**喝汤，不吃饭。
Xiǎo Wáng chángcháng zhǐ hē tāng, bù chī fàn.
Xiao Wang often only has soup, but no rice.

小张和小丁**也都常常只**喝汤，不吃饭。
Xiǎo Zhāng hé Xiǎo Dīng yě dōu chángcháng zhǐ hē tāng, bù chī fàn.
Both Xiao Zhang and Xiao Li also often only have soup, but no rice.

张：我爸妈**常一起**去看电影。
Zhāng: Wǒ bàmā cháng yìqǐ qù kàn diànyǐng.
丁：我爸妈**也常一起**去看电影。
Dīng: Wǒ bàmā yě cháng yìqǐ qù kàn diànyǐng.
Zhang: My parents often go to see a movie together.
Ding: My parents also often go to see a movie together.

Negative adverb 不: As a general rule, 不 appears before the word it negates. Therefore, the word order of a negative sentence affects its meaning.

我爸爸妈妈**都不**是老师。
Wǒ bàba māma dōu bú shì lǎoshī.
Neither of my parents is a teacher.
Compare:　我爸爸妈妈**不都**是老师。
　　　　　Wǒ bàba māma bù dōu shì lǎoshī.
　　　　　My parents are not both teachers. (One is; the other isn't.)

你身体不好，**不可以**喝酒。
Nǐ shēntǐ bù hǎo, bù kěyǐ hē jiǔ.
Your health is not good; you cannot drink (= you are not allowed to drink).
Compare:　你酒量不好，**可以不**喝酒。
　　　　　Nǐ jiǔliàng bù hǎo, kěyǐ bù hē jiǔ.
　　　　　You get drunk easily; you don't have to drink (= it's OK if
　　　　　you don't drink).

我的法文老师是日本人，他的法文**不太好**。
Wǒde Fǎwén lǎoshī shì Rìběn rén, tāde Fǎwén bú tài hǎo.
My French teacher is Japanese; his French is not very good (literally: not too good).
Compare:　我的英文老师是中国人，他的英文**很不好**。
　　　　　Wǒde Yīngwén lǎoshī shì Zhōngguó rén, tāde Yīngwén hěn bù hǎo.
　　　　　My English teacher is Chinese; his English is very bad.

☞ Do **not** place an adverb immediately before a noun/noun phrase, pronoun or proper noun.

English:　　Both Xiao Wang and Xiao Li are my good friends.
Chinese:　　小王和小李**都**是我的好朋友。
　　　　　　Xiǎo Wáng hé Xiǎo Lǐ dōu shì wǒde hǎo péngyǒu.
(Incorrect:　都小王和小李是我的好朋友。)

English: Mrs Wang has only one son.
Chinese: 王太太**只**有一个儿子。
Wáng tàitai zhǐ yǒu yí ge érzi.
(Incorrect: 王太太有只一个儿子。)

(f) Placement of direct objects and indirect objects

Some verbs can take two objects: one is the direct object and the other, the indirect object. The indirect object, which is usually a person, immediately follows the verb. The direct object, which is usually a non-person, follows the indirect object.

Such verbs in Chinese are limited and the most common ones are: 给 (*gěi*: 'to give'), 送 (*sòng*: 'to give something as a gift'), 借 (*jiè*: 'to lend'), 还 (*huán*: 'to return something'), 教 (*jiāo*: 'to teach'), 问 (*wèn*: 'to ask questions'), 告诉 (*gàosù*: 'to tell information'), 通知 (*tōngzhī*: 'to notify').

> 上星期我借**小王**三本词典，这星期他还**我**一本。（小王 and 我 are the indirect objects.)
> *Shàng xīngqī wǒ jiè Xiǎo Wáng sān běn cídiǎn, zhè xīngqī tā huán wǒ yì běn.*
> Last week I lent Xiao Wang three dictionaries; this week, he returned one to me.

> 王老师教**我们**语法，他每天都问**我们**很多问题。（我们 is the indirect object.)
> *Wáng lǎoshī jiāo wǒmen yǔfǎ, tā měi tiān dōu wèn wǒmen hěn duō wèntí.*
> Teacher Wang teaches us grammar; every day, he asks us many questions.

It should be noted that the direct object in the 'V + indirect O + direct O' structure tends to be non-definite. When the direct object is definite, it is frequently pre-posed or the 把 structure is preferred.

☞ See Chapter 21 for the 把 structure.

> 他送了我一辆自行车。（一辆自行车 is non-definite.)
> *Tā sòng le wǒ yí liàng zìxíngchē.*
> He gave me a bicycle (as a gift).

> 那辆自行车，他送我了。（– 他把那辆自行车送我了。）（那辆自行车 is definite.)
> *Nà liàng zìxíngchē, tā sòng wǒ le.*
> He gave me that bicycle (as a gift).

🕭 In English, the indirect object of an action can be expressed with a prepositional phrase using 'to' or 'for'. In Chinese, such an option does not exist.

> English: I bought a dictionary for my sister. = I bought my sister a dictionary.
> Chinese: 我给妹妹买了一本词典。
> *Wǒ gěi mèimei mǎi le yì běn cídiǎn.*
> (Incorrect: 我买妹妹一本词典。)

> English: I wrote a letter to my mother. = I wrote my mother a letter.
> Chinese: 我给妈妈写了一封信。
> *Wǒ gěi māma xiě le yì fēng xìn.*
> (Incorrect: 我写妈妈一封信。)

(g) Subordinate clauses and main clauses

In a complex sentence, the subordinate clause (the dependent clause) should appear before the main clause (the independent clause).

When the subordinate clause is ……的时候 (when)，……以前 (before) or ……以后 (after), it must always appear before the main clause. ☯ In English, the order is flexible.

☞ See Chapter 27 for more information on 以前, 以后 and 时候.

English: I had a glass of wine when I ate dinner yesterday.
            = When I ate dinner yesterday, I had a glass of wine.
Chinese: 昨天我吃晚饭的时候， 喝了一杯酒。
                      ↓   ↓
            Subordinate clause   Main clause
            Zuótiān wǒ chī wǎnfàn de shíhòu, hē le yì bēi jiǔ.
(Incorrect: 昨天我喝了一杯酒，吃晚饭的时候。)

When the subordinate clause and the main clause are connected by a conjunctive pair, which indicates the relationship between the two clauses, such as 因为……, 所以……; 虽然……, 但是……; 不但……, 而且……, it is important to recognize the main clause since the first word in the conjunctive pair is sometimes omissible.

☞ See Chapter 29 for more information on conjunctive pairs.

English: Although the weather is nice, I don't feel like going out.
            = I don't feel like going out although the weather is nice.
Chinese: (虽然)今天天气不错，   可是我不想出去。
                      ↓   ↓
            Subordinate clause   Main clause
            (Suīrán) jīntiān tiānqì búcuò, kěshì wǒ bù xiǎng chūqù.
(Incorrect: 我不想出去，虽然今天天气不错。)

Exercises

Rearrange the words or phrases given to form complete sentences.

Level 1

1 Neither Mr Wang nor his girlfriend likes to go to movies.
   不   喜欢   女朋友   看电影   王先生   他   都   跟

2 Mr Ding also teaches English in China.
   中国   英文   丁先生   在   教   也

3 My sons are both studying Chinese in China right now.
   中国   中文   都   学   在   我儿子   现在

4 I often go to the flower shop to buy flowers for my mother.
   妈妈   去   买   花店   我   花   常   为

5 He went to China in March (and) he went to Beijing from Shanghai in June.
   三月   去中国   去北京   六月   他   从上海

Level 2

6 It is not a secret that Mr Wang likes Miss Li.
   李小姐   不   王先生   是   喜欢   秘密

7 I always watch TV at home when the weather is bad.

看电视　我　不好　在家　的时候　天气　总是

8 The kitchen of this house is too small; also, its price is too expensive. (topic–comment structure)

厨房　这个　价钱　房子　也　小　贵　太 (twice)

9 Not all my friends are Chinese. I also have Japanese friends.

中国人　日本朋友　都　我的　也　是　有　朋友　不　我

10 Yesterday Xiao Wang lent two books to Miss Li; today she only returned one to him.

今天　昨天　小王 (twice)　李小姐　借　还　两本书　一本　只　她

2 The eleven types of question in Chinese

Questions can be converted from statements without a change of word order. Basically, a question can be formed by (i) adding a modal particle at the end of the statement, or (ii) replacing the part that indicates the answer in the statement with an interrogative pronoun. Based on these two rules, as well as another type of question termed the 'alternative question' using 还是 (háishì), eleven types of question can be formed in Chinese.

Question type	Example
1 Questions with the modal particle 吗	你是中国人吗? *Nǐ shì Zhōngguó rén ma?* Are you Chinese?

2 Questions with the modal particle 呢	1 我是中国人，你呢?
	  Wǒ shì Zhōngguó rén, nǐ ne?
	  I am Chinese. How about you?
	
	2 我的书呢?
	  Wǒde shū ne?
	  Where is (what happened to) my book?

3 Questions with the modal particle 吧	你也是中国人吧? *Nǐ yě shì Zhōngguó rén ba?* You must also be Chinese, aren't you?
4 Questions with the modal particle 了	你们都姓李，那你们是姐妹了? *Nǐmen dōu xìng Lǐ, nà nǐmen shì jiěmèi le?* Both of you have the same last name, Li, then you must be sisters, aren't you?
5 Affirmative–negative questions	你是不是中国人? *Nǐ shì bú shì Zhōngguó rén?* Are you (or are you not) Chinese?
6 Affirmative–negative questions: verb (or verbal phrase) + (了) + 没有	你吃饭了没有? *Nǐ chī fàn le méiyǒu?* Have you eaten (lunch/dinner)?
7 Alternative questions (using 还是)	你想喝茶还是喝咖啡? *Nǐ xiǎng hē chá háishì hē kāfēi?* Do you want to drink tea or coffee?
8 Tag questions	你是中国人，对不对? *Nǐ shì Zhōngguó rén, duì bú duì?* You are Chinese, right?

Question type	Example
9 Questions with interrogative pronouns	你叫什么名字？ *Nǐ jiào shénme míngzì?* What is your name?
10 Rhetorical questions	我这么忙，怎么有时间出去玩？ *Wǒ zhème máng, zěnme yǒu shíjiān chū qù wán?* I am so busy, how do I have time to go out and have fun?
11 Unmarked questions	你才写了五分钟，就写完了？ *Nǐ cái xiě le wǔ fēnzhōng, jiù xiě wán le?* You only spent five minutes writing it, and you are done?

Level 1

2.1 Questions with the modal particle 吗

Without a specific context, this type of question is used to elicit a yes-or-no answer.

☞ See 28.2 for more information.

张：你是老师**吗**？
Zhāng: Nǐ shì lǎoshī ma?
王：我不是老师，是学生。
Wáng: Wǒ bú shì lǎoshī, shì xuéshēng.
Zhang: Are you a teacher?
Wang: I am not a teacher; I am a student.

老师：你们有问题**吗**？
Lǎoshī: Nǐmen yǒu wèntí ma?
丁：我有。
Dīng: Wǒ yǒu.
李：我没有。
Lǐ: Wǒ méiyǒu.
Teacher: Do you (plural) have questions?
Ding: I do.
Li: I don't.

(a) Positive questions

Frequently 吗 is used (instead of an affirmative–negative question ☞ See 2.5 for affirmative–negative questions) when the person asking the question expects the answer to be 'yes'.

(Situation: Seeing a friend getting out of a new car, you ask him if he has just bought a new car.)

你买新车了**吗**？ (An affirmative–negative question (你买新车了没有？) would not be proper in this context since there is a strong indication that he did.)
Nǐ mǎi xīn chē le ma?
Did you buy a new car? (You bought a new car?)

(b) Negative questions

When the person asking the question expects the answer to be 'no', 吗 is used at the end of a negative statement to make it a negative question.

(Situation: Seeing Wang refusing to eat spinach, Li has the impression that Wang does not like spinach.)

李：你不喜欢吃菠菜吗？
Lǐ: Nǐ bù xǐhuān chī bōcài ma?
王：（对,）（我）不喜欢。
Wáng: (Duì,) (wǒ) bù xǐhuān.
Li: You don't like spinach?
Wang: (That's right,) I don't like it.

2.2 Questions with the modal particle 呢

呢 does not only appear in questions. When it does appear in questions, it usually follows an elliptical sentence with the part that is understood being omitted. Therefore, it is only used in context.

☞ See 28.3 for more information.

(a) Asking the same question without repeating it

王：你在哪里工作？
Wáng: Nǐ zài nǎlǐ gōngzuò?
李：在中国银行。你呢？(= 你在哪里工作？)
Lǐ: Zài Zhōngguó Yínháng. Nǐ ne?
Wang: Where do you work?
Li: At the Bank of China. How about you? (Meaning: Where do you work?)

(b) Omitting the predicate

The predicate can be omitted from a question if it is understood.

八的一半是四，六的一半呢？(= 六的一半是多少？)
Bā de yí bàn shì sì, liù de yí bàn ne? (= Liù de yí bàn shì duōshǎo?)
Half of eight is four; what about half of six? (Meaning: What is half of six?)

老师：这个问题，李明、张力都会回答。王安，你呢？(= 你会不会回答？)
Lǎoshī: Zhè ge wèntí, Lǐ Míng, Zhāng Lì dōu huì huídá. Wáng Ān, nǐ ne? (= Nǐ huì bú huì huídá?)
Teacher: Both Li Ming and Zhang Li can answer this question. Wang An, how about you? (Meaning: Wang An, can you answer it?)

(c) Asking about 'whereabouts'

When one does not see who or what one is expecting to see, 呢 is used to ask 'what happened to . . . ?' or 'where did . . . go?'

◐ It should be noted that sometimes this question is translated as 'where is . . . ?' However, it is different from ……在哪里? which is a question about the 'location' of something, not its 'whereabouts'.

(Situation: Mei Ying and her boyfriend are always seen together. But today you have bumped into her in the cinema and her boyfriend is not with her.)

梅英，你一个人来看电影吗？你男朋友呢？
Méi Yīng, nǐ yí ge rén lái kàn diànyǐng ma? Nǐ nán péngyǒu ne?
Mei Ying, you came to see the movie by yourself? Where is your boyfriend?
(= What happened to him?)

(Situation: You are back in a town you left years ago. You are standing in front of a shop which used to be your favourite coffee shop, but now it's something else.)

> 咦，咖啡馆**呢**？ (咦 is an interjection, indicating curiosity or puzzlement.)
> *Yí, kāfēiguǎn ne?*
> Hey, where is the coffee shop? (What happened to the coffee shop? Where did the coffee shop go?)

To ask the physical location of someone or something, use 在哪里？

(Situation: You are new in town and you ask someone where the post office is.)

> 请问，邮局**在哪里**？
> *Qǐng wèn, yóujú zài nǎlǐ?*
> Excuse me. Where is the post office?

2.3 Questions with the modal particle 吧

Level 2

A question with 吧 indicates that the speaker is almost certain of the situation, but not 100% sure. Frequently, adverbs such as 一定 (*yídìng*: 'definitely') and 大概 (*dàgài*: 'probably') can be used in such a question, but 吧 alone can serve the function of indicating near certainty.

(a) 吧! or 吧?

It is acceptable to use an exclamation mark instead of a question mark after 吧.

> 你工作了一整天，（一定）累了**吧**!
> *Nǐ gōngzuò le yì zhěngtiān, (yídìng) lèi le ba!*
> You worked all day; you must be tired, aren't you?

> 这本书上写着你的名字，是你的**吧**？
> *Zhè běn shū shàng xiě zhe nǐde míngzì, shì nǐde ba?*
> This book has your name written in it. It must be yours, isn't it?

(b) 吗 or 吧?

Although questions with 吧 and 吗 both indicate that the speaker has made an assumption of the situation and has an expectation as to what the answer will be, 吧 shows a stronger assumption or expectation than 吗.

(Situation: Someone has bought several French textbooks and two French dictionaries at a bookshop. The cashier could ask any of the following:)

> 你是学法文的**吧**?
> *Nǐ shì xué Fǎwén de ba?* (Near certainty.)
> You must be studying French, aren't you?
> 你是学法文的**吗**？
> *Nǐ shì xué Fǎwén de ma?* (Expecting 'yes' to be the answer.)
> Are you studying French?
> 你**是不是**学法文的？
> *Nǐ shì bú shì xué Fǎwén de?* (No assumption.)
> Are you (or are you not) studying French?

2.4 Questions with the modal particle 了

Level 2

了 in this type of question is sometimes represented by other characters with similar pronunciations, such as 咯 (*lo*) or 啰 (*lo*). Such a question is used to make inferences about a situation; therefore, an optional 那/那么 (*nà/nàme*: 'in that case') is frequently used.

☞ See 28.5(f) for more examples.

李：那个女孩跟你很象，她是谁？

Lǐ: Nà ge nǚhái gēn nǐ hěn xiàng, tā shì shéi?

王：我跟她同姓，可是她不是我姐姐。

Wáng: Wǒ gēn tā tóng xìng, kěshì tā bú shì wǒ jiějie.

李：那她是你妹妹了？

Lǐ: Nà tā shì nǐ mèimei le?

Li: That girl looks very much like you. Who is she?

Wang: We have the same last name, but she is not my older sister.

Li: Then (in that case) she must be your younger sister, isn't she?

2.5 Affirmative–negative questions: 'verb 不 verb' or 'adjective 不 adjective'

Level 1

This type of question is used to elicit an answer of either yes or no. It should be noted that an auxiliary verb (☞ see Chapter 11) can be used this way as well.

(a) Monosyllabic verbs/adjectives/auxiliary verbs

When the verb, the adjective or the auxiliary verb contains only one character:

王：你们明天**去不去**他家？

Wáng: Nǐmen míngtiān qù bú qù tā jiā?

张：我去，我太太不去。

Zhāng: Wǒ qù, wǒ tàitai bú qù.

Wang: Are you (plural) going to his house tomorrow?

Zhang: I am going; my wife is not.

丁：你**累不累**？

Dīng: Nǐ lèi bú lèi?

陈：不太累。

Chén: Bú tài lèi.

Ding: Are you tired?

Chen: I am not too tired.

李：明天**会不会**下雨？

Lǐ: Míngtiān huì bú huì xiàyǔ?

张：不会。

Zhāng: Bú huì.

Li: Will it rain tomorrow?

Zhang: It won't.

(b) Disyllabic verbs/adjectives/auxiliary verbs

When the verb, the adjective or the auxiliary verb contains two characters, the second character of the affirmative part is optional, especially in casual speech.

李：你**高(兴)不高兴**？

Lǐ: Nǐ gāo(xìng) bù gāoxìng?

张：我很高兴。

Zhāng: Wǒ hěn gāoxìng.

Li: Are you happy?

Zhang: I am happy.

王：那件事，我们**应(该)不应该**告诉他？

Wáng: Nà jiàn shì, wǒmen yīng(gāi) bù yīnggāi gàosù tā?

丁：不应该。

Dīng: Bù yīnggāi.

Wang: Should we tell him about that matter?

Ding: We should not.

(c) The verb 有

When the verb is 有, the affirmative–negative question is 有没有.

李：你今天**有没有**空？

Lǐ: Nǐ jīntiān yǒu méiyǒu kòng?

王：我下午有空，晚上没有。

Wáng: Wǒ xiàwǔ yǒu kòng, wǎnshàng méiyǒu.

Li: Are you free today? (= Do you have free time today?)

Wang: I am free in the afternoon; I am not free in the evening.

2.6 Affirmative–negative questions: verb (or verbal phrase) + (了) + 没有?

This type of affirmative–negative question can be interchangeable with 'verb (or verbal phrase) + 了 + 吗?'

☞ See 9.9 for more on this type of question.

(a) When 了 is optional

When 没有 is used to ask the affirmative–negative question, 了 is optional if the verb has two characters or has an object following it.

你吃饭**(了)没有**？ (= 你吃饭**了**吗？)

Nǐ chī fàn (le) méiyǒu?

Have you eaten?

你爸爸退休**(了)没有**？ (= 你爸爸退休**了**吗？) (退休 is a disyllabic verb.)

Nǐ bàba tuìxiū (le) méiyǒu?

Has your father retired?

(b) When 了 is necessary

了 is necessary if the verb is monosyllabic and does not have an object following it.

小李做的菜，你吃**了没有**？ (= 小李做的菜，你吃**了**吗？)

Xiǎo Lǐ zuò de cài, nǐ chī le méiyǒu?

Have you eaten the food Xiao Li made?

(Do **not** say 小李做的菜，你吃没有？ since the object of 吃 has been pre-posed.)

2.7 Alternative questions

还是 is used to offer choices and it should be thought of as '(whether) . . . or . . .'.

主人：我们有咖啡，也有茶；你想喝咖啡**还是**(喝)茶？

Zhǔrén: Wǒmen yǒu kāfēi, yě yǒu chá; nǐ xiǎng hē kāfēi háishì (hē) chá?

客人：我想喝茶。

Kèrén: Wǒ xiǎng hē chá.

Host: We have coffee and we also have tea. Would you like to drink coffee or tea?

Guest: I would like to drink tea.

(a) More than two options

Sometimes, more than two options are offered; 还是 is used between the last two options.

你喜欢日本车、美国车**还是**德国车？
Nǐ xǐhuān Rìběn chē, Měiguó chē háishì Déguó chē?
Do you like Japanese cars, American cars or German cars?

(b) Choosing all/none

When no choice is made, the options are either omitted or pre-posed, and 都 is used.

👁 Learners who are English speakers should pay special attention to this word-order rule.

李：你们喜欢吃中国菜还是法国菜？
Lǐ: Nǐmen xǐhuān chī Zhōngguó cài háishì Fǎguó cài?
丁：(中国菜跟法国菜，)我**都**喜欢吃。
Dīng: (Zhōngguó cài gēn Fǎguó cài,) wǒ dōu xǐhuān chī.
王：(中国菜跟法国菜，)我**都不**喜欢吃。 (Incorrect: 我都喜欢中国菜跟法国菜 or 我都不喜欢吃中国菜跟法国菜。)
Wáng: (Zhōngguó cài gēn Fǎguó cài,) wǒ dōu bù xǐhuān chī.
Li: Do you like to eat Chinese food or French food?
Ding: I like both.
Wang: I like neither.

(c) 还是 or 或者?

Do not confuse 还是 with 或者 (*huòzhě*: 'either . . . or . . .'). 或者 is used in a statement.

👁 Since both 还是 and 或者 can be translated as 'or' in English, learners who are English speakers should pay special attention to the distinction between these two words.

请你给我一杯茶**或者**咖啡。
Qǐng nǐ gěi wǒ yì bēi chá huòzhě kāfēi.
Please give me (either) a cup of tea or a cup of coffee.

- When 或者 is used in a question, it is an affirmative–negative question or a question with the modal particle 吗

王：我很渴，想喝一点饮料。**有没有**茶**或者**汽水？ (= 有茶**或者**汽水吗？)
Wáng: Wǒ hěn kě, xiǎng hē yìdiǎn yǐnliào. Yǒu méiyǒu chá huòzhě qìshuǐ?
李：有。要汽水**还是**要茶？ (This is an alternative question offering choices.)
Lǐ: Yǒu. Yào qìshuǐ háishì yào chá?
Wang: I am thirsty; I want to drink something. Is there tea or soda?
Li: Yes. Do you want soda or tea?

Level 1
2.8 Questions with interrogative pronouns

Interrogative pronouns are similar to *wh*-question words in English. They are 谁 (*shéi*: 'who/whom'), 哪 (*nǎ*: 'which'), 什么 (*shénme*: 'what'), 哪里/哪儿 (*nǎlǐ/nǎr*: 'where'), 怎么 (*zěnme*: 'how; how come'), 怎么样 (*zěnmeyàng*: 'how'), 为什么 (*wèishénme*: 'why'), 多 (*duō*: 'how (+ adjective)'), 多少 (*duōshǎo*: 'how many/how much'), 几 (*jǐ*: 'how many (+ measure word)'), 干嘛 (*gànmá*: 'what for'). It should be noted that 'when' is 什么时候 (*shénme shíhòu*), and 'what time' is 几点 (*jǐ diǎn*).

This type of question can be converted from a statement by replacing the part that indicates the answer with an interrogative pronoun; that is, there is no change in word order.

☞ See Chapter 33 for detailed discussions on the use of interrogative pronouns.

Level 1

2.9 Tag questions

After a statement is made, a tag question can be attached. Such a question is used to seek confirmation/agreement/approval or to make a suggestion.

(a) Confirming a statement

对不对/对吗？ is used to confirm a statement. It is similar to a question with the modal particle 吧.

那个人跟你很象；他是你哥哥，**对不对**？ (= 他是你哥哥**吧**？)

Nà ge rén gēn nǐ hěn xiàng; tā shì nǐ gēge, duì bú duì?

That person looks very much like you. He is your brother, right?

(b) Making a suggestion

好不好/好吗？ or 怎么样？ is used to make a suggestion.

李：下课以后，我们一起去吃饭、看电影，**好不好**？

Lǐ: Xià kè yǐhòu, wǒmen yìqǐ qù chī fàn, kàn diànyǐng, hǎo bù hǎo?

丁：好啊！电影票，你买；吃午饭，我请客，**怎么样**？

Dīng: Hǎo a! Diànyǐng piào, nǐ mǎi; chī wǔfàn, wǒ qǐngkè, zěnmeyàng?

Li: Let's go have lunch and see a movie together after class, OK?

Ding: Sure! How about you pay for the movie tickets and I'll treat you to lunch?

(c) Seeking approval/permission

可(以)不可以/可以吗？ or 行不行/行吗？ is used to seek approval/permission.

儿子：妈，我想跟朋友去游泳，**行不行**？

Érzi: Mā, wǒ xiǎng gēn péngyǒu qù yóuyǒng, xíng bù xíng?

Son: Mother, I want to go swimming with my friends; is it OK?

Level 3

2.10 Rhetorical questions

A rhetorical question is used not to seek an answer or reply but to make a statement. Generally, a positive question denotes a negative statement, whereas a negative question denotes a positive statement. Rhetorical questions with interrogative pronouns may have specific meanings.

☞ See Chapter 34 for detailed discussions on rhetorical questions.

Level 1

2.11 Unmarked questions

Structurally, this type of question is identical to a statement. In speech, the sentence ends with a raised pitch. In writing, the sentence ends with a question mark. This type of question is used either to indicate doubt or to convey mild surprise.

儿子：妈，我功课写完了，我要跟朋友出去玩。

Érzi: Mā, wǒ gōngkè xiě wán le, wǒ yào gēn péngyǒu chūqù wán.

妈妈：你功课写完了？你才写了十分钟，就写完了？

Māma: Nǐ gōngkè xiě wán le? Nǐ cái xiě le shí fēnzhōng, jiù xiě wán le?

Son: Mother, I have finished my homework; I want to go out with my friends.

Mother: You have finished your homework? You only spent ten minutes writing (= doing your homework) and you already finished?

Level

2

2.12 Direct questions and indirect questions

Since the word order in a question and in a statement is basically the same, there is no distinction between a direct question and an indirect question in Chinese. In addition, a question mark is acceptable in an indirect question.

👁 Learners who are English speakers should pay special attention to this rule.

> English: Go ask Xiao Li if he has eaten.
> 你去问一下小李，吃饭**了没有**？ (This is an indirect question with a question mark.)
> *Nǐ qù wèn yíxià Xiǎo Lǐ, chī fàn le méiyǒu?*
>
> 李：他跟你说了些什么？
> *Lǐ: Tā gēn nǐ shuō le xiē shénme?*
> 张：他问我**能不能**帮他一个忙？ (This is an indirect question, but a question mark is correct.)
> *Zhāng: Tā wèn wǒ néng bù néng bāng tā yí ge máng?*
> Li: What did he say to you?
> Zhang: He asked whether I could help him (or not).

Exercises

Form proper questions based on the given situations.

Level

1

1 You want to introduce a woman you know to a friend. But first you want to find out from him whether he already has a girlfriend.

2 Observing your roommate leaving the house with an umbrella, you ask her if this means it will rain today.

3 A man is taking his girlfriend out for dinner. They usually eat either Chinese or French food. He asks her which she feels like (eating) today.

4 A host asks her guest if he feels like (drinking) a cup of tea or coffee. (And the guest replies, 'Sure.')

5 After explaining the class policy to the students, the teacher asks if anyone has any questions.

6 You have an appointment to see Teacher Li, but you have forgotten to ask him where his office is located. So you ask a classmate if she knows where Teacher Li's office is.

Level

2

7 Xiaoming and his younger sister arrive at the same class together every day. But today he arrives alone. The teacher asks what has happened to his sister (meaning: her whereabouts).

8 You are cleaning a messy desk and see a French book which does not belong to you. You are pretty sure it belongs to your roommate since he is studying French. What question would you ask him to ascertain this fact?

9 (a) After announcing to his wife that he has been promoted, Mr Wang asks if she is happy.

   (b) Mrs Wang begins to cry upon hearing this good news and cannot immediately answer. Puzzled, Mr Wang asks if she is not happy about it.

10 A mother reminds her son that he should take out the trash, but he says he has done it. The mother is incredulous. She points at the trash and sarcastically asks what it is. (Ask two questions. The first one is to show her incredulity, and the second one is to show her sarcasm.)

3 The use of 是, 在 and 有 and the definiteness of nouns

Each of the three words 是, 在 and 有 has more than one usage in Chinese. In this chapter, the focus is on sentences using these three words whose English counterparts all involve the copula verb 'be'. Because of this similarity in English, it is important to examine and compare these three types of sentence in Chinese.

3.1 The basic functions of 是, 在 and 有

是 (shì)	Identification	我爸爸是老师。 *Wǒ bàba shì lǎoshī.* My father is a teacher.
在 (zài)	Location	你家在哪里? *Nǐ jiā zài nǎlǐ?* Where is your house?
有 (yǒu)	1 Possession 2 Existence	1 我有一辆自行车。 *Wǒ yǒu yí liàng zìxíngchē.* I have a bicycle. 2 桌上有一本书。 *Zhuō shàng yǒu yì běn shū.* There is a book on the desk.

(a) 是 (identification)

是 is used to identify the subject.

> 昨天是我的生日。
> *Zuótiān shì wǒde shēngrì.*
> Yesterday was my birthday.

(b) 在 (location)

在 is used to indicate where the subject is located. What follows 在 is a word or phrase indicating a location.

> 我家在学校对面。
> *Wǒ jiā zài xuéxiào duìmiàn.*
> My house is across from the school.

(c) 有 (possession/existence)

有 is used to indicate possession (to have; to own) or existence (there is/are).

Possession: 我有自行车，他没有。
Wǒ yǒu zìxíngchē, tā méiyǒu.
I have a bicycle; he does not (have one).

Existence: 教室(里)有三十把椅子。
Jiàoshì lǐ yǒu sānshí bǎ yǐzi.
There are 30 chairs in the classroom.

3.2 The definiteness of nouns

Level 3

In order to make effective comparisons between 是, 在 and 有 sentences and their counterparts in English, it is necessary to first clarify the concept of 'definiteness' in Chinese grammar.

(a) Definite nouns

A noun or noun phrase is definite when the interlocutors both know about its existence/identity or it has been mentioned in their exchanges.

A proper noun such as 王先生 (*Wáng xiānsheng*: 'Mr Wang'), 天安门 (*Tiān'ānmén*) or 上海 (*Shànghǎi*); a pronoun such as 他 (*tā*: 'he'), 我们 (*wǒmen*: 'we') or 你 (*nǐ*: 'you'); a noun phrase with 这 or 那, such as 这些 (*zhèxiē*: 'these'), 那个 (*nà ge*: 'that') or 那三个 (*nà sān ge*: 'those three'); as well as what follows the possessive case of the above three forms, such as 王先生的家 (*Wáng xiānsheng de jiā*: 'Mr Wang's home'), 上海的居民 (*Shànghǎi de jūmín*: 'residents of Shanghai'), 你的书 (*nǐde shū*: 'your book') and 那个人的车 (*nà ge rén de chē*: 'that person's car'), are considered 'definite'.

(b) Indefinite nouns

A noun phrase is indefinite when neither of the interlocutors knows its identity or when only the speaker knows about its existence. Such a noun phrase is either 'unnamed' or can be thought of as '(a) certain + noun' in English.

我认识很多中国人。
Wǒ rènshì hěnduō Zhōngguó rén.
I know many Chinese people. (很多中国人 is 'unnamed'.)

我认识一个姓白的中国人。
Wǒ rènshì yí ge xìng Bái de Zhōngguó rén.
I know a (certain) Chinese person whose last name is Bai.

(c) When indefinite nouns become definite

An indefinite noun phrase usually becomes definite after it has been mentioned once. The second time it is mentioned, it is definite.

我认识一个姓白的中国人，**他是我的中文老师。** (他 is definite.)
Wǒ rènshì yí ge xìng Bái de Zhōngguó rén, tā shì wǒde Zhōngwén lǎoshī.
I know a Chinese person whose last name is Bai; he is my Chinese (language) teacher.

(d) Subjects

As a general rule, in the Chinese language, the subject in a sentence should be definite. However, an indefinite noun that is generic can serve as the subject as well.

一个人不能没有良心。（一个人 means 'any man', not 'a certain man'. It is 'generic'
and can serve as the subject.)
Yí ge rén bù néng méiyǒu liángxīn.
A man cannot be without conscience.

(Incorrect: 一个人在等你。)
Correct: 有一个人在等你。（一个人 means 'a certain man'. It is indefinite;
            therefore, it cannot serve as the subject.)
            Yǒu yí ge rén zài děng nǐ.
            A man is waiting for you.

 See 20.7 for more information.

学生应该用功。（学生 is generic.)
Xuéshēng yīnggāi yònggōng.
Students should be diligent.

那个学生很用功。（那个学生 is definite.)
Nà ge xuéshēng hěn yònggōng.
That student is diligent.

熊猫很可爱。（熊猫 is generic.)
Xióngmāo hěn kě'ài.
Pandas are cute.

(e) Noun phrases with numbers

Generally, a noun phrase with a number but without 这 or 那 is considered indefinite.
However, note that such a noun phrase, when in context, can actually be definite.

桌上有两本书；**一本**是我的，**一本**是他的。
Zhuō shàng yǒu liǎng běn shū, yì běn shì wǒde, yì běn shì tāde.
There are two books on the table; one (of them) is mine; one (of them) is his.
(两本书 is indefinite. In this context, 一本 is definite and, therefore, can serve as the
subject of the sentence 一本是我的.)

Level
/2/3

3.3 是, 在 and 有 sentences and the definiteness of nouns

(a) 是 sentences

In a 是 sentence, the subject is either definite or generic. The subject complement (what
follows 是) can be definite or non-definite (indefinite or generic).

人是感情的动物。（人 and 感情的动物 are both generic.)
Rén shì gǎnqíng de dòngwù.
Human beings are creatures of emotions.

那个人是个冷血动物。（那个人 is definite; 一个冷血动物 is indefinite.)
Nà ge rén shì ge lěngxuě dòngwù.
That man is a cold-blooded creature.

那个人是我的英文老师。（那个人 and 我的英文老师 are both definite.)
Nà ge rén shì wǒde Yīngwén lǎoshī.
That man is my English teacher.

(b) 在 sentences

In a 在 sentence, the subject is definite. The word or phrase indicating the location can be either definite or indefinite.

English: A book is on the table.
Chinese: 桌上有一本书。
              Zhuō shàng yǒu yì běn shū.
(Incorrect: 一本书在桌上。 (一本書 is indefinite; it cannot be the subject.))
(This sentence is not to indicate 'location', but to indicate 'existence'. Therefore, it is not a 在 sentence in Chinese.)

我的车在那棵树下。
Wǒde chē zài nà kē shù xià.
My car is under that tree.
我的车在一棵树下。
Wǒde chē zài yì kē shù xià.
My car is under a tree (a certain tree).
English: A car is under the tree.
Chinese: 那棵树下有一辆车。
              Nà kē shù xià yǒu yí liàng chē.
(Incorrect: 一辆车在那棵树下。)
(我的车 and 那棵树 are both definite; 一棵树 and 一辆车 are both indefinite.)

(c) 有 sentences

In a 有 sentence, the subject is definite or generic; what follows 有, whether 有 is indicating possession or existence, must be non-definite (indefinite or generic).

人应该有良心。 (人 and 良心 are generic.)
Rén yīnggāi yǒu liángxīn.
Man should have a conscience.

我有三本英文詞典，没有中文词典。
Wǒ yǒu sān běn Yīngwén cídiǎn, méiyǒu Zhōngwén cídiǎn.
I have three English dictionaries; I don't have any Chinese dictionaries.

◗ It should be noted that, in English, a definite noun or noun phrase can follow the verb 'to have/to own'. Such an English sentence should not be translated literally into Chinese since its Chinese counterpart would not be a 有 sentence.

(Situation: Li is looking for his dictionary. He wants to know where his dictionary is, not in terms of its physical location, but in terms of its temporary possession.)

Li: Who **has** my dictionary? Please return it to me.
Zhang: I **have** it. I am still using it.
李：我的词典**在谁那儿**？请还我。
Lǐ: Wǒde cídiǎn zài shéi nàr? Qǐng huán wǒ.
张：(**你的词典**)**在我这儿**。我还在用呢。
Zhāng: (Nǐde cídiǎn) zài wǒ zhèr. Wǒ hái zài yòng ne.
(It is incorrect to say 谁有我的词典 or 我有你的词典。我的 (or 你的) 词典 is definite; it cannot follow 有。Since 有 indicates 'possession', it would be illogical to say 'I own your dictionary'.)

☝ When the subject is a definite person and the verb is 有, what follows 有 in the Chinese sentence must be of indefinite nature regardless of how the English sentence is worded.

(Situation: Wang was in a bookshop. He saw a book and wanted to point out that he owned a copy of that particular book.)

English:	I have that book. (Meaning: I have a copy of that book.)
Chinese:	那本书，我也有一本。 (一本 is indefinite and can follow 有.)
	Nà běn shū, wǒ yě yǒu yì běn.
(Incorrect:	我有那本书。 (那本书 is definite; it cannot follow 有.))

(Situation: Ding bought a nice car from Chen.)

English:	I own this car now.
Chinese:	这辆车是我的了。
	Zhè liàng chē shì wǒde le.
(Incorrect:	我有这辆车了。 (这辆车 is definite; it cannot follow 有.))

When 有 indicates existence, the sentence generally starts with a definite location. What follows 有 must be indefinite.

☞ See 20.9 for similar structures.

我家前面有一个很大的院子，院子里有很多漂亮的花。
Wǒ jiā qiánmiàn yǒu yí ge hěn dà de yuànzi, yuànzi lǐ yǒu hěn duō piàoliàng de huā.
There is a big garden in front of my house; there are many pretty flowers in the garden.

(Situation: A tourist feels like eating French food but does not have a specific French restaurant in mind, so he asks the hotel receptionist where he can find a French restaurant.)

请问，**哪里有**法国餐馆？ (法国餐馆 is indefinite in this sentence.)
Qǐng wèn, nǎlǐ yǒu Fǎguó cānguǎn?
Excuse me, where is there a French restaurant? (Meaning: where can I find a French restaurant?)

(Situation: You know the hotel you are staying at has a French restaurant, but you cannot locate it, so you ask the hotel receptionist.)

请问，法国餐馆**在哪里**？ (法国餐馆 is definite in this sentence.)
Qǐng wèn, Fǎguó cānguǎn zài nǎlǐ?
Excuse me, where is the French restaurant?

(d) Many

☝ When an English sentence includes 'to have/there be' and 'many', its Chinese counterpart usually does not use 有; instead, 很多/不少 is used as the predicate. This is particularly the case when the sentence is negative since 没有 and 很多/不少 together can make the sentence sound awkward or incorrect.

English:	There are many study-abroad students at this school.
Chinese:	这个学校有很多留学生。
	Zhè ge xuéxiào yǒu hěn duō liúxuéshēng.
	= 这个学校(的)留学生很多。
	Zhè ge xuéxiào (de) liúxuéshēng hěnduō.

English: I don't have many Chinese friends.
Chinese: 我的中国朋友不多。
               Wǒde Zhōngguó péngyǒu bù duō.
(Awkward: 我没有很多中国朋友。)
(Incorrect: 我没有不少中国朋友。)

(e) Combining existence and identification

It is possible to combine existence and identification in one sentence. The word order indicates existence since the sentence starts with a location, whereas the verb used is 是. What follows 是 can be either indefinite or definite.

> 我家前面是一条大马路，后面是一个小树林。（一条大马路 and 一个小树林 are indefinite.）
> *Wǒ jiā qiánmiàn shì yì tiáo dà mǎlù, hòumiàn shì yí ge xiǎo shùlín.*
> (What's) in front of my house is a big street; (what's) at the back is a small wooded area.

(Situation: Wang is showing her family's new house to a friend.)

> 王：这是厨房；厨房左边是我的房间，右边是我爸妈的房间。（我的房间 and 我爸妈的房间 are definite.）
> *Wáng: Zhè shì chúfáng; chúfáng zuǒbiān shì wǒde fángjiān, yòubiān shì wǒ bàmā de fángjiān.*
> Wang: This is the kitchen. On the left of the kitchen is my room; on the right is my parents' room.

3.4 Summary of the use of 是, 在 and 有

Level 2

The following is a summary of the use of 是, 在 and 有 and the definiteness of nouns.

Definite	是	Definite	王小英是我的女朋友。 *Wáng Xiǎoyīng shì wǒde nǚ péngyǒu.* Wang Xiaoying is my girlfriend.
Definite	是	Indefinite	这是一个没有用的东西。 *Zhè shì yí ge méiyǒu yòng de dōngxi.* This is a useless thing.
Generic	是	Generic	人是理性的动物。 *Rén shì lǐxìng de dòngwù.* Humans are creatures of rationality.
Definite	在	Definite	你的书在那张桌子上。 *Nǐde shū zài nà zhāng zhuōzi shàng.* Your book is on that desk.
Definite	在	Indefinite	我家在一条大马路旁边。 *Wǒ jiā zài yì tiáo dà mǎlù pángbiān.* My house is on a big street.

Definite	有	Indefinite	那棵树下有一辆车。 *Nà kē shù xià yǒu yí liàng chē.* There is a car under that tree. 我有三本语法书。 *Wǒ yǒu sān běn yǔfǎ shū.* I have three grammar books.
Generic	有	Generic	人都有理性跟良心。 *Rén dōu yǒu lǐxìng gēn liángxīn.* All humans have rationality and conscience.

Exercises

Translate the following sentences into Chinese. Be precise about the use of 是, 在 and 有.

1 There are five people in my family. These five people are my parents, my older brother, my younger sister and me.

2 There are two books on the table. One is mine; one is my younger brother's.

3 My boyfriend is Chinese. He is in the UK right now.

4 Wang: Where is your Chinese dictionary? May I borrow it?
   Zhang: I don't have a Chinese dictionary.

5 Wang: Is this Japanese car yours?
   Li: I have two cars; one is an American car and one is a German car. I don't have a Japanese car.

6 Li: There is a car under the tree. Is it yours?
   Zhang: It is not. My car is in the garage.

7 Ding: Where is my Chinese dictionary? Do you have my dictionary, Wang Zhong?
   Wang: No, Li Ming has it now.

8 Wang: There is a computer here. Whose is it? Is it yours?
   Ding: No, my computer is in my dormitory. Li Ming, is it yours?
   Li: It's not mine either. I don't have a computer.

9 New student: Excuse me, where is the toilet?
   Teacher: It's on the fifth floor. There isn't one on this floor.
   New student: Isn't this the fifth floor?
   Teacher: No, we are on the fourth floor right now.

10 Wang: There are two grammar books here. Which is yours?
   Li: Neither is mine. I don't have any grammar books.

4 The functions of 的, relative clauses and noun clauses

A basic rule to remember about the use of 的 (*de*) is that a 的 phrase, in most cases, is used attributively. This means that it appears before a noun or noun phrase, even though the noun or noun phrase sometimes is omitted from the sentence.

Level 1

4.1 Possessive 的

的 can be used to indicate possession.

> 王先生**的**新房子很大。
> *Wáng xiānsheng de xīn fángzi hěn dà.*
> Mr Wang's new house is big.

> **我的**车坏了。
> *Wǒde chē huàn le.*
> My car has broken down.

> 这是**谁的**书？
> *Zhè shì shéi de shū?*
> Whose book is this?

(a) When possessive 的 can be omitted

After a personal pronoun (你 (*nǐ*), 我 (*wǒ*), 他/她 (*tā*), etc.), 的 is frequently omitted, especially in casual speech, when what follows is a family member. This rule can also apply to nouns such as 家 (*jiā*) and 男朋友 (*nán péngyǒu*)/女朋友 (*nǚ péngyǒu*).

> **我家**有三个卧室；**我爸妈**的卧室最大，**我弟弟**的最小。
> *Wǒ jiā yǒu sān ge wòshì; wǒ bàmā de wòshì zuì dà, wǒ dìdi de zuì xiǎo.*
> My house has three bedrooms; my parents' room is the biggest, my younger brother's is the smallest.

> **我女朋友**的哥哥是**我妹妹**的男朋友。
> *Wǒ nǚ péngyǒu de gēge shì wǒ mèimei de nán péngyǒu.*
> My girlfriend's older brother is my younger sister's boyfriend.

(b) English vs. Chinese word order

👁 In English, the word 'of' is sometimes used in a sentence whose Chinese counterpart uses 的. It is important to note the difference in word order between English and Chinese in such sentences.

English: The colour of this skirt is ugly.
Chinese: 这条裙子的颜色不好看。
           Zhè tiáo qúnzi de yánsè bù hǎokàn.

English: The author of this book is a good friend of mine.
Chinese: 这本书的作者是我的好朋友。
           Zhè běn shū de zuòzhě shì wǒde hǎo péngyǒu.

我妹妹的男朋友是大学生。
Wǒ mèimei de nán péngyǒu shì dàxuéshēng.
The boyfriend of my younger sister is a university student.

我男朋友的妹妹是大学生。
Wǒ nán péngyǒu de mèimei shì dàxuéshēng.
The younger sister of my boyfriend is a university student.

(c) Location phrases with possessive 的

👁 In English, the phrase 'in/at/on + location' should sometimes be thought of as a 的 phrase in Chinese when such a phrase is used to modify a noun or noun phrase. To translate such an English phrase into a prepositional phrase with 在 (*zài*) is a common mistake made by learners of Chinese whose native language is English.

English: Students at Beijing University are all good students.
Chinese: 北京大学的学生都是好学生。
           Běijīng dàxué de xuéshēng dōu shì hǎo xuéshēng.
(Incorrect: 学生在北京大学都是好学生。)

English: Wow! The scenery here is really beautiful!
Chinese: 哇！这里的风景真美啊！
           Wà! Zhèlǐ de fēngjǐng zhēn měi a!
(Incorrect: 哇！风景在这里真美啊！)

(d) Omission of noun after possessive 的

When the context is clear, the noun after the possessive 的 can be, and frequently is, omitted.

王：这本书是**谁的**？
Wáng: Zhè běn shū shì shéi de?
李：不是**我的**；可能是**张文的**。
Lǐ: Bú shì wǒde; kěnéng shì Zhāng Wén de.
Wang: Whose is this book? (= To whom does this book belong?)
Li: It's not mine; it's probably Zhang Wen's.

Level 2   4.2 的 with disyllabic modifiers

When a disyllabic modifier is used attributively to describe a noun (meaning the modifier appears before a noun or noun phrase), 的 is needed.

李：你知道吗？王老师有一个**很大的**房子呢！(很大 is disyllabic.)
Lǐ: Nǐ zhīdào ma? Wáng lǎoshī yǒu yí ge hěn dà de fángzi ne!
张：是吗？我不知道呢。可是我知道他有一辆**新**车。(新 is monosyllabic.)
Zhāng: Shì ma? Wǒ bù zhīdào ne. Kěshì wǒ zhīdào tā yǒu yí liàng xīn chē.
Li: Did you know? Teacher Wang has a very big house!
Zhang: Is that so? I didn't know. But I know he has a new car.

(a) Exception: 很多/不少

When 很多/不少 appears before a noun or noun phrase, 的 is not used even though each is disyllabic.

他去过很多国家。(= 他去过不少国家。)
Tā qù guo hěn duō guójiā.
He has been to many countries.

In casual speech, however, 的 is acceptable after 很多/不少.

今天他带了很多(的)钱，所以买了不少(的)好东西。
Jīntiān tā dài le hěn duō (de) qián, suǒyǐ mǎi le bù shǎo (de) hǎo dōngxi.
Today he brought a lot of money, so he bought a lot of good stuff.

(b) Exception: When monosyllabic modifiers take 的

When a monosyllabic adjective is used attributively for the purpose of making a distinction, 的 is needed.

家里有两个苹果，两个桃子。妈妈上午把**大的**苹果给了我，所以下午就给我**小的**桃子。
Jiā lǐ yǒu liǎng ge píngguǒ, liǎng ge táozi. Māma shàngwǔ bǎ dà de píngguǒ gěi le wǒ, suǒyǐ xiàwǔ jiù gěi wǒ xiǎo de táozi.
There were two apples and two peaches at home. My mother gave me the bigger apple in the morning, so she gave me the smaller peach in the afternoon.
(大 and 小 are both monosyllabic; 大的 and 小的 are used because 大 and 小 are used to distinguish the two apples from the two peaches.)

(Situation: A photographer is arranging a group of people to be in a photo.)

高的人站后面；**矮的**人站前面。
Gāo de rén zhàn hòumiàn; ǎi de rén zhàn qiánmiàn. (高人 and 矮人 would be incorrect.)
Taller people stand at the back; shorter people stand in front.

(c) Omission of noun

When the context is clear, the noun after the adjective can be omitted. In this case, 的 must be attached to the adjective regardless of the number of characters the adjective has.

妈妈：这里有两条**漂亮的**裙子；是谁的？
Māma: Zhèlǐ yǒu liǎng tiáo piàoliàng de qúnzi, shì shéi de?
女儿：**红的**是我的；**蓝的**是姐姐的。
Nǚ'er: Hóng de shì wǒde; lán de shì jiějie de.
Mother: There are two pretty skirts here. Whose (skirts) are they?
Daughter: The red one is mine; the blue one is (my) older sister's.

4.3 Relative clauses

Level 3

A relative clause is also called an adjectival clause since it functions as an adjective. A relative clause in Chinese appears before the noun or noun phrase; therefore, 的 is needed even in rare cases where there is only a monosyllabic verb before it.

In Chinese, a relative clause appears before the noun or noun phrase it modifies.
In English, a relative clause follows the noun or noun phrase.

(a) Verbs and verbal phrases

A relative clause can be a verb or a verbal phrase.

> 李：昨天我家有一个派对。
> *Lǐ: Zuótiān wǒ jiā yǒu yí ge pàiduì.*
> 王：哦，是吗？**来**的人多不多？
> *Wáng: Ó, shì ma? Lái de rén duō bù duō?*
> Li: Yesterday there was a party at my house.
> Wang: Oh, is that so? Were there many people who came (to your party)?

> **喜欢看中国电影**的人应该学中文。
> *Xǐhuān kàn Zhōngguó diànǐng de rén yīnggāi xué Zhōngwén.*
> People who like to see Chinese movies should study Chinese.

> 昨天**跟我去看电影**的那个女孩子是我妹妹。
> *Zuótiān gēn wǒ qù kàn diànyǐng de nà ge nǚ háizi shì wǒ mèimei.*
> The girl who went to see a movie with me yesterday was my younger sister.

(b) Subject + verb

A relative clause can be 'subject + verb'.

> 王：**我**昨天**看**的那个电影真不错。
> *Wáng: Wǒ zuótiān kàn de nà ge diànyǐng zhēn búcuò.*
> 张：是不是上星期**李老师给我们介绍**的那个电影？
> *Zhāng: Shì bú shì shàng xīngqī Lǐ lǎoshī gěi wǒmen jièshào de nà ge diànyǐng?*
> Wang: The movie which I saw yesterday was really good.
> Zhang: Was it the movie which Teacher Li recommended last week?

> 陈：请告诉我，这几个字是什么意思？
> *Chén: Qǐng gàosù wǒ, zhè jǐ ge zì shì shénme yìsi?*
> 丁：这些都是**你学过**的字，你不应该来问我。
> *Dīng: Zhè xiē dōu shì nǐ xué guo de zì, nǐ bù yīnggāi lái wèn wǒ.*
> Chen: Please tell me: what are the meanings of these few words?
> Ding: All these are words (that) you have learned; you should not ask me.

(c) Subject + verb + object

A relative clause can be 'subject + verb + object'. The object in this case must be an indirect object and the noun/noun phrase being modified by the relative clause is the direct object.

☞ See 1.5 for more information on direct objects and indirect objects.

> 你看，这是**我男朋友送我**的生日礼物。
> *Nǐ kàn, zhè shì wǒ nán péngyǒu sòng wǒ de shēngrì lǐwù.*
> Look! This is the birthday gift (that) my boyfriend gave me.

> 我把**他告诉我**的秘密都写在日记里了。
> *Wǒ bǎ tā gàosù wǒ de mìmì dōu xiě zài rìjì lǐ le.*
> I wrote all the secrets he told me in my diary.

(d) Complete sentences

◉ It may sound awkward in Chinese, although deemed acceptable by some, if the relative clause is a complete sentence with a prepositional phrase (subject + prepositional phrase + verb + object); however, its counterpart in English is perfectly acceptable.

English:	The girl whom I went to the movie with is Miss Bai.
Awkward but acceptable:	我跟她去看电影的那个女孩子是白小姐。
	Wǒ gēn tā qù kàn diànyǐng de nà ge nǚ háizi shì Bái xiǎojiě.
Should be:	The girl who went to the movie with me is Miss Bai.
	跟我去看电影的那个女孩子是白小姐。
	Gēn wǒ qù kàn diànyǐng de nà ge nǚ háizi shì Bái xiǎojiě.
English:	The person to whom I wrote a letter last week is here.
Awkward but acceptable:	上星期我给他写信的那个人现在来了。
	Shàng xīngqī wǒ gěi tā xiě xìn de nà ge rén xiànzài lái le.

(e) 这/那 + measure word

➲ It is useful to know that '那 + measure word', which appears before the noun/noun phrase after the relative clause, normally does not literally mean 'that', but is only used to clearly indicate the singular number of the noun.

• Without '那 + measure word' in front of the noun, the meaning can be ambiguous.

> 我上星期提到的**那个**女孩子今天没有来参加舞会。
> *Wǒ shàng xīngqī tídào de nà ge nǚ háizi jīntiān méiyǒu lái cānjiā wǔhuì.*
> **The** girl I mentioned last week didn't come to the dance party today.
> (Without 那个, it would not be clear how many girls the speaker mentioned last week.)

> 我昨天买的书在哪里?
> *Wǒ zuótiān mǎi de shú zài nǎli?*
> Where is the book I bought yesterday? *or* Where are the books I bought yesterday?

• When 这/那 appears before the relative clause, it usually literally means 'this/that'.

> **那个**穿绿裙子的女孩就是我昨天提到的**那个**留学生。
> *Nà ge chuān lǜ qúnzi de nǚhái jiù shì wǒ zuótiān tídào de nà ge liúxuéshēng.*
> **That** girl (over there) who's wearing a green skirt is **the** exchange student I mentioned yesterday.
> (The speaker is likely to be pointing at the girl while speaking.)

> **这件**让大家都不愉快的事,我们忘了吧!
> *Zhè jiàn ràng dàjiā dōu bù yúkuài de shì, wǒmen wàng le ba.*
> Let's forget this matter, which has upset everybody.
> (Improper: 让大家都不愉快的这件事,我们忘了吧!)

(f) Number + measure word

When 'a number + measure word' is used with a relative clause, it *tends* to appear before the relative clause, not immediately before the noun/noun phrase. It is indefinite and it means '(a) certain'. (When it appears immediately before the noun/noun clause, the sentence is still correct but may have a slightly different implication.)

> 昨天我收到**一个**爸爸寄给我的**礼物**。
> *Zuótiān wǒ shōudào yí ge bàba jì gěi wǒ de lǐwù.*
> Yesterday I received a present that my father sent me.

> 这是**一件**大家都已经知道的**事**,你不用说了。
> *Zhè shì yí jiàn dàjiā dōu yǐjīng zhīdào de shì, nǐ búyòng shuō le.*
> This is a matter (that) everybody already knew about. You don't have to say it any more.

(g) Particle 了

了, whether a modal particle or a perfective aspect particle, is rarely included in a relative clause.

☞ See Chapter 9 for more information on the use of 了.

这件事，大家都**已经知道了**。
Zhè jiàn shì, dàjiā dōu yǐjīng zhīdǎo le.
Everybody already knew about this matter.
Compare: 这是一件大家都**已经知道的**事。
Zhè shì yí jiàn dàjiā dōu yǐjīng zhīdào de shì.
This is a matter that everybody already knew about.

我**昨天买了**一辆日本车。
Wǒ zuótiān mǎi le yí liàng Rìběn chē.
I bought a Japanese car yesterday.
Compare: 这就是我**昨天买的**那辆日本车。
Zhè jiù shì wǒ zuótiān mǎi de nà liàng Rìběn chē.
This is the Japanese car that I bought yesterday.

◉ In certain cases when 了 is needed in the relative clause, it must follow the verb.

你是**结了婚**的人，怎么还出去交女朋友呢？ (结婚的人 or 结婚了的人 would not be correct.)
Nǐ shì jié le hūn de rén, zěnme hái chūqù jiāo nǚ péngyǒu ne?
You are a married man; how can you still go out and date another woman?

(h) More formal with use of 所

When the relative clause is 'subject + verb' and the noun which the relative clause modifies is the object of the verb, then an optional 所 (*suǒ*) can be used before the verb in a more formal style of speech.

老师(所)**说的话**，你们都懂了吗？
Lǎoshī (suǒ) shuō de huà, nǐmen dōu dǒng le ma?
Did you all understand the words (which) the teacher said?
(话 is the object of the verb 说; therefore, an optional 所 can appear before 说.)

人口太多(所)**带来的问题**，是很不容易解决的。
Rénkǒu tài duō (suǒ) dàilái de wèntí, shì hěn bù róngyì jiějué de.
The problem (which) excessive population has brought is very difficult to solve.
(问题 is the object of the verb 带来; therefore, an optional 所 can appear before 带来.)

When the relative clause is 'subject + verb + indirect object', an optional 所 can be used as well.

我(所)**告诉你**的那个秘密，请你不要告诉别人。
Wǒ (suǒ) gàosù nǐ de nà ge mìmì, qǐng nǐ bú yào gàosù biérén.
Please do not tell others the secret I told you.

4.4 的 and noun clauses

Level 3

(a) Omission of noun

When the context is clear, the noun following the relative clause is often omitted. The 的 phrase, thus, becomes a noun clause.

上个月，我哥哥，弟弟各买了一辆新车；**哥哥买的**是日本车；**弟弟买的**是
美国车。

*Shàng ge yuè, wǒ gēge, dìdi gè mǎi le yí liàng xīn chē; gēge mǎi de shì Rìběn chē; dìdi mǎi
de shì Měiguó chē.*

Last month, my older brother and my younger brother each bought a new car; what
my older brother bought was a Japanese car; what my younger brother bought was
an American car.

王：你的中文老师姓什么？

Wáng: Nǐde Zhōngwén lǎoshī xìng shénme?

李：我有两个中文老师；**教语法的**姓白；**教会话的**姓丁。

Lǐ: Wǒ yǒu liǎng ge Zhōngwén lǎoshī; jiāo yǔfǎ de xìng Bái; jiāo huìhuà de xìng Dīng.

Wang: What is the last name of your Chinese teacher?

Li: I have two Chinese teachers. The one who teaches grammar is (last name is) Bai;
the one who teaches conversation is (last name is) Ding.

昨天的舞会，没有**吃的**，没有**喝的**，真没有意思。

Zuótiān de wǔhuì, méiyǒu chī de, méiyǒu hē de, zhēn méiyǒu yìsi.

At yesterday's dance party, there was no **food** and there were no **drinks**; it was really
boring.

(b) Another type of noun clause

There is another type of noun clause, whose surface structure looks identical to that of a
'relative clause + noun'. However, unlike a relative clause, this type of clause does not function
as an adjective, but serves to provide the 'content' of the noun.

👁 In English, the conjunction 'that' is used to connect the clause with the noun.

女人结了婚就应该待在家里**的**观念早就过时了。

Nǚrén jié le hūn jiù yīnggāi dāi zài jiā lǐ de guānniàn zǎo jiù guòshí le.

The concept **that** women should stay home once they are married has long been
outdated.

李先生马上就要当上总裁**的**消息还没有正式发布呢。

Lǐ xiānsheng mǎshàng jiùyào dāng shàng zǒngcái de xiāoxí hái méiyǒu zhèngshì fābù ne.

The news **that** Mr Li will soon be promoted to CEO has not been officially announced.

- 的 in a relative clause is not omissible, but 的 in the above-mentioned noun clause can be
  omitted if '那/这 + measure word' is used

女人结了婚就应该待在家里(的)**这个**观念早就过时了。

Nǚrén jié le hūn jiù yīnggāi dāi zài jiā lǐ (de) zhè ge guānniàn zǎojiù guòshí le.

The concept **that** woman should stay home once they are married has long been
outdated.

Compare: 结了婚**的**女人还是可以有自己的事业。(的 in 结了婚的女人
　　　　　is not omissible.)
　　　　　Jié le hūn de nǚrén háishì kěyǐ yǒu zìjǐ de shìyè.
　　　　　Married women (women **who** are married) can still have
　　　　　professional careers.

李先生马上就要当上总裁(的)**这个**消息还没有正式发布呢。

*Lǐ xiānsheng mǎshàng jiùyào dāng shàng zǒngcái (de) zhè ge xiāoxí hái méiyǒu zhèngshì
fābù ne.*

The news **that** Mr Li will soon be promoted to CEO has not been officially announced.

Compare:　　上星期当上总裁**的**那位先生姓什么？(的 is not omissible.)

Shàng xīngqī dāng shàng zǒng cái de nà wèi xiānsheng xìng shénme?

What is the last name of the gentleman **who** was promoted to CEO last week?

Level 2

4.5 When 的 is not used

(a) 'Belonging' not 'owning'

When one 'belongs to' a group or an organization but does not 'own' it, 的 is not used, and the plural form of a personal pronoun (你们, 我们, 他们) is used, although the possessive case is used in such an expression in English. For example, 我们家 (= 我家), 我们国家, 他们班, 你们学校.

我们国家的足球队又输了。

Wǒmen guójiā de zúqiú duì yòu shū le.

The football team of **our country** lost again.

他们班只有男生，没有女生。

Tāmen bān zhǐ yǒu nánshēng, méiyǒu nǚshēng.

There are only male students in their class; there are no female students.

你们学校对面有一家书店，对不对？

Nǐmen xuéxiào duìmiàn yǒu yì jiā shūdiàn, duì bú duì?

There is a bookshop across from your school; is that right?

(b) 'Disyllabic adjective + noun' without 的

Certain words may appear to be 'disyllabic adjective + noun' without 的 after the adjective. This is because they are considered to be one word, not two words. Examples: 年轻人 (*niánqīng rén*: 'youth; young person'), 古典音乐 (*gǔdiǎn yīnyuè*: 'classical music'); 流行歌曲 (*liúxíng gēqǔ*: 'pop songs'), etc.

(c) When attributive is a noun

When the attributive is a noun, 的 frequently is not used. This is because it is considered to be one word, not two words. Examples: 汉英词典 (*Hàn Yīng cídiǎn*: 'Chinese–English dictionary'), 日本车 (*Rìběn chē*: 'Japanese car'), 法国菜 (*Fǎguó cài*: 'French food'), 女权主义 (*nǚquán zhǔyì*: 'feminism').

(d) More than one 的

Given the various functions of 的, it is not unusual to find several 的 in one sentence. In this case, one can omit some of them to make the speech flow more smoothly.

Some general rules for this type of omission are: (i) 的 in a relative clause should not be omitted, (ii) 的 after a disyllabic adjective should not be omitted, (iii) 的 indicating possession can be omitted if necessary, and (iv) when more than one 的 is used to connect a series of nouns, the one that is closest to the beginning of the sentence is generally omitted first.

我(的)[iii] 那个漂亮的[ii] 同屋是我(的)[iv] 男朋友(的)[iv] 弟弟的女朋友。

Wǒ(de) nà ge piàoliàng de tóngwū shì wǒ(de) nán péngyǒu (de) dìdi de nǚ péngyǒu.

That pretty roommate of mine is the girlfriend of my boyfriend's younger brother.

现在在跟王先生跳舞的[i] 那个漂亮的[ii] 女孩是李老师(的)[iv] 妹妹的同屋。

Xiànzài zài gēn Wáng xiānsheng tiàowǔ de nà ge piàoliàng de nǚhái shì Lǐ lǎoshī (de) mèimei de tóngwū.

The pretty girl (who is) dancing with Mr Wang is the roommate of Teacher Li's younger sister.

Exercises

Insert 的 into the following sentences. The number in parentheses indicates the number of times that 的 will be used. If 的 could be optional, the optional one(s) should be omitted.

Example   我女朋友爸爸有一家很大公司。（2）

Answer   我女朋友**的**爸爸有一家很大**的**公司。
Wǒ nǚ péngyǒu de bàba yǒu yì jiā hěn dà de gōngsī.
My girlfriend's father has a very big company.

Level
2

1   我有很多喜欢听古典音乐朋友。（1）
I have many friends who like classical music.

2   这么可爱小男孩，是你儿子吗？（1）
Such a cute little boy! Is he your son?

3   你看，这就是我上星期买新车。（1）
Look! This is the new car I bought last week.

4   这是谁日本车？是新还是二手？（3）
Whose Japanese car is this? Is it new or second-hand?

5   今年爸爸送我生日礼物是一辆新车。（1）
The birthday present my father gave me this year was a new car.

Level
3

6   我听说那家新开书店有很多从日本来杂志。（2）
I heard that that newly opened bookstore has many magazines from Japan.

7   张：昨天我去看了了一个很好看中国电影。（1）
李：是不是老师上星期给我们介绍那个？（1）
Zhang: Yesterday I went to see a very good Chinese movie.
Li: Was is the one that our teacher recommended last week?

8   王太太：昨天我儿子在家办了一个非常大舞会。（1）
李太太：哦，是吗？来人多不多？（1）
王太太：相当多。都是他在学校认识年轻人。（1）
Mrs Wang: Yesterday my son had a very big dance party at home.
Mrs Li: Oh, is that so? Were there many people who came?
Mrs Wang: Quite a lot. They were all young people he knows from school.

9 丁：你看，我买了一本王老师写语法书。（1）

李：我也买了一本王老师书。可是，我买是他写一本小说。（3）

Ding: Look! I bought a grammar book by Teacher Wang.

Li: I also bought a book by Teacher Wang. But what I bought was a novel he wrote.

10 妹妹昨天买那条裙子颜色不好看。（1）

The colour of the skirt my younger sister bought yesterday is not pretty.

11 二十一世纪中国人已经没有"重男轻女"观念了。（2）

Chinese people of the 21st century do not have the concept of 'valuing boys and thinking little of girls' anymore.

5 Position words

5.1 Position words

边、面 (biān, miàn)	前边、前面 Front	后边、后面 Back	上边、上面 Top; above	下边、下面 Below, beneath	里边、里面 Inside	外边、外面 Outside
边 only	左边 Left side	右边 Right side	旁边 Side; around			
Without 边	中间 Between; middle	对面 The other side; across from				

* In casual speech, 头 (tóu) can replace 边/面 in 前/后/上/下/里/外.

5.2 The use of 在, 有, 是 and position words

☞ See Chapter 3 for more information on the use of 在, 有 and 是.

- 在: location

    我家在银行和花店(的)中间。
    Wǒ jiā zài yínháng hé huādiàn (de) zhōngjiān.
    My house is (located) between the bank and the flower shop.

- 有: existence

    卧室(的)里边有一张床、一张书桌，没有椅子。
    Wòshì (de) lǐbiān yǒu yì zhāng chuáng, yì zhāng shūzhuō, méiyǒu yǐzi.
    There is a bed and a desk inside the bedroom; there is no chair.

- 是: identification

    客厅(的)旁边是不是厨房？
    Kètīng (de) pángbiān shì bú shì chúfáng?
    Is it the kitchen next to the living room?

5.3 Word order

The following explains the relationship in terms of word order between position words and nouns/pronouns.

(a) Focus on the position word

When the focus is the position word, the noun/pronoun appears first. The 的 between the noun/pronoun and the position word is optional, and is, in fact, frequently omitted.

我家(的)　　　前边　　　是一个小花园，　　花园(的)　　里边　　有很多花。
Wǒ jiā (de)　　qiánbiān　　shì yí ge　　　　huāyuán (de)　lǐbiān　　yǒu hěn
　　　　　　　　　　　　　　xiǎo huāyuán,　　　　　　　　　　　　　duō huā.
　　　　　　　　　↓　　　　　　　　　　　　　　　　　　　　↓
　　　　　　　focus　　　　　　　　　　　　　　　　　　　focus

In front of my house is a small garden; there are many flowers in(side) the garden.

我的卧室在书房(的)　　　左边，　　卧室(的)　　里边　　有一张大书桌，
Wǒde wòshì　　　　　　zuǒbiān,　wòshì (de)　lǐbiān　yǒu yì zhāng
zài shūfáng (de)　　　　　　　　　　　　　　　　　dà shūzhuō,
　　　　　　　　　　　↓　　　　　　　　　↓
　　　　　　　　　focus　　　　　　　focus

书桌(的)　　　上边　　　总是有几本书。
shūzhuō (de)　shàngbiān　zǒngshì yǒu jǐ běn shū.
　　　　　　　↓
　　　　　focus

My bedroom is to the left of the study; inside the bedroom, there is a big desk; there are always a few books on top of the desk.

(b) Focus on the noun

When the focus is the noun, the position word appears first. The 的 between the noun and the position word is not optional. A pronoun (你, 我, 他, 这儿, 那儿, etc.) rarely follows a position word.

王：我们去对面的　　　　　咖啡馆　　喝咖啡，怎么样？
Wáng: Wǒmen qù duìmiàn de　kāfēiguǎn　hē kāfēi, zěnmeyàng?
　　　　　　　　　　　　　↓
　　　　　　　　　　　　focus
李：对面有两家店，都有咖啡；我们去哪家？
Lǐ: Duìmiàn yǒu liǎng jiā diàn, dōu yǒu kāfēi; wǒmen qù nǎ jiā?
王：
左边的　　　茶馆　　有茶，也有咖啡；　右边的　　　咖啡馆　　有咖啡，也有啤酒。
Wáng:
Zuǒbiān de　cháguǎn　yǒu chá, yě yǒu kāfēi;　yòubiān de　kāfēiguǎn　yǒu kāfēi, yě yǒu píjiǔ.
　　↓　　　　　　　　　　　　　　　　　　　　↓
　focus　　　　　　　　　　　　　　　　　　focus
李：太好了！今天我想喝啤酒。我们去右边的那家吧。
Lǐ: Tài hǎo le! Jīntiān wǒ xiǎng hē píjiǔ. Wǒmen qù yòubiān de nà jiā ba.
Wang: How about going to the coffee shop across from here to have some coffee?
Li: There are two shops across from here. Which one shall we go to?
Wang: The tea shop on the left has tea and they also have coffee; the coffee shop on the right has coffee and they also have beer.
Li: Great! I feel like drinking beer today. Let's go to the one on the right.

(c) Focus on '这/那 + noun'

When the focus is the noun and 这 or 那 precedes the noun, the 的 between the position word and the noun becomes optional.

银行(的)对面有两家花店；左边(的)那家花多，右边(的)那家价钱便宜，所以两家的顾客都很多。

Yínháng (de) duìmiàn yǒu liǎng jiā huādiàn; zuǒbiān (de) nà jiā huā duō, yòubiān (de) nà jiā jiàqián piányí, suǒyǐ liǎng jiā de gùkè dōu hěn duō.
There are two flower shops across from the bank; the one on the left has more flowers; the one on the right has cheaper prices; therefore, both shops have many customers.

(d) General rule: Focus comes last

👁 It is not unusual to have 'noun/pronoun + position word + 的 + noun'. The general rule is: The expression starts with the information that is furthest away and the focus comes last. Therefore, the Chinese word order is a reverse of the English word order.

Example: the French restaurant on the left side of the bank
(The French restaurant is the focus; the bank is the information that is furthest away.)

银行旁边的	法国餐馆	or	银行旁边	那家法国餐馆
yínháng pángbiān de	*Fǎguó cānguǎn*	or	*yínháng pángbiān*	*nà jiā Fǎguó cānguǎn*
	↓			↓
	focus			focus

(e) Omission of the noun

The noun after 的 can be omitted if the context is clear.

房间里面有三张床；**左边的**是哥哥的，**右边的**是弟弟的，**中间的**是我的。
Fángjiān lǐmiàn yǒu sān zhāng chuáng; zuǒbiān de shì gēge de, yòubiān de shì dìdi de, zhōngjiān de shì wǒde.
There are three beds in(side) the bedroom. The one on the left is my older brother's; the one on the right is my younger brother's; the one in the middle is mine.

(f) When 边/面/头 is optional

When the position word 前边, 后边, 上边, 下边, 里边, 外边 or 旁边 is the focus, the character 边/面/头 can be optional. In this case, what precedes the position word must be a regular noun, not a pronoun or a measure word. Also, 的 must be omitted.

桌子(的)上边 = 桌子上 = 桌上
zhuōzi (de) shàngbiān = zhuōzi shàng = zhuō shàng
on (top of) the table

厨房(的)里边 = 厨房里
chúfáng (de) lǐbiān = chúfáng lǐ
in(side) the kitchen

教室(的)旁边 = 教室旁
jiàoshì (de) pángbiān = jiàoshì páng
next to the classroom

他(的)旁边有一张桌子。
Tā(de) pángbiān yǒu yì zhāng zhuōzi.
There is a table next to him.
(他旁有一张桌子 would be incorrect since 他 is a pronoun.)

那个图书馆里有一间杂志阅览室，这个里边也有一间。
Nà ge túshūguǎn lǐ yǒu yì jiān zázhì yuèlǎnshì, zhè ge lǐbiān yě yǒu yì jiān.
There is a magazine room inside that library; there is also one inside this (library).
(这个里也有一间 would be incorrect since 个 is a measure word.)

(g) Compass points

There is another group of position words (东, 西, 南, 北) whose meanings vary depending on the suffixes. The suffixes can be either 边, 方 or 部.

太阳每天从东边出来, 从西边下去。
Tàiyáng měi tiān cóng dōngbiān chūlái, cóng xībiān xiàqù.
The sun rises (comes out) in the east every day and sets (goes down) in the west.

美国(的)东边是大西洋, 西边是太平洋。
Měiguó de dōngbiān shì Dàxīyáng, xībiān shì Tàipíngyáng.
To the east of the USA is the Atlantic Ocean; to the west is the Pacific Ocean.

张先生是南方人, 李先生是北方人; 所以他们的口音不一样。
Zhāng xiānsheng shì nánfāng rén, Lǐ xiānsheng shì běifāng rén; suǒyǐ tāmen de kǒuyīn bù yíyàng.
Mr Zhang is a southerner; Mr Li is a northerner; therefore, their accents are different.

东方人跟西方人(的)文化, 思想都很不一样。
Dōngfāng rén gēn Xīfāng rén (de) wénhuà, sīxiǎng dōu hěn bù yíyàng.
Oriental people and Occidental (Western) people are different in culture and thought.

这个国家东部是海岸, 西部是高山。
Zhè ge guójiā dōngbù shì hǎiàn, xībù shì gāoshān.
The eastern part of the country is coast; the western part is high mountains.

(h) When 里 is not used

A proper noun indicating a place does not need 里 in a sentence with 在. Other nouns indicating a place may or may not need 里 in such a sentence, depending on whether the place has a well-defined boundary or not. (Normally 里 is used when there is a clear boundary.)

他现在在中国学中文。
Tā xiànzài zài Zhōngguó xué Zhōngwén.
He is studying Chinese in China now.
(Incorrect: 他现在在中国里学中文。)

我女儿在北京工作。
Wǒ nǚ'ér zài Běijīng gōngzuò.
My daughter works in Beijing.
(Incorrect: 我女儿在北京里工作。)

我妈妈现在没有工作, 她在家(里)给人看孩子。
Wǒ māma xiànzài méiyǒu gōngzuò, tā zài jiā (lǐ) gěi rén kān háizi.
My mother does not have a job now. She babysits for people at home.

妈妈在厨房(里)做饭, 爸爸在客厅(里)看电视, 弟弟在房间(里)写功课。
Māma zài chúfáng (lǐ) zuòfàn, bàba zài kètīng (lǐ) kàn diànshì, dìdi zài fángjiān (lǐ) xiě gōngke.
My mother is cooking in the kitchen; my father is watching TV in the living room; my younger brother is doing homework in the bedroom.

妈妈: 爸爸跟弟弟回家了吗?
Māma: Bàba gēn dìdi huí jiā le ma?
女儿: 没有, 爸爸还在办公室, 弟弟还在学校呢!
Nǚ'er: Méiyǒu, bàba hái zài bàngōngshì, dìdi hái zài xuéxiào ne!
Mother: Have your father and younger brother come home?
Daughter: No. Father is still at the office, and younger brother is still at school.

Exercises

Rearrange the words or phrases to form complete sentences.

Level
1

1 There is a bank between the coffee shop and the flower shop.

有　银行　一家　中间　咖啡馆　花店　跟

2 There are three houses on this road. The one in the middle is my home.

这条路　中间　我家　上　有　是　那个　房子　三个

3 The student dormitory is between the library and the bookshop.

学生　中间　跟　图书馆　宿舍　的　在　书店

4 There are two books on the table. The one on top is mine.

桌子　两本　上　有　书　上面　我的　是　那本

5 **(a)** There are two coffee shops across from the student dormitory.

两家　宿舍　咖啡馆　有　对面　学生

(b) I work at the one on the right.

工作　我　那家　在　右边

Level
2

6 **(a)** There are three bedrooms in my house. Two are on the second floor.

卧房　二楼　有　在　我家　三个　两个

(b) The one on the first floor is mine.

那个　的　在　一楼　我的　是

(c) Next to my bedroom is a small kitchen. There is a dining table in the middle of the kitchen.

小厨房　中间　厨房　卧房　我的　一张　一个　旁边　是　有　饭桌

7 On the left side of my house is a flower shop; on the right is a bank.

右边　左边　我家　花店　银行　是 (twice)　一家 (twice)

8 The building next to the library is the student dormitory.

是　图书馆　大楼　的　宿舍　旁边　学生

9 There is a coffee shop inside the bookshop across from here.

里　对面　一个　那家　书店　咖啡馆　有

10 The coffee shop inside this bookshop also has tea.

茶　的　咖啡馆　有　书店　里面　也　这家

6 Prepositional constructions

Many prepositions in Chinese share similarities with verbs or can be used as verbs; therefore, they are also referred to as 'coverbs' by some grammarians. This chapter will adopt the term 'preposition'.

A preposition together with the object (a noun or a pronoun) that follows it forms a prepositional phrase. The following shows the basic word-order rules of a sentence with a preposition.

In modern Chinese, a prepositional phrase is used before the verb. 👁 In English, a prepositional phrase normally appears after the verb.	我儿子在北京学中文。 *Wǒ érzi zài Běijīng xué Zhōngwén.* My son studied Chinese in Beijing. 他从图书馆走路回家。 *Tā cóng túshūguǎn zǒulù huí jiā.* He walked home from the library.
In formal usage, some prepositional phrases can appear after the verb.	我父母来自农村。 *Wǒ fùmǔ lái zì nóngcūn.* My parents come from farming villages.
Many disyllabic prepositional phrases appear at the beginning of the sentence.	根据天气预报，明天会下雨。 *Gēnjù tiānqì yùbào, míngtiān huì xià yǔ.* According to the weather forecast, it will rain tomorrow.
Some prepositions can be used as the complement of result; these prepositions appear after the verb.	这封信，请你交给他。 *Zhè fēng xìn, qǐng nǐ jiāo gěi tā.* Please hand this letter to him.

Level 1

6.1 Indicating location, direction, space, etc.

(a) 在 + location + verb

张：他爸爸妈妈**在哪里**工作？
Zhāng: Tā bàba māma zài nǎlǐ gōngzuò?
王：他爸爸**在银行**工作；他妈妈没有工作，她**在家**看孩子。
Wáng: Tā bàba zài yínháng gōngzuò; tā māma méiyǒu gōngzuò, tā zài jiā kān háizi.
Zhang: Where do his parents work?
Wang: His father works at a bank; his mother does not have a job; she cares for the children at home.

李：王先生的孩子都**在外国**留学吗？
Lǐ: Wáng xiānsheng de háizi dōu zài wàiguó liúxué ma?
丁：对，他儿子现在**在中国**学中文；女儿**在法国**学设计。
Dīng: Duì, Tā érzi xiànzài zài Zhōngguó xué Zhōngwén; nǚ'er zài Fǎguó xué shèjì.

Li: Are both Mr Wang's children studying in foreign countries?
Ding: That's right. His son is studying Chinese in China right now; his daughter is studying design in France.

👁 A prepositional phrase in English with the preposition 'at' or 'in' may not be a 在 phrase in Chinese. When the verb of the sentence does not show an activity, but is 是 or when the predicate is an adjective, a prepositional phrase is not used in Chinese.

English:	My mother is an English teacher **at** this school.
Chinese:	我妈妈是这个学校**的**英文老师。(是 is a verb that does not show an activity.)
	Wǒ māma shì zhè ge xuéxiào de Yīngwén lǎoshī.
Or:	我妈妈**在这个学校**当英文老师。(当 is a verb that shows an activity.)
	Wǒ māma zài zhè ge xuéxiào dāng Yīngwén lǎoshī.
English:	Business at this restaurant is good.
Chinese:	这家餐馆的生意很好。
	Zhè jiā cānguǎn de shēngyì hěn hǎo.
(Incorrect:	生意在这家餐馆很好。)

(b) 从 + location + verb

Note that 由 can replace 从 in more formal situations.

从我家骑车去图书馆只要十分钟。
Cóng wǒ jiā qí chē qù túshūguǎn zhǐ yào shí fēnzhōng.
It only takes ten minutes from my house to the library by bicycle.

他下个月要**从北京**搬到上海。
Tā xià ge yuè yào cóng Běijīng bān dào Shànghǎi.
He is going to move to Shanghai from Beijing next month.

(c) Forming location words

👁 In English, a non-location word can follow the preposition 'at' or 'from'; however, only words indicating locations can follow 在 or 从 in modern Chinese. Therefore, it is necessary to convert the non-location word into a location word to meet this grammar requirement.

The word 这儿/这里 or 那儿/那里 can be attached to a person to convert the person into a location. It should be noted that 的 is not used.

我们从**王老师那儿**学到了很多宝贵的知识。
Wǒmen cóng Wáng lǎoshī nàr xué dào le hěn duō bǎoguì de zhīshí.
We learned a lot of precious knowledge **from Teacher Wang**.

王：下星期的会，在**谁那儿**开？(Compare: 下星期的会在哪儿开？)
Wáng: Xià xīngqī de huì, zài shéi nàr kāi?
李：在**我们这儿**开吧。
Lǐ: Zài wǒmen zhèr kāi ba.
Wang: At whose place will the meeting be held next week? (Where will the meeting be held next week?)
Li: Why don't we have it at our place?

The word 身上 is frequently used to convert a person into a location. 的 is optional in this case.

王立的爸妈在他(的)身上放了很多责任跟压力。
Wáng Lì de bàmā zài tā(de) shēnshàng fàng le hěn duō zérèn gēn yālì.
Wang Li's parents placed a lot of responsibility and pressure on him.

(d) 往/向 + direction + verb

Note that 往 can be pronounced *wǎng* or *wàng*. 向 and 往 are often interchangeable.

外地人：请问，去邮局怎么走？
Wàidì rén: Qǐng wèn, qù yóujú zěnme zǒu?
本地人：你先**往前**走两、三分钟，再**往右拐**，就到了。
Běndì rén: Nǐ xiān wǎng qián zǒu liǎng, sān fēnzhōng, zài wǎng yòu guǎi, jiù dào le.
Out-of-towner: Excuse me, how do I get to the post office?
Local person: Go straight ahead for two or three minutes, turn right, and you will be there.

他**往屋子里**看了半天，没看到一个人。
Tā wǎng wūzi lǐ kàn le bàntiān, méi kàndào yí ge rén.
He looked (towards) inside the house for quite a while and didn't see anybody.

(e) 朝 + direction + verb

The direction used in this structure is usually 东, 西, 南, 北, 上 or 下.

他**朝南**走了半个小时才发现方向错了，所以又回头**朝北**走。
Tā cháo nán zǒu le bàn ge xiǎoshí cái fāxiàn fāngxiàng cuò le, suǒyǐ yòu huítóu cháo běi zǒu.
He walked (towards) south for half an hour and finally realized the direction was wrong, so he turned back and walk (towards) north.

(f) Verb + 自 + location

This structure is more formal, and the verb appears before the prepositional phrase. 自 means 'from' and the verb is frequently 来, 出 or 发.

今天我想说几句**发自**(or **出自**)**内心**的话。
Jīntiān wǒ xiǎng shuō jǐ jù fā zì (chū zì) nèixīn de huà.
Today I want to say a few words that come from deep in my heart.

我爸妈都**来自农村**，没有受过教育。
Wǒ bàmā dōu lái zì nóngcūn, méiyǒu shòu guo jiàoyù.
My parents both come from agricultural villages; they never had any education.

6.2 Indicating time

(a) 从 + time + verb

Note that 自 sometimes replaces 从 in more formal situations.

他每天**从早**忙到晚，很少休息。
Tā měi tiān cóng zǎo máng dào wǎn, hěnshǎo xiūxí.
Every day, he is busy from morning until night; he rarely takes a break.

这个电影**从两点**演到五点，真太长了。
Zhè ge diànyǐng cóng liǎng diǎn yǎn dào wǔ diǎn, zhēn tài cháng le.
This movies runs from 2 o'clock until 5 o'clock; it's really too long.

小王跟小李从小(= 自小)一起长大。
Xiǎo Wáng gēn Xiǎo Lǐ cóng xiǎo (= zì xiǎo) yìqǐ zhǎngdà.
Xiao Wang and Xiao Li grew up together since childhood.

(b) 在 + time + verb

It is usually not necessary to have 在 before a time phrase; however, 在 is used when a word such as 要, 想, 会 or 将 precedes the time phrase. 要, 想, 会 or 将 is used to indicate that the event or action will take place in the future.

Note that 于 (*yú*) can replace 在 in more formal situations.

我下星期五要在法院结婚；我们**将在星期六**请客。 (Because of 将, 在 is used before 星期六.)
Wǒ xià xīngqī wǔ yào zài fǎyuàn jiéhūn; wǒmen jiāng zài xīngqī liù qǐngkè.
I am getting married next Friday at the court house; we will have a reception on Saturday.
(Compare: 我们下星期五结婚，星期六请客。)

老师**会在明天上课的时候**告诉我们下次考试的重点。
Lǎoshī huì zài míngtiān shàng kè de shíhòu gàosù wǒmen xià cì kǎoshì de zhòngdiǎn.
The teacher will tell us the focus of the next test during class time tomorrow.
(Compare: 明天上课的时候，老师会告诉我们下次考试的重点。)

Level 2

6.3 Indicating target, object or interaction

(a) 跟 + person + verb

彼得很喜欢**跟他的中国朋友**练习说中文。
Bǐdé hěn xǐhuān gēn tāde Zhōngguó péngyǒu liànxí shuō Zhōngwén.
Peter likes to practise speaking Chinese with his Chinese friends.

王：请问会议室在哪里？
Wáng: Qǐng wèn huìyìshì zài nǎlǐ?
张：请**跟我**来。
Zhāng: Qǐng gēn wǒ lái.
Wang: Excuse me, where is the meeting room?
Zhang: Please come with me.

(b) 给 + person/object + verb

- Meaning 'for', indicating the action is a service or an act of kindness (为 can replace 给 in a more formal situation)

小王来了，你快去**给他**开门。
Xiǎo Wáng lái le, nǐ kuài qù gěi tā kāimén.
Xiao Wang is here. Hurry and go open the door for him.

我要去书店**给我妹妹**买两本书。
Wǒ yào qù shūdiàn gěi wǒ mèimei mǎi liǎng běn shū.
I am going to the bookshop to buy two books for my younger sister. (This can either mean an act of service – going to the bookshop for her – or an act of kindness – buying the books as gifts for her.)

如果你们选我当市长，我一定努力地**为你们**服务。
Rúguǒ nǐmen xuǎn wǒ dāng shìzhǎng, wǒ yídìng nǔlì de wèi nǐmen fúwù.
If you elect me to be mayor, I will definitely serve you (work for you) diligently.

- Meaning 'to', indicating the person is the target or recipient of the action (为 cannot be used to replace 给)

  我常**给家人**发短信，但是不常**给他们**打电话。
  Wǒ cháng gěi jiā rén fā duǎnxìn, dànshì bù cháng gěi tāmen dǎ diànhuà.
  I often send text messages to my family, but I don't often call them.

(c) 对 + person/object + verb/adjective

你**对历史**、**文学**有没有兴趣？
Nǐ duì lìshǐ, wénxué yǒu méiyǒu xìngqù?
Are you interested in history or literature?

他**对朋友**很大方。
Tā duì péngyǒu hěn dàfāng.
He is generous to his friends.

他**对你**说了些什么？快告诉我。
Tā duì nǐ shuō le xiē shénme? Kuài gàosù wǒ.
What did he say to you? Tell me quickly.

(d) 为 + noun/pronoun + verb

- Meaning 'for/for the sake of' (为 can be replaced by 为了)

  妈妈**为(了)我们**牺牲了她的一辈子。
  Māma wèi(le) wǒmen xīshēng le tāde yíbèizi.
  Mother has sacrificed her whole life for us.

  弟弟功课不好，爸妈**为他的将来**担心得要命。
  Dìdi gōngkè bù hǎo, bàmā wèi tāde jiānglái dānxīn de yàomìng.
  My younger brother's grades in school are bad; my parents worry about his future a lot.

- When a verb follows the preposition, only 为了 'in order to' can be used.

  他**为了**赚零用钱，去餐厅找了一份洗碗的工作。 (赚 is a verb; 为赚零用钱 would be improper.)
  Tā wèile zhuàn língyòngqián, qù cāntīng zhǎo le yí fèn xǐ wǎn de gōngzuò.
  He went to a restaurant to get a dishwasher's job in order to make some pocket money.

- Meaning 'on behalf of/in place of' (can be replaced by 替 in less formal situations)

  别担心，该办的手续，他都**为你**办好了。
  Bié dānxīn, gāi bàn de shǒuxù, tā dōu wèi nǐ bàn hǎo le.
  Don't worry. He has taken care of all the necessary paperwork for you.

(e) 替 + noun/pronoun + verb

替 can be replaced by 帮 in very casual speech.

为什么我跟她吵架的时候，你总是**替她**说话？
Wèishénme wǒ gēn tā chǎojià de shíhòu, nǐ zǒngshì tì tā shuōhuà?
Why do you always speak for her (meaning: take her side) when I argue with her?

今天我没空，你**替我**去邮局拿包裹，好不好？
Jīntiān wǒ méi kòng, nǐ tì wǒ qù yóujú ná bāoguǒ, hǎo bù hǎo?
I don't have time today. Could you go to the post office to pick up the parcel for me?

Level 2

6.4 Other commonly used prepositions

(a) 用 + noun/pronoun (indicating a tool) + verb

中国人**用筷子**吃饭。
Zhōngguó rén yòng kuàizi chī fàn.
Chinese people eat with chopsticks.

上中文课的时候，老师常常**用中文**问我们问题。
Shàng Zhōngwén kè de shíhòu, lǎoshī chángcháng yòng Zhōngwén wèn wǒmen wèntí.
Our teacher often asks us questions in Chinese during class.

(b) 依, 照, 按 + noun (indicating a rule/policy/advice) + verb

不**按规定**办事的人会被处罚。
Bú àn guīdìng bànshì de rén huì bèi chǔfá.
People who do not handle business according to regulations will be punished.

(c) 靠 + noun (indicating resources/support) + verb

我们学校每年都有很多**靠奖学金**来留学的外国学生。
Wǒmen xuéxiào měi nián dōu yǒu hěn duō kào jiǎngxuéjīn lái liúxué de wàiguó xuéshēng.
Every year, there are many foreign students who come to study at our school on scholarships.

Level 2

6.5 Disyllabic prepositions

(a) Compared to monosyllabic counterparts

Although they are similar in meaning and usage to their monosyllabic counterparts, disyllabic prepositions frequently appear at the beginning of a sentence. In this case, a comma often follows the prepositional phrase.

- 对于 and 对

  我**对(于)你的建议**不感兴趣。 or **对于你的建议**，我不感兴趣。
  Wǒ duìyú nǐde jiànyì bù gǎn xìngqù.
  I am not interested in your suggestions.

- 为了 and 为

  他**为(了)儿女**操劳了一辈子。 or **为了儿女**，他操劳了一辈子。
  Tā wèile érnǚ cāoláo le yíbèizi.
  For the sake of his children, he has worked exhaustedly all his life.

- 跟着 and 跟

  我们**跟(着)王老师**访问了不少农村。 or **跟着王老师**，我们访问了不少农村。
  Wǒmen gēnzhe Wáng lǎoshī fǎngwèn le bùshǎo nóngcūn.
  We visited many agricultural villages with Teacher Wang.

- 根据 and 据: 'according to; based on'

  根据天气预报，今天应该不会下雨。
  Gēnjù tiānqì yùbào, jīntiān yīnggāi bú huì xiàyǔ.
  According to yesterday's weather forecast, it should not rain today.

那位作家**根据历史事实**写了一部小说。
Nà wèi zuòjiā gēnjù lìshǐ shìshí xiě le yí bù xiǎoshuō.
The author wrote a novel according to historical facts.

- 按照 and 按: 'according to' (regulations, rules, policy)

守法的老百姓每年都**按(照)**政府规定缴税。
Shǒufǎ de lǎobǎixìng měi nián dōu àn (zhào) zhèngfǔ guīdìng jiǎoshuì.
Law-abiding citizens pay taxes every year according to government regulations.

(b) The use of disyllabic prepositions

These disyllabic prepositions normally appear at the beginning of a sentence. Their functions are similar to those of conjunctions or to serve as transitions in communication. The following is a list of such disyllabic prepositions that are commonly used.

- 关于: to bring up a new topic

关于我们上次讨论的那件事，我已经做了决定了。
Guānyú wǒmen shàngcì tǎolùn de nà jiàn shì, wǒ yǐjīng zuò le juédìng le.
Regarding the matter we discussed last time, I have already made a decision.

- 至于: to bring up another topic (that already exists in context)

你说的那两件事，第一件，我赞成；**至于**第二件，我还要考虑一下。
Nǐ shuō de nà liǎng jiàn shì, dì yī jiàn, wǒ zànchéng; zhìyú dì èr jiàn, wǒ hái yào kǎolǜ yíxià.
About those two matters you mentioned, I support the first one; as to the second, I still need to think about it.

- 由于: to introduce a reason

Since 由于 is similar in meaning and usage to 因为, it can be followed by a complete sentence. In this case, it functions as a conjunction, not a preposition.

☞ See Chapter 29 for more on conjunctive pairs.

由于各种因素，原来的计划取消了。(由于 is a preposition.)
Yóuyú gèzhǒng yīnsù, yuánlái de jìhuà qǔxiāo le.
Due to all kinds of factors, the original plan has been cancelled.

由于老师病了，**因此**我们今天没有上课。(由于 and 因此 are a conjunctive pair.)
Yóuyú lǎoshī bìng le, yīncǐ wǒmen jīntiān méiyǒu shàngkè.
Because the teacher was sick, we didn't have class today.

Level 2

6.6 Complements of result

A prepositional phrase that appears after a verb is a complement of the verb.

☞ See 21.5 for more on prepositions used after the verb.

(a) Verb + 在 + location

他把我的书**放在桌子**上。
Tā bǎ wǒde shū fàng zài zhuōzi shàng.
He put my book on the table.

我的车，你**停在哪里**了？
Wǒde chē, nǐ tíng zài nǎlǐ le?
Where did you park my car?

(b) Verb + 往 + location (destination)

这班飞机是**飞往伦敦**的。
Zhè bān fēijī shì fēi wǎng Lúndūn de.
This flight is bound for London.

(c) Verb + 给 + person

请把这封信**交给他**。
Qǐng bǎ zhè fēng xìn jiāo gěi tā.
Please hand this letter to him.

那辆日本车，他已经**卖给我**了。
Nà liàng Rìběn chē, tā yǐjīng mài gěi wǒ le.
He already sold that Japanese car to me.

Level
2

6.7 More than one prepositional phrase: Word order

It is not unusual to have more than one prepositional phrase in a sentence. The general rule is that a prepositional phrase indicating time precedes one indicating location.

王英**从小**就**在家**跟爸妈说中文，所以她中文说得不错。
Wáng Yīng cóngxiǎo jiù zài jiā gēn bàmā shuō Zhōngwén, suǒyǐ tā Zhōngwén shuō de búcuò.
Wang Ying has been speaking Chinese with her parents at home since childhood, so she speaks Chinese quite well.

王先生跟李小姐将**于下星期五在法院**结婚，他们并且会**在那天晚上在饭馆**请客。
Wáng xiānsheng gēn Lǐ xiǎojiě jiāng yú xià xīngqī wǔ zài fǎyuàn jiéhūn, tāmen bìngqiě huì zài nà tiān wǎnshàng zài fànguǎn qǐngkè.
Mr Wang and Miss Li will get married at the court house next Friday; they will also have a dinner celebration at a restaurant that evening.

Exercises

I   Fill in the blanks using the most appropriate preposition (在, 给, 从, 用 or 跟).

Level
1

1   今天晚上我没空，我要 _____ 家 _____ 我爸妈写信。

2   _____ 我家走路去图书馆要十五分钟。

3   彼得常常 _____ 他的中国朋友练习说中文。

4   我男朋友现在 _____ 中国学中文，昨天他 _____ 北京寄来几张照片。

5   那个人不是中国人吗？为什么我 _____ 中文 _____ 他说话，他不懂呢？

6   张：小王，你要去哪里？
    王：去 _____ 我女朋友买生日礼物；明天是她的生日。

7 我来中国以后，每天都 _____ 筷子吃饭，现在我已经习惯了。

8 我们 _____ 王老师那里学到很多有用的知识。

9 小王上课的时候常常 _____ 手机给他的朋友发短信。

10 上午我男朋友 _____ 我打电话，请我 _____ 他去公园玩，可是我告诉他，今天天气不好，我想 _____ 家看电视。

11 我 _____ 法国学中文，所以没有中国人 _____ 我练习说中文。昨天我的中文老师说，她下星期会 _____ 我介绍一个中国朋友，以后我可以常常 _____ 中文说话。

12 李明 _____ 咖啡馆工作。他每天下课以后，就 _____ 教室走路去咖啡馆工作。

II Fill in each blank, choosing the most appropriate preposition from those given in parentheses.

1 外地人：请问火车站在哪里？
本地人：你 _____ 前走，差不多五分钟就到了。(跟，对，往)

2 我 _____ 学习外语非常有兴趣，所以我会说日文跟法文。(对，为，向)

3 他 _____ 亲戚朋友借他的钱念完了大学。(按，靠，替)

4 我 _____ 他做了这么多事，他居然也没有说一声"谢谢"，真气人！(为，对，靠)

5 老王很不诚实，他 _____ 我说的话，我完全不相信。(为，对，替)

6 _____ 赚一些零用钱，我去一家中国餐馆当服务员。(对于，为了，根据)

7 _____ 你上次开会提出的问题，我们已经想到了一个解决的办法。(根据，关于，按照)

8 那位作家 _____ 他自己亲身的经历写了一篇很有名的短篇小说。(关于，根据，为了)

7 Imperative sentences and the use of 别

An imperative sentence is used to express a command, order or request, or to give a warning, suggestion or advice.

Level 1 ## 7.1 Imperative sentences with/without 你/你们

An imperative sentence in English rarely starts with the subject 'you' unless the speaker wants to adopt an emphatic tone. In Chinese, the omission of the subject 你 (*nǐ*) or 你们 (*nǐmen*) is optional. The presence or absence of 你 or 你们 has no effect on the tone adopted by the speaker.

> **你看**! 车来了。快跑。
> *Nǐ kàn! Chē lái le. Kuài pǎo.*
> Look! The bus is coming. Hurry and run.

> **听**! 好像有人在敲门。**你去**看看是谁。
> *Tīng! Hǎoxiàng yǒu rén zài qiāo mén. Nǐ qù kàn kàn shì shéi.*
> Listen! It sounds like someone is knocking on the door. Go take a look to see who it is.

When one gives different commands to more than one person, 你 is used in each command.

> 老王，**你**扫地；小张，**你**擦窗户；小李，**你**抹桌子。
> *Lǎo Wáng, nǐ sǎodì; Xiǎo Zhāng, nǐ cā chuānghù; Xiǎo Lǐ, nǐ mǒ zhuōzi.*
> Lao Wang, you sweep the floor; Xiao Zhang, you clean the windows; Xiao Li, you wipe the tables.

Level 1 ## 7.2 Imperative sentences with 请

请 (*qǐng*) can be used at the beginning of an imperative sentence to soften the tone of a command and make the speaker sound more polite or courteous.

Note that, in English, 'please' can appear at the end of the imperative sentence, whereas 请 cannot.

English:	Come in, please. Have a seat, please. Have some tea, please.
Chinese:	请进。请坐。请喝茶。
	Qǐng jìn. Qǐng zuò. Qǐng hē chá.
(Incorrect:	进，请。坐，请。喝茶，请。)

(a) 请你 vs. 你请

请 is also a verb, meaning 'to invite, to politely request'. When both 请 and 你 are used in an imperative sentence, '请你 + action' may have a different connotation from '你请 + action'.

你请 or 请你 can imply an invitation:

> 啊，王老师，您好！**您请**进来坐。……**请您**喝杯茶。
> *À, Wáng lǎoshī, nín hǎo! Nín qǐng jìnlái zuò. …… Qǐng nín hē bēi chá.*
> Ah, Teacher Wang, how are you! Please come in and have a seat. . . . Please have some tea.

When a command (but not an invitation) is given in a polite way, 你请 is not appropriate. Only 请你 is proper in this context:

> 王：**请你**给我去邮局买几张邮票。
> *Wáng: Qǐng nǐ gěi wǒ qù yóujú mǎi jǐ zhāng yóupiào.*
> 丁：好，不过**请你**先把买邮票的钱给我。
> *Dīng: Hǎo, búguò qǐng nǐ xiān bǎ mǎi yóupiào de qián gěi wǒ.*
> Wang: Please go to the post office and buy some stamps for me.
> Ding: OK. But please give me the money for the stamps first.

(b) 请你 = 麻烦你

When a command is given in a polite way, 麻烦你 can be used to replace 请你. 你 is not optional.

> **麻烦你**给我拿杯水来。
> *Máfán nǐ gěi wǒ ná bēi shuǐ lái.*
> Would you please fetch a glass of water for me?

7.3 Imperative sentences with 吧

Level 1

The modal particle 吧 can be used at the end of an imperative sentence to express a suggestion. An exclamation mark is frequently used.

> 饭做好了，来吃饭**吧**！
> *Fàn zuò hǎo le, lái chī fàn ba!*
> The meal is ready. Come and eat!

> 你有意见吗？现在就提出来**吧**！
> *Nǐ yǒu yìjiàn ma? Xiànzài jiù tí chūlái ba!*
> You have some opinions? Why don't you raise them now!

吧 can also be used to soften the tone of a command while making the sentence sound more casual than an imperative sentence with 请.

> 啊！老王，是你！好久不见！进来**吧**！
> *À! Lǎo Wáng, shì nǐ! Hǎo jiǔ bú jiàn! Jìn lái ba!*
> Ah, Lao Wang, it's you! Long time no see! Come in!

7.4 Suggestions with 吧

Level 1

An imperative sentence in English can begin with 'let's + verb'; its counterpart in Chinese does not, however, start with 让 (*ràng*: 'to let'). Instead, it is a suggestion with the modal particle 吧. 我们/咱们 is the subject of the sentence, which can be omitted if the context is clear.

> 老师来了！咱们进教室**吧**！
> *Lǎoshī lái le! Zánmen jìn jiàoshì ba!*
> The teacher is here. **Let's** go into the classroom.

明天星期六，一起去看场电影**吧**！
Míngtiān xīngqī liù, yìqǐ qù kàn chǎng diànyǐng ba!
Tomorrow is Saturday. **Let's** go see a movie together.

7.5 Suggestions or requests with 怎么样?/好不好?

An imperative sentence used to express a request or a suggestion is frequently followed by a tag question such as 怎么样? or 好不好?

你去邮局帮我寄封信，**好不好？** (Request)
Nǐ qù yóujú bāng wǒ jì fēng xìn, hǎo bù hǎo?
Go to the post office and mail a letter for me, OK?

晚上你有空吗？一起去看场电影，**怎么样？** (Suggestion)
Wǎnshàng nǐ yǒu kòng ma? Yìqǐ qù kàn chǎng diànyǐng, zěnmeyàng?
Are you free this evening? Let's go to a movie together, how's that?

7.6 Negative imperative sentences

别 is used in a negative imperative sentence to express 'don't'. 别 and 不要 are interchangeable in this case. In this chapter, only 别 will be used.

请别把我的秘密告诉别人。
Qǐng bié bǎ wǒde mìmì gàosù biérén.
Please don't tell others my secret.

老王不是好人；**别**跟他交朋友。
Lǎo Wáng bú shì hǎo rén; bié gēn tā jiāo péngyǒu.
Lao Wang is not a good person; don't be friends with him.

(a) Negative imperative sentences with/without 你/你们

If 你/你们 is used in a negative imperative sentence, it always appears before 别.

你们别相信他说的话；他常说谎。
Nǐmen bié xiāngxìn tā shuō de huà; tā cháng shuōhuǎng.
Don't believe what he says; he often lies.

你别光在那里坐着，过来帮忙。
Nǐ bié guāng zài nàlǐ zuò zhe, guòlái bāngmáng.
Don't just sit over there. Come over here and help.

(b) Negative imperative sentences with 你/你们 and 请

If 请 and 你/你们 are both used in a negative imperative sentence, 请 normally appears before 你/你们.

请你们别说话，别人在看书呢。
Qǐng nǐmen bié shuō huà, biérén zài kànshū ne.
Please don't talk. Other people are reading.

7.7 Adjectives and imperative sentences

(a) Adjectives in negative imperative sentences

An adjective/adjectival phrase can appear after 别.

别难过，他不是在批评你。
Bié nánguò, tā bú shì zài pīpíng nǐ.
Don't be (so) sad. He wasn't criticizing you.

别那么高兴，比赛还没有结束呢！
Bié nàme gāoxìng, bǐsài hái méiyǒu jiéshù ne!
Don't be so happy. The game is not over yet.

(b) Lone adjectives in positive imperative sentences

An adjective alone rarely appears in a positive imperative sentence unless it is used to issue a warning. In this case, an exclamation mark is necessary:

- Seeing that someone is about to step in front of a moving car, you say: 小心！(*Xiǎoxīn*: 'Careful!')

- To sternly quiet down a noisy group, one might loudly say: 安静！(*Ānjìng*: 'Quiet!')

(c) 'Adjective + 一点' in positive imperative sentences

'Adjective + 一点' can form a positive imperative sentence. Such an imperative sentence is usually used to urge the listener to make changes or improve.

快一点，大家都在等你一个人呢！
Kuài yìdiǎn, dàjiā dōu zài děng nǐ yí ge rén ne!
Hurry up. Everybody's waiting for you.

马虎一点吧！不必那么严格。
Mǎhū yìdiǎn ba! Búbì nàme yán'gé.
Be a little bit sloppier. There is no need to be so strict.

(d) '不 + adjective' in negative imperative sentences

'不 + adjective' can be in a negative imperative sentence, but not in a positive one.

别不识相，他不欢迎咱们，咱们走吧！
Bié bú shíxiàng, tā bù huānyíng zánmen, zánmen zǒu ba!
Don't be clueless. We are not welcome here. Let's go.

别不好意思，上来表演一下吧！
Bié bù hǎo yìsi, shànglái biǎoyǎn yíxià ba!
Don't be shy. Come up here and perform (a song, a dance, etc.)!

7.8 别……了

Level 2

In this case, 了 has two different meanings.

(a) Indicating a change of situation

Used to urge or order the listener(s) to stop doing something, 了 here indicates a change of situation.

他已经向你道歉了；别哭了。(The listener is crying.)
Tā yǐjīng xiàng nǐ dàoqiàn le; bié kū le.
He already apologized to you; don't cry any more.

我要告诉你一个坏消息；你听了以后，别哭。(The listener is not crying.)
Wǒ yào gàosù nǐ yí ge huài xiāoxí; nǐ tīng le yǐhòu, bié kū.
I am going to tell you some bad news. Don't cry after you hear it.

(b) Indicating the result of an action

了 can also indicate the result of an action. In this case, the imperative sentence can be a positive one as well.

别忘了把这封信交给他。（了 does not indicate a change of situation; it is the result of 忘.)
Bié wàng le bǎ zhè fēng xìn jiāo gěi tā.
Don't forget to hand this letter to him.
Compare: 忘了他吧！像他这种人，不值得你爱。
　　　　　Wàng le tā ba! Xiàng tā zhè zhǒng rén, bù zhíde nǐ ài.
　　　　　Forget him! Someone like him does not deserve your love.

儿子：这么多空瓶子，怎么办?
Érzi: Zhème duō kōng píngzi, zěnme bàn?
妈妈：丢了，别留那种没有用的东西。
Māma: Diū le. Bié liú nà zhǒng méiyǒu yòng de dōngxi.
Son: So many empty bottles. What are we going to with them?
Mother: Throw them away. Don't keep those kinds of useless things.
Compare: 这样东西很重要，拿好，别丢了。
　　　　　Zhè yàng dōngxi hěn zhòngyào, ná hǎo, bié diū le.
　　　　　This is something very important; hold on to it; don't lose it.

7.9 Indirect imperative sentences

Level 2

(a) Indirect imperative sentences with 叫, 请, 让 and 要

A command/suggestion/piece of advice conveyed through a third person is an indirect imperative sentence. Words such as 叫, 请, 让 and 要 are used.

老师：王小明，站起来。
Lǎoshī: Wáng Xiǎomíng, zhàn qǐlái.
王：小丁，老师说什么?
Wáng: Xiǎo Dīng, lǎoshī shuō shénme?
丁：他叫你站起来。
Dīng: Tā jiào nǐ zhàn qǐlái.
Teacher: Wang Xiaoming, stand up.
Wang: Xiao Ding, what did the teacher say?
Ding: He told you to stand up.

(b) Indirect imperative sentences with 劝 and 希望

A command/suggestion/advice can be conveyed indirectly when the speaker urges the listener to follow his/her command/suggestion/piece of advice with verbs such as 劝 and 希望.

这么重要的事，我劝你再考虑考虑。
Zhème zhòngyào de shì, wǒ quàn nǐ zài kǎolǜ kǎolǜ.
This is such an important matter. I urge you to think more about it.

(c) Negative indirect imperative sentences

Do not use 不 in a negative indirect imperative sentence; instead, use 别.

◐ Using 不 in a negative indirect imperative sentence is a mistake frequently made by learners who are English speakers.

妈妈**叫你别**看电视，你为什么还在看？

Māma jiào nǐ bié kàn diànshì, nǐ wèishénme hái zài kàn?

Mother has told you not to watch TV; why are you still watching?

小王不是好人，我**劝你别**跟他交往。

Xiǎo Wáng bú shì hǎo rén, wǒ quàn nǐ bié gēn tā jiāowǎng.

Xiao Wang is not a good person. I urge you not to be friends with him.

你这次考得不好没关系，可是我**希望你**下次**别**又不及格。

Nǐ zhè cì kǎo de bù hǎo méi guānxi, kěshì wǒ xīwàng nǐ xià cì bié yòu bù jígé.

It's all right if you didn't do well this time; but I hope that you won't fail again next time.

7.10 **Other uses of** 别

Although 别 is generally regarded as the negative word in a negative imperative sentence, in which 你/你们 before 别 is optional, there is another type of '别 + verb' sentence that does not imply an omitted subject 你/你们.

(a) Expressing a wish or hope with 别

Such a sentence starts with 别 and can be used to express the speaker's **wish or hope**. The speaker hopes that **an undesirable situation** will not turn out to be true. The expression is usually 别是 or 别是……吧.

(Situation: You just got rid of Xiao Wang five minutes ago and someone is knocking at the door now. You hope it's not Xiao Wang again.)

哎哟！怎么又有人敲门？**别**又**是**小王！(= 我希望不是小王。)

Āiyō! Zěnme yòu yǒu rén qiāo mén? Bié yòu shì Xiǎo Wáng.

Hey! How come someone is at the door again? Don't let it be Xiao Wang again!

(Situation: You go on a blind date and see a very unattractive person who might be your date.)

糟糕！**别是**这个人吧。

Zāogāo! Bié shì zhè ge rén ba.

Oh, no! Don't let it be this person.

(b) Expressing an assumption with 别

A similar structure can be used to express one's **assumption**, which is **an undesirable situation**. But because the speaker is not personally involved in the situation, such an expression does not carry the connotation of the speaker's hope or wish.

(Situation: You observe someone you don't know acting extremely strangely.)

这么奇怪。**别是**疯了**吧**！

Zhème qíguài. Bié shì fēng le ba.

So strange. Could it be that he's crazy?

(c) Expressing a wish or hope with 别 and 希望 or 但愿

希望 or 但愿 can be used with 别 to express one's hope or wish that an undesirable event won't happen.

但愿明天**别**下雨，否则，运动会就会被取消。

Dànyuàn míngtiān bié xiàyǔ, fǒuzé, yùndòng huì jiù huì bèi qǔxiāo.

I hope it won't rain tomorrow; otherwise, the sports competition will be called off.

昨天没准备功课，**希望**今天老师**别**叫我回答问题。

Zuótiān méi zhǔnbèi gōngkè, xīwàng jīntiān lǎoshī bié jiào wǒ huídá wèntí.

I didn't do the preparation homework yesterday. I hope the teacher won't ask me to answer questions today.

Level 1

7.11 Negative imperative sentences without 别

There are also negative imperative sentences that do not start with 别. When the listener is forbidden to do something, the imperative sentence can start with 不许, 不准 or 不可以. Such a sentence is stronger in tone than one that starts with 别.

不许说话！同学们都在看书呢！

Bùxǔ shuōhuà! Tóngxuémen dōu zài kànshū ne!

Don't talk! Other students are reading.

不准插嘴！大人在说话呢！

Bùzhǔn chāzuǐ! Dàrén zài shuōhuà ne!

Don't interrupt! Grown-ups are talking!

Level 2

7.12 Imperative sentences, subjectless sentences and elliptical sentences compared

These three types of sentence share similarities on the surface in the sense that each may appear to be without a subject.

(a) Imperative sentences

An imperative sentence may not always start with a verb since the object of the verb may be pre-posed or the sentence may be in the 把 structure. In addition, it is possible for an imperative sentence to start with a prepositional phrase.

妈妈：把眼睛**闭**上，**睡**觉。

Māma: Bǎ yǎnjīng bì shàng, shuìjiào.

女儿：好，你出去的时候，把灯关了。

Nǚ'er: Hǎo, nǐ chūqù de shíhòu, bǎ dēng guān le.

Mother: Close your eyes. Go to sleep.

Daughter: OK. Turn off the light when you leave.

妈妈：小明，**你看**，妹妹哭了。**跟她说**《对不起》。

Māma: Xiǎomíng, nǐ kàn, mèimei kū le. Gēn tā shuō 'duìbùqǐ'.

小明：妹妹，对不起，**别**哭了。

Xiǎomíng: Mèimei, duìbùqǐ, bié kū le.

Mother: Xiaoming, look, your sister is crying. Say 'sorry' to her.

Xiaoming: Sorry, little sister. Don't cry anymore.

(b) Subjectless sentences

A subjectless sentence may begin with a verb since no subject is used in such a sentence.

☞ See Chapter 20 for more information on the subjectless sentence.

下雨了！真讨厌！

Xià yǔ le! Zhēn tǎoyàn!

It's raining. How annoying!

(c) Elliptical sentences

The subject of an elliptical sentence is omitted because the context is clear and the meaning can be understood without the subject being present.

王：小张呢？
Wáng: Xiǎo Zhāng ne?
丁：走了。(= 他走了。)
Dīng: Zǒu le.
Wang: Where is Xiao Zhang?
Ding: He left.

Exercises

Fill in the blanks with 别 or 不.

1 这件事虽然 _____ 是秘密，但是请你 _____ 告诉任何人。

Although this matter is not a secret, please don't tell anybody.

2 王：我要告诉你一个秘密，但是请你 _____ 告诉小张。

李：好，我 _____ 告诉他，请快告诉我这个秘密。

Wang: I am going to tell you a secret, but please don't tell Xiao Zhang.

Li: OK, I won't tell him. Please tell me this secret now.

3 老师：彼得，这是中文课， _____ 可以说英文。

彼得：安娜，老师说什么？

安娜：他叫你 _____ 说英文。

Teacher: Peter, this is a Chinese class. You must not speak English.

Peter: Anna, what did the teacher say?

Anna: He told you not to speak English.

4 妈妈：我叫你 _____ 跟小王交朋友，你为什么 _____ 听？

儿子：你 _____ 管我跟谁交朋友。

妈妈：我是你妈妈，我 _____ 管你，谁管你？

Mother: I have told you not to be friends with Xiao Wang. Why wouldn't you listen?

Son: Don't control who I am friends with.

Mother: I am you mother. If I don't take care of you, who will?

5 王先生：奇怪，汽车怎么发动不了了？ _____ 是坏了。

王太太：我看 _____ 是坏了，是没油了。

Mr Wang: Strange! How come the car won't start? I hope this doesn't mean that it's broken down.

Mrs Wang: I don't think it's broken down. It's out of petrol.

6 女儿：希望明天 _____ 下雨，如果下雨，我跟小王就不能去野餐了。

妈妈：不管明天下不下雨，我都 _____ 希望你跟小王出去。

女儿：我已经不是小孩了，我希望你 _____ 管我的事。

Daughter: I hope it won't rain tomorrow. If it rains, Xiao Wang and I won't be able to go on a picnic.

Mother: Whether it rains or not tomorrow, I don't want you to go out with Xiao Wang.

Daughter: I am not a child any more. I wish you'd keep out of my business (= I hope that you will not mind my business).

7 王：下班以后，我们一起去啤酒馆喝啤酒，好不好？

李：医生叫我 _____ 喝酒，我 _____ 去。

丁：我太太 _____ 让我喝酒，我也 _____ 去。

王：_____ 告诉你太太，我也 _____ 告诉她。你跟我去，好吗？

Wang: Let's go to a pub to have some beer after work, OK?

Li: My doctor has told me not to drink. I am not going.

Ding: My wife does not allow me to drink. I am not going, either.

Wang: Don't tell your wife and I won't tell her, either. You go with me, OK?

8 The progressive aspect and the continuous aspect

The Chinese language does not employ tenses to indicate the time (present, past or future) of an event's happening; instead, there are aspects, which indicate the stages of the event. For example, an event can be viewed as being in progress, in continuation or as having been completed.

A. The progressive aspect

The first part of this chapter focuses on the use of the progressive aspect, which indicates an action in progress. Since there are no tenses in Chinese, an action in progress might be happening in the past, at present or in the future. The actual time of the event's happening is indicated by a time phrase, an independent clause or is not mentioned at all if it is understood in the context.

8.1 Basic form of the progressive aspect

There are three basic ways to show an action in progress:

正	在	Verb	呢	Example
✓		✓	Optional	下午我正睡觉(呢)，他就打电话来了。 *Xiàwǔ wǒ zhèng shuìjiào (ne), tā jiù dǎ diànhuà lái le.* In the afternoon, I was sleeping and he called.
	✓	✓	Optional	爸爸在睡觉(呢)，别去吵他。 *Bàba zài shuìjiào (ne), bié qù chǎo tā.* Your father is sleeping. Don't go and disturb him.
✓	✓	✓	Optional	大地震发生的时候，我正在吃晚饭(呢)。 *Dà dìzhèn fāshēng de shíhòu, wǒ zhèng zài chī wǎnfàn (ne).* When the big earthquake occurred, I was eating dinner.

(a) 正 + verb + (呢)

A sentence using '正 + verb + (呢)' normally does not stand alone; therefore, its usage is quite limited. It is most frequently used to express the time when another action takes/took place. It is also used with an action that does not last (see (f) below for more on this).

今天下午我**正**看电视**呢**，他就来了。

Jīntiān xiàwǔ wǒ zhèng kàn diànshì ne, tā jiù lái le .

This afternoon he arrived when I was watching TV.

昨天我到他家的时候，他**正**从家里出来(呢)。 (出来 is an action that does not last.)

Zuótiān wǒ dào tā jiā de shíhòu, tā zhèng cóng jiā lǐ chūlái (ne).

Yesterday when I arrived at his home, he was coming out from his house.

(b) When 呢 is used

When the optional 呢 is used, the speech sounds more casual.

(Situation: Zhang and Wang are chatting over the phone. It's a very informal situation.)

张：你**在**做什么？

Zhāng: Nǐ zài zuò shénme?

王：我(**正**)**在**看电视(呢)。

Wáng: Wǒ (zhèng) zài kàn diànshì (ne).

Zhang: What are you doing?

Wang: I am watching TV.

(c) When 呢 is not used (1)

Since 呢 is a modal particle that appears at the end of a sentence, it should not be used mid-sentence.

李：你们**在**做什么？

Lǐ: Nǐmen zài zuò shénme?

王：我**在**吃水果，他**在**写功课(呢)。

Wáng: Wǒ zài chī shuǐguǒ, tā zài xiě gōngkè (ne).

Li: What are you (plural) doing?

Wang: I am eating fruit; he is doing homework.

(Improper: 我在吃水果呢，他在写功课呢。)

(d) When 呢 is not used (2)

Likewise, 呢 is never used when the action in progress is in a relative clause.

(**正**)**在**跟王老师说话**的**那个人是谁？

(Zhèng) zài gēn Wáng lǎoshī shuōhuà de nà ge rén shì shéi?

Who is the person that is talking to Teacher Wang?

(Improper: (正)在跟王老师说话呢的那个人是谁？)

(e) 正在/在 + verb + (呢)

Although '正在 + verb + (呢)' and '在 + verb + (呢)' are generally viewed as being interchangeable, '正在 + verb + (呢)' carries a more emphatic tone than '在 + verb + (呢)'. Therefore, when the speaker mentions a specific moment of time, 正在 tends to be used.

昨天下午他来我家**的时候**，我**正在**洗澡；给他开门的人是我妹妹。

Zuótiān xiàwǔ tā lái wǒ jiā de shíhòu, wǒ zhèng zài xǐzǎo; gěi tā kāimén de rén shì wǒ mèimei.

When he came to my house yesterday afternoon, I was taking a bath. The person who opened the door for him was my younger sister.

张：你**在**想什么？（你正在想什么？ would be less common since no specific time is mentioned.)
Zhāng: Nǐ zài xiǎng shénme?
王：**在**想王老师要我们回答的那个问题。
Wáng: Zài xiǎng Wáng lǎoshī yào wǒmen huídá de nà ge wèntí.
Zhang: What are you thinking about?
Wang: (I am) thinking about the question Teacher Wang wanted us to answer.

昨天老师叫到我**的时候**，我正在做白日梦(呢)。
Zuótiān lǎoshī jiào dào wǒ de shíhòu, wǒ zhèng zài zuò báirì mèng ne.
Yesterday when the teacher called on me, I was daydreaming.

(f) Actions that do not last

Verbs in the '正在 + verb + (呢)' and '在 + verb + (呢)' structures must indicate actions that can last. For actions that do not last, use 正 + verb + (呢) to emphasize that the action is in progress.

老师**正**进教室的时候，火警的警铃响起来了。（进 is considered an action that does not last.)
Lǎoshī zhèng jìn jiàoshì de shíhòu, huǒjǐng de jǐnglíng xiǎng qǐlái le.
When the teacher was entering the classroom, the fire alarm went off.

老师**正在**骂学生的时候，下课的铃声响了。(骂 is an action that can last.)
Lǎoshī zhèng zài mà xuéshēng de shíhòu, xià kè de líng shēng xiǎng le.
When the teacher was scolding her students, the bell for the end of class rang.

8.2 Yes–no questions in the progressive aspect

To form a yes–no question about an action in progress, use '(正) 在 + verb 吗?' or '是不是 (正) 在?' 呢 should not appear in a yes–no question. Use 对 to confirm and use 没有 or 不是 to give a short answer 'no'.

妈妈：你听！他们的房间里有音乐；他们(正)**在**跳舞**吗**?
Māma: Nǐ tīng! Tāmen de fángjiān lǐ yǒu yīnyuè; tāmen (zhèng) zài tiàowǔ ma?
爸爸：我去看看。……**对**，他们(正)**在**唱歌、跳舞(呢)。
Bàba: Wǒ qù kàn kàn. . . . Duì, tāman (zhèng) zài chànggē, tiàowǔ (ne).
Mother: Listen! There is music in their room. Are they dancing?
Father: I'll go take a look. . . . That's right. They are singing and dancing.

妈妈：小明，你又**在**上网**吗**？（With 又, 正 should not be used.)
Māma: Xiǎomíng, nǐ yòu zài shàngwǎng ma?
小明：**没有**，我**在**写功课；今天的功课是要用电脑写的。
Xiǎomíng: Méiyǒu, wǒ zài xiě gōngkè; jīntiān de gōngkè shì yào yòng diànnǎo xiě de.
Mother: Xiaoming, are you surfing the Internet again?
Xiaoming: No, I'm not. I am doing homework. We have to use the computer for today's homework.

王：你**在**看房屋出售的广告？你**是不是在**找房子？
Wáng: Nǐ zài kàn fángwū chūshòu de guǎnggào? Nǐ shì búshì zài zhǎo fángzi?
张：**不是**，我**在**研究房屋的市价。
Zhāng; Búshì, wǒ zài yánjiū fángwū de shìjià.
Wang: You are looking at ads for houses for sale? Are you looking for a house (to buy)?
Zhang: No, I'm not. I am researching market prices for houses.

8.3 Negative sentences in the progressive aspect

To form a negative sentence, use '没 (有) 在 + verb' or '不是在 + verb'.

> 妈妈：小明，你在洗澡间里做什么？在洗澡吗？
> *Māma: Xiǎomíng, nǐ zài xǐzǎojiān lǐ zuò shénme? Zài xǐzǎo ma?*
> 小明：我不是在洗澡，我在上厕所。
> *Xiǎomíng: Wǒ bú shì zài xǐzǎo, wǒ zài shàng cèsuǒ.*
> Mother: Xiaoming, what are you doing in the bathroom? Are you taking a bath?
> Xiaoming: I'm not taking a bath. I am using the toilet.

> 王：老张，真对不起，这么晚给你打电话。你在睡觉吗？
> *Wáng: Lǎo Zhāng, zhēn duìbùqǐ, zhème wǎn gěi nǐ dǎ diànhuà. Nǐ zài shuìjiào ma?*
> 张：没关系，我没有在睡觉，我在看电视呢。
> *Zhāng: Méi guānxi, wǒ méiyǒu zài shuìjiào, wǒ zài kàn diànshì ne.*
> Wang: Lao Zhang, terribly sorry to call you so late. Were you sleeping?
> Zhang: It's all right. I wasn't sleeping; I was watching TV.

8.4 Locations in the progressive aspect

When a location is combined with an action in progress, 在 can appear only once. If 正在 is used, it appears before the location.

> 昨天发生大地震的时候，我正在家睡觉。(Do not say 我在家正睡觉.)
> *Zuótiān fāshēng dà dìzhèn de shíhòu, wǒ zhèng zài jiā shuìjiào.*
> Yesterday when the earthquake occurred, I was sleeping at home.

8.5 从 prepositional phrases in the progressive aspect

When a prepositional phrase with 从 is used, 正 appears before the prepositional phrase. Neither 正在 nor 在 is proper in this case.

> 我到他家的时候，他正从家里出来。
> *Wǒ dào tā jiā de shíhòu, tā zhèng cóng jiā lǐ chūlái.*
> When I reached his house, he was just coming out from inside the house.

8.6 Other prepositional phrases in the progressive aspect

Prepositional phrases (other than a 从 phrase) can appear after either 正在 or 在.

> 昨天他打电话来的时候，我正在给他写信。
> *Zuótiān tā dǎ diànhuà lái de shíhòu, wǒ zhèngzài gěi tā xiěxìn.*
> Yesterday when he called me, I was (just in the middle of) writing him a letter.

> 别插嘴，我在跟王老师说话呢。
> *Bié chāzuǐ, wǒ zài gēn Wáng lǎoshī shuōhuà ne.*
> Don't interrupt. I am talking to Teacher Wang.

8.7 现在 in the progressive aspect

When 现在 is used, it is possible for 在 to appear twice.

> 张：你知不知道王老师在哪里？我想问他一个问题。
> *Zhāng: Nǐ zhī bù zhīdào Wáng lǎoshī zài nǎlǐ? Wǒ xiǎng wèn tā yī ge wèntí.*
> 李：他现在在开会呢。

Lǐ: Tā xiànzài zài kāihuì ne.
Zhang: Do you know where Teacher Wang is? I want to ask him a question.
Li: He is in a meeting right now.

8.8 Adjectives in the progressive aspect

Level 1

It is possible to have an adjective after 正在 or 在 if such an adjective can indicate a **temporary psychological state or feeling**. Adjectives such as 高 (*gāo*: 'tall'), 聪明 (*cōngmíng*: 'clever'), 冷 (*lěng*: cold), etc. that indicate a permanent state or a physical feeling cannot be used with the progressive aspect.

(Situation: An international soccer tournament.)

观众以为美国队一定会赢，**正在高兴**的时候，德国队踢进了两球，美国队输了。
Guānzhòng yǐwéi Měiguó duì yídìng huì yíng, zhèngzài gāoxìng de shíhòu, Déguó duì tī jìn le liǎng qiú, Měiguó duì shū le.
The audience thought that the US team definitely would win. (Just) when they were (feeling) happy, the German team scored two points. The US team lost.

有人说她儿子死了；她**正在难过**的时候，儿子回家了。
Yǒu rén shuō tā érzi sǐ le; tā zhèng zài nánguò de shíhòu, érzi huí jiā le.
Someone said that her son had died. While she was grieving, her son came home.

8.9 Actions about to happen

Level 2

'正要/正想 + verb' (but not 正在要/正在想) does not indicate an action in progress; it indicates an action that is just **about to** happen. The expression can also be 正打算/正准备.

妈妈：小明，你在做什么？去洗碗！
Māma: Xiǎomíng, nǐ zài zuò shénme? Qù xǐ wǎn!
小明：我**正在准备**明天上课要作的口头报告呢。让爸爸去洗吧，好吗？
Xiǎomíng: Wǒ zhèng zài zhǔnbèi míngtiān shàng kè yào zuò de kǒutóu bàogào ne. Ràng bàba qù xǐ ba, hǎo ma?
妈妈：我和爸爸**正准备**出门去看电影呢。(正在准备 and 正准备 have different meanings.)
Māma:Wǒ hé bàba zhèng zhǔnbèi chū mén qù kàn diànyǐng ne.
Mother: Xiaoming, what are you doing? Go do the dishes.
Xiaoming: I am preparing an oral presentation for tomorrow's class. Ask Father to do it, OK?
Mother: Your father and I are just about to go out and see a movie.

张：小王，你要去哪里？
Zhāng: Xiǎo Wáng, nǐ yào qù nǎlǐ?
王：啊！老张，是你！我**正要**（or 正想/正打算）去找你呢。
Wáng: À! Lǎo Zhāng, shì nǐ! Wǒ zhèng yào (or zhèng xiǎng/zhèng dǎsuàn) qù zhǎo nǐ ne.
Zhang: Xiao Wang, where are you going?
Wang: Ah! Lao Zhang, it's you! I was just about to go and see you.

B. The continuous aspect

While an action in progress and an action in continuation share some similarities, a progressive aspect (正在/正) is used when the verbs or adjectives indicate activities or an active state, whereas the continuous aspect of an action refers to a static/inactive situation.

<table>
<tr><td>Level
2</td></tr>
</table>

8.10 Basic form of the continuous aspect

The aspect particle 着, which can only appear immediately after a verb or adjective, is used to indicate the continuous aspect of an action. An optional 呢 can appear at the end of the sentence.

> 你看，邮局的门**开着呢**。邮局还**在营业**，我要去买几张邮票。
> *Nǐ kàn, yóujú de mén kāi zhe ne. Yóujú hái zài yíngyè, wǒ yào qù mǎi jǐ zhāng yóupiào.*
> Look, the door of the post office is open. The post office is still doing business.
> I am going to buy a few stamps.
> (开着 shows an inactive situation, whereas 在营业 shows an active activity.)

> 小王的眼睛**闭着**，我想他大概**在睡觉**，所以没有跟他打招呼。
> *Xiǎo Wáng de yǎnjīng bì zhe, wǒ xiǎng tā dàgài zài shuìjiào, suǒyǐ méiyǒu gēn tā dǎ zhāohū.*
> Xiao Wang's eyes were closed. I thought he might be sleeping, so I didn't greet him.

<table>
<tr><td>Level
2</td></tr>
</table>

8.11 Simultaneous actions

When two actions happen at the same time, the main verb appears after the secondary verb. 着 should follow the secondary verb.

(a) Indicating manner

The secondary verb indicates the manner in which the main verb is performed.

> 老师**笑着说**："你们这次都考得很好。"
> *Lǎoshī xiào zhe shuō: 'Nǐmen zhè cì dōu kǎo de hěn hǎo.'*
> The teacher said with a smile (= said while smiling): 'All of you did well in the test this time.'
> (说 is the main verb; 笑 is the secondary verb.)

> 妹妹每天晚上都**抱着**娃娃**睡觉**。
> *Mèimei měi tiān wǎnshàng dōu bào zhe wáwa shuìjiào.*
> Every night, my little sister sleeps while holding her doll.
> (睡觉 is the main verb; 抱 is the secondary verb.)

(b) Indicating purpose

The main verb indicates the purpose for the action of the secondary verb.

> 丁：那些人在那里做什么？
> *Dīng: Nàxiē rén zài nàlǐ zuò shénme?*
> 王：他们都在**等着买**火车票呢。
> *Wáng: Tāmen dōu zài děng zhe mǎi huǒchē piào ne.*
> Ding: What are those people doing over there?
> Wang: They are all waiting to buy train tickets.
> (买火车票 is the purpose of 等.)

<table>
<tr><td>Level
3</td></tr>
</table>

8.12 The use of placement verbs and 着

There is a group of verbs that will be termed as 'placement verbs' in this book. The use of placement verbs frequently involves the use of 着.

☞ See 20.10 and 20.11 for more information on this.

Exercises

Translate the following sentences into Chinese. Pay special attention to the use of the progressive and continuous aspects.

Level
1

1 Wang: What are those people doing?

Li: They are waiting for the bus.

2 Li: Wang Zhong, sorry to call you at this time. Were you sleeping?

Wang: It's OK, I wasn't sleeping; I was doing homework. Were you also doing homework?

Li: No, I was watching TV.

3 Wang: Are you watching TV right now?

Li: No. I am surfing the Internet.

Wang: Hurry and turn on the TV. Teacher Wang is singing. (Teacher Wang is performing on TV.)

4 When I returned home, the TV was on, but everybody at home was sleeping; nobody was watching TV.

5 Every day when I return home, my mother is always cooking dinner. Sometimes, my father is reading the newspaper, and sometimes he is watching TV.

Level
2

6 Zhang: Why are there so many people over there? What are they doing?

Li: All of them are waiting to buy movie tickets.

7 Pointing at the photos on the wall, the teacher said, 'Now please answer my questions while looking at these photos.'

8 Wang: Are you reading the newspaper? Is there any big news?

Li: I don't know. I am not reading news; I am looking for jobs.

Wang: You are looking for a job? 'The Great Wall' Chinese restaurant is looking for a waiter.

Li: I know, but they are looking for someone who has experience.

9 Manager: All employees please come to my office.

Mr Wang: Manager, some people are in a meeting right now.

Manager: All those who are not in a meeting, please come to my office immediately.

10 When I was about to enter the lift, I saw that all four people in the lift were talking on their phones. So I decided to wait for the next lift.

9 The use of 了 (the perfective aspect particle and modal particle)

As stated in the previous chapter, the Chinese language does not have tenses; instead, there are aspects, which indicate the stages of an event. The focus of the first part of this chapter will be on the perfective aspect, which is indicated with the perfective aspect particle 了 (*le*) immediately following the verb.

Since 了 can also function as a modal particle, which appears at the end of a sentence, the use of 了 as a modal particle will be the focus of the second part of this chapter.

A. The perfective aspect particle 了

The perfective aspect is used to indicate the completion of an action; it is, however, not equivalent to the past tense in English. The completion of an action may have occurred in the past, but it may occur in the future as well. Also, a past event may or may not need a perfective aspect particle 了.

> English: Yesterday was my boyfriend's birthday; so I treated him to a movie. (Past event)
> Chinese: 昨天是我男朋友的生日，所以我请他去看(了一场)电影。
> *Zuótiān shì wǒ nán péngyǒu de shēngrì, suǒyǐ wǒ qǐng tā qù kàn (le yì chǎng) diànyǐng.*

> English: After you have arrived in China, you must write to me often. (Future event)
> Chinese: 你到了中国(以后)，一定要常常给我写信。
> *Nǐ dào le Zhōngguó (yǐhòu), yídìng yào chángcháng gěi wǒ xiě xìn.*

> English: After he arrived in China, he immediately found a job. (Past event)
> Chinese: 他到了中国(以后)，马上找了一份工作。
> *Tā dào le Zhōngguó (yǐhòu), mǎshàng zhǎo le yí fèn gōngzuò.*

Level 1 | 9.1 Habitual past events

A past event that is habitual does **not** take the perfective particle 了.

> 我小时候每天早上都喝一杯牛奶。
> *Wǒ xiǎo shíhòu měi tiān zǎoshàng dōu hē yì bēi niúnǎi.*
> When I was very young, I drank a glass of milk every morning.

> 我在中国的时候，每星期都去看(一场)中国电影。
> *Wǒ zài Zhōngguó de shíhòu, měi xīngqī dōu qù kàn (yì chǎng) Zhōngguó diànyǐng.*
> When I was in China, I went to a Chinese movie every week.

9.2 Quantified past events

A quantified past event (i.e., the object of the verb includes either a number or 很多/不少)
usually takes the perfective particle 了.

> 昨天我跟妈妈去外面吃饭。我们叫了**一条**鱼跟**一只**烤鸭。
> *Zuótiān wǒ gēn māma qù wàimiàn chī fàn. Wǒmen jiào le yì tiáo yú gēn yì zhī kǎoyā.*
> Yesterday my mother and I went out to eat. We ordered a fish and a roast duck.

> 我在中国留学的时候，认识了**不少**中国朋友。
> *Wǒ zài Zhōngguó liúxué de shíhòu, rènshì le bùshǎo Zhōngguó péngyǒu.*
> When I was studying in China, I made many Chinese friends.

9.3 Definite or specific past events

A definite or specific past event usually takes the perfective particle 了.

(a) When the object of the verb has a modifier

> 老师接受了**我们的**建议，取消了**今天的**考试。
> *Lǎoshī jiēshòu le wǒmen de jiànyì, qǔxiāo le jīntiān de kǎoshì.*
> The teacher accepted our suggestions and cancelled today's test.

> 张：你怎么知道今天会下雨？
> *Zhāng: Nǐ zěnme zhīdào jīntiān huì xiàyǔ?*
> 王：因为我昨晚看了**天气**预报。
> *Wáng: Yīnwèi wǒ zuówǎn kàn le tiānqì yùbào.*
> Zhang: How did you know it would rain today?
> Wang: Because I watched the weather forecast yesterday evening.

(b) When the object of the verb is a proper noun or pronoun

> 李：昨天我在路上遇见了**老王**。
> *Lǐ: Zuótiān wǒ zài lù shàng yùjiàn le Lǎo Wáng.*
> 张：真巧！我今天也在路上遇见了**他**。
> *Zhāng: Zhēn qiǎo! Wǒ jīntiān yě zài lù shàng yùjiàn le tā.*
> Li: I ran into Lao Wang on the street yesterday.
> Zhang: What a coincidence! I also ran into him on the street today.

(c) When the object of the verb is 什么/哪 (*shénme/nǎ*) or the answer to a question with 什么/哪

> 王：下午我去你家找你，你妈说你去超级市场买东西(了)。你买了**什么**？
> *Wáng: Xiàwǔ wǒ qù nǐ jiā zhǎo nǐ, nǐ mā shuō nǐ qù chāojíshìchǎng mǎi dōngxi (le). Nǐ mǎi le shénme?*
> 李：买了**水果**、面包跟牛奶。
> *Lǐ: Mǎi le shuǐguǒ, miànbāo gēn niúnǎi.*
> Wang: In the afternoon I went to your house to see you; your mother said you had gone to the supermarket to buy some things. What did you buy?
> Li: I bought fruit, bread and milk.

9.4 Two verbs: One action after another

When a situation includes two actions, and the second action takes place immediately after
the completion of the first, the aspect particle 了 is used to indicate the completion of the first

action even if the object of the verb is not quantified or does not have a modifier. These two actions may or may not be past events.

(a) The use of 就

It should be noted that 就 (*jiù*, implying 'immediately') or another adverb is frequently used to link the two actions. Without such an adverb, the sentence may not sound correct.

> 我爸爸每天**吃了**饭就吃胃药。 (吃胃药 is a habitual event. 就 is necessary.)
> *Wǒ bàba měi tiān chī le fàn jiù chī wèiyào.*
> My father takes acid-reducing medicine right after dinner every day.

> 小王跟客人**说了再见**就把门关上了。 (把门关上了 is a past event. 就 is necessary.)
> *Xiǎo Wáng gēn kèrén shuō le zàijiàn jiù bǎ mén guān shàng le.*
> Xiao Wang closed the door right after saying goodbye to his guests.

> 明天咱们**下了**课一起去看场电影，怎么样？ (看电影 is a future event.)
> *Míngtiān zánmen xià le kè yìqǐ qù kàn chǎng diànyǐng, zěnmeyàng?*
> How about if we go to a movie after class tomorrow?

(b) Modal particle 了 instead of perfective aspect particle 了

In a simple sentence, the perfective aspect particle 了 is not used if the object of the verb is not quantified or does not have a modifier; instead, modal particle 了 is used at the end of the sentence.

(☞ See 9.3(b) and (c) above for exceptions.)

English:	Mr Wang bought a car。 (This is a simple sentence.)
Chinese #1:	王先生**买车了**。 (了 is a modal particle since it appears at the end of the sentence.)
	Wáng xiānsheng mǎi chē le.
Chinese #2:	王先生**买了一辆**车。 (了 is the perfective aspect particle since it follows the verb.)
	Wáng xiānsheng mǎi le yí liàng chē.
(Incorrect:	王先生买了车 or 王先生买一辆车了.)

> 王先生**买了车**就跟王太太去兜风了。 (This is a complex sentence.)
> *Wáng xiānsheng mǎi le chē jiù gēn Wáng tàitai qù dōufēng le.*
> Mr Wang and Mrs Wang went for a ride right after he bought the car (bought a car).

An optional perfective aspect particle 了 and a necessary modal particle 了 can be used together in a simple sentence.

> 王先生买**了**车**了**。 (= 王先生买车**了**。)
> *Wáng xiānsheng mǎi le chē le.*
> (Incorrect: 王先生买了车。)

(Situation: Wang's roommate Zhang asks Wang to join him for a late-night snack.)

> 张：我要吃宵夜，你要不要吃一些？
> *Zhāng: Wǒ yào chī xiāoyè, nǐ yào bú yào chī yì xiē?*
> 王：谢谢，我不吃，我刷**了**牙**了**。
> *Wáng: Xièxiè, wǒ bù chī, wǒ shuā le yá le.*
> Zhang: I am going to have a late-night snack. Would you like some?
> Wang: No, thanks. I already brushed my teeth.

Level 2

9.5 Two verbs: One indicating purpose

When a simple sentence has two verbs and the second verb indicates the purpose of the first verb, such as 来 (*lái*), 去 (*qù*) and 用 (*yòng*), the perfective aspect particle 了 follows the second verb if it is a past event.

下午我**去**超级市场**买了**一些水果和面包。
Xiàwǔ wǒ qù chāojíshìchǎng mǎi le yìxiē shuǐguǒ hé miànbāo.
I went to the supermarket to buy some fruit and bread in the afternoon.
(Incorrect: 下午我去了超级市场买一些水果和面包。)

我**用**手机给我妈妈**发了**一个短信，告诉她我不能回家吃饭。
Wǒ yòng shǒujī gěi wǒ māma fā le yí ge duǎnxìn, gàosù tā wǒ bù néng huí jiā chī fàn.
I used my mobile phone to send my mother a text message, telling her I would not be home for dinner.
(Incorrect: 我用了手机给我妈妈发一个短信，告诉她我不能回家吃饭。)

B. The modal particle 了

A modal particle appears at the end of a sentence. As a modal particle, 了 does not indicate the completion of an action, it indicates the emergence of a new situation or a change of situation. It can also be used to imply 'already'.

Level 3

9.6 When the meaning of sentence-ending 了 is ambiguous

When a sentence ends with a verb that does not have an object, 了 following the verb (aspect particle) can be viewed as appearing at the end of the sentence (modal particle) as well, rendering the meaning of 了 ambiguous. In this case, the context in which the sentence is uttered decides the meaning of 了.

*(Situation: At a party Zhang is throwing, Zhang wants to know if Wang Ming **has arrived**.)*

张：王明**来了**没有？
Zhāng: Wáng Míng lái le méiyǒu?
丁：(他)来了。
Dīng: (Tā) lái le.
Zhang: Has Wang Ming arrived? (Meaning: **Is** Wang Ming here?)
Ding: He has arrived. (Meaning: He is here.)

*(Situation: Li and Ding are discussing the party they threw the night before. Since it was a big party, Li did not see Wang Ming among the guests. He asks Ding if Wang Ming **was there**.)*

张：王明**来了**没有？
Zhāng: Wáng Míng lái le méiyǒu?
丁：(他)来了。
Dīng: (Tā) lái le.
Zhang: Did Wang Ming come? (Meaning: **Was** Wang Ming here?)
Ding: He came. (Meaning: He was here.)

(Situation: You have been waiting for the bus. When you see the bus approaching the bus stop from a distance, you say:)

啊！车**来了**！
À! Chē lái le.
Ah! Here comes the bus. (了 indicates the '**emergence**' of the bus.)

(Situation: You and your friend are walking towards the bus stop. Before you arrive at the stop, the bus is already there picking up passengers. You say to your friend:)

> 啊！车**来了**！快跑！
> *À! Chē lái le. Kuài pǎo!*
> Ah! The bus is (already) here. Hurry and run! (了 indicates the '**completion**' of the action and it can imply '**already**' as well.)

9.7 Indicating a new situation or change of situation

Level 2

The modal particle 了 is typically used to indicate the emergence of a new situation or a change of situation although the line between the two can be blurred.

(a) Indicating the emergence of a new situation

> 春天到了，花都开了。
> *Chūntiān dào le, huā dōu kāi le.*
> Spring is here. Flowers are blooming.

> 你看，外面下雨了。
> *Nǐ kàn, wàimiàn xià yǔ le.*
> Look, it's raining outside. (Note: This implies it wasn't raining earlier.)

(b) Indicating a change of situation

> 天黑了，风也大了，我们回家吧。
> *Tiān hēi le, fēng yě dà le, wǒmen huí jiā ba.*
> It's dark now and the wind is stronger. Let's go home.

> 秋天了，枫叶都红了。咱们可以去城外看红叶了。
> *Qiūtiān le, fēng yè dōu hóng le. Zánmen kěyǐ qù chéngwài kàn hóng yè le.*
> It's autumn now, all the maple leaves have turned red. Now we can go outside the city to see red leaves. (Note: 'Now' in the English sentences implies this is a new situation, which is indicated by 了 in Chinese.)

> 下雨了，咱们不能去公园了。
> *Xià yǔ le, zánmen bù néng qù gōngyuán le.*
> It's raining now. We cannot go to the park (as we originally planned).

(c) 不/别……了: 'not . . . anymore'

Here 了 indicates a change of situation.

> 昨天我跟老王吵了一架，我决定以后**不**跟他说话了。
> *Zuótiān wǒ gēn Lǎo Wáng chǎo le yí jià, wǒ juédìng yǐhòu bù gēn tā shuōhuà le.*
> I had a fight with Lao Wang yesterday. I have decided that I will not talk to him anymore.

> 对不起，我向你道歉，**别**哭了。
> *Duìbùqǐ, wǒ xiàng nǐ dàoqiàn, bié kū le.*
> Sorry. I apologize. Don't cry any more (= stop crying).
> Compare:　我要告诉你一个坏消息，你听了以后请**别**哭。
> 　　　　　*Wǒ yào gàosù nǐ yī ge huài xiāoxí, nǐ tīng le yǐhòu qǐng bié kū.*
> 　　　　　I am going to tell you some bad news. Please don't cry when you hear it.

<table>
<tr><td>Level 2</td></tr>
</table>

9.8 Implying 'already'

(a) With 已经 or 都

A sentence with the adverb 已經 (*yǐjīng*) or 都 (*dōu*, when 都 means 'already') should have 了 at the end of the sentence.

都十点了，小明怎么还在睡觉？
Dōu shí diǎn le, Xiǎomíng zěnme hái zài shuìjiào?
It's already ten o'clock. How come Xiaoming is still sleeping?

安娜来北京已经半年了，可是只认识了一、两个中国朋友。
Ānnà lái Běijīng yǐjīng bàn nián le, kěshì zhǐ rènshì le yī, liǎng ge Zhōngguó péngyǒu.
Anna has already been in Beijing for half a year; but she has only met one or two Chinese people.

Compare: 安娜来北京才半年，可是中国话已经说得非常流利了。
Ānnà lái Běijīng cái bàn nián, kěshì Zhōngguóhuà yǐjīng shuō de fēicháng liúlì le.
Anna has only been in Beijing for half a year, but she already speaks Chinese fluently.

(b) Without 已经 or 都

Since 了 at the end of the sentence can imply 'already', 已经 or 都 can be omitted without affecting the meaning of the sentence.

下课二十分钟了，老师还在不停地说话呢。
Xià kè èrshí fēnzhōng le, lǎoshī hái zài bùtíng de shuōhuà ne.
Class has been over for 20 minutes already, but the teacher is still talking non-stop.

Compare: 下课还不到一分钟，同学们就都走了。
Xià kè hái bú dào yī fēnzhōng, tóngxué men jiù dōu zǒu le.
Class has not been over for more than one minute and all the students are gone.

王：你爸爸多大年纪？
Wáng: Nǐ bàba duō dà niánjì?
张：他七十多了，已经退休了。你爸爸呢？
Zhāng: Tā qīshí duō le, yǐjīng tuìxiū le. Nǐ bàba ne?
王：五十出头，还在工作呢。
Wáng: Wǔshí chūtóu, hái zài gōngzuò ne.
Wang: How old is your father?
Zhang: He's (already) in his 70s and he has already retired. How about your father?
Wang: A little over 50; he is still working.

<table>
<tr><td>Level 2</td></tr>
</table>

9.9 Forming questions

To form a yes–no question or an affirmative–negative question, use '…… 了吗?' or '…… 了没有?'

(a) Verbs with objects

If the verb has an object, the object usually is not quantified or does not have a modifier.

妈妈：你吃晚饭了没有？(你吃晚饭了吗？)
Māma: Nǐ chī wǎnfàn le méiyǒu? (Nǐ chī wǎnfàn le ma?)

儿子：吃了。
Érzi: Chī le.
Mother: Did you eat dinner? (The translation could also be: Have you eaten dinner?)
Son: Yes, I did. (Yes, I have.)

谢：你买车**了没有**？(你买车**了吗**？)
Xiè: Nǐ mǎi chē le méiyǒu?
王：买了一辆二手车。
Wáng: Mǎi le yí liàng èrshǒu chē.
Xie: Have you bought a car?
Wang: I have bought a second-hand car.

(b) Pre-posing the object

If the object has a longish modifier, it is better to pre-pose the object.

爸爸：妈妈作的鱼汤，你喝**了没有**？(= 你喝了妈妈作的鱼汤没有？)
Bàba: Māma zuò de yú tāng, nǐ hē le méiyǒu?
小明：喝了三碗(了)。
Xiǎomíng: Hē le sān wǎn le.
Father: Did you have any of the fish soup your mother made?
Xiaoming: I had three bowls (already).

(c) When to use 了 with 没有/吗

没有 can be used at the end of a question with or without 了 if the verb has an object or is a disyllabic word. When 吗 is used, 了 must always be used.

☞ See 2.6 for more on these types of question.

Subject	Verb	了	没有	吗	Example
✓	Monosyllabic	✓	✓		这道菜，你尝了没有？ *Zhè dào cài, nǐ cháng le méiyǒu?* Have you tried the dish?
✓	Monosyllabic	✓		✓	这道菜，你尝了吗？ *Zhè dào cài, nǐ cháng le ma?* Have you tried the dish?
✓	Disyllabic	Optional	✓		你爸爸退休(了)没有？ *Nǐ bàba tuìxiū (le) méiyǒu?* Is your father retired?
✓	Disyllabic	✓		✓	你爸爸退休了吗？ *Nǐ bàba tuìxiū le ma?* Is your father retired?
✓	Monosyllabic + object	Optional	✓		爸爸回家(了)没有？ *Bàba huí jiā (le) méiyǒu?* Has father come home?
✓	Monosyllabic + object	✓		✓	爸爸回家了吗？ *Bàba huí jiā le ma?* Has father come home?

妈妈：爸爸**回家**(了)没有？ (= 爸爸回家了吗？) (But it is incorrect to say 爸爸回家吗？)

Māma: Bàba huíjiā (le) méiyǒu?

小明：回了。

Xiǎomíng: Huí le.

Mother: Has your father come home?

Xiaoming: Yes.

你爸爸**退休**(了)没有？ (= 你爸爸退休了吗？)

Nǐ bàba tuìxiū (le) méiyǒu?

Has your father retired?

他借你的钱，你**还**了没有？ (= 你还了吗？ or 你还他没有？) (But 你还没有？ is incorrect.)

Tā jiè nǐ de qián, nǐ huán le méiyǒu?

Did you return the money he lent you?

Level 2

9.10 Negative sentences

To make a negative sentence, use 没(有) before the verb without 了.

(a) Short negative answers

A short negative answer can simply be 没有.

爸爸：妈妈今天做了很多菜，你吃了没有？ (= 你吃了吗？)

Bàba: Māma jīntiān zuò le hěn duō cài, nǐ chī le méiyǒu?

儿子：我吃了青菜，**没**(有)吃肉。

Érzi: Wǒ chī le qīngcài, méiyǒu chī ròu.

Father: Your mother made lots of dishes today. Did you eat any?

Son: I had vegetables; I didn't have the meat dishes.

张：你给王先生打电话(了)没有？ (= 你给王先生打电话了吗？)

Zhāng: Nǐ gěi Wáng xiānsheng dǎ diànhuà (le) méiyǒu?

丁：**没有**。

Dīng: Méiyǒu.

Zhang: Did you call Mr Wang? (Have you called Mr Wang?)

Ding: No. (I didn't call him.)

(b) Negative answers with 还

Another negative answer can be 还没有 (+ verb) 呢! 呢 is frequently used, but is, in fact, optional. When 还 is used, it implies 'not yet'.

王：老师叫我们看的那本书，你看了没有？ (= 你看了吗？)

Wáng: Lǎoshī jiào wǒmen kàn de nà běn shū, nǐ kàn le méiyǒu?

李：**还没有**(呢)！

Lǐ: Hái méiyǒu (ne)!

Wang: Have you read the book the teacher asked us to read?

Li: Not yet! (I have not read it yet.)

(c) 了 and 没有 in the same sentence

When 了 and 没有 appear in the same sentence, 了 indicates a change of situation. 没有 in this case is usually used to indicate 'non-existence' or the negative progressive aspect.

王：我想喝杯咖啡，有没有咖啡？
Wáng: Wǒ xiǎng hē bēi kāfēi, yǒu méiyǒu kāfēi?
李：**没有**咖啡**了**，喝杯茶，好不好？
Lǐ: Méiyǒu kāfēi le, hē bēi chá, hǎo bu hǎo?
Wang: I want to have a cup of coffee. Is there any coffee?
Li: There is no more coffee. (We ran out of coffee.) Have a cup of tea, OK?

妈妈：小明，你还在看电视吗？
Māma: Xiǎomíng, nǐ hái zài kàn diànshì ma?
小明：没有，我**没有在**看**了**。
Xiǎomíng: Méiyǒu, wǒ méiyǒu zài kàn le.
Mother: Xiaoming, are you still watching TV?
Xiaoming: No, I'm not watching any more. (I have stopped.)

9.11 Impending events

Level 2

The following patterns are used to indicate that an event is going to happen very soon.

(a) The basic patterns

There are four basic patterns for an impending event; they are considered interchangeable.

就	快	要	……了	
		✓	✓	要下雨了，咱们回家吧！ *Yào xià yǔ le, zánmen huíjiā ba!* It's about to rain. Let's go home.
	✓		✓	我女儿**快**两岁**了**。 *Wǒ nǚ'ér kuài liǎng suì le.* My daughter is almost two years old.
	✓	✓	✓	**快要**下课**了**。 *Kuài yào xià kè le.* The class is going to be over soon.
✓		✓	✓	我下个月**就要**毕业**了**。 *Wǒ xià ge yuè jiù yào bìyè le.* I am (soon) going to graduate next month.

(b) A specific moment

When a specific moment is mentioned; only 就要……了 can be used.

你**六月就要**毕业了，为什么还没有开始找工作呢？
Nǐ liùyuè jiù yào bìyè le, wèishénme hái méiyǒu kāishǐ zhǎo gōngzuò ne?
You are about to graduate in June; why haven't you started to look for a job?

还有两个星期就要考期末考了，你开始准备了没有？
Hái yǒu liǎng ge xīngqī jiù yào kǎo qímòkǎo le, nǐ kāishǐ zhǔnbèi le méiyǒu?
Final exams are coming (soon) in only two weeks; have you started to prepare?

(c) Implying 'already'

When 'already' is implied in an impending action, 都 is used more often than 已经; also, 快……了, 要……了 or 快要……了 is used with 都; 就要……了 is rarely used in this situation.

王先生**都快**四十**了**，怎么还没有结婚呢？
Wáng xiānsheng dōu kuài sìshí le, zěnme hái méiyǒu jiéhūn ne?
Mr Wang is already close to 40 years old; how come he is not married yet?

咱们亏了这么多钱，我**都快要**哭**了**，你怎么还在笑？
Zánmen kuī le zhème duō qián, wǒ dōu kuài yào kū le, nǐ zěnme hái zài xiào?
We lost so much money; I am already about to cry; how come you are still laughing?

(d) A specific point in time about to be reached

When a specific point in time is about to be reached, and usually the expression involves a number, 快……了 or 快要……了 is the best choice of the four.

王太太的儿子快（要）**两岁了**。
Wáng tàitai de érzi kuài (yào) liǎng suì le.
Mrs Wang's son is going to be two years old soon.

妈妈：**快十二点了**，你怎么还不上床睡觉？
Māma: Kuài shí'èr diǎn le, nǐ zěnme hái bú shàng chuáng shuìjiào?
儿子：我还在学习呢。大考**就要**到**了**。
Érzi: Wǒ hái zài xuéxí ne. Dà kǎo jiùyào dào le.
Mother: It's almost 12 o'clock, how come you are not in bed yet?
Son: I am still studying. The big exam is coming soon.

(e) Relative clauses or expressions before nouns

When the impending event is in a relative clause or is an expression before a noun, 了 is not used. This sometimes results in confusion on the part of the learner, especially when 快 is used in the expression since 快 has several other meanings.

李：音乐会的票你买到没有？
Lǐ: Yīnyuèhuì de piào, nǐ mǎi dào méiyǒu?
王：真倒霉！我排了**快**两小时的队，**快**轮到我的时候，票就卖完了。
Wáng: Zhēn dǎoméi! Wǒ pái le kuài liǎng xiǎoshí de duì, kuài lún dào wǒ de shíhòu, piào jiù mài wán le.
Li: Did you get the tickets for the concert?
Wang: Really bad luck. I was in line for almost two hours. When it was about to be my turn, the tickets sold out.

李老师教了**快**四十年书，他一共教过**快**三千个学生。
Lǐ lǎoshī jiāo le kuài sìshí nián shū, tā yígòng jiāo guò kuài sān qiān ge xuéshēng.
Teacher Li has taught for almost 40 years. He has taught almost 3,000 students.

Level
1

9.12 Quoting direct or indirect speech

It should be noted that when one quotes either directly or indirectly something someone said, 了 should not be used after words such as 说, 告诉 and 问.

我带小王参观了我的新房子以后，**他说**："哇！你家真大！"
Wǒ dài Xiǎo Wáng cānguān le wǒde xīn fángzi yǐhòu, tā shuō, 'Wà, nǐ jiā zhēn dà!'
After I had shown Xiao Wang my new house, he said, 'Wow, your house is really big!'

昨天我去检查身体，医生**告诉我**，我的心脏跳得太快，血压也太高，**他说**我不应该吸烟、喝酒。
Zuótiān wǒ qù jiǎnchá shēntǐ, yīshēng gàosù wǒ, wǒde xīnzàng tiào de tài kuài, xuěyā yě tài gāo, tā shuō wǒ bù yīnggāi xī yān, hē jiǔ.

Yesterday I went to have a physical check-up. The doctor told me that my heart beats too fast and that my blood pressure is also too high; he said I should not smoke or drink (alcohol).

Exercises

Decide which of the sentences is correct.

Level
1

1 Yesterday Mr Wang invited me to eat.
   (a) 昨天王先生请我吃饭。
   (b) 昨天王先生请我吃了饭。
   (c) 昨天王先生请了我吃饭。

2 In the past, I often drank coffee. I drank two or three cups every day.
   (a) 以前我常喝咖啡，每天都喝两、三杯了。
   (b) 以前我常喝咖啡，每天都喝了两、三杯。
   (c) 以前我常喝咖啡，每天都喝两、三杯。

3 Did you read the books the teachers wanted us to read?
   (a) 老师要我们看的那些书，你看了吗？
   (b) 老师要我们看的那些书，你看没有？
   (c) 老师要我们看的那些书，你看没有看？

4 Why did you do so poorly in this test? Did you study (prepare)?
   (a) 这次考试，你为什么考得这么差，你准备没有？
   (b) 这次考试，你为什么考得这么差，你准备吗？
   (c) 这次考试，你为什么考得这么差，你准备不准备？

5 I did not sleep last night because I was doing homework the entire night.
   (a) 昨天晚上我不睡觉了，因为我整个晚上都在写功课。
   (b) 昨天晚上我没有睡觉，因为我整个晚上都在写功课。
   (c) 昨天晚上我没有睡觉了，因为我整个晚上都在写功课。

Level
2

6 Mr Zhang took his girlfriend for a ride right after he bought a car.
   (a) 张先生买车了就带他女朋友去兜风了。
   (b) 张先生买了车就带他女朋友去兜风了。
   (c) 张先生买车就带他女朋友去兜风了。

7 How about if we go to a movie tomorrow after class?
   (a) 我们明天下课了一起去看电影，好不好？
   (b) 我们明天下了课一起去看电影，好不好？
   (c) 我们明天下课一起去看电影，好不好？

8 Anna goes to the library to study right after she eats lunch every day.

   (a) 安娜每天吃午饭就去图书馆学习。

   (b) 安娜每天吃午饭了就去图书馆学习。

   (c) 安娜每天吃了午饭就去图书馆学习。

9 I am (soon) going to Beijing to study Chinese next month.

   (a) 我下个月快去北京学中文了。

   (b) 我下个月就要去北京学中文了。

   (c) 我下个月快要去北京学中文了。

10 The use of 过 (the experiential aspect particle)

This chapter will focus on the use of 过 (*guo*), which is sometimes referred to as the experiential aspect particle. It is used to indicate an action that took place in the past or has taken place before. Its function in a sentence is to indicate experience, influence, impact/effect, etc. from a past action.

10.1 Verb + 过

过 must immediately follow a verb in a sentence.

Experience	王：你去过哪些国家？ *Wáng: Nǐ qù guo nǎ xiē guójiā?* 李：我去过英国跟法国。 *Lǐ: Wǒ qù guo Yīngguó gēn Fǎguó.* Wang: Which countries have you been to? Li: I have been to the UK and France.
Influence/effect	我跟你说过他不是好人，你为什么还跟他交朋友？ *Wǒ gēn nǐ shuō guo tā bú shì hǎo rén, nǐ wèishénme hái gēn tā jiāo péngyǒu?* I have told you he is not a good person. Why are you still friends with him?
Impact/result	妈妈：小明，来吃晚饭。 *Māma: Xiǎomíng, lái chī wǎnfàn.* 小明：我在外面吃过了。 *Xiǎomíng: Wǒ zài wàimiàn chī guo le.* Mother: Xiaoming, come and eat dinner. Xiaoming: I have eaten outside (when I was out).

10.2 Adjective + 过

It is possible for 过 to follow an adjective in a sentence.

上星期我们全家打扫屋子，我家**干净过**几天，现在又脏了。
Shàng xīngqī wǒmen quánjiā dǎsǎo wūzi, wǒjiā gānjìng guo jǐ tiān, xiànzài yòu zāng le.
Last week our whole family cleaned up our house, so our house was clean for a couple of days, but now it's dirty again.

Level 1

10.3 Forming questions and answers

(a) Affirmative–negative questions

To form an affirmative–negative/yes–no question, use 'verb + 过 (+ object) 没有/吗?'

你们**吃过**北京烤鸭没有？(= 你们吃过北京烤鸭吗？)
Nǐmen chī guo Běijīng kǎo yā méiyǒu?
Have you had (eaten) Beijing duck?

(b) Short answers

To give a short positive answer, use 'verb + 过'. To give a short negative answer, use '没有 + verb + 过' or simply '没有'.

李：你们**看过**《哈利波特》吗？
Lǐ: Nǐmen kàn guo 'Hālì Bōtè' ma?
张：我**没有**看**过**。
Zhāng: Wǒ méiyǒu kàn guo.
丁：我也**没有**。
Dīng: Wǒ yě méiyǒu.
Li: Have you read *Harry Potter*?
Zhang: I have not read it.
Ding: I have not, either.

Level 2

10.4 Two verbs with 过

When there are two verbs in a simple sentence, 过 should follow the second verb. In this case, the second verb usually indicates the purpose of the first verb. So the first verb is most likely to be 来, 去, 用, etc.

☞ See 9.5 for a similar use of 了.

张：你**去过**王先生的家吗？
Zhāng: Nǐ qù guo Wáng xiānsheng de jiā ma?
李：**去过**。我**去**他家**吃过**两次饭。
Lǐ: Qù guo. Wǒ qù tā jiā chī guo liǎng cì fàn.
Zhang: Have you been to Mr Wang's house?
Li: Yes, I have. I have been there twice to eat.

(Situation: At a dinner party where Chinese food is being served.)

主人：你们要用筷子还是刀叉？
Zhǔrén: Nǐmen yào yòng kuàizi háishì dāochā?
客人甲：我用刀叉吧。我没有**用**筷子**吃过**饭。
Kèrén jiǎ: Wǒ yòng dāochā ba. Wǒ méiyǒu yòng kuàizi chī guo fàn.
客人乙：咱们都用筷子吧。我也没有**用过**筷子，一起试试，好吗？
Kèrén yǐ: Zánmen dōu yòng kuàizi ba. Wǒ yě méiyǒu yòng guo kuàizi, yìqǐ shì shì, hǎoma?
Host: Would you like to use chopsticks or a knife and fork?
Guest A: Let me use a knife and fork. I've never used chopsticks to eat.
Guest B: Let's use chopsticks. I have never used chopsticks, either. Let's try together, OK?

10.5 Adverbial time phrases with 过

Level 3

A sentence with 过 can have an adverbial phrase indicating a past time.

(a) Specific time phrases

❧ It should be noted that while a sentence with 过 is frequently translated into the perfect tense in English to indicate one's experiences, it could also be translated into the past tense on many occasions, especially when the specific time of the action is mentioned.

王：你去过长城吗？
Wáng: Nǐ qù guo Chángchéng ma?
张：去过，你呢？
Zhāng: Qù guo, nǐ ne?
王：去年去过一次，今年还没去过。
Wáng: Qùnián qù guo yí cì, jīnnián hái méi qù guo.
Wang: Have you been to the Great Wall?
Zhang: Yes, I have. How about you?
Wang: I went there once last year. I haven't been there this year.

(*Situation: A doctor inquires about a patient's medical history.*)

医生：你得过什麼病？
Yīshēng: Nǐ dé guo shénme bìng?
病人：小时候得过两次肺炎，上中学以后，没有得过大病。
Bìngrén: Xiǎo shíhòu dé guo liǎng cì fèiyán, shàng zhōngxué yǐhòu, méiyǒu dé guo dà bìng.
Doctor: What illnesses have you had (before)?
Patient: I had pneumonia twice when I was little. I have not had anything serious since I entered middle school.

(b) Negative 过 sentences with 以前

When an optional 以前 (*yǐqián*: 'in the past; before') is used in a negative sentence with 过, the sentence implies that although the speaker has not had a certain experience before, he/she is experiencing it or is about to experience it for the first time.

我没有坐过飞机，我很希望以后能有机会坐坐看。
Wǒ méiyǒu zuò guo fēijī, wǒ hěn xīwàng yǐhòu néng yǒu jīhuì zuò zuò kàn.
I have never flown. I hope I will have the opportunity to try it in the future.

我(以前)没有坐过飞机，这是我第一次，所以现在我很兴奋。
Wǒ (yǐqián) méiyǒu zuò guo fēijī, zhè shì wǒ dì yí cì, suǒyǐ xiànzài wǒ hěn xīngfèn.
I have never flown before; this is my first time; so I am very excited now.

10.6 还没有 + verb + 过 + (呢): 'not yet'

Level 2

'还没有 + verb + 过 + (呢)' indicates 'not yet'; it can be used to imply that an action is likely to happen at a future time. 呢 is optional but is frequently used in conversation.

(*Situation: Both Wang and Zhang **are currently in** Beijing.*)

王：你来北京以后，去过长城没有？
Wáng: Nǐ lái Běijīng yǐhòu, qù guo Chángchéng méiyǒu?
张：我还没有去过呢。 (or 还没有呢。)
Zhāng: Wǒ hái méiyǒu qù guo ne.

Wang: Have you been to the Great Wall since you came to Beijing?

Zhang: I have not been there yet. (Implied: But I probably will sometime in the future.)

*(Situation: Zhang is **currently not** in Beijing; therefore, he would not say 还没有去过. Note that the way Wang asks the 过 question in both situations is the same.)*

王：你住在北京的时候，**去过**长城**没有**？

Wáng: Nǐ zhù zài Běijīng de shíhòu, qù guo Chángchéng méiyǒu?

张：我**没有**去过。(or **没有**。)

Zhāng: Wǒ méiyǒu qù guo.

Wang: When you lived in Beijing, did you ever go to the Great Wall?

Zhang: I never did.

Level
3

10.7 从来没有 + verb + 过

'从来没有 + verb + 过' is stronger in tone than '没有 + verb + 过' and they are similar in meaning.

我**从来没有**听**过**这么奇怪的事。

Wǒ cónglái méiyǒu tīng guo zhème qíguài de shì.

I have never heard anything so strange.

小王去了北京以后，给我打过两次电话，可是他**从来没有**给我写**过**信。

Xiǎo Wáng qù le Běijīng yǐhòu, gěi wǒ dǎ guo liǎng cì diànhuà, kěshì tā cónglái méiyǒu gěi wǒ xiě guo xìn.

Ever since Xiao Wang went to Beijing, he has called me twice, but he has never written to me.

👁 Learners who are English speakers frequently associate '从来没有 + verb + 过' with the present perfect tense or past perfect tense in English. Actually, the context will decide which English tense '从来没有 + verb + 过' is equal to. It can even simply be past tense.

*(Situation: The narrator **is currently** in China.)*

我来中国以前，**从来没有**迷**过**路，因为我的方向感很好；可是来中国以后，常常迷路，因为我不认识中国字，看不懂路标。

Wǒ lái Zhōngguó yǐqián, cónglái méiyǒu mí guo lù, yīnwèi wǒde fāngxiàng gǎn hěn hǎo; kěshì lái Zhōngguó yǐhòu, chángcháng mílù, yīnwèi wǒ bú rènshì Zhōngguó zì, kàn bù dǒng lùbiāo.

Before I came to China, I **had never got lost** because I had a good sense of direction. But since I came to China, I have often got lost because I don't know Chinese characters and so I cannot understand street signs.

*(Situation: The narrator **is currently not** in China.)*

我在中国的时候，**从来没有**迷**过**路，因为我找不到路的时候，中国人总是热情地帮助我。

Wǒ zài Zhōngguó de shíhòu, cónglái méiyǒu mí guo lù, yīnwèi wǒ zhǎo bú dào lù de shíhòu, Zhōngguó rén zǒngshì rèqíng de bāngzhù wǒ.

When I was in China, I never **got lost** because Chinese people always helped me warmly when I could not find my way.

Level 1

10.8 过 with modal particle 了

A sentence with 过 can have modal particle 了 at the end to emphasize 'already'.

> 王：明天我们一起去看《阿凡达》吧。
> *Wáng: Míngtiān wǒmen yìqǐ qù kàn 'Ā Fán Dá' ba.*
> 李：那个电影，我看过了。(= 我已经看过了。)
> *Lǐ: Nà ge diànyǐng, wǒ kàn guo le. (= wǒ yǐjīng kàn guo le.)*
> Wang: Shall we go see *Avatar* together tomorrow?
> Li: I have already seen that movie.

Level 2

10.9 过 with 曾经

An optional word, 曾经 (*céngjīng*), can be used with 过 to make the speech sound more formal. 曾经 can be shorted to 曾. The negative form is '不曾/未曾 + verb + 过'.

> 王先生曾(经)出过两本诗集，现在他改写小说了。
> *Wáng xiānsheng céngjīng chū guo liǎng běn shījí, xiànzài tā gǎi xiě xiǎoshuō le.*
> Mr Wang published two collections of poetry; now he has switched to writing fiction.

> 我不曾(= 未曾 = 没有)见过象王小姐这么美貌的女子。
> *Wǒ bù céng (= wèi céng = méiyǒu) jiàn guo xiàng Wáng xiǎojiě zhème měimào de nǚzi.*
> I have not met a lady as beautiful as Miss Wang.

Level 3

10.10 Comparing the use of 过 and 了

(a) Different emphases

Sometimes, 过 and 了 can be interchangeable, but the sentences may have slightly different emphases.

> English: I lived in England for two years when I was little.
> Chinese #1: 我小时候在英国住了两年。
> *Wǒ xiǎo shíhòu zài Yīngguó zhù le liǎng nián.*
> This is to **state the fact** about a past event.
> Chinese #2: 我小时候在英国住过两年。
> *Wǒ xiǎo shíhòu zài Yīngguó zhù guo liǎng nián.*
> This is to **indicate the experience** of living abroad.

(b) Stating fact vs. indicating impact

To state the fact about a past event, use 了. To indicate the impact of a past event, use 过.

> 王：老师叫我们看的那本书，你们看了没有？
> *Wáng: Lǎoshī jiào wǒmen kàn de nà běn shū, nǐmen kàn le méiyǒu?*
> 张：我看了。
> *Zhāng: Wǒ kàn le.*
> 丁：那本书，我小时候就看过了。
> *Dīng: Nà běn shū, wǒ xiǎo shíhòu jiù kàn guo le.*
> Wang: Did you read (*or*: have you read) the book the teacher assigned us to read?
> Zhang: I did. (or: I have.)

Ding: I had already read that book before (when I was a young child.) (了 implies that he had no need to read the book again since he had read it before. 过 is used to indicate the impact of a previous action.)

王：你今年夏天去了哪些地方？
Wáng: Nǐ jīnnián xiàtiān qù le nǎ xiē dìfāng?
张：我**去了**两趟北京。
Zhāng: Wǒ qù le liǎng tàng Běijīng.
Wang: Where did you go this past summer?
Zhang: I went to Beijing twice. (Stating what he did in summer.)

王：下个月咱们一起去北京玩玩，怎么样？
Wáng: Xià ge yuè, zánmen yìqǐ qù Běijīng wán wán, zěnmeyàng?
张：我不想去，因为我今年夏天**去过**两趟北京。
Zhāng: Wǒ bù xiǎng qù, yīnwèi wǒ jīnnián xiàtiān qù guo liǎng tàng Běijīng.
Wang: How about if we go to Beijing for a holiday next month?
Zhang: I don't want to go because I went there twice this past summer. (Emphasizing the impact of having been to Beijing earlier – he does not want to go again next month.)

(c) Indicating completion vs. emphasizing experience

了 indicates the completion of an action at a specific moment; 过 emphasizes previous experience, impact, effect, etc.

李：昨天我去你家的时候，你不在，你**去**哪里**了**？
Lǐ: Zuótiān wǒ qù nǐ jiā de shíhòu, nǐ bú zài, nǐ qù nǎlǐ le?
丁：我跟朋友**去**看电影**了**。
Dīng: Wǒ gēn péngyǒu qù kàn diànyǐng le.
Li: Yesterday when I went to your house, you weren't in. Where did you go?
(*or*: Where had you gone?)
Ding: I went to a movie with a friend. (*or*: I had gone to a movie.)

昨天我去看病。医生说，我**得了**肺炎。我**小时候**也**得过**两次肺炎。
Zuótiān wǒ qù kàn bìng. Yīshēng shuō, wǒ dé le fèiyán. Wǒ xiǎo shíhòu yě dé guo liǎng cì fèiyán.
I went to see the doctor yesterday. The doctor said that I have pneumonia. I had pneumonia twice when I was young.

(d) Past vs. current events

Since 了 indicates the completion of an action, it may or may not be about a past event. 过 basically indicates that the action took place in the past.

病人的妈妈：医生，请告诉我，我儿子**得了**什么病？
Bìngrén de māma: Yīshēng, qǐng gàosù wǒ, wǒ érzi dé le shénme bìng?
医生：他**得了**肺炎。他**以前得过**肺炎吗？
Yīshēng: Tā dé le fèiyán. Tā yǐqián dé guo fèiyán ma?
病人的妈妈：**小时候得过**两次。
Bìngrén de māma: Xiǎo shíhòu dé guo liǎng cì.
Patient's mother: Doctor, please tell me what illness my son has? (What illness did he get?)
Doctor: He has pneumonia. Has he had pneumonia before?
Patient's mother: He had it twice when he was little.

王：丁先生在哪里？他**来了**吗？
Wáng: Dīng xiānsheng zài nǎlǐ? Tā lái le ma?
张：他**来了**，正在客厅里等你呢。
Zhāng: Tā lái le, zhèng zài kètīng lǐ děng nǐ ne.
Wang: Where is Mr Ding? Is he here? (Has he come?)
Zhang: He is here. (He has come.) He is waiting for you in the living room.

丁：王先生在哪里？他**来了**吗？
Dīng: Wáng xiānsheng zài nǎlǐ? Tā lái le ma?
李：他**来过了**，可是十分钟以前**走了**。
Lǐ: Tā lái guo le, kěshì shí fēnzhōng yǐqián zǒu le.
Ding: Where is Mr Wang? Is he here?
Li: He was here, but he left ten minutes ago.

(e) Negative sentences

In a negative sentence, 了 is not used, but 过 should be used if the verb is said.

王：**上星期**你**去**李老师家了吗？
Wáng: Shàng xīngqī nǐ qù Lǐ lǎoshī jiā le ma?
张：我**没有去**。(or **没有**。) (Incorrect: 我没有去了。)
Zhāng: Wǒ méiyǒu qù.
Wang: Did you go to Teacher Li's house last week?
Zhang: I didn't.

丁：你**去过**李老师家吗？
Dīng: Nǐ qù guo Lǐ lǎoshī jiā ma?
王：**没有去过**。(or **没有**。) (Incorrect: 我没有去。)
Wáng: Méiyǒu qù guo.
Ding: Have you been to Teacher Li's house?
Wang: I haven't.

(f) Same meaning

Occasionally, a sentence with 过 (+ object) and a sentence with 了 share the same meaning, especially when one asks if someone has eaten (a traditional way to greet someone around meal time).

王：你们**吃过饭了**吗？(= 你们**吃饭了**吗？)
Wáng: Nǐmen chī guo fàn le ma?
张：**吃过了**。(= **吃了**。)
Zhāng: Chī guo le.
丁：我**还没吃**。(But rarely 我还没吃过。)
Dīng: Wǒ hái méi chī.
Wang: Have you eaten (lunch/dinner)?
Zhang: I have.
Ding: I haven't (yet).

<table>
<tr><td>Level</td></tr>
<tr><td>2</td></tr>
</table>

10.11 Related information

(a) 没有 or 没?

没有 can be shortened to 没, especially when a verb follows. However, when giving a short negative answer without a verb or an adverb, 没有 is more frequently used than simply 没.

李：谁去过长城？

Lǐ: Shéi qù guo Chángchéng?

王：我**没**去过。小张，你呢？

Wáng: Wǒ méi qù guo. Xiǎo Zhāng, nǐ ne?

张：也还**没**，不过我打算下星期去。

Zhāng: Yě hái méi, búguò wǒ dǎsuàn xià xīngqī qù.

Li: Who has been to the Great Wall?

Wang: I haven't. Xiao Zhang, what about you?

Zhang: I have not yet been there, either. But I plan to go next week.

(b) 过: *guo or guò?*

过 as an experiential aspect particle is normally pronounced in the neutral tone. However, when the emphasis is on the effect or impact of an action, 过 can be pronounced in the fourth tone. Therefore, in this chapter, 过 in many sentences can be pronounced in the fourth tone.

妈妈：小明，你才**吃过**午饭，现在不可以吃点心。（过 is used to emphasize **the effect** of 吃.)

*Māma: Xiǎomíng, nǐ cái chī **guò** wǔfàn, xiànzài bù kěyǐ chī diǎnxīn.*

Mother: Xiaoming, you just ate lunch; you are not allowed to eat any snacks now.

王：你**吃过**印度菜没有？想不想一起去吃？（过 indicates **experience**; it is in the neutral tone)

*Wáng: Nǐ chī **guo** Yìndù cài méiyǒu? Xiǎng bù xiǎng yìqǐ qù chī?*

李：我昨天刚跟朋友去**吃过**，今天吃中国菜吧！（过 indicates **impact**; it is in the fourth tone.)

*Lǐ: Wǒ zuótiān gāng gēn péngyǒu qù chī **guò**, jīntiān chī Zhōngguó cài ba!*

Wang: Have you had Indian food before? Would you like to go get some (Indian food) together?

Li: I just had Indian food with some friends yesterday. How about if we have Chinese food today?

Exercises

Fill in the blanks using 了, 过 or nothing. (Answers in some of the blanks can be flexible.)

1 那本书我已经看 ＿＿＿＿ 两遍 ＿＿＿＿，我不想再看 ＿＿＿＿。

   I have already read that book twice. I don't want to read it any more.

2 王：你以前用 ＿＿＿＿ 筷子吗？

   Wang: Have you used chopsticks before?

   李：我没用 ＿＿＿＿。

   Li: I have not.

3 老师：你用 ＿＿＿＿ 毛笔写 ＿＿＿＿ 字吗？

   Teacher: Have you ever used brush pen to write characters?

   学生：没有 ＿＿＿＿。

   Student: No.

Level

1

4 他们来 _____ 北京一个多星期 _____，参观 _____ 很多地方。

They have been to Beijing for more than a week and have visited many places.

5 我十岁的时候，去 _____ 英国，在那里住 _____ 三个月 _____。

When I was ten years old, I went to England and I lived there for three months.

6 昨天我去 _____ 医院看医生的时候，医生说，我得 _____ 肺炎。他问我以前得 _____ 肺炎没有，我告诉 _____ 他，我小时候也得 _____ 一次。

When I went to the hospital to see a doctor, the doctor said that I had pneumonia. He asked me if I had had pneumonia before and I told him that I had had it once when I was young.

7 妈妈：今天的功课，你写 _____ 没有？

Mother: Have you done today's homework?

儿子：我写 _____，可是弟弟没有写 _____。

Son: I have, but little brother hasn't.

8 昨天我在王先生家吃 _____ 饭的时候，用 _____ 一下儿筷子。用 _____ 筷子吃 _____ 饭真有意思，我从来没有用 _____ 筷子吃 _____ 饭。

When I ate at Mr Wang's house yesterday, I used chopsticks. Eating with chopsticks (using chopsticks to eat) was really fun. I had never eaten with chopsticks before.

9 我小时候身体不好，得 _____ 两次肺炎。上中学的时候，没有得 _____ 大病；可是上个月我又得 _____ 一次肺炎，到现在还没有好 _____。

When I was young, I was not healthy and I had pneumonia twice. When I was in middle school, I never had any serious illnesses. But last month, I once again got pneumonia and I have not yet recovered so far.

10 客人：你爸爸去哪里 _____？

Guest: Where did your father go?

男孩：他去日本 _____。

Boy: He went to Japan.

客人：他以前去 _____ 日本吗？

Guest: Has he been to Japan before?

男孩：没有 _____。但是他去 _____ 很多别的国家。

Boy: He has not. But he has been to many other countries.

11 王：我没有来 _____ 你们学校，请你带我参观一下儿，好不好？

Wang: I have never been to your school. Would you please show me around?

张：我们等一下儿吧。李先生也没有来 _____，可是他现在还没来 _____，他来 _____ 我就带你们一起参观。

Zhang: Let's wait for a while. Mr Li has not been here either. But he is not here yet. As soon as he arrives, I will show the two of you around together.

11 Auxiliary verbs

Auxiliary verbs in Chinese are similar to auxiliary verbs in English. Some grammarians term this group of words 'modal verbs'.

The following table shows the most common auxiliary verbs and their functions. Some of the auxiliary verbs can have more than one meaning and some of them share similar meanings; therefore, it is important to take into consideration the context when deciding which auxiliary verb is the proper one to use in a situation.

Volition, intention	要 (yào), 想 (xiǎng)
Willingness	愿意 (yuànyì), 肯 (kěn)
Obligation, moral duty	要, 得 (děi), 应该 (yīnggāi), 应当 (yīngdāng), 应, 该
Assumption, estimation	应该
Necessity, requirement	要, 必须 (bìxū), 得, 不必 (búbì), 不用 (búyòng)
Ability	能 (néng), 能够 (nénggòu), 会 (huì), 可以 (kěyǐ)
Possibility	会, 能, (可能 (kěnéng))
Permission	能, 可以, 行 (xíng)

An auxiliary verb should be followed by a regular verb unless it is a short answer to a question. Only 应该 can be followed by another auxiliary verb. ☞ See 11.9 for details.

不, not 没有, is used before the auxiliary verb as the negative form. When 不 appears after the auxiliary verb, it is used to negate the main verb. The two patterns have different meanings.

> 不 + auxiliary verb + main verb ≠ auxiliary verb + 不 + main verb

11.1 Volition or intention (要, 想)

Level
1/2

要 is stronger in meaning than 想. Therefore, 要 is similar to 'will, to be going to', whereas 想 is similar to 'would like' or 'to feel like'. 要 indicates one's strong will to make something happen; 想 indicates one's wish, plan, etc.

(a) The negative form of 要 and 想

Normally, the negative form for both 要 and 想 is 不想. Although 不要 can also be the negative form for 要, it carries a very strong negative tone and is used less frequently.

> 王：今年八月我**要**去中国。
> *Wáng: Jīnnián bāyuè wǒ yào qù Zhōngguó.*
> 张：太好了！以后我也**想**去中国学中文。
> *Zhāng: Tài hǎo le! Yǐhòu wǒ yě xiǎng qù Zhōngguó xué Zhōngwén.*

Wang: I **am going to** China in August this year.

Zhang: That's great! In the future, I **would like to** go to China to study Chinese, too.

李：明天晚上小张家有一个舞会，你**要**不**要**去？

Lǐ: Míngtiān wǎnshàng Xiǎo Zhāng jiā yǒu yí ge wǔhuì, nǐ yào bú yào qù?

丁：我**不想**去，我不喜欢跳舞。

Dīng: Wǒ bù xiǎng qù, wǒ bù xǐhuān tiàowǔ.

Li: There will be a dance party at Xiao Zhang's house tomorrow evening; **will** you go?

Ding: I **don't feel like** going. I don't like to dance.

张：桌上有很多点心，你吃一点吧！

Zhāng: Zhuō shàng yǒu hěn duō diǎnxīn, nǐ chī yìdiǎn ba.

李：我**不要**吃那种会让我发胖的东西。

Lǐ: Wǒ bú yào chī nà zhǒng huì ràng wǒ fāpàng de dōngxī.

Zhang: There are lots of snacks on the table; why don't you have some?

Li: I **will not** eat that kind of fattening food.

(b) Adverbs indicating degree

Adverbs indicating degree, such as 很, 真 and 非常 can only appear before 想, not 要. However, 一定 can only go with 要, not 想.

我**很想**(or **非常想**)学中文，可是一直没有时间；明年我**一定要**开始学。

Wǒ hěn xiǎng (or fēicháng xiǎng) xué Zhōngwén, kěshì yìzhí méiyǒu shíjiān; míngnián wǒ yídìng yào kāishǐ xué.

I **would like to** learn Chinese **very much**, but I have not had the time; I **will definitely** begin to take Chinese lessons next year.

(c) 要 and 想 as regular verbs

Both 要 and 想 can be used as regular verbs. As regular verbs, 要 means 'to want', and 想 means 'to think' or 'to miss'. Furthermore, 不要 is interchangeable with 别 in a negative imperative sentence.

老师**要**我们回家去**想一想**这两个问题。

Lǎoshī yào wǒmen huí jiā qù xiǎng yì xiǎng zhè liǎng ge wèntí.

The teacher **wanted** us to go home and **think about** these two questions.

妈妈**要**我到了中国以后**不要**(= **别**)太想家。

Māma yào wǒ dào le Zhōngguó yǐhòu búyào (= bié) tài xiǎng jiā.

My mother **wants** me to not **miss** home too much after I go to China.

Level 1

11.2 Willingness (愿意, 肯)

小李很倔强，从来**不肯**让步，所以没有人**愿意**跟他合作。

Xiǎo Lǐ hěn juéjiàng, cónglái bù kěn ràngbù, suǒyǐ méiyǒu rén yuànyì gēn tā hézuò.

Xiao Li is stubborn; he is **never willing** to back down, so nobody is **willing to** work with him.

Level 1/2

11.3 Obligation or moral duty (要, 得, 应该, 应当, 应, 该)

(a) 要 and 得

要 and 得 both mean 'must, to have to'; 得 is pronounced *děi* and is more casual than 要.

明天有考试，今晚我**得**准备考试。

Míngtiān yǒu kǎoshì, jīn wǎn wǒ děi zhǔnbèi kǎoshì.

There will be a test tomorrow. This evening I **have to** study for the test.

(Situation: Two parents give advice to their children. 要 can be replaced by 得 to make the tone more casual. 要 can also be replaced by 应该/应当/应/该 to mean 'should' instead of 'must'.)

爸爸：做人**要**诚实，做事**要**负责，学习**要**认真。

Bàba: Zuòrén yào chéngshí, zuòshì yào fùzé, xuéxí yào rènzhēn.

妈妈：对，而且还**要**爱护弟妹，帮助朋友。

Māma: Duì, érqiě hái yào àihù dìmèi, bāngzhù péngyǒu.

Father: You **must** be honest in dealing with people, you **must** be responsible in dealing with work and you **must** be conscientious in studying.

Mother: That's right. Also, you **must** take care of your younger siblings and help your friends.

(b) 应该, 应当, 应 and 该

应该, 应当, 应 and 该 all mean 'should, ought to' and are interchangeable, but 应 is more formal than 应该/应当, whereas 该 is more casual. Neither 应 nor 该 should be used to give a short answer without the verb following. In giving a short answer, use 应该 or 不应该.

王：我们**应不应该**把这件事告诉他？

Wáng: Wǒmen yīng bù yīnggāi bǎ zhè jiàn shì gàosù ta?

李：**不应该**。(我们**不该**告诉他。)

Lǐ: Bù yīnggāi.

Wang: **Should** we tell him about this matter?

Li: We **should not**. (*or* We should not tell him.)

(c) The negative forms of 要 and 得

The negative forms of 要 and 得 are **not** 不要 and 不得; they are 不用 or 不必, meaning 'no need to'. Furthermore, 得 cannot be used in asking an affirmative–negative question; i.e. 得不得 is incorrect.

王：今天我没有去上课。请告诉我，今天**要不要**作语法练习？

Wáng: Jīntiān wǒ méiyǒu qù shàng kè. Qǐng gàosù wǒ, jīntiān yào bú yào zuò yǔfǎ liànxí?

李：老师说，今天**不用**(= **不必**)作语法练习，但是**得**念课文。

Lǐ: Lǎoshī shuō, jīntiān búyòng (= búbì) zuò yǔfǎ liànxí, dànshì děi niàn kèwén.

Wang: I didn't go to class today. Please tell me: **do we have to** do grammar exercises today?

Li: The teacher said we **don't have to** do grammar exercises today, but we **have to** read the text.

11.4 Assumption or estimation (应该)

The assumption/estimation in these sentences is based on reason or experience.

(a) The negative form (1)

When 应该 indicates assumption, its negative form is 应该不, **not** 不应该.

我家只有我爸懂英文，这本英文书**应该**是他的。

Wǒ jiā zhǐ yǒu wǒ bà dǒng Yīngwén, zhè běn Yīngwén shū yīnggāi shì tāde.

In my family only my father knows English; this English book **should** be his.

王明不懂英文，这本英文书**应该不**是他的。

Wáng Míng bù dǒng Yīngwén, zhè běn Yīngwén shū yīnggāi bú shì tāde.

Wang Míng does not know English; this English book **shouldn't** be his.

张：王小兰**不应该**说别人坏话。（不应该说: moral duty)

Zhāng: Wáng Xiǎolán bù yīnggāi shuō biérén huàihuà.

李：我很了解王小兰，她**应该不**是那种人。（应该不是: assumption/estimation)

Lǐ: Wǒ hěn liǎojiě Wáng Xiǎolán, tā yīnggāi bú shì nà zhǒng rén.

Zhang: Wang Xiaolan **should not** have said bad things about other people.

Li: I know Wang Xiaolan very well. She **shouldn't** be that type of person.

(b) The negative form (2)

When 应该 indicates assumption, its negative form can also be 应该没有. But when it indicates obligation, it is never 没有应该 and is always 不应该.

(Situation: Two teachers are talking about a student's attendance.)

张老师：昨天王中来上课了没有？

Zhāng lǎoshī: Zuótiān Wáng Zhōng lái shàng kè le méiyǒu?

李老师：**应该没有**，因为出席表上没有他的签名。

Lǐ lǎoshī: Yīnggāi méiyǒu, yīnwèi chūxí biǎo shàng méiyǒu tāde qiānmíng.

张老师：他昨天**不应该**缺席，因为医生说他的病已经好了。

Zhāng lǎoshī: Tā zuótiān bù yīnggāi xuēxí, yīnwèi yīshēng shuō tāde bìng yǐjīng hǎo le.

Teacher Zhang: Did Wang Zhong come to class yesterday?

Teacher Li: I **gathered that he did not** because his signature was not on the attendance sheet.

Teacher Zhang: He **should not** have been absent yesterday because the doctor said that he had recovered from his illness already.

Level 1/2   11.5 Necessity (要, 必须, 得)

This includes requirements, needs, etc. 得 is casual.

(Situation: Two parents are giving their children advice on safety.)

妈妈：过马路的时候，**要**记得先看看两边有没有车。

Māma: Guò mǎlù de shíhòu, yào jìde xiān kàn kàn liǎng biān yǒu méiyǒu chē.

爸爸：对，而且还**要**等绿灯亮了才过去。

Bàba: Duì, érqiě hái yào děng lǜdēng liàng le cái guòqù.

Mother: When you are about to cross the street, you **have to** remember to look if there are cars coming from either side.

Father: That's right. Also, you **have to** wait for the green light (to be on) before crossing.

这个学校的学生毕业以前**必须**学两年的外语课。

Zhè ge xuéxiào de xuéshēng bìyè yǐqián bìxū xué liǎng nián de wàiyǔ kè.

Students at this school **must** (= **are required to**) study a foreign language for two years before graduating.

The negative form is 不必 or 不用 'no need to', **not** 不必须 or 不得. 不要 means 别 ('don't' in a negative imperative sentence); therefore, it is not considered to be in the form of an auxiliary verb.

张：小王，你**得**帮帮我，这几个问题，我都不懂。

Zhāng: Xiǎo Wáng, nǐ děi bāng bāng wǒ, zhè jǐ ge wèntí, wǒ dōu bù dǒng.

王：**不必**着急，我现在就来帮你。
Wáng: Búbì zháojí, wǒ xiànzài jiù lái bāng nǐ.
Zhang: Xiao Wang, you **have to** help me. I don't understand any of these questions.
Wang: **No need to** be anxious. I'll come and help you right now.

Level 2/3

11.6 Ability (能, 能够, 会, 可以)

The ability can be either one's competence or one's ability to do something afforded by the situation.

(a) 能, 能够 and 可以

能 and 能够 are interchangeable, but 能 is used more frequently than 能够.

王：李明的腿摔伤了，明天的比赛，他**能(够)**跑吗？(= **可以**跑吗？)
Wáng: Lǐ Míng de tuǐ shuāi shāng le, míngtiān de bǐsài, tā néng(gòu) pǎo ma?
张：他说他的伤不严重，他**能**(= **可以**)跑。
Zhāng: Tā shuō tāde shāng bù yánzhòng, tā néng (= kěyǐ) pǎo.
Wang: Li Ming has injured his leg. **Can** he run in tomorrow's race?
Zhang: He says that his injury is not serious and that he **can** run.

李英**能**唱，**能**跳，请她表演一下吧。
Lǐ Yīng néng chàng, néng tiào, qǐng tā biǎoyǎn yíxià ba.
Li Ying **can** sing and **can** dance. Let's ask her to perform.

(b) The negative form of 能/能够/可以

The negative form of 能/能够/可以 is 不能, **not** 不可以. 不可以 means 'mustn't; to be forbidden'.

今晚我的家人**要**一起去看电影，可是明天我有个考试，所以我**不能**跟他们去。
Jīnwǎn wǒde jiā rén yào yìqǐ qù kàn diànyǐng, kěshì míngtiān wǒ yǒu ge kǎoshì, suǒyǐ wǒ bù néng gēn tāmen qù.
My family **is going to** see a movie this evening, but I have an exam tomorrow, so I **can't** go with them.

(c) 会: acquired skill

会 indicates having an acquired skill. It is frequently translated as 'to know how to'.

我妹妹才一岁，还**不会走路**。
Wǒ mèimei cái yī suì, hái bú huì zǒulù.
My younger sister is only one year old; she **can't** (= **hasn't learned how to**) walk yet.
Compare: 小王的腿摔伤了，他现在暂时**不能走路**。
Xiǎo Wáng de tuǐ shuāi shāng le, tā xiànzài zhànshí bù néng zǒulù.
Xiao Wang has injured his leg. He **cannot** walk for the time being.

老师：李明，这个问题你**会不会**回答？你来回答一下，好不好？
Lǎoshī: Lǐ Míng, zhè ge wèntí, nǐ huì bú huì huídá? Nǐ lái huídá yíxià, hǎo bù hǎo?
丁：老师，李明喉咙痛，他今天**不能说话**。
Dīng: Lǎoshī, Lǐ Míng hóulóng tòng, tā jīntiān bù néng shuōhuà.
Teacher: Li Ming, **can you** (= **do you know how to**) answer this question? Why don't you answer it?
Ding: Sir, Li Ming has a sore throat. He **cannot** talk today.

(d) 会: 'good at'

会 can mean 'good at', especially when it is modified by degree adverbs such as 很, 真 or 非常.

我妈妈**非常会**做菜；可是她**不太会**做家事。
Wǒ māma fēicháng huì zuò cài, kěshì tā bú tài huì zuò jiāshì.
My mother is **very good at** cooking; but she is **not too good at** doing housework.

王：听说你**很会**唱歌，你教我唱中国民歌《茉莉花》，好不好？（很会: 'good at')
Wáng: Tīngshuō nǐ hěn huì chànggē, nǐ jiāo wǒ chàng Zhōngguó míngē 'Mòlì huā', hǎo bù hǎo?
李：我**不会**唱《茉莉花》，我教你唱《康定情歌》吧！（不会: 'don't know how')
Lǐ: Wǒ bú huì chàng 'Mòlì huā', wǒ jiāo nǐ chàng 'Kāngdìng qínggē' ba!
Wang: I heard that you are **good at** singing. Would you teach me how to sing the Chinese folk song *Jasmine Flowers*?
Li: I **don't know how to** sing *Jasmine Flowers*. Let me teach you *Kangding Love Song*.

11.7 Possibility (会, 能, 可能)

Some grammarians consider 可能 an adverb, which means 'probably, perhaps'. From this perspective, 可能 can appear before another auxiliary verb.

(a) Future event with 会

会 indicates the possibility of something happening more or less naturally without anyone consciously exercising control to make it happen.

天气预报说，明天**不会**下雨，但是**可能会**很冷。
Tiānqì yùbào shuō, míngtiān bú huì xiàyǔ, dànshì kěnéng huì hěn lěng.
The weather forecast says that it will not rain tomorrow, but it might be very cold.

(Situation: A dialogue between a man and his girlfriend.)

男：明天是我第一次跟你爸妈见面，他们**会不会**不喜欢我？
Nán: Míngtiān shì wǒ dì yí cì gēn nǐ bàmā jiànmiàn, tāmen huì bú huì bù xǐhuān wǒ?
女：你放心，他们一定**会**很喜欢你的。
Nǔ: Nǐ fàngxīn, tāmen yídìng huì hěn xǐhuān nǐ de.
Male: Tomorrow will be the first time I meet your parents. **Will** they dislike me?
Female: Don't worry. They **will** definitely like you very much.

(b) 会 vs. 要 for future event

👁 As auxiliary verbs, both 会 and 要 are frequently translated as 'to be going to' or 'will'. When the main verb indicates a future action that cannot be controlled by a person's will, such as 下雨 'to rain', or when the speaker does not want to emphasize a person's will to control it, 会 is used.

王：明天**会**是个好天气，我**要**去公园走走，你**想不想**去？
Wáng: Míngtiān huì shì ge hǎo tiānqì, wǒ yào qù gōngyuán zǒu zǒu, nǐ xiǎng bù xiǎng qù?
李：明天我**会**很忙，我**不能**去。
Lǐ: Míngtiān wǒ huì hěn máng, wǒ bù néng qù.
Wang: Tomorrow **will** be a nice day. I **am going to** the park for a walk. **Would you like** to go?
Li: I **will** be busy tomorrow. I **won't be able to** go.

(c) Indicating 'possibility'

能 indicates the possibility of one's doing something. In this case, 能 is frequently followed by 不. Also, 不能不 means 'must, to have to'.

李：对不起，晚上**不能**来你家吃饭了。我**得**去王先生家给他看孩子。
Lǐ: Duìbùqǐ, wǎnshàng bù néng lái nǐ jiā chī fàn le. Wǒ děi qù Wáng xiānsheng jiā gěi tā kān háizi.

张：你**能**不去吗？ (or 你**能不能**不去？)
Zhāng: Nǐ néng bú qù ma?

李：老板叫我做的事，我**不能**不做。
Lǐ: Lǎobǎn jiào wǒ zuò de shì, wǒ bù néng bú zuò.

Li: Sorry, I **can't** come to your house for dinner (as I promised I would). I **have to** go to Mr Wang's house to babysit.

Zhang: **Can you not** go? (Is it **possible** for you not to go?)

Li: It is **not possible** for me to **not** do what my boss asks me to do. (= I **have to** do what my boss asks me to do.)

Level 2

11.8 Permission (能, 可以, 行)

The distinction between ability and permission can be vague. Both can be 能 or 可以, and both of those are translated as 'can, to be able to'. 行 is more casual or conversational than 能/可以. Also, 行 is not normally used to express ability.

不可以/不行 is used to indicate 'to not be allowed/permitted; to be forbidden'.

李：我想学游泳，你**可不可以**教我？ (When asking a favour, 可以 is better than 能.)
Lǐ: Wǒ xiǎng xué yóuyǒng, nǐ kě bù kěyǐ jiāo wǒ?

张：对不起，我**不能**教你，因为我也**不会**游泳。(不能: inability)
Zhāng: Duìbùqǐ, wǒ bù néng jiāo nǐ, yīnwèi wǒ yě bú huì yóuyǒng.

Li：I **would like to** learn swimming. **Can** you teach me?

Zhang: Sorry, I **can't** teach you. I **don't know how to** swim, either.

儿子：我**可(以)不可以**跟朋友去河边玩？
Érzi: Wǒ kě(yǐ) bù kěyǐ gēn péngyǒu qù hébiān wán?

妈妈：**不行**，你还**不会**游泳，你**不可以**去。
Māma: Bù xíng, nǐ hái bú huì yóuyǒng, nǐ bù kěyǐ qù.

Son: **Can** I go with my friends to the river(side) and have some fun?

Mother: No, you **can't**. You **don't know how to** swim yet. You **are not allowed** to go.

Level 3

11.9 Related information

(a) 应该 + another auxiliary verb

应该 is the only auxiliary verb that can appear before another auxiliary verb (unless 可能 is considered an auxiliary verb). When it appears before another auxiliary verb, its meaning is 'assumption' or 'estimation', not 'moral duty' or 'obligation'. Therefore, its negative form is 应该不, not 不应该.

张：明天晚上的饭局，你**会不会**去？
Zhāng: Míngtiān wǎnshàng de fànjú, nǐ huì bú huì qù?

李：**应该会**，明天我没有事。你呢？ (应该会: estimation)
Lǐ: Yīnggāi huì, míngtiān wǒ méiyǒu shì. Nǐ ne?

张：我**应该不能**去，我太太出国了，我**得**在家照顾孩子。(应该不能: estimation)
Zhāng: Wǒ yīnggāi bù néng qù, wǒ tàitai chūguó le, wǒ děi zài jiā zhàogù háizi.

李：你**应该**找人来帮你看孩子。明天是老板的生日，咱们都**应该**去。
(应该: duty, obligation)
Lǐ: Nǐ yīnggāi zhǎo rén lái bāng nǐ kān háizi. Míngtiān shì lǎobǎn de shēngrì, zánmen dōu yīnggāi qù.

Zhang: **Will** you be at tomorrow evening's dinner party?

Li: I **should be there (I estimate that I will be there)**. I am free tomorrow. How about you?

Zhang: I **estimate** that I **won't be able to** go. My wife is out of the country; I **have to** stay home and take care of the kids.

Li: You **should** get someone to babysit. Tomorrow is our boss's birthday; we **should** all go.

(b) 该不会……吧/该不是……吧

In casual speech, 该不会……吧 (but usually not 应该不) or 该不是……吧 indicates the speaker's assumption of an undesirable situation. The subject before 该不 is **not** the person making the assumption.

(Situation: Mr Wang has a date with Miss Li. He has been waiting for more than half an hour, but she has not shown up.)

> 李小姐**该不会**改变主意了**吧**！
> *Lǐ xiǎojiě gāi bú huì gǎibiàn zhǔyì le ba!*
> Could it be that Miss Li has changed her mind?

(Situation: Ding Xiaolan has never missed a class, but today she is absent. Her teacher thinks this probably means she is sick.)

> 老师：丁小兰今天怎么没来上课？她**该不是**病了**吧**！
> *Lǎoshī: Dīng Xiǎolán jīntiān zěnme méi lái shàng kè? Tā gāi bú shì bìng le ba!*
> Teacher: How come Ding Xiaolan didn't come to class today? Could it be that she is sick?

(c) 不能不 and 不得不

不能不 and 不得不 both mean 'to have to'. 得 in 不得不 is pronounced *dé*.

> 下雨了，所以我们**不得不**改变去野餐的计划，而留在家里看电视。
> *Xià yǔ le, suǒyǐ wǒmen bù dé bù gǎibiàn qù yěcān de jìhuà, ér liú zài jiā lǐ kàn diànshì.*
> It was raining. So we **had to** change our plan to go for a picnic and stayed home to watch TV.

> 王：明天晚上的饭局，你去不去？
> *Wáng: Míngtiān wǎnshàng de fànjú, nǐ qù bú qù?*
> 李：我**不想**去，可是老板过生日，所以**不能不**去。
> *Lǐ: Wǒ bù xiǎng qù, kěshì lǎobǎn guò shēngrì, suǒyǐ bù néng bú qù.*
> Wang: Are you going to tomorrow evening's dinner party?
> Li: I **don't feel like** going, but it's our boss's birthday, so I **have to** go (I **cannot not** go).

Exercises

Choose the proper auxiliary verb for each of the blanks and decide whether the auxiliary verb should be in the **positive**, **negative** or **interrogative** form.

Level
1

1 丁：图书馆里 _____ （可以，得，必须）吸烟。

张：好，我不吸烟。_____ （可以，应该，能够）喝水呢？

丁：我想 _____ （应该，愿意，能够） _____ （要，必须，可以）喝水。

2 张： 今天下午，我和小李 _____ （要，应该，肯）去河边玩，你 _____
（想，会，应该）一起去？

王： 我很 _____ （要，想，能）去，可是我想我不 _____ （能，要，得）
去，因为我妈妈说，我还不 _____ （能，可以，会）游泳，所以 _____
（可以，愿意，必须）去河边玩。

3 李： 小王，你妹妹真漂亮，你 _____ （可以，要，会）给我们介绍一下？

王： 你 _____ （想，愿意，能）认识我妹妹吗？没问题，我给你们介绍。
可是，我妹妹不 _____ （可以，能，会）说中文，你只 _____
（会，能，要）跟她说英文。

4 王： 老师今天问的那个问题，你 _____ （会，得，肯）回答？

李： 那个问题很容易，我 _____ （会，要，行）回答。

5 张： 我家有咖啡，也有矿泉水，你 _____ （想，能，应）喝哪个？

丁： 我 _____ （想，肯，应）喝酒，有没有啤酒？

张： 医生说，你身体不好，_____ （该，肯，想）喝 酒。你忘了吗？

Level
2

6 丁： 桌上有咖啡，你 _____ （要，可以，必须）喝杯咖啡？

王： 有没有牛奶？我不 _____ （肯，必，想）喝没有牛奶的咖啡。

丁： _____ （应该，愿意，必须）有。你去厨房找一找。

7 丁： 你知道不知道王老师在哪里？

李： 现在两点半，我想他现在 _____ （愿意，必须，应该）在教室里教书。

丁： 我 _____ （想，能，会）问他一个问题；你想，我 _____ （可以，
必须，愿意）现在进教室问他？

李： 我想，别人正在上课的时候，我们 _____ （应当，想，必须）进他们的
教室。

8 张： 朋友请我跟他们一起去游泳的时候，我总是不 _____ （能，该，得）去，
因为我 _____ （要，会，行）游泳。我真 _____ （要，想，能）学，
你 _____ （可以，要，应该）教我？

王： 对不起，我很 _____ （要，愿意，可以）教你，可是我 _____ （可以，
能，应该）教你，因为我太忙了。小丁，你 _____ （应该，能，会）
教小张？

丁： 我也 _____ （该，会，能）教他，因为我也 _____ （该，会，能）
游泳。

9 张： 老王很 _____ （会，可以，肯）作菜，他作的法国菜特别好吃。

李： 那我 _____ （应该，能够，愿意）请他教我作几道他的拿手菜，因为我
正想学作菜呢。

10 奇怪，车怎么 _____ （能，必，可以）动了，_____ （该，会，能）不是坏
了吧！

12 The complement of state and the complement of degree

A complement is generally defined as a word or phrase that follows a verb or adjective to complete or expand the meaning of that verb or adjective.

Some grammarians do not make the distinction between the complement of degree and the complement of state; they use only the term 'complement of degree'. This is because both are used to indicate the extent to which an action (a verb) is/was/has been performed or the status an adjective has reached.

For those who care to make the distinction, this is how this book distinguishes between the two: a complement of state generally follows a verb; a complement of degree generally follows an adjective (or a verb with the qualities of an adjective).

A. The complement of state

The complement of state is usually used to describe (i) the outcome of an action, and (ii) an action that is/was habitual.

得 (*de*) must immediately follow the verb, and the complement that follows 得 is frequently an adjective. In a simple positive statement, a degree adverb such as 很 (*hěn*), 真 (*zhēn*), 非常 (*fēicháng*), 太 (*tài*), 最 (*zuì*) or 更 (*gèng*) should precede the adjective. In a negative statement, a degree adverb is optional.

Level 2   12.1 The basic pattern

When the verb is a single word that does not need an object, the word order is:
verb + 得 + complement. This is the basic pattern.

> 张：昨天的百米比赛，王中**跑得怎么样**？（怎么样: asking about the outcome）
> *Zhāng: Zuótiān de bǎimǐ bǐsài, Wáng Zhōng pǎo de zěnmeyàng?*
> 李：他**跑得非常快**，所以他是第一名。
> *Lǐ: Tā pǎo de fēicháng kuài, suǒyǐ tā shì dì yī míng.*
> Zhang: How (well) did Wang Zhong perform in yesterday's 100 m race?
> Li: He ran extremely fast; therefore, he came first.

> 老师：这个问题，你**回答得不对**，你再想一下。（回答 is a disyllabic word.）
> *Lǎoshī: Zhè ge wèntí, nǐ huídá de bú duì, nǐ zài xiǎng yíxià.*
> 学生：对不起，我昨天晚上**睡得(很)不好**，现在我的脑子不清楚。
> *Xuéshēng: Duìbùqǐ, wǒ zuótiān wǎnshàng shuì de (hěn) bù hǎo, xiànzài wǒde nǎozi bù qīngchǔ.*

Teacher: You answered this question incorrectly. Think again.
Student: Sorry, I slept badly last night. Right now, my brain is not clear. (I can't think clearly.)

12.2 When the verb takes an object

When the verb needs or has an object, the complement should not follow the object, but should still follow the verb. There are four different patterns. All four patterns show that 得 is immediately after the verb.

(a) The verb-repetition pattern

The verb-repetition pattern is: subject + **verb** + object + **verb** + 得 + complement.

王老师**说话说得太快**，所以我总是不懂他在说什么。
Wáng lǎoshī shuōhuà shuō de tài kuài, suǒyǐ wǒ zǒngshì bù dǒng tā zài shuō shénme.
Teacher Wang speaks too fast, so I never understand what he is saying.

小李**游泳游得非常好**，想学游泳的人，去找他。
Xiǎo Lǐ yóuyǒng yóu de fēicháng hǎo, xiǎng xué yóuyǒng de rén, qù zhǎo tā.
Xiao Li swims extremely well. Those who want to take swimming lessons, go see him.

(b) The verb-omission pattern

The verb-omission pattern is: subject + **object** + **verb** + 得 + complement.

Because the verb must appear before 得, it can be omitted before it is repeated. Therefore, it would seem as though the object appears before the verb when this pattern is used.

王明**(学)语法学得很认真**，**(写)字写得很好看**；真是个好学生。
Wáng Míng (xué) yǔfǎ xué de hěn rènzhēn, (xiě) zì xiě de hěn hǎokàn; zhēn shì ge hǎo xuéshēng.
Wang Ming studies grammar conscientiously and he writes characters well. He really is a good student.

李：小丁**(唱)歌唱得不错**，**(跳)舞**也**跳得很好**；他真有才华。
Lǐ: Xiǎo Dīng (chàng)gē chàng de búcuò, (tiào)wǔ yě tiào de hěn hǎo; tā zhēn yǒu cáihuá.
王：你知道吗？他**(打)网球**也**打得相当好**呢。
Wáng: Nǐ zhīdào ma? Tā (dǎ) wǎngqiú yě dǎ de xiāngdāng hǎo ne.
Li: Xiao Ding sings (songs) well and he dances well, also. He is really talented.
Wang: Did you know? He also plays tennis quite well.

(c) The 的-insertion pattern

The 的-insertion pattern is: subject + (的) **object** + **verb** + 得 + complement. This pattern is used when the verb is omitted. The inserted 的 is optional.

小李学过日文跟法文。**他(的)日文说得**很不错，可是**他(的)法文说得**不太好。
Xiǎo Lǐ xué guo Rìwén gēn Fǎwén. Tā(de) Rìwén shuō de hěn búcuò, kěshì tā(de) Fǎwén shuō de bú tài hǎo.
Xiao Li has studied Japanese and French. He speaks Japanese quite well; but he does not speak French very well.

我妈妈(的)中国菜作得非常好，**她(的)法国点心作得**更好。
Wǒ māma (de) Zhōngguó cài zuò de fēicháng hǎo, tā(de) Fǎguó diǎnxīn zuò de gèng hǎo.
My mother makes Chinese food very well; she makes French pastries even better.
(Meaning: My mother makes good Chinese food; she makes even better French pastries.)

(d) The pre-position pattern

In the pre-position pattern, the object can be moved to the beginning of the sentence (pre-posed). This leaves 得 immediately after the verb.

The pre-position pattern is normally used to emphasize the prominence of the object or to show a contrast between two objects. It is not unusual to have a comma after the pre-posed object.

> 中文，李明说得好；法文，王中说得好。 (Both a contrast and a comparison are implied.)
> *Zhōngwén, Lǐ Míng shuō de hǎo; Fǎwén, Wáng Zhōng shuō de hǎo.*
> Li Ming speaks Chinese better (than Wang Zhong); Wang Zhong speaks French better (than Li Ming).

• When the object is considered long (such as when a relative clause is used), the pre-position pattern is preferred

> 老师问的问题，你回答得十分好。 (老师问的问题 is the object of 回答.)
> *Lǎoshī wèn de wèntí, nǐ huídá de shífēn hǎo.*
> You answered the question that the teacher asked extremely well.

(e) Summary of patterns: Complement of state

The following table is a summary of these patterns.

Patterns	Object	Subject	Verb	Object	Verb	得 + complement	Examples
Basic		✓ 我	✓ 跑			✓ 得 + 非常慢	我跑得非常慢。 *Wǒ pǎo de fēicháng màn.* I run extremely slowly.
Verb-repetition		✓ 他	✓ 游	✓ 泳	✓ 游	✓ 得 + 很快	他游泳游得很快。 *Tā yóuyǒng yóu de hěn kuài.* He swims fast.
Verb-omission		✓ 她		✓ 舞	✓ 跳	✓ 得 + 不错	她舞跳得不错。 *Tā wǔ tiào de búcuò.* She dances quite well.
的-insertion		✓ 我	(的)	✓ 英文	✓ 说	✓ 得 + 不流利	我的英文说得不流利。 *Wǒde Yīngwén shuō de bù liúlì.* I do not speak English fluently.
Pre-position	✓ 中国菜	✓ 他	✓ 作			✓ 得 + 很好	中国菜，他作得很好。 *Zhōngguó cài, tā zuò de hěn hǎo.* He makes Chinese food well.

Level 2/3

12.3 Related information

(a) The negative form

👁 The negativity of a sentence in English and the negativity of a sentence with the complement of state in Chinese are expressed differently. In English, the negative word 'not' goes with the verb, whereas 不 in a Chinese sentence appears in the complement.

English: Mr Wang **does not speak** English very fluently.
Chinese: 王先生(的)英文说得**不太流利**。
              Wáng xiānsheng (de) Yīngwén shuō de bú tài liúlì.
(Incorrect: 王先生不说英文说得很流利。)

English: I **didn't sleep** well last night.
Chinese: 我昨天晚上**睡得不好**。
              Wǒ zuótiān wǎnshàng shuì de bù hǎo.
(Incorrect: 我昨天晚上没有睡得很好。)

(b) Placement of adverbs

Adverbs (such as 都, 也, 总是, 一定 and 常常) other than degree adverbs (such as 很, 非常, 太 and 真) should appear before the repeated verb or before the complement. Do **not** put adverbs before the object or before the verb that can be omitted.

English: Both Xiao Wang and Xiao Li play tennis quite well.
Verb-repetition: 小王、小李(打)网球**都打**得不错。 (都 is before the repeated verb.)
                  Xiǎo Wáng, Xiǎo Lǐ dǎ wǎngqiú dōu dǎ de búcuò.
                  小王、小李(打)网球打得**都不错**。 (都 is before the complement.)
                  Xiǎo Wáng, Xiǎo Lǐ dǎ wǎngqiú dǎ de dōu búcuò.
Incorrect: 小王、小李都打网球打得不错。 (都 is before the omissible verb.)
Verb-omission: 小王、小李网球**都打**不错。 (= 小王，小李网球**打得**都不错。)
Incorrect: 小王、小李都网球打得不错。 (都 is before the object.)

(c) Implied comparison

When no degree adverb precedes the adjective, a comparison between two situations is implied.

张：我应该请谁教我游泳？小王还是小李？
Zhāng: Wǒ yīnggāi qǐng shéi jiāo wǒ yóuyǒng? Xiǎo Wáng háishì Xiǎo Lǐ?
丁：小李**游得快**，请他教你。
Dīng: Xiǎo Lǐ yóu de kuài. Qǐng tā jiāo nǐ.
Zhang: Whom should I ask to be my swimming coach? Xiao Wang or Xiao Li?
Ding: Xiao Li swims faster. Ask him to teach you.

(d) Relative clauses

A degree adverb is not necessary when the complement of state is in a relative clause unless the meaning of the degree word is necessary.

晚上**睡得晚的人**往往早上也**起得比较晚**。 (No need to say 晚上睡得很晚的人.)
Wǎnshàng shuì de wǎn de rén wǎngwǎng zǎoshàng yě qǐ de bǐjiào wǎn.
Those who go to bed late at night usually get up rather late as well.

篮球教练：我们需要**长得高的人**来参加篮球队。
Lánqiú jiàoliàn: Wǒmen xūyào zhǎng de gāo de rén lái cānjiā lánqiú duì.
王老师：我们班的李明**长得很高**。我去叫他来跟你谈。
Wáng Lǎoshī: Wǒmen bān de Lǐ Míng zhǎng de hěn gāo. Wǒ qù jiào tā lái gēn nǐ tán.
Basketball coach: We need people who are tall (literally: grow tall) to join the basketball team.
Teacher Wang: Li Ming in my class is tall (grows tall). I will ask him to come and talk to you.

(e) The complement of state vs. the complement of potential

In cases where no degree adverb is present and, at the same time, the sentence does not imply a comparison or does not contain a relative clause, the adjective may be functioning as a complement of potential.

☞ See 17.1 for the basic structure of the complement of potential.

妈妈：小明，去洗碗。
Māma: Xiǎomíng, qù xǐ wǎn.
爸爸：别叫他去洗！他总是洗得不干净。我洗得干净，我去洗吧！(洗得不干净 is the complement of state. 洗得干净 is the complement of potential.)
Bàba: Bié jiào tā qù xǐ! Tā zǒngshì xǐ de bù gānjìng. Wǒ xǐ de gānjìng, wǒ qù xǐ ba!
Mother: Xiaoming, go wash the dishes.
Father: Don't ask him to wash the dishes. He never does a good job. (He never gets them clean.) I can do a good job. (I **can** get them clean.) Let me go do the dishes.

(f) The complement of state vs. adverbial modifier

👁 The majority of sentences with a complement of state can be translated into English sentences with an adverb; however, not all English sentences with an adverb will be translated into Chinese sentences with a complement of state.

我爷爷岁数大了，他走路**走得很慢**。(This is habitual.)
Wǒ yéye suìshù dà le, tā zǒulù zǒu de hěn màn.
My grandfather is old; he **walks slowly**.
Compare: 别急，时间还很多，今天咱们可以**慢慢地走**。(This is **not** habitual.)
Bié jí, shíjiān hái hěn duō, jīntiān zánmen kěyǐ mànmàn de zǒu.
Don't be in such a hurry. There is still plenty of time. Today we can **walk slowly**.

Since a complement of state is used to describe the outcome of an action or a habitual action, the expression 'slowly' in 'today we can walk slowly' is not represented by a complement of state in Chinese. Instead, it is an adverbial modifier.

☞ See 18.5 for detailed explanations and comparisons.

(g) The complement of state vs. the complement of result

In cases where the adjective follows the verb without 得, the adjective is not functioning as the complement of state and may be functioning as a complement of result. The complement of result should not have a degree adverb such as 很.

☞ See 16.7 for more information on the complement of result.

English: I've heard what he said clearly. You don't have to repeat it.
Chinese #1: 他说的话，我**听得很清楚**，你不必重复。(很清楚 is the complement of state.)
Tā shuō de huà, wǒ tīng de hěn qīngchǔ, nǐ búbì chóngfù.
(The negative of 听得很清楚 is 听得不清楚.)
Chinese #2: 他说的话，我**听清楚**了，你不必重复。(清楚 is the complement of result.)
Tā shuō de huà, wǒ tīng qīngchǔ le, nǐ búbì chóngfù.
(The negative of 听清楚了 is 没有听清楚.)

(h) The use of 多 and 少 after a verb

- When 多 and 少 function as adjectives, they can be used in the complement of state

我今天午饭**吃得太多**，所以下午上课的时候，很想睡觉。
Wǒ jīntiān wǔfàn chī de tài duō, suǒyǐ xiàwǔ shàng kè de shíhòu, hěn xiǎng shuìjiào.
Today I ate too much for lunch, so I was sleepy when I was in class in the afternoon.

- When 多 and 少 function as nouns, 得 is not used after the verb

(Situation: A host urges her guest to eat more.)

主人：怎么**吃得这么少**？再吃一些吧！（这么少 is the complement of state. 少 is an adjective.）
Zhǔrén: Zěnme chī de zhème shǎo? Zài chī yìxiē ba!
客人：不了，谢谢，我已经**吃了很多**了。（很多 is functioning as a noun, meaning 很多东西.）
Kèrén: Bù le, xièxie, wǒ yǐjīng chī le hěn duō le.
Host: How come you ate so little? Eat some more!
Guest: No, thanks! I already ate a lot (of food).

B. The complement of degree

The complement of degree is used to describe the extent (or degree) that an emotional or physical status has reached. The emotional and physical status is usually indicated by an adjective (or a verb that has the qualities of an adjective, such as 喜欢).

12.4 Two basic patterns

In most cases, 得 precedes the complement of degree. And such a sentence is usually translated into English as 'so + adjective + that + complement'. The complement is usually a complete sentence or a verbal phrase. There are also many fixed expressions with or without 得.

(a) Some examples of the 'so + adjective + that' expression in English

When the subject of the entire sentence and the subject of the complement of degree are the same, do not repeat the subject in the complement.

王中看到一个老朋友，**高兴得跳起来**。（跳起来 is a verbal phrase.）
Wáng Zhōng kàndào yí ge lǎo péngyǒu, gāoxìng de tiào qǐlái.
Wang Zhong saw an old friend; he was **so happy that he jumped up**.
(Incorrect: 王中看到一个老朋友，高兴得他跳起来. 他 is 王中; therefore, it can't be used.)

这里的风景**美得象一幅画**。（象一幅画 is a verbal phrase.）
Zhèlǐ de fēngjǐng měi de xiàng yì fú huà.
The scenery here is **so beautiful that it's like a painting**.
(Incorrect: 这里的风景美得它象一幅画. 它 is 风景; therefore, it can't be used.)

公共汽车**挤得我简直没办法呼吸**。（我简直没办法呼吸 is a sentence.）
Gōnggòng qìchē jǐ de wǒ jiǎnzhí méi bànfǎ hūxī.
The bus was **so crowded that I practically could not breathe**.

天气**热得大家都没有胃口吃饭**。（大家都没有胃口吃饭 is a sentence.）
Tiānqì rè de dàjiā dōu méiyǒu wèikǒu chī fàn.
The weather is **so hot that no one has any appetite**.

(b) Some fixed expressions

There are many **fixed expressions** with or without 得 that are considered the complements of degree.

• The following are some expressions that are commonly used with 得

> 我**忙得要命**，别来烦我。
> *Wǒ máng de yàomìng, bié lái fán wǒ.*
> I am **busy to death**. Don't bother me.

> 我整天工作，现在**累得要死**。
> *Wǒ zhěngtiān gōngzuò, xiànzài lèi de yàosǐ.*
> I worked all day long. Now I am **tired to death**.

> 这件大衣还**好得很**，你为什么不要了？(好得很 = 很好)
> *Zhèjiàn dàyī hái hǎo de hěn, nǐ wèishénme bú yào le?*
> This coat is **still good**. Why don't you want it anymore?

> 我听了老王的话以后，**气得不得了**，决定以后不再跟他说话。
> *Wǒ tīng le Lǎo Wáng de huà yǐhòu, qì de bùdeliǎo, juédìng yǐhòu bú zài gēn tā shuōhuà.*
> After I heard what Lao Wang said, I was **angry beyond description**. I decided that I won't talk to him anymore.

• The following are some expressions that are commonly used without 得

> 我**饿死了**，咱们找家饭馆吃饭吧！
> *Wǒ è sǐ le, zánmen zhǎo jiā fànguǎn chī fàn ba.*
> I am **hungry to death** (= starving). Let's find a restaurant to eat in.

> 今天我跑马拉松，**累死我了**。
> *Jīntiān wǒ pǎo mǎlāsōng, lèi sǐ wǒ le.*
> I ran a marathon today. I was **tired to death**.

> 老师说，小明最近进步了很多，他爸妈听了，**高兴极了**。
> *Lǎoshī shuō, Xiǎoming zuìjìn jìnbù le hěn duō, tā bàmā tīng le, gāoxìng jí le.*
> The teacher said that Xiaoming had improved a lot recently. Hearing this, his parents were **extremely happy**.

Exercises

Translate the following sentences into Chinese using the patterns suggested in parentheses.

Level
1

1 I <u>didn't sleep well</u> last night, so I <u>got up late</u> this morning. (the basic pattern)

2 Wang Zhong <u>studies diligently</u>. (the basic pattern) So he always <u>answers the teacher's questions correctly</u>. (the pre-position pattern)

3 Both Anna and Wang Zhong <u>dance quite well (= not bad)</u>. (the verb-repetition pattern) But I <u>dance even better</u>. (the basic pattern)

4 Mrs Li: I heard that both of your children are taking cooking classes (= are learning to cook). Who <u>cooks better</u>? (the 的-insertion pattern)

Mrs Wang: My son <u>cooks French food better</u> and my daughter <u>cooks Chinese food better</u>. (the pre-position pattern)

5 My younger brother <u>does not run fast</u>. (the basic pattern) But he <u>swims fast</u>. (the verb-repetition pattern)

Level
2

6 Wang: Li Ming told me that you <u>speak English fluently</u>. (the verb-omission pattern) Will you teach me (how) to speak English?

Ding: Actually, I <u>speak English poorly</u>. (the 的-insertion pattern) You should go ask someone who <u>speaks fluently</u> to teach you. (the basic pattern)

7 Mrs Li: <u>How well</u> does my son <u>learn Chinese</u>? (the verb-omission pattern)

Teacher: He <u>studies conscientiously</u>. (the basic pattern) So, he <u>writes characters beautifully</u>; (the 的-insertion pattern) he also <u>learns grammar well</u>; (the verb-omission pattern); but he still <u>does not speak daily conversation fluently</u>. (the pre-position pattern)

8 Mother: You <u>ate too much</u>. (The basic pattern) Don't eat any more. Your father hasn't eaten.

Son: I was hungry to death. You <u>cooked too little food</u> today. (the verb-omission pattern)

9 He always <u>drives too fast</u>. (the verb-repetition pattern) His mother told him not to <u>drive too fast</u>; (the basic pattern) he was unhappy.

10 He was <u>well-prepared</u> for today's test, (the pre-position pattern) so he <u>did extremely well</u>. (the basic pattern)

13 The complement of duration

The complement of duration is used to indicate the period of time or length of time during which an action is/was lasting.

It is useful to know that 多久 (*duō jiǔ*) or 多长时间 (*duō cháng shíjiān*) is used to ask 'how long?' in terms of time, and is frequently used in asking a question with the complement of duration. In addition, 几 (*jǐ*) can be used to mean 'how many?' as in 几天 (*jǐ tiān*: 'how many days'), 几年 (*jǐ nián*: 'how many years'), 几分钟 (*jǐ fēnzhōng*: 'how many minutes'), 几个钟头 (*jǐ ge zhōngtóu*: 'how many hours'), etc.

Level
2

13.1 Word order

There are four patterns and, in all of them, the verb appears before the complement. The verb in this case must indicate an action that can last. The patterns are very similar to those for the complement of state.

☞ See 12.1 and 12.2 for detailed information on the complement of state.

(a) The basic pattern

The basic pattern is: verb + complement. This pattern is used when the verb does not have an object.

我们每天**工作**八个小时，**休息**一个小时。(工作 and 休息 are disyllabic words.)
Wǒmen měi tiān gōngzuò bā ge xiǎoshí, xiūxí yī ge xiǎoshí.
Every day we work for eight hours and we take a break for one hour.

史密斯先生在北京**住**了十年，所以他的中国话说得很流利。(住了 can be 住过.)
Shǐmìsī xiānsheng zài Běijīng zhù le shí nián, suǒyǐ tāde Zhōngguóhuà shuō de hěn liúlì.
Mr Smith lived in Beijing for ten years, so he speaks Chinese fluently.

(b) The verb-repetition pattern

The verb-repetition pattern is: **verb** + object + **verb** + complement. When the verb has an object, the verb must be repeated before the complement of duration appears.

昨天他**跳舞跳**了一个晚上，所以今天早上起得很晚。
Zuótiān tā tiàowǔ tiào le yī ge wǎnshàng, suǒyǐ jīntiān zǎoshàng qǐ de hěn wǎn.
He danced all night last night, so he got up late this morning.

张：王老师**教书教**了多长时间了？ (To teach is 教书 when the subject matter is not mentioned.)
Zhāng: Wáng lǎoshī jiāoshū jiāo le duō cháng shíjiān le?

李：他教了快十五年了。（书 does not have to be mentioned when the situation is in context.)
Lǐ: Tā jiāo le kuài shíwǔ nián le.
Zhang: How long has Teacher Wang been teaching?
Li: He has been teaching for almost 15 years.

(c) The verb-omission pattern

The verb-omission pattern is: **object + verb** + complement.

小李中文学了三年了，他日文也学了快一年。
Xiǎo Lǐ Zhōngwén xué le sān nián le, tā Rìwén yě xué le kuài yì nián.
Xiao Li has studied Chinese for three years; he has also studied Japanese for almost a year.

(d) The insertion pattern

The insertion pattern is: verb + complement + (的) + **object**.

- When the verb has an object, the complement of duration can be inserted between the verb and the object. An optional 的 can be used after the complement

妈妈：小明，你已经看了两小时(的)电视了，别再看了。
Māma: Xiǎomíng, nǐ yǐjīng kàn le liǎng xiǎoshí (de) diànshì le, bié zài kàn le.
小明：让我再看半小时，好不好？
Xiǎomíng: Ràng wǒ zài kàn bàn xiǎoshí, hǎo bù hǎo?
Mother: Xiaoming, you have already watched TV for two hours; don't watch it anymore.
Xiaoming: Let me watch another half hour, OK?

从美国去中国，要坐十几个钟头(的)飞机。（坐飞机: 'to fly')
Cóng Měiguó qù Zhōngguó, yào zuò shí jǐ ge zhōngtóu (de) fēijī.
One will have to fly for over ten hours to get to China from the USA.

- The insertion pattern is used when the object is indefinite or generic. When the object is definite (for example: a word following 这 or 那), it is not proper to use the insertion pattern

English: I waited for that person for ten minutes.
Chinese: 我等那个人等了十分钟。
             Wǒ děng nà ge rén děng le shí fēnzhōng.
(Incorrect: 我等了十分钟(的)那个人。)

(e) The pre-position pattern

In the pre-position pattern, the object of the verb is moved to the beginning of the sentence.

老师问的问题，他想了半天，还是不会回答。（老师问的问题 is the object of 想.)
Lǎoshī wèn de wèntí, tā xiǎng le bàntiān, háishì bú huì huídá.
He thought for quite a while about the question that the teacher had asked and he still didn't know how to answer it.

(f) Summary: Complement of duration

The following table gives a summary of the complement of duration patterns.

Pattern	Object	Subject	Verb	Object	Verb	Complement	Object	Example
Basic		✓ 我	✓ 工作			✓ 十小时		我每星期工作十小时。 *Wǒ měi xīngqī gōngzuò shí xiǎoshí.* I work ten hours each week.
Verb-repetition		✓ 我	✓ 看	✓ 电视	✓ 看	✓ 两小时		我看电视看了两小时。 *Wǒ kàn diànshì kàn le liǎng xiǎoshí.* I watched TV for two hours.
Verb-omission		✓ 我		✓ 法文	✓ 学	✓ 两年		我法文学了两年。 *Wǒ Fǎwén xué le liǎng nián.* I studied French for two years.
Insertion		✓ 他	✓ 教			✓ 三年(的)	✓ 书	他教了三年(的)书。 *Tā jiāo le sān nián (de) shū.* He taught for three years.
Pre-position	✓ 那本书	✓ 我	✓ 找			✓ 三天		那本书，我找了三天。 *Nà běn shū, wǒ zhǎo le sān tiān.* I searched for the book for three days.

Level 2

13.2 Adjective + complement of duration

The complement of duration can also follow an adjective.

今天这个考试太重要了，为了这个考试，我**紧张**了三个月呢。
Jīntiān zhè ge kǎoshì tài zhòngyào le, wèile zhè ge kǎoshì, wǒ jǐnzhāng le sān ge yuè ne.
Today's exam is too important. I have been nervous about this exam for three months.

Level 3

13.3 Perfective aspect particle 了 and modal particle 了

The perfective aspect particle 了 can appear after the (repeated) verb to indicate completion; this means the period of time indicated in the complement has elapsed. In addition, a modal particle 了 can appear at the end of the sentence to indicate 'already'. The modal particle 了 also implies a current status.

史密斯先生在北京**住**了三年**了**，所以他会说一点(儿)中国话。
Shǐmìsī xiānsheng zài Běijīng zhù le sān nián le, suǒyǐ tā huì shuō yìdiǎn(er) Zhōngguóhuà.
Mr Smith has been living in Beijing for three years already, so he can speak a little Chinese. (This implies that Mr Smith is currently living in Beijing.)

妈妈：小明，你自己说，你**看**了几个小时的电视**了**？
Māma: Xiǎomíng, nǐ zìjǐ shuō, nǐ kàn le jǐ ge xiǎoshí de diànshì le? (The modal particle 了 at the end of the sentence indicates that Xiaoming is watching TV as his mother speaks.)
小明：我下午**念**了四小时书，晚上为什么不能看电视？ (There is no 了 after 四小时书.)
Xiǎomíng: Wǒ xiàwǔ niàn le sì xiǎoshí shū, wǎnshàng wèishénme bù néng kàn diànshì?
Mother: Xiaoming, you tell me, for how many hours have you been watching TV?
Xiaoming: I studied for four hours in the afternoon; why can't I watch TV in the evening?

13.4 Experiential aspect particle 过

The experiential aspect particle 过 can follow the (repeated) verb. In this case, a modal particle 了 is rarely used. This is because 过 indicates past action, whereas the modal particle 了 implies a current situation.

(Situation: Mr Zhang comes back to Beijing, where he lived for several years before.)

张先生以前在北京**住过**好几年，所以他对北京的街道很熟。

Zhāng xiānsheng yǐqián zài Běijīng zhù guo hǎo jǐ nián, suǒyǐ tā duì Běijīng de jiēdào hěn shóu.

Mr Zhang lived in Beijing for quite a few years, so he is very familiar with Beijing's streets.

13.5 Perfective aspect particle 了

A perfective aspect particle 了 after the (repeated) verb can imply a past action when no modal particle 了 appears in the sentence.

我上大学的时候，**学了**一学期法文，成绩很不好。

Wǒ shàng dàxué de shíhòu, xué le yì xuéqī Fǎwén, chéngjī hěn bù hǎo.

When I was at university, I took French for one term; my grades were very bad.

13.6 Points in time

A length of time (or duration of time) should not be confused with a point in time. A length of time frequently serves as the complement of duration, whereas a point in time serves as an adverb. The complement of duration appears after the verb; whereas an adverb indicating a point in time is either at the beginning of the sentence or before the verbal phrase.

English: Two years ago, I lived in Shanghai for half a year.
Chinese: **两年以前**，我在上海住了 (**or 住过**) **半年**。
           Liǎng nián yǐqián, wǒ zài Shànghǎi zhù le (or zhù guo) bàn nián.
           (两年以前 is a time phrase indicating a point in time. 半年 is a complement of duration.)

13.7 Negative sentences

When an action has **not** happened in a certain length of time or will **not** happen for a certain length of time, the sentence is no longer one with the complement of duration. In this case, the length of time appears before the verb, not after. This word order is very different from that of an English sentence with a similar meaning.

好久**不**见！

Hǎo jiǔ bú jiàn!

Long time no see!

为了准备这个重要的考试，我已经**两天没有**睡觉了。

Wèile zhǔnbèi zhè ge zhòngyào de kǎoshì, wǒ yǐjīng liǎng tiān méiyǒu shuìjiào le.

In order to study for this important exam, I have not slept in two days.

我决定从今天开始，我要**三天不**吃肉。

Wǒ juédìng cóng jīntiān kāishǐ, wǒ yào sān tiān bù chī ròu.

I have decided that, starting today, I won't eat meat for three days.

13.8 When the object is a pronoun or proper noun

There are cases where the complement of duration does not follow the verb. When the object of the verb is a pronoun or a proper noun, the complement of duration follows the object.

请你在这里**等我**五分钟，我去跟王老师说几分钟话。（等五分钟我 is incorrect.）
Qǐng nǐ zài zhèlǐ děng wǒ wǔ fēnzhōng, wǒ qù gēn Wáng lǎoshī shuō jǐ fēnzhōng huà.
Please wait for me here for five minutes. I'm going to talk to Teacher Wang for a few minutes.

我**劝**了**他**几个小时，他还是不肯改变主意。（我劝了几个小时他 is incorrect.）
Wǒ quàn le tā jǐ ge xiǎoshí, tā háishì bù kěn gǎibiàn zhǔyì.
I tried to persuade him for a couple of hours; he still would not change his mind.

13.9 Instantaneous actions

Certain actions, for example, 来 (*lái*: 'to come'), 去 (*qù*: 'to go'), 到 (*dào*: 'to arrive'), 进 (*jìn*: 'to enter'), 出 (*chū*: 'to exit'), 离开 (*líkāi*: 'to leave'), 下课 (*xiàkè*: 'class is over'), 结婚 (*jiéhūn*: 'to get married'), 离婚 (*líhūn*: 'to divorce'), cannot last. The complement of duration follows the object of the verb if there is an object to the verb. These actions are sometimes referred to as 'instantaneous actions' because they mark clear 'before' and 'after' states.

了 is not used after these verbs. But a modal particle 了 can be used if 'already' is implied.

下课十分钟了，你们为什么还坐在教室里？（十分钟 does not follow the verb 下.）
Xiàkè shí fēnzhōng le, nǐmen wèishénme hái zuò zài jiàoshì lǐ?
Class has been over for ten minutes, why are you still sitting in the classroom?

我**来**北京才三个星期，有很多有名的地方我还没去过呢。（三个星期 does not follow 来.）
Wǒ lái Běijīng cái sān xīngqī, yǒu hěn duō yǒumíng de dìfāng wǒ hái méi qù guo ne.
I have only in Beijing for three weeks; there are many famous places I have not been to yet.

王先生跟王太太**结婚**十年了，才生第一个孩子。（婚 is a noun. 十年 does not follow 结.）
Wáng xiānsheng gēn Wáng tàitai jiéhūn shí nián le, cài shēng dìyī ge háizi.
Mr and Mrs Wang have been married for ten years already; they just had their first child.

13.10 Verb + complement vs. object + complement

Occasionally, in a sentence with an action that can last, the complement of duration still follows the object, not the verb. In this case, the sentence is interpreted slightly differently.

他**学**了三年的**中文**了，可是只会写几个简单的汉字。
Tā xué le sān nián de Zhōngwén le, kěshì zhǐ huì xiě jǐ ge jiǎndān de Hànzì.
He has studied Chinese for three years, but he only knows how to write a few simple characters.

Compare: 你**学中文**都三年了，怎么还不会写自己的中文名字呢?
Nǐ xué Zhōngwén dōu sān nián le, zěnme hái bú huì xiě zìjǐ de Zhōngwén míngzì ne?
It's been three years since you started to study Chinese; how come you still don't know how to write your own name?

Exercises

Translate the following sentences into Chinese using the patterns suggested in parentheses. Pay attention to the use of 了.

Level 2

1 Ding: For how many months did you live in Beijing before? (the basic pattern)

Li: I never lived in Beijing. But I have been living in Shanghai for eight months now. (the basic pattern)

2 Wang: I studied Chinese for four and half years when I was at university. (the insertion pattern)

Ding: Really? How many years of university did you attend? (the insertion pattern)

Wang: I was at (= attended) university for five years in total. (the basic pattern)

3 Wang: I have been thinking about this problem for five hours (the pre-position pattern) and I still don't know how to answer it.

Li: Really? I only thought about it for five minutes before I knew the answer. (the basic pattern)

4 Mother: You have been watching TV for almost four hours. (the insertion pattern) Don't watch anymore.

Son: I did homework for the entire afternoon. (the insertion pattern) Please let me watch another half hour. (the basic pattern)

5 Chinese: You speak Chinese very well. How long has it been since you came to China?

Foreigner: No, not really. I have been in China for five months. Before coming to China, I studied Chinese for two years. (the insertion pattern)

Level 3

6 Li: How long will it take to get to school from here by bus (= riding the bus)? (the insertion pattern)

Wang: I don't know. I always ride my bicycle to school. I have to ride for 20 minutes every day. (the basic pattern)

7 Zhang: I heard that you have studied foreign languages for many years. (the insertion pattern) Is that true?

Li: It's true. I have studied French, Japanese and Spanish. I studied French for ten years. I have studied Japanese for five years and Spanish for three years now. (the pre-position pattern)

8 Xiao Wang and his girlfriend have known each other for three years. Lately, they have often fought. His girlfriend has not been talking to him for three weeks.

9 It had not been raining for three months. Unexpectedly, it started to rain this week. But once it rained, it rained for three days.

14 The complement of quantity

The complement of quantity can be broken down into two types of complement; each involves a number or an amount. The two types are: the complement of occurrence and the complement of quantitative difference.

It should be noted that (i) some grammarians consider the complement of duration a type of complement of quantity (☞ see Chapter 13 for discussions on the complement of duration) and that (ii) grammarians may use different terminology to refer to the complements of quantity.

A. The complement of occurrence

The complement of occurrence is used to indicate how many times an action occurs.

Level 2

14.1 Common words used in the complement of occurrence

次, 遍 and 趟 (cì, biàn, tàng) are the most common words used in the complement of occurrence. All of these words can mean 'time(s)' as in 'twice' and 'three times'.

(a) 次 and 遍

次 is usually used for an instantaneous action that does not last, whereas 遍 is used to indicate an action that has an obvious beginning and end. Also, 遍 indicates the same process or experience each time an action is repeated; 次 is used when the process or outcome is not entirely the same.

> 这本书我已经看了**两遍**了，有空的时候，我想再看**一遍**。
> *Zhè běn shū wǒ yǐjīng kàn le liǎng biàn le, yǒu kòng de shíhòu, wǒ xiǎng zài kàn yí biàn.*
> I have read this book twice already. When I have free time, I want to read it one more time.

> 李：你**去**过**几次**中国？ （去 is an instantaneous action.）
> *Lǐ: Nǐ qù guo jǐ cì Zhōngguó?*
> 张：**去**过**三次**，我还去过两次香港。
> *Zhāng: Qù guo sān cì, wǒ hái qù guo liǎng cì Xiānggǎng.*
> Li: How many times have you been to China?
> Zhang: Three times and I have also been to Hong Kong twice.

(b) 趟

趟 (and 回) is used to indicate the number of trips one makes to a place.

王：《阿凡达》真太好看了，我已经**看**过**两遍**了，你呢？（看《阿凡达》 is a specific experience; each time the experience or process is the same since it is the same movie.)
Wáng: 'Ā Fán Dá' zhēn tài hǎokàn le, wǒ yǐjīng kàn guo liǎng biàn le, nǐ ne?
李：上星期**跑**了**两趟（两回）**电影院，都没有买到票。
Lǐ: Shàng xīngqī pǎo le liǎng tàng (liǎng huí) diànyǐng yuàn, dōu méiyǒu mǎi dào piào.
Wang: *Avatar* is truly wonderful. I have seen it twice. How about you?
Li: I made two trips to the cinema last week, (but) I didn't get tickets.

14.2 'Bodily movement' words used in the complement of occurrence

A group of words, which are associated with bodily movements, are frequently used in the complement of occurrence. These words are 眼 (*yǎn*: 'eye', associated with 看/瞪 *kàn/dèng*: 'to look/to glare'), 脚 (*jiǎo*: 'foot', associated with 踢 *tī*: 'to kick'), 拳 (*quán*: 'fist', associated with 打 *dǎ*: 'to hit'), 声 (*shēng*: 'sound, voice', associated with 叫 *jiào*: 'to call'), 口 (*kǒu*: 'mouth', associated with 咬 *yǎo*: 'to bite' or 吃/喝 *chī/hē*: 'to eat/to drink'), 下 (*xià*: usually showing a nod or tapping movement), etc.

> 老张真可恶，我恨不得**踢**他**一脚**，**打**他**两拳**。
> *Lǎo Zhāng zhēn kěwù, wǒ hèn bù dé tī tā yì jiǎo, dǎ tā liǎng quán.*
> Lao Zhang is really nasty. I really wish I could kick him (once) and hit him with my fist (twice).

> 我问老师可不可以下课了；他**看**了**一眼**墙上的钟，**点**了**两下**头。
> *Wǒ wèn lǎoshī kě bù kěyǐ xià kè le; tā kàn le yì yǎn qiáng shàng de zhōng, diǎn le liǎng xià tóu.*
> I asked the teacher if the class could be dismissed; he took a glance at the clock on the wall and nodded twice.

14.3 Word order

The word-order rules involving the complement of occurrence are complicated and are dependent on the nature of the object. The following are some basic principles:

(a) When the object is a pronoun or proper name

When the object of the verb is a pronoun or a proper name, the complement of occurrence follows the pronoun or the proper name. (Note that 这里 (*zhèlǐ*) and 那里 (*nàlǐ*) are considered pronouns in Chinese.)

> 我**看**了他**一眼**，就觉得我不喜欢他。（他 is a pronoun; 一眼 does not immediately follow 看.)
> *Wǒ kàn le tā yì yǎn, jiù juéde wǒ bù xǐhuān tā.*
> I took one look at him and I immediately felt that I didn't like him.

> 我**帮**过小明好几次，可是他只**帮**过我一次。
> *Wǒ bāng guo Xiǎomíng hǎo jǐ cì, kěshì tā zhǐ bāng guo wǒ yí cì.*
> I have helped Xiaoming quite a few times, but he has only helped me once.

(b) When the object is a place

When the object of the verb indicates a place, it can follow either the verb or the complement of occurrence.

王：你去过北京几次？(= 你去过几次北京？)
Wáng: Nǐ qù guo Běijīng jǐ cì?
李：我没去过北京，可是我去过三次上海。(= 我去过上海三次。)
Lǐ: Wǒ méi qù guo Běijīng, kěshì wǒ qù guo sān cì Shànghǎi.
Wang: How many times have you been to Beijing?
Li: I have not been to Beijing, but I have been to Shanghai three times.

上个月我去了三次长城，两次北京动物园。下星期我想再去动物园一次。
Shàng ge yuè wǒ qù le sān cì Chángchéng, liǎng cì Běijīng dòngwùyuán. Xià xīngqī wǒ xiǎng zài qù dòngwùyuán yí cì.
Last month I went to the Great Wall three times and to Beijing Zoo twice. Next week I want to go to the zoo one more time.

(c) When the object is definite

When the object of the verb is definite, some flexibility is allowed depending on whether the sentence has a perfect aspect particle 了 or not. Therefore, it is best to pre-pose the definite object when possible, or use the 把 structure.

☞ See Chapter 21 for the 把 structure.

老师：今天的功课，你得再写一遍。(今天的功课 is the pre-posed object.)
Lǎoshī: Jīntiān de gōngkè, nǐ děi zài xiě yí biàn.
学生：求您别叫我再写一遍这个功课。(= 把这个功课再写一遍。)
Xuéshēng: Qiú nín bié jiào wǒ zài xiě yí biàn zhè ge gōngkè.
Teacher: You have to rewrite today's homework.
Student: I beg you to not make me rewrite this homework.

我看了一眼那张风景明信片(= 我看了那张风景明信片一眼)，就知道我去过那里好几次。(那里 is a pronoun; therefore, 好几次 does not follow the verb 去.)
Wǒ kàn le yì yǎn nà zhāng fēngjǐng míngxìnpiàn, jiù zhīdào wǒ qù guo nàlǐ hǎo jǐ cì.
I took one look at that scenery postcard and I knew that I had been there several times.

(d) When the object is indefinite

☺ When the object is indefinite or the verb and the object form one word, such as 结婚 and 离婚, the complement of occurrence should follow the verb.

王先生结过三次婚，也离过三次婚；下个月他又要再结一次。
Wáng xiānsheng jié guo sān cì hūn, yě lí guo sān cì hūn; xià ge yuè tā yòu yào zài jié yí cì.
Mr Wang has been married three times and also divorced three times. Next month, he is going to get married again (one more time).
(Incorrect: 王先生结婚过三次 or 王先生结过婚三次.)

我叫了好几声《救命》，可是没有人来救我。
Wǒ jiào le hǎo jǐ shēng 'Jiù mìng', kěshì méiyǒu rén lái jiù wǒ.
I called out 'Help!' several times, but no one came to rescue me.

B. The complement of quantitative difference

The complement of quantitative difference is used to indicate the difference after a comparison has been made. ☺ It should be noted that English sentences of similar meaning have quite a different word order.

☞ See 23.4 for detailed information on the complement of quantitative difference.

Level
3

14.4 Precise differences

The difference can be precise and indicated by a number.

我比小李高十公分。
Wǒ bǐ Xiǎo Lǐ gāo shí gōngfēn. (Do not say 我比小李十公分高.)
I am 10 cm taller than Xiao Li.

这栋房子比那栋贵**好几倍**。
Zhè dòng fángzi bǐ nà dòng guì hǎo jǐ bèi.
This house is several times more expensive than that house.

Level
3

14.5 Vague differences

The difference can be vague and indicated either by 'a lot/many/much' or 'a little'. The complement of quantitative difference must have at least two characters except when the difference is 一点 or 一些, which can be shortened to 点 or 些.

这本书比那本贵**很多**(= 贵**得多**，贵**多了**)。
Zhè běn shū bǐ nà běn guì hěn duō (= guì de duō = guì duō le).
This book is much more expensive than that book.
(It is incorrect to say 这本书比那本贵多 since 多 is only one character.)

新宿舍设备比旧宿舍好(一)**些**，但价钱贵**太多**(**了**)，所以我住旧宿舍。
Xīn sùshè shèbèi bǐ jiù sùshè hǎo (yì) xiē, dàn jiàqián guì tài duō (le), suǒyǐ wǒ zhù jiù sùshè.
The new dormitory's facilities are a little better than the old dormitory's, but the price is too much more expensive, so I live in the old dormitory.

Level
3

14.6 多 and 少 as adjectives

Special attention must be paid to comparisons of which the adjective is 多 or 少. 👁 Learners are often confused about the juxtaposition of 多 and 少.

我有三百本书，他只有十几本。我的书比他(的)**多得多**(= **多很多**，**多多了**)。
= 他的书比我(的)**少得多**(= **少很多**，**少多了**)。
Wǒ yǒu sān bǎi běn shū, tā zhǐ yǒu shí jǐ běn. Wǒde shū bǐ tā(de) duō de duō (= duō hěn duō, duō duō le).
= *Tāde shū bǐ wǒ(de) shǎo de duō (= shǎo hěn duō, shǎo duō le).*
I have 300 books; he only has 10–20. I have a lot more books than he has.
= He has a lot fewer books than I have.

Exercises

Translate the following sentences into Chinese.

Level
1

1 Wang: How many times have you read *The Old Man and the Sea*?
   Li: I have read the English version twice and I have also read the Chinese version once.

2 Ding: Have you seen *Crouching Tiger Hidden Dragon*?
   Li: I caught (watched) it on TV twice, but each time I didn't finish watching it.

3 Yesterday I made two trips to his house, but each time he was not there. Today I will go there one more time.

4 Wang Ming was sleeping in class. The teacher called on him twice (meaning: The teacher called his name twice); he didn't hear it. I kicked him twice and he finally woke up.

5 Yesterday I wasn't feeling well, and I went to the toilet five or six times.

6 Last month, I was ill twice. I went to the hospital to see a doctor five times.

7 We asked the teacher to sing that song one more time. He nodded once, took two sips of water and then began to sing.

8 I have helped Miss Zhang many times, but she has only thanked me once.

Level
2

9 Mr and Mrs Wang have been married only half a year, but they have fought ten times already.

10 He lied to me a few times, but I decide to trust him one more time.

11 That vendor has cheated tourists quite a few times; therefore, the police have arrested him quite a few times as well.

12 Mr Li has been divorced twice. I don't understand why he is planning to marry again (= one more time).

15 The complement of direction

There are two types of complement of direction: the simple complement of direction and the complex complement of direction. The complement of direction is a word that follows the verb to indicate the direction in which the subject is proceeding.

A. The simple complements of direction

The simple complements of direction consist of 来 (*lái*) and 去 (*qù*). It should be noted that although 来 and 去 can be verbs, as complements, they must follow another verb. The sentence can involve a place or a non-place (person or object/thing).

15.1 With places

When the sentence involves a place, the verb that precedes 来 or 去 is 上 (*shàng*), 下 (*xià*), 进 (*jìn*), 出 (*chū*), 回 (*huí*), 过 (*guò*) or 到 (*dào*). (The usage of 到 is slightly different from that of the other verbs.) The place can be optional if the context is clear. When it is present, it must appear between the verb and the complement.

上来 to come up	下来 to come down	出来 to come out	进来 to come in	过来 to come over	回来 to come back	到……来 to come
上去 to go up	下去 to go down	出去 to go out	进去 to go in	过去 to go over	回去 to go back	到……去 to go

他们都在楼上，咱们也**上(楼)去**吧。 (It is incorrect to say 咱们也上去楼吧.)
Tāmen dōu zài lóushàng, zánmen yě shàng lóu qù ba.
They are all upstairs. Let's **go up(stairs)**, too.

李：老王，你怎么还不**出来**？我在这外面等了十分钟了。
Lǐ: Lǎo Wáng, nǐ zěnme hái bù chū lái? Wǒ zài zhè wàimiàn děng le shí fēnzhōng le.
张：老王不在这儿，他已经**回(家)去**了。 (It is incorrect to say 回去家.)
Zhāng: Lǎo Wáng bú zài zhèr, tā yǐjīng huí (jiā) qù le.
Li: Lao Wang, how come you still haven't **come out**? I have been waiting here outside for ten minutes already.
Zhang: Lao Wang is not here. He **went back home** already.

(a) 来 or 去? (Based on the location of the speaker)

Whether to use 来 or 去 depends on where the speaker (我, *wǒ*) is located. When the person spoken to is moving towards where the speaker (我) is, 来 should be used. When either the speaker or the person spoken to is moving away from where the speaker is, 去 should be used.

(Situation: Xiao Li and Xiao Zhang are outside the classroom; Xiao Wang is inside.)

王：小李、小张，老师已经**进**教室**来**了，你们也**进来**吧。
Wáng: Xiǎo Lǐ, Xiǎo Zhāng, lǎoshī yǐjīng jìn jiàoshì lái le, nǐmen yě jìn lái ba.
张：小李，小王说，老师到了，咱们**进**教室**去**吧。
Zhāng: Xiǎo Lǐ, Xiǎo Wáng shuō, lǎoshī dào le, zánmen jìn jiàoshì qù ba.
Wang: Xiao Li, Xiao Zhang, the teacher has **come into** the classroom. You two **come in**, too.
Zhang: Xiao Li, Xiao Wang said that the teacher has arrived. Let's **go into** the classroom.

小丁，请你**过来**，我有话要跟你说。
Xiǎo Dīng, qǐng nǐ guò lái, wǒ yǒu huà yào gēn nǐ shuō.
Xiao Ding, please come over (here). I have something to say to you.

(b) 来 or 去? (Based on the location of the subject)

When the utterance is made from a third person's point of view, and there is no 我 present in the situation, the use of 来 or 去 is based on where the subject or focus of the sentence is.

小王一看见他女朋友在街对面，就立刻**过(街)去**跟她说话。（小王 is the subject.）
Xiǎo Wáng yí kànjiàn tā nǔ péngyǒu zài jiē duìmiàn, jiù lìkè guò jiē qù gēn tā shuōhuà.
The moment Xiao Wang noticed that his girlfriend was across from the street, he immediately went across the street to speak to her.

昨天小明告诉妈妈他今天不会**出去**，可是他上午十点起来以后就**出(门)去**了；他妈妈买菜**回来**的时候，没人给她开门，她很不高兴。
Zuótiān Xiǎomíng gàosù māma tā jīntiān bú huì chū qù, kěshì tā shàngwǔ shí diǎn qǐ lái yǐhòu jiù chū mén qù le; tā māma mǎi cài huí lái de shíhòu, méi rén gěi tā kāi mén, tā hěn bù gāoxìng.
Yesterday Xiaoming had told his mother that he would not **go out** today. But he **got up** at 10 o'clock in the morning and then **went out** (of the door). When his mother **came back** from grocery shopping, nobody opened the door for her; she was unhappy.

(c) Exception

When the place in question is the home (or the base) of one of the interlocutors, 来 can be used where 去 normally would be used.

(Situation: Wang is at home and he calls Zhang on the phone.)

王：小张，你今天有没有空？可不可以**过来**一趟？
Wáng: Xiǎo Zhāng, nǐ jīntiān yǒu méiyǒu kòng? Kě bù kěyǐ guò lái yí tàng?
张：我晚上有空，我八点**过来**，可以吗？（过去 is also acceptable.）
Zhāng: Wǒ wǎnshàng yǒu kòng, wǒ bā diǎn guò lái, kěyǐ ma?
Wang: Xiao Zhang, do you have time today? Can you **come over**?
Zhang: I have time in the evening. I'll **come over** at 8 o'clock, is that OK?

(d) When the verb is 到

When the verb is 到, a place (the destination in this case) must be inserted between 到 and 来/去. Otherwise, simply use 来 or 去 as the verb without 到.

张：你什么时候要**到中国去**？（到中国**去** = **去**中国）
Zhāng: Nǐ shénme shíhòu yào dào Zhōngguó qù?
李：我下个月去。欢迎你有空的时候**到北京来**看我。（**到北京来** = **来**北京）
Lǐ: Wǒ xià ge yuè qù. Huānyíng nǐ yǒu kòng de shíhòu dào Běijīng lái kàn wǒ.
Zhang: When do you plan to go to China?
Li: I am going next month. You are welcome to come to Beijing to visit me when you have time.

15.2 With non-places

When the sentence involves a person or an object (a thing), verbs frequently used in such a sentence are 拿 (*ná*: 'to hold'), 带 (*dài*: 'to carry'), 搬 (*bān*: 'to move'), 寄 (*jì*: 'to mail'), 送 (*sòng*: 'to deliver'), 借 (*jiè*: 'to borrow'), 打 (电话) (*dǎ diànhuà*: 'to make phone call'), 开 (车) (*kāichē*: 'to drive'), 骑 (车/马) (*qí chē/mǎ*: 'to ride bicycle/horse'), 买 (*mǎi*: 'to buy'), etc.

(a) Word order

The following table shows three word-order patterns. The word order is slightly more flexible when the sentence has 了 than when the sentence does not have 了. The person/object tends to be indefinite.

Pattern #1 (with 了)	Verb	了	Person/object	来 or 去
Pattern #2 (with 了)	Verb	来 or 去	了	Person/object
Pattern #3 (without 了)	Verb	∅	Person/object	来 or 去

我一说口渴，他就给我**拿了**一杯水**来**。(= 他就给我**拿来了**一杯水。)
Wǒ yì shuō kǒu kě, tā jiù gěi wǒ ná le yì bēi shuǐ lái.
As soon as I said I was thirsty, he immediately **brought** a glass of water to me.

我口渴，请你给我**拿**一杯水**来**，好不好？(Pattern #3)
Wǒ kǒu kě, qǐng nǐ gěi wǒ ná yì bēi shuǐ lái, hǎo bù hǎo?
I'm thirsty, please **bring** me a glass of water, OK?

小王请人从法国给我**带来了**一瓶香水(= **带了**一瓶香水**来**)，所以明天我要给他**寄**五十块钱**去**。(寄五十块钱去 is pattern #3.)
Xiǎo Wáng qǐng rén cóng Fǎguó gěi wǒ dài lái le yì píng xiāngshuǐ, suǒyǐ míngtiān wǒ yào gěi tā jì wǔshí kuài qián qù.
Xiao Wang asked someone to **bring** me a bottle of perfume from France; so I am going to **mail** $50 **to him** tomorrow.

(b) When the verb is 送

Since 送 has several meanings, it should be noted that when 送 appears before the complement of direction 来/去, it means 'to deliver something' or 'to take someone to a place'.

王先生，你的司机下午有没有空？可不可以请他**送**我**去**机场？
Wáng xiānsheng, nǐde sījī xiàwǔ yǒu méiyǒu kòng? Kě bù kěyǐ qǐng tā sòng wǒ qù jīchǎng?
Mr Wang, is your chauffeur free this afternoon? Can I ask him to **take** me to the airport?

那家店服务真好，我**打了**一个电话**去**，他们就**送来**了我要买的东西。

Nà jiā diàn fúwù zhēn hǎo, wǒ dǎ le yí ge diànhuà qù, tāmen jiù sòng lái le wǒ yào mǎi de dōngxī.

That shop's service was really good. I **made a phone call (to them)** and they immediately **delivered (to me)** what I wanted to buy.

(c) When the verb is 买 or 借

Words such as 买 and 借, which do not carry the meaning of transporting someone or something, can go with 来/去 with the meaning of 'bring' being implied. 👁 Two verbs might be necessary in English, but only one is used in Chinese.

妈妈：你五点就**出去**了，为什么现在才**回来**？你去哪里了？

Māma: Nǐ wǔ diǎn jiù chū qù le, wèishénme xiànzài cái huí lái? Nǐ qù nǎlǐ le?

儿子：我**到**图书馆**去**了。现在我要**上楼去**看我**借来**的漫画书。(借来: to borrow and bring)

Érzi: Wǒ dào túshūguǎn qù le. Xiànzài wǒ yào shàng lóu qù kàn wǒ jiè lái de mànhuà shū.

Mother: You **went out** at 5 o'clock? Why did you only **come back** now? Where were you?

Son: I **went** to the library. Now I am **going upstairs** to read the comic books that I **checked out** (and **brought** back with me).

The following two examples illustrate the difference between 买 and 买来.

张：我知道你没有词典，所以我昨天去给你**买了**一本。

Zhāng: Wo zhīdào nǐ méiyǒu cídiǎn, suǒyǐ wǒ zuótiān qù gěi nǐ mǎi le yì běn.

李：太好了，谢谢。让我看看。

Lǐ: Tài hǎo le, xièxie. Ràng wǒ kàn kàn.

张：对不起，我今天忘了**带来**。

Zhāng: Duìbùqǐ, wǒ jīntiān wàng le dài lái.

Zhang: I knew you didn't have a dictionary, so I went and **bought** one for you yesterday.

Li: Great! Thank you. Let me see it.

Zhang: Sorry, I forgot to **bring** it today.

王英，我知道你没有汉英词典，所以我去书店给你**买了**一本**来**。

Wáng Yīng, wǒ zhīdào nǐ méiyǒu Hàn Yīng cídiǎn, suǒyǐ wǒ qù shūdiàn gěi nǐ mǎi le yì běn lái.

Wang Ying, I knew you didn't have a Chinese–English dictionary, so I went to the bookshop and **bought** one for you (and I **brought** it).

B. The complex complements of direction

The complex complements of direction are based on the simple complements of direction. There are 13 of them in total.

上来	下来	进来	出来	回来	过来	起来
上去	下去	进去	出去	回去	过去	∅

Since these 13 words are complements, each of them should follow a verb. Similar to the usage of the simple complements of direction, the use of the complex complements of direction can involve a place or a non-place (person/object).

evel
2/3

15.3 With places

The verbs that are frequently used in such sentences are 走 (*zǒu*: 'to walk'), 跑 (*pǎo*: 'to run'), 游 (*yóu*: 'to swim'), 跳 (*tiào*: 'to jump'), 穿 (*chuān*: 'to cross'), 骑 (*qí*: 'to ride horse or bicycle'), 开 (*kāi*: 'to drive'), 坐 (*zuò*: 'to sit; to ride public transportation'), 站 (*zhàn*: 'to stand'), etc.

- With the use of a verb, a sentence with a complex complement of direction can convey more information than one with a simple complement of direction

(Situation: Wang and Zhang are talking about how late a park is open to the public.)

王：十点以后，汽车还能**进去**吗？(进 is the verb; 去 is the simple directional complement.)
Wáng: Shí diǎn yǐhòu, qìchē hái néng jìn qù ma?
张：车不能**开进去**了，不过人还是可以**走进去**。
Zhāng: Chē bù néng kāi jìnqù le, búguò rén háishì kěyǐ zǒu jìnqù.
Wang: Can cars go in after 10 o'clock?
Zhang: You cannot drive a car in, but people can still walk in.

- Certain verbs that are used with the complex complement of direction do not convey more meaning than a simple complement of direction. They are just different ways to say the same thing

他一看绿灯亮了，就立刻**穿过**马路**来**跟我说话。(**穿过**马路**来** = **过**马路**来**)
Tā yí kàn lǜ dēng liàng le, jiù lìkè chuān guò mǎlù lái gēn wǒ shuōhuà.
As soon as he noticed that the green light was on (the light was green), he immediately crossed the street to talk to me.

因为这座山不太高，所以我们就决定**爬上**山**去**照相。(**爬上**山**去** = **上**山**去**)
Yīnwèi zhè zuò shān bú tài gāo, suǒyǐ wǒmen jiù juédìng pá shàng shān qù zhàoxiàng.
Because this mountain is not very tall, we decided to climb up to the top to take some photos.

(a) Word-order

When the place is mentioned, it should appear between the two characters forming the complement.

(Situation: Two friends are on top of a mountain.)

王：咱们**跑下**(山)**去**吧！
Wáng: Zánmen pǎo xià (shān) qù ba!
李：我光是**走上来**就累死了，怎么可能有力气跑？
Li: Wǒ guāngshì zǒu shànglái jiù lèi sǐ le, zěnme kěnéng yǒu lìqì pǎo?
Wang: Let's **run down** the hill.
Li: Just **walking up here**, I am already tired to death. How can I possibly have the energy to run?

河上虽然有桥，可是他决定**游过**(河)**去**，再从桥上**走回来**。
Hé shàng suīrán yǒu qiáo, kěshì tā juédìng yóu guò (hé) qù, zài cóng qiáo shàng zǒu huílái.
Although there was a bridge on the river, he decided to **swim across** (**to the other side**) and to **walk back** on the bridge later.

(b) 起来 and 上来

起来 does not have a counterpart 起去. Its counterpart is 下去. The difference between 起来 and 上来 lies in the fact that 起来 usually does not indicate an obvious change of altitude, whereas 上来 does.

> 病人看到医生**走进病房来**，就**坐起来**跟他说话。(The patient had been lying down.)
> *Bìngrén kàndào yīshēng zǒu jìn bìngfáng lái, jiù zuò qǐlái gēn tā shuōhuà.*
> The patient saw the doctor enter the room, so he **sat up** and talked to him.

> 小王一听到这么好的消息，就高兴得**跳起来**。
> *Xiǎo Wáng yì tīngdào zhème hǎo de xiāoxi, jiù gāoxìng de tiào qǐlái.*
> Once Xiao Wang heard such good news, he was so happy that he **jumped up**.
> Compare:　小兰一看到地上有一只蟑螂，就吓得**跳上椅子去**。
> 　　　　　*Xiǎolán yí kàndào dìshàng yǒu yì zhī zhāngláng, jiù xià de tiào shàng yǐzi qù.*
> 　　　　　Seeing a cockroach on the floor, Xiaolan was so scared that she **jumped onto** a chair at once.

(c) 坐下来 and 坐下去

坐下来 and 坐下去 both mean 'to sit down'. Whether to use 下来 or 下去 depends on whether the speaker is sitting or standing. If the description is given from a third person's point of view, then either 下来 or 下去 can be used.

(Situation: During class, the teacher is standing whereas the students are sitting.)

> 老师：王中，请你**站起来**回答下一个问题。回答完了，你就可以**坐下去**。
> *Lǎoshī: Wáng Zhōng, qǐng nǐ zhàn qǐlái huídá xià yí ge wèntí. Huídá wán le, nǐ jiù kěyǐ zuò xiàqù.*
> Teacher: Wang Zhong, please **stand up** and answer the next question. When you are done answering the question, you can **sit down**.

(Situation: Wang Zhong has finished answering the question, but he is still standing. Student Li, who is sitting, reminds him that he can sit down.)

> 李：王中，你可以**坐下来**了。
> *Lǐ: Wáng Zhōng, nǐ kěyǐ zuò xiàlái le.*
> Li: Wang Zhong, you can **sit down** now.

Level 2/3

15.4 With non-places

When the sentence with the complex complement of direction involves a non-place (person/object), the verbs are the same as those used in the simple complement of direction, e.g. 拿, 带, 搬, 寄, 送, 借, 打 (电话), 开 (车), 骑 (车/马), 买, etc.

(a) Word order with 了

If 了 is used in the sentence, the word order basically follows the following rules:

Pattern #1	Verb	了		Person/object	Complement	Ø
Pattern #2	Verb	Complement		了	Person/object	Ø
Pattern #3	Verb	First character in the complement		了	Person/object	来 or 去

昨天爸爸下班的时候，**请**了两个同事**回来**吃晚饭。 (Pattern #1)
Zuótiān bàba xiàbān de shíhòu, qǐng le liǎng ge tóngshì huílái chī wǎnfàn.
Yesterday when my father got off work, he invited (brought) two co-workers home to eat dinner.

教室里本来只有三把椅子，刚才小王**搬进来**了两把，现在有五把了。
(Pattern #2)
Jiàoshì lǐ běnlái yǒu sān bǎ yǐzi, gāngcái Xiǎo Wáng bān jìnlái le liǎng bǎ, xiànzài yǒu wǔ bǎ le.
There were originally three chairs in the classroom; just now, Xiao Wang moved (brought) in two more; so there are five chairs now.

刚才老张忽然**说出**了一句很奇怪的话**来**。 (Pattern #3)
Gāngcái Lǎo Zhāng hūrán shuō chū le yí jù hěn qíguài de huà lái.
Lao Zhang suddenly uttered (spoke out) a very strange sentence just now.

(b) Word order without 了

When the sentence does not need 了, Pattern #2 is not proper. Pattern #1 might be the best choice.

老师：同学们，请你们每个人都**拿**一支笔**出来**(= 拿出一支笔来)。
Lǎoshī: Tóngxué men, qǐng nǐmen měi ge rén dōu ná yì zhī bǐ chūlái (= ná chū yì zhī bǐ lái).
Teacher: Students, everybody please **take** a pen **out** (of your backpack, pencil case, etc.).

(c) When the object is definite

The three patterns above apply best to indefinite objects. If the object/person is definite, it would be better to pre-pose the object/person or to use the 把 structure.

外面有两张桌子，园的那张，请你**搬进来**，好吗？ (The object is pre-posed.)
Wàimiàn yǒu liǎng zhāng zhuōzi, yuán de nà zhāng, qǐng nǐ bān jìnlái, hǎo ma?
There are two tables here. Would you please move the round one inside?

医生：你爷爷可以出院了，你现在就可以把他**带回家去**了。
Yīshēng: Nǐ yéye kěyǐ chūyuàn le, nǐ xiànzài jiù kěyǐ bǎ tā dài huí jiā qù le.
Doctor: Your grandfather can leave the hospital. You can take him home now.

C. Extended or abstract meanings of the complex complement of direction

15.5 Extended or abstract meanings based on the idea of direction

Some of the complex complements of direction have extended or abstract meanings which do not explicitly indicate a direction but are based on the idea of direction.

医生们花了十几个小时，终于把他的命**救回来**了。
Yīshēng men huā le shí jǐ ge xiǎoshí, zhōngyú bǎ tāde mìng jiù huílái le.
The doctors spent over ten hours and finally saved him (**brought** his life **back**).

妈妈叫我把圣诞礼物都**包起来**。

Māma jiào wǒ bǎ Shèngdàn lǐwù dōu bāo qǐlái.

My mother asked me to **wrap up** all the Christmas gifts.

15.6 Frequently used complements of direction with extended or abstract meanings

The following are some of the frequently used complex complements of direction that have extended or abstract meanings:

(a) 起来: beginning something unexpected

起来 can indicate the beginning of an action; the subtle implication is that it is somewhat unexpected for this to happen. The object, if there is one, appears between 起 and 来.

老师话还没有说完，学生就**鼓起掌来**。

Lǎoshī huà hái méiyǒu shuō wán, xuéshēng jiù gǔ qǐ zhǎng lái.

The teacher had not finished talking and the students already **began to applaud**.

王小姐学了二十年芭蕾舞，最近却**跳起**现代舞**来**。

Wáng xiǎojiě xué le èrshí nián bāléiwǔ, zuìjìn què tiào qǐ xiàndài wǔ lái.

Miss Wang studied ballet for 20 years; but she has recently **started to do** modern dance.

(b) 起来: bringing something to a focused point

起来 can imply bringing things or people to a focused point or a fixed position.

他贪污了一笔钱，现在被**关起来**了。

Tā tānwū le yì bǐ qián, xiànzài bèi guān qǐlái le.

He embezzled a large sum of money. Now he's been **locked up**.

咱们把脑力**集中起来**，一定可以**想出**好办法**来**。

Zánmen bǎ nǎolì jízhōng qǐlái, yídìng kěyǐ xiǎng chū hǎo bànfǎ lái.

Let's gather together our brain power. We can definitely think of a good solution.

(c) Verb + 起来 + adjective

Verb + 起来 can be followed by an adjective to imply what it's like when the action is being performed. It is possible to have an object between 起 and 来.

爷爷虽然八十岁了，可是**说起**话**来**还很大声，**走起路来**也很快。

Yéye suīrán bāshí suì le, kěshì shuō qǐ huà lái hái hěn dàshēng, zǒu qǐ lù lái yě hěn kuài.

My grandfather is already 80 years old, but he is loud when speaking and fast when walking.

这件事**说起来**简单，**做起来**很不容易。

Zhè jiàn shì shuō qǐlái jiǎndān, zuò qǐlái hěn bù róngyì.

This matter is simple when you talk about it, but is very difficult when you (try to) do it.

(d) Verb indicating a sense + 起来 + adjective

Verbs indicating senses, such as to look (看: *kàn*), to smell (闻: *wén*), to taste (尝: *cháng*), to touch (摸: *mō*), to listen (听: *tīng*), can appear before 起来 to form a verbal phrase which will be followed by an adjective.

⟨➍⟩ Learners who are English speakers tend to forget the use of 起来 in such phrases since verbs indicating senses are immediately followed by adjectives in English.

他做的菜，**看起来**漂亮，**闻起来**也很香，可是**吃起来**不好吃。
Tā zuò de cài, kàn qǐlái piàoliàng, wén qǐlái yě hěn xiāng, kěshì chī qǐlái bù hǎochī.
The food he made looked appealing, smelled good, but tasted bad.

这件大衣，**摸起来**很软，可是**穿起来**不舒服。
Zhè jiàn dàyī, mō qǐlái hěn ruǎn, kěshì chuān qǐlái bù shūfú.
This coat feels soft (when you touch it), but it's not comfortable when you wear it.

(e) 下去: continuation

下去 can indicate the continuation of a situation or action. In this case, 下去 must immediately follow the verb.

你别插嘴，让他**说下去**(= 让他把话**说下去**)。
Nǐ bié chāzuǐ, ràng tā shuō xiàqù.
Don't interrupt! Let him continue (talking).

只要是一个生命，就有**活下去**的权利。
Zhǐyào shì yí ge shēngmìng, jiù yǒu huó xiàqù de quánlì.
As long as it's a life, it has the right to continue living.

(f) 下来: gradual change from light to dark, etc.

下来 can indicate a change from an earlier status to a current status. The change is usually gradual and from a brighter, higher, faster, etc. status to a darker, lower, slower, etc. status.

过了下午六点，天就**黑下来**了。
Guò le xiàwǔ liù diǎn, tiān jiù hēi xiàlái le.
After 6 p.m., the sky (gradually) becomes dark.

火车进了站，速度就会**慢下来**。
Huǒchē jìn le zhàn, sùdù jiù huì màn xiàlái.
After the train has entered the station, the speed will slow down.

(g) 起来: gradual change from dark to light, etc.

If the change goes from a darker, lower, slower, etc. status to a brighter, higher, faster, etc. status, the complement is usually 起来.

我最近太忙，没空做饭，天天在外面吃，所以没多久就**胖起来**了。
Wo zuìjìn tài máng, méi kòng zuòfàn, tiāntiān zài wàimiàn chī, suǒyǐ méi duō jiǔ jiù pàng qǐlái le.
Recently, I have been too busy. I have no time to cook and eat out every day. So I soon put on weight.

我妈妈一生气，说话的声音就会**大起来**。
Wǒ māma yì shēngqì, shuōhuà de shēngyīn jiù huì dà qǐlái.
As soon as my mother gets angry, her voice will become louder.

Exercises

I Fill in the blanks using a verb and a simple complement of direction (来/去) based on the context provided in the sentence.

Example 你看，安娜跟王明从山上 <u>下 来</u> 了。

Nǐ kàn, Ānnà gēn Wáng Míng cóng shān shàng <u>xià lái</u> le.

Look, Anna and Wang Ming have come down from the mountain.

Level 1

1 安娜：你的男朋友**在对面**叫你，你为什么不 ＿＿ ＿＿ 呢？

小兰：他是男的，应该他 ＿＿ ＿＿。

安娜：要是你不 ＿＿ ＿＿ ，他也不 ＿＿ ＿＿ ，你们就不能谈话了。

2 你看，他们都**在山上**，我们也 ＿＿ ＿＿ 吧！

3 (妈妈给小明打电话。)

妈妈：小明，大家都**在家里**等你一起吃饭，你为什么还不 ＿＿ ＿＿ 呢？

4 上星期我的好朋友李中**从上海** ＿＿ ＿＿ 了一封**信**，他在信上问我什么时候可以 ＿＿ ＿＿ ＿＿ ＿＿(= 去那里)看他。

5 我听说你喜欢吃法国点心，所以我**去店里**给你 ＿＿ ＿＿ 了一些，都在厨房里，你去吃吧！

6 上星期我给爸爸 ＿＿ ＿＿ 了一封**信**，请他下个月来中国看我的时候，给我 ＿＿ 一本汉英词典 ＿＿。昨天爸爸 ＿＿ 了一个**电话** ＿＿ ，告诉我他不能 ＿＿ ＿＿ ＿＿ ＿＿(= 来中国)看我了，所以我要的词典，他会 ＿＿ ＿＿。(send by mail)

7 今天我请几个朋友来我家开派对，每个朋友都 ＿＿ ＿＿了一个他们在家做的菜，但是小李**去店里** ＿＿ 了一瓶酒 ＿＿。

II Fill in the blanks using a verb and a complex complement of direction, based on the context provided in the sentence. The choice of the verb may be flexible in some cases.

Example 他一看到我在楼下，就从楼上 <u>走(**or** 跑)</u> <u>下 来</u> 了。

Tā yí kàn dào wǒ zài lóu xià, jiù cóng lóu shàng <u>zǒu (or pǎo)</u> <u>xià lái</u> le.

As soon as he saw that I was downstairs, he immediately walked (*or* ran) down (from upstairs).

Level 2

1 你别**站**在那里了，快 ＿＿ ＿＿ ＿＿ 休息休息吧！(说话的人也站着。)

2 这家小吃店人太多了，我不想在这里吃，我们 ＿＿ 一些小吃 ＿＿ 家 ＿＿ 吃，好不好？

3 这个人**从十楼** ＿＿ ＿＿ ＿＿ ，所以他很快就死了。(说话的人在大楼外面。)

4 十点了，饭馆里还有很多客人在吃饭，**从外面**又 ____ ____ ____ 几个人，今天生意真好！

5 我每天下午都 ____ 我的狗 ____ ____ 玩。

6 在中国，老师一进教室，小学生就会**从椅子上** ____ ____ ____ 说"老师好。"

7 你看，**山上**有一个漂亮的亭子，咱们 ____ ____ 山 ____ 照几张相吧！

8 爸爸每次**出国**，都会给我 ____ 礼物 ____ ____。

9 河上有一条桥，我打算 ____ (swim) ____ ____，再从**桥上** ____ ____ ____。

16 The complement of result

In Chinese, there are some disyllabic words that are actually composed of a verb and a complement of result. The verb indicates the effort; the verb and the complement following it together show that the effort has produced a result. The complement of result is generally either another verb or an adjective.

Nothing should be inserted between the verb and the complement of result unless a complement of potential is formed. (☞ See 17.1 for details of the complement of potential.) Should the sentence need an aspect particle 了/过 (le/guo), or if the verb has an object, the 了/过 or the object should appear after the complement of result, not after the verb. Sometimes, the object can be pre-posed.

Level 2

16.1 Effort vs. effort and result

◉ The difference between an effort and an effort plus its result is frequently indicated by using two different words in English. In Chinese, the difference is indicated by the presence of the complement of result.

王：你在做什么？
Wáng: Nǐ zài zuò shénme?
张：我在**找**我的笔记本。（找 indicates the effort.）
Zhāng: Wǒ zài zhǎo wǒde bǐjìběn.
（五分钟以后）
(Wǔ fēnzhōng yǐhòu)
王：笔记本，你**找到**了吗？（到 indicates the result.）
Wáng: Bǐjìběn, nǐ zhǎo dào le ma?
张：**找到**了。
Zhāng: Zhǎodào le.
Wang: What are you doing?
Zhang: I am **looking for** my notebook.
(Five minutes later)
Wang: Did you **find** that notebook? (Have you **found** that notebook?)
Zhang: I **found** it.

李：你**看**，树上有一只彩色的鸟。（看 indicates the effort.）
Lǐ: Nǐ kàn, shùshàng yǒu yì zhī cǎisè de niǎo.
丁：是吗？我怎么没有**看见**？（见 indicates the result.）
Dīng: Shìma? Wǒ zěnme méiyǒu kàn jiàn?
Li: **Look**! There is a multi-coloured bird in the tree.
Ding: Is that so? How come I can't **see** it?

Level
1
16.2 The negative form

The negative form of 'verb + result' is normally '没 (有) (*méiyǒu*) + verb + result'. To ask an affirmative–negative (or yes–no) question, use 'verb + result + (了) 没有?' or 'verb + result + 了吗 (*le ma*)?'

王小姐上个星期才开始**学**开车，她还没有**学会**呢。 (学 is the effort; 会 is the result.)
Wáng xiǎojiě shàng ge xīngqī cái kāishǐ xué kāichē, tā hái méiyǒu xué huì ne.
Miss Wang only started to take driving lessons last week; she hasn't learned how to drive yet.

李：老师问的问题，你**答对**(了)没有? (答 is the effort; 对 is the result.)
Lǐ: Lǎoshī wèn de wèntí, nǐ dá duì (le) méiyǒu?
张：唉! **答错**了。你呢? (错 is the result.)
Zhāng: Ài! Dá cuò le. Nǐ ne?
李：我也没有**答对**。
Lǐ: Wǒ yě méiyǒu dá duì.
Li: Did you correctly answer the question that the teacher asked?
Zhang: Sigh! I answered it wrong. How about you?
Li: I didn't answer it correctly either.

王：老师说的话，你**听清楚**了吗? （听 is the effort; 清楚 is the result.)
Wáng: Lǎoshī shuō de huà, nǐ tīng qīngchǔ le ma?
丁：他说得太小声了，我没(有)**听清楚**。
Dīng: Tā shuō de tài xiǎoshēng le, wǒ méi(yǒu) tīng qīngchǔ.
Wang: Did you hear clearly what the teacher said?
Ding: He spoke too softly; I did not hear it clearly.

Level
1
16.3 Use of 不 in the negative form

Occasionally, 不 (*bù*) can be used in the negative form of 'verb + result'. This is usually used to indicate a lack of good effort, which leads to a lack of result.

王：你在做什么?
Wáng: Nǐ zài zuò shénme?
张：我在**记**生词呢。要是我今晚**不**把这些生词都**记住**，明天的考试，我一定会考得很差。 (记 is the effort of trying to remember; 住 is the result of actually remembering.)
Zhāng: Wǒ zài jì shēngcí ne. Yàoshì wǒ jīnwǎn bù bǎ zhè xiē shēngcí dōu jì zhù, míngtiān de kǎoshì, wǒ yídìng huì kǎo de hěn chà.
Wang: What are you doing?
Zhang: I am trying to memorize vocabulary words. If I don't actually memorize all these words this evening, I will definitely do badly in tomorrow's test.

Level
2
16.4 Placement of objects

The object of the verb should follow the complement of result or be pre-posed. It should not immediately follow the verb.

昨天我**收到**(了)一封小王寄来的信。
Zuótiān wǒ shōu dào (le) yì fēng Xiǎo Wáng jì lái de xìn.
Yesterday I received a letter from Xiao Wang.

那本畅销书，我一直没有**买到**，因为早就**卖完**了。
Nà běn chàngxiāo shū, wǒ yìzhí méiyǒu mǎi dào, yīnwèi zǎo jiù mài wán le.
I have not succeeded in purchasing that best-selling book because it had been long
sold out.

16.5 Placement of aspect particles

The aspect particle 过/了 (*guo/le*) follows the complement of result, not the verb. Also, 了 can
be optional when the object follows the complement.

法文老师说的故事，我以前从来没**听懂过**，可是他今天说的，我居然**听懂**了。
*Fǎwén lǎoshī shuō de gùshì, wǒ yǐqián cónglái méiyǒu tīng dǒng guò, kěshì tā jīntiān shuō
de, wǒ jūrán tīng dǒng le.*
I had never understood the stories my French teacher told. But, surprisingly,
I understood the one he told today.

那三个小偷，警察只**抓住**(了)两个，还有一个**跑走**了。
Nà sān ge xiǎotōu, jǐngchá zhǐ zhuā zhù (le) liǎng ge, háiyǒu yí ge pǎo zǒu le.
The police only caught two of the three thieves; the other one ran away.

16.6 Words commonly used as a complement of result

Verbs and adjectives that can be used to indicate the result of an action are numerous. It is
impossible to provide a complete list of such verbs and adjectives. The following are examples
of words commonly used as a complement of result.

(a) 懂 (*dǒng*)

懂 means 'to understand'. The verbs (effort) associated with 懂 are 看 (*kàn*) and 听 (*tīng*).

老师刚才说的话，你**听懂**了没有？
Lǎoshī gāngcái shuō de huà, nǐ tīng dǒng le méiyǒu?
Did you understand what the teacher just said?

牌子上那五个字，我只**看懂**三个。
Páizi shàng nà wǔ ge zì, wǒ zhǐ kàn dǒng sān ge.
I only understand three of the five characters on that sign.

(b) 会 (*huì*)

会 means 'to know how to do something'. The verb (effort) associated with 会 is 学 (*xué*).

自行车，我只**学**了三小时就**学会**了；可是我**学**游泳**学**了半年了，还是没有**学会**。
*Zìxíngchē, wǒ zhǐ xué le sān xiǎoshí jiù xué huì le; kěshì wǒ xué yóuyǒng xué le bàn nián
le, háishì méiyǒu xué huì.*
I learned to ride a bike in only three hours; but I have been taking swimming lessons
for half a year already and I still haven't learned how to swim.

(c) 见 (*jiàn*)

见 means 'to perceive'. The verbs most frequently associated with 见 are 听 (*tīng*) and 看
(*kàn*). 见 can also be the result for 遇 (*yù*) and 碰 (*pèng*); 遇见 and 碰见 both mean 'to run
into someone'.

张：听，有人在敲门。

Zhāng: Tīng, yǒu rén zài qiāo mén.

王：有人在敲门？我怎么没有**听见**？

Wáng: Yǒu rén zài qiāo mén? Wǒ zěnme méiyǒu tīng jiàn?

Zhang: Listen, someone is knocking at the door.

Wang: Someone is knocking at the door? How come I didn't hear it?

昨天我在街上**遇见**一个很久没有**看见**的老朋友。

Zuótiān wǒ zài jiē shàng yùjiàn yí ge hěn jiǔ méiyǒu kànjiàn de lǎo péngyǒu.

Yesterday I ran into an old friend whom I hadn't seen in a long time.

(d) 完 (*wán*)

完 means 'to finish'; it primarily serves as a complement of result and is rarely used as an independent verb. 👁 Therefore, expressions such as 'Did you finish?' and 'I am done' in English cannot be directly translated into Chinese. Such an expression in Chinese must contain the verb that indicates the actual action.

(Situation: Mr Wang is complaining that Mrs Wang nags too much.)

王先生：你到底**说完**了没有？

Wáng xiānsheng: Nǐ dàodǐ shuō wán le méiyǒu?

王太太：别插嘴，我还没**说完**呢。

Wáng tàitai: Bié chāzuǐ, wǒ hái méi shuō wán ne.

Mr Wang: Are you done (talking) or not?

Mrs Wang: Don't interrupt. I am not done (talking) yet.

完 can also be used to indicate that something is all gone. In this case, 完 is interchangeable with 光 (*guāng*).

妈妈：小明，锅里的汤，你别**喝完**，留一些给爸爸喝。(喝完 = 喝光)

Māma: Xiǎomíng, guō lǐ de tāng, nǐ bié hē wán, liú yìxiē gěi bàba hē.

小明：你说得太晚了，我已经把它**喝完**了。

Xiǎomíng: Nǐ shuō de tài wǎn le, wǒ yǐjīng bǎ tā hē wán le.

Mother: Xiaoming, don't drink all of the soup in the pot. Save some for your father.

Xiaoming: Too late. I already finished it.

要看这个电影的人太多了，所有的票一小时就**卖完**了。(卖完 = 卖光)

Yào kàn zhè ge diànyǐng de rén tài duō le, suǒyǒu de piào yì xiǎoshí jiù mài wán le.

Too many people wanted to see this movie. All the tickets were sold out within one hour.

(e) 到 (*dào*)

- 到 can indicate 'to reach' a certain point or the availability of something. Verbs showing actions of movement or progress can be associated with 到 to show the point reached. Some of these verbs are 走 (*zǒu*), 跑 (*pǎo*), 开 (车) (*kāichē*), 骑 (*qí*), 游 (*yóu*), 说 (*shuō*), 讲 (*jiǎng*), 学 (*xué*), etc.

你往前走，**走到**红绿灯那里，往右转，就会**看见**火车站了。

Nǐ wàng qián zǒu, zǒu dào hónglǜdēng nàlǐ, wàng yòu zhuǎn, jiù huì kànjiàn huǒchēzhàn le.

Walk ahead until you **reach** the traffic lights, turn right and you will **see** the train station.

昨天他**写完**功课就开始看电视，**看到**十二点才去睡觉。

Zuótiān tā xiě wán gōngkè jiù kāishǐ kàn diànshì, kàn dào shí'èr diǎn cái qù shuìjiào.

Yesterday he began to watch TV right after he **finished writing** his homework. He **watched until** 12 o'clock before he finally went to bed. (It is incorrect to say 他看电视 到十二点 because 到 must follow the verb 看.)

这本书有三十课，但是这学期我们只能**学到**第二十四课。

Zhè běn shū yǒu sānshí kè, dànshì zhè xuéqī wǒmen zhǐ néng xué dào dì èrshí sì ke.

This book has 30 lessons, but we can only **study up to** Lesson 24 this term.

- 到 can also indicate the 'availability' or 'presence' of someone or something. Verbs associated with this definition are 找 (*zhǎo*), 买 (*mǎi*), 请 (*qǐng*), 看 (*kàn*), 听 (*tīng*), 遇 (*yù*), 碰 (*pèng*), 见 (*jiàn*), etc. Expressions such as 看见, 听见, 遇见 and 碰见 can be 看到, 听到, 遇到 and 碰到 respectively. However, when 到 specifically indicates 'availability/presence', 看到, 听到, 遇到 and 碰到 must be used.

真没想到，在这么偏僻的法国小镇还能**看到**最新的中国电影，**吃到**地道的 中国菜。

Zhēn méi xiǎngdào, zài zhème piānpì de Fǎguó xiǎo zhèn hái néng kàndào zuì xīn de Zhōngguó diànyǐng, chī dào dìdào de Zhōngguó cài.

I really didn't expect that I could actually get to see the newest Chinese movie and get to eat authentic Chinese food in such an out-of-place small French town.

昨天我在路上**碰到**(= 碰见)了一个老朋友，他说他最近**遇到**(**cannot be** 遇见)了 很多困难。

Zuótiān wǒ zài lù shàng pèng dào (= pèng jiàn) le yí ge lǎo péngyǒu, tā shuō tā zuìjìn yùdào le hěn duō kùnnán.

I ran into an old friend yesterday. He said that he had **encountered** many difficulties lately.

(f) 住 (*zhù*)

住 as a complement of result means 'to stay, to stop the movement of something or someone'.

太太：你**留**客人了没有？

Tàitai: Nǐ liú kèrén le méiyǒu?

先生：**留**了，可是只**留住**了三个，另外两个没有**留住**。 (留 is the effort; 住 is the result.)

Xiānsheng: Liú le, kěshì zhǐ liú zhù le sān ge, lìngwài liǎng ge méiyǒu liú zhù.

Wife: Did you **ask** our guests **to stay**?

Husband: I did, but I only **succeeded in getting** three **to stay**. I didn't **succeed in getting** the other two **to stay**.

那场比赛，美国队输了，因为有两个球，他们没有**接住**。 (接 is the effort, 住 is the result.)

Nà chǎng bǐsài, Měiguó duì shū le, yīnwèi yǒu liǎng ge qiú, tāmen méiyǒu jiē zhù.

The US team lost the game because they missed (did not catch) two balls.

站住！我还没说**完**话，你怎么可以走？

Zhàn zhù! Wǒ hái méi shuō wán huà, nǐ zěnme kěyǐ zǒu?

Stop walking away and stand still! I have not finished talking; how can you leave?

(g) 掉 (*diào*)

掉 means 'to drop or to lose something'. As a complement of result, it indicates that the action causes something to be gone forever. If the expression is followed by 了 (*le*), 掉 is optional since 了 can serve a similar function.

> 哥哥：桌上的巧克力糖去哪里了？
> *Gēge: Zhuō shàng de qiǎokèlì táng qù nǎlǐ le?*
> 弟弟：我**吃掉**了。
> *Dìdi: Wǒ chī diào le.*
> Older brother: Where did the chocolate on the table go?
> Younger brother: I ate it.

> 太太：冰箱里的剩菜呢？
> *Tàitai: Bīngxiāng lǐ de shèngcài ne?*
> 先生：那些菜都已经**坏掉**了，所以我把它们都**倒掉**了。
> *Xiānsheng: Nà xiē cài dōu yǐjīng huài diào le, suǒyǐ wǒ bǎ tāmen dōu dào diào le.*
> Wife: What happened to the leftovers in the refrigerator?
> Husband: Those dishes had all gone bad already, so I threw them out.

(h) 死 (*sǐ*)

死 means 'to die'. It is the result of any action or situation that can cause death. It is also often used to indicate an exaggeration.

> 大家都以为王先生是**病死**的，其实他是被人**杀死**的。
> *Dàjiā dōu yǐwéi Wáng xiānsheng shì bìng sǐ de, qíshí tā shì bèi rén shā sǐ de.*
> Everybody mistakenly thinks Mr Wang died of an illness; actually, he was murdered.

> 先生：我**饿死**了，什么时候吃饭？
> *Xiānsheng: Wǒ è sǐ le, shénme shíhòu chī fàn?*
> 太太：我上了一天班，**累死**了，哪里有力气做饭？
> *Tàitai: Wǒ shàng le yì tiān bān, lèi sǐ le, nǎlǐ yǒu lìqì zuòfàn?*
> Husband: I am hungry to death (= starving). When are we going to eat?
> Wife: I worked all day and I am tired to death. How do I have the energy to cook?

(i) 好 (*hǎo*)

As a complement of result, 好 can have two meanings; one indicates that the action is done properly, securely or well, and the other indicates the 'completion' of a task.

- Verbs associated with 好 meaning 'properly' or 'securely' are 学 (*xué*), 坐 (*zuò*), 放 (*fàng*), 带 (*dài*), 拿 (*ná*), 准备 (*zhǔnbèi*), etc.

> 各位旅客，请在座位上**坐好**，并且**系好**安全带，飞机就要起飞了。
> *Gèwèi lǚkè, qǐng zài zuòwèi shàng zuòhǎo, bìngqiě xì hǎo ānquán dài, fēijī jiù yào qǐfēi le.*
> All passengers, please sit properly (securely) in your own seats and fasten your seatbelts securely. The airplane will take off soon.

> 大家都**准备好**了吗？可以出发了吧？（准备: to prepare; 准备好: ready）
> *Dàjiā dōu zhǔnbèi hǎo le ma? Kěyǐ chūfā le ba?*
> Is everybody ready? We can set off now, right?

- When 好 indicates the completion of a task, an assignment or a piece of work, it shares similarities with 完 (*wán*); therefore, sometimes they can be interchangeable. However, 好 tends to mean the completed work can be shown, whereas 完 indicates that once something is done, it's gone. The verbs associated with this meaning are 作 (*zuò*: 'to do'), 写 (*xiě*: 'to write'), 画 (*huà*: 'to paint'), 修 (*xiū*: 'to repair'), 洗 (*xǐ*: 'to wash'), 翻译 (*fānyì*: 'to translate'), etc.

> 王老师花了三年才把那本语法书**写好**。
> *Wáng lǎoshī huā le sān nián cái bǎ nà běn yǔfǎ shū xiě hǎo.*
> Teacher Wang spent three years and finally completed the grammar book.
> Compare:　今天的功课真多，我写了三个多小时还没**写完**。
> 　　　　　*Jīntiān de gōngkè zhēn duō, wǒ xiě le sān ge duō xiǎoshí hái méi xiě wán.*
> 　　　　　There is so much homework today. I have worked on it for over three hours but I still have not finished (writing it).

(j) 对 (*duì*) and 错 (*cuò*)

It should be noted that when the verb has an object, 错 is not used to modify the object, but should follow the verb to serve as a complement of result.

> 糟糕！咱们**坐错**车了。
> *Zāogāo! Zánmen zuò cuò chē le.* (咱们坐了错的车 is incorrect.)
> Oh no! We got on the wrong bus.

> 别着急，你一着急就会**说错**话。　(Do not say 你会说错的话.)
> *Bié zháojí, nǐ yì zháojí jiù huì shuō cuò huà.*
> Don't be anxious. The moment you get anxious, you will say the wrong thing.

> 这个问题很难，**回答对**的人不多。
> *Zhè ge wèntí hěn nán, huídá duì de rén bù duō.*
> This question is very difficult. Not many people answered it correctly.

(k) 够 (*gòu*)

As an adjective, 够, which means 'enough', very rarely appears before a noun. It is used after the verb to serve as the complement of result. If the verb has an object, it should appear after 够 or be pre-posed.

> 我打算一**赚够**了钱就退休。
> *Wǒ dǎsuàn yí zhuàn gòu le qián jiù tuìxiū.*
> I plan to retire as soon as I have made enough money.

> 张：你以前那么喜欢旅行，这几年怎么很少出门了?
> *Zhāng: Nǐ yǐqián nàme xǐhuān lǚxíng, zhè jǐ nián zěnme hěn shǎo chūmén le?*
> 王：这个世界我已经**看够**了。现在我想在家多休息休息。
> *Wáng: Zhè ge shìjiè wǒ yǐjīng kàn gòu le. Xiànzài wǒ xiǎng zài jiā duō xiūxí xiūxí.*
> Zhang: You used to like travelling so much. How come you rarely leave your house now?
> Wang: I have seen enough of this world. Now I just want to stay home and rest more.

Level
3

16.7 Adjectives as the complements of state, result and potential compared

Since an adjective can serve as the complement of result, the complement of state (☞ see Chapter 12) and the complement of potential (☞ see Chapter 17), it is important to note the difference in structures and meanings among the three.

Types of complement	Word order for positive form	Word order for negative form
Complement of state	Verb + 得 + 很 (太, 真, etc.) + adjective	Verb + 得 + 不 + adjective
Complement of result	Verb + adjective	没有/不 + verb + adjective
Complement of potential	Verb + 得 + adjective	Verb + 不 + adjective

The following table gives some examples.

Complement	Positive form	Negative form
State	他说的话，我听得很清楚。 *Tā shuō de huà, wǒ tīng de hěn qīngchǔ.* I heard clearly what he said.	他说的话，我听得不清楚。 *Tā shuō de huà, wǒ tīng de bù qīngchǔ.* I didn't hear clearly what he said.
Result	他说的话，我听清楚了。 *Tā shuō de huà, wǒ tīng qīngchǔ le.* I heard clearly what he said.	他说的话，我没有听清楚。 *Tā shuō de huà, wǒ méiyǒu tīng qīngchǔ.* I didn't hear clearly what he said.
Potential	他说的话，我听得清楚。 *Tā shuō de huà, wǒ tīng de qīngchǔ.* I can hear clearly what he says.	他说的话，我听不清楚。 *Tā shuō de huà, wǒ tīng bù qīngchǔ.* I cannot hear clearly what he says.

张：房子**打扫干净**以前，咱们都不可以去睡觉。快继续打扫。（干净 is the complement of result. It follows the verb 打扫。）
Zhāng: Fángzi dǎsǎo gānjìng yǐqián, zánmen dōu bù kěyǐ qù shuìjiào. Kuài jìxù dǎsǎo.
李：什么？我打扫了一下午，已经**打扫得这么干净**了，还打扫什么？
Lǐ: Shénme? Wǒ dǎsǎo le yí xiàwǔ, yǐjīng dǎsǎo de zhème gānjìng le, hái dǎsǎo shénme?
（这么干净 is the complement of state. 得 is needed after the verb 打扫。)
Zhang: Before (= until) we clean up the house, we can't go to bed. So hurry and continue to clean it.
Li: What? I spent all afternoon cleaning. It's already been cleaned so well. What more is there to do?

(Situation: A teacher is giving a student feedback on his performance of question-answering.)

第一个问题，你回答**得**相当对；（相当对: the complement of state）
Dì yī ge wèntí, nǐ huídá de xiāngdāng duì;
You answered the first question quite correctly;
第二个问题，你也回答**得**不错；（不错 = 很好: the complement of state）
dì èr ge wèntí, nǐ yě huídá de búcuò;
you also answered the second question quite well;
第三个问题，你回答**错**了，（错: the complement of result）
dì sān ge wèntí, nǐ huídá cuò le,
you answered the third question incorrectly,
第四个问题，你也没有回答**对**。（对: the complement of result）
dì sì ge wèntí, nǐ yě méiyǒu huídá duì.
you also did not answer the fourth question correctly.

Exercise

Fill in the blanks using the proper complement of result based on the context provided in the sentence.

Level
1

1 王：墙上有一个牌子，你看 ＿＿ 了没有？
李：我看 ＿＿ 了，可是上面写的字，我没有看 ＿＿。

2 他学游泳只学了两个多小时就学 ＿＿ 了。

3 我的车修 ＿＿ 了，今天我们可以开车出去玩了。

4 今天的功课太多了，我写了两个多小时，还没有写 ＿＿。

5 我告诉他我姓张，可是他听 ＿＿ 了，所以他叫我常先生。

6 我的英文不好，所以那个英国人说的话，我没有听 ＿＿。

Level
2

7 要买那本畅销书的人太多了，我去了两趟书店，都没有买 ＿＿。

8 站 ＿＿，别走！我是老师，我还没说 ＿＿ 话呢，你怎么可以走？

9 今天的比赛，德国队输了，因为有两个球，他们没有接 ＿＿。

10 妈妈：这种巧克力糖很贵，你要慢慢地吃。
儿子：这么一小块，我一口就吃 ＿＿ 了。

11 大家都准备 ＿＿ 了吗？咱们上飞机吧！自己的行李，一定要拿 ＿＿！

12 今天我收 ＿＿ 一封王小姐去年寄给我的信，因为她把地址写 ＿＿ 了，所以过了一年这封信才寄 ＿＿ 我家。

17 The complement of potential

The complement of potential is primarily based on the complement of direction and the complement of result. It is used to indicate the possibility or probability of something happening. It can also indicate someone's ability to achieve something. Therefore, it nearly always carries the meaning of 'can/could' or 'cannot/could not' without having to actually use 能/可以 (*néng/kěyǐ*) or 不能 (*bù néng*). ◉ Because similar structures are not found in English, learners who are speakers of English should pay special attention to this chapter.

17.1 Forming the complement of potential

得 (*de*) is inserted between the verb and the complement to mean 能; 不 is inserted between the verb and the complement to mean 不能.

Affirmative form	Verb	得	Complement
Negative form	Verb	不	Complement

王：那个牌子上的字，你**看得见**吗？
Wáng: Nà ge páizi shàng de zì, nǐ kàn de jiàn ma?
李：**看得见**，不过那些字太小了，所以我**看不清楚**。
Lǐ: Kàn de jiàn, búguò nà xiē zì tài xiǎo le, suǒyǐ wǒ kàn bù qīngchǔ.
Wang: **Can** you **see** those words on that sign?
Li: Yes, I **can**. But those words are too small, so I **cannot see** them **clearly**.

张：今天老师用英文说的那个故事，你**听得懂**吗？
Zhāng: Jīntiān lǎoshī yòng Yīngwén shuō de nà ge gùshì, nǐ tīng de dǒng ma?
李：我应该**听得懂**，可是我没注意听，所以**没有听懂**。
Lǐ: Wǒ yīnggāi tīng de dǒng, kěshì wǒ méi zhùyì tīng, suǒyǐ méiyǒu tīng dǒng.
Zhang: **Could** you **understand** the story the teacher told in English today?
Li: I should have been **able to understand**, but I wasn't paying attention; so I **didn't understand** it.

Level 2

17.2 Forming questions

There are three way to form a yes–no question.

Modal particle 吗	Verb + 得 + complement	吗	?
Affirmative–negative construction	Verb + 得 + complement	Verb + 不 + complement	?
*Alternative affirmative–negative construction	Verb + 不	Verb + 得 + complement	?

(a) Questions using modal particle 吗

李：听说你很会修车，我这辆旧车，你**修得好吗**？
Lǐ: Tīngshuō nǐ hěn huì xiū chē, wǒ zhè liàng jiù chē, nǐ xiū de hǎo ma?
王：没问题，我一定**修得好**。
Wáng: Méi wèntí, wǒ yídìng xiū de hǎo.
Li: I heard that you are good at repairing cars. **Can** you **fix** this old car of mine?
Wang: No problem, I can definitely fix it.

你早上六点**起得来吗**？如果**起不来**，就别买七点的火车票。
Nǐ zǎoshàng liù diǎn qǐ de lái ma? Rúguǒ qǐ bù lái, jiù bié mǎi qī diǎn de huǒchē piào.
Can you get up at 6 o'clock in the morning? If you can't, then don't buy a train ticket for 7 o'clock.

(b) Questions using the affirmative–negative construction

老师：我刚才说的话，你们**听得懂听不懂**？（= 听得懂吗？）
Lǎoshī: Wǒ gāngcái shuō de huà, nǐmen tīng de dǒng tīng bù dǒng?
学生：不知道，您说得太小声了，我们都**听不清楚**您在说什么。
Xuéshēng: Bù zhīdào, nín shuō de tài xiǎoshēng le, wǒmen dōu tīng bù qīngchǔ nín zài shuō shénme.
Teacher: **Can** you **understand** what I just said?
Student: I don't know. You spoke too softly; we **could not hear clearly** what you were saying.

(c) Questions using the alternative affirmative–negative construction

It is acceptable to use 'verb + 不 + verb + 得 + complement' as an alternative form for the affirmative–negative construction. This alternative form is frequently used in casual speech.

张：这座山相当高，你**上不上得去**？（= 上得去上不去？= 上得去吗？）
Zhāng: Zhè zuò shān xiāngdāng gāo, nǐ shàng bú shàng de qù?
王：应该**上得去**。咱们开始往上爬吧。
Wáng: Yīnggāi shàng de qù. Zánmen kāishǐ wǎng shàng pá ba.
Zhang: This mountain is quite high; will you **be able to go up**?
Wang: I should be able to go up. Let's start climbing up.

丁：今天的功课，你八点以前**写不写得完**？
Dīng: Jīntiān de gōngkè, nǐ bā diǎn yǐqián xiě bù xiě de wán?
李：太多了，恐怕**写不完**呢。
Lǐ: Tài duō le, kǒngpà xiě bù wán ne.
Ding: **Can you finish** (**writing**) today's homework by 8 o'clock?
Li: There is too much. I am afraid I **won't be able to finish** (it by then).

Level
3

17.3 Word order

得 or 不 in the complement of potential should always follow the verb. This renders the complement of potential based on the simple complement of direction and one based on the complex complements of direction quite different in terms of word order.

☞ See Chapter 15 for more information on the complement of direction.

王：晚上十点以后，那个公园，咱们还**进得去**吗？ (进 is the verb; 去 is the complement.)
Wáng: Wǎnshàng shí diǎn yǐhòu, nà ge gōngyuán, zánmen hái jìn de qù ma?
李：汽车**开不进去**，不过自行车还**骑得进去**。 (开 and 骑 are verbs; 进去 is the complement. It is incorrect to say 汽车开进不去 or 自行车骑得进去.)
Lǐ: Qìchē kāi bú jìnqù, búguò zìxíngchē hái qí de jìnqù.
Wang: **Can** we still **go into** the park after 10 p.m.?
Li: (We) **can't drive in**, but (we) **can ride** bikes **in**.

(Situation: Many people are trying to get on the bus.)

哥哥：要坐这班车的人太多了，咱们一定**上不去**，还是走路回家吧。
Gēge: Yào zuò zhè bān chē de rén tài duō le, zánmen yídìng shàng bú qù, háishì zǒulù huí jiā ba.
弟弟：咱们去跟别人挤，一定**挤得上去**的。 (It is incorrect to say 一定挤上得去.)
Dìdi: Zánmen qù gēn biérén jǐ, yídìng jǐ de shàngqù de.
Older brother: Too many people want to take this bus. We definitely **won't be able to get on**. We might as well walk home.
Younger brother: Let's go join the crowd. We definitely **can push our way onto** the bus.

Level
2

17.4 Adding auxiliary verbs 能 and 可以

The auxiliary verbs 能 and 可以 can be placed before the affirmative form (but not the negative form) and the meaning of the sentence remains unchanged. However, 不能 cannot be used this way.

老师：这个教室太大了，坐在后面的人，（可以）**听得见**我说的话吗？
Lǎoshī: Zhè ge jiàoshì tài dà le, zuò zài hòumiàn de rén, (kěyǐ) tīng de jiàn wǒ shuō de huà ma?
王同学：（可以）**听得见**。
Wáng tóngxué: (Kěyǐ) tīng de jiàn.
李同学：我**听不清楚**。
Lǐ tóngxué: Wǒ tīng bù qīngchǔ.
(我不能听得清楚 or 我能听不清楚 is incorrect since this is a negative sentence.)
Teacher: This classroom is too big. **Can** those sitting in the back **hear** what I'm saying?
Student Wang: I **can hear** you.
Student Li: I **cannot hear** you **clearly**.

你明天八点有课，现在都十二点了，你还不去睡觉，明天早上你（能）**起得来**吗？
Nǐ míngtiān bā diǎn yǒu kè, xiànzài dōu shí'èr diǎn le, nǐ hái bú qù shuìjiào, míngtiān zǎoshàng nǐ (néng) qǐ de lái ma?
You have a class at 8 o'clock tomorrow. It's already 12 o'clock now and you are still not in bed. **Can** you **get up** tomorrow morning?

Level
2

17.5 When the complement of potential cannot be used

The complement of potential cannot be used to indicate permission or a request.

别人在上课呢，咱们**不可以进去**。 (In this situation, it is incorrect to say
咱们进不去.)
Biérén zài shàng kè ne, zánmen bù kěyǐ jìnqù.
Other people are having a class now. We **cannot go in**.

Compare: 他把门锁上了，所以咱们都**进不去**。
Tā bǎ mén suǒ shàng le, suǒyǐ zánmen dōu jìn bú qù.
He locked the door, so we **cannot get in**.

小王，你**能不能下来**？我在楼下等了你十分钟了。(It is incorrect to say
你下不下得来.)
Xiǎo Wáng, nǐ néng bù néng xiàlái? Wǒ zài lóuxià děng le nǐ shí fēnzhōng le.
Xiao Wang, can you come down? I have been waiting for you downstairs for ten
minutes.

Level
3

17.6 Words commonly used as complements of potential

The following are some of the frequently used complements of potential that are not based on
the complement of direction or the complement of result.

(a) 下 (*xià*)

下 is used to indicate there is/isn't enough room to accommodate a certain amount/quantity
of things/people. Verbs associated with 下 are 放 (*fàng*: 'to put'), 摆 (*bǎi*: 'to put'), 坐 (*zuò*:
'to sit'), 站 (*zhàn*: 'to stand'), 住 (*zhù*: 'to live; to stay'), 停 (车) (*tíngchē*: 'to park'), 挤 (*jǐ*:
'to squeeze'), 写 (*xiě*: 'to write'), etc. There is usually a number to indicate the capacity of the
space.

王：这个教室**坐得下**二十五个学生吗？
Wáng: Zhè ge jiàoshì zuò de xià èrshí wǔ ge xuéshēng ma?
李：这个教室只**放得下**二十把椅子，所以**坐不下**二十五个学生。
Lǐ: Zhè ge jiàoshì zhǐ fàng de xià èrshí bǎ yǐzi, suǒyǐ zuò bú xià èrshí wǔ ge xuéshēng.
Wang: **Can** this classroom **seat** 25 students?
Li: This classroom **can** only **accommodate** 20 chairs, so it **cannot seat** 25 students.

这家电影院**坐得下**五百个观众，可是他们的停车场只**停得下**一百多辆车，所以
我们**找不到**停车的地方。
*Zhè jiā diànyǐngyuàn zuò de xià wǔ bǎi ge guānzhòng, kěshì tāmen de tíngchēchǎng zhǐ
tíng de xià yì bǎi duō liàng chē, suǒyǐ wǒmen zhǎo bú dào tíngchē de dìfāng.*
This cinema **can seat** 500 viewers, but their parking lot **can hold** only 100 or so cars, so
we **cannot find** a place to park.

下 can also be the complement of potential for the verbs 吃 and 喝. In this case, the space is
replaced by a person and a number may not be necessary.

我爷爷虽然八十了，可是每餐都还**吃得下**三碗饭呢。
Wǒ yéye suīrán bāshí le, kěshì měi cān dōu hái chī de xià sān wǎn fàn ne.
Although my grandfather is already 80 years old, he **can** still **eat** three bowls of rice at
every meal.

主人：再吃一点菜吧！
Zhǔrén: Zài chī yìdiǎn cài ba!
客人：我实在**吃不下**了。

Kèrén: Wǒ shízài chī bú xià le.
主人：那你还**喝得下**一碗汤吗？
Zhǔrén: Nà nǐ hái hē de xià yì wǎn tāng ma?
客人：汤我也**喝不下**了。
Kèrén: Tāng wǒ yě hē bú xià le.
Host: Have some more food.
Guest: I truly **cannot eat** any more. (I **have no room** for any more food.)
Host: Then **can** you still **have** a bowl of soup?
Guest: I **cannot have** any soup, either. (I **have no room** for soup, either.)

(b) 动 (*dòng*)

动 is used to indicate there is/isn't enough energy/strength to cause movement. The verbs associated with 动 are those that show movements, such as 拿 (*ná*: 'to hold'), 搬 (*bān*: 'to move'), 走 (*zǒu*: 'to walk'), 跑 (*pǎo*: 'to run'), 跳 (*tiào*: 'to jump, to dance'), 游 (*yóu*: 'to swim'), 骑 (*qí*: 'to ride bicycle/horse'), etc.

王：这个箱子很重，你**拿得动拿不动**？要不要我来帮你一下？
Wáng: Zhè ge xiāngzi hěn zhòng, nǐ ná de dòng ná bú dòng? Yào bú yào wǒ lái bāng nǐ yíxià?
张：不重，不重，我 (可以) **拿得动**。
Zhāng: Bú zhòng, bú zhòng, wǒ (kěyǐ) ná de dòng.
Wang: This box is very heavy, **can** you **carry** it? (**Do you have the strength** to carry it?) Do you want me to help you?
Zhang: No, no, it's not heavy. I **can carry** it. (I **have the strength** to carry it.)

李：咱们跑下山去，好不好？
Lǐ: Zánmen pǎo xià shān qù, hǎo bù hǎo?
丁：我走了两小时才走上来，现在已经**走不动**了，你想我怎么还**跑得动**？
Dīng: Wǒ zǒu le liǎng xiǎoshí cái zǒu shànglái, xiànzài yǐjīng zǒu bú dòng le, nǐ xiǎng wǒ zěnme hái pǎo de dòng?
Li: Let's run down the hill, OK?
Ding: I walked for two hours before I finally came up; now I **don't have any energy to walk** anymore. How **can** I **have the energy to run**?

(c) 了 (*liǎo*) #1

了 as the complement of potential 了 of complement has two functions. One function of 了 is to indicate one's ability to handle a large amount/quantity all at once. In this case, 多 in the context is the key word.

这么多书，你一次**拿得了**吗？今天拿几本，明天再拿几本吧。
Zhème duō shū, nǐ yí cì ná de liǎo ma? Jīntiān ná jǐ běn, míngtiān zài ná jǐ běn ba.
There are so many books. **Can** you **take all of them all at once**? Why don't you take a few today and take a few more tomorrow?

你买太多了，我一个人**吃不了**，你带一些回家吧。
Nǐ mǎi tài duō le, wǒ yí ge rén chī bù liǎo, nǐ dài yìxiē huíjiā ba.
You bought too much; I **can't eat it all** by myself. Why don't you take some home with you?

• The difference between 吃不下 and 吃不了 can be subtle. 吃不下 is sometimes interpreted as 'having no appetite'; it does not have to do with the amount of food. 吃不了 always implies there is a lot

这两天我不舒服，胃口不好，常常**吃不下**。

Zhè liǎng tiān wǒ bù shūfú, wèikǒu bù hǎo, chángcháng chī bú xià.

These days I am not feeling well; I have had no appetite and I often cannot eat.

- 吃不了 and 吃不完 may share similarities. Generally, 吃不了 is used before one begins to eat, whereas 吃不完 refers to the portion one cannot finish

(Situation: At a to-go food counter.)

太太：哎呀！你买太多了。 咱们两个人怎么**吃得了**这么多？

Tàitai: Āiyā! Nǐ mǎi tài duō le. Zánmen liǎng ge rén zěnme chī de liǎo zhème duō?

先生：没关系，今天**吃不完**的，可以明天吃。

Xiānsheng: Méi guānxi, jīntiān chī bù wán de, kěyǐ míngtiān chī.

Wife: Aiya! You ordered too much. How **can** the two of us **eat so much**?

Husband: It's OK. Tomorrow we can eat what we **cannot finish** (the leftover) today.

- When the money or time allocated for an activity is too much for such an activity, the phrase 花不了 or 用不了 is used to describe such a situation. Hence, 用不了 has become an expression to mean 'no need for so much' or 'it won't take so much'

今天的功课不多，**用不了**(or 花不了)两小时就**写得完**。

Jīntiān de gōngkè bù duō, yòng bù liǎo (or huā bù liǎo) liǎng xiǎoshí jiù xiě de wán.

There isn't much homework today. It **won't take** two hours before I **can finish** (writing it).

这本书很便宜，**用不了**两块钱就**买得到**。

Zhè běn shū hěn piányí, yòng bù liǎo liǎng kuài qián jiù mǎi de dào.

This book is inexpensive. You **can get it** for **less than** $2 (it **won't cost** $2).

(d) 了 (liǎo) #2

了 also has the function of serving as the complement for verbs that are already 'complete' in meaning; in other words, these verbs do not need a complement to complete their meanings. When such a verb is used in a potential structure, 了 serves as the complement to fulfill the grammatical requirement.

张：图书馆还有半小时关门，咱们现在走，关门以前**到得了到不了**？

(= 能到吗？)

Zhāng: Túshūguǎn hái yǒu bàn xiǎoshí guānmén, zánmen xiànzài zǒu, guānmén yǐqián dào de liǎo dào bù liǎo?

王：从这里走路去图书馆只要十分钟，关门以前一定**到得了**。

Wáng: Cóng zhèlǐ zǒulù qù túshūguǎn zhǐ yào shí fēnzhōng, guānmén yǐqián yídìng dào de liǎo.

Zhang: There is half an hour before the library closes. If we leave now, **can** we **arrive** before it closes?

Wang: It takes only ten minutes to walk from here to the library. We **can** definitely **arrive** before it closes.

李：热死了，真不知道谁**受得了**这种天气？ (受 can mean 'to tolerate'.)

Lǐ: Rè sǐ le, zhēn bù zhīdào shéi shòu de liǎo zhè zhǒng tiānqì?

王：现在才六月，你就**受不了了**，到了八月你怎么办？

Wáng: Xiànzài cái liùyuè, nǐ jiù shòu bu liǎo le, dào le bāyuè nǐ zěnmebàn?

Li: It's hot to death. I really don't know who **can stand** this kind of weather.

Wang: It's only June now and you already **can't stand** it. What are you going to do in August?

(e) 起 (qǐ)

起 is most frequently used to indicate whether one can afford something financially. The verb 买 is the most common one that is associated with 起. Other verbs that imply paying for it can be used with 起 as well.

(Situation: The property salesperson is about to show Mr Zhang a big house.)

张先生：这么大的房子，我恐怕**买不起**。
Zhāng xiānsheng: Zhème dà de fángzi, wǒ kǒngpà mǎi bù qǐ.
房地产商：没关系，**买不起**的人也可以进去看看。
Fángdìchǎn shāng: Méi guānxi, mǎi bù qǐ de rén yě kěyǐ jìn qù kàn kàn.
Mr Zhang: Such a big house, I am afraid that I cannot afford (to buy) it.
Property salesperson: It's OK. Those who cannot afford it can also go in to take a look.

(Situation: Mr. and Mrs. Li are talking about their vacation plans.)

李太太：我在一个五星级的饭店订了一个房间。
Lǐ tàitai: Wǒ zài yí ge wǔ xīng jí de fàndiàn dìng le yí ge fángjiān.
李先生：咱们**住得起**五星级的饭店吗？
Lǐ xiānsheng: Zánmen zhù de qǐ wǔ xīng jí de fàndiàn ma?
Mrs Li: I made reservation for a room at a five-star hotel.
Mr Li: Can we afford (to stay in) a five-star hotel?

Do not confuse 买得起/买不起 (affordability) with 买得到/买不到 (availability). Therefore, the subject for 买得起/买不起 is a person, whereas the subject for 买得到/买不到 does not have to be a person.

李先生：这么大的房子，没有一百万，一定**买不到**。
Lǐ xiānsheng: Wà! Zhème dà de fángzi, méiyǒu yì bǎiwàn, yídìng mǎi bú dào.
房地产商：您说得很对！**买得起**这个房子的人不多。
Fángdìchǎn shāng: Nín shuō de hěn duì! Mǎi de qǐ zhè ge fángzi de rén bù duō.
Mr Li: Such a big house! It is definitely not available to those without $1 million.
Property salesperson: You said it right! There are not many people who can afford this house.

It should be noted that 起 in the expressions 看得起/看不起 does not imply financial affordability. 看得起 indicates one's high regard for a person, whereas 看不起 indicates one's contempt for a person.

王先生：李小兰喜欢在朋友背后讨论他们，我最**看不起**这种人。
Wáng xiānsheng: Lǐ Xiǎolán xǐhuān zài péngyǒu bèi hòu tǎolùn tāmen, wǒ zuì kàn bù qǐ zhè zhǒng rén.
王太太：世界上好像没有你**看得起**的人。
Wáng tàitai: Shìjiè shàng hǎoxiàng méiyǒu nǐ kàn de qǐ de rén.
Mr Wang: Li Xiaolan likes to discuss her friends behind their back. I really despise such people.
Mrs Wang: It seems that there is not anybody in this world that you regard highly.

17.7 The complement of result and the complement of potential compared

The complement of potential indicates whether the result 'can' or 'cannot' be produced; whereas the complement of result only indicates whether or not there is a result.

王：你昨天下午在**找**的那本书，**找到**了没有？

Wáng: Nǐ zuótiān xiàwǔ zài zhǎo de nà běn shū, zhǎodào le méiyǒu?

李：我**找**了好几个小时，还是**没有找到**。我看大概**找不到**了。

Lǐ: Wǒ zhǎo le hǎo jǐ ge xiǎoshí, háishì méiyǒu zhǎodào. Wǒ kàn dàgài zhǎo bú dào le.

Wang: Did you **find** the book you were **looking for** yesterday afternoon?

Li: I **searched** several hours and I still **did not find** it. I think I probably **won't be able to find** it.

老师：小王，你怎么又**不把**功课**写完**就交来？

Lǎoshī: Xiǎo Wáng, nǐ zěnme yòu bù bǎ gōngkè xiě wán jiù jiāo lái?

小王：昨天的功课实在太多了，我不是**不写完**，是**写不完**。

Xiǎo Wáng: Zuótiān de gōngkè shízài tài duō le, wǒ bú shì bù xiě wán, shì xiě bù wán.

Teacher: Xiao Wang, how come you once again turned in homework **without finishing** it?

Xiao Wang: There was truly too much homework yesterday. It is not that I **would not finish** it; it is that I **could not finish** it.

<table>
<tr><td>Level</td></tr>
<tr><td>3</td></tr>
</table>

17.8 Adjectives as the complement of state and the complement of potential compared

☞ See Chapter 12 for more information on the complement of state.

Affirmative form					Examples
Complement of state	Verb	得	Degree adverb (很, 真, 太, etc.)	Adjective	跑得很快
Complement of potential	Verb	得	∅	Adjective	跑得快
Negative form					
Complement of state	Verb	得	不	Adjective	跑得不快
Complement of potential	Verb	∅	不	Adjective	跑不快

(a) Affirmative form

Both complements need 得 after the verb in the affirmative form; for the complement of state, a degree adverb such as 很 (*hěn*), 太 (*tài*), 真 (*zhēn*) or 非常 (*fēicháng*), etc. is needed before the adjective. A degree adverb cannot be used in the complement of potential.

老师说的话，我听得**很清楚**。（很清楚 is the complement of state.）

Lǎoshī shuō de huà, wǒ tīng de hěn qīngchǔ.

I **heard clearly** what the teacher said.

Compare: 老师说的话，我听得**清楚**。（清楚 is the complement of potential.）

Lǎoshī shuō de huà, wǒ tīng de qīngchǔ.

I **could hear clearly** what the teacher said.

这件衬衫本来非常脏，现在洗得**真干净**。（真干净 is the complement of state.）

Zhè jiàn chènshān běnlái fēicháng zāng, xiànzài xǐ de zhēn gānjìng.

The shirt originally was extremely dirty, now it's been **washed really clean**.

Compare: 用这种洗衣粉，多脏的衣服都洗得**干净**。（干净 is the complement of potential.)
Yòng zhèzhǒng xǐyī fěn, duō zāng de yīfú dōu xǐ de gānjìng.
With this laundry powder, no matter how dirty the clothes are, they **can be washed clean**.

(b) When a comparison is implied

When a comparison is implied, a degree adverb is not used before the adjective. Therefore, sometimes the context must be taken into consideration in order to decide whether it is a complement of state or a complement of potential.

让小王参加比赛吧，他跑得**快**，我跑得**慢**。（Both 快 and 慢 are the complements of state.)
Ràng Xiǎo Wáng cānjiā bǐsài ba, tā pǎo de kuài, wǒ pǎo de màn.
Let Xiao Wang run in the race (instead of me). He runs **faster**; I run **more slowly**. (= He runs faster than I do.)

跑得慢的人不能参加比赛。
Pǎo de màn de rén bù néng cānjiā bǐsài.
Those who **run slowly** (or more slowly than others) cannot run in the race.
(慢 is the complement of state and a comparison is implied even without a clear context. Since the complement of potential is used to indicate one's ability, to run slowly cannot be considered an ability.)

(c) Negative form

得 and 不 are both needed in the negative form for the complement of state; only 不 is used in the negative form for the complement of potential.

小王不能参加比赛，因为他**跑得不快**。（= 他跑得**很慢**. 不快 is the complement of state.)
Xiǎo Wáng bù néng cānjiā bǐsài, yīnwèi tā pǎo de bú kuài.
Xiao Wang cannot run in the race because he **does not run fast** enough (= he **runs slowly**).

Compare: 我以前**跑得很快**，后来腿受伤了，现在我**跑不快**了。（很快 is the complement of state; 不快 is the complement of potential.)
Wǒ yǐqián pǎo de hěn kuài, hòulái tuǐ shòu shāng le, xiànzài wǒ pǎo bú kuài le.
I used to **run fast**; later on, my leg was injured; now I **cannot run fast** anymore.

我儿子不用功，所以考试总是**考得不好**。（不好 is the complement of state.)
Wǒ érzi bú yònggōng, suǒyǐ kǎoshì zǒngshì kǎo de bù hǎo.
My son is not hardworking, so he always **does poorly** in tests.

Compare: 这孩子又笨又懒，所以考试总是**考不好**。（不好 is the complement of potential.)
Zhè háizi yòu bèn yòu lǎn, suǒyǐ kǎoshì zǒngshì kǎo bù hǎo.
This kid is stupid and lazy; therefore, he **can never do well** in any tests.

Exercises

Fill in the blanks using the proper complement of potential based on the context provided. You also must decide whether the structure should be in the positive or negative form.

Examples   这座山太高了，我上<u>不</u>去。
Zhè zuò shān tài gāo le, wǒ shàng <u>bú qù</u>.
This mountain is too high, I cannot go up.

今天的功课这么多，半小时怎么写<u>得</u> 完?
Jīntiān de gōngkè zhème duō, bàn xiǎoshí zěnme xiě <u>de wán</u>?
There's so much homework today. How am I to finish it in half an hour?

Level
1

1   这个教室只有二十把椅子，坐 ＿＿＿ ＿＿＿ 三十个人。

2   这么重的桌子，你一个人搬 ＿＿＿ ＿＿＿ 吗？要不要我来帮你一下？

3   英文小说我看 ＿＿＿ ＿＿＿，因为我的英文不好。

4   听说那本书非常畅销，想买的人很多，你快去买吧，去晚了，就买 ＿＿＿ ＿＿＿ 了。

5   老师：坐在后面的同学，听 ＿＿＿ ＿＿＿ 我说的话吗？
    学生：听 ＿＿＿ ＿＿＿，可是黑板上的字，我们看 ＿＿＿ ＿＿＿。

6   主人：还有很多菜，再吃一点吧！
    客人：不了，谢谢，我吃 ＿＿＿ ＿＿＿ 了。

7   那本书，我已经找了三天了，我想，可能找 ＿＿＿ ＿＿＿ 了。

Level
2

8   汽车在路上坏了，飞机起飞以前我到 ＿＿＿ ＿＿＿ 机场了。

9   王：昨天我在街对面叫了你五、六次，你怎么不过来呢？
    张：因为那时候街上车太多了，我过 ＿＿＿ ＿＿＿。

10 香港的房价太高了，所以我只买 ＿＿＿ ＿＿＿ 一个很小的房子。

11 我一个人只有两只手，你想我怎么拿 ＿＿＿ ＿＿＿ 这么多东西？你快过来帮我拿一些。

12 我听说那本书很便宜，用 ＿＿＿ ＿＿＿ 两块钱就买 ＿＿＿ ＿＿＿。

13 我们学校的宿舍住 ＿＿＿ ＿＿＿ 一千多个学生，可是宿舍的停车场只停 ＿＿＿ ＿＿＿ 五百辆车，所以我常常找 ＿＿＿ ＿＿＿ 停车的地方。

14 张先生：今天是你的生日，咱们叫一只龙虾吧！
    张太太：龙虾？咱们怎么吃 ＿＿＿ ＿＿＿ 龙虾？

18 The adverbial modifier with 地

An adjective followed by the particle 地 (pronounced *de*) forms an adverbial modifier. An adverbial modifier should appear before the verb or the verbal phrase it modifies. It can also appear before an adjective to modify the adjective. ◉ Similar structures in English can have more flexibility in terms of word order.

火车快离站了，妈妈**难过地**跟我说再见。
Huǒchē kuài lízhàn le, māma nánguò de gēn wǒ shuō zàijiàn.
The train was about to take off, my mother **sadly** said goodbye to me.

老王的脾气**出名地**坏，没有人喜欢跟他做朋友。
Lǎo Wáng de píqì chūmíng de huài, méiyǒu rén xǐhuān gēn tā zuò péngyǒu.
Lao Wang is **notoriously** bad-tempered; no one likes to be his friend.

18.1 Structure

Level 2

At least two characters are needed before 地.

(a) When the adjective is monosyllabic

If an adjective is monosyllabic, 很 (*hěn*) can be added or the adjective can be reduplicated. Whether to repeat the monosyllabic adjective or to add 很 is a matter of fixed expressions, not grammar rules. For example, 慢 (*màn*) and 好 (*hǎo*) are frequently reduplicated, whereas 快 (*kuài*) tends to become 很快.

他一看公共汽车快开了，就**很快地**跑去上车。
Tā yí kàn gōnggòng qìchē kuài kāi le, jiù hěn kuài de pǎo qù shàng chē.
He noticed that the bus was about to leave the bus stop, so he **quickly** ran over to get on the bus.

今天咱们时间很多，可以**慢慢地**走，不必急。
Jīntiān zánmen shíjiān hěn duō, kěyǐ màn màn de zǒu, búbì jí.
Today we have lots of time; we can walk **slowly**. There is no need to hurry.

(b) Adjectives with more than one character

老王**心甘情愿地**为李小姐服务。
Lǎo Wáng xīngānqíngyuàn de wèi Lǐ xiǎojiě fúwù.
Lao Wang works **willingly** for Miss Li.

An adjective with two or more characters can still have a degree adverb (很, 非常, 十分, etc.) in an adverbial modifier.

柜台的服务人员总是**很热情地**回答访客的问题。

Guìtái de fúwù rényuán zǒngshì hěn rèqíng de huídá fǎngkè de wèntí.

The service personnel at the counter always answer visitors' questions **very warmly**.

老师**非常愤怒地**把作弊的学生骂了一顿。

Lǎoshī fēicháng fènnù de bǎ zuòbì de xuéshēng mà le yí dùn.

The teacher scolded the cheating students **extremely angrily**.

<table><tr><td>Level
3</td></tr></table>

18.2 When 地 can be optional

地 can be optional in the following situations:

(a) Reduplicated adjectives

When a monosyllabic adjective is repeated or if each of the characters in a disyllabic adjective is reduplicated, 地 becomes optional. (Not all disyllabic adjectives can be repeated.)

放学了，我**慢慢(地)**走回家去。

Fàngxué le, wǒ màn màn (de) zǒu huí jiā qù.

After classes were over, I **slowly** walked home.

我期末考得了一百分，这**大大(地)**提高了我这学期的平均分数。

Wǒ qīmòkǎo dé le yì bǎi fēn, zhè dà dà(de) tígāo le wǒ zhè xuéqí de píngjūn fēnshù.

I got 100 in the final exam. This **greatly** raised my average score for the term.

放学了，小朋友都**高高兴兴(地)**回家去。(Do not say 高兴高兴地回家去。)

Fàngxué le. Xiǎo péngyǒu dōu gāo gāo xìng xìng (de) huí jiā qù.

Classes were over. All the school children went home **happily**.

这件事，老师**清清楚楚(地)**说了三遍，他还是没记住。

Zhè jiàn shì, lǎoshī qīng qīng chǔ chǔ (de) shuō le sān biàn, tā háishì méi jìzhù.

The teacher said it **clearly** three times, but he still didn't remember.

(b) Sequential/individual action

When describing an action being performed sequentially or individually, '一 + measure word' must be reduplicated. In this case, 地 becomes optional.

别挤，先排好队，再**一个一个(地)**上去。(Sequentially)

Bié jǐ, xiān pái hǎo duì, zài yī ge yī ge (de) shàngqù.

Don't push each other. Form a line first and then get on (the bus) **one by one**.

你们每个人都先找好一个练习伙伴，再**一组一组(地)**练习。(Individually)

Nǐmen měi ge rén xiān zhǎo hǎo yī ge liànxí huǒbàn, zài yì zǔ yì zǔ (de) liànxí.

Each of you first find a partner and then practise **in groups**.

<table><tr><td>Level
2</td></tr></table>

18.3 Adjectives functioning as adverbs

Some adjectives, such as 大声 (*dàshēng*: 'loud'), 努力 (*nǔlì*: 'diligent'), 仔细 (*zǐxì*: 'careful'), 注意 (*zhùyì*: 'attentive'), 小心 (*xiǎoxīn*: 'careful'), can function as adverbs. In this case, 地 is optional.

王太太**不停地**说话，王先生受不了了，**大声(地)**叫她闭嘴。

Wáng tàitai bùtíng de shuōhuà, Wáng xiānsheng shòu bù liǎo le, dàshēng (de) jiào tā bì zuǐ.

Mrs Wang talked **(constantly) without stopping**. Mr Wang could not stand it anymore, so he **loudly** told her to shut up.

老师问的问题，你要**注意(地)**听，然后**大声(地)**回答。

Lǎoshī wèn de wèntí, nǐ yào zhùyì (de) tīng, ránhòu dàshēng (de) huídá.

You have to listen **attentively** to the teacher's question and then answer **loudly**.

18.4 True adverbs

Some words are adverbs by nature; these words cannot be followed by 地, even though their English counterparts may be 'adjective + ly'. 马上 (*mǎshàng*: 'immediately'), 立刻 (*lìkè*: 'immediately'), 显然 (*xiǎnrán*: 'obviously'), 非常 (*fēicháng*: 'extremely'), 居然 (*jūrán*: 'surprisingly') are some of these adverbs.

春天一到，天气**马上**就暖和起来了。 (It is incorrect to say 马上地 for 'immediately'.)

Chūntiān yí dào, tiānqì mǎshàng jiù nuǎnhuo qǐlái le.

As soon as spring arrives, the weather **immediately** begins to warm up.

小明考得很差，他**显然**很难过，所以妈妈决定不骂他。

Xiǎomíng kǎo de hěn chà, tā xiǎnrán hěn nánguò, suǒyǐ māma juédìng bú mà tā.

Xiaoming did poorly in the test; he was **obviously** sad, so his mother decided not to scold him.

18.5 Adverbial modifier and complement of state compared

👁 Since the complement of state is frequently translated into an adverb in English, it is important to distinguish between the usages of the complement of state and the adverbial modifier.

☞ See Chapter 12 for more information on the complement of state.

(a) Habitual behaviour vs. specific occasion

The complement of state (with 得) is normally used to describe a habitual behaviour. The adverbial modifier (with 地) is used to describe an action on one specific occasion.

小王写字**写得太快**，所以常常写错。 (写得太快 is habitual.)

Xiǎo Wáng xiě zì xiě de tài kuài, suǒyǐ chángcháng xiě cuò.

Xiao Wang writes characters too **quickly**, so he frequently makes mistakes.

小王**很快地**在纸上写了几个字就离开了。 (很快地写 is one specific occasion.)

Xiǎo Wáng hěn kuài de zài zhǐ shàng xiě le jǐ ge zì jiù líkāi le.

Xiao Wang **quickly** wrote a few characters on the paper and then left.

爷爷年纪大了，走路**走得很慢**。可是他刚听到孙儿在叫救命，就**很快地**跑去救他。 (走得很慢 is habitual. 很快地跑去 is one specific occasion.)

Yéye niánjì dà le, zǒulù zǒu de hěn màn. Kěshì tā gāng tīngdào sūn'ér zài jiào jiùmìng, jiù hěn kuài de pǎo qù jiù tā.

Grandfather is old; he walks **slowly**. But just now he heard his grandson calling for help, so he **quickly** ran to help him.

(b) Outcomes vs. conscious effort

To describe the outcome of an event, use the complement of state (with 得), even though it may not be habitual; therefore, it is an action that is often not intentional or beyond one's control. For an action one can control or can put in conscious effort to achieve, use the adverbial modifier (with 地).

上次的考试，我**考得很差**，因为我没有**好好地**准备。（考得很差 refers to the outcome of the test. 好好地准备 refers to conscious effort.）

Shàngcì de kǎoshì, wǒ kǎo de hěn chà, yīnwèi wǒ méiyǒu hǎo hǎo de zhūnbèi.

I did **poorly** in the last test because I did not **do a good job studying** for it.

昨天的比赛，小王**跑得最快**，所以他得了第一名。从今天起，我天天都要**认真地**练习，下次我一定要得第一名。（跑得最快 is the outcome of the race. 认真地练习 refers to conscious effort.）

Zuòtiān de bǐsài, Xiǎo Wáng pǎo de zuì kuài, suǒyǐ tā dé le dìyī míng. Cóng jīntiān qǐ, wǒ tiān tiān dōu yào rènzhēn de liànxí, xiàcì wǒ yídìng yào dé dìyī míng.

In yesterday's race, Xiao Wang ran the **fastest**, so he won first place. From today, I will train **conscientiously** every day. I will definitely win first place next time.

妈妈**着急地**说：“小明，你**开得太快**了。”（开得太快 describes the outcome of an act.）

Māma zháojí de shuō, 'Xiǎomíng, nǐ kāi de tài kuài le.'

小明**很不情愿地**说：“好吧，我**慢慢地开**。”（慢慢地开 is an act that can be controlled.）

Xiǎomíng hěn bù qíngyuàn de shuō, 'hǎo ba, wǒ màn màn de kāi'.

Mother said **anxiously**, 'Xiaoming, you are driving **too fast**.'

Xiaoming **very reluctantly** said, 'All right, I'll drive **slowly**.'

最近我忙死了，下个月我要休假，跟家人去欧洲**好好地玩**一玩。（好好地玩 refers to an act one can make an effort to achieve.）

Zuìjìn wǒ máng sǐ le, xià ge yuè wǒ yào xiūjià, gēn jiārén qù Ōuzhōu hǎo hǎo de wán yì wán.

Recently I have been busy to death. Next month, I am going to take a holiday and go to Europe with family to **really have a good time**.

王：听说上个月你跟家人去欧洲度假，**玩得怎么样**？（怎么样 is used to ask about the outcome.）

Wáng: Tīngshuō shàng ge yuè nǐ gēn jiārén qu Ōuzhōu dùjià, wán de zěnmeyàng?

李：大家都**玩得十分高兴**。

Lǐ: Dàjiā dōu wán de shífēn gāoxìng.

Wang: I heard that you went to Europe with your family for a holiday last month. How did you enjoy yourself? (Did you **have a good time?**)

Li: Everybody **had an extremely good time**.

(c) Use of degree adverbs

Degree adverbs such as 太 (*tài*), 真 (*zhēn*), 更 (*gèng*), 最 (*zuì*), 这么 (*zhème*), 那么 (*nàme*) and 够 (*gòu*) only go with the complement of state; they rarely appear in the adverbial modifier. (Adverbs indicating various degrees of 'very' such as 很 (*hěn*), 非常 (*fēicháng*), 十分 (*shífēn*) are exceptions; they can be used in adverbial modifiers.)

前天我去找王家三兄弟的时候，他们都在**认真地**准备考试。后来，听说老三**准备得最充分**，所以他**考得**比两个哥哥**更好**。

Qiántiān wǒ qù zhǎo Wáng jiā sān xiōngdì de shíhòu, tāmen dōu zài rènzhēn de zhǔnbèi kǎoshì. Hòulái, tīngshuō lǎo sān zhǔnbèi de zuì chōngfèn, suǒyǐ tā kǎo de bǐ liǎng ge gēge gèng hǎo.

When I went to see the Wang family's three brothers the day before yesterday, they were all studying conscientiously for the test. Later on, I heard that the youngest was the most fully prepared, so he did even better than his two older brothers.

王：他**开得这么慢**，为什么还被警察拦下来？

Wáng: Tā kāi de zhème màn, wèishénme hái bèi jǐngchá lán xiàlái?

李：在高速公路上**开得太慢**也是很危险的。

Lǐ: Zài gāosù gōnglù shàng kāi de tài màn yě shì hěn wéixiǎn de.

Wang: He drove so slowly. Why was he still pulled over by the police?

Li: Driving too slowly on the highway is also very dangerous.

(d) No significant difference in meaning

Some situations can be described by using either the adverbial modifier (with 地) or the complement of state (with 得) without any significant difference in meaning. These tend to be acts on specific occasions (地) that are not intentionally controlled (得).

他一听到这个坏消息，就**难过地哭**了。 (adverbial modifier 地)

Tā yì tīngdào zhè ge huài xiāoxí, jiù nánguò de kū le.

他一听到这个坏消息，就**哭得很难过**。 (complement of state)

Tā yì tīngdào zhè ge huài xiāoxí, jiù kū de hěn nánguò.

The moment he heard the bad news, he cried sadly.

Compare:　他一听到这个坏消息，就难过**得哭**了。 (complement of degree)

　　　　　　Tā yì tīngdào zhè ge huài xiāoxí, jiù nánguò de kū le.

　　　　　　The moment he heard the bad news, he was **so** sad **that** he cried.

他一听到这个好消息，就**开心地笑**了。 (adverbial modifier 地)

Tā yì tīngdào zhè ge hǎo xiāoxí, jiù kāixīn de xiào le.

他一听到这个好消息，就**笑得很开心**。 (complement of state)

Tā yì tīngdào zhè ge hǎo xiāoxí, jiù xiào de hěn kāixīn.

The moment he heard the good news, he smiled happily.

Compare:　他平常很少笑，可是他刚才听到这个好消息，就开心**得笑**了。

　　　　　　(complement of degree)

　　　　　　Tā píngcháng hěn shǎo xiào, kěshì tā gāngcái tīngdào zhè ge
　　　　　　hǎo xiāoxí, jiù kāixīn de xiào le.

　　　　　　Ordinarily, he rarely smiles. But when he heard this good news
　　　　　　just now, he was **so** happy **that** he smiled.

(e) Summary

The following table provides a summary of the usages of the complement of state and the adverbial modifier.

Habitual action	Complement of state	我爷爷走路走得很慢。 *Wǒ yéye zǒulù zǒu de hěn màn.* My grandfather walks (or walked) slowly.
Specific incident (Non-habitual)		
Describing outcome	Complement of state	上次考试，我考得很差。 *Shàng cì kǎoshì, wǒ kǎo de hěn chà.* I did poorly in the last test.
Describing an intentional action	Adverbial modifier	下课了，他慢慢地走回家。 *Xià kè le, tā màn màn de zǒu huí jiā.* Class was over. He slowly walked home.
Action involving conscious effort	Adverbial modifier	下次考试，我会认真地准备。 *Xià cì kǎoshì, wǒ huì rènzhēn de zhǔnbèi.* I will study conscientiously for the next test.

Use of degree adverbs		
太, 真, 更, 最, 这么, 那么, 够	Complement of state	你开车开得太快了。 *Nǐ kāi chē kāi de tài kuài le.* You are driving too fast. (You drive too fast.)
很, 非常, 十分, 不太	Both	他跑得非常慢。 (Habitual) *Tā pǎo de fēicháng màn.* He runs extremely slowly. 他很高兴地向我问好。 (Intentional) *Tā hěn gāoxìng de xiàng wǒ wèn hǎo.* He happily said hello to me.

Exercises

Level 3

Translate the following sentences into Chinese. Be sure to make the distinction between the complement of state (with 得) and the adverbial modifier (with 地).

1 Mr Wang is old; therefore, he walks slowly.

2 I got up early this morning. So I can walk to school slowly now. (Meaning: I can take my time.)

3 Wang Ming studies conscientiously, so he always does well in tests.

4 When I was young, I ran fast. Now I can only jog (= run slowly) for half an hour every day because my doctor says that I need exercise.

5 Mr Wang gave Miss Li a gift that was wrapped beautifully. Miss Li happily said, 'Thank you.'

6 Mrs Li felt that Mr Li was driving too fast, so she said anxiously, 'Don't drive so fast. We have plenty of time. You should drive slowly.'

7 Hearing this, Mr Li said unhappily, 'Look! Everybody else is driving even faster than I am.'

8 When my older brother and I returned home, our mother was angrily scolding our younger brother. My older brother said nervously, 'I also did badly in today's test. Mother will be so angry that she won't let me watch TV.'

9 Beijing's traffic is notoriously bad. When you are driving, you must watch the traffic signs carefully.

10 Because Mrs Wang is a good cook (= cooks well), Mr Wang has gradually (= slowly) gained weight (= become fat) since he got married.

19 The 是……的 structure

The 是 (shì)……的 (de) structure has several quite different functions. The element between 是 and 的 can be a sentence, a verbal phrase (which might include a time phrase or a prepositional phrase), an adjective or even an auxiliary verb. When what is between 是 and 的 is a noun or a pronoun, the noun/pronoun and 的 form the possessive, (for example, 这本书是我的 (Zhè běn shū shì wǒ de)), which is not the concern of this chapter.

Since the 是……的 structure is used when an event has taken place, 了 cannot be used.

The affirmative–negative question is 是不是……的? (Or 是……的吗?) The negative form is 不是……的.

A. Providing focus

The 是……的 structure can be used to give information on the 'who, where, how and when' of an event that has already taken place. It is used in context, meaning the fact that the event has taken place must be either mentioned first or it should be a pre-existent situation understood by each of the interlocutors.

👁 Learners who are English speakers should pay special attention to the distinction between the 是……的 structure and a sentence with 了 since both frequently share only one English sentence.

> 张：客人呢？
> *Zhāng: Kèrén ne?*
> 王：都走了。
> *Wáng: Dōu zǒu le.*
> 张：哦？他们**是**几点走**的**？
> *Zhāng: Ò? Tāmen shì jǐ diǎn zǒu de?*
> 王：两个**是**九点走**的**，还有一个**是**十点才走**的**。
> *Wáng: Liǎng ge shì jiǔ diǎn zǒu de, háiyǒu yī ge shì shí diǎn cái zǒu de.*
> Zhang: Where are the guests?
> Wang: They all left.
> Zhang: Oh? **When** did they leave?
> Wang: Two left at 9 o'clock and another one left at 10 o'clock.

The following passage describes the activities, none of which is in context yet. This passage does not focus on giving information on the time when the guests left; therefore, the 是……的 structure is not used.

> 昨天我家请客，饭后我们聊天、打牌，大家都玩得很高兴，所以客人**半夜才回家**。
> *Zuótiān wǒ jiā qǐngkè, fàn hòu wǒmen liáotiān, dǎ pái, dàjiā dōu wán de hěn gāoxìng, suǒyǐ kèrén bànyè cái huíjiā.*
> Yesterday I had guests over. We chatted and played cards after dinner; everybody had a good time, so my guests didn't leave until midnight.

19.1 Focus on 'who'

When the focus is on asking about or giving information on 'who', it is possible to start the sentence with 是. This is because the person following 是 is the focus.

王：听说你昨天跟一个很漂亮的女孩去参加颁奖典礼。
Wáng: Tīngshuō nǐ zuótiān gēn yí ge hěn piàoliàng de nǚhái qù cānjiā bānjiǎng diǎnlǐ.
李：你听错了，我**是跟我妈妈去**的。
Lǐ: Nǐ tīng cuò le. Wǒ shì gēn wǒ māma qù de.
Wang: I heard that you went with a pretty girl to the award ceremony yesterday.
Li: You heard it wrong. I went with my mother.

张：这件事，**是谁**告诉你**的**？
Zhāng: Zhè jiàn shì, shì shéi gàosù nǐ de?
丁：**是老王**告诉我**的**。（老王是告诉我的 is ungrammatical.)
Dīng: Shì Lǎo Wáng gàosù wǒ de.
Zhang: Who told you about this matter?
Ding: Lao Wang told me about it.

张：这个消息，你**是怎么**知道**的**？
Zhāng: Zhè ge xiāoxí, nǐ shì zěnme zhīdào de?
丁：**是老王**打电话告诉我**的**。
Dīng: Shì Lǎo Wáng dǎ diànhuà gàosù wǒ de.
(It would be incorrect to say 老王是打电话告诉我的 as the response to this question.)
Zhang: How did you know about this news?
Ding: Lao Wang called and told me.

Compare: 张：这个消息，老王**是怎么**通知你**的**？（The focus is 'how', not 'who'.)
Zhāng: Zhè ge xiāoxí, Lǎo Wáng shì zěnme tōngzhī nǐ de?
丁：他**是**打电话来告诉我**的**。
Dīng: Tā shì dǎ diànhuà lái gàosù wǒ de.
Zhang: How did Lao Wang notify you of this news?
Ding: He called and told me. (He notified me by phone.)

19.2 Focus on 'where'

When the focus is on 'where', the element between 是 and 的 usually contains a prepositional phrase with 在 (*zài*) or 从 (*cóng*).

我爸妈**是在中国**认识、结婚**的**；但是我**是在英国**生**的**。
Wǒ bàmā shì zài Zhōngguó rènshì, jiéhūn de; dànshì wǒ shì zài Yīngguó shēng de.
My parents met and married in China, but I was born in the UK.

这些家具都**是从外国**进口**的**，所以非常贵。
Zhè xiē jiājù dōu shì cóng wàiguó jìnkǒu de, suǒyǐ fēicháng guì.
All the furniture was imported from foreign countries, so it is very expensive.

19.3 Focus on 'how'

When the focus is on giving information on 'how' something happened, two verbs might be necessary, with the first verb being used to indicate the method.

王：你们**是怎么**知道这件事**的**？
Wáng: Nǐmen shì zěnme zhīdào zhè jiàn shì de?

张：是小王打电话告诉我的。
Zhāng: Shì Xiǎo Wáng dǎ diànhuà gàosù wǒ de.
丁：我是从老李那里听说的。
Dīng: Wǒ shì cóng Lǎo Lǐ nàlǐ tīngshuō de.
Wang: How did you know about this incident?
Zhang: Xiao Wang called and told me.
Ding: I heard it from Lao Li.

李：下这么大的雨，你是怎么来学校的？
Lǐ: Xià zhème dà de yǔ, nǐ shì zěnme lái xuéxiào de?
丁：我是开车来的。（我是开车的 would be incorrect.）
Dīng: Wǒ shì kāichē lái de.
Li: It rained so hard today. How did you come to school?
Ding: I drove here.

The following passage describes a habitual act, it does not focus on giving information on how a specific event took place; therefore, the 是……的 structure is not used.

不管晴天还是下雨，我每天都走路去学校。
Bùguǎn qíngtiān háishì xià yǔ, wǒ měi tiān dōu zǒulù qù xuéxiào.
Whether it's sunny or it rains, I walk to school every day.

In the following passage, the 是……的 structure is again not used; therefore, 怎么 has a different meaning.

李：今天下这么大的雨，而且又没课，你怎么来了？
Lǐ: Jīntiān xià zhème dà de yǔ, érqiě yòu méi kè, nǐ zěnme lái le?
王：上星期跟老师约定了今天见面，谁知道今天会下大雨？
Wáng: Shàng xīngqī gēn lǎoshī yuēdìng le jīntiān jiànmiàn, shéi zhīdào jīntiān huì xià dà yǔ?
Li: It's raining so hard today; besides, there is no class, **how come** you are here?
Wang: I made an appointment to meet with the teacher today. Who would have known it would rain so hard today?

<table>
<tr><td>Level
3</td></tr>
</table>

19.4 Focus on 'when'

The 是……的 structure may be used to focus on giving information on 'when', with the time phrase following 是.

张：昨天的派对，你去了吗？
Zhāng: Zuótiān de pàiduì, nǐ qù le ma?
李：去了。
Lǐ: Qù le.
张：我怎么没看到你？你是几点走的？
Zhāng: Wǒ zěnme méi kàndào nǐ? Nǐ shì jǐ diǎn zǒu de?
李：我是八点半走的。
Lǐ: Wǒ shì bā diǎn bàn zǒu de.
张：难怪，我是九点才到的。
Zhāng: Nánguài, wǒ shì jiǔ diǎn cái dào de.
Zhang: Did you go to yesterday's party?
Li: Yes, I did?
Zhang: How come I didn't see you? What time did you leave?
Li: I left at 8.30.
Zhang: No wonder (I didn't see you). I didn't arrive until 9 o'clock.

这座大楼是八十年前盖的，不过后面的游泳池是去年才加的。

Zhè zuò dàlóu shì bāshí nián qián gài de, búguò hòumiàn de yóuyǒngchí shì qùnián cái jiā de.

This building was built 80 years ago, but the swimming pool behind it was only added last year.

19.5 Focus on 'purpose' of coming or going somewhere

Level 3

来 (*lái*) or 去 (*qù*) can follow 是 to indicate one's purpose of coming/going to a place. The 是来/去……的 structure is usually used to imply that one is/was not here/there for another purpose.

(Situation: Wang and Zhang have recently had a falling-out.)

王：我又没有请你，你来做什么？

Wáng: Wǒ yòu méiyǒu qǐng nǐ, nǐ lái zuò shénme?

张：我**是来**向你道歉**的**。(Implied: **不是来**找麻烦**的**。)

Zhāng: Wǒ shì lái xiàng nǐ dàoqiàn de.

Wang: I did not invite you, why are you here?

Zhang: I am here to apologize to you. (Implied: I am not here to look for trouble.)

去年我去了一趟上海，大家都以为我**是去**旅游**的**，其实我**是去**找工作**的**。

Qùnián wǒ qù le yí tàng Shànghǎi, dàjiā dōu yǐwéi wǒ shì qù lǚyóu de, qíshí wǒ shì qù zhǎo gōngzuò de.

Last year, I made a trip to Shanghai. Everybody thought I went to travel; actually, I went there to look for a job.

👁 The 不是来/去……的 structure may have a very different English counterpart.

English: I **didn't come** to argue with you; I came to apologize to you.
Chinese: 我**不是来**跟你吵架**的**，**是来**向你道歉**的**。
           Wǒ bú shì lái gēn nǐ chǎojià de, shì lái xiàng nǐ dàoqiàn de.

(Situation: A college student has failed all his classes. His father is angry.)

爸爸：别忘了，你**不是去**浪费我的血汗钱**的**，**是去**受教育**的**。

Bàba: Bié wàng le, nǐ bú shì qù làngfèi wǒde xuèhàn qián de, shì qù shòu jiàoyù de.

Father: Don't forget that you **didn't go** to college to waste my hard-earned money; you went to get an education.

19.6 Placement of objects

Level 3

When the element between 是 and 的 ends with 'verb + object', the object can be moved after 的. However, the object should not be a pronoun.

张：昨天你妈妈做了哪些菜？

Zhāng: Zuótiān nǐ māma zuò le nǎ xiē cài?

王：昨天我们**是**在外面吃**的晚饭**，(= 昨天我们**是**在外面**吃晚饭的**，)**不是**在家吃**的**。

Wáng: Zuótiān wǒmen shì zài wàimiàn chī de wǎnfàn, bú shì zài jiā chī de.

Zhang: What dishes did your mother make yesterday?

Wang: Yesterday we ate dinner out; we didn't eat at home.

丁：你去邮局的时候，怎么没把我下午写的那封信也寄了？

Dīng: Nǐ qù yóujú de shíhòu, zěnme méi bǎ wǒ xiàwǔ xiě de nà fēng xìn yě jì le?

李：我是上午去的邮局。(= 我是上午去邮局的。)
Lǐ: Wǒ shì shàngwǔ qù de yóujú.
Ding: Why didn't you also mail the letter I wrote this afternoon when you went to the post office?
Li: I went to the post office in the morning.

19.7 When 是 is optional

是 is optional in a positive sentence (particularly when the statement starts with 是), but 的 is never optional. Without 是, the sentence may sound more casual.

王：这个秘密，(是)谁告诉老张的？
Wáng: Zhè ge mìmì, (shì) shéi gàosù Lǎo Zhāng de?
李：(是)老张自己发现的，不是别人告诉他的。
Lǐ: (Shì) Lǎo Zhāng zìjǐ fāxiàn de, bú shì biérén gàosù tā de.
Wang: Who told Lao Zhang this secret?
Li: Lao Zhang discovered it himself; it was not revealed to him by anybody.

张：今天是你的生日，对不对？祝你生日快乐！
Zhāng: Jīntiān shì nǐde shēngrì, duì bú duì? Zhù nǐ shēngrì kuàilè.
李：对，谢谢，可是，你(是)怎么知道的？
Lǐ: Duì, xièxie, kěshì, nǐ (shì) zěnme zhīdào de?
张：(是)小王告诉我的。
Zhāng: (Shì) Xiǎo Wáng gàosù wǒ de.
Zhang: Today is your birthday, right? Happy birthday!
Li: That's right, thanks. But how did you know?
Zhang: Xiao Wang told me.

19.8 Mysteries and crimes

When there is a mystery or when a crime has occurred, the 'who, where, how and when' **are** the focus of interest; therefore, 是......的 is used in discussing these situations.

李明的电脑被偷了。他知道是他同屋偷的，可是他提不出证明。
Lǐ Míng de diànnǎo bèi tōu le. Tā zhīdào shì tā tóngwū tōu de, kěshì tā tí bù chū zhèngmíng.
Li Ming's computer was stolen. He knew his roommate had stolen it, but he could not prove it.

警察已经知道王先生是在这个屋子里被谋杀的，可是他们不知道他是怎么死的。
Jǐngchá yǐjīng zhīdào Wáng xiānsheng shì zài zhè ge wūzi lǐ bèi móushā de, kěshì tāmen bù zhīdào tā shì zěnme sǐ de.
The police already know Mr Wang was murdered in this room, but they don't know how he died.

张：没有人知道这件奇怪的事是什么时候发生的。
Zhāng: Méiyǒu rén zhīdào zhè jiàn qíguài de shì shì shénme shíhòu fāshēng de.
王：(是)谁说的？大家都知道这件事是上个星期发生的。
Wáng: (Shì) shéi shuō de? Dàjiā dōu zhīdào zhè jiàn shì shì shàng ge xīngqī fāshēng de.
Zhang: No one knows when this strange incident happened.
Wang: Who said so? Everybody knows that it happened last week.

<table>
<tr><td>Level
3</td></tr>
</table>

19.9 Focus on 'origin'

Sentences with the 是……的 structure can be translated into the passive voice in English when it shows the 'origin' of the subject. A sentence showing 'origin' can also be in the present tense in English since it indicates a fact, not a specific event that has taken place.

张：豆腐**是**用什么做**的**？
Zhāng: Dòufu shì yòng shénme zuò de?
李：豆腐主要**是**用黄豆做**的**。
Lǐ: Dòufu zhǔyào shì yòng huángdòu zuò de.
Zhang: What **is** tofu **made** from?
Li: Tofu is made mainly from soya beans.

丁：你的中文老师**是不是**从中国来**的**？
Dīng: Nǐde Zhōngwén lǎoshī shì bú shì cóng Zhōngguó lái de?
王：不是，他**是**在英国生**的**，不过他爸妈**是**从中国来**的**。
Wáng: Bú shì, tā shì zài Yīngguó shēng de, búguò tā bàmā shì cóng Zhōngguó lái de.
Ding: **Is** your Chinese teacher **from** China? (Did your Chinese teacher come from China?)
Wang: No, he was born in the UK. But his parents **are from** China (= came from China).

张：这本食谱**是**你写**的**吗？
Zhāng: Zhè běn shípǔ shì nǐ xiě de ma?
李：不是，**是**我妈妈写**的**；不过我最近也**写**了一本食谱，还没出版。
Lǐ: Bú shì, shì wǒ māma xiě de, búguò wǒ zuìjìn yě xiě le yì běn shípǔ, hái méi chūbǎn.
Zhang: Was this cookbook written by you? (**Did** you write this cookbook?)
Li: No, it is by my mother. (It was written by my mother). But I **have** recently **written** a cookbook, too; it has not been published yet.

<table>
<tr><td>Level
3</td></tr>
</table>

19.10 Subjects in context

👁 In the absence of English structures completely equivalent to the 是……的 structure, it is important to keep in mind that the subject of the 是……的 structure should be 'in context', meaning its existence is known to both or all of the people engaged in the conversation.

English: Who wrote those words on the wall?
Chinese: 墙上的那些字**是谁**写**的**？
 Qiáng shàng de nà xiē zì shì shéi xiě de?
 (It would be incorrect to say 谁写了那些字在墙上？since 那些字 is the 'known information'.)

English: Who moved away my chair?
Chinese: 谁把我的椅子搬走了？
 Shéi bǎ wǒde yǐzi bān zǒu le?
 (This is not the 是……的 structure since 我的椅子 is not in context yet.)

English: Who moved **this chair** here?
Chinese: 这把椅子**是谁**搬来**的**？
 Zhè bǎ yǐzi shì shéi bān lái de?
 (这把椅子 is the 'known information' in this sentence, and is considered 'in context'.)

妈妈：谁把冰箱里的牛奶喝完了？

Māma: Shéi bǎ bīngxiāng lǐ de niúnǎi hē wán le?

（没有人回答。）

(Méiyǒu rén huídá.)

妈妈：快说，冰箱里的牛奶**是**谁喝完**的**？

Māma: Kuài shuō, bīngxiāng lǐ de niúnǎi shì shéi hē wán de? (The fact that someone drank the milk is now 'in context', and the focus is now on 'who'.)

Mother: Who drank the milk in the refrigerator?

(Nobody answers.)

Mother: Tell me now, **who** drank the milk in the refrigerator?

B. Identifying people

Level 3

The element between 是......的 can be a verbal phrase used to identify a person by the person's profession/job, academic specialty or native place.

王中和李明都是北京大学的学生，王中**是学**历史**的**，李明**是学**哲学**的**。

Wáng Zhōng hé Lǐ Míng dōu shì Běijīng Dàxué de xuéshēng, Wáng Zhōng shì xué lìshǐ de, Lǐ Míng shì xué zhéxué de.

Both Wang Zhong and Li Ming are students at Beijing University. Wang Zhong is a history student; Li Ming is a philosophy student.

王先生跟李先生都是司机，王先生**是开**公共汽车**的**，李先生**是开**出租汽车**的**。

Wáng xiānsheng gēn Lǐ xiānsheng dōu shì sījī, Wáng xiānsheng shì kāi gōnggòng qìchē de, Lǐ xiānsheng shì kāi chūzū qìchē de.

Both Mr Wang and Mr Li are drivers. Mr Wang drives buses (= is a bus driver); Mr Li drives a taxi (= is a taxi driver).

张：你爸爸**是做**什么**的**？　(It would be improper to say 你爸爸做什么？)

Zhāng: Nǐ bàba shì zuò shénme de?

王：他**是教**英文**的**。你爸爸呢？

Wáng: Tā shì jiāo Yīngwén de. Nǐ bàba ne?

张：他也**是教**书**的**。

Zhāng: Tā yě shì jiāoshū de.

Zhang: What (kind of work) does your father do?

Wang: He teaches English. (= He is an English teacher.) How about your father?

Zhang: He also teaches. (= He is also a teacher.)

C. Stating facts

Level 3

 The element between 是......的 can be an adjective. Such an adjective is used to indicate a fact, not an opinion, and therefore, does not follow a degree adverb. For example, 这件大衣**很贵** (*Zhè jiàn dàyī hěn guì*: 'This coat **is expensive**') is an opinion, whereas 这件大衣**是蓝的** (*Zhè jiàn dàyī shì lán de*: 'This coat **is blue**') is a fact.

(Situation: A mother and her daughter are shopping for a coat for the daughter.)

妈妈：你不是说想买红色的大衣吗？这件**是红的**，就买这件吧！

Māma: Nǐ bú shì shuō xiǎng mǎi hóngsè de dàyī ma? Zhè jiàn shì hóng de, jiù mǎi zhè jiàn ba!

女儿：这件**太红了**，我不喜欢。

Nǚ'ér: Zhè jiàn tài hóng le, wǒ bù xǐhuān.

(这件大衣是红的 is a fact; 这件太红了 is an opinion.)

Mother: Didn't you say you wanted to buy a red coat? This one **is red**; buy this one!

Daughter: This one **is too red**. I don't like it.

19.11 Using mutually exclusive adjectives

Level 3

The adjective in the 是……的 structure is frequently one of two adjectives whose meanings are mutually exclusive.

贿赂**是非法的**，但是送礼**是合法的**，所以你可以送礼，不可以贿赂。

(It is incorrect to say 贿赂很非法，送礼很合法. 非法 and 合法 are mutually exclusive.)

Huìlù shì fēifǎ de, dànshì sònglǐ shì héfǎ de, suǒyǐ nǐ kěyǐ sònglǐ, bù kěyǐ huìlù.

Bribery is illegal, but giving gifts is legal; so you can give gifts, (but you) cannot bribe.

我们学校老师跟学生的地址、电话号码都**是公开的**，(**不是秘密的**)。

Wǒmen xuéxiào lǎoshī gēn xuéshēng de dìzhǐ, diànhuà hàomǎ dōu shì gōngkāi de, (bú shì mìmì de.)

At our school, teachers' and students' addresses and telephone numbers are open to the public (not confidential).

妈妈：你的中文老师**是男的**还是**女的**？ (It is rude to call an individual 男人 or 女人.)

Māma: Nǐde Zhōngwén lǎoshī shì nán de háishì nǚ de?

儿子：我们有两个中文老师，一个**是男的**，一个**是女的**。

Érzi: Wǒmen yǒu liǎng ge Zhōngwén lǎoshī, yí ge shì nán de, yí ge shì nǚ de.

Mother: Is your Chinese teacher male or female?

Son: We have two Chinese teachers; one is male; one is female.

19.12 Using auxiliary verbs

Level 3

Some auxiliary verbs can be placed between 是 and 的. 应该 (*yīnggāi*)/不应该, 可以 (*kěyǐ*)/不可以 and 不行 (*bù xíng*) can be used this way. 👁 Auxiliary verbs in English are rarely used this way.

(Situation: Xiao Wang gave his seat to an old man on the bus. The old man said, 'Thank you.')

小王：哪里，这**是应该的**。

Xiǎo Wáng: Nǎli, zhè shì yīnggāi de.

Xiao Wang: Don't mention it. This **is the way it should be**.

学外语的时候，只记生词、不学语法，**是不行的**。

Xué wàiyǔ de shíhòu, zhǐ jì shēngcí, bù xué yǔfǎ, shì bùxíng de.

When one studies a foreign language, only memorizing vocabulary without studying grammar **won't do**. (It won't do to only memorize vocabulary without studying grammar.)

D. Emphatic expressions

The 是……的 structure can be optional when used in an emphatic expression.

<table>
<tr><td>Level 2</td></tr>
</table>

19.13 Emphasizing a point

The element between 是 and 的 can be an adjective with a degree adverb such as 很 (*hěn*) or 非常 (*fēicháng*) to emphasize the point. In this case, 是……的 is an emphatic expression and it is optional.

李明：老师，请问，这两个句子，哪一句**是错的**？ (错 is an adjective that cannot go with a degree adverb such as 很; therefore, 是……的 is not optional.)
Lǐ Míng: Lǎoshī, qǐng wèn, zhè liǎng ge jùzi, nǎ yí jù shì cuò de?
老师：同学们，李明的这个问题，**(是)**十分值得讨论**(的)**。
Lǎoshī: Tóngxuémen, Lǐ Míng de zhè ge wèntí (shì) shífēn zhíde tǎolùn (de).
Li Ming: Sir, would you please tell me which of these two sentences is incorrect?
Teacher: Everyone, Li Ming's question is very much worth discussing.

学生：我认为，多学一种外语对将来找工作**(是)很有帮助(的)**。
Xuéshēng: Wǒ rènwéi, duō xué yì zhǒng wàiyǔ duì jiānglái zhǎo gōngzuò (shì) hěn yǒu bāngzhù (de).
老师：你的这个看法**(是)**相当正确**(的)**。
Lǎoshī: Nǐde zhè ge kànfǎ (shì) xiāngdāng zhèngquè (de).
Student: I think that to learn one more foreign language is helpful for getting a job in the future.
Teacher: This viewpoint of yours is quite accurate.

<table>
<tr><td>Level 2</td></tr>
</table>

19.14 Emphasizing one's confidence/certainty

An optional 是……的 can be used to emphasize one's confidence about a prediction or the certainty of the happening of a future event; in this case, the element between 是 and 的 should include words such as 会 (*huì*), 要 (*yào*) and 可能 (*kěnéng*), and an optional 一定 (*yídìng*) is often used to make the point even stronger.

这件事这么重要，我想，他**是(一定)不会**忘记**的**。(= 他一定不会忘记。)
Zhè jiàn shì zhème zhòngyào, wǒ xiǎng, tā shì (yídìng) bú huì wàngjì de.
This matter is so important; I think he definitely won't forget.

小王犯了这么大的错，他**是(一定)**要负责**的**。(= 他一定要负责。)
Xiǎo Wáng fàn le zhème dà de cuò, tā shì (yídìng) yào fùzé de.
Xiao Wang made such a big mistake; he definitely will have to be responsible for it.

<table>
<tr><td>Level 2</td></tr>
</table>

19.15 Emphasizing the negative

It should be noted that when 是……的 is used for the purpose of emphasis and what is being emphasized is negative, the structure is 是不……的, not 不是……的.

李明非常诚实，他**是不**可能说谎**的**。(Do not say 他不是可能说谎的.)
Lǐ Míng fēicháng chéngshí, tā shì bù kěnéng shuōhuǎng de.
Li Ming is extremely honest. It is **not** possible that he would lie.

E. Summary of the functions of 是......的

Functions	Examples
Focus	
Who	这件事是谁告诉你的？ *Zhè jiàn shì shì shéi gàosù nǐ de?* Who told you about this matter?
Where	我爸妈是在法国认识的。 *Wǒ bàmā shì zài Fǎguó rènshì de.* My parents met in France.
How	今天我是走路来的。 *Jīntiān wǒ shì zǒulù lái de.* Today I walked here.
When	昨天晚上客人是几点走的？ *Zuótiān wǎnshàng kèrén shì jǐ diǎn zǒu de?* What time did the guests leave last night?
Purpose (of coming or going to a place)	我是来问问题的，不是来聊天的。 *Wǒ shì lái wèn wèntí de, bú shì lái liáotiān de.* I came to ask questions, not to chat.
Origin (often passive voice in English)	这本书是我妈妈写的。 *Zhè běn shū shì wǒ māma xiě de.* My mother wrote this book. (= This book was written by my mother.)
Identification and fact	
Verb	王先生是开公共汽车的。 *Wáng xiānsheng shì kāi gōnggòng qìchē de.* Mr Wang is a bus driver.
Adjective	贿赂是非法的。 *Huìlù shì fēifǎ de.* Bribery is illegal.
Emphatic expression	
Adjective	多运动对身体是很有好处的。 *Duō yùndòng duì shēntǐ shì hěn yǒu hǎochù de.* Exercising more **is** beneficial to one's health.
会, 要, 可能	这么重要的事，我是不会忘记的。 *Zhème zhòngyào de shì, wǒ shì bú huì wàngjì de.* I won't forget such an important matter.

Exercises

Choose the correct sentence based on the scenario.

1 Mr Zhang tells Mr Smith that he is a native of Beijing, not Shanghai.
   (a) 是从北京我来的，不是上海。
   (b) 我是从北京来的，不是上海。
   (c) 从北京我是来的，不是上海。

2 Miss Zhang and Miss Wang ran into each other after many years. Miss Wang asked Miss Zhang what she had been doing. Miss Zhang told her that she had written a novel. Miss Zhang would say:
   (a) 一本小说是我写的。
   (b) 我是写了一本小说的。
   (c) 我写了一本小说。

3 Mr Ding says 'Happy Birthday' to Anna and Anna asks him how he found out it was her birthday. What would Mr Ding say?
   (a) 你的男朋友告诉我的。
   (b) 你的男朋友告诉我了。
   (c) 你的男朋友是告诉我的。

4 Miss Li tells Mr Wang that she had a party at her house yesterday and that her guests went home late. And Mr Wang asks her what time they left. Mr. Wang would say:
   (a) 哦，是吗？他们是几点走的?
   (b) 哦，是吗？他们几点走了?
   (c) 哦，是吗？他们是几点走了?

5 Mrs Li tells a friend that she and her husband were in China when they married.
   (a) 我跟我先生是在中国结的婚。
   (b) 是我跟我先生在中国结婚的。
   (c) 我跟我先生在中国是结婚的。

6 Pointing at a book on her bookshelf, Miss Chen tells a visitor that her mother is the author of that book.
   (a) 我妈妈写了这本书。
   (b) 是我妈妈写这本书的。
   (c) 这本书是我妈妈写的。

7 How would you ask someone what her father's line of work was before his retirement?
   (a) 你爸爸退休以前，是做了什么?
   (b) 你爸爸退休以前，是做什么的?
   (c) 你爸爸退休以前，做什么工作了?

8 You have just learned that Wang Zhong knows a secret of yours and you want
   to know how he has come to know it.

   (a) 是谁把我的秘密告诉你的?

   (b) 谁是把我的秘密告诉你的?

   (c) 我的秘密是谁告诉的你?

9 At a department store, you saw a coat that you really liked, but you didn't buy it
   because you felt that it was too expensive. Your friend has asked you why you
   didn't buy it. How would you tell her the reason?

   (a) 因为那件大衣是太贵的，我买不起。

   (b) 因为那件大衣太贵了，我买不起。

   (c) 因为那件大衣是贵的，我买不起。

10 On the first day of school, Wang Ming tells his teacher his birth year and birth
   place.

   (a) 我一九九六年在中国是生的。

   (b) 我一九九六年是在中国生的。

   (c) 我是一九九六年在中国生的。

11 Mr Wang is found dead in his house. But nobody knows how he died.

   (a) 没有人知道王先生怎么死了。

   (b) 王先生是怎么死的，没有人知道。

   (c) 王先生是死的，可是没有人知道怎么。

12 Wang Zhong has been hospitalized. He is surprised when Zhang Ming shows
   up to visit him. What would Wang Zhong say when he sees Zhang Ming?

   (a) 张明，是你! 你怎么来了?

   (b) 张明，是你! 你是怎么来的?

   (c) 张明，是你! 你是怎么来了?

13 Wang Zhong also asks Zhang Ming if he drove there because he knows that
   Zhang Ming lives in another town. Zhang Ming tells him that he rode the train.
   Zhang Ming says:

   (a) 我来是坐火车的。

   (b) 我是来坐火车的。

   (c) 我是坐火车来的。

14 Xiaoming's mother asks him how he found out that he will soon have a sibling
   because she has not told him about her pregnancy. Xiaoming says that his
   father told him about it.

   (a) 爸爸告诉我的。

   (b) 我是爸爸告诉的。

   (c) 爸爸是告诉我的。

20 Subjectless sentences and existential sentences

Both subjectless sentences and existential sentences are unique grammatical structures in Chinese. These two types of sentence share similar grammatical features. The unique features and the similarities will be the focus of this chapter.

In addition, a group of verbs termed 'placement verbs' in this book will be introduced in this chapter. The use of placement verbs and existential sentences are closely related. ☜ Another unique sentence type which will be termed as sentences with the subject 'hidden' will be discussed, although it should not be confused with a subjectless sentence.

Both subjectless sentences and existential sentences are used to indicate the **emergence** of a new situation. Also, what emerges in the situation should be of an **indefinite nature**.

☜ Since the definiteness of a noun does not play an important role in English, what is discussed in this chapter merits special attention for learners who are English speakers.

☞ See 3.2 for more information on the definiteness of nouns.

A. Subjectless sentences

As the term indicates, a subjectless sentence is a sentence without an obvious subject. Therefore, a subjectless sentence frequently starts with a verb. However, elliptical sentences or imperative sentences are not considered subjectless sentences.

☞ See Chapter 7 for more information on the imperative sentence and 1.3 for elliptical sentences.

张：告诉我，你想吃什么？（告诉我 is an imperative sentence.）
Zhāng: Gàosù wǒ, nǐ xiǎng chī shénme?
王：想吃牛肉面。（想吃牛肉面 is an elliptical sentence, meaning 我想吃牛肉面.）
Wáng: Xiǎng chī niúròu miàn.
Zhang: Tell me, what do you want to eat?
Wang: I want to eat beef noodles.

20.1 The emergence of meteorological or natural phenomena

A subjectless sentence is used to indicate the emergence of a meteorological or natural phenomenon, that is, phenomena that are related to the weather or seasons. It is important to note that, when a subjectless sentence is used, it is usually **the first observation** or **the first mentioning** of the phenomenon.

你看，下雨了。咱们不能去公园了。

Nǐ kàn, xià yǔ le. Zánmen bù néng qù gōngyuán le.

Look, it's raining. We can't go to the park any more.

('It's raining' is being mentioned for the first time. Both occurrences of 了 indicate a new situation.)

冬天了，所以天天刮风、下雪。

Dōngtiān le, suǒyǐ tiāntiān guā fēng, xià xuě.

It's winter now. So the wind blows and it snows every day.

(冬天了 can be considered a subjectless sentence since 冬天 in this sentence is not the subject.)

Level 3

20.2 Indefinite nouns

In a subjectless sentence, what is being mentioned must be an indefinite noun.

早上下大雨，现在出大太阳，这种天气真奇怪。

Zǎoshàng xià dà yǔ, xiànzài chū dà tàiyáng, zhè zhǒng tiānqì zhēn qíguài.

It was raining hard this morning, and there is strong sunlight now. Such weather is really strange.

(太阳 in this sentence does not mean 'the sun'; it means 'sunlight'. Therefore, it is indefinite.)

Compare: 太阳每天从东边出来。

Tàiyáng měi tiān cóng dōngbiān chūlái.

The sun rises from the east every day.

(太阳 in this sentence refers to 'the sun'; it is definite. Therefore, a subjectless sentence should not be used in this case. It is incorrect to say 每天早上出来太阳.)

张：昨天天气怎么样？

Zhāng: Zuótiān tiānqì zěnmeyàng?

李：下了一场大雨，下雨的时候，还闪电、打雷呢。

(一场大雨 and 电/雷 are indefinite; therefore, it would be incorrect to say 一场大雨下了, 电闪 or 雷打.)

Lǐ: Xià le yì chǎng dà yǔ; xià yǔ de shíhòu, hái shǎn diàn, dǎ léi ne.

Zhang: How was the weather yesterday?

Li: There was a bout of heavy rain. When it was raining, there was also thunder and lightning.

Level 3

20.3 Meteorological phenomenon as definite noun

Not all meteorological or natural phenomena should be in subjectless sentences. When the phenomenon has been mentioned (and thus has become definite) or already exists in the context, the sentence should have a subject.

张：昨天又下了一场雨，恐怕要闹水灾了。（一场雨 and 水灾 are indefinite.）

Zhāng: Zuótiān yòu xià le yì chǎng yǔ, kǒngpà yào nào shuǐzāi le.

李：你放心，那场雨下得不大，不会闹水灾的。（那场雨 is definite.）

Lǐ: Nǐ fàngxīn, nà chǎng yǔ xià de bú dà, bú huì nào shuǐzāi de.

Zhang: It rained (There was rain) again yesterday. I am afraid there will soon be a flood.

Li: Don't worry. Yesterday's rain was not heavy; there won't be any flood.

王：真气人！又下雪了，咱们不能去公园了。（又下雪了 is a subjectless sentence.）

Wáng: Zhēn qìrén! Yòu xià xuě le, zánmen bù néng qù gōngyuán le.

李：这场雪大概不会下太久，雪一停咱们就走。

Lǐ: Zhè chǎng xuě dàgài bú huì xià tài jiǔ, xuě yì tíng zánmen jiù zǒu.

Wang: How annoying! It's snowing again. We can't go to the park any more.

Li: The snow probably won't last for too long. As soon as it stops, we will go.

20.4 Activities on fixed schedules

A phenomenon or an event that happens **regularly** according to a **fixed schedule** can be described by using the subjectless sentence. The schedule can be natural or man-made; also, the event should be **indefinite** or being **mentioned for the first time**.

(a) School-related activities

For example, regular school-related activities which follow a fixed schedule are frequently described by using the subjectless sentence.

王：快**期中考**了，咱们应该多学习、少玩。(快期中考了 is a subjectless sentence.)

Wáng: Kuài qīzhōngkǎo le, zánmen yīnggāi duō xuéxí, shǎo wán.

李：什么？刚**开学**怎么就要期中考了呢？(开学 is a subjectless sentence.)

Lǐ: Shénme? Gāng kāixué zěnme jiù yào qīzhōngkǎo le ne?

Wang: Mid-term exams are going to be here soon. We should study more and have less fun.

Li: What? How come school has just started and mid-term exams are coming already?

我女儿说一**放寒假**她就会回家；现在**寒假**都快**放**完了，她还没回来。
(放寒假 is subjectless; 寒假 is the subject in 寒假快放完了.)

Wǒ nǚ'ér shuō, yí fàng hánjià tā jiù huì huí jiā; xiànzài hánjià dōu kuài fàng wán le, tā hái méi huí lái.

My daughter said that she would come home as soon as the winter holidays started. But now the winter holidays are about to end and she has not come back yet.

(b) Seasons and seasonal activities

Seasons and **seasonal activities or events** can be described by using subjectless sentences.

到了夏天，总是会**出现**很多苍蝇、蚂蚁，真讨厌！(夏天 and 苍蝇，蚂蚁 are indefinite; therefore, both sentences are subjectless.)

Dào le xiàtiān, zǒngshì huì chūxiàn hěnduō cāngyíng, mǎyǐ, zhēn tǎoyàn!

When summer comes, there will always be lots of flies and ants. How annoying!

Compare:　夏天到了，苍蝇、蚂蚁也多起来了，真讨厌！
(夏天 in this sentence is definite since the sentence is uttered during summer.)
Xiàtiān dào le, cāngyíng, mǎyǐ yě duō qǐlái le, zhēn tǎoyàn.
Summer is here. Flies and ants have begun to gather. How annoying!

20.5 The emergence of a situation

As a general rule, when the verb of the sentence indicates **the emergence** of a situation and what emerges is an **indefinite noun**, the sentence is a subjectless sentence.

你开车的时候，一定要小心，否则会**出事**。(出事 is subjectless.)

Nǐ kāichē de shíhòu, yídìng yào xiǎoxīn, fǒuzé huì chū shì.

When you drive, you must be careful; otherwise, there will be accidents.

Compare:　现在**事发**了，大家都有责任。(事 is definite and is the subject in 事发了.)
Xiànzài shì fā le, dàjiā dōu yǒu zérèn.
Now the incident has occurred, everybody will bear some responsibility.

昨天晚上我正在看电视的时候，忽然**停电**了。半小时以后，**电来**了，可是我在看的那个节目已经演完了。 (停电 is subjectless; 电 in 电来了 is the subject.)

Zuótiān wǎnshàng wǒ zhèng zài kàn diànshì de shíhòu, hūrán tíng diàn le. Bàn xiǎoshí yǐhòu, diàn lái le, kěshì wǒ zài kàn de nà ge jiémù yǐjīng yǎn wán le.

Yesterday evening when I was watching TV, there was suddenly a blackout. Half an hour later, the electricity came back, but the show I had been watching was already finished.

(Situation: A restaurant owner inquires about how business is going.)

老板：昨天生意怎么样？

Lǎobǎn: Zuótiān shēngyì zěnmeyàng?

经理：很差，只**来了三位**客人。不过，**那三位**客人今天又**来了**。 (三位客人 is indefinite; 那三位客人 becomes definite.)

Jīnglǐ: Hěn chà, zhǐ lái le sān wèi kèrén. Búguò, nà sān wèi kèrén jīntiān yòu lái le.

Owner: How was business yesterday?

Manager: Not good. Only three customers came. But, those three customers came again today.

Level 3

20.6 Placement of time and location

It should be noted that a subjectless sentence does not always start with a verb. A **time phrase** or a **location** can appear before the verb. A phrase indicating time or location is not considered the subject of the sentence.

张：这里每年夏天都会**刮**几场飓风。 (这里 is the location; 每年夏天 is the time phrase.)

Zhāng: Zhèlǐ měi nián xiàtiān dōu huì guā jǐ chǎng táifēng.

李：是啊！上个月刚**刮**了一场，听说下个星期还会**刮**一场呢！

Lǐ: Shì a! Shàng ge yuè gāng guā le yì chǎng, tīngshuō xià ge xīngqī hái huì guā yì chǎng ne!

Zhang: Every year in the summer there are several typhoons here.

Li: That's right! There was one just last month. I heard that there will be another one next week!

你看，**外面**在下冰雹，咱么别去了吧。 (外面 is the location.)

Nǐ kàn, wàimiàn zai xià bīngbào, zánmen bié qù le ba.

Look, it's hailing outside. Let's not go any more.

Level 3

20.7 有/有些 + indefinite noun

A sentence can begin with 有 or 有些 followed by an **indefinite noun**. 👁 Since an English sentence can start with an indefinite noun, 有 should not be thought of as 'there be'; instead, it should be though of as 'some; certain' to indicate the indefinite nature of the subject.

有人在唱歌，你听见了没有？

Yǒu rén zài chàng gē, nǐ tīngjiàn le méiyǒu?

Someone is (*or* Some people are) singing; did you hear it?

有一个姓白的人下午打了一个电话来，你要不要给他回个电话？

Yǒu yí ge xìng Bái de rén xiàwǔ dǎ le yí ge diànhuà lái, nǐ yào bú yào gěi tā huí ge diànhuà?

Someone whose last name is Bai called you this afternoon. Do you want to call him back?

有些人以为中文很难，所以他们不敢学。 (Do not translate 有些 into 'a few'.)

Yǒu xiē rén yǐwéi Zhōngwén hěn nán, suǒyǐ tāmen bù gǎn xué.

Some people think that Chinese is difficult, so they dare not study it.

(Situation: Two teachers are discussing students' test results.)

王老师：这次考试，你们班**有没有人不及格**？
Wáng lǎoshī: Zhè cì kǎoshì, nǐmen bān yǒu méiyǒu rén bù jígé?
李老师：**没有人不及格**，有两个得到满分。
Lǐ lǎoshī: Méiyǒu rén bù jígé, yǒu liǎng ge rén dédào mǎn fēn.
Teacher Wang: Is there anyone in your class who failed the test?
Teacher Li: No one failed. Two got perfect scores.

B. Existential sentences

Existential sentences include two types of sentence. One type indicates the **emergence** or **disappearance** of a situation (and what emerges/disappears is of an **indefinite nature**); the other indicates the **existence** of something, which is also of an **indefinite nature**. The first type is very similar to the subjectless sentence discussed earlier.

20.8 The emergence or disappearance of a situation

This sentence pattern is very similar to that of the subjectless sentence. A minor difference between an existential sentence and a subjectless sentence is the fact that an existential sentence frequently starts with a location or a time phrase, whereas a subjectless sentence can begin directly with a verb.

There are three basic elements for an existential sentence indicating emergence/disappearance, and the word order for these three elements is: Location/time + verb + indefinite noun.

It should be noted that (i) the preposition 在 usually does not appear before the location/time, (ii) the verb must be one that indicates the emergence or disappearance of the noun and (iii) the noun that follows the verb must be indefinite.

我们班这学期**转走**了三个学生，**转来**了**两个**，所以这学期少了一个学生。(转走 indicates disappearance; 转来 indicates emergence.)
Wǒmen bān zhè xuéqī zhuǎn zǒu le sān ge xuéshēng, zhuǎn lái le liǎng ge, suǒyǐ zhè xuéqī shǎo le yí ge xuéshēng.
This term, three students transferred out of our class and two transferred into our class. So there is one fewer student this term.

昨天**我家来**了三位客人，妈妈说，明天还会**来**三个。(来 indicates emergence.)
Zuótiān wǒ jiā lái le sān wèi kèrén, māma shuō, míngtiān hái huì lái sān ge.
Yesterday three guests came to our house. My mother said that three more will come tomorrow.

这个地区常常**发生战争**；一打仗就会**死很多**老百姓。(发生 indicates emergence; 死 indicates disappearance.)
Zhè ge dìqū chángcháng fāshēng zhànzhēng; yì dǎzhàng jiù huì sǐ hěn duō lǎobǎixìng.
Wars frequently occur in this area. Once a war breaks out, many civilians will die.

我家对面**开了**一家中国餐馆。(开了 indicates emergence.)
Wǒ jiā duìmiàn kāi le yì jiā Zhōngguó cānguǎn.
A Chinese restaurant opened across from my house.
Compare:
(Incorrect: 桥对面**开了**一辆日本车。)(开 does **not** indicate emergence.)
Correct: 桥对面**开来**了一辆日本车。(开来 indicates emergence.)
Qiáo duìmiàn kāilái le yí liàng Rìběn chē.
A Japanese car came over from the other side of the bridge.

Level 3

20.9 The existence of a situation

There are four basic elements in this pattern. The word order for these four elements is:

Location	Placement verb	了 or 着	Indefinite noun

When the verb is 有, it is not necessary to have the particle 了 or 着. For practical purposes, 了 and 着 can be considered interchangeable in the existential sentence.

> 我家后边**有**一个菜园，菜园里**种了**各种蔬菜。
> *Wǒ jiā hòubiān yǒu yí ge càiyuán, càiyuán lǐ zhòng le gè zhǒng shūcài.*
> There is a vegetable garden behind my house; all kinds of vegetable are planted in the garden.

> 门口**停着**一辆汽车，车上**坐着**两个人。
> *Ménkǒu tíng zhe yí liàng chē, chēshàng zuò zhe liǎng ge rén.*
> A car is parked outside the door; two people are sitting in the car.

Level 3

20.10 Placement verbs

A placement verb indicates that someone or something is not actively engaged in an action, but is **in a state of rest** at a certain location as the result of that action. Frequently used placement verbs are 放 (*fàng*: 'to put'), 摆 (*bǎi*: 'to put'), 挂 (*guà*: 'to hang'), 贴 (*tiē*: 'to paste'), 坐 (*zuò*: 'to sit'), 站 (*zhàn*: 'to stand'), 躺 (*tǎng*: 'to lie'), 住 (*zhù*: 'to live'), 写 (*xiě*: 'to write'), 画 (*huà*: 'to paint; to draw'), 种 (*zhòng*: 'to plant'), 装 (*zhuāng*: 'to hold'), 停 (*tíng*: 'to park'), etc.

In an existential sentence, the placement verb + 着/了 can be replaced by 有 without seriously affecting the meaning of the sentence.

> 门上**贴着**一张纸，纸上**写着**四个我不认识的字。
> *Mén shàng tiē zhe yì zhāng zhǐ, zhǐ shàng xiě zhe sì ge wǒ bú rènshì de zì.*
> A piece of paper is pasted on the door; four characters that I don't recognize are written on the paper. (= There is a piece of paper on the door; there are four characters on the paper.)

> 墙上**挂了**一幅画，画上除了**画着**山水以外，还**写着**一首古诗。
> *Qiáng shàng guà le yì fú huà, huà shàng chúle huà zhe shānshuǐ yǐwài, hái xiě zhe yì shǒu gǔshī.*
> A painting is hanging on the wall; in addition to the landscapes painted on the painting, an ancient poem is written on it.

(a) Regular verb + indefinite subject ≠ existential sentence

A sentence with a regular verb (meaning: It is not a placement verb) cannot be used in an existential sentence, even if the subject (in its English counterpart) is indefinite.

> English: A boy is standing under the tree. (This is an existential sentence.)
> Chinese: 树下**站**着一个小男孩。
> *Shùxià zhàn zhe yí ge xiǎo nánhái.*

> English: A boy is crying under the tree. ('To cry' is not a placement verb.)
> Chinese: 有一个小男孩在树下**哭**。
> *Yǒu yí ge xiǎo nánhái zài shùxià kū.*
> (It is incorrect to say 树下哭着一个小男孩.)

(b) Placement verb + definite subject ≠ existential sentence

A sentence with a placement verb but a definite noun cannot be in an existential sentence.

English:	A man is sitting behind the table. (This is an existential sentence.)
Chinese:	桌子后面**坐着一个人**。
	Zhuōzi hòumiàn zuò zhe yí ge rén.

English:	Mr Wang is sitting behind the table. ('Mr Wang' is definite.)
Chinese #1:	**王先生**在桌子后面坐着。
	Wáng xiānsheng zài zhuōzi hòumiàn zuò zhe.
Chinese #2:	**王先生**坐在桌子后面。
	Wáng xiānsheng zuò zài zhuōzi hòumiàn.
(Incorrect:	桌子后面坐着王先生。)

(c) Unknown information

Occasionally, it is possible for a sentence with a definite noun and a placement verb to be an existential sentence if the definite noun is something/someone that the speaker **did not expect to encounter** when uttering the sentence. In other words, it is 'unknown information'.

王小姐给了我一张条子，我打开一看，上面写着**她的电话号码**。
Wáng xiǎojiě gěi le wǒ yì zhāng tiáozi, wǒ dǎkāi yí kàn, shàngmiàn xiě zhe tāde diànhuà hàomǎ.
Miss Wang handed me a note. I opened it and saw that her phone number was written on it.

Compare:	李：王小姐的电话号码**写在**哪里？
	Lǐ: Wáng xiǎojiě de diànhuà hàomǎ xiě zài nǎlǐ?
	张：她的手机号码就**写在**这张纸上；我没有她家的号码。
	Zhāng: Tāde shǒujī hàomǎ jiù xiě zài zhè zhāng zhǐ shàng; wǒ méiyǒu tā jiā de hàomǎ.
	Li: Where is Miss Wang's phone number written?
	Zhang: Her mobile phone number is written right on this piece of paper. I don't have her home phone number.

20.11 Forming sentences with definite/indefinite nouns and placement verbs

There are four scenarios when forming these kinds of sentence.

(a) Placement verb + indefinite noun

The sentence has a **placement verb** and an **indefinite noun**: Such a sentence should be an **existential sentence**.

墙上贴了**两张**小学生画的画；一张上面**画着**马，一张上面**画着**房子。
Qiáng shàng tiē le liǎng zhāng xiǎo xuéshēng huà de huà; yì zhāng shàngmiàn huà zhe mǎ, yì zhāng shàngmiàn huà zhe fángzi.
On the wall were pasted two drawings by school pupils; one had a horse drawn on it; the other had a house drawn on it.

(b) Placement verb + definite noun

The sentence has **a placement verb** and a **definite noun**. There are **two ways** to construct such a sentence: the location can appear before the verb, or it can appear after the verb.

| Definite noun | 在 + location | Placement verb | 着 | Example: 我的车在树下停着。
Wǒ de chē zài shù xià tíng zhe. |
| Definite noun | | Placement verb | 在 + location | Example: 我的车停在树下。
Wǒ de chē tíng zài shù xià. |

- When the location appears before the verb, 着 must follow the placement verb

  我们新买的沙发就在客厅里**摆着**，爸爸却在地板上**坐着**，真奇怪！
  Wǒmen xīnmǎi de shāfā jiù zài kètīng lǐ bǎi zhe, bàba què zài dìbǎn shàng zuò zhe, zhēn qíguài!
  The newly purchased couch is placed right there in the living room, but my father is sitting on the floor. This is really strange.

- When the location appears after the verb, 着 should not be used

  李家的两个儿子都还**住在**家里；老大跟他太太住在二楼，老二睡在客房里。
  Lǐ jiā de liǎng ge érzi dōu hái zhù zài jiā lǐ; lǎodà gēn tā tàitai zhù zài èrlóu, lǎo'èr shuì zài kèfáng lǐ.
  Both sons of the Li family still live at home. The elder son and his wife live on the second floor; the younger son sleeps in the guest room.

(c) Subject, placement verb + indefinite noun

The sentence has a **placement verb**, an **indefinite noun** and a **subject** that performs the action of the placement verb. This would be considered a **regular sentence** and the placement verb would not play a special role in arranging the word order.

English:	Mr Wang wrote many characters on this piece of paper. (写 is a placement verb.)
Chinese:	王先生在这张纸上写了很多字。 *Wáng xiānsheng zài zhè zhāng zhǐ shàng xiě le hěn duō zì.*
Compare:	Mr Wang made many Chinese friends in the USA. (认识 is not a placement verb.) 王先生在美国认识了很多中国朋友。 *Wáng xiānsheng zài Měiguó rènshì le hěn duō Zhōngguó péngyǒu.*

(d) Subject, placement verb + definite noun

The sentence has a **placement verb**, a **definite noun** and a **subject** that performs the action of the placement verb. Either the 把 **structure** (☞ see Chapter 21) can be used or the definite noun should be **pre-posed**.

王：我昨天买的那两本词典，你们**放在**哪里了？
Wáng: Wǒ zuótiān mǎi de nà liǎng běn cídiǎn, nǐmen fàng zài nǎlǐ le?
张：我**把**那本中文的**放在**你的书房里；他**把**英文的**放在**这个书架上。
Zhāng: Wǒ bǎ nà běn Zhōngwén de fàng zài nǐde shūfáng lǐ; tā bǎ Yīngwén de fàng zài zhè ge shūjià shàng. (Do not say 我放那本中文的在你的书房里/他放那本英文的在书架上.)
Wang: Where did you (plural) put the two dictionaries that I bought yesterday?
Zhang: I put the Chinese one in your study; he put the English one on this bookshelf.

王：你把张小姐的电话号码**写在**哪里？
Wáng: Nǐ bǎ Zhāng xiǎojiě de diànhuà hàomǎ xiě zài nǎlǐ?

李：她的手机号码，我**写在**这张纸上；她家的号码，我**写在**电话本子里了。

Lǐ: Tāde shǒujī hàomǎ, wǒ xiě zài zhè zhāng zhǐ shàng; tā jiā de hàomǎ, wǒ xiě zài diànhuà běnzi lǐ le.

Wang: Where did you write down Miss Zhang's phone number?

Li: I wrote her mobile phone number on this piece of paper and her home number in the phonebook.

(e) Summary

The following table gives a summary of the four placement verb scenarios.

Two major components	Word orders and examples
1 Placement verb + indefinite noun	Location + verb + 着/了 + indefinite noun 树下停着（or 停了）一辆车。 *Shù xià tíng zhe (or tíng le) yí liàng chē.* A car is parked under the tree.
2 Placement verb + definite noun	(a) Definite noun + verb + 在 + location 我的车停在树下。 *Wǒde chē tíng zài shù xià.* My car is parked under the tree. (b) Definite noun + 在 + location + verb + 着 我的车在树下停着。 *Wǒde chē zài shù xià tíng zhe.* My car is parked under the tree.
Three major components	
3 Subject, placement verb + indefinite noun	Subject + 在 + location + verb 他在花园里种了很多花。 *Tā zài huāyuán lǐ zhòng le hěn duō huā.* He planted many flowers in the garden.
4 Subject, placement verb + definite noun	(a) Definite noun + subject + verb + 在 + location 那本书，他放在书架上了。 *Nà běn shū, tā fàng zài shūjià shàng le.* He put that book on the bookshelf. (b) Subject + 把 + definite noun + verb + 在 + location 他把那本书放在书架上了。 *Tā bǎ nà běn shū fàng zài shūjià shàng le.* He put that book on the bookshelf.

C. Sentences with the subject 'hidden'

In a sentence with the subject 'hidden', the subject can be identified but is not used. In a subjectless sentence, no obvious subject can be identified. Also, a sentence with the subject 'hidden' does not involve any special word order.

When the subject is the '**generic public**' or the '**general public**' (meaning: 'everyone') and the predicate has an **auxiliary verb** indicating '**can, must, need**' or a **potential structure** (☞ see Chapter 17), the subject is usually 'hidden'. In English, the subject is frequently 'you' or 'one', referring to the 'generic public'.

王：请问，这里**可不可以**停车？ (The 'hidden' subject is the general public.)
Wáng: Qǐng wèn, zhèlǐ kě bù kěyǐ tíngchē?
停车场管理员：**你**不可以在这里停，因为你没有停车证。 (The subject 你 is not 'hidden' since it is specifically about Wang.)
Tíngchē chǎng guǎnlǐ yuán: Nǐ bù kěyǐ zài zhèlǐ tíng, yīnwèi nǐ méiyǒu tíngchē zhèng.
Wang: Excuse me, can one park here? (Is parking allowed here?)
Parking attendant: You cannot park here because you don't have a parking permit.

张：这里**可以不可以**游泳？
Zhāng: Zhèlǐ kěyǐ bù kěyǐ yóuyǒng?
李：水太深了，这里**不可以**游泳。
Lǐ: Shuǐ tài shēn le, zhèlǐ bù kěyǐ yóuyǒng.
(There are no subjects for these sentences since the 'hidden' subject is the general public.)
Zhang: Can I swim here? (Meaning: Can anyone swim here?)
Li: The water is too deep. You cannot swim here. (Meaning: No one is allowed to swim here.)

(一个人)只要多听、多读、多说，就**能**学好外语。 (一个人 is optional since it is generic.)
(Yí ge rén) zhǐyào duō tīng, duō dú, duō shuō, jiù néng xuéhǎo wàiyǔ.
As long as **one** listens more, reads more and speaks more, one can master a foreign language.

在中国，**大家**都喜欢熊猫。
Zài Zhōngguó, dàjiā dōu xǐhuān xióngmāo.
(大家 is not 'hidden' since there is no auxiliary verb indicating 'can, must, need, etc.')
In China, everybody likes pandas.
Compare:　在中国，去动物园就**看得到**熊猫。
　　　　　　Zài Zhōngguó, qù dòngwùyuán jiù kàn de dào xióngmāo.
　　　　　　(The subject is 'hidden' since there is a potential phrase 看得到.)
　　　　　　In China, one can see pandas as long as one goes to the zoo.

D.　Summary: Subjectless sentences and existential sentences

The following tables show the word orders and grammatical requirements for, and some examples of, subjectless and existential sentences.

Structure	Location/time	Verb	Third element	Noun
Subjectless				
Meteorological or natural phenomena	Optional	Yes	Optional	Indefinite
Event on regular, fixed schedule	Optional	Yes	Optional	Indefinite
有/没有	Optional	有/没有	No	Indefinite

Existential				
Emergence (or disappearance)	Yes (can be skipped in context)	Showing emergence or disappearance	Yes (if verb does not show emergence or disappearance)	Indefinite
Existence	Yes (can be skipped in context)	Placement verb	了 or 着	Indefinite

Structure	Example
Subjectless	
Meteorological or natural phenomena	1 昨天下了一场雨。 *Zuótiān xià le yì chǎng yǔ.* It rained yesterday. 2 这个地区常常下雨。 *Zhè ge dìqū chángcháng xià yǔ.* It often rains here.
Event on regular, fixed schedule	1 到了夏天，蚊虫会很多。 *Dào le xiàtiān, wénchóng huì hěn duō.* When summer comes, there will be many insects. 2 下个星期就要开学了。 *Xià ge xīngqī jiù yào kāi xué le.* School will open next week. (The term will start next week.)
有/没有	1 这个教室里有三十把椅子。 *Zhè ge jiàoshì lǐ yǒu sānshí bǎ yǐzi.* There are 30 chairs in this classroom. 2 没有人会回答这个问题。 *Méiyǒu rén huì huídá zhè ge wèntí.* No one knows how to answer this question.
Existential	
Emergence (or disappearance)	1 昨天来了三个客人，明天还会来三个。 *Zuótiān lái le sān ge kèrén, míngtiān hái huì lái sān ge.* Three guests came yesterday; three more will come tomorrow. 2 我家门口开来一辆车，车上下来几个人。 *Wǒ jiā ménkǒu kāi lái yí liàng chē, chē shàng xià lái jǐ ge rén.* A car came to my front door; a couple of people emerged from the car.
Existence	墙上贴了一张纸，纸上写着几个字。 *Qiáng shàng tiē le yì zhāng zhǐ, zhǐ shàng xiě zhe jǐ ge zì.* A piece of paper is pasted on the wall, some characters are written on it.

Exercises

Write sentences in Chinese based on the given situations. Use subjectless sentences or existential sentences whenever possible.

Level

3

1 Only three customers came to a newly opened restaurant yesterday; but the same three customers came again today. The restaurant owner asks the manager how business is. How would the manager describe the situation to him?

2 Anna moved to a new town during winter, where there was strong wind every day and it sometimes snowed as well. How would she describe the winter in a letter to a friend?

3 In a subsequent letter, Anna tells her friend that it's spring time now and that although it rains sometimes, it is rarely windy. How would she describe this situation?

4 On a rainy day, Miss Wang calls Li Ming to cancel their date because it is raining too heavily and she does not like going out when it's pouring. How would she use two sentences to explain this to Li Ming?

5 Mr Wang asks his wife where she has written down Mr Zhang's mobile phone number. His wife tells him that two numbers are written on the calendar, but she does not know which one is Mr Zhang's. Create a short dialogue between Mr and Mrs Wang.

6 Mrs Li had been taking a nap in the bedroom upstairs. Her young son woke her up and informed her that two strangers had just arrived and were downstairs. What would the little boy have said to his mother?

7 Upon seeing bird droppings on her new car, Mrs Zhang angrily asks her son why he parked her car under the tree again. Her son explains that there were several huge boxes stored (= placed) in their garage when he came home and that he could not park the car in the garage. Create a short dialogue between Mrs Zhang and her son.

8 Mr Zhang met a young woman at a party yesterday evening. She wrote something (a few words) on a piece of paper before she left the party and put that note into Mr Zhang's pocket. Upon unfolding (opening) the piece of paper, Mr Zhang realized that she had written her name and phone number on it. How would Mr Zhang describe this to his roommate?

9 Wang Ming comes to visit Li Zhong at his house. He sees an expensive car outside Li Zhong's house. He remembers having heard that Li Zhong has just bought an expensive car. When he enters Li Zhong's house, he says that an expensive car is parked right outside and asks if it is his new car. But Li Zhong says that his car is parked in his garage now and that he would not park his new car on the street. Create a dialogue between Wang Ming and Li Zhong.

10 Anna has just moved into a new building. She has recently met an old man whose last name is Zhang and he and his wife live on the third floor. Mr Zhang has told her that two Americans are living above her on the second floor and that altogether five families live in the building. How would Anna describe her building to a friend?

21 The 把 structure

The 把 (bǎ) structure is a structure unique to Chinese; it requires the object of the verb to be placed before the verb. In terms of word order, there is no equivalent in English; learners who are English speakers should pay special attention to this structure. The following is the basic word order:

Subject	把	Object (definite noun)	Verb	Other element

21.1 The three basic rules when forming a 把 sentence

The following three rules must be kept in mind before constructing a 把 sentence.

(a) Verb restrictions

Not all verbs can be used in a 把 sentence. Verbs that **do not indicate actions**, such as 有 (yǒu), 在 (zài) and 是 (shì), cannot be used in a 把 sentence; neither can verbs that indicate **emotional feelings**, such as 喜欢 (xǐhuān: 'to like'), 讨厌 (tǎoyàn: 'to dislike'), 希望 (xīwàng: 'to hope') and 怕 (pà: 'to fear'), **mental status**, such as 相信 (xiāngxìn: 'to believe') 知道 (zhīdào: 'to know'), 同意 (tóngyì: 'to agree'), 懂 (dǒng: 'to understand') and 了解 (liǎojiě: 'to understand') or **senses**, such as 看见 (kànjiàn: 'to see'), 听到 (tīngdào: 'to hear') and 闻到 (wéndào: 'to smell'). Verbs indicating **going to places** (来 (lái), 去 (qù), 回 (huí), 进 (jìn), 到 (dào), etc.) cannot be used in a 把 sentence, either.

王小姐**喜欢**小张，**讨厌**小李。
Wáng xiǎojiě xǐhuān Xiǎo Zhāng, tǎoyàn Xiǎo Lǐ.
Miss Wang likes Xiao Zhang and dislikes Xiao Li.
(Incorrect: 王小姐把小张喜欢了，把小李讨厌了。)

上个月我**去**了一趟北京。
Shàng ge yuè wǒ qù le yí tàng Běijīng.
I made a trip to Beijing last month.
(Incorrect: 上个月我把北京去了一趟。)

(b) Definite objects

The object after 把 should **not** be indefinite.

王老师写了**一本**语法书。 (一本语法书 is indefinite.)
Wáng lǎoshī xiě le yì běn yǔfǎ shū.
Teacher Wang wrote a grammar book.
(Incorrect: 王老师把一本语法书写了。)

(c) Need 'other element' after verb

A 把 sentence should not end with a verb. Another element must follow the verb.
(☞ See 21.3 for elaboration.)

妈妈：小明，来，吃药。

Māma: Xiǎo Míng, lái, chī yào.

= 小明，来，把药**吃了**。 (It would be incorrect to say 把药吃 since 吃 is a verb.)

= *Xiǎoming, lái, bǎ yào chī le.*

Mother: Xiaoming, come and take the medicine.

老师：哪位同学愿意回答这个问题？

Lǎoshī: Nǎ wèi tóngxué yuànyì huídá zhè ge wèntí?

= 哪位同学愿意把这个问题回答一下？ (Do not say 把这个问题回答。)

= *Nǎ wèi tóngxué yuànyì bǎ zhè ge wèntí huídá yíxià?*

Teacher: Which of you is willing to answer this question?

21.2 The 把 structure vs. S + V + O/O + S + V structures

In many instances, a sentence with 把 can be considered interchangeable with a regular (subject + verb + definite object) sentence or a sentence with a pre-posed object (pre-posed object + subject + verb).

(a) Nuanced differences

In the actual use of the language, the three structures may have nuanced differences and thus be used in difference contexts/situations.

张：昨天是星期天，你做了些什么？

Zhāng: Zuótiān shì xīngqī tiān, nǐ zuò le xiē shénme?

王：下午**洗衣服**，晚上**看书**，没有做别的事。

Wáng: Xiàwǔ xǐ yīfú, wǎnshàng kàn shū, méiyǒu zuò biéde shì.

(洗衣服 and 看书 are considered two activities with no emphasis on either 衣服 or 书.)

Zhang: Yesterday was Sunday; what did you do?

Wang: I did the laundry (= I washed my clothes) in the afternoon and I read in the evening. I didn't do anything else.

妈妈：咦？房间里的脏衣服、脏床单呢？

Māma: Yí? Fángjiān lǐ de zāng yīfú, zāng chuángdān ne?

儿子：我**把**衣服洗了，爸爸**把**床单送到干洗店了。(把 is used to show what happened to the two items previously mentioned. 衣服 and 床单 can be pre-posed as well.)

Érzi: Wǒ bǎ yīfú xǐ le, bàba bǎ chuángdān sòng dào gānxǐ diàn le.

Mother: Hey? What happened to those dirty clothes and dirty bed sheets that were in the bedroom?

Son: I washed the clothes and Father took the bed sheets to the dry cleaner.

妈妈：小明，交待你洗的那两样东西，你都洗了吗？

Māma: Xiǎomíng, jiāodài nǐ xǐ de nà liǎng yàng dōngxi, nǐ dōu xǐ le ma?

小明：衣服我洗了，碗还没洗。

Xiǎomíng: Yīfú wǒ xǐ le, wǎn hái méi xǐ.

(In this situation, 衣服 and 碗 are **pre-posed** to show the **contrast** between the two.)

Mother: Xiaoming, did you wash those two things I asked you to wash?

Xiaoming: I washed the clothes, but I haven't washed the dishes.

(b) No distinction necessary

When the object of the verb is in context, it may not be necessary to make the distinction between a 把 sentence and a sentence with the pre-posed object. In spontaneous speeches, the choice between the two by a native speaker of Chinese may not be a conscious one.

妈妈：咦？房间里的脏衣服、脏床单呢？

Māma: Yí? Fángjiān lǐ de zāng yīfú, zāng chuángdān ne?

儿子：衣服，我洗了；床单，爸爸送到干洗店了。

Érzi: Yīfú, wǒ xǐ le; chuángdān, bàba sòng dào gānxǐ diàn le.

Mother: Hey? What happened to those dirty clothes and dirty bed sheets that were in the bedroom?

Son: I washed the clothes and Father took the bed sheets to the dry cleaner.

21.3 The 'other element'

evel
3

A 把 sentence cannot end with a verb, but must end with something other than a verb. The 'other element' that appears after the verb can be one of the following.

(a) A complement

A complement (of state, direction, quantity or result) is the most frequently used element that follows the verb in a 把 sentence.

☞ See Chapter 12 for the complement of state, Chapter 14 for the complement of quantity, Chapter 15 for the complement of direction and Chapter 16 for the complement of result.

上床以前，别忘了把窗户关**起来**，把门锁**好**。

Shàngchuáng yǐqián, bié wàng le bǎ chuānghù guān qǐlái, bǎ mén suǒ hǎo.

Before going to bed, don't forget to close the windows and lock the door.

(起来 is the complement of direction; 好 is the complement of result.)

妈妈：小明，你先把碗洗**干净**，再把垃圾拿**出去**。

Māma: Xiǎomíng, nǐ xiān bǎ wǎn xǐ gānjìng, zài bǎ lājī ná chūqù.

小明：我在写功课呢。让我先把功课写**完**。

Xiǎomíng: Wǒ zài xiě gōngkè ne. Ràng wǒ xiān bǎ gōngkè xiě wán.

(干净 and 完 are the complements of result; 出去 is the complement of direction.)

Mother: Xiaoming, first wash the dishes (clean) and then take out the garbage.

Xiaoming: I am doing homework. Let me finish doing homework first.

他把送女朋友的生日礼物包得**非常漂亮**，可是他女朋友竟然把这个礼物退**回来**了。

Tā bǎ sòng nǚ péngyǒu de shēngrì lǐwù bāo de fēicháng piàoliàng, kěshì tā nǚ péngyǒu jìngrán bǎ zhè ge lǐwù tuì huílái le.

He wrapped up his birthday gift for his girlfriend beautifully, but surprisingly his girlfriend returned this gift (to him).

(非常漂亮 is the complement of state; 回来 is the complex complement of direction.)

你先把这篇文章看**几遍**，再把你的看法写**下来**。

Nǐ xiān bǎ zhè piān wénzhāng kàn jǐ biàn, zài bǎ nǐde kànfǎ xiě xiàlái.

Read this article a few times and then write down your opinions.

(几遍 is the complement of quantity; 下来 is the complex complement of direction.)

昨天妈妈把小明骂了**一顿**，因为他没有把功课写**完**就出去玩了。

Zuótiān māma bǎ Xiǎomíng mà le yí dùn, yīnwèi tā méiyǒu bǎ gōngkè xiě wán jiù chūqù wán le.

Yesterday Xiaoming's mother scolded him because he went out to play without finishing doing his homework.

(一顿 is the complement of quantity; 完 is the complement of result.)

👁 It should be noted that a verb plus the complement of result frequently forms only one word in English. Such a combination should not be mistaken for one verb.

English: I must **break** Xiao Wang's record today.

Chinese: 我今天一定要把小王的记录打**破**。 (打 is the verb; 破 is the complement of result.)

Wǒ jīntiān yídìng yào bǎ Xiǎo Wáng de jìlù dǎ pò.

English: You must **answer** this question today.

Chinese: 你今天一定要把这个问题**回答**一下。 (回答 is the verb. 回 and 答 cannot be separated.)

Nǐ jīntiān yídìng yào bǎ zhè ge wèntí huídá yíxià.

今天你不把这件事解释一下，就不准你回家。

Jīntiān nǐ bù bǎ zhè jiàn shì jiěshì yíxià, jiù bù zhǔn nǐ huíjiā.

If you don't explain this matter today, I won't allow you to go home.

(解释 is the verb; 解 and 释 cannot be separated.)

Compare: 今天你不把那本书找**到**，就不准你吃饭。

Jīntiān nǐ bù bǎ nà běn shū zhǎodào, jiù bù zhǔn nǐ chīfàn.

If you don't find that book today, I won't allow you to eat.

(找 is the verb 'to look'; 到 is the complement of result; 找到 means 'to find'.)

The **complement of potential cannot** be used in a 把 sentence.

☞ See Chapter 17 for more information on the complement of potential.

你八点以前能不能把这件事做**完**?

Nǐ bā diǎn yǐqián néng bù néng bǎ zhè jiàn shì zuò wán?

Can you finish doing this thing by 8 o'clock?

(It is incorrect to say 你八点以前把这件事做得完做不完?)

(b) 了

If the verb does not need a complement to complete its meaning, 了 can be used after the verb. When the action has taken place, 了 can be used as the other element following the verb.

他把妈妈的劝告全忘了，离开家没多久，就把钱都花了。

Tā bǎ māma de quàngào quán wàng le, líkāi jiā méi duō jiǔ, jiù bǎ qián dōu huā le.

He forgot his mother's advice. Soon after he left home, he spent all the money.

王先生本来欠了不少钱；上个月他把房子卖了，所以把欠的债都还了。

Wáng xiānsheng běnlái qiàn le bùshǎo qián; shàng ge yuè tā bǎ fángzi mài le, suǒyǐ bǎ qiàn de zhài dōu huán le.

Originally Mr Wang owed a lot of money; he sold his house last month and so he has settled all his debt (returned all the money he owed).

Even if the action has not taken place, 了 can still be used to indicate that, as the result of the action, something will be **gone** or **reach the finale**. In this case, 了 has a function similar to the complement of result.

把电视关了，不许再看了。

Bǎ diànshì guān le, bù xǔ zài kàn le.

Turn off the TV. You are not allowed to watch any more.

快把瓶子里的水喝了，喝完以后，就可以把瓶子扔了。

Kuài bǎ píngzi lǐ de shuǐ hē le, hē wán yǐhòu, jiù kěyǐ bǎ píngzi rēng le.

Hurry and finish the water in the bottle. After you are done, you can throw away the bottle.

(c) A reduplicated verb or 'verb + 一下(儿)'

If neither a complement nor 了 can be used in the sentence, the verb can be reduplicated or 一下(儿) can be used after the verb. ☞ See Chapter 26 for more on verb reduplication.

老师：请大家回家去把这个问题的答案**想(一)想**。
Lǎoshī: Qǐng dàjiā huí jiā qù bǎ zhè ge wèntí de dá'àn xiǎng (yì) xiǎng.
学生：您可不可以把这个问题先**说明一下(儿)**。（说明 is a two-character word.）
Xuéshēng: Nín kě bù kěyǐ bǎ zhè ge wèntí xiān shuōmíng yíxià(r).
Teacher: Everybody please go home to think (for a while) about the answer to this question.
Student: Could you first explain the question a little bit?

你先把这个报告**看一下(儿)**，看完以后，再把你的意见**说一说**。
Nǐ xiān bǎ zhè ge bàogào kàn yíxià(r), kàn wán yǐhòu, zài bǎ nǐde yìjiàn shuō yì shuō.
First you read this report. State your opinions after you are done reading it.

(d) An indirect object

When the verb has two objects (a direct object and an indirect object), the direct object appears after 把 and the **indirect object** appears after the verb as **the other element**. Normally, a person would be the indirect object.

☞ See 1.5 for more information on direct objects and indirect objects.

王：你打算什么时候把这本书还**他**？
Wáng: Nǐ dǎsuàn shénme shíhòu bǎ zhè běn shū huán tā?
李：他已经把这本书送**我**了，所以我不用还他。
Lǐ: Tā yǐjīng bǎ zhè běn shū sòng wǒ le, suǒyǐ wǒ búyòng huán tā.
Wang: When do you plan to return this book to him?
Li: He has already given this book to me; so I don't have to return it to him.

丁：老张，我上星期去面谈的那家公司已经把结果通知**我**了，他们录取我了。
Dīng: Lǎo Zhāng, wǒ shàng xīngqī qù miàntán de nà jiā gōngsī yǐjīng bǎ jiéguǒ tōngzhī wǒ le, tāmen lùqǔ wǒ le.
张：哦，是吗？太好了！你打算什么时候把现在的工作辞**了**？
Zhāng: Ò, shìma? Tài hǎo le. Nǐ dǎsuàn shénme shíhòu bǎ xiànzài de gōngzuò cí le?
丁：还没决定，所以请你暂时别把这件事告诉**别人**。
Dīng: Hái méi juédìng. Suǒyǐ qǐng nǐ zànshí bié bǎ zhè jiàn shì gàosù biérén.
Ding: Lao Zhang, the company I went to have an interview with already notified me of the result; they have decided to hire me.
Zhang: Oh, is that so? Great! When do you plan to quit your current job?
Ding: I have not decided yet. So, for the time being, please don't tell anybody about this matter.

21.4 Exception: When 把 sentences *can* end with a verb

In rare situations, it is possible to end a 把 sentence with a verb.

(a) Prepositional phrase + verb

Occasionally a verb following a prepositional phrase can end a 把 sentence.

小王叫我不要把他的秘密**跟任何人**说。
Xiǎo Wáng jiào wǒ bú yào bǎ tāde mìmì gēn rènhé rén shuō.
Xiao Wang asked me not to tell anybody his secrets.

小明，你真可恶！你怎么可以把香蕉皮**往我身上扔**？

Xiǎomíng, nǐ zhēn kěwù! Nǐ zěnme kěyǐ bǎ xiāngjiāo pí wǎng wǒ shēnshàng rēng?

Xiaoming, you are really nasty! How can you throw the banana peel onto me?

(b) 一 + verb

Sometimes a verb with 一 before it can end a 把 sentence. 一 implies that the action is done with determination or strong force.

你只要把这个按钮用力**一按**，抽屉就会自动打开。

Nǐ zhǐyào bǎ zhè ge ànniǔ yònglì yí àn, chōutì jiù huì zìdòng dǎkāi.

As long as you push this button hard once, the drawer will open automatically.

老王每次看到让他不舒服的事，就把眼睛**一闭**，假装没有看到。

Lǎo Wáng měi cì kàndào ràng tā bù shūfú de shì, jiù bǎ yǎnjīng yí bì, jiǎzhuāng méiyǒu kàndào.

Every time Lao Wang sees something that annoys him, he closes his eyes and pretends not to have seen it.

Level 3

21.5 Some special 把 sentences

Five types of special 把 sentence will be discussed in the following section. Each of these kinds of 把 sentence **cannot** be converted into a regular S + V + O sentence. However, the object can be pre-posed.

(a) 在 + a location

In this kind of sentence, the other element is 在 + **a location** and the verb indicates an action that causes something (of a definite nature) to be **fixed in the location**. Such a verb is a placement verb and can include 放 (*fàng*: 'to put'), 挂 (*guà*: 'to hang'), 写 (*xiě*: 'to write'), 画 (*huà*: 'to paint'), 停 (车) (*tíngchē*: 'to park cars'), 拿 (*ná*: 'to hold'), 忘 (*wàng*: 'to forget'), 留 (*liú*: 'to leave behind'), 种 (*zhòng*: 'to plant'), 藏 (*cáng*: 'to hide'), etc.

☞ See 20.10 for more information on the use of placement verbs.

王太太：我叫你别把我的车**停在**树下，你为什么不听？ (Do not say 别停我的车在树下.)

Wáng tàitai: Wǒ jiào nǐ bié bǎ wǒde chē tíng zài shù xià, nǐ wèishénme bù tīng?

王先生：你把旧家具都**放在**车库里，车库已经满了，要是我不把车**停在**树下，还有什么地方可以停呢？ (Do not say 你放旧家具在车库里.)

Wáng xiānsheng: Nǐ bǎ jiù jiājù dōu fàng zài chēkù lǐ, chēkù yǐjīng mǎn le, yàoshi wǒ bù bǎ chē tíng zài shù xià, hái yǒu shénme dìfāng kěyǐ tíng ne?

Mrs Wang: I told you not to park my car under the tree; why wouldn't you listen?

Mr Wang: You put all the old furniture in the garage; the garage is already full. If I don't park the car under the tree, where else can I park?

老师：我把出席表**摆在**这张桌子上；别忘了来把自己的名字**写在**出席表上。

Lǎoshī: Wǒ bǎ chūxíbiǎo bǎi zài zhè zhāng zhuōzi shàng; bié wàng le lái bǎ zìjǐ de míngzi xiě zài chūxíbiǎo shàng.

(Do not say 我摆出席表在这张桌子上/写自己的名字在出席表上.)

学生：老师，你不是已经把今天的出席表**贴在**墙上了吗？

Xuéshēng: Lǎoshī, nǐ bú shì yǐjīng bǎ jīntiān de chūxíbiǎo tiē zài qiáng shàng le ma?

(Do not say 你已经贴今天的出席表在墙上了.)

Teacher: I'll put the attendance form on this desk. Don't forget to write your own names on the attendance form before leaving the classroom.

Student: Sir, didn't you already paste today's attendance form on the wall?

(b) 到 + a location

In this type of sentence, the other element is **到 + a location** and the verb indicates the action of **shifting** something or someone (of a definite nature) **from one location to another**. Such verbs include 搬 (*bān*: 'to move'), 拿 (*ná*: 'to hold'), 带 (*dài*: 'to carry'), 送 (*sòng*: 'to deliver'), 寄 (*jì*: 'to mail'), 开 (车) (*kāichē*: 'to drive'), 骑 (*qí*: 'to ride bicycle/horse'), 放 (*fàng*: 'to put'), etc. Such an expression is the same in meaning as when the other element is a complement of direction.

> 请把这张桌子搬**到楼上去**。(= 请把这张桌子搬上楼去。)
> *Qǐng bǎ zhè zhāng zhuōzi bān dào lóushàng qù.*
> Please move this table upstairs.

> 那个地方不能停车，你快去把你的车开**到收费停车场去**吧！
> *Nà ge dìfāng bù néng tíngchē, nǐ kuài qù bǎ nǐde chē kāi dào shōufèi tíngchēchǎng qù ba!*
> That place is a no-parking zone. Hurry and go move (drive) your car to the pay car park.

> 小明忽然昏倒了，老师立刻叫来救护车把他**送到医院去**。(= 把他送去医院)
> *Xiǎomíng hūrán hūndǎo le, lǎoshī lìkè jiào lái jiùhùchē bǎ tā sòng dào yīyuàn qù.*
> Xiaoming suddenly passed out. The teacher immediately called for an ambulance to take him to hospital.

(c) 给 + a person

In these sentences, the other element is **给 + a person** and the verb indicates an action that causes something (of a definite nature) to **change hands** or certain information (of a definite nature) to **be conveyed**. Such verbs include 带 (*dài*: 'to carry'), 拿 (*ná*: 'to hold'), 寄 (*jì*: 'to mail'), 交 (*jiāo*: 'to hand'), 送 (*sòng*: 'to give a present'), 借 (*jiè*: 'to lend'), 还 (*huán*: 'to return'), 留 (*liú*: 'to leave behind'), 介绍 (*jièshào*: 'to introduce'), etc.

> 请你帮我把这封信交**给王小姐**，好不好？
> *Qǐng nǐ bāng wǒ bǎ zhè fēng xìn jiāo gěi Wáng xiǎojiě, hǎo bù hǎo?*
> Could you please hand this letter to Miss Wang for me?

> 张先生打算把遗产全部都留**给他女儿**。
> *Zhāng xiānsheng dǎsuàn bǎ yíchǎn quánbù dōu liú gěi tā nǚ'ér.*
> Mr Zhang plans to leave all his estate to his daughter.

> 小王没有女朋友，所以我想把我妹妹介绍**给他**。
> *Xiǎo Wáng méiyǒu nǚ péngyǒu, suǒyǐ wǒ xiǎng bǎ wǒ mèimei jièshào gěi tā.*
> Xiao Wang does not have a girlfriend; so I am thinking of introducing my younger sister to him.

(d) 成 + a noun

When the other element is **成 + a noun**, there are two implications:

• The action of the verb results in the **transformation** or **creation** of something

> 小李把他妈妈的一生**写成**了一本小说。
> *Xiǎo Lǐ bǎ tā māma de yìshēng xiě chéng le yì běn xiǎoshuō.*
> Xiao Li wrote his mother's life into a novel. (= Xiao Li wrote a novel based on his mother's life.)

> 我打算把这本英文书**翻译成**中文。
> *Wǒ dǎsuàn bǎ zhè běn Yīngwén shū fānyì chéng Zhōngwén.*
> I plan to translate this English book into Chinese.

今天的语法练习是把肯定句**改成**问句。

Jīntiān de yǔfǎ liànxí shì bǎ kěndìng jù gǎi chéng wèn jù.

Today's grammar exercise is to change positive sentences into questions.

- 成 can imply that the action of the verb **results in a mistake**. Verbs frequently used in this situation are 看 (*kàn*: 'to look'), 说 (*shuō*: 'to say'), 叫 (*jiào*: 'to call'), 想 (*xiǎng*: 'to think'), 想像 (*xiǎngxiàng*: 'to imagine'), 当 (*dāng*: 'to treat'), 写 (*xiě*: 'to write'), etc.

昨天我把小王**看成**了小张，今天又把他的名字**叫成**小黄，我觉得很不好意思。

Zuótiān wǒ bǎ Xiǎo Wáng kàn chéng le Xiǎo Zhāng, jīntiān yòu bǎ tāde míngzì jiào chéng Xiǎo Huáng, wǒ juéde hěn bù hǎoyìsi.

Yesterday I mistook Xiao Wang for Xiao Zhang; today I called him by the name Xiao Huang; I feel embarrassed.

他不但把"太"字**念成**"大"，而且还把它**写成**了"犬"字。

Tā búdàn bǎ 'tài' zì niàn chéng 'dà', érqiě hái bǎ tā xiě chéng le 'quǎn' zì.

Not only did he pronounce the character *tài* like *dà* but he also wrote it like the character *quǎn*.

(e) 作 + a noun

When the other element is 作 + **a noun** and the verb indicates an action that causes **transformation**, a 把 sentence should be used. However, unlike 成, 作 **does not imply a mistake** since the transformation is the result of an intentional act to equate the two. Verbs frequently used in this situation are 看 (*kàn*: 'to look'), 叫 (*jiào*: 'to call'), 念 (*niàn*: 'to read'), 当 (*dāng*: 'to treat'), 选 (*xuǎn*: 'to elect'), 留 (*liú*: 'to keep'), 用 (*yòng*: 'to use'), etc.

请别把那些照片扔了，我想把它们**留作**纪念。

Qǐng bié bǎ nàxiē zhàopiàn rēng le, wǒ xiǎng bǎ tāmen liú zuò jìniàn.

Please don't throw away those photos. I want to keep them as mementos.

王太太把小李**看作**(or **当作**)自己的儿子。

Wáng tàitai bǎ Xiǎo Lǐ kàn zuò (or dāng zuò) zìjǐ de érzi.

Mrs Wang views (*or* treats) Xiao Li like her own son.

(It is also acceptable to say 王太太把小李**看成**自己的儿子. In this case, 成 does not imply a mistake, but shows some type of transformation.)

李小姐很喜欢小王，可是小王已经有女朋友了，所以他只把李小姐**看作**他妹妹。昨天他没戴眼镜，把李小姐**看成**了他女朋友，所以对李小姐说："我爱你。"后来他觉得很不好意思。

Lǐ xiǎojiě hěn xǐhuān XiǎoWáng, kěshì Xiǎo Wáng yǐjīng yǒu nǚ péngyǒu le, suǒyǐ tā zhǐ bǎ Lǐ xiǎojiě kàn zuò tā mèimei. Zuótiān tā méi dài yǎnjìng, bǎ Lǐ xiǎojiě kàn chéng le tā nǚ péngyǒu, suǒyǐ duì Lǐ xiǎojiě shuō: 'Wǒ ài nǐ.' Hòulái tā juéde hěn bùhǎo yìsi.

Miss Li likes Xiao Wang (romantically), but Xiao Wang already has a girlfriend, so he only views Miss Li as his sister. Yesterday he did not wear his glasses, so he mistook Miss Li for his girlfriend and so he said 'I love you' to her. Later, he felt embarrassed.

(f) Summary

The following table gives a summary of the five special types of 把 sentence.

The other element	Verb	Example
1 在 + location	放, 挂, 写, 画, 停 (车), 拿, 忘, 留, 种, 藏, etc.	你把我的车停在哪里? *Nǐ bǎ wǒde chē tíng zài nǎlǐ?* Where did you park my car?
2 到 + location	搬, 拿, 带, 送, 寄, 开 (车), 骑, 放, etc.	请把这张桌子搬到外面。 *Qǐng bǎ zhè zhāng zhuōzi bān dào wàimiàn.* Please move this table outside.
3 给 + person	带, 拿, 寄, 交, 送, 借, 还, 留, 介绍, etc.	王先生要我把这封信交给你。 *Wáng xiānsheng yào wǒ bǎ zhè fēng xìn jiāo gěi nǐ.* Mr Wang wanted me to hand this letter to you.
4 成 + noun		
Transformation or creation	设计, 发展, 翻译, 换, 改, 做, 当, etc.	我要把这篇文章翻译成英文。 *Wǒ yào bǎ zhè piān wénzhāng fānyì chéng Yīngwén.* I will translate this article into English.
Implying a mistake	看, 说, 叫, 想, 想像, 当, 写, etc.	昨天我把小王看成了小张。 *Zuótiān wǒ bǎ Xiǎo Wáng kàn chéng le Xiǎo Zhāng.* Yesterday I mistook Xiao Wang for Xiao Zhang.
5 作 + noun (intentional act to equate two)	看, 叫, 念, 当, 选, 留, 用, etc.	他把出差当作旅游的机会。 *Tā bǎ chūchāi dāng zuò lǚyóu de jīhuì.* He regards business trips as opportunities to travel.

(g) 成 vs. 作

In some situations, 成 and 作 are considered the same. These usually involve verbs such as 看 (*kàn*) and 当 (*dāng*). 成 in these cases is not used to implied a mistake, but to indicate a transformation.

王家的人对我非常好，他们简直把我**当作**(or **当成**)家人.
Wáng jiā de rén duì wǒ fēicháng hǎo, tāmen jiǎnzhí bǎ wǒ dāng zuò (or dāng chéng) jiā rén.
The Wang family is very nice to me; they practically treat me like (as if I were) family.

(h) Pre-posing the object

When the other element is 在 + a location, 到 + a location + or 给 + a person(s), the object after 把 can be pre-posed. However, when the other element is 作/成 + noun, the 把 structure is considered the best choice. The noun after 把 is usually not pre-posed.

他把那封信**藏在**床垫中间，(= 那封信，他**藏在**床垫中间,)没有人找得到。
Tā bǎ nà fēng xìn cáng zài chuángdiàn zhōngjiān, méiyǒu rén zhǎo de dào.
He hid that letter between the mattresses; nobody could find it.

你快把我的书**放到**书架上去吧！你可以把你自己的**留在**桌子上。(= 我的书，你快**放到**书架上去吧！你自己的，你可以**留在**桌子上。)
Nǐ kuài bǎ wǒde shū fàng dào shūjià shàng qù ba! Nǐ kěyǐ bǎ nǐ zìjǐ de liú zài zhuōzi shàng.
Hurry and put my book on the bookshelf. You can leave your own on the table.

王：你可不可以把昨天买的那本词典**借给**我？

Wáng: Nǐ kě bù kěyǐ bǎ zuótiān mǎi de nà běn cídiǎn jiè gěi wo?

李：对不起，那本词典，我已经**借给**小张了。（= 我已经把那本词典**借给**小张了。）

Lǐ: Duìbùqǐ, nà běn cídiǎn, wǒ yǐjīng jiè gěi Xiǎo Zhāng le.

Wang: Can you lend me the dictionary you bought yesterday?

Li: Sorry, I already lent that dictionary to Xiao Zhang.

21.6 The negative form
Level 2

A **negative word**, 不, 没有 or 别, should appear **before** 把.

李：他把欠你的钱还你没有？

Lǐ: Tā bǎ qiàn nǐ de qián huán nǐ méiyǒu?

王：他**没有把**钱还我，不过他把向我借的书还我了。

Wáng: Tā méiyǒu bǎ qián huán wǒ, búguò tā bǎ xiàng wǒ jiè de shū huán wǒ le.

Li: Did he return to you the money he owed you?

Wang: He didn't return the money to me, but he returned to me the book he borrowed from me.

要是你**不把**这些生词记住，明天的考试你一定会考得很差。

Yàoshì nǐ bù bǎ zhèxiē shēngcí jì zhù, míngtiān de kǎoshì nǐ yídìng huì kǎo de hěn chà.

If you don't memorize these vocabulary words, you will definitely do poorly in tomorrow's test.

别把车停在这里，这里不可以停车。

Bié bǎ chē tíng zài zhèlǐ, zhèlǐ bù kěyǐ tíngchē.

Don't park your car here. This is a no-parking zone.

21.7 Placement of time phrases
Level 2

A **time phrase** should appear **before** 把.

请你**明天把**这封信送到王先生家去。

Qǐng nǐ míngtiān bǎ zhè fēng xìn sòng dào Wáng xiānsheng jiā qù.

Please deliver this letter to Mr Wang's house tomorrow.

(It would not be proper to say 请你把这封信明天送到王先生家去。)

我**下午三点**就**把**今天的功课写完了。

Wǒ xiàwǔ sān diǎn jiù bǎ jīntiān de gōngkè xiě wán le.

I finished writing today's homework at 3 o'clock in the afternoon.

(It would not be proper to say 我把今天的功课下午三点就写完了。)

21.8 Formal: 将
Level 2

把 can be replaced by 将 (*jiāng*) when the style is **formal**.

现在我们请王先生**将**这个问题解说一下。

Xiànzài wǒmen qǐng Wáng xiānsheng jiāng zhè ge wèntí jiěshuō yíxià.

Now we will ask Mr Wang to explain this issue.

21.9 Use of 它/它们
Level 2

它 (*tā*) or 它们 (*tāmen*) can follow 把 even though 它 is normally not used when it is not a 把 sentence unless it is referring to an animal.

桌上有一碗**芝麻糊**，你**把它**喝了吧。

Zhuōshàng yǒu yì wǎn zhīmáhú, nǐ bǎ tā hē le ba.

There is a bowl of sesame drink on the table; why don't you drink it?

(你把它喝了吧 can be 你喝了吧, but it would not be proper to say 你喝了它吧.)

小明：冰箱里的那几个**剩菜**呢？

Xiǎomíng: Bīngxiāng lǐ de nà jǐ ge shèngcài ne?

妈妈：早就坏了，我昨天就**把它们**都扔了。

Māma: Zǎo jiù huài le, wǒ zuótiān jiù bǎ tāmen dōu rēng le.

Xiaoming: What happened to those leftover dishes in the refrigerator?

Mother: They were long bad. I threw them away yesterday.

(It would be improper to say 它们早就坏了，我昨天就扔了它们了.)

21.10 Casual: 给 + verb

Level 3

An **optional** 给 (*gěi*) can appear before the verb in a 把 sentence. It should be noted that 给 **does not have a meaning** and should not be interpreted as 'to give'. When 给 is used, the sentence sounds **casual**.

你怎么把我的眼镜(**给**)打破了？

Nǐ zěnme bǎ wǒde yǎnjìng (gěi) dǎpò le?

How come you broke my glasses?

他一出门就把妈妈对他说的话全都(**给**)忘了。

Tā yì chūmén jiù bǎ māma shuō de huà quán dōu (gěi) wàng le.

As soon as he left the house, he immediately forgot everything his mother had said to him.

请你小声一点，要不然，你会把我爸爸(**给**)吵醒。

Qǐng nǐ xiǎoshēng yìdiǎn, yàobùrán, nǐ huì bǎ wǒ bàba (gěi) chǎo xǐng.

Please quieten down a little bit; otherwise, you will wake up my father.

Exercises

Convert the following sentences into the 把 structure if possible.

Level 2

1 王：那封信你给丁小姐了没有？

   李：还没有呢，因为昨天我没有看到她。

   Wang: Did you give that letter to Miss Ding?

   Li: Not yet because I didn't see her yesterday.

2 现在我要去图书馆借一本小说。

   I am going to the library to check out a novel.

3 王：请记住我说的话。

   李：请放心，那些话，我已经写在一个本子上了。

   Wang: Please remember those words I said.

   Li: Please don't worry. I already wrote those words in a notebook.

4 明天别忘了带一个照相机来。

Don't forget to bring a camera tomorrow.

5 丁：我说的话，你不可以告诉小王。

李：我根本不认识小王。

Ding: You cannot tell Xiao Wang what I said.

Li: I don't know Xiao Wang at all.

Level

3

6 小明：你包了太多饺子了，我一个人吃不了一百个饺子。

妈妈：你吃不完的，我们可以留到明天吃。

Xiaoming: You made too many dumplings. I cannot eat 100 dumplings by myself.

Mother: We can save those you cannot finish until tomorrow and eat them then.

7 我听说王老师住院了；我想去医院看他。

I heard that Teacher Wang has been hospitalized. I want to go to the hospital to visit him.

8 你说的话，我听不清楚。那些话，你可不可以再说一遍？

I cannot hear clearly what you said. Can you repeat it?

9 我忘了新秘书的名字，所以我请李先生再告诉我一次她的名字。

I had forgotten our new secretary's name, so I asked Mr Li to tell me her name one more time.

10 王：你弟弟病了三天了，你怎么还不送他去医院？

李：昨天送去了，可是医生说他只是感冒，所以叫我带他回家来休息。

Wang: Your younger brother has been sick for three days. How come you have not taken him to the hospital?

Li: I did yesterday. But the doctor said that he only had a cold, so he told me to bring him home and let him rest.

11 他去那家新开的百货公司给他女朋友买了一个很贵的礼物。

He went to that newly opened department store to buy a very expensive gift for his girlfriend.

22 Passive structures

In a passive sentence, the subject does not perform the action indicated by the verb, but is the 'receiver' of the action. The passive voice in English can be represented by several different ways in Chinese depending on the nature of the sentence. The focus of this chapter is on the distinction between these different passive structures in Chinese.

Level 2

22.1 Passive in English, but not in Chinese

A sentence in the passive voice in English may not be a passive sentence in Chinese. 👁 For example, the English expression 'I was told that . . .' would not be a passive structure when translated into Chinese; instead, it would be 有人告诉我…… (*Yǒu rén gàosu wǒ . . .*: 'Someone told me that . . .'). The following are some English fixed expressions in the passive voice whose counterparts in Chinese are not passive sentences.

English: I was impressed.
Chinese: 我觉得……很不错(非常好，很了不起, etc.)。
Wǒ juéde … hěn búcuò (fēicháng hǎo, hěn liǎobùqǐ, etc.).

English: I was interested.
Chinese: 我很感兴趣。 (or 我有兴趣。)
Wǒ hěn gǎn xìngqù. (or Wǒ yǒu xìngqù.)

English: I was surprised.
Chinese: 我感到很意外。 (or 我没想到。)
Wǒ gǎndào hěn yìwài. (or Wǒ méi xiǎngdào.)

Level 3

22.2 The 是……的 structure

Although the 是 (*shì*) ……的 (*de*) structure is not considered a passive structure in Chinese, its counterpart in English oftentimes is a sentence in the passive voice. 👁 Therefore, it is important to know that when such an English sentence is used to indicate the **origin** of someone or something, its counterpart in Chinese should be in the 是……的 structure.

☞ See 19.9 for more information.

English: I **was born** in Shanghai.
Chinese: 我**是**在上海生**的**。
Wǒ shì zài Shànghǎi shēng de.

English: This book **is written** by my mother.
Chinese: 这本书**是**我妈妈写**的**。
Zhè běn shū shì wǒ māma xiě de.

English: Tofu **is made** from soya beans.
Chinese: 豆腐**是**用黄豆做**的**。
Dòufu shì yòng huángdòu zuò de.

22.3 The unmarked passive

A passive sentence can be 'unmarked'; that is, the sentence is **passive in 'notion'**, but not in structure. An unmarked passive sentence is sometimes referred to as a 'notional' passive sentence.

In an unmarked passive sentence, the subject is not the 'performer' of the action indicated by the verb, but is the 'receiver'. Such a sentence is understood as passive since it is obvious that the subject is not able to perform the action indicated by the verb.

The performer is not mentioned either because who the performer is is understood or unknown or because it is not necessary to mention the performer.

> 电影票都**卖**完了。
> *Diànyǐng piào dōu mài wán le.*
> All the movie tickets **are sold** out. (电影票 is unable to perform the action of 'selling'.)

> 这篇文章**写**得真好，**翻译**成外文没有？
> *Zhè piān wénzhāng xiě de zhēn hǎo, fānyì chéng wàiwén méiyou?*
> This article **is** really well-**written**. Has it **been translated** into foreign languages?

> 儿子：我的自行车**送**去修了没有？
> *Érzi: Wǒde zìxíngchē sòngqù xiū le méiyǒu?*
> 妈妈：送去了，可是还没有**修**好，所以你走路去吧。
> *Māma: Sòngqù le, kěshì hái méiyǒu xiū hǎo, suǒyǐ nǐ zǒulù qù ba.*
> Son: Has my bicycle **been sent** for repairing?
> Mother: It has been sent, but it has not **been fixed** yet, so why don't you walk.

> 王太太：菜都**吃**光了，可是客人还没吃饱，怎么办？
> *Wáng tàitai: Cài dōu chī guāng le, kěshì kèrén hái méi chī bǎo, zěnme bàn?*
> 王先生：打电话去叫几个披萨。披萨**送**来以后，问题就**解决**了。
> *Wáng xiānsheng: Dǎ diànhuà qù jiào jǐ ge pīsà. Pīsà sòng lái yǐhòu, wèntí jiù jiějué le.*
> Mrs Wang: The dishes are all gone (have **been eaten**), but our guests are not full (have not eaten enough) yet. What are we going to do?
> Mr Wang: Call and order a couple of pizzas. After the pizzas **are delivered**, the problem will **be solved**.

22.4 The 被 structure

被 (*bèi*) is sometimes referred to as the passive marker. The word order in a 被 sentence is:

Subject	被	Performer (can be optional)	Verb	Other element (can be optional)

(a) 把 vs. 被

In terms of word order, the 把 (*ba*) structure and the 被 structure share similarities on the surface. However, the subject of the 把 sentence is the 'performer' of the action, whereas the subject of the 被 sentence is the 'receiver' of the action. What can serve as the 'other element' in both structures is similar as well.

> 瓶里的水都**被我**喝光了。(= **我把**瓶里的水都喝光了。)
> *Píng lǐ de shuǐ dōu bèi wǒ hē guāng le. (= Wǒ bǎ píng lǐ de shuǐ dōu hē guāng le.)*
> All the water in the bottle was consumed (drunk) by me. (= I drank all the water in the bottle.)

王明**被我们**推举为班长。(= **我们把**王明推举为班长。)

Wáng Míng bèi wǒmen tuījǔ wéi bānzhǎng. (= Wǒmen bǎ Wáng Míng tuījǔ wéi bānzhǎng.)

Wang Ming was elected (as) the class leader by us. (= We elected Wang Ming our class leader.)

昨天他在埋怨公司的制度，没想到他说的话**被经理**听见了，所以今天他**被经理**叫去谈话。

Zuótiān tā zài mányuàn gōngsī de zhìdù, méi xiǎngdào tā shuō de huà bèi jīnglǐ tīngjiàn le, suǒyǐ jīntiān tā bèi jīnglǐ jiào qù tánhuà.

Yesterday he was complaining about the company's system. He would not have thought that his words were heard (overheard) by the manager. So today he was asked by the manager to go have a talk with him.

老师：小明，功课交了没有？ (Unmarked passive)

Lǎoshī: Xiǎomíng, gōngkè jiāo le méiyǒu?

小明：没有，因为功课昨晚**被狗**吃了。

Xiǎomíng: Méiyǒu, yīnwèi gōngkè zuówǎn bèi gǒu chī le.

Teacher: Xiaoming, has you homework been turned in?

Xiaoming: No, because my homework was eaten by the dog last night.

头发才刚梳好，一出门就**被风**吹得乱七八糟。(头发刚梳好 is unmarked passive.)

Tóufǎ cái gāng shū hǎo, yì chūmén jiù bèi fēng chuī de luànqībāzāo.

My hair had just been combed nicely, but once I got out of the door, it was immediately blown by the wind to the point that it became totally messy.

(b) When the 'other element' is not necessary

A 被 sentence may not always need the 'other element'; that is, it can end with a verb. Such a sentence usually indicates a habitual situation or a future situation and cannot be converted into a 把 sentence. This is because a 把 sentence, with rare exceptions, does not end with a verb.

☞ See 21.3 for more information on the 'other element' used in a 把 sentence.

老王非常怕太太，所以他总是**被朋友笑**。

Lǎo Wáng fēicháng pà tàitai, suǒyǐ tā zǒngshì béi péngyǒu xiào.

Lao Wang is extremely afraid of his wife, so he is always teased (laughed at) by his friends.

小明成绩很差；每次他考不及格，不是**被爸爸骂**，就是**被妈妈打**。

Xiǎomíng chéngjī hěn chà; měi cì tā kǎo bù jígé, búshì béi bàba mà, jiùshì bèi māma dǎ.

Xiaoming's performance at school is poor. Every time he fails in a test, he is either scolded by his father or hit by his mother.

他的自行车停在户外，每天**被风吹**，**被日晒**，**被雨淋**，不久就坏了。

Tāde zìxíngchē tíng zài hùwài, měi tiān bèi fēng chuī, běi rì shài, běi yǔ lín, bùjiǔ jiù huài le.

His bicycle was parked outdoors. Every day, it was blown by the wind, shone on by the sun and rained on by the rain; it soon broke.

(c) Omitting the 'performer'

When the performer is unknown or when it is not necessary to mention the performer, either 人 can be used as the performer or the performer can be omitted without altering the meaning of the sentence.

我的电脑**被(人)**偷了。
Wǒde diànnǎo bèi (rén) tōu le.
My computer was stolen (by someone).

王先生**被(人)**谋杀了。
Wáng xiānshēng bèi (rén) móushā le.
Mr Wang was murdered (by someone).

图书馆的工作人员告诉我，我想借的那本书已经**被(人)**借走了。
Túshūguǎn de gōngzuò rényuán gàosǔ wǒ, wǒ xiǎng jiè de nà běn shū yǐjīng bèi (rén) jiè zǒu le.
The library employee told me the book I wanted to borrow had already been borrowed (by someone else).

👁 In English, when the performer is not mentioned, the preposition 'by' is not used. Learners who are English speakers should pay attention to this difference between English and Chinese.

唉！这次考试，又不及格；回家以后，大概又会**被骂**。
Ài! Zhè cì kǎoshì, yòu bù jígé; huí jiā yǐhòu, dàgài yòu huì bèi mà.
Oh no! I failed the test again. After I get home, I will probably be scolded again.

今天上课的时候，小王又**被赞美**了；因为这次考试，又是他考得最好。
Jīntiān shàngkè de shíhòu, Xiǎo Wáng yòu bèi zànměi le, yīnwèi zhè cì kǎoshì, yòu shì tā kǎo de zuì hǎo.
Today in class, Xiao Wang was praised again because once again he did the best in the test.

(d) Casual: 叫 or 让

被 can be replaced by 叫 (*jiào*) or 让 (*ràng*) when **the performer is mentioned**. When the performer is not mentioned, neither 叫 nor 让 can be used. The use of 叫 or 让 makes the utterance sound more casual.

观光客到了外国常常**被骗**。
Guānguāngkè dào le wàiguó chángcháng bèi piàn.
(观光客到了外国常常叫骗/让骗 is incorrect since the performer is not mentioned.)
Tourists are often cheated (ripped off) when they go to foreign countries.

我住在那个国家的时候，**被**(or 叫/让)当地人骗过好多次。
Wǒ zhù zài nà ge guójiā de shíhòu, bèi (or jiào/ràng) dāngdì rén piàn guò hǎo duō cì.
When I lived in that country, I was cheated by the locals many times.

- Since 叫 and 让 have other definitions, it is important to make the correct interpretation when 叫 or 让 appears in a sentence

妈妈包的饺子都**叫**弟弟吃完了，所以妈妈**叫**我打电话去**叫**一个披萨。
Māma bāo de jiǎozi dōu jiào dìdi chī wán le, suǒyǐ māma jiào wo dǎ diànhuà qù jiào yí ge pīsà.
All the dumplings that Mother made were eaten **by** little brother, so Mother **asked** me to call and **order** a pizza.

新买的电动玩具，昨天**让**弟弟弄坏了。他想再买一个，妈妈不**让**他再买，这**让**他非常不高兴。

Xīnmǎi de diàndòng wánjù, zuótiān ràng dìdi nòng huài le. Tā xiǎng zài mǎi yí ge, māma bú ràng tā zài mǎi, zhè ràng tā fēicháng bù gāoxìng.

The newly purchased video game was broken **by** little brother yesterday. He wanted to buy another one, but Mother would not **let** him and this **made** him very upset.

(e) Very casual: 给

In **very casual** speech, 给 (*gěi*) sometimes is used **in place of** 被 whether or not the performer is mentioned.

那本畅销书一到图书馆就**给(人)**借走了。

*Nà běn chàngxiāo shū yí dào túshūguǎn jiù **gěi (rén)** jiè zǒu le.*

That best-selling book was borrowed as soon as it arrived at the library.

我上星期才买的电脑，这星期就**给偷**了。

*Wǒ shàng xīngqī cái mǎi de diànnǎo, zhè xīngqī jiù **gěi tōu** le.*

The computer I bought only last week has already been stolen this week.

(f) Optional 给

An **optional** 给 can appear before the verb in a sentence with '被/叫/让 + performer'.

我今天一大早就**被**邻居的狗叫声**(给)**吵醒了。

*Wǒ jīntiān yí dà zǎo jiù **bèi** línjū de gǒu jiàoshēng **(gěi)** chǎo xǐng le.*

Today, very early in the morning, I was awoken by the barking of my neighbour's dog.

老王的儿子这学期每次考试都不及格，老王快**叫**他儿子**(给)气死**了。

*Lǎo Wáng de érzi zhè xuéqī měi cì kǎoshì dōu bù jígé, Lǎo Wáng kuài **jiào** tā érzi **(gěi)** qì sǐ le.*

Lao Wang's son has failed every test this term. Lao Wang has been highly upset by his son (literally: to the point that he is about to die).

Level
3

22.5 The use of 受到

When the **verb** used in a 被 sentence has an **identical noun**, 被 can be replaced by 受到 (*shòudào*). In this case, **the verb** usually does not indicate an active action and has **more than one character**. For example, 我的电脑被偷了 (*Wǒ de diànnǎo bèi tōu le*) cannot be converted into a sentence with 受到 because 偷 is a monosyllabic verb.

在男女平等的社会里，女人不会**被歧视**。(= 女人不会**受到歧视**。)

*Zài nán nǚ píngděng de shèhuì lǐ, nǚrén bú huì **bèi qíshì**.*

(歧视 is both 'to discriminate' and 'discrimination'. The verb and the noun are identical.)

In a society where men and women are equal, women will not be discriminated again.

我的车坏了，可是坐公共汽车很方便，所以生活没有**被影响**。(= 生活没有**受到影响**。)

Wǒde chē huài le, kěshì zuò gōnggòng qìchē hěn fāngbiàn, suǒyǐ shēnghuó méiyǒu bèi yǐngxiǎng.

(影响 is both 'to influence; to affect' and 'the influence'.)

My car had broken down, but riding the bus is convenient, so my life was not affected.

(a) 受到 + performer (的) + noun

When the performer is mentioned in the 被 sentence, the performer and an optional 的 are used before the noun in the 受到 sentence.

小王提出的建议**被全班同学**反对。(= 小王提出的建议受到**全班同学(的)**反对。)
Xiǎo Wáng tíchū de jiànyì bèi quán bān tóngxué fǎnduì. (= Xiǎo Wáng tíchū de jiànyì shòudào quán bān tóngxué (de) fǎnduì.)
The suggestion Xiao Wang made was opposed by the entire class.
(反对 is both 'to oppose' and 'opposition'.)

小明在学校里总是**被同学欺负**。(= 小明在学校里总是**受到同学(的)**欺负。)
Xiǎomíng zài xuéxiào lǐ zǒngshì bèi tóngxué qīfù. (= Xiǎomíng zài xuéxiào lǐ zǒngshì shòudào tóngxué (de) qīfù.)
Xiaoming is always bullied by his classmates at school.
(欺负 is both a verb and a noun in Chinese.)

(b) 受到 + adjective 的 + noun

The complement of degree (with 得) or an adverbial modifier (with 地) in a 被 sentence will be converted into an adjective used attributively (with 的 before the noun) in a corresponding 受到 sentence.

近几年来，许多大城市的环境都被污染**得很严重**。 (污染 is 'to pollute' and 'pollution'.)
Jìn jǐ nián lái, xǔduō dà chéngshì de huánjìng dōu bèi wūrǎn de hěn yánzhòng.
(= 近几年来，许多大城市的环境都受到**严重的**污染。)
(= *Jìn jǐ nián lái, xǔduō dà chéngshì de huánjìng dōu shòudào yánzhòng de wūrǎn.*)
In recent years, the environment in many big cities has been polluted severely.

(c) Undesirable situations

When an **undesirable situation** is being described, 遭到 (*zāodào*) or 遭受 (*zāoshòu*) is frequently used in place of 受到.

在中国的文化大革命期间，许多无辜的人**遭到迫害**。(遭到迫害 = 受到迫害)
Zài Zhōngguo de wénhuà dà gémìng qījiān, xǔduō wúgū de rén zāodào pòhài.
During China's Cultural Revolution, many innocent people were persecuted.

小兰才上高中，就想搬出去住；她的这个想法，**遭到**她爸妈强烈的**反对**。
Xiǎolán cái shàng gāozhōng, jiù xiǎng bān chūqù zhù; tāde zhè ge xiǎngfǎ, zāodào tā bàmā qiángliè de fǎnduì.
Xiaolan is only in high school and she already wants to move out of home. This idea of hers is strongly opposed by her parents.

(d) Desirable situations

When a **desirable situation** is being described, 获得 (*huòdé*) or 得到 (*dédào*) is frequently used in place of 受到.

最近小明的成绩有很大的进步，所以他上星期**获得**老师的**夸奖**。小明**得到**了老师的**鼓励**，决定要更努力地学习。
Zuìjìn Xiǎomíng de chéngjī yǒu hěn dà de jìnbù, suǒyǐ tā shàng xīngqī huòdé lǎoshī de kuājiāng. Xiǎomíng dédào le lǎoshī de gǔlì, juédìng yào gèng nǔlì de xuéxí.
Recently, Xiaoming has had huge improvement in his schoolwork, so he **was praised** by the teacher last week. After **being encouraged** by the teacher, Xiaoming decided that he will study even harder.

小张精心设计的海报**获得**了老师的**赞赏**。

Xiǎo Zhāng jīngxīn shèjì de hǎibào huòdé le lǎoshī de zànshǎng.

The poster Xiao Zhang had carefully designed was praised by the teacher.

22.6 No subject

Occasionally, a sentence can start with '被 + the performer' **without a subject**. In this case, the element following the verb is an **indefinite noun**. This can be considered a type of subjectless sentence that indicates the '**emergence**' of something. The meaning of such a sentence remains unchanged even if 被 is not used.

老李当记者的时候，（**被他**）发掘出**一件**轰动一时的贪污案。

Lǎo Lǐ dāng jìzhě de shíhòu, (bèi tā) fājué chū yí jiàn hōngdòng yìshí de tānwū àn.

When Lao Li was a journalist, a sensational embezzlement case was uncovered by him.

她的运气真好，竟然（**被她**）中了**一百万**。

Tāde yùnqì zhēn hǎo, jìngrán bèi tā zhòng le yì bǎiwàn.

She was really lucky; she unexpectedly won $1 million.

22.7 Preposition 由

A sentence with the preposition 由 (*yóu*) can be translated into an English sentence in the passive voice. However, the **passivity** indicated in a 由 sentence is **not strong**. Such a sentence emphasizes that the performer will be **in charge of** or be **responsible for** the event or action.

The following are the two types of word order involving 由.

(a) Subject + 由 performer (来/去) + verb

This word order is similar to the word order for a 被 sentence. (Note that the 由 sentence in this word order usually does not have the 'other element'.)

这件事**由**老张（**来**）**负责**，别人不用管。

Zhè jiàn shì yóu Lǎo Zhāng (lái) fùzé, biérén búyòng guǎn.

This matter will be taken care of by Lao Zhang (meaning: Lao Zhang will be responsible for this matter); others do not have to worry about it.

昨天你请我看电影，今天这顿饭**由**我（**来**）**请**吧。

Zuótiān nǐ qǐng wǒ kàn diànyǐng, jīntiān zhè dùn fàn yóu wǒ (lái) qǐng ba.

You treated me to a movie yesterday. Today's meal will be paid by me. (Meaning: I will be responsible for paying for this meal.)

(b) 由 performer (来/去) + verb + subject

The **subject** of the 由 sentence can be moved to **follow the verb** without altering the meaning of the sentence. This results in a sentence beginning with 由.

他是我的律师，**由**他来**处理**我的法律问题吧！

Tā shì wǒde lǜshī, yóu tā lái chǔlǐ wǒde fǎlǜ wèntí ba!

He is my lawyer. My legal matters will be handled by him. (Meaning: he will be in charge.)

你是这方面的专家，**由**你来**决定**问题的解决方法。

Nǐ shì zhè fāngmiàn de zhuānjiā, yóu nǐ lái juédìng wèntí de jiějué fāngfǎ.

You are the expert in this area. The solution to the problem will be decided by you. (Meaning: you will be responsible for deciding on the solution.)

Level 3 — 22.8 Formal: Subject + 为 performer + 所 verb

In a **formal** style, 'subject + 为 (*wéi*) performer + 所 (*suŏ*) verb' is used in place of a sentence with 被.

> 王先生一向**为**部属**所**尊重，没想到他竟做出这种事。
> *Wáng xiānsheng yíxiàng wéi bùshǔ suŏ zūnzhòng, méi xiăngdào tā jìng zuò chū zhè zhŏng shì.*
> Mr Wang had always **been respected** by his subordinates. No one would have thought that he would have done such a thing.

> 他写的小说，生前大多不**为人所**知，死后却都成了畅销书。
> *Tā xiě de xiăoshuō, shēng qián dàduō bù wéi rén suŏ zhī, sĭ hòu què dōu chéng le chăngxiāo shū.*
> Most of the novels he wrote were unknown to people when he was alive; but all his books became best-sellers after he died.

Level 3 — 22.9 Summary of passive structures

The following table gives a summary of the passive structures in Chinese.

Structure	Grammatical features	Examples
1 是……的	Showing origin	这本书是他写的。 *Zhè běn shū shì tā xiě de.* This book was written by him.
2 Unmarked passive	Subject is receiver of the action Performer is unknown or unimportant	我的车修好了没有？ *Wŏde chē xiū hăo le méiyŏu?* Has my car been fixed?
3 被/给 sentence		
Performer is mentioned	Subject + 被 (or 给) performer + verb	他常被（or 给）老师骂。 *Tā cháng bèi (or gěi) lăoshī mà.* He is often scolded by the teacher.
Performer is not mentioned	Subject + 被 (or 给) + verb	他六点就被（or 给）吵醒了。 *Tā liù diăn jiù bèi (or gěi) chăo xĭng le.* He was woken up at 6 o'clock.
4 让/叫 = 被	Performer must be mentioned	纸让风吹走了。 *Zhĭ ràng fēng chuī zŏu le.* The paper was blown away by the wind. 我叫那个摊贩骗了。 *Wŏ jiào nà ge tānfàn piàn le.* I was cheated by that vendor.
5 受到/遭到/获得 + noun	Verb and noun must be identical and have more than one character	我的建议受到反对。 *Wŏde jiànyì shòudào fănduì.* My suggestion was opposed.
6 由 sentence	Subject + 由 performer + verb Performer is in charge of action	这件事由他处理吧。 *Zhè jiàn shì yóu tā chŭlĭ ba.* This matter will be handled by him.

Exercises

evel
2

I   Translate the following sentences into Chinese.

1   This essay was well-written, so it has been posted (= placed) on our class blog by the teacher.

2   This novel was written by a famous Chinese writer.

3   Her computer was stolen, so her life has been greatly affected.

4   Li: Ever since I came to China, I have been ripped off (= cheated) by street vendors several times.
    Zhang: I have been ripped off, too.
    Wang: I have never been ripped off.

5   This morning my mother was awoken by the music I played. So I was scolded.

6   I was bothered by him to the point that I could not do a thing.

evel
3

II Translate the following sentences into Chinese. Only use 被 if there is no other option.

1   Those sheets of paper were blown away by the wind.

2   Wang Li's father is a doctor. Wang Li has been influenced by him and has decided to be a doctor, too.

3   The antique flower vase I bought last week was broken by my son.

4   Wang Ming has been elected our class leader.

5   Li Zhong's suggestion was opposed by all the classmates in the class.

6   Mr Wang is our representative. Your questions will be answered by him.

7   Because the water in this river has been polluted severely, the fish from this river are not edible.

8   Lately Wang Zhong has been often praised by the teacher.

23 Making comparisons (1)

There are basically two types of comparison. One indicates which of the two items is stronger (or weaker) in the feature being compared; the other indicates whether or not two items are similar/identical. Although certain patterns can imply both, the focus of this chapter will be on the first type of comparison. The second type is covered in Chapter 24.

23.1 Simple sentences with contrasting adjectives

Level 2

One or two simple sentences with **adjectives of opposite meanings** can be used to imply that a comparison is being made. In this case, the adjectives cannot have 很 (*hěn*) or other degree adverbs.

> 我们班，男生**多**，女生**少**。
> *Wǒmen bān, nánshēng duō, nǚshēng shǎo.*
> There are **more** males students than female students in my class.

> 哥哥的房间**大**，我的房间**小**；他的东西**多**，所以爸妈把大的房间给了他。
> *Gēge de fángjiān dà, wǒde fángjiān xiǎo, tāde dōngxī duō, suǒyǐ bàmā bǎ dà de fángjiān gěi le tā.*
> My older brother's room is **bigger** than mine. He has **more** stuff, so my parents gave him the bigger room.

23.2 The use of 比

Level 2/3

When 比 (*bǐ*) is used to make comparisons, only the **subjects** or **time phrases** can be compared. In other words, 比 cannot be used to compare the two objects in a sentence.

👁 The topic–comment structure is used to compare two objects.

☞ See 1.4 for more information on the topic–comment structure.

English: I like physics more than (I like) chemistry.
('Physics' and 'chemistry' are the two **objects** of the verb 'like'.)
Chinese: 物理跟化学，我(比较)喜欢物理。
Wùlǐ gēn huàxué, wǒ (bǐjiào) xǐhuān wùlǐ.

English: I like Mr Wang more than (I like) Mr Zhang.
('Mr Wang' and 'Mr Zhang' are the two **objects** of the verb 'like'.)
Chinese: 王先生和张先生，我(比较)喜欢王先生。
Wáng xiānsheng hé Zhāng xiānsheng, wǒ bǐjiào xǐhuān Wáng xiānsheng.

English: I like Mr Wang more than Mr Zhang (likes him.)
('I' and 'Mr Zhang' are the two **subjects**. Mr Wang is the object.)
Chinese: 我比张先生喜欢王先生。
Wǒ bǐ Zhāng xiānsheng xǐhuān Wáng xiānsheng.

English: I am busier this year than last year.
          (This is comparing the two **time phrases** 'this year' and 'last year'.)
Chinese: 我今年比去年忙。
          Wǒ jīnnián bǐ qùnián máng.

23.3 Word order of 比 sentences

The basic word order for a 比 sentence is 'A 比 B + feature being compared'. The feature being compared is usually an adjective, a complement of state, a verb (which has the quality of an adjective or which can indicate increase/decrease, etc.) or, occasionally, an auxiliary verb.

(a) Adjectives

It is important to keep in mind that the feature being compared cannot include 不 (*bù*), 很 (*hěn*), 真 (*zhēn*), 太 (*tài*), 非常 (*fēicháng*), etc.

我比我弟弟**高**。 (高 is an adjective and is the feature being compared.)
Wǒ bǐ wǒ dìdi gāo.
I am taller than my younger brother.
= 我弟弟比我**矮**。
Wǒ dìdi bǐ wǒ ǎi.
My younger brother is shorter than I.
(Incorrect: 我比我弟弟很高 or 我弟弟比我不高.)

王先生家**比**李先生家**大**。 (大 is an adjective and is the feature being compared.)
Wáng xiānsheng jiā bǐ Lǐ xiānsheng jiā dà.
Mr Wang's house is bigger than Mr Li's house.
= 李先生家**比**王先生家**小**。
Lǐ xiānsheng jiā bǐ Wáng xiānsheng jiā xiǎo.
Mr Li's house is smaller than Mr Wang's house.
(Incorrect: 王先生家比李先生家很大 or 李先生家比王先生家不大.)

(b) Complements of state

When the feature being compared is a complement of state, the word order can be slightly flexible.

☞ See Chapter 12 for more information on the complement of state.

小王**比**小李跑得**快**。 (跑得快 is a complement of state and is the feature being compared.)
Xiǎo Wáng bǐ Xiǎo Lǐ pǎo de kuài.
= 小王跑得**比**小李**快**。
= *Xiǎo Wáng pǎo de bǐ Xiǎo Lǐ kuài.*
Xiao Wang runs faster than Xiao Li.
= 小李**比**小王跑得**慢**。
Xiǎo Lǐ bǐ Xiǎo Wáng pǎo de màn.
= 小李跑得**比**小王**慢**。
Xiǎo Lǐ pǎo de bǐ Xiǎo Wáng màn.
Xiao Li runs slower than Xiao Wang.
(Incorrect: 小王比小李跑得很快 or 小李跑得比小王不快.)

(c) Placement of objects

When the verb has an object, such as 唱歌 and 跳舞, it is not proper to put 比 before the object.

妹妹舞跳得**比**我**好**，可是我歌唱得**比**她**好**。
Mèimei wǔ tiào de bǐ wǒ hǎo, kěshì wǒ gē chàng de bǐ tā hǎo.
= 妹妹舞**比**我跳得**好**，可是我歌**比**她唱得**好**。
= *Mèimei wǔ bǐ wǒ tiào de hǎo, kěshì wǒ gē bǐ tā chàng de hǎo.*
My younger sister dances better than I do, but I sing better than she does.
(Do not say 妹妹比我舞跳得好，可是我比她歌唱得好.)

(d) Verbs

When the feature being compared is a verb, the **verb** must have **the quality of an adjective**; normally, these verbs can take degree adverbs, such as 很, 真 and 非常, before them.

我比小明**喜欢**数学。(喜欢 is a verb with the quality of an adjective.)
Wǒ bǐ Xiǎomíng xǐhuān shùxué.
I like mathematics more than Xiaoming does.

妈妈**比**爸爸**爱**看小说。(爱 is a verb with the quality of an adjective.)
Māma bǐ bàba ài kàn xiǎoshuō.
My mother likes to read novels more than my father does.

- Verbs without the quality of an adjective cannot be directly compared

English: I miss home more than my sister does. (= I am more homesick.)
Chinese: 我**比**姐姐**想**家。(想 is a verb with the quality of an adjective.)
Wǒ bǐ jiějie xiǎng jiā.

English: I walk more than you do. (Meaning: I walk more frequently than you do.)
Chinese: 我**比**你**常**走路。(走路 is a verb without the quality of an adjective.)
Wǒ bǐ nǐ cháng zǒulù.

English: I walk more than you do. (Meaning: I walk longer distances than you do.)
Chinese: 我走的路**比**你走的**长**。
Wǒ zǒu de lù bǐ nǐ zǒu de cháng.
(It is incorrect to say 我比你走路 in either of the above sentences since 'to walk' is a verb without the quality of an adjective.)

- Verbs that indicate **increase/elevation** or **decrease/decline** can be compared

我今年的收入**比**去年**增加**了。
Wǒ jīnnián de shōurù bǐ qùnián zēngjiā le.
My income this year is more than my income last year.

今年的入学标准**比**去年**降低**了。
Jīnnián de rùxué biāozhǔn bǐ qùnián jiàngdī le.
This year's admission standard is lower than last year's.

- Auxiliary verbs such as 想 (*xiǎng*), 会 (*huì*) and 愿意 (*yuànyì*), which can follow degree adverbs such as 很, 真, 非常, can be used in a 比 sentence. 想 in this case means 'would like'; and 会 means 'to be good at'

小李**比**小王**会**跳舞。
Xiǎo Lǐ bǐ Xiǎo Wáng huì tiàowǔ.
Xiao Li is better at dancing than Xiao Wang (is).

小丁**比**小张**愿意**帮助人。
Xiǎo Dīng bǐ Xiǎo Zhāng yuànyì bāngzhù rén.
Xiao Ding is more willing to help others than Xiao Zhang (is).

我**比**她**想**去中国留学。
Wǒ bǐ tā xiǎng qù Zhōngguó liúxué.
I would like to go to China to study more than she would like to.

👁 The verb 有 cannot be used in a 比 sentence unless 有 is part of an adjective.

这本书**比**那本**有意思**得多。 (有意思 means 'interesting'.)
Zhè běn shū bǐ nà běn yǒu yìsi de duō.
This book is much more interesting than that book.

王家**比**李家**有钱**。 (有钱 means 'wealthy'.)
Wáng jiā bǐ Lǐ jiā yǒuqián.
The Wang family is wealthier than the Li family.

English: I have more books than he does.
Chinese: 我的书**比**他的**多**。
             Wǒde shū bǐ tāde duō.
(Incorrect: 我有比他多书。)

English: Xiao Wang has more questions than Xiao Li.
Chinese: 小王的问题**比**小李的**多**。
             Xiǎo Wáng de wèntí bǐ Xiǎo Lǐ de duō.
(Incorrect: 小王有比小李很多问题。)

23.4 Complements of quantitative difference

After making a comparison with 比, **a complement of quantity** (☞ referred to as 'complement of quantitative difference' in Chapter 14) can follow to indicate **the difference**.

👁 The word orders for this structure in English and in Chinese are quite dissimilar; therefore, learners who are English speakers should pay special attention to avoid mistakes.

(a) Forming questions about the difference

多少 or '几 + **measure word**' is used in questions to **ask about the difference**.

这本书比那本**贵多少(钱)**？
Zhè běn shū bǐ nà běn guì duōshǎo (qián)?
How much more expensive is this book than that book?

你们班比他们班**多几个人**？
Nǐmen bān bǐ tāmen bān duō jǐ ge rén?
How many more people are there in your class than in his class?

你家比他家**大多少**？
Nǐ jiā bǐ tā jiā dà duōshǎo?
How much bigger is your house than his house?

(b) Vague differences vs. precise differences

There are two types of difference, a **vague** difference and a **precise** difference. **At least two characters are necessary** to indicate the difference. Only 一些 (*yìxiē*) or 一点 (*yìdiǎn*) can be shortened to 些 or 点.

- When a **vague** difference is indicated, the difference is either 'a lot/much/many' or 'a little'

  English:　　Xiao Wang is **much taller** than his younger brother.
  Chinese:　　小王比他弟弟**高很多**(= 高得多 = 高多了)。
  　　　　　　Xiǎo Wáng bǐ tā dìdi gāo hěn duō (= gāo de duō = gāo duō le).
  (Incorrect:　小王比他弟弟高多。) (多 is monosyllabic.)

  English:　　My house is **a little smaller** than his house.
  Chinese:　　我家比他家**小一些**(= 小一点)。
  　　　　　　Wǒ jiā bǐ tā jiā xiǎo yìxiē (= xiǎo yìdiǎn).

  这次考试，我考得比王明**好**(一)**些**。
  Zhè cì kǎoshì, wǒ kǎo de bǐ Wáng Míng hǎo (yì) xiē.
  I did a little better than Wang Ming in this test.

- When the adjective being compared is 多 (*duō*) or 少 (*shǎo*) and the complement of quantitative difference is 很多/得多/多了, the resulting sentence can be confusing to learners due to the juxtaposition of 多 and 少

(Situation: Mr Wang has five students; Mr Zhang has eight students; Mr Li has 80 students.)

  王先生的学生比李先生的**少很多**(= 少多了 = 少得多)。
  Wáng xiānsheng de xuéshēng bǐ Lǐ xiānsheng de shǎo duō le.
  = 李先生的学生比王先生的**多多了**(= 多得多 = 多很多)。
  Lǐ xiānsheng de xuéshēng bǐ Wáng xiānsheng de duō duō le.
  王先生的学生比张先生的**少一点**(= 少一些 = 少点 = 少些)。
  Wáng xiānsheng de xuéshēng bǐ Zhāng xiānsheng de shǎo yìdiǎn.
  = 张先生的学生比王先生的**多一些**(= 多一点 = 多些 = 多点)。
  Zhāng xiānsheng de xuéshēng bǐ Wáng xiānsheng de duō yìxiē.

- The vague difference can be '几 + measure word' if what is being compared is countable

  王先生的学生只比张先生的**少几个**。 ('几个' means 'a few' here.)
  Wáng xiānsheng de xuéshēng zhǐ bǐ Zhāng xiānsheng de shǎo jǐ ge.

- The complement of quantitative difference can also indicate a **precise** difference. The actual difference should have **at least two characters**, except when it is an arithmetic question

  老师：十五比十二大**多少**？
  Lǎoshī: Shíwǔ bǐ shí'èr dà duōshǎo?
  小学生：大三。
  Xiǎoxuéshēng: Dà sān.
  Teacher: **How much** bigger is 15 than 12?
  Pupil: It's bigger **by 3**.

  我今年十五，我哥哥十八，弟弟十三。我比哥哥**小三岁**，比弟弟**大两岁**。
  Wǒ jīnnián shíwǔ, wǒ gēge shíbā, dìdi shísān. Wǒ bǐ gēge xiǎo sān suì, bǐ dìdi dà liǎng suì.
  I am 15 this year; my older brother is 18; my younger brother is 13. I am three years younger than my older brother, two years older than my younger brother.
  (三岁 and 两岁 are the precise differences. Although it is acceptable to say 我今年十五 without using 岁, it is incorrect to say 我比哥哥小三，比弟弟大二.)

  我一百八十公分，他一百六十五公分；我比他**高十五公分**。
  Wǒ yì bǎi bāshí gōngfēn, tā yì bǎi liùshí wǔ gōngfēn; wǒ bǐ tā gāo shíwǔ gōngfēn.
  I am 180 cm tall; he is 165 cm tall. I am 15 cm taller than he is.

23.5 更: 'even more'

更 (*gèng*) can appear before the feature being compared to indicate '**even more**'. The use of 更 must be in proper context, in which B already possesses the feature, but A is even stronger in that feature.

(a) The use of 更, 还, and 还要

When 比 is used in making the comparison, 还 (*hái*), 还要 (*háiyào*) and 更 are interchangeable. When 比 is not used, only 更 can be used.

> English: Xiao Wang is tall; Xiao Zhang is even taller (than he is).
> Chinese: 小王很高，小张比他**更**高。
> *Xiǎo Wáng hěn gāo, Xiǎo Zhāng bǐ tā gèng gāo.*
> = 小王很高，小张**比**他**还**(**要**)高。
> = *Xiǎo Wáng hěn gāo, Xiǎo Zhāng bǐ tā hái(yào) gāo.*
> = 小王很高，小张**更**高。
> *Xiǎo Wáng hěn gāo, Xiǎo Zhāng gèng gāo.*
> (Incorrect: 小王很高，小张还高。)

> 昨天的考试，我考得不错，可是小李考得(比我)**更**好。
> *Zuótiān de kǎoshì, wǒ kǎo de búcuò, kěshì Xiǎo Lǐ kǎo de (bǐ wǒ) gèng hǎo.*
> I did quite well in yesterday's test, but Xiao Li did even better (than I did).

> 昨天的考试，我考得不好，小李考得比我**还**(**要**)差。
> *Zuótiān de kǎoshì, wǒ kǎo de bù hǎo, Xiǎo Lǐ kǎo de bǐ wǒ hái(yào) chà.*
> I did not do well in yesterday's test; Xiao Li did even worse than I did.

(b) Negative sentences with 更

It is acceptable to have '不 + the feature being compared' if 更 is used.

> 上次考试，我考得非常不好，没想到这次我考得**更不好**。
> *Shàng cì kǎoshì, wǒ kǎo de fēicháng bùhǎo, méi xiǎngdào zhè cì wǒ kǎo de gèng bù hǎo.*
> I did extremely poorly in the last test; I didn't expect that I would do even more poorly this time.
> (Do not say 这次考试我考得比上次不好. One can only say 这次考试我比上次考得差.)

(c) 'Much more' vs. 'even more'

Do not confuse '**much more**' with '**even more**'.

(Situation: Mr Wang is a multi-millionaire. Mr Li is a billionaire.)

> 王先生非常有钱，李先生比他**更**有钱。
> *Wáng xiānsheng fēicháng yǒuqián, Lǐ xiānsheng bǐ tā gèng yǒuqián.*
> Mr Wang is very wealthy; Mr. Li is even wealthier than he (is).

(Situation: Teacher Zhang shows you and Mr Ding some homework written by Xiao Li and Xiao Wang and asks you whose handwriting is better. Both of you give him your opinions.)

> 你：我觉得小王的字写得马马虎虎，小李的字写得比他**好多了**。
> *Nǐ: Wǒ juéde Xiǎo Wáng de zì xiě de mǎmǎhūhū, Xiǎo Lǐ de zì xiě de bǐ tā hǎo duō le.*

丁：我觉得两个人都写得不错，不过小李比小王写得**更好**。

Dīng: Wǒ juéde liǎng ge rén dōu xiě de búcuò, búguò Xiǎo Lǐ bǐ Xiǎo Wáng xiě de gèng hǎo.

You: I feel that Xiao Wang's handwriting is **average**; Xiao Li's handwriting is **much better**.

Ding: I feel **both** of them have **good** handwriting, but Xiao Li's is **even better** than Xiao Wang's.

这本书相当有意思，那本比这本**更有意思**。

Zhè běn shū xiāngdāng yǒu yìsi, nà běn bǐ zhè běn gèng yǒu yìsi.

This book is quite interesting; that book is even more interesting than this one.

Compare: 这本书不太有意思，那本比这本**有意思得多**。

Zhè běn shū bú tài yǒu yìsi, nà běn bǐ zhè běn yǒu yìsi de duō.

This book is not very interesting; that book is much more interesting than this one.

(d) Adding 还 or 还要

还 or 还要 can be combined with the complement of quantitative difference to indicate the difference. 还要更 can be used to indicate the 'vague' difference. 👁 A sentence such as this would be unusual in English; therefore, learners who are English speakers should be aware of such situations in Chinese.

张太太：苹果一斤三块！这么贵！香蕉呢？

Zhāng tàitai: Píngguǒ yì jīn sān kuài, zhème guì! Xiāngjiāo ne?

摊贩：一斤五块。

Tānfàn: Yì jīn wǔ kuài.

张太太：什么! 香蕉比苹果**还要贵两块**！ (两块 is the precise difference; 更 cannot be used.)

Zhāng tàitai: Shénme! Xiāngjiāo bǐ píngguǒ háiyào guì liǎng kuài!

Mrs Zhang: Apples are $3 per Chinese pound! So expensive! How about bananas?
Vendor: $5 per Chinese pound.
Mrs Zhang: What! Bananas are **even more expensive** than apples **by $2**!

小兰：这条蓝裙子不好看，也太贵；让我看看那条绿的。

Xiǎolán: Zhè tiáo lán qúnzi bù hǎokàn, yě tài guì; ràng wǒ kàn kàn nà tiáo lǜ de.

店员：可是那条绿的比这条蓝的**还要(更)贵一点**呢！ (一点 is a vague difference.)

Diànyuán: Kěshì nà tiáo lǜ de bǐ zhè tiáo lán de háiyào gèng guì yìdiǎn ne!

Xiaolan: This blue skirt is not pretty and it's too expensive. Let me take a look at that green one.

Sales clerk: But the green one is **even a little bit more** expensive than the blue one.

(e) Adding auxiliary verbs

Some auxiliary verbs, such as 想 (*xiǎng*), 会 (*huì*), 应该 (*yīnggāi*) and 可以 (*kěyǐ*), can appear in a 比 sentence with 更.

小王不应该喝酒，你比他**更不应该**喝。 (你比小王不应该喝酒 is incorrect.)

Xiǎo Wáng bù yīnggāi hē jiǔ, nǐ bǐ tā gèng bù yīnggāi hē.

Xiao Wang is not supposed to drink alcohol; you are even less supposed to drink.

(f) Comparing time phrases

Two time phrases can be compared by using 比.

我这星期比上星期忙，下星期会比这星期更忙。
Wǒ zhè xīngqī bǐ shàng xīngqī máng; xià xīngqī huì bǐ zhè xīngqī gèng máng.
I am busier this week than last week and I will be even busier next week than this week.

23.6 Comparisons with '早/晚/多/少 + verb'

Level 3

When 早 (*zǎo*), 晚 (*wǎn*), 多 or 少 appears **before a verb**, a comparison is being made whether or not the sentence has 比. The difference can be indicated by using a complement of quantitative difference after the comparison has been made.

张：你比我早走十分钟，怎么比我晚到五分钟？
Zhāng: Nǐ bǐ wǒ zǎo zǒu shí fēnzhōng, zěnme bǐ wǒ wǎn dào wǔ fēnzhōng?
李：因为我的自行车比你的旧得多，所以我骑得比你慢。
Lǐ: Yīnwèi wǒde zìxíngchē bǐ nǐde jiù de duō, suǒyǐ wǒ qí de bǐ nǐ màn.
Zhang: You **left** ten minutes **earlier** than I did; how come you **arrived** five minutes **later** (than I did)?
Li: Because my bicycle is much older than yours, I rode more slowly than you.

王：我买了五张票，可是只有四个人要去，我多买了一张。
Wáng: Wǒ mǎi le wǔ zhāng piào, kěshì zhǐ yǒu sì ge rén yào qù, wǒ duō mǎi le yì zhāng.
丁：不对，你少买了一张，因为我弟弟跟妹妹也要去。
Dīng: Bú duì, nǐ shǎo mǎi le yì zhāng, yīnwèi wǒ dìdi gēn mèimei yě yào qù.
Wang: I bought five tickets, but only four people are going. I bought **one more** (than needed).
Ding: Wrong! You bought **one ticket fewer** (than needed) because my younger brother and younger sister also want to go.

23.7 The use of '先/晚 + verb'

Level 2

先 (*xiān*) can appear **before the verb** in a 比 sentence to indicate **the first in a sequence of two actions**. The **opposite** of 先 in this situation is usually 晚.

(Situation: Wang and a friend get on the bus and they are about to sit down.)

王：我会比你先下车，所以你坐靠窗的座位吧。
Wáng: Wǒ huì bǐ nǐ xiān xiàchē, suǒyǐ nǐ zuò kào chuāng de zuòwèi ba.
I will get off before you, so why don't you sit in the window seat.

李明比他弟弟先进大学，却比弟弟晚毕业。
Lǐ Míng bǐ tā dìdi xiān jìn dàxué, què bǐ dìdi wǎn bìyè.
Li Ming entered college before his younger brother, but graduated later than his brother.

23.8 Forming yes–no and alternative questions with 比

Level 2

Use 吗 to ask a yes–no question. Otherwise, use 还是 to ask an alternative question.

你比你弟弟高吗？
Nǐ bǐ nǐ dìdi gāo ma?
(Do not say 你比你弟弟高不高？)
Are you taller than your younger brother?

你比你弟弟高**还是**比他矮？
Nǐ bǐ nǐ dìdi gāo háishì bǐ tā ǎi?
Are you taller (or shorter) than your younger brother?

你家比他家大**还是**他家比你家大？ (Do not say 你家比他家大不大？)
Nǐ jiā bǐ tā jiā dà háishì tā jiā bǐ nǐ jiā dà?
Is your house bigger than his house or is his house bigger (than yours)?

Level
3

23.9 The use of 有 in comparisons

The word order is 'A 有 B (这么/那么) + feature being compared'. When 有 is used in comparison, **the status of B is known** and is used **as a standard** to describe whether A has reached that level. Therefore, A and B can be equal or A is possibly stronger in that feature. Since the status of B is already known, 这么/那么 is frequently used before the feature being compared.

去年弟弟比我矮，今年他**有**我这么高了。
Qùnián dìdi bǐ wǒ ǎi, jīnnián tā yǒu wǒ zhème gāo le.
Last year, my younger brother was shorter than I am; this year, he is already (at least) as tall as I am.

我家前面的那棵大树**有**三层楼高。
Wǒ jiā qiánmiàn de nà kē dà shù yǒu sān céng lóu gāo.
The big tree in front of my house is as tall as (and possibly a little taller than) three storeys.

(a) Forming questions

Use 有没有 or 有......吗 to ask a question only when the status of B is already known.

王：我跑百米只要十二秒，你跑得**有**我**快**吗？
Wáng: Wǒ pǎo bǎi mǐ zhǐ yào shí'èr miǎo, nǐ pǎo de yǒu wǒ kuài ma?
李：我跑得当然**有**你**快**，而且我跑得**比**你**更快**。我的百米纪录是十一秒。
Lǐ: Wǒ pǎo de dāngrán yǒu nǐ kuài, érqiě wǒ pǎo de bǐ nǐ gèng kuài. Wǒde bǎi mǐ jìlù shì shíyī miǎo.
Wang: It takes me only 12 seconds to run 100 m. Do you run as fast as I do?
Li: Of course I do. And I run even faster than you. My record for 100 m is 11 seconds.

王太太：我儿子今年八岁，你儿子**有没有**我儿子大？
Wáng tàitai: Wǒ érzi jīnnián bā suì, nǐ érzi yǒu méiyǒu wǒ érzi dà?
张太太：我儿子**比**你儿子**小**一岁。
Zhāng tàitai: Wǒ érzi bǐ nǐ érzi xiǎo yī suì.
Mrs Wang: My son is eight years old this year. Is your son as old as my son?
Mrs Zhang: My son is one year younger than your son.

(b) Adding 那么/这么

那么 or 这么 can appear before the feature being compared when 有 or 没有 is used.

(Situation: Talking about promotions at work.)

张：我跟王中的学历，资历都一样，为什么他升级了，我没升呢？
Zhāng: Wǒ gēn Wáng Zhōng de xuélì, zīlì dōu yíyàng, wèishénme tā shēngjí le, wǒ méi shēng ne?
经理：你**有**王中**那么**能干吗？ (The implication is Wang Zhong's competence is known.)

Jīnglǐ: Nǐ yǒu Wáng Zhōng nàme nénggàn ma?
Zhang: Wang Zhong and I have the same educational background and seniority. Why is it that Wang Zhong has been promoted, but I haven't?
Manager: Are you as competent as Wang Zhong?

23.10 Negative comparisons

The negative comparison can be either a sentence with 不比 (*bùbǐ*) or a sentence with 没有. These two types of sentence have **different connotations**.

(a) Negative comparisons with 不比

'A 不比 B + the feature being compared' indicates that 'A is not more/less . . . than B'. For example, 我家不比你家小 means 'My house is not (any) smaller than yours' and the implication is that my house is possibly even bigger or at least the same size.

张：你出三十块，我出二十块，好不好？
Zhāng: Nǐ chū sānshí kuài, wǒ chū èrshí kuài, hǎo bù hǎo?
李：我**不比**你有钱，为什么要**比**你多出？
Lǐ: Wǒ bù bǐ nǐ yǒuqián, wèishénme yào bǐ nǐ duō chū?
Zhang: You pay $30 and I pay $20, OK?
Li: I am not richer (I don't have more money) than you; why do I have to pay more?
(This implies that Li and Zhang may be equally well-off or Li may be poorer.)

王：你看，上次考试我考得不错，这是老师给我的奖品。
Wáng: Nǐ kàn, shàngcì kǎoshì wǒ kǎo de búcuò, zhè shì lǎoshī gěi wǒ de jiǎngpǐn.
丁：我考得**不比**你差，怎么老师没有给我奖品？
Dīng: Wǒ kǎo de bù bǐ nǐ chà, zěnme lǎoshī méiyǒu gěi wǒ jiǎngpǐn?
Wang: Look! I did quite well in the last test. This is the prize the teacher gave me.
Ding: I didn't do worse than you. How come the teacher didn't give me a prize?
(The implication is that Ding did equally well or possibly even better in the test.)

(b) Negative comparisons with 没有

'A 没有 B + the feature being compared' indicates 'A is not as . . . as B'. In other words, 'B is more . . . than A'. For example, 我没有我弟弟高 (*Wǒ méiyǒu wǒ dìdi gāo*: 'I am not as tall as my younger brother') means 我弟弟比我高 (*Wǒ dìdi bǐ wǒ gāo*: 'My younger brother is taller than I am').

我家**没有**他家大，可是他家地点**没有**我家好，所以房价也**没有**我家高。
Wǒ jiā méiyǒu tā jiā dà, kěshì tā jiā dìdiǎn méiyǒu wǒ jiā hǎo, suǒyǐ fángjià yě méiyǒu wǒ jiā gāo.
My house is not as big as his house, but the location of his house is not as good as the location of my house; therefore, the price of his house is not as high as the price of my house.

张：你为什么要搬家？
Zhāng: Nǐ wèishénme yào bān jiā?
王：因为那里的冬天**没有**这里冷，夏天也**没有**这里热。
Wáng: Yīnwèi nàlǐ de dōngtiān méiyǒu zhèlǐ lěng, xiàtiān yě méiyǒu zhèlǐ rè.
Zhang: Why are you going to move away?
Wang: Because the winter over there is not as cold as it is here and summer there is not as hot as it is here.

(c) Adding 这么/那么 to a negative comparison with 没有

Sometimes, 这么/那么 can appear before the feature being compared. The implication is that B is already strong in that feature.

我跑得相当快，可是还是**没有**小王跑得**那么**快。 (Implication: Xiao Wang runs really fast.)
Wǒ pǎo de xiāngdāng kuài, kěshì háishì méiyǒu Xiǎo Wáng pǎo de nàme kuài.
I run pretty fast, but I still don't run as fast as Xiao Wang.

妈妈：这次考试，你怎么又**没有**小李考得好？
Māma: Zhè cì kǎoshì, nǐ zěnme yòu méiyǒu Xiǎo Lǐ kǎo de hǎo?
小明：因为我**没有**小李**那么**聪明。 (Implication: Xiao Li is really smart.)
Xiǎomíng: Yīnwèi wǒ méiyǒu Xiǎo Lǐ nàme cōngmíng.
妈妈：不对，真正的原因是你**没有**他**那么**努力。 (Implication: Xiao Li is really hardworking.)
Māma: Bú duì, zhēnzhèng de yuányīn shì nǐ méiyǒu tā nàme nǔlì.
Mother: How come you once again didn't do as well as Xiao Li did in the test?
Xiao Ming: Because I am not as smart as Xiao Li.
Mother: Wrong! The real reason is you are not as hardworking as he is.

(d) A common mistake

Do not use 'A 没有比 B + feature being compared'. This is a common mistake made by learners.

English: Yesterday was not colder than today.
Chinese: 昨天**不比**今天冷。
            Zuótiān bù bǐ jīntiān lěng.
(Incorrect: 昨天没有比今天冷。)

English: My younger brother is not as tall as I am, but I am not as fat as he is.
Chinese: 我弟弟**没有**我高，可是我**没有**他胖。
            Wǒ dìdi méi yǒu wǒ gāo, kěshì wǒ méi yǒu tā pàng.
(Incorrect: 我弟弟没有比我高，可是我没有比他胖。) (The meanings are not clear.)

(e) Negative future comparisons with 不会有 and 不会比

Occasionally, 没有 can be replaced by **不会有** and 不比 can be replaced by **不会比** when the statement is about a **future situation** or a **hypothetical situation**.

今天真冷！听说明天**不会有**今天这么冷。 (future situation)
Jīntiān zhēn lěng! Tīngshuō míngtiān bú huì yǒu jīntiān zhème lěng.
Today is really cold! I heard that tomorrow **will not be as cold** as today.

昨天真冷，今天没有昨天(那么)冷，我想明天也**不会比**昨天冷。 (future situation)
Zuótiān zhēn lěng, jīntiān méiyǒu zuótiān nàme lěng, wǒ xiǎng míngtiān yě bú huì bǐ zuótiān lěng.
Yesterday was really cold; today is not as cold as yesterday. I think tomorrow **won't be colder** than yesterday either.

小李非常聪明，就算他不花功夫准备考试，我的成绩也**不会比**他的高。
(hypothetical situation)
Xiǎo Lǐ fēicháng cōngmíng, jiùsuàn tā bù huā gōngfū zhǔnbèi kǎoshì, wǒde chéngjī yě bú huì bǐ tāde gāo.

Xiao Li is extremely smart. Even if he didn't spend time preparing for the exam, my score still would **not** be **higher** than his.

我没有小李聪明，就算今天晚上我不睡觉，明天的考试也**不会有**他考得好。
Wǒ méiyǒu Xiǎo Lǐ cōngmíng, jiùsuàn wǒ jīntiān wǎnshàng bù shuìjiào, míngtiān de kǎoshì yě bú huì yǒu tā kǎo de hǎo.
I am not as smart as Xiao Li. Even if I don't go to bed tonight, I will not **do as well** as he will in tomorrow's test.

(f) Negative comparisons with 不如

When the feature being compared denotes a **positive value**, 不如 (*bùrú*) can be used in place of 没有.

> 王小姐**不如**李小姐**漂亮**，但李小姐**不如**王小姐**聪明**。
> *Wáng xiǎojiě bùrú Lǐ xiǎojiě piàoliàng, dàn Lǐ xiǎojiě bùrú Wáng xiǎojiě cōngmíng.*
> Miss Wang is not as pretty as Miss Li, but Miss Li is not as smart as Miss Wang.

> 我英文说得**不如**小兰**流利**，不过她的发音**不如**我的**清楚**。
> *Wǒ Yīngwén shuō de bùrú Xiǎolán liúlì, búguò tāde fāyīn bùrú wǒde qīngchǔ.*
> I don't speak English as fluently as Xiaolan does, but her pronunciation is not as clear as mine.

• Do not use 不如 when the feature being compared is not considered a 'positive' value

> 我弟弟**不如**我**高**。＝我弟弟**没有**我**高**。 (高 is considered a positive value.)
> *Wǒ dìdi bùrú wǒ gāo. = Wǒ dìdi méiyǒu wǒ gāo.*
> My younger brother is not as tall as I am.
> (Do not say 我不如我弟弟矮 since 矮 is not considered a positive value.)

> 这个房间**不如**那个**大**。＝这个房间**没有**那个**大**。 (大 is considered a positive value.)
> *Zhè ge fángjiān bùrú nà ge dà. = Zhè ge fángjiān méiyǒu nà ge dà.*
> This room is not as big as that one.
> (Do not say 这个房间不如那个小 since 小 is not considered a positive value.)

• When the feature being compared is 好, 好 can be optional when 不如 is used

> 王先生的儿子在各方面都**不如**李先生的儿子。
> *Wáng xiānsheng de érzi zài gè fāngmiàn dōu bùrú Lǐ xiānsheng de érzi.*
> Mr Wang's son is not as outstanding as Mr Li's son in all respects.

> 中国人常说："来得早**不如**来得巧。"
> *Zhōngguó rén cháng shuō: 'Lái de zǎo bùrú lái de qiǎo.'*
> Chinese people often say, 'To arrive early is not as good as to arrive timely.'

23.11 Omitting information

Level 2

Once full information about A is given, the information about B does not have to be complete as long as the meaning is clear. This frequently results in a topic–comment structure.

> 这本书(的)作者比那本有名，所以价钱也比那本贵。(Without 的, 这本书 is the topic.)
> *Zhè běn shū (de) zuòzhě bǐ nà běn yǒumíng, suǒyǐ jiàqián yě bǐ nà běn guì.*
> The author of this book is more famous than (the author of) that book, so the price (of this book) is also more expensive than (the price of) that book.

我学习得比他努力，所以考试成绩也比他高(= 比他的高)。
Wǒ xuéxí de bǐ tā nǔlì, suǒyǐ kǎoshì chéngjī yě bǐ tā gāo (= bǐ tā de gāo).
I study harder (more diligently) than he does, so my test scores are higher than his.

23.12 The need for balance

Level 3

Both A and B need to be the same type of word or phrase in Chinese.

English: My test score is not as good as I hoped.
Chinese: 我的考试**成绩**没有我**希望的**好。 (My test score is not as good as what I hoped for.)
            Wǒde kǎoshì chéngjī méiyǒu wǒ xīwàng de hǎo.
(Improper: 我的考试成绩没有我希望好。)(成绩 is a noun and 希望 is a verb.)

他到了那个小镇以后才发现**那个地方**比他**想象中**更落后。
Tā dào le nà ge xiǎo zhèn yǐhòu cái fāxiàn nà ge dìfāng bǐ tā xiǎngxiàng zhōng gèng luòhòu.
Only after he arrived at that small town did he discover that that place was even more backward than what he had imagined.
(想象中 can be 想象的, but it is improper to say 那个地方比他想象更落后 since 地方 is a noun and 想象 is a verb.)

派小王出国比**派小张**合适得多，因为**小张**英文说得没有**小王**好。
Pài Xiǎo Wáng chūguó bǐ pài Xiǎo Zhāng héshì de duō, yīnwèi Xiǎo Zhāng Yīngwén shuō de méiyǒu Xiǎo Wáng hǎo.
Sending Xiao Wang overseas is much more fitting than sending Xiao Zhang because Xiao Zhang does not speak English as well as Xiao Wang does.

23.13 Implied comparisons without 比

Level 2

A comparison can be implied without using 比.

(a) Implied comparisons with 比较

When the two items being compared have been mentioned or are existent in the context, 比较 (*bǐjiào*) is used to imply a comparison.

小王跟小李都很聪明，但是小李**比较**用功(= 小李比小王用功)。
Xiǎo Wáng gēn Xiǎo Lǐ dōu hěn cōngmíng, dànshì Xiǎo Lǐ bǐjiào yònggōng.
Both Xiao Wang and Xiao Li are smart, but Xiao Li is more diligent.

张：明天的讨论会，应该在你家举行还是在他家举行？
Zhāng: Míngtiān de tǎolùn huì, yīnggāi zài nǐ jiā jǔxíng háishì zài tā tiā jǔxíng?
王：我家**比较**大(= 我家比他家大)，在我家吧。
Wáng: Wǒ jiā bǐjiào dà, zài wǒ jiā ba.
Zhang: Should we hold tomorrow's discussion at your house or at his house?
Wang: My house is bigger. Let's do it at my house.

(b) Implied comparisons with (一) 点 and (一) 些

Level
3

When (一) 点 (*diǎn*) or (一) 些 (*xiē*) appears **after an adjective**, a comparison is implied. This pattern is often used in giving others **advice or commands**.

那条街车子特别多，过马路的时候要**小心(一)点**。
Nà tiáo jiē chēzi tèbié duō, guò mǎlù de shíhòu yào xiǎoxīn (yì)diǎn.
That street has a lot of traffic; you must be **a little bit more careful** when crossing the street.

你说什么？我听不清楚，**大声一点**，好不好？
Nǐ shuō shénme? Wǒ tīng bù qīngchǔ, dàshēng yìdiǎn, hǎo bù hǎo?
What did you say? I can't hear you clearly. **A little louder**, OK?

Level
3

23.14 Summary of the basic comparison structures

The following table summarizes the basic structures in making comparisons.

Structure	Basic word order	Basic grammatical features	Examples
比	A 比 B + feature being compared (FC)	1 FC cannot have 不 or an adverb except 更/还. 2 A complement of quantity can follow FC to indicate the difference between A and B.	1. 我比他高。(他比我不高 is wrong.) *Wǒ bǐ tā gāo.* I am taller than he is. 2. 我比他高得多。(我比他很高 is incorrect.) *Wǒ bǐ tā gāo de duō.* I am much taller than he is.
有	A 有 B + FC	1 The status of B is known. 2 An optional 那么/这么 can appear before FC.	我儿子八岁，你儿子有我儿子(这么)大吗? *Wǒ érzi bā suì, nǐ érzi yǒu wǒ érzi (zhème) dà ma?* My son is eight years old. Is your son as old (as my son)?
没有	A 没有 B + FC	1 A is not as FC as B (B is more). 2 An optional 那么/这么 can appear before FC.	我儿子七岁，他儿子八岁，我儿子没有他儿子(那么)大。 *Wǒ érzi qī suì, tā érzi bā suì, wǒ érzi méiyǒu tā érzi (nàme) dà.* My son is seven; his son is eight. My son as not as old as his son.
不比	A 不比 B + FC	1 A is not more FC than B. 2 A and B are possibly equal and B could possibly be more FC.	他不比我聪明，可是我的成绩总是不比他的好。 *Tā bù bǐ wǒ cōngmíng, kěshì wǒde chéngjī zǒngshì bù bǐ tāde hǎo.* He is not smarter than I am; but my test scores are never better than his.

Exercises

Use 比, 不比 or 没有 to make comparisons based on the situations.

Example: I am 1.78 m tall; my younger brother is 1.82 m tall. (Use 没有.)

我没有我弟弟高。

Wǒ méiyǒu wǒ dìdi gāo.

Level

3

1 I did well in yesterday's test because I got 95. Wang Zhong got 98. (Only one comparison can best describe this situation.)

2 Everybody says that Wang Zhong runs fast because he can run 8 km in half an hour. I can run 8 km in about as much time. (Use 不比.)

3 My house is 140 m^2 and Mr Li's house is 170 m^2. But my house is worth 20,000 *yuan* and his house is worth 15,000 *yuan*. (Use 没有 and 比 to make two comparisons.)

4 Li Ming is the smartest student in our class. (Use 没有.)

5 Both my older brother and I are about 1.8 m tall. My brother is 90 kg and I am only 70 kg. (Use 不比 and 比 to make two comparisons.)

6 Yesterday's temperature was about 10°C and today's is about 2°C. (Use 没有.)

7 I work ten hours a day and Mr Zhang works seven hours a day. He makes 500 *yuan* a week, but I only make 300 *yuan* a week. (Use 比 and 没有 to make two comparisons.)

8 My house has five bedrooms and Mr Li's house has three bedrooms. Also, I have a huge kitchen and his kitchen is of medium size. (Use 没有 twice to make two comparisons.)

9 None of Li Zhong's classmates studies as diligently as he does; therefore, his test scores are always the highest in the class. (Use 比 twice to make two comparisons.)

10 Teacher Wang likes to complain that he has too many students. Actually both Teacher Wang and Teacher Li have between 250 and 260 students. But Teacher Li does not like to complain that much. (Use 不比 and 比 to make two comparisons.)

24 *Making comparisons (2)*

The focus of this chapter will be on comparisons indicating whether two items are similar/identical or different.

24.1 Making comparisons using 跟

The basic word order is 'A 跟 (*gēn*) B (不) (*bù*) 一样 (*yíyàng*)'. There might be more than one way to translate such a comparison into English, but there is only one sentence pattern in Chinese. Also, 不一样 can be replaced by 不同 (*bùtóng*).

> 我的做法跟你的一样，但是(我的)成果跟你的却不一样。
> *Wǒde zuòfǎ gēn nǐde yíyàng, dànshì (wǒde) chéngguǒ gēn nǐde què bù yíyàng.*
> #1 My method **and** yours are the same, but my outcome and yours are not the same.
> #2 My method is the same **as** yours, but my outcome is different from yours.

> 这条裙子的颜色跟那条一样，但是价钱跟那条不同。
> = 这条裙子跟那条颜色一样，但是价钱不同。
> *Zhè tiáo qúnzi de yánsè gēn nà tiáo yíyàng, dànshì jiàqián gēn nà tiáo bù tóng.*
> The colour of this skirt is the same as that one, but the price is not the same.

(a) Unquantifiable differences

If the difference is not quantifiable, 很 or another degree adverb (非常, 十分, 相当, etc.) can appear before 不一样/不同. But 很 should not appear before 一样.

> 你跟小李虽然**年纪**一样，但是你的**个性**跟他的**很不同**。 (年纪 is quantifiable; 个性 is not.)
> *Nǐ gēn Xiǎo Lǐ suīrán niánjì yíyàng, dànshì nǐ de gèxìng gēn tāde hěn bùtóng.*
> Although your age and Xiao Li's are the same, your personality is very different from his.

(b) The 'feature being compared'

The feature being compared in a 跟......一样 sentence is similar to what might be in a 比 (*bǐ*) sentence. That is, the feature can be an adjective, a complement of state or a verb with the quality of an adjective. Certain auxiliary verbs can also be the feature being compared.

> 小王跟小李一样**高**，他跑得也跟小李一样**快**。
> *Xiǎo Wáng gēn Xiǎo Lǐ yíyàng gāo, tā pǎo de yě gēn Xiǎo Lǐ yíyàng kuài.*
> Xiao Wang is as tall as Xiao Li; he also runs as fast as Xiao Li.
> (This means Xiao Wang and Xiao Li are of the same height and they run equally fast.)

> 小兰跟她姐姐一样会唱歌，也跟姐姐一样爱跳舞。
> *Xiǎolan gēn tā jiějie yíyàng huì chànggē, yě gēn jiějie yíyàng ài tiàowǔ.*
> Xiaolan is as good at singing as her older sister; she also loves dancing as much as her older sister.

(c) Negative form

When 'A 跟 B 不一样 + feature being compared' is used, it only indicates A and B are **not equal** or not the same, but does not indicate which is stronger (or weaker) in the feature being compared.

这次演讲比赛，王明**跟**李中准备得**一样认真**，但是他们的表现却**不一样好**。
Zhè cì yǎnjiǎng bǐsài, Wáng Míng gēn Lǐ Zhōng zhǔnbèi de yíyàng rènzhēn, dànshì tāmen de biǎoxiàn què bù yíyàng hǎo.
Wang Ming prepared as conscientiously as Li Zhong did for the speech contest, but their performances were not equally good. (This does not explicitly indicate whose performance was better.)

这次考试，我准备的时间**跟**小李**一样多**，但是我的表现**没有**他的好。
Zhè cì kǎoshì, wǒ zhǔnbèi de shíjiān gēn Xiǎo Lǐ yíyàng duō, dànshì wǒde biǎoxiàn méiyǒu tāde hǎo.
The time I spent studying for the test was as much as the time Xiao Li spent, but my performance was not as good as his. (This indicates Xiao Li's performance was better.)

(d) When the feature being compared is a noun

When the feature being compared is a noun, the word order can be slightly flexible. The noun can be part of A or part of B; and 的 can be optional.

这件毛衣**跟**那件(的)**颜色不一样**，但是(跟那件)**大小一样**，你自己决定想买哪件。
Zhè jiàn máoyī gēn nà jiàn (de) yánsè bù yíyàng, dànshì (gēn nàjiàn) dàxiǎo yíyàng, nǐ zìjǐ juédìng xiǎng mǎi nǎ jiàn.
= 这件毛衣(的)**颜色跟**那件**不一样**，但是**大小跟**那件**一样**，你自己决定想买哪件。
This sweater's colour is different from that one's, but the size is the same as that one's. You yourself decide which one you want to buy.

张：王先生**跟**李先生的**学历、经历都一样**，为什么薪水却**不一样高**呢？
Zhāng: Wáng xiānsheng gēn Lǐ xiānsheng de xuélì, jīnglì dōu yíyàng, wèi shénme xīnshuǐ què bù yíyàng gāo ne?
(= 王先生的**学历、经历**都**跟**李先生**一样**，......)
丁：因为王先生的**职位跟**李先生的**不一样**。(= 因为王先生**跟**李先生的**职位不一样**。)
Dīng: Yīnwèi Wáng xiānsheng de zhíwèi gēn Lǐ xiānsheng de bù yíyàng.
Zhang: Mr Wang's educational background and experiences are both the same as Mr Li's; why is it that their salaries are not the same (not equally high)?
Ding: Because Mr Wang's position is different from Mr Li's. (= Because Mr Wang's position is not the same as Mr Li's.)

(e) Making more than one comparison

When more than one comparison is made on the same two items, 'A 跟 B' does not have to be repeated each time. Pronouns (你们 (*nǐmen*), 我们 (*wǒmen*), 他们 (*tāmen*), etc.) can be used or nothing at all.

小兰**跟**她姐姐**一样聪明**，(她们)钢琴也弹得**一样好**。
Xiǎolán gēn tā jiějie yíyàng cōngmíng, (tāmen) gāngqín yě tán de yíyàng hǎo.
Xiaolan is as smart as her older sister; they also play the piano as well as each other (equally well).

(f) Using 和 or 与 in place of 跟

和 or 与 can be used in place of 跟. 与 tends to be more formal than 跟 or 和.

> 小李**和**他弟弟一样高，可是(他)却**和**他哥哥一样胖。
> *Xiǎo Lǐ hé tā dìdi yíyàng gāo, kěshì (tā) què hé tā gēge yíyàng pàng.*
> Xiao Li is as tall as his younger brother, but he is as fat as his older brother.

> 张经理学历、经验都**与**陈经理一样，因此薪资也**与**陈经理一样。
> *Zhāng jīnglǐ xuélì, jīngyàn dōu yǔ Chén jīnglǐ yíyàng, yīncǐ xīnzī yě yǔ Chén jīnglǐ yíyàng.*
> Manager Zhang's education and experiences are both the same as Manager Chen's; therefore, his salary is also the same as Manager Chen's.

24.2 Making comparisons with 差不多 and 差很多

Level 2

(a) 差不多: Approximately the same

'A 跟 B 差不多 (*chàbùduō*) (一样)' or 'A 跟 B 差不多 (一样) + feature being compared' can be used to indicate A and B are approximately the same.

> 我的意见**跟**你的**差不多**。
> *Wǒde yìjiàn gēn nǐde chàbùduō.*
> My opinion is **about the same** as yours.

After 差不多, an adjective can follow. In this case, '一样 + adjective' can be used.

> 王： 你大还是小李大？
> *Wáng: Nǐ dà háishì Xiǎo Lǐ dà?*
> 张： 我**跟**他年纪**差不多**(大)，而且我们也**差不多**一样高。
> *Zhāng: Wǒ gēn tā niánjì chàbùduō (dà), érqiě wǒmen yě chàbùduō yíyàng gāo.*
> Wang : Are you older or is Xiao Li older?
> Zhang: He and I are about the same age; we are also about the same height.

(b) 差很多: Very different

'A 跟 B 差很多' is used to mean there is a big difference between A and B or 'A 跟 B 很不一样'.

> 这件蓝衬衫**跟**那件绿的，质料、花色都**差不多**，可是价钱**差很多**。
> *Zhè jiàn lán chènshān gēn nà jiàn lǜ de, zhìliào, huāsè dōu chàbùduō, kěshì jiàqián chà hěn duō.*
> The fabric and pattern on this blue shirt and that green one are about the same, but there is a big difference in their prices.

> 小明**跟**他哥哥的个性**差很多**(= 很不一样)，可是他们的兴趣、爱好却**差不多**。
> *Xiǎoming gēn tā gēge de gèxìng chà hěn duō (= hěn bù yíyàng), kěshì tāmen de xìngqù, àihào què chàbùduō.*
> Xiaoming's personality is very different from his older brother's, but their interests and hobbies are about the same.

24.3 Making comparisons using 象

Level 2/3

象 (*xiàng*) means 'to be like'; it implies a certain kind of resemblance.

(a) Physical resemblances

When A resembles (or does not resemble) B in features that are obvious in context, the pattern is simply 'A (不) 象 B'.

大家都说小明**不象**我哥哥，反而**象**我弟弟。

Dàjiā dōu shuō Xiǎomíng bú xiàng wǒ gēge, fǎn'ér xiàng wǒ dìdi.

Everyone says that Xiaoming is not like my older brother; instead, he is like my younger brother.

(The obvious context is that Xiaoming is, in fact, my older brother.)

老王很注意保养，所以**不象**五十多岁的人。

Lǎo Wáng hěn zhùyì bǎoyǎng, suǒyǐ bú xiàng wǔshí duō suì de rén.

Lao Wang pays attention to maintaining his looks, so he does not look like someone in his 50s.

在王家，儿子都**象**妈妈，女儿都**象**爸爸；真有意思。

Zài Wáng jiā, érzi dōu xiàng māma, nǚ'ér dōu xiàng bàba; zhēn yǒu yìsi.

In the Wang family, all the sons resemble their mother; all the daughters resemble their father. This is really interesting.

(b) Non-physical resemblances

When the resemblance is not about physical features, then 'A 象 B 一样' can be used.

小王**象**他爸爸**一样**，也不喜欢吃鱼。

Xiǎo Wáng xiàng tā bàba yíyàng, yě bù xǐhuān chī yú.

Xiao Wang is like his father; he does not like to eat fish, either.

这个地方的风景真美，简直**象**幅画儿**一样**。

Zhè ge dìfāng de fēngjǐng zhēn měi, jiǎnzhí xiàng fǔ huàr yíyàng.

The scenery here is really beautiful. It's practically like a painting.

(c) The use of 那么/这么

When it is necessary to mention the feature being compared, **B's status must be already known**. Therefore, 那么/这么 (*nàme/zhème*) appears before the feature being compared. The pattern is 'A (不) 象 B 那么/这么 + feature being compared'.

这件事派我去做吧，别叫老张做。我**不象**老张**那么忙**(= 我**没有**老张**那么忙**)。

Zhè jiàn shì pài wǒ qù zuò ba, bié jiào Lǎo Zhāng zuò. Wǒ bú xiàng Lǎo Zhāng nàme máng.

Why don't you assign me to do this job? Don't assign it to Lao Zhang. I am not as busy as Lao Zhang. (This implies that Lao Zhang is very busy.)

您的体力真好！如果我**象**你**这么忙**，早就累病了！(Do not say 如果我象你忙……)

Nínde tǐlì zhēn hǎo! Rúguǒ wǒ xiàng nǐ zhème máng, zǎo jiù lèi bìng le!

You are really energetic. If I were as busy as you are, I would have been ill (from exhaustion).

(d) Adding a 'feature being compared' after 一样

The sentence pattern can also be 'A 象 B 一样 + feature being compared'. This pattern usually is not a negative statement.

已经十一月了，怎么天气还**象**夏天**一样热**？

Yǐjīng shíyī yuè le, zěnme tiānqì hái xiàng xiàtiān yíyàng rè?

It's already November. How come the weather is still as hot as summer?

如果我长得**象**你**一样**帅，那么我的女朋友大概也会**象**你的**一样**多。

Rúguǒ wǒ zhǎng de xiàng nǐ yíyàng shuài, nàme wǒde nǚ péngyǒu dàgài yě huì xiàng nǐde yíyàng duō.

If I were as handsome as you are, then I probably would have as many girlfriends as you do.

24.4 Comparisons with 跟 vs. comparisons with 象

'A 跟 B 一样 + feature being compared' and 'A 象 B 一样 + feature being compared' oftentimes can be interchangeable. When 象 is used, the status of B must be already known, but when 跟 is used, the status of B may or may not be already known.

王小姐非常漂亮，我真希望我能**跟**她**一样**漂亮(= 象她一样漂亮)。

Wáng xiǎojiě fēicháng piàoliàng, wǒ zhēn xīwàng wǒ néng gēn tā yíyàng piàoliàng.

Miss Wang is extremely pretty. I really wish I could be as pretty as she is.

李： 小王比较帅还是小张比较帅？

Lǐ: Xiǎo Wáng bǐjiào shuài háishì Xiǎo Zhāng bǐjiào shuài?

丁： 小王**跟**小张**一样**帅。

Dīng: Xiǎo Wáng gēn Xiǎo Zhāng yíyàng shuài.

(It is not proper in this case to say 小王象小张一样帅 since 小张's status is unknown.)

Li: Is Xiao Wang more handsome or is Xiao Zhang more handsome?

Ding: Xiao Wang and Xiao Zhang are **equally handsome**.

24.5 Comparisons with 有 vs. comparisons with 象

'A 有 (*yǒu*) B 这么/那么 + feature being compared' and 'A 象 B 这么/那么 + feature being compared' are similar in meaning, **the status of B must be already known** in both patterns. But the use of 有 implies 'A has reached the level of B and may even be higher in level' whereas the use of 象 implies A and B are similar in status.

张： 王小姐非常漂亮，李小姐**有**她**那么**漂亮吗？

Zhāng: Wáng xiǎojiě fēicháng piàoliàng, Lǐ xiǎojiě yǒu tā nàme piàoliàng ma?

丁： 李小姐不但**有**她**(那么)**漂亮，而且**比**她**更**漂亮。

Dīng: Lǐ xiǎojiě búdàn yǒu tā (nàme) piàoliàng, érqiě bǐ tā gèng piàoliàng.

Zhang: Miss Wang is very pretty. Is Miss Li as pretty as she is?

Ding: Miss Li is not just as pretty; she is even prettier.

张： 经理，老王加薪了，为什么我没加呢？

Zhāng: Jīnglǐ, Lǎo Wáng jiāxīn le, wèishénme wǒ méi jiā ne?

经理： 如果你**有**他**那么**能干，那么你当然也会加。

Jīnglǐ: Rúguǒ nǐ yǒu tā nàme nénggàn, nàme nǐ dāngrán yě huì jiā.

张： 如果我的工作**象**他的**那么**轻松，那么我也会显得很能干。

Zhāng: Rúguǒ wǒde gōngzuò xiàng tāde nàme qīngsōng, nàme wǒ yě huì xiǎnde hěn nénggàn.

Zhang: Manager, Lao Wang got a pay rise, how come I didn't get one?

Manager: If you were as competent as he is (if you could reach his level of competence), then of course you would have had a pay rise, too.

Zhang: If my job was as easy as his, then I would appear to be very competent.

24.6 Negative comparisons with 没有 vs. negative comparisons with 不象

Level 2

'A 没有 (*méiyǒu*) B 那么 + feature being compared' and 'A 不象 (*bú xiàng*) B 那么 + feature being compared' can be considered **interchangeable** all the time. Also, when 没有 B is used, 'B' becomes optional if it has previously been mentioned.

我的朋友都说《阿凡达》很好看。可是我去看了以后，发现这个电影**没有**(他们说的)**那么**好看(= 这个电影**不象**他们说的**那么**好看)。

Wǒde péngyǒu dōu shuō 'Ā Fán Dá' hěn hǎokàn. Kěshì wǒ qù kàn le yǐhòu, fāxiàn zhè ge diànyǐng méiyǒu (tāmen shuō de) nàme hǎokàn (= zhè ge diànyǐng bú xiàng tāmen shuō de nàme hǎokàn).

All my friends said that *Avatar* was good. But after I went to see it, I found that this movie was not as good as they had said.

昨天真冷，今天**没有**昨天**那么**冷(= 今天**没有那么**冷 = 今天**不象**昨天**那么**冷)。

Zuótiān zhēn lěng, jīntiān méiyǒu zuótiān nàme lěng (= jīntiān méiyǒu nàme lěng = jīntiān bú xiàng zuótiān nàme lěng).

Yesterday was really cold; today is not as cold as yesterday.

24.7 The use of 那么 explained

Level 2

Although 'A 没有 B 那么 + feature being compared' and 'A 没有 B + feature being compared' are similar in meaning, the former implies that the status of B is already known, whereas the latter does not always imply the same.

王先生的房子非常贵，李先生的**没有**(王先生的)**那么**贵。

Wáng xiānsheng de fángzi fēicháng guì, Lǐ xiānsheng de méiyǒu (Wáng xiānsheng de) nàme guì.

Mr Wang's house is very expensive. Mr Li's house is not as expensive (as Mr Wang's).

我的书八块钱，你的**没有**我的**贵**。(Whether 八块钱 is considered expensive is not clear.)

Wǒde shū bā kuài qián, nǐde méiyǒu wǒde guì.

My book is $8. Yours is not as expensive as mine.

24.8 Comparisons with 跟 vs. comparisons with 象

Level 2

When the feature being compared is **measureable**, or A and B are **exactly the same** or **identical**, the use of 跟 would be more proper than the use of 象.

(a) Positive forms

象 implies the two are similar, whereas 跟 implies the two are identical.

我**跟**我哥哥**一样高**，也**一样胖**。(Height and weight are measurable.)

Wǒ gēn wǒ gēge yíyàng gāo, yě yíyàng pàng.

My height and the weight are the same as my older brother's.

这条绳子**跟**那条**一样长**。(Length is measurable.)

Zhè tiáo shéngzi gēn nà tiáo yíyàng cháng.

This rope is as long as that one. (This rope is the same length as that one.)

他虽然吃了退烧药，可是体温还是**跟**(or 象)吃药以前**一样高**。

Tā suīrán chī le tuìshāo yào, kěshì tāde tǐwēn háishì gēn (or xiàng) chī yào yǐqián yíyàng gāo.

Although he has taken fever-reducing medicine, his body temperature is still as high as before he took the medicine.

(b) Negative forms

The negative form for a 象 sentence is 'A 不象 B + 那么/这么 + feature being compared',
whereas the negative form for a 跟 sentence is 'A 跟 B + 不一样'.

> 这件红大衣**不象**那件绿的**那么**贵，所以我买了红的。
> *Zhè jiàn hóng dàyī bú xiàng nà jiàn lǜ de nàme guì, suǒyǐ wǒ mǎi le hóng de.*
> This red coat is not as expensive as that green one, so I bought the red one.

> 这件大衣**跟**那件**不一样**贵，你知不知道哪件比较贵？
> *Zhè jiàn dàyī gēn nà jiàn bù yíyàng guì, nǐ zhī bù zhīdào nà jiàn bǐjiào guì?*
> This coat and that one are not equally expensive. Do you know which one is more
> expensive?

Level 3

24.9 Relative clauses in sentences of comparison

Only B is mentioned. The basic word order is '比 B + feature being compared + 的' or '跟/象
B 一样/那么 + feature being compared + 的'.

> 这条裙子太贵了，有没有**比这条**便宜**的**？
> *Zhè tiáo qúnzi tài guì le, yǒu méiyǒu bǐ zhè tiáo piànyí de?*
> This skirt is too expensive. Are there any that are cheaper than this one?

> 我英文说得不够好，你去请一个说得**比我好的**人教你吧！
> *Wǒ Yīngwén shuō de bú gòu hǎo, nǐ qù qǐng yí ge shuō de bǐ wǒ hǎo de rén jiāo nǐ ba!*
> I don't speak English well enough. Why don't you go ask someone who speaks better
> than I do to teach you?

> 小王相当聪明，可是我们班还有两个**比他**更聪明**的**(学生)。
> *Xiǎo Wáng xiāngdāng cōngmíng, kěshì wǒmen bān háiyǒu liǎng ge bǐ tā gèng cōngmíng de.*
> Xiao Wang is quite smart, but there are two even smarter students in our class.

> 我从来没有看过**象小兰这么漂亮的**女孩子。
> *Wǒ cónglái méiyǒu kàn guò xiàng Xiǎolán zhème piàoliàng de nǚ háizi.*
> I have never seen a girl (who is) as pretty as Xiaolan.

> 我想买一件**跟你那件**一样**的**大衣。
> *Wǒ xiǎng mǎi yí jiàn gēn nǐ nà jiàn yíyàng de dàyī.*
> I want to buy a coat that is the same as yours.

> 昨天我认识了一个**跟你女朋友一样漂亮的**女孩。
> *Zuótiān wǒ rènshì le yí ge gēn nǐ nǚ péngyǒu yíyàng piàoliàng de nǚhái.*
> Yesterday I met a girl who is as pretty as your girlfriend.

Exercises

Translate the following sentences into Chinese. (There may be more than one way to
translate some of them.)

Level 3

1   Teacher Zhang: I have never taught a student as smart as Wang Ming.

    Teacher Li: I have taught students as smart as him, but I have not taught anyone
    even smarter than him.

2 Li Zhong and his younger brother are the same height, but (Li Zhong) is not as thin as his younger brother.

3 These two coats are the same colour and style, but the material is not the same, so their prices are very different.

4 Li: Mr Zhang's girlfriend is really pretty. Mr Wang's girlfriend is not as pretty as she is.

Ding: But I know she is as kind as Mr Zhang's girlfriend.

Chen: If I knew a girlfriend as pretty as Mr Wang's girlfriend, I would be very happy.

5 Li: Today is really cold. If tomorrow is as cold as today, I will stay home.

Wang: Tomorrow is not going to be as cold; it will be even colder.

6 Female: When are you coming to visit me?

Male: How about next year? Next year I will not be as busy as I am this year.

Female: All right, but don't be like last time again. Last time, you cancelled your flight the day before departure.

7 The scenery here is as beautiful as a painting.

8 Wang: If I were as rich as he is, I could also buy a house as big as his.

Ding: That house is not that big. Although I am not as rich as he is, I already have a house even bigger than his.

9 Although Anna is not as smart as Wang Zhong, she is also not as lazy as he is; therefore, their test scores are always about the same.

Section 2

25 Measure words

A measure word appears after a number, 这 (*zhè*), 那 (*nà*), 哪 (*nǎ*), 几 (*jǐ*) or 每 (*měi*) and before a noun. (半 (*bàn*) and 多少 (*duōshǎo*) can precede a measure word as well.) Although the choice of the measure word for each noun can be associated with the shape, function, form, etc. of the noun, to categorize measure words is not within the scope of this chapter.

To a certain degree, the choice of the measure word is arbitrary. ☉ Therefore, when a noun is acquired by the learner as a new vocabulary word, its matching measure word should be learned at the same time. For example, the phrase 'a pair of' can involve different measure words depending on the nouns being described: 'a pair of chopsticks' is 一双筷子 (*yì shuāng kuàizi*), whereas 'a pair of earrings' is 一付耳环 (*yí fù ěrhuán*).

There are over 100 words that can be used as measure words. This chapter will not list all these words and their nouns. Instead, the focus will be on the grammar rules concerning the use of measure words.

25.1 Nouns that do not need measure words

Level 1/2

Only a few nouns do not need measure words. The most common ones are those regarding 'time'; they are 年 (*nián*: 'year'), 天 (*tiān*: 'day'), 分钟 (*fēnzhōng*: 'minute'), 秒钟 (*miǎozhōng*: 'second') and 周 (*zhōu*: 'week').

> 一年有三百六十五天。 (Do not say 一个年有三百六十五个天.)
> *Yì nián yǒu sān bǎi liùshí wǔ tiān.*
> A year has 365 days.

> 一分钟有六十秒(钟)。 (Do not say 一个分钟有六十个秒钟.)
> *Yì fēnzhōng yǒu liùshí miǎo(zhōng).*
> One minute has 60 seconds.

> 一周有七天。 (Do not say 一个周有七个天.)
> *Yì zhōu yǒu qī tiān.*
> A week has seven days.

(a) 'Time' nouns with optional measure words

Certain nouns regarding 'time' can have an optional measure word (个: *ge*). These words are 星期 (*xīngqī*: 'week'), 小时 (*xiǎoshí*: 'hour'), 学期 (*xuéqī*: 'term/semester').

> 一年有五十二(个)星期；一(个)星期有七天。
> *Yì nián yǒu wǔshí èr (ge) xīngqī; yì (ge) xīngqī yǒu qī tiān.*
> A year has 52 weeks; a week has seven days.

> 这(个)学期功课特别多，我每天都要花三(个)小时才能把功课写完。
> *Zhè (ge) xuéqī gōngkè tèbié duō, wǒ měi tiān dōu yào huā sān (ge) xiǎoshí cái néng bǎ gōngkè xiě wán.*

This term, I have an inordinate amount of homework. It takes me three hours every day to finally finish doing my homework.

(b) Special case: 礼拜, 钟头 and 日子

It should be noted that, although 星期 and 礼拜 (*lǐbài*) share the same meaning, and 小时 and 钟头 (*zhōngtóu*) also share the same meaning, the measure word (个) for 礼拜 and for 钟头 is **not** optional. Likewise, 日子 (*rìzi*) shares a similar meaning to 天, but the measure word (个) for 日子 is **not** optional.

(c) Special case: 月

The measure word for 月 (*yuè*: 'month') is 个 and it is **not** optional.

> 一个月有几天？
> *Yí ge yuè yǒu jǐ tiān?*
> How many days are there in **a month**?
> Compare: 一月有几天？
> > *Yīyuè yǒu jǐ tiān?*
> > How many days are there in **January**?

(d) Other nouns with optional measure words

Other nouns that do not always need measure words tend to be one-character words that indicate some form of organization, such as 班 (*bān*: 'class'), 家 (*jiā*: 'family'), 组 (*zǔ*: 'team'), 队 (*duì*: 'team'), 州 (*zhōu*: 'state'), 省 (*shěng*: 'province'), 国 (*guó*: 'country'), etc.

- As soon as any of these words is expressed by a two-character word (if possible), the measure word becomes necessary. One-character words that can be expressed in two characters are 班 (班级: *bānjí*), 家 (家庭: *jiātíng*), 国 (国家: *guójiā*), 队 (队伍: *duìwǔ*), etc. These two-character words must use measure words

   > 东亚主要有三个国家--中国、日本和韩国；这三国的语言各不相同。
   > *Dōng Yà zhǔyào yǒu sān ge guójiā – Zhōngguó, Rìběn hé Hánguó; zhè sān guó de yǔyán gè bù xiāngtóng.*
   > East Asia mainly has three countries – China, Japan and Korea. The languages of these three countries are different from one another.

- As one-character words, the measure word (个) is optional (国 and 家 are exceptions to this rule)

   > 这个学校有六个年级，每个年级有三(个)班，所以一共有十八(个)班。
   > *Zhè ge xuéxiào yǒu liù ge niánjí, měi ge niánjí yǒu sān (ge) bān, suǒyǐ yígòng yǒu shíbā (ge) bān.*
   > This school has six grades; each grade has three classes, so altogether there are 18 classes.

   > 这次比赛，有几(个)队报名参加？
   > *Zhè cì bǐsài, yǒu jǐ (ge) duì bàomíng cānjiā?*
   > How many teams have entered this competition?

   > 在中国，一家(= 一个家庭)只能有一个孩子。(Improper: 一个家)
   > *Zài Zhōngguó, yì jiā (= yí ge jiātíng) zhǐ néng yǒu yí ge háizi.*
   > In China, one family can have only one child.

- Although 国 and 家 are exceptions to the above-mentioned rule, when 家 refers to one's own home, the measure word 个 becomes necessary

王先生有**两个家**，一个在中国，一个在日本。 (Incorrect: 王先生有两家.)

Wáng xiānsheng yǒu liǎng ge jiā, yí ge zài Zhōngguó, yí ge zài Rìběn.

Mr Wang has two homes; one is in China, one is in Japan.

(e) Special case: 人

The measure word for 人 is 个 and it is optional. When the number of people is large, 个 is hardly ever used.

老师：今天我带来的课件不够，所以**两人**一张(= **两个人**一张)。

Lǎoshī: Jīntiān wǒ dàilái de kèjiàn bú gòu, suǒyǐ liǎng rén yì zhāng (= liǎng ge rén yì zhāng).

学生：**两(个)人**一张也还是不够，可能要三**(个)人**一张。

Xuéshēng: Liǎng (ge) rén yì zhāng yě hái shì bú gòu, kěnéng yào sān (ge) rén yì zhāng.

Teacher: I didn't bring enough handouts today, so one piece for every two people.

Student: It's still not enough even if every two people share one piece. Probably every three people have to share one piece.

Level 1

25.2 Nouns that can have more than one measure word

Many nouns can have more than one measure word. The choice of measure word may depend on who the speaker is or in what context the speech is uttered. There are many such cases; the following are only a few examples.

一**个**卧室 = 一**间**卧室

yí ge wòshì = yì jiān wòshì

one bedroom

一**个**工作 = 一**份**工作

yí ge gōngzuò = yí fèn gōngzuò

one job

两**辆**车 = 两**部**车 = 两**台**车

liǎng liàng chē = liǎng bù chē = liǎng tái chē

two cars

两**首**歌 = 两**条**歌 = 两**只**歌

liǎng shǒu gē = liǎng tiáo gē = liǎng zhī gē

two songs

三**个**房子 = 三**栋**房子 = 三**幢**房子

sān ge fángzi = sān dòng fángzi = sān zhuàng fángzi

three houses

三**个**记者 = 三**位**记者 = 三**名**记者

sān ge jìzhě = sān wèi jìzhě = sān míng jìzhě

three reporters

四**家**书店 = 四**个**书店

sì jiā shūdiàn = sì ge shūdiàn

four bookshops

四**座**大楼 = 四**栋**大楼

sì zuò dà lóu = sì dòng dà lóu

four tall buildings

<table>
<tr><td>Level
1</td></tr>
</table>

25.3 The use of measure words with 多少

When 多少 means 'how many', the measure word is optional and is more often than not omitted. When 多少 means 'how much', there is usually no measure word.

你们班有**多少(个)**学生？**多少(个)**男的？**多少(个)**女的？
Nǐmen bān yǒu duōshǎo (ge) xuéshēng? Duōshǎo (ge) nán de? Duōshǎo (ge) nǚ de?
How many students are there in your class? How many male? How many female?

王老师教了二十几年书，连他自己也不知道教过**多少**学生。
Wáng lǎoshī jiāo le èrshí jǐ nián shū, lián tā zìjǐ yě bù zhīdào jiāo guo duōshǎo xuéshēng.
Teacher Wang taught for more than 20 years. Even he himself does not know how many students he has taught.

太太：你喝了**多少**啤酒？
Tàitai: Nǐ hē le duōshǎo píjiǔ?
先生：我喝得不多。
Xiānsheng: Wǒ hē de bù duō.
太太：你到底喝了**多少**瓶？
Tàitai: Nǐ dàodǐ hē le duōshǎo píng?
Wife: **How much beer** did you drink?
Husband: I didn't drink much.
Wife: Exactly **how many bottles** did you drink?

<table>
<tr><td>Level
1</td></tr>
</table>

25.4 The use of measure words with 很多

Grammatically, it is not necessary to use a measure word after 很多 (hěn duō). However, it is not unusual to use one in casual speech.

安娜来中国才半年，可是已经交了**很多**中国朋友。
Ānnà lái Zhōngguó cái bàn nián, kěshì yǐjīng jiāo le hěn duō Zhōngguó péngyǒu.
Anna has only been in China for half a year, but she has made many Chinese friends.

这学期我们念了**很多**篇鲁迅写的文章。
Zhè xuéqī wǒmen niàn le hěn duō piān Lǔ Xùn xiě de wénzhāng.
This term, we read many articles written by Lu Xun.

<table>
<tr><td>Level
1/2</td></tr>
</table>

25.5 The use of measure words with 半

半 can appear either before or after the measure word. Different word orders result in different meanings.

史密斯先生在北京住了**半年**，在南京也住了**半年**，后来又到上海去住了**一年半**才回国，所以他一共在中国住了**两年半**。
Shǐmìsī xiānsheng zài Běijīng zhù le bàn nián, zài Nánjīng yě zhù le bàn nián, hòulái yòu dào Shànghǎi qù zhù le yì nián bàn cái huí guó, suǒyǐ tā yígòng zài Zhōngguó zhù le liǎng nián bàn.
Mr Smith lived in Beijing for **half a year** and he also lived in Nanjing for **half a year**. Afterwards, he went to Shanghai and lived there for **a year and a half** before he finally returned to his own country. So altogether he lived in China for **two and a half years**.

我天天早上都吃**半个**苹果，可是今天觉得特别饿，就多吃了一个，所以一共吃了**一个半**。
Wǒ tiān tiān zǎoshàng dōu chī bàn ge píngguǒ, kěshì jīntiān juéde tèbié è, jiù duō chī le yí ge, suǒyǐ yígòng chī le yí ge bàn.

I eat half an apple every morning, but today I felt particularly hungry, so I ate one more (apple), eating one and a half apples in total.

25.6 The use of 大 and 小 with measure words

An adjective cannot immediately precede a measure word, except 大 (*dà*) and 小 (*xiǎo*). In this case, neither 大 nor 小 refers to size; rather, they refer to amount or quantity.

一**小**群狗 *yì xiǎo qún gǒu*   vs.   一群**小**狗 *yì qún xiǎo gǒu*
a small group of dogs   a group of small dogs

他说了**一大堆**话，可是我一句也不懂。（一大堆: 'a huge amount')
Tā shuō le yí dà duī huà, kěshì wǒ yí jù yě bù dǒng.
He said a whole lot of things, but I didn't understand even one sentence.
Compare: 他说了一堆**大话**，所以我一句也不信。（大话: 'exaggerated words')
                    Tā shuō le yì duī dàhuà, suǒyǐ wǒ yí jù yě bú xìn.
                    He made a lot of exaggerated statements, so I don't believe even one sentence.

我肚子不太饿，但是口很渴，所以只吃了**一小碗**饭，不过喝了**两大碗**汤。
Wǒ dùzi bú tài è, dànshì kǒu hěn kě, suǒyǐ zhǐ chī le yì xiǎo wǎn fàn, búguò hē le liǎng dǎ wǎn tāng.
I was not very hungry, but I was thirsty. So I only had a small bowl of rice, but I had two full bowls of soup.
(小 and 大 may or may not refer to the size of the bowls, but their main function in the sentence is to tell the amount of rice and soup consumed.)

安娜做了布丁跟蛋糕。布丁不好吃，蛋糕还不错；我吃了**一小口**布丁，却吃了**一大块**蛋糕。
Ānnà zuò le bùdīng gēn dàngāo. Bùdīng bù hǎochī, dàngāo hái búcuò, wǒ chī le yì xiǎo kǒu bùdīng, què chī le yí dà kuài dàngāo.
Anna made pudding and cake. The pudding was not good and the cake is not bad.
I had a small bite of the pudding, but I ate a large piece of the cake.

25.7 No 的 after measure words

的 (*de*) should not be used between a measure word and a noun.

我**哪种人**都见过，就是没见过象小王**这样的人**。（种 is a measure word; 样 is not.)
Wǒ nǎ zhǒng rén dōu jiàn guò, jiùshi méi jiàn guò xiàng Xiǎo Wáng zhèyàng de rén.
= 我**什么样的人**都见过，就是没见过象小王**这种人**。
= *Wǒ shénme yàng de rén dou jiàn guò, jiùshì méi jiàn guò xiàng Xiǎo Wáng zhè zhǒng rén.*
I have seen all kinds of people, but I have not seen a person like Xiao Wang.

25.8 Reduplicating measure words

Many measure words can be reduplicated to give the meaning 'every'. One-character words that do not need measure words can perform the same function if reduplicated.

- These reduplicated measure words can serve as an adverbial phrase or the subject of a sentence

小李**天天**准时来上课。
Xiǎo Lǐ tiān tiān zhǔnshí lái shàngkè.
Every day, Xiao Li comes to class on time.

停在这个停车场上的车，**辆辆**都是进口的高级车。

Tíng zài zhè ge tíngchēchǎng shàng de chē, liàng liàng dōu shì jìnkǒu de gāojí chē.

Every car that is parked in this car park is an imported high-class car.

这个社区，都是有钱人，所以**家家**都有昂贵的进口车。

Zhè ge shèqū, dōu shì yǒuqián rén, suǒyǐ jiā jiā dōu yǒu ángguì de jìnkǒu chē.

The people in this community are all rich, so every family has expensive imported cars.

- However, the reduplicated measure words cannot be the object of a verb

王老师：我的学生，**个个**都很努力，所以我要送**每个人**一本词典。

Wáng lǎoshī: Wǒde xuéshēng, gè gè dōu hěn nǔlì, suǒyǐ wǒ yào sòng měi ge rén yì běn cídiǎn.

李老师：现在几乎**人人**都用网络词典了。

Lǐ lǎoshī: Xiànzǎi jīhū rén rén dōu yòng wǎngluò cídiǎn le.

Teacher Wang: Every one of my students is diligent, so I want to give each a dictionary.

Teacher Li: Nowadays almost everyone is using dictionaries on the Internet.

- Although 人 is not considered a measure word, 人人 can be used in the same way

在中国，**人人**都喜欢熊猫。

Zài Zhōngguó, rén rén dōu xǐhuān xióngmāo.

In China, everybody likes pandas.

Level 1/2 25.9 Omitting the noun after a measure word

When the noun is omitted from a sentence in order to avoid repetition, the measure word must remain.

(Situation: Two sisters are shopping for clothes. Note that the word 'blouse' only appears once, but its measure word 件 appears every time a blouse is mentioned.)

姐姐：我打算买**两件衬衫**，你呢？

Jiějie: Wǒ dǎsuàn mǎi liǎng jiàn chènshān, nǐ ne?

妹妹：我只要买**一件**。你觉得**这件**好不好看？

Mèimei: Wǒ zhǐ yào mǎi yí jiàn. Nǐ juéde zhè jiàn hǎo bù hǎokàn?

姐姐：**这件**不好，那个架子上**那几件**好像还不错。

Jiějie: Zhè jiàn bù hǎo, nà ge jiàzi shàng nà jǐ jiàn hǎoxiàng hái búcuò.

妹妹：对，**这几件**都不错。我们去问问**那个店员**，一人每次可以试穿**几件**？

Mèimei: Duì, zhè jǐ jiàn dōu bú cuò. Wǒmen qù wèn wèn nà ge diànyuán, yì rén měi cì kěyǐ shìchuān jǐ jiàn?

Older sister: I plan to buy two blouses. How about you?

Younger sister: I only want to buy one. Do you think this one is pretty?

Older sister: This one is not good. Those on that rack seem quite nice.

Younger sister: You are right. All these are quite nice. Let's go ask that sales clerk over there how many blouses a person can try on at a time.

Level 1 25.10 Omitting 一 before a measure word

In casual speech, the 一 before a measure word can usually be omitted as long as it is not at the beginning of the sentence. Also, the omitted 一 should not be being used to put emphasis on the number.

张：我给你介绍**个**女朋友吧！

Zhāng: Wǒ gěi nǐ jièshào ge nǚ péngyǒu ba!

李：女朋友越多越好，一个哪里够，你给我介绍**两个**吧！

Lǐ: Nǚ péngyǒu yuè duō yuè hǎo, yí ge nǎlǐ goù, nǐ gěi wǒ jièshào liǎng ge ba!

张：不行，我只能给你介绍一个，因为我女朋友只有一个妹妹。（Neither 一 can be omitted in this sentence since both mean 'one'.)

Zhāng: Bù xíng, wǒ zhǐ néng gěi nǐ jièshào yí ge, yīnwèi wǒ nǚ péngyǒu zhǐ yǒu yí ge mèimei.

Zhang: How about if I introduce a girl (to be your girlfriend) to you?

Li: The more girlfriends, the better. One is not enough. How about if you introduce two to me?

Zhang: No, I can't. I can introduce only one to you because my girlfriend has only one sister.

25.11 Words that can be both nouns and measure words

Words indicating containers, such as 杯 (*bēi*: 'cup; glass'), 碗 (*wǎn*: 'bowl'), 盘 (*pán*: 'plate'), 瓶 (*píng*: 'bottle'), 壶 (*hú*: 'pot'), 盆 (*pén*: 'pot') and 罐 (*guàn*: 'can'), can often be both nouns and measure words. ☜ In English, the expressions may sound very similar. As nouns, the measure word for these words is 个.

太太：你喝了**几瓶**？（Meaning: 几瓶啤酒. 瓶 is the measure word.)

Tàitai: Nǐ hē le jǐ píng?

先生：你去看看厨房里有**几个瓶子**，（个 is the measure word）就会知道我喝了**几瓶**。

Xiānsheng: Nǐ qù kàn kàn chúfáng lǐ yǒu jǐ ge píngzi, jiù huì zhīdào wǒ hē le jǐ píng.

Wife: How **many bottles** (of beer) did you drink?

Husband: If you go take a look to see how **many bottles** there are in the kitchen, then you will know how **many bottles** I drank.

张：桌上本来有**两杯咖啡**，都被你喝了吗？

Zhāng: Zhuōshàng běnlái yǒu liǎng bēi kāfēi, dōu bèi nǐ hē le ma?

李：我只喝了**一杯**，因为我来的时候，只剩一杯了，不过我看到一个空**杯子**。

Lǐ: Wǒ zhǐ hē le yì bēi, yīnwèi wǒ lái de shíhòu, zhǐ shèng yì bēi le, búguò wǒ kàndào yí ge kōng bēizi.

Zhang: There were **two cups** of coffee on the table. Did you drink both?

Li: I only drank **one cup** because there was only one cup left when I came. But I saw **an** empty **cup**.

Exercises

Correct the mistake in each of the following sentences.

1   这个房子非常大，有五间卧房、三半个洗澡间。

2   一星期有七个天，我天天都学习中文。

3   我每天都喝三个杯子咖啡。

4   桌子上面那本的英文书是谁的？

5   我们班每人都有一中文名字。

6 这一群小只狗真可爱。

7 这件大衣不是我的，我的件新大衣是黑色的。

8 王明不是个好人，你怎么会认识这样人？

9 我在上海住过三星期，也在北京住过一半年。

10 我喜欢蓝色，所以昨天买了三蓝条裙子。

11 桌上有两大个杯子，我跟弟弟口渴，所以一人喝了一大杯水。

12 你说，你喝了多少个瓶啤酒？

13 你看过哪些本有名的中国小说？

26 Verb reduplication and adjective reduplication

Some verbs and adjectives in Chinese can be reduplicated, meaning the verb or adjective can be repeated to have a slightly different connotation from the original word. There are specific formulae for the reduplications.

A. Verb reduplication

Only verbs indicating actions (including mental actions such as 想 (*xiǎng*: 'to think'), 考虑 (*kǎolǜ*: 'to consider'), 分析 (*fēnxī*: 'to analyse')) can be reduplicated. Verbs indicating feelings (such as 怕 (*pà*: 'to fear'), 喜欢 (*xǐhuān*: 'to like')) or mental states (such as 知道 (*zhīdào*: 'to know'), 觉得 (*juéde*: 'to feel')) cannot be reduplicated. Auxiliary verbs cannot be reduplicated, either.

26.1 Forming reduplicated verbs

Level 1

A monosyllabic verb is reduplicated by being repeated once. A disyllabic verb is reduplicated by repeating the entire word once, not character by character. For example, the reduplicated form of 休息 (*xiūxi*) is 休息休息, not 休休息息.

When the verb is reduplicated, it implies that the action will be performed quickly or briefly and in an informal manner. Therefore, verb reduplication and 'verb + 一下 (儿) (*yíxiàr*)' frequently share similar meanings. 儿 in 一下儿 is optional.

26.2 Inserting 一 within the verb reduplication

Level 1

一 (*yī*) can be inserted between the verb and the repeated verb without changing the meaning, but only when the original verb is monosyllabic. 一 cannot be inserted if the original verb is disyllabic.

张：下课了，一起去吃中饭吧！
Zhāng: Xiàkè le, yìqǐ qù chī zhōngfàn ba.
王：你在这里等(一)等，我去厕所洗(一)洗手就来。
Wáng: Nǐ zài zhèlǐ děng (yì) děng, wǒ qù cèsuǒ xǐ (yì) xǐ shǒu jiù lái.
Zhang: Class is over. Let's go have lunch together.
Wang: Wait here for a moment. I'll go to the bathroom to quickly wash my hands and then be right back.
(等等 = 等一等 = 等一下；洗洗手 = 洗一洗手 = 洗一下手)

(Situation: Televisions are on sale in a shop, but Mr Wang cannot decide whether he should buy a new TV or not.)

售货员：价钱这么便宜，您不买太可惜了。
Shòuhuòyuán: Jiàqián zhème piányí, nín bù mǎi tài kěxí le.

王：我回家去**考虑考虑**。（考虑考虑 = 考虑一下, but 考虑一考虑 is incorrect.）
Wáng: Wǒ huí jiā qù kǎolù kǎolù.
售货员：考虑什么？今天不买，明天就不是这个价钱了。
Shòuhuòyuán: Kǎolù shénme? Jīntiān bù mǎi, míngtiān jiù bú shì zhè ge jiàqián le.
王：我得跟我太太**商量商量**。（商量商量 = 商量一下，but 商量一商量 is
incorrect.）
Wáng: Wǒ děi gēn wǒ tàitai shāngliáng shāngliáng.
Sales clerk: The price is so cheap. It would be a pity if you don't buy one.
Wang: Let me go home to (spend some time and) think about it.
Sales clerk: Think about what? If you don't buy one today, it won't be this price
tomorrow.
Wang: I have to (spend some time and) discuss it with my wife.

<table>
<tr><td>Level</td></tr>
<tr><td>1</td></tr>
</table>

26.3 Softening the tone

Verb reduplication can soften the tone to make the speaker sound more polite or less blunt.
This is particularly relevant when the speaker is making a request or suggestion.

> 这件事我一个人做不了，你可不可以来**帮帮我**？（帮帮我 sounds more polite than
> 帮我.）
> *Zhè jiàn shì wǒ yí ge rén zuò bù liǎo, nǐ kě bù kěyǐ lái bāng bāng wǒ?*
> I cannot handle this matter by myself. Can you come and help me?

> 这么重要的事，咱们应该先**讨论讨论**再做决定。（讨论讨论 sounds less blunt than
> simply 讨论.）
> *Zhème zhòngyào de shì, zánmen yīnggāi xiān tǎolùn tǎolùn zài zuò juédìng.*
> This is such an important matter. We should discuss it first before making a decision.

<table>
<tr><td>Level</td></tr>
<tr><td>1</td></tr>
</table>

26.4 Implying 'to give something a try'

Verb reduplication can be used to imply that the action should be performed as a trial.

> 这是我做的菜，你**尝(一)尝**，然后告诉我好吃不好吃。
> *Zhè shì wǒ zuò de cài, nǐ cháng (yì) cháng, ránhòu gàosù wǒ hǎochī bù hǎochī.*
> This dish was made by me. Taste it and then tell me whether it is delicious or not.

> 我没坐过云霄飞车，咱们去**坐(一)坐**，怎么样？
> *Wǒ méi zuò guo yúnxiāo fēichē, zánmen qù zuò (yí) zuò, zěnmeyàng?*
> I have never ridden a rollercoaster before. How about if we go try it?

<table>
<tr><td>Level</td></tr>
<tr><td>1/2</td></tr>
</table>

26.5 Placement of 了

If 了 (*le*) is necessary, it can be inserted between the verb and the repeated verb whether the
verb is monosyllabic or disyllabic.

When the verb is disyllabic, 了 and 一 cannot be used together. However, it is acceptable to
use 了 and 一 together when the verb is monosyllabic.

> 爸爸下班回家以后，**休息了休息**，**看了看**电视，又出门去做他的兼职了。
> *Bàba xiàbān huí jiā yǐhòu, xiūxí le xiūxí, kàn le kàn diànshì, yòu chūmén qù zuò tāde
> jiānzhí le.*
> After my father got off work and came home, he rested a little bit, watched TV for a
> short while and then left the house again to work his second job.
> (休息了休息 = 休息了一下, but 休息了一休息 is incorrect since 休息 is disyllabic.
> 看了看电视 = 看了一下电视 = 看了一看电视)

王先生跟王太太都很喜欢这个新房子，所以他们只简单地**讨论了讨论**就决定买了。

Wáng xiānsheng gēn Wáng tàitai dōu hěn xǐhuān zhè ge xīn fángzi, suǒyǐ tāmen zhǐ jiǎndān de tǎolùn le tǎolùn jiù juédìng mǎi le.

Both Mr and Mrs Wang like this new house, so they only briefly discussed it before deciding to buy.

26.6 Adding 看 after a reduplicated verb

When 看 (*kàn*) follows a reduplicated verb, it implies 'to try' something, or to see what will happen. In this case, 一 or 了 cannot be used.

If the verb being used is already 看, then a third 看 cannot be used. When the verb is 试 (*shì*: 'to try'), 看 can follow 试试 without adding more meaning.

李：张经理在不在？有一件事，我要跟他**谈(一)谈**。

Lǐ: Zhāng jīnglǐ zài bú zài? Yǒu yī jiàn shì, wǒ yào gēn tā tán (yì) tán.

秘书：您**坐坐**，我去**看看**他电话打完了没有。（坐坐 cannot be 坐坐看 in this sentence.）

Mìshū: Nín zuò zuò ,wǒ qù kàn kàn tā diànhuà dǎ wán le méiyǒu.

Li: Is Manager Zhang in? There is something I want to talk to him about (briefly and informally).

Secretary: Have a seat (and sit for a bit). I will go and see if he is finished talking on the phone or not.

(Situation: Two tourists are discussing whether they should go by public transport.)

王：咱们坐公共汽车去，好不好？

Wáng: Zánmen zuò gōnggòng qìchē qù, hǎo bù hǎo?

李：听说这里的公共汽车又挤又乱，我不想坐。

Lǐ: Tīngshuō zhèlǐ de gōnggòng qìchē yòu jǐ yòu luàn, wǒ bù xiǎng zuò.

王：不**坐坐看**怎么知道？（不坐坐 and 不坐坐看 have similar meanings.）

Wáng: Bú zuò zuò kàn zěnme zhīdào?

李：好吧，去**试试看**吧。（试试看 = 试试）

Lǐ: Hǎo ba, qù shì shì kàn ba.

Wang: Let's ride the bus, shall we?

Li: I heard that buses here are both crowed and chaotic.

Wang: If we don't try (to ride) it, how will we know?

Li: All right, let go try it.

26.7 Verbs that cannot be reduplicated

Normally, verbs indicating moving in a direction or going to a place (such as 来 (*lái*), 回 (*huí*), 进 (*jìn*), 出 (*chū*)) cannot be reduplicated, but 去 is an exception; that is, 去 can be reduplicated.

李：下课了，一起走路回家吧。

Lǐ: Xià kè le, yìqǐ zǒulù huí jiā ba.

王：老师叫我下课以后到他的办公室拿功课，我**去去**就来。（去去 = 去一去 = 去一下）

Wáng: Lǎoshī jiào wǒ xià kè yǐhòu dào tāde bàngōngshì ná gōngkè, wǒ qù qù jiù lái.

Li: Class is over. How about if we walk home together?

Wang: The teacher asked me to go to his office to pick up my homework. I will quickly go over there and will be right back.

While a reduplicated verb has a similar meaning to 'verb + 一下', 来一下 or 过来一下 is acceptable, but 来来 or 过来过来 would be improper.

> 张：小王，你**来一下**，好不好？有一个问题，我想**问问**你。（来一下 cannot be 来来。）
>
> *Zhāng: Xiǎo Wáng, nǐ lái yíxià, hǎo bù hǎo? Yǒu yí ge wèntí, wǒ xiǎng wèn wèn nǐ.*
>
> 王：你**等一下**（= 等等），那里有一个牌子，我要先过去**看一看**（= 看一下）牌子上的字。
>
> *Wáng: Nǐ děng yíxià (= děng děng), nàlǐ yǒu yí ge páizi, wǒ yào xiān guòqù kàn yí kàn (= kàn yíxià) páizi shàng de zì.*
>
> Zhang: Xiao Wang, will you come here for a minute? There is a question I would like to quickly ask you.
>
> Wang: Wait a moment. There is a sign over there. I want to go over there first to take a look at those characters on the sign.

B. Adjective reduplication

Not all adjectives can be reduplicated. Sentences with reduplicated adjectives tend to sound more informal and perhaps more personal. Sometimes descriptions with reduplicated adjectives may convey a sense of vividness.

> Level
> 1

26.8 Forming reduplicated adjectives

To reduplicate a disyllabic adjective, each character is repeated before the next. This is different from the reduplication of a disyllabic verb. For example, the reduplicated form of 清楚 (*qīngchǔ*) is 清清楚楚, not 清楚清楚.

> 王先生的新家，是一栋**小小的**木造房子，屋顶上有一个**高高的**烟囱；屋子里总是收拾**得干干净净**(的)。
>
> *Wáng xiānsheng de xīn jiā, shì yí dòng xiǎoxiǎo de mùzào fángzi, wūdǐng shàng yǒu yí ge gāogāo de yāncōng; wūzi lǐ zǒngshì shōushí de gāngānjìngjìng (de).*
>
> Mr Wang's new home is a small wood house; there is a tall chimney on the roof. The rooms are always spotlessly clean.

> Level
> 1

26.9 No degree adverbs with reduplicated adjectives

When a reduplicated adjective is used attributively (meaning it appears before a noun) or used in a complement of state, a degree adverb (such as 很 (*hěn*), 太 (*tài*), 真 (*zhēn*), 非常 (*fēicháng*)) cannot be used. 不 (*bù*) cannot be used either.

> 那个**胖胖的**小女孩，有一双**大大的**眼睛，一头**卷卷的**金发，真可爱，是谁家的小孩？
>
> *Nà ge pàngpàng de xiǎo nǚhái, yǒu yì shuāng dàdà de yǎnjīng, yì tóu juǎnjuǎn de jīn fǎ, zhēn kě'ài, shì shéi jiā de xiǎohái?*
>
> That chubby little girl has a pair of big eyes and a head of curly blonde hair – really cute. Whose daughter is she?

> Level
> 2

26.10 The use of 的 with reduplicated adjectives

(a) Monosyllabic adjectives

When a monosyllabic adjective is reduplicated and used as a predicate or in a complement of state, 的 (*de*) should follow the reduplicated adjective.

李：你知不知道小王的女朋友长什么样子？
Lǐ: Nǐ zhī bù zhīdào Xiǎo Wáng de nǚ péngyǒu zhǎng shénme yàngzi?
丁：**瘦瘦的**，脸**圆圆的**，头发**长长的**，皮肤**白白的**，非常漂亮。（Every 的 is necessary.）
Dīng: Shòushòu de, liǎn yuányuán de, tóufà chángcháng de, pífū báibái de, fēicháng piàoliàng.
Li: Do you know what Xiao Wang's girlfriend looks like?
Ding: Thin, round face, long hair, fair skin, extremely pretty.

(b) Disyllabic adjectives

When a disyllabic adjective is reduplicated and used as a predicate or in a complement of state, 的 is optional.

张小姐对人**客客气气(的)**，说话的时候，也总是**小小声声(的)**，难怪大家都喜欢她。
Zhāng xiǎojiě duìrén kèkèqìqì (de), shuōhuà de shíhòu, yě zǒngshì xiǎoxiǎoshēngshēng (de), nánguài dàjiā dōu xǐhuān tā.
Miss Zhang is courteous towards people. When she talks, she is always soft spoken. No wonder everybody likes her.

咱们上山去吧。站在山顶上，整座城都可以看得**清清楚楚(的)**。
Zánmen shàng shān qù ba. Zhàn zài shāndǐng shàng, zhěng zuò chéng dōu kěyǐ kàn de qīngqīngchǔchǔ de.
Let's go up the mountain. When you stand on top of the mountain, the whole town can be seen clearly.

26.11 The use of 地 with reduplicated adjectives

When a reduplicated adjective is followed by 地 (*de*) to form an adverbial modifier, 地 becomes optional.

☞ See Chapter 18 for more information on adverbial modifiers.

老王一看到小李，就**急急忙忙(地)**跑过来向他借钱；小李听了，**慢慢(地)**从口袋里拿了二十块钱出来借他。
Lǎo Wáng yí kàn dào Xiǎo Lǐ, jiù jíjímángmáng (de) pǎo guòlái xiàng tā jiè qián. Xiǎo Lǐ tīng le, màn màn (de) cóng kǒudài lǐ ná le èrshí kuài qián chūlái jiè tā.
As soon as Lao Wang saw Xiao Li, he hurriedly ran over to borrow some money from him. After listening to his request, Xiao Li slowly took $20 out from his pocket and lent it to him.

上次考试，他没有**好好(地)**准备，所以不及格。现在他天天都**认认真真(地)**学习，希望下次能考得好一点。
Shàng cì kǎoshì, tā méiyǒu hǎo hǎo (de) zhǔnbèi, suǒyǐ bù jígé. Xiànzài tā tiān tiān dōu rènrènzhēnzhēn (de) xuéxí, xīwàng xià cì néng kǎo de hǎo yìdiǎn.
He did not do a good job studying for the previous test; therefore, he failed the test. Now he is studying conscientiously every day and he hopes to do better next time.

26.12 Reduplicating adjectives that function as verbs

Some adjectives can function as verbs and can be reduplicated. When such an adjective is a disyllabic word, the entire word is repeated, not the individual characters.

放学了，小朋友**高高兴兴(地)**回家去。(高高兴兴地 is an adverbial modifier.)
Fàngxué le, xiǎo péngyǒu gāogāoxìngxìng (de) huí jiā qù.
School was out. The children went home happily.

你快把那个好消息告诉他，让他**高兴高兴**。(高兴高兴 is a reduplicated verb.)
Nǐ kuài bǎ nà ge hǎo xiāoxí gàosù tā, ràng tā gāoxìng gāoxìng.
Hurry and tell him that good news and cheer him up a little bit.

Exercises

Level 2

Choose the sentence that is grammatically correct.

1 Mother: Xiaoming, dinner is ready. Go quickly and wash your hands first, then come to dinner.
   (a) 妈妈：小明，饭已经做好了，你先去洗手洗手再来吃。
   (b) 妈妈：小明，饭已经做好了，你先去洗洗手再来吃。
   (c) 妈妈：小明，饭已经做好了，你先去洗手一下再来吃。

2 Can you wait for me here for a while? I have to quickly go to the bathroom.
   (a) 你可不可以在这里等一下我？我要去一下洗手间。
   (b) 你可不可以在这里等我等我？我要去一下洗手间。
   (c) 你可不可以在这里等等我？我要去一下洗手间。

3 I waited at the bus stop for a while. The bus didn't come, so I decided to walk to school.
   (a) 我在车站等了等，车没来，我就决定走路去学校了。
   (b) 我在车站等一等，车没来，我就决定走路去学校了。
   (c) 我在车站等一下，车没来，我就决定走路去学校了。

4 We should carefully discuss this issue. We can't make the decision now.
   (a) 这个问题，我们应该好好地讨讨论论，不能现在就决定。
   (b) 这个问题，我们应该好好地讨论一讨论，不能现在就决定。
   (c) 这个问题，我们应该好好地讨论讨论，不能现在就决定。

5 I was tired today. After dinner, I watched TV for a while and then went to bed.
   (a) 昨天我很累，吃完晚饭，看了看电视，就去睡觉了。
   (b) 昨天我很累，吃完晚饭，看看了电视，就去睡觉了。
   (c) 昨天我很累，吃完晚饭，看一看了电视，就去睡觉了。

6 Mr Li, do you know Miss Wang? Let me introduce you to each other.
   (a) 李先生，你认识王小姐吗？我来给你们介绍一介绍。
   (b) 李先生，你认识王小姐吗？我来给你们介一介绍。
   (c) 李先生，你认识王小姐吗？我来给你们介绍一下。

7 Sales assistant: This coat is of the highest quality. Touch it and see how it feels.

   (a) 店员：这件大衣是最上等的质量，你摸摸一下。

   (b) 店员：这件大衣是最上等的质量，你摸摸看。

   (c) 店员：这件大衣是最上等的质量，你摸了摸。

8 As soon as Xiaoming saw his father coming home, he happily went to open the door for him.

   (a) 小明一看到爸爸回家了，就高高兴兴地去给爸爸开门。

   (b) 小明一看到爸爸回家了，就高兴高兴地去给爸爸开门。

   (c) 小明一看到爸爸回家了，就高兴高兴去给爸爸开门。

9 Look, the tall building in front is our school's student dormitory.

   (a) 你看，前面那个建筑高高，就是我们学校的学生宿舍。

   (b) 你看，前面那个高高的建筑，就是我们学校的学生宿舍。

   (c) 你看，前面那个很高高的建筑，就是我们学校的学生宿舍。

27 *The use of* 以前, 以后 *and* 时候

以前 (*yǐqián*), 以后 (*yǐhòu*) and 时候 (*shíhòu*) are three important words used to form time phrases. 👁 Although their counterparts can be found in English, the word order of such phrases is quite different in Chinese.

A. The use of 以前 and 以后

以前 and 以后 can appear after a sentence, verb/verbal phrase or duration of time to form a time phrase. Each of these words can also be a stand-alone adverb.

Level 1

27.1 以前 and 以后 as stand-alone adverbs

When 以前 and 以后 are used as stand-alone adverbs, they mean 'in the past; previously' and 'in the future' respectively. Their grammatical features are similar to those of 现在 (*xiànzài*). They can appear either at the beginning of a sentence or after the subject.

A casual word for 以前 is 过去 (*guòqù*). 以后 can be replaced by 将来 (*jiānglái*) or 未来 (*wèilái*); but 将来 and 未来 seem more formal than 以后.

> 我**以前**在银行工作，**现在**在上研究所，**以后**我想当教授。
> *Wǒ yǐqián zài yínháng gōngzuò, xiànzài zài shàng yánjiūsuǒ, yǐhòu wǒ xiǎng dāng jiàoshòu.*
> Previously, I worked at a bank; now I am attending graduate school; in the future, I want to be a professor.

> **过去**大家都认为学中文没有用，所以**以前**学中文的人不多。**现在**中国的经济发展得很快，**以后**(= **将来**)一定会有很多人想学中文。
> *Guòqù dàjiā dōu rènwéi xué Zhōngwén méiyǒu yòng, suǒyǐ yǐqián xué Zhōngwén de rén bù duō. Xiànzài Zhōngguó de jīngjì fāzhǎn de hěn kuài, yǐhòu (= jiānglái) yídìng huì yǒu hěn duō rén xiǎng xué Zhōngwén.*
> In the past, everybody thought that studying Chinese was useless; therefore, there were not many people studying Chinese. Now China's economy is developing rapidly; in the future, there will definitely be many people wanting to study Chinese.

Level 2

27.2 以前 and 以后 in time phrases

When 以前 or 以后 is used to form a time phrase, it must appear after a sentence, a verb/verbal phrase or duration of time. 👁 In this regard, the English and Chinese word orders are opposite and thus merit special attention. 以 can be optional.

The time phrase must appear before the main clause. 👁 In English, the main clause can appear either before or after the time phrase.

小明每天晚上**睡觉**(以)**前**，妈妈都会给他讲一个故事。
Xiǎomíng měitiān wǎnshàng shuìjiào yǐqián, māma dōu huì gěi tā jiǎng yí ge gùshì.
Every night before Xiaoming goes to sleep, his mother will tell him a story.

王先生成绩、人品都好；他**毕业**(以)**后**，很多大公司想请他去工作。
Wáng xiānsheng chéngjī, rénpǐn dōu hǎo; tā bìyè yǐhòu, hěn duō dà dōngsī xiǎng qǐng tā qù gōngzuò.
Mr Wang's (university) results and his moral character were both good. After he graduated, many big companies wanted to hire him.

27.3 Placement of the subject in a sentence with a 以前/以后 time phrase

If the time phrase and the main clause share the same subject, the subject should not be repeated. It is best to use the subject in the time phrase although it is acceptable to use it in the main clause.

她吃晚饭(以)前，喜欢喝一杯鸡尾酒；吃晚饭(以)后，常常喝一杯咖啡。
Tā chī wǎnfàn (yǐ)qián, xǐhuān hē yì bēi jīwěijiǔ; chī wǎnfàn (yǐ)hòu, chángcháng hē yì bēi kāfēi.
She likes to drink a cocktail before eating dinner; after eating dinner, she often has a cup of coffee.
(吃晚饭以前，她喜欢喝一杯鸡尾酒 is considered acceptable, but 她吃晚饭以前，她喜欢喝一杯鸡尾酒 is improper.)

王先生退休(以)前，只知道工作，没有任何嗜好，所以他退休(以)后，不知道怎么过日子。
Wáng xiānsheng tuìxiū (yǐ)qián, zhǐ zhīdào gōngzuò, méiyǒu rènhé shìhào, suǒyǐ tā tuìxiū (yǐ)hòu, bù zhīdào zěnme guò rìzi.
Before Mr Wang retired, he only knew about his work and didn't have any hobbies; therefore, after he retired, he didn't know how to spend his days.

27.4 以前 and 以后 with a duration of time

以前 or 以后 can follow duration of time to mean '. . . ago/before' or '. . . later/in . . .'. In this case, 以 is frequently omitted.

杰夫两个月(以)前才开始学中文，现在他已经会写几百个汉字了。
Jiéfū liǎng ge yuè (yǐ)qián cái kāishǐ xué Zhōngwén, xiànzài tā yǐjīng huì xiě jǐ bǎi ge Hànzì le.
Jeff only started to study Chinese two months ago; now he already knows how to write several hundred Chinese characters.

(Situation: This is a phone conversation.)

张：请问，王先生在不在？
Zhāng: Qǐng wèn, Wáng xiānsheng zài bú zài?
王太太：他在洗澡，请你十分钟(以)后再打来，好不好？
Wáng tàitai: Tā zài xǐzǎo, qǐng nǐ shí fēnzhōng (yǐ)hòu zài dǎ lái, hǎo bù hǎo?
Zhang: May I ask, is Mr Wang home?
Mrs Wang: He is taking a shower. Will you please call back in ten minutes (= ten minutes later)?

27.5 Duration of time + 以后 = 过 + during of time

'Duration of time + 以后' is interchangeable with '过 + duration of time'.

王：请问，张经理回国没有？

Wáng: Qǐng wèn, Zhāng jīnglǐ huí guó méiyǒu?

秘书：还没有。他一个星期以后才会回来。(= 他再过一个星期才会回来。)

Mìshū: Hái méiyǒu. Tā yī ge xīngqī yǐhòu cái huì huílái. (= Tā zài guò yí ge xīngqī cái huì huílái).

Wang: May I please ask if Manager Zhang is back in the country?

Secretary: Not yet. He won't be back until a week later.

27.6 Negative sentences with 以前

A negative sentence can appear before 以前 without a negative meaning. This is a unique feature of the use of 以前. The expression is considered correct in Chinese.

功课**还没有写完**以前 (= 功课**写完**以前)，你不可以跟朋友出去玩。

*Gōngkè **hái méiyǒu xiě wán** yǐqián, nǐ bù kěyǐ gēn péngyǒu chūqù wán.*

Before you finish your homework, you are not allowed to go out with your friends.

王先生已经二十五岁了，还住在他爸妈的家里。他**不能独立生活**以前，也不能考虑跟女朋友结婚的事。

Wáng xiānsheng yǐjīng èrshí wǔ suì le, hái zhù zài tā bàmā de jiā lǐ. Tā bù néng dúlì shēnghuó yǐqián, yě bù néng kǎolǜ gēn nǚ péngyǒu jiéhūn de shì.

Mr Wang is already 25 years old and he still lives at his parents' house. **Before he can be** independent, he cannot consider marriage with his girlfriend.

27.7 Omitting 以后

以后 can be omitted when the perfective aspect 了 (*le*) is used in the time phrase. (The perfective aspect 了 must follow the verb immediately.)

下课以后，我们一起去看电影，怎么样？(= 我们**下了课**一起去看电影，怎么样？)

Xiàkè yǐhòu, wǒmen yìqǐ qù kàn diànyǐng, zěnmeyàng?

How about if we go to a movie together after class?

(It would be improper to say 我们下课了一起去看电影，怎么样？)

王太太结婚以前，在一家银行当经理；**结婚**以后 (= 结了婚)，就辞职在家做家庭主妇了。

Wáng tàitai jiéhūn yǐqián, zài yì jiā yínháng dāng jīnglǐ; jié hūn yǐhòu (= jié le hūn), jiù cízhí zài jiā zuò jiātíng zhǔfù le.

Before Mrs Wang got married, she was a manager at a bank; after she got married, she quit her job and became a housewife.

27.8 后来 vs. 以后

后来 (*hòulái*) and 以后 overlap in meaning in the sense that both can be used to mean 'later on' or 'afterwards', and both are used to refer to an action that has already taken place.

(a) Actions that have already taken place

For events that have already taken place, 后来 may sound better than 以后, although 以后 is acceptable.

昨天下午我跟我女朋友一起去看了一场电影；**后来**(= 以后)，我们又一起去
一家中国餐馆吃晚饭。

*Zuótiān xiàwǔ wǒ gēn wǒ nǚ péngyǒu yìqǐ qù kàn le yì chǎng diànyǐng; hòulái (= yǐhòu),
wǒmen yòu yìqǐ qù yì jiā Zhōngguó cānguǎn chī wǎnfàn.*

Yesterday afternoon, I went to see a movie with my girlfriend; afterwards, we also went
to a Chinese restaurant to have dinner.

小明以前喜欢欺负弟弟，所以被妈妈罚了几次，**后来**(= 以后)他就不敢了。

*Xiǎomíng yǐqián xǐhuān qīfù dìdi, suǒyǐ bèi māma fá le jǐ cì; hòulái (= yǐhòu) tā jiù bù
gǎn le.*

Xiaoming used to like to bully his younger brother, so he was punished by his mother
a couple of times. After that, he dared not do it again.

(b) Actions that are yet to take place

For actions that will take place in the future, only 以后 can be used.

妈妈：小明，你又欺负弟弟了。今天不许你吃点心，看你**以后**还敢不敢欺负他。

*Māma: Xiǎomíng, nǐ yòu qīfù dìdi le. Jīntiān bù xǔ nǐ chī diǎnxīn, kàn nǐ yǐhòu hái gǎn
bù gǎn qīfù tā.*

小明：我**以后**不敢了。（后来 would not be correct here.）

Xiǎomíng: Wǒ yǐhòu bù gǎn le.

Mother: Xiaoming, you bullied your younger brother again. I will not allow you to eat
dessert today. I'll see if you dare to bully him again in the future.

Xiaoming: In the future, I dare not do it again.

27.9 以前 and 以后 as adjectives

以前 (or 过去) and 以后 (or 将来/未来) can be used as adjectives before a noun. In this case,
they mean 'previous' and 'future' respectively; and 的 (*de*) must follow 以前/以后.

以前的错误，咱们忘了吧。**以后的**计划，才是最要紧的。

Yǐqián de cuòwù, zánmen wàng le ba. Yǐhòu de jìhuà, cái shì zuì yàojǐn de.

Let's forget about previous mistakes. Our future plans are the most important.

B. The use of 时候

27.10 什么时候 vs. 几点 vs. 时间: 'when', 'what time' and 'time'

As a noun, 时候 normally refers to a point of time, not a duration of time, which should be
时间 (*shíjiān*).

您今天下午有没有**时间**？我想来您的办公室问您几个问题。

Nín jīntiān xiàwǔ yǒu méiyǒu shíjiān? Wǒ xiǎng lái nínde bàngōngshì wèn nín jǐ ge wèntí.

Do you have time this afternoon? I would like to come to your office to ask you a few
questions.

(It would be improper to ask 您今天有没有时候？)

Since 时候 refers to a point of time, 什么时候? means 'when?' ◑ Although 什么时候
literally means 'what time?' the Chinese expression for 'what time?' should be 几点？ (*jǐ diǎn?*)

学生：老师，您下午**有没有时间**？我想来您的办公室问几个问题。

*Xuéshēng: Lǎoshī, nín xiàwǔ yǒu méiyǒu shíjiān? Wǒ xiǎng lái nínde bànggōngshì wèn jǐ
ge wèntí.*

老师：对不起，我今天下午恐怕没有空。
Lǎoshī: Duìbùqǐ, wǒ jīntiān xiàwǔ kǒngpà méiyǒu kòng.
学生：没关系，您**什么时候**有空呢？
Xuéshēng: Méi guānxi, nín shénme shíhòu yǒu kòng ne?
老师：你明天下午来吧！
Lǎoshī: Nǐ míngtiān xiàwǔ lái ba!
学生：好，您要我**几点**来？
Xuéshēng: Hǎo, nín yào wǒ jǐ diǎn lái?
Student: Sir, do you have time in the afternoon? I would like to come to your office to ask a few questions.
Teacher: Sorry, I am afraid that I don't have time this afternoon.
Student: That's OK. When will you have time?
Teacher: Why don't you come tomorrow afternoon?
Student: OK. What time do you want me to come?

27.11 时候 and the measure word 个

Level 1

时候 can have an optional measure word, 个 (*ge*). It is frequently omitted.

(a) 这 (个) 时候 and 那 (个) 时候

这 (个) 时候 means 'at this time'; 那 (个) 时候 means 'at that time', which can refer to either a previous time frame or a future time frame.

昨天晚上我错过了最后一班公共汽车，站在车站不知道应该怎么办。**这(个)时候**，我的同屋开车经过车站，所以他 "救" 了我。
Zuótiān wǎnshàng wǒ cuòguò le zuìhòu yì bān gōnggòng qìchē, zhàn zài chēzhàn bù zhīdào yīnggāi zěnme bàn. Zhè (ge) shíhòu, wǒde tóngwū kāi chē jīngguò chēzhàn, suǒyǐ tā 'jiù' le wǒ.
Last night I missed the last bus; I stood at the bus stop not knowing what I should do. At this time, my roommate drove by, so he 'saved' me.

我以前在中国住过两年；**那(个)时候**，我还不会说中文，所以没有交到中国朋友。
Wǒ yǐqián zài Zhōngguó zhù guo liǎng nián; nà (ge) shíhòu, wǒ hái bú huì shuō Zhōngwén, suǒyǐ méiyǒu jiāo dào Zhōngguó péngyǒu.
I lived in China for two years before. At that time, I didn't know how to speak Chinese yet, so I did not make friends with any Chinese people.

(b) 那 (个) 时候 and 到时候

When 那 (个) 时候 refers to a future time frame, it is interchangeable with 到时候. The 候 can be omitted in all these phrases.

我女儿明年就要进大学了，**那(个)时候**(= **到时候**)，我们会需要一大笔钱，所以我打算下个月去找个工作。
Wǒ nǚ'ér míngnián jiù yào jìn dàxué le, nà (ge) shíhòu (= dào shíhòu), wǒmen huì xūyào yí dà bǐ qián, suǒyǐ wǒ dàsuàn xià ge yuè qù zhǎo ge gōngzuò.
My daughter is going to enter university next year. At that time, we will need a large sum of money, so I plan to go and get a job next month.

27.12 ⋯⋯的时候

Level 2

⋯⋯的时候 is also translated as 'when' in English, but this construction is a time phrase, not a question. The ⋯⋯的时候 phrase must appear before the main clause. Its grammatical feature is similar to that of ⋯⋯以前 or ⋯⋯以后.

张：昨天我给你打电话**的时候**，你太太说你在睡觉。
Zhāng: Zuótiān wǒ gěi nǐ dǎ diànhuà de shíhòu, nǐ tàitai shuō nǐ zài shuìjiào.
王：哦，是吗？你是几点打来的？
Wáng: Ò, shìma? Nǐ shì jǐ diǎn dǎlái de?
Zhang: **When** I called you yesterday, your wife said that you were taking a nap.
Wang: Oh, is that so? What time did you call?

李：上中文课**的时候**，我们老师不让我们说英文。你们老师呢？
Lǐ: Shàng Zhōngwén kè de shíhòu, wǒmen lǎoshī bú ràng wǒmen shuō Yīngwén. Nǐmen lǎoshī ne?
丁：我们老师上课**的时候**不说英文，下课**以后**也不说。
Dīng: Wǒmen lǎoshī shàng kè de shíhòu bù shuō Yīngwén, xià kè yǐhòu yě bù shuō.
Li: Our teacher does not allow us to speak English **when** we are in Chinese class. How about your teacher?
Ding: Our teacher does not speak English (when we are) in class, nor after class.

王：今年的交换学生**什么时候**来？
Wáng: Jīnnián de jiāohuàn xuéshēng shénme shíhòu lái?
李：下个月。
Lǐ: Xià ge yuè.
王：他们来**的时候**，谁去机场接他们？
Wáng: Tāmen lái de shíhòu, shéi qù jīchǎng jiē tāmen?
Wang: **When** will this year's exchange students arrive?
Li: Next month.
Wang: Who will go to the airport to pick them up **when** they arrive?

27.13 ⋯⋯的时候 and the progressive aspect

Level 2

When using the ⋯⋯的时候 phrase and describing an action in progress, '正 (在) + verb' is used more often than '在 + verb'.

☞ See Chapter 8 for more on the progressive aspect.

昨天发生大地震**的时候**，我**正在**吃晚饭（呢）。
Zuótiān fāshēng dà dìzhèn de shíhòu, wǒ zhèng zài chī wǎnfàn (ne).
When a strong earthquake occurred yesterday, I was eating dinner.

早上我出门**的时候**，外面**正下着**大雨呢（＝**正在**下大雨呢）。
Zǎoshàng wǒ chūmén de shíhòu, wàimiàn zhèng xià zhe dà yǔ ne (= zhèng zài xià dà yǔ ne).
When I left the house this morning, it was raining hard.

27.14 The use of 以前 or 以后 with ⋯⋯的时候

Level 2

When 以前 or 以后 is used as a stand-alone adverb, it can be used together with the ⋯⋯的时候 phrase. 👁 This structure can be confusing to learners.

我现在是吃素的。我**以前**还吃肉**的时候**，很喜欢吃牛排。
Wǒ xiànzài shì chī sù de. Wǒ yǐqián hái chī ròu de shíhòu, hěn xǐhuān chī niúpái.
I am a vegetarian now. When I used still to eat meat, I liked steak very much.

我爸妈不了解我。**以后**我自己当了妈妈**的时候**，一定要想办法了解我的孩子。
Wǒ bàmā bù liǎojiě wǒ. Yǐhòu wǒ zìjǐ dāng le māma de shíhòu, yídìng yào xiǎng bànfǎ liǎojiě wǒde háizi.
My parents don't understand me. In the future, when I myself become a mother, I definitely will try to understand my children.

十几年**(以)前**我住在中国**的时候**，中国不象现在这么进步。
Shí jǐ nián yǐqián wǒ zhù zài Zhōngguó de shíhòu, Zhōngguó bú xiàng xiànzài zhème jìnbù.
When I lived in China more than ten years ago, China was not as advanced as it is now.

Level 2 — 27.15 The use of nouns/verbs in 以前, 以后 and ......的时候 phrases

(a) When verbs are necessary

In ......以前, ...以后 or ......的时候 phrases, what appears before 以前, 以后 or 的时候 usually includes a verb unless a number is involved. 👁 Learners who are English speakers should be aware of this difference between English and Chinese – in English, the same phrases can include nouns only.

我爸爸每天**吃晚饭以前**都喝一瓶啤酒；**吃饭的时候**，他常喝一杯白葡萄酒。
Wǒ bàba měi tiān chī wǎnfàn yǐqián dōu hē yì píng píjiǔ; chī fàn de shíhòu, tā cháng hē yì bēi bái pútáo jiǔ.
My father drinks a bottle of beer every day **before dinner**; **during dinner**, he often has a glass of white wine.
(It is odd to simply say 每天晚饭以前 and is incorrect to say 饭的时候.)

老师：**上中文课的时候**，你们不应该说英文；**下课以后**，最好也别说。这样，你们的中文才会进步。
Lǎoshī: Shàng Zhōngwén kè de shíhòu, nǐmen bù yīnggāi shuō Yīngwén. Xià kè yǐhòu, zuìhǎo yě bié shuō. Zhèyàng, nǐmen de Zhōngwén cái huì jìnbù.
Teacher: **During Chinese class**, you should not speak English. It is best that you also don't speak English **after class**. This way, your Chinese will improve.
(Do not say 中文课的时候 or 课以后.)

你明天早上**六点以前**一定要起床。 (六点 has a number; 六点以前 is correct.)
Nǐ míngtiān zǎoshàng liù diǎn yǐqián yídìng yào qǐchuáng.
You have to get up **before 6 o'clock** tomorrow morning.

(b) Nouns acceptable when 以 is dropped

If 以 is not used in 以前/以后, it is acceptable to have nouns without verbs before 前/后.

医生：这个药，你**饭前**吃两粒，**饭后**吃一粒。
Yīshēng: Zhè ge yào, nǐ fàn qián chī liǎng lì, fàn hòu chī yí lì.
You take two pills of this medicine before meals and one pill after meals.

Exercises

Translate the following sentences into Chinese. Be sure to use 以前, 以后 or 时候 in each of the sentences.

Level
2

1 Yesterday I was busy. I studied at the library before class; and went to the coffee shop to work after class. In the evening after dinner, I had to study for a test next week.

2 When I was in my teens, I had already decided that I wanted to be a writer in the future.

3 Li: Mrs Wang, when are you free? I would like to come to your house and visit you.

   Wang: I am free every day after dinner. Why don't you come tomorrow evening?

   Li: Great! What time do you want me to come over?

   Wang: My daughter goes to bed at 8.30. Before she goes to bed, I have to bathe her. So please come before 7.30.

4 Wang: Do you know when Mr Zhang will come to Shanghai?

   Li: He will be here next month after he has attended an international conference in Beijing.

   Wang: When he comes, who will go to meet him at the airport?

   Li: Let's talk about it when the time comes.

Level
3

5 Ten years ago, not many people had mobile phones. Ten years from now (= ten years later), there probably won't be too many people who don't have mobile phones.

6 Li Ming and I used to be good friends. At that time, we talked on the phone almost every day. But later I discovered that he had lied to me a few times; now we no longer talk. In the future, I will be careful when choosing friends.

7 In the past when I was still eating meat, I would eat hamburgers three times a week. Later on, I became a vegetarian. Nowadays when my boyfriend and I go to a hamburger place, I only eat French fries.

8 Before my parents were divorced, they fought almost every day. At that time, I told myself that, in the future, for the sake of my children, after I get married I will never fight with my husband.

28 Modal particles

Modal particles are also called 'sentential particles' because they appear at the end of a sentence. Some of the modal particles have grammatical functions and specific meanings; these particles are thus definable. However, many of them are used to convey certain attitudes, moods, etc. and are used intuitively by native speakers of Chinese. These modal particles cannot be clearly defined. In this chapter, the most commonly used modal particles with definable meanings and usages will be discussed.

28.1 The different moods conveyed by 了, 吧, 啊 after 好

Level 2

The following examples show how modal particles (here, 了 (*le*), 吧 (*ba*) and 啊 (*a*) after 好 (*hǎo*)) can be used to convey different moods and attitudes.

(a) 好了!

好了! can be used to mean 'enough!', 'stop!' or 'no more!' and is used to show one's impatience. Since one of the meanings of 了 as a modal particle is to indicate a 'change of situation', 了 in this case can be considered a modal particle with a definable meaning.

> 王太太：你要自己注意身体；别吸烟，别喝酒。
> *Wáng tàitai: Nǐ yào zìjǐ zhùyì shēntǐ; bié xīyān, bié hējiǔ.*
> 王先生：**好了**，别再唠叨了。 (Both 了 imply a change of situation.)
> *Wáng xiānsheng: Hǎo le, bié zài lāodāo le.*
> Mrs Wang: You have to pay attention to your own health. Don't smoke; don't drink.
> Mr Wang: Enough! Stop nagging.

> 妈妈：你到了国外，要自己注意身体。
> *Māma: Nǐ dào le guówài, yào zìjǐ zhùyì shēntǐ.*
> 女儿：**好**，我一定会注意。 (好 and 好了 convey very different meanings.)
> *Nü'ér: Hǎo, wǒ yídìng huì zhùyì.*
> Mother: After you are abroad, you must take care of your own health.
> Daughter: OK, I definitely will.

(b) 好吧!

好吧! is used to shows one's reluctance or lack of enthusiasm in agreeing to do something.

> 张：一起去看《铁达尼号》，怎么样？
> *Zhāng: Yìqǐ qù kàn 'Tiě dá ní hào', zěnmeyàng?*
> 王：我看过了，没什么意思。
> *Wáng: Wǒ kàn guo le, méi shénme yìsi.*
> 张：我有两张免费的票。
> *Zhāng: Wǒ yǒu liǎng zhāng miǎnfèi de piào.*
> 王：**好吧**！反正没什么事，在家也无聊。
> *Wáng: Hǎo ba! Fǎnzhèng méi shénme shì, zài jiā yě wúliáo.*

Zhang: How about if we go see *Titanic* together?
Wang: I have seen it. It's not very interesting.
Zhang: I have two free tickets.
Wang: All right. Anyway, I don't have much to do; it's boring staying at home.

(c) 好啊!

好啊! can be used to show one's enthusiasm in agreeing to do something.

李：要不要一起去看《铁达尼号》？我有两张免费的票。
Lǐ: Yào bu yào yìqǐ qù kàn 'Tiě dá ní hào'? Wǒ yǒu liǎng zhāng miǎnfèi de piào.
丁：**好啊**！听说这个电影很好看。
Dīng: Hǎo a! Tīngshuō zhè ge diànyǐng hěn hǎokàn.
Li: Would you like to go see *Titanic* with me? I have two free tickets.
Ding: OK! I've heard that this movie is good.

28.2 The use of 吗

吗 (*ma*) is used to ask a yes–no question. It is sometimes interchangeable with an affirmative–negative question.

☞ See 2.1 for more information on the use of 吗.

你学了两年中文，有中文名字吗？（= 有没有中文名字？）
Nǐ xué le liǎng nián Zhōngwén, yǒu Zhōngwén míngzì ma?
You have studied Chinese for two years. Do you have a Chinese name?

(a) Use 吗 in questions with adverbs

When the question has an adverb, such as 也 (*yě*), 都 (*dōu*), 已经 (*yǐjīng*), etc., only 吗 can be used.

你的同学都有中文名字吗？（It is incorrect to say 你的同学都有没有中文名字？）
Nǐde tóngxué dōu yǒu Zhōngwén míngzì ma?
Do all of your classmates have Chinese names?

(b) Use 吗 in questions when one has an expectation of the answer

When one has an expectation of the answer, 吗 is used to ask the question.

(Situation: Wang visits his classmate Zhang at home and sees many thick volumes of medical books.)

王：这些是谁的书？
Wáng: Zhè xiē shì shéide shū?
张：都是我爸爸的。
Zhāng: Dōu shì wǒ bàba de.
王：你爸爸是医生吗？
Wáng: Nǐ bàba shì yīshēng ma?
(你爸爸是不是医生？ would not be the best choice in this situation since Wang expects the answer to be 'yes'.)
Wang: Whose books are these?
Zhang: They are my father's.
Wang: Is your father a doctor?

(Situation: A telephone conversation.)

> 张：请问，王先生在家吗？(= 王先生在不在家？)
> *Zhāng: Qǐng wèn, Wáng xiānsheng zài jiā ma?*
> 王太太：他在睡觉，有事**吗**？(有没有事？would not be the best choice in this case.)
> *Wáng tàitai: Tā zài shuìjiào, yǒu shì ma?*
> Zhang: May I ask, is Mr Wang home?
> Mrs Wang: He is sleeping. Do you have anything (important)?

(Situation: A student sleeps in class.)

> 老师：小王，你为什么在睡觉？你昨天晚上**没有**睡觉吗？(你昨天晚上有没有
> 睡觉？or 你昨天晚上睡觉了没有？would not be proper in this context.)
> *Lǎoshī: Xiǎo Wáng, nǐ wèishénme zài shuìjiào? Nǐ zuótiān wǎnshàng méiyǒu shuìjiào ma?*
> 小李：老师，您**不**知道**吗**？小王家昨天晚上闹了一场火灾。(您知不知道？would
> not be proper in this context.)
> *Xiǎo Lǐ: Lǎoshī! Nín bù zhīdào ma? Xiǎo Wáng jiā zuótiān wǎnshàng nào le yì chǎng huǒzāi.*
> Teacher: Xiao Wang, why are you sleeping? Did you not sleep last night?
> Xiao Li: Sir, didn't you know that there was a fire at Xiao Wang's house last night?

<table>
<tr><td>Level
1/2</td></tr>
</table>

28.3 The use of 呢

(a) Asking a question in context with 呢

呢 (*ne*) is used to either ask a previously asked question without repeating it or to ask a question when the context clearly indicates what that question is.

> 老师：小王，这是什么字？
> *Lǎoshī: Xiǎo Wáng, zhè shì shénme zì?*
> 王：那是"大"字。
> *Wáng: Nà shì 'dà' zì.*
> 老师：对，很好！这个**呢**？(= 这个是什么字？)
> *Lǎoshī: Duì, hěn hǎo! Zhè ge ne? (= Zhè ge shì shénme zì?)*
> 王：我不知道。
> *Wáng: Wǒ bù zhīdào.*
> 老师：小王不认识这个字；小李，你**呢**？(= 你认识不认识这个字？)
> *Lǎoshī: Xiǎo Wáng bú rènshì zhè ge zì; Xiǎo Lǐ, nǐ ne? (= Nǐ rènshì bú rènshì zhè ge zì?)*
> Teacher: Xiao Wang, what character is this?
> Wang: That is the character 'big'.
> Teacher: Correct, good! How about this one? (= What character is this one?)
> Wang: I don't know.
> Teacher: Xiao Wang does not recognize this character. Xiao Li, how about you?
> (= Xiao Li, do you recognize this character?)

(b) 如果/要是......呢: 'what if . . . ?'

如果/要是......呢 is used to ask 'what if . . .'.

> 职员：经理，今年的迎新会，要办什么活动？
> *Zhíyuán: Jīnglǐ, jīnnián de yíngxīn huì, yào bàn shénme huódòng?*
> 经理：室外烤肉。
> *Jīnglǐ: Shìwài kǎoròu.*

职员：如果下雨**呢**？

Zhíyuán: Rúguǒ xiàyǔ ne?

Staff: Manager, what kind of activity are we going to have for this year's welcome party?

Manager: An outdoor BBQ.

Staff: What if it rains?

(c) Asking about 'whereabouts' with 呢

呢 can be used to ask about 'whereabouts'. When you expect to see someone or something, but what you expect to see is not there, you can use 呢 to ask 'what has happened to . . . ?' Although such a phrase is sometimes translated into 'where is . . . ?' its connotation is different from a question with 哪里 (*nǎlǐ*), which is used to ask the physical location of someone or something.

(Situation: Xiao Wang and his girlfriend are nearly always together, but today you ran into him outside the cinema and he was alone.)

你：小王！怎么今天一个人来看电影？你女朋友**呢**？ (It would not be 你女朋友**在哪里**? since the real meaning of the question is 'why is she not with you?')

Nǐ: Xiǎo Wáng! Zěnme jīntiān yí ge rén lái kàn diànyǐng? Nǐ nǚ péngyǒu ne?

小王：她今天不太舒服。

Xiǎo Wáng: Tā jīntiān bú tài shūfú.

You: Xiao Wang! How come you came to the movie by yourself today? Where is your girlfriend?

Xiao Wang: She is not feeling well today.

(Situation: You are new in town and want to know where the library and Bank of China are.)

你：请问，图书馆**在哪里**？

Nǐ: Qǐng wèn, túshūguǎn zài nǎlǐ?

当地人：前面那栋白色的大楼就是图书馆。

Dāngdì rén: Qiánmiàn nà dòng báisè de dà lóu jiù shì túshūguǎn.

你：谢谢。中国银行**呢**？ (= 中国银行在哪里？)

Nǐ: Xièxie. Zhōngguó yínháng ne? (= Zhōngguó yínháng zài nǎlǐ?)

当地人：本市没有中国银行。

Dāngdì rén: Běn shì méiyǒu Zhōngguó yínháng.

You: Excuse me. **Where** is the library?

Local person: That white building up ahead is the library.

You: Thanks. **What about** the Bank of China?

Local person: There is no Bank of China in this city.

(Situation: You have returned to the town you left years ago and you are standing in front of the place where your favourite coffee shop used to be. Now it's something else.)

你：我以前常去的那家咖啡馆**呢**？

Nǐ: Wǒ yǐqián cháng qù de nà jiā kāfēiguǎn ne?

当地的朋友：那家咖啡馆已经搬走了。

Dāngdì de péngyǒu: Nà jiā kāfēiguǎn yǐjīng bān zǒu le.

你：是吗？搬到**哪里**了？

Nǐ: Shì ma? Bān dào nǎlǐ le?

You: What happened to the coffee shop that I often used to go?

Local friend: That coffee shop has moved.

You: Is that so? Where did it move to?

(d) Softening the tone of a question with 呢

呢 can be used at the end of a question (other than a 吗 question) to soften the tone and make the question sound less harsh or blunt. In this case, 呢 does not have a grammatical function; its use is optional.

李小姐：王先生，真对不起，明天的约会，我不能来了。
Lǐ xiǎojiě: Wáng xiānsheng, zhēn duìbùqǐ, míngtiān de yuēhuì, wǒ bù néng lái le.
王先生：哦？为什么呢？ (Without 呢, the utterance sounds harsh.)
Wáng xiānsheng: Ò? Wèishénme ne?
Miss Li: Mr Wang, I am really sorry. I can't make it to our date tomorrow.
Mr Wang: Oh? Why's that?

你不是说六点就会回家吗？怎么现在才回来呢？ (Without 呢, the question may sound like an accusation.)
Nǐ búshì shuō liù diǎn jiù huì huí jiā ma? Zěnme xiànzài cái huí lái ne?
Didn't you say you would be home by 6 o'clock? How come you only came back now?

(e) 还……呢!

An optional 呢 is often used when the sentence has 还 (hái) in it, although its connotation is indefinable.

李太太：你儿子大学毕业了没有？
Lǐ tàitai: Nǐ érzi dàxué bìyè le méiyǒu?
张太太：还没有呢！他还有两年呢！你儿子呢？ (= 你儿子大学毕业了吗？)
Zhāng tàitai: Hái méiyǒu ne! Tā hái yǒu liǎng nián ne! Nǐ érzi ne? (= Nǐ érzi dàxué bìyè le ma?)
李太太：我儿子还在上高中呢！
Lǐ tàitai: Wǒ érzi hái zài shàng gāozhōng ne.
Mrs Li: Has your son graduated from university?
Mrs Zhang: Not yet. He still has two years. How about your son?
Mrs Li: My son is still in high school.

王先生: 这个房子不错，够大！五个卧房、三个洗手间。
Wáng xiānsheng: Zhè ge fángzi bú cuò, gòu dà! Wǔ ge wòfáng, sān ge xǐshǒujiān.
房地产商：您看，后面还有一个大花园呢！
Fángdìchǎn shāng: Nín kàn, hòumiàn hái yǒu yí ge dà huāyuán ne!
Mr Wang: This house is not bad, big enough! Five bedrooms and three bathrooms.
Property salesperson: Look! There is also a big garden behind it.

(f) Using 呢 with the progressive aspect

An optional 呢 can be used when the sentence indicates an action in progress.

妈妈：小明，怎么还不去洗碗？你在做什么？
Māma: Xiǎomíng, zěnme hái bú qù xǐ wǎn? Nǐ zài zuò shénme?
爸爸：他在写功课呢。我去洗吧。
Bàba: Tā zài xiě gōngkè ne. Wǒ qù xǐ ba.
Mother: Xiaoming, how come you still have not washed the dishes? What are you doing?
Father: He is doing his homework. Let me go do the dishes.

(Situation: You have a date with your girlfriend. She is waiting for you to pick her up at her house. You arrive at her house, but her younger brother is the one who opens the door.)

你：你好！你姐姐**呢**？ （呢 in this question is asking the 'whereabouts' of his older sister, not her actual physical location, since you expected to see her.)
Nǐ: Nǐ hǎo! Nǐ jiějie ne?
弟弟：她**在化妆呢**！
Dìdi: Tā zài huàzhuāng ne!
You: Hello! Where is your sister?
Little brother: She is putting on make-up.

28.4 The use of 吧

Level 1/2

吧 has two definable usages: when making suggestions and when making assumptions.

(a) Making suggestions with 吧

吧 can be used to make a suggestion or to urge someone to do something.

张：天气这么好，咱们去郊外走走**吧**！
Zhāng: Tiānqì zhème hǎo, zánmen qù jiāowài zǒu zǒu ba!
李：今天我很忙，你一个人去**吧**！
Lǐ: Jīntiān wǒ hěn máng, nǐ yí ge rén qù ba!
Zhang: The weather is so nice. Let's go out to the countryside for a walk!
Li: Today I am busy. Why don't you go by yourself?

王：下课了，一起去吃午饭**吧**！
Wáng: Xiàkè le, yìqǐ qù chī wǔfàn ba!
丁：好，走**吧**！
Dīng: Hǎo, zǒu ba!
Wang: Class is over. Shall we go have lunch together?
Ding: OK, let's go!

(b) Making strong assumptions with 吧

吧 can be used to indicate near certainty or a strong guess/assumption, which means that the speaker is quite sure of what s/he believes to be true, but is not 100% certain. Such a sentence sometimes includes 一定 (*yídìng*) or words such as 大概 (*dàgài*) and 可能 (*kěnéng*), but 吧 alone can be enough to convey the feeling of certainty. A question mark, full stop or exclamation mark can be used at the end of the sentence.

(Situation: Miss Zhang is half an hour late for her date with Mr Wang.)

张：对不起，来晚了，你等了很久了**吧**！
Zhāng: Duìbùqǐ, lái wǎn le, nǐ děng le hěn jiǔ le ba!
王：没关系，路上堵车，是**吧**？
Wáng: Méi guānxi, lùshàng dǔchē, shì ba?
Zhang: Sorry I am late. You must have waited a long time.
Wang: It's OK. There must have been a traffic jam, right?

李：听说小兰跟她男朋友分手了。
Lǐ: Tīngshuō Xiǎolán gēn tā nán péngyǒu fēnshǒu le.
丁：什么？不会**吧**！上星期她告诉我，他们快要结婚了。
Dīng: Shénme? Bú huì ba! Shàng xīngqī tā gàosù wǒ, tāmen kuài yào jiéhūn le.
Li: I heard that Xiaolan and her boyfriend broke up.
Ding: What? It can't be true! She told me last week they were about to get married.

(c) 吧 not used in a narrative

It should be noted that when 吧 is used to imply a strong assumption or near certainty, it is usually used in a dialogue, not in a narrative. In a narrative, only 一定, 可能 or 大概 is used.

最近小李的女朋友总是不跟他见面，也不接他的电话，所以小李认为，她一定交了新的男朋友。(一定 indicates a strong assumption, but 吧 should not be used in this narrative.)

Zuìjìn Xiǎo Lǐ de nǚ péngyǒu zǒngshì bù gēn tā jiànmiàn, yě bù jiē tāde diànhuà, suǒyǐ Xiǎo Lǐ rènwéi, tā yídìng jiāo le xīn de nán péngyǒu.

Recently, Xiao Li's girlfriend would never meet with him and she also would not answer his phone calls. So Xiao Li thinks that she must have met someone new.

28.5 The use of 了

Level 2/3

了 can be used as a perfective aspect marker (after a verb) to indicate the completion of an action. As a modal particle (at the end of a sentence), 了 has at least three major meanings.

☞ See Chapter 9 for more information on 了.

(a) Indicating 'already' with 了

了 as a modal particle can indicate 'already'. Therefore, when a sentence contains the adverb 已经 (*yǐjīng*), 了 should be used at the end of the sentence. Since the modal particle 了 can, by itself, serve the function of indicating 'already', 已经 is optional.

Compare the following dialogues to see the difference between a sentence with 了 and one without 了.

张：今天我忘了戴手表，请问，现在(是)几点？
Zhāng: Jīntiān wǒ wàng le dài shǒubiǎo, qǐng wèn, xiànzài (shì) jǐ diǎn?
王：六点半。
Wáng: Liù diǎn bàn.
Zhang: I forgot to bring my watch today. May I ask what time it is now?
Wang: It's 6.30.

Compare: 张：几点了？小李怎么还没来？
Zhāng: Jǐ diǎn le? Xiǎo Lǐ zěnme hái méi lái?
王：六点半了，他大概不来了。
Wáng: Liù diǎn bàn le, tā dàgài bù lái le.
Zhang: What time is it **already**? How come Xiao Li is still not here?
Wang: It's **already** 6.30. He probably won't come.

(了 in 几点了 and 六点半了 indicates that it's getting late; therefore, the meaning of 'already' is implied. 了 in 不来了 indicates a change of situation. See below.)

他来中国半年了，一个好玩的地方也没去过。
Tā lái Zhōngguó bàn nián le, yí ge hǎowán de dìfāng yě méi qù guo.
He has **already** been in China for half a year; (but) he has not been anywhere fun.
(Because 了 implies 'already', 'half a year' is considered quite a long time in this sentence.)

Compare: 他来中国才半年，所以还不太习惯。
Tā lái Zhōngguó cái bàn nián, suǒyǐ hái bú tài xíguàn.
He has been in China for only half a year, so he is not used to it yet.
(Because 才 means 'only', this sentence cannot have 了.)

(b) Some other expressions that should take 了

In addition to 已经, some other expressions that have a similar meaning to 已经, such as 早就 (zǎojiù: 'long ago') and 好久 (hǎojiǔ: 'for a long time') should take a modal particle 了.

李：你知道吗？小王跟张小姐要结婚了。（要……了 indicates an impending action.）
Lǐ: Nǐ zhīdào ma? Xiǎo Wáng gēn Zhāng xiǎojiě yào jiéhūn le.
丁：这件事我**早就**知道了。
Dīng: Zhè jiàn shì wǒ zǎojiù zhīdào le.
Li: Did you know? Xiao Wang and Miss Zhang are going to get married.
Ding: I have long known about this.

王：今天想吃什么菜？
Wáng: Jīntiān xiǎng chī shénme cài?
张：**好久**没吃法国菜了，吃法国菜吧！
Zhāng: Hǎo jiǔ méi chī Fǎguó cài le, chī Fǎguó cài ba!
Wang: What kind of food do you feel like eating today?
Zhang: I have not had French food in quite a while. Let's have French food!

(c) Indicating a change of situation with 了

了 as a modal particle can imply a change of situation or the emergence of a new situation.

下雨了，咱们不能去公园了。
Xià yǔ le, zánmen bù néng qù gōngyuán le.
It's raining. We cannot go to the park (as we planned).
（了 in 下雨了 indicates the emergence of a new situation. 了 in 咱们不能去公园了 indicates a change of situation.）

医生：今天觉得怎么样？
Yīshēng: Jīntiān juéde zěnmeyàng?
病人：好一点了。头不疼了，也不发烧了。
Bìngrén: Hǎo yìdiǎn le. Tóu bù téng le, yě bù fāshāo le.
医生：我想，你的病再过两天就会**好了**。（好 + 了 = to feel fine + new situation = to recover）
Yīshēng: Wǒ xiǎng, nǐde bìng zài guò liǎng tiān jiù huì hǎo le.
Doctor: How do you feel today?
Patient: A little better. （了 implies this is a new situation.) I don't have a headache any more and I don't have a fever any more, either.
Doctor: I think you will recover from your illness in two days.

(d) 别……了

别 (bié) ……了 is a negative imperative sentence used to urge the listener to stop doing something. The expression can also be 别再 (zài) ……了. The implication of 了 here is a change of situation.

别哭了，赶快想解决问题的办法吧。
Bié kū le, gǎnkuài xiǎng jiějué wèntí de bànfǎ ba.
Stop crying. (= Don't cry anymore.) Hurry and try to think of a solution to the problem.
Compare: 现在我要告诉你一个坏消息；你听了以后，**别**哭。
Xiànzài wǒ yào gàosù nǐ yí ge huài xiāoxí; nǐ tīng le yǐhòu, bié kū.
I am going to tell you some bad news. When you've heard it, don't cry.
（Without 了 after 别哭, it indicates the listener is not crying.)

既然他总骗你，以后你就**别再**相信他说的话了。

Jìrán ta zǒng piàn nǐ, yǐhòu nǐ jiù bié zài xiāngxìn tā shuō de huà le.

Since he always lies to you, **don't** believe what he says **any more**.

(e) 太……了

The 了 in 太 (*tài*) …… 了 is optional, but it is frequently used. In a negative sentence, the 了 is no longer used.

王先生：这个房子**太**小(了)，也**太**贵(了)。

Wáng xiānsheng: Zhè ge fángzi tài xiǎo (le), yě tài guì (le).

房地产商：那我再带你去看一个；那个房子**不太**贵，不过那里的交通**不太**方便。

Fángdìchǎn shāng: Nà wǒ zài dài nǐ qù kàn yí ge; nà ge fángzi bú tài guì, búguò nàlǐ de jiāotōng bú tài fāngbiàn.

Mr Wang: This house is too small and it's also too expensive.

Property salesperson: Then I will take you to see another one. That one is not very expensive, but the transportation there is not very convenient.

(f) Making an inference

了 can be used to make an inference according to a given situation. 那 (*nà*) or 那么 (*nàme*), meaning 'in that case' is frequently used in such a sentence. It is not unusual to see a different character, such as 咯 or 啰, both pronounced *lo*, in place of 了. Either a full stop or a question mark can be used.

李：我们班，男的都是美国人，女的都是英国人。

Lǐ: Wǒmen bān, nán de dōu shì Měiguó rén, nǚ de dōu shì Yīngguó rén.

张：**那么**史密斯先生是美国人了？

Zhāng: Nàme Shǐmìsī xiānsheng shì Měiguó rén le.

Li: In our class, all the males are American and all the females are British.

Zhang: In that case, Mr Smith must be an American.

王太太：我儿子考上了最好的大学。

Wáng tàitai: Wǒ érzi kǎo shàng le zuì hǎo de dàxué.

李太太：**那**你现在一定很高兴**咯**。

Lǐ tàitai: Nà nǐ xiànzài yídìng hěn gāoxìng lo.

Mrs Wang: My son has passed the entrance exam into the best university.

Mrs Li: Then you must be happy now.

<table>
<tr><td>Level
2</td></tr>
</table>

28.6 The use of 的 as a modal particle

(a) Emphasizing the 'certainty' of a future event with 会……的

的 can be used as a modal particle to emphasize 'certainty' of a future event. It is used in a sentence with 会 (*huì*) to reassure the listener.

妈妈：要记得，你到了外国，一定要常常打电话回家。

Māma: Yào jìde, nǐ dào le wàiguó, yídìng yào chángcháng dǎ diànhuà huí jiā.

爸爸：别担心了，她不**会**忘记**的**。（了 indicates a change of situation; 的 goes with 会 and is used to reassure the listener of the certainty of a future event.）

Bàba: Bié dānxīn le, tā bú huì wàngjì de.

女儿：对，妈妈，您放心吧，我**会**常常给你们打**的**。（Another 会……的.）

Nǚ'ér: Duì, māma, nín fàngxīn ba, wǒ huì chángcháng gěi nǐmen dǎ de.

Mother: Don't forget to call us often while you are abroad.

Father: Stop worrying. She **won't** forget.

Daughter: That's right, Mother, don't worry! I definitely will call you often.

(b) 挺......的/满......的: 'quite'

An optional 的 is used in 挺 (*tǐng*) ......的 or 满 (*mǎn*) ......的, meaning 'quite'.

> 李：听说王老师昨天请你去参观他新买的房子。他的新房子怎么样？
>
> *Lǐ: Tīngshuō Wáng lǎoshī zuótiān qǐng nǐ qù cānguān tā xīn mǎi de fángzi. Tāde xīn fángzi zěnmeyàng?*
>
> 张：**满**大、也**满漂亮**(的)，不过离市区**挺远**(的)。
>
> *Zhāng: Mǎn da, yě mǎn piàoliàng (de), búguò lí shìqū tǐng yuǎn (de).*
>
> Li: I heard that Teacher Wang invited you to visit his newly bought house. How is his new house?
>
> Zhang: Quite big and quite pretty, but it is quite far away from the city.

Exercises

Fill in each of the blanks with a proper modal particle (吗, 呢, 吧, 了 or 的). If no modal particle should be used from a grammatical perspective, use Ø.

Not all modal particles have grammatical functions; some only have pragmatic functions. Try to decide on a proper one for each blank, even if it is not grammatically required.

Level 2

1 妈妈：小明，你为什么又在吃点心？你已经这么胖 ____，别再吃 ____！

爸爸：好 ____，让他吃 ____，别唠叨 ____。

2 这本词典上面写着你的名字，是你的 ____！借我用一下，好 ____？

3 妈妈：爸爸 ____？他回家了 ____？

儿子：他在客厅里看电视 ____。

4 李：最近我快忙死 ____，天天都半夜以后才上床睡觉 ____。

王：那明天晚上的舞会，你不能去 ____？

李：我还没有决定 ____！因为后天是星期天，所以星期六晚上，我想轻松一下。

Level 3

5 妈妈：现在几点 ____？小明怎么还没回来 ____？平常这个时候，他早就回来 ____。大家都在等他回来吃饭 ____。

爸爸：不用急，还不到八点 ____！咱们再等十分钟 ____！

女儿：如果十分钟以后他还是没回来 ____？我饿死 ____。

爸爸：那我们就不等 ____。

6 男：星期六晚上一起去吃饭，好 ____？

女：对不起，我不能去外面吃饭。

男：哦？为什么 ____？

女：你大概不知道 ____，我最近正在减肥 ____！

男：那我们星期六晚上做什么 ____？

女：去看场电影 ____！我好久没看电影 ____。

男：哦，那你还没看过《哈利波特》 ____？去看《哈利波特》 ____！

女：我对这个电影没有兴趣。

男：那《阿凡达》 ____？

女：太好 ____！听说这个电影不错，咱们就去看《阿凡达》 ____。

7 老师：这是什么字？谁知道？王中，你知道 ____？

王中：老师，我们还没有学过那个字 ____！

老师：哦，是 ____？好，那我问你另外一个。……这个 ____？学过了 ____？

王中：学过 ____，可是我想不起来那个字的意思。

老师：王中不认识这个字，李明，你 ____？

8 女：你到了中国以后，可能会很忙 ____，可是一定要记得常常给我打电话 ____。

男：没问题，我一定会打 ____。

29 Conjunctive pairs

Conjunctions are used to connect two words, two phrases or two clauses. The relationship between the words, the phrases or the clauses is indicated by the meaning of the conjunction. In Chinese, a conjunction can be a word or a pair of words. The focus of this chapter will be on the most commonly used conjunctions that are used in pairs. Such conjunctions will thus be referred to as 'conjunctive pairs'.

Basic grammatical features	Examples
1 The subordinate clause appears before the main clause.	因为天气不错，所以我要出去走走。 *Yīnwèi tiānqì bú cuò, suǒyǐ wǒ yào chū qù zǒu zǒu.* Because the weather is nice, I am going out for a walk.
2 A comma should be used between the subordinate clause and the main clause.	虽然天气不错，可是我不想出去。 *Suīrán tiānqì bú cuò, kěshì wǒ bù xiǎng chū qù.* Although the weather is nice, I don't feel like going out.
3 The subject can appear before the first word of the conjunctive pair.	这个考试虽然很难，但是我考得很好。 *Zhè ge kǎoshì suīrán hěn nán, dànshì wǒ kǎo de hěn hǎo.* Although the test was hard, I did well.
4 The subject should not be repeated if the subordinate clause and the main clause have the same subject.	如果你明天还是不舒服，就不必来开会了。 *Rúguǒ nǐ míngtiān háishì bù shūfú, jiù bú bì lái kāi huì le.* If you still don't feel well tomorrow, you don't have to come to the meeting.

Level
2

29.1 The use of 因为......，所以......

因为今天天气不错，所以我打算到公园去走走。（所以 is not optional.）
Yīnwèi jīntiān tiānqì bú cuò, suǒyǐ wǒ dǎsuàn dào gōngyuán qù zǒu zǒu.
Because the weather is nice today, I plan to go to the park for a walk.

因为他昨天没有写功课，所以今天被老师骂了一顿。（Do not repeat 他 after 所以.）
Yīnwèi tā zuótiān méiyǒu xiě gōngkè, suǒyǐ jīntiān bèi lǎoshī mà le yí dùn.
Because he did not do his homework yesterday, he was scolded by the teacher today.

他因为欠了一大笔债，所以只好把房子卖了来还债。（The subject can appear before 因为.）
Tā yīnwèi qiàn le yí dà bǐ zhài, suǒyǐ zhǐhǎo bǎ fángzi mài le lái huán zhài.
Because he owed a large sum of money, he had no choice but to sell his house to settle the debt.

(a) Omitting 因为

It is acceptable to use 所以 without 因为. In this case, 因此 (*yīncǐ*) can be used in place of 所以 to make the speech sound more formal.

小李跟他的女朋友分手了，**所以**最近他心情不好，常常发脾气。
Xiǎo Lǐ gēn tāde nǚ péngyǒu fēnshǒu le, suǒyǐ zuìjìn tā xīnqíng bù hǎo, chángcháng fā píqì.
Xiao Li has broken up with his girlfriend; therefore, he has been in a bad mood lately, and often lost his temper.

最近经济很不景气，**因此**失业的人很多。
Zuìjìn jīngjì hěn bù jǐngqì, yīncǐ shīyè de rén hěn duō.
Recently, the economy has been in a recession; therefore, there are many unemployed people.

(b) Omitting 所以

It is possible to have 因为 without 所以, but in this case the 因为 clause must follow the main clause, and a comma should be used between the two clauses. Also, the 因为 clause should have a subject whether or not it is the same as the subject in the main clause.

今天小王心情特别好，**因为**老师在全班同学的面前夸奖他。 (The comma is not optional.)
Jīntiān Xiǎo Wáng xīnqíng tèbié hǎo, yīnwèi lǎoshī zài quán bān tóngxué de miànqián kuājiǎng tā.
Today Xiao Wang is in a particularly good mood because his teacher praised him in front of the entire class.

我跟我男朋友分手了，**因为我**发现他骗我。 (我 before 发现 is necessary even though both clauses share the same subject.)
Wǒ gēn wǒ nán péngyǒu fēnshǒu le, yīnwèi wǒ fāxiàn tā piàn wǒ.
I've broken up with my boyfriend because I found out that he lied to me.

<table><tr><td>Level
3</td></tr></table>

29.2 The use of '因为......就/而 + verb or verbal phrase'

The subject must appear only once and it must appear before 因为. 就 (*jiù*) is used to imply that the reason is insufficient; 而 (*ér*) does not have such an implication. Whether or not the reason is sufficient is sometimes subjective.

(a) When 因为......而...... and 因为......所以 can be interchangeable

The following examples show that some 因为......而...... sentences can be interchangeable with 因为......所以...... sentences.

今天小李**因为**身体不舒服**而**不能来上课。 (= 今天小李**因为**身体不舒服，**所以**不能来上课。)
Jīntiān Xiǎo Lǐ yīnwèi shēntǐ bù shūfú ér bù néng lái shàngkè.
Today Xiao Li could not come to class because he was not feeling well.

小王的女朋友**因为**他脾气太坏**而**决定跟他分手。 (= **因为**小王的脾气太坏，**所以**他女朋友决定跟他分手。)
Xiǎo Wáng de nǚ péngyǒu yīnwèi tā píqì tài huài ér juédìng gēn tā fēnshǒu.
Xiao Wang's girlfriend decided to break up with him because he is bad-tempered.

(b) When 因为......而...... and 因为......所以 are not interchangeable

The following examples show that 因为......而...... sentences may not always be interchangeable with 因为......所以...... sentences.

小王常常**因为**天气不好**就**不去上课。
Xiǎo Wáng chángcháng yīnwèi tiānqì bù hǎo jiù bú qù shàng kè.
Xiao Wang frequently skips classes (**simply**) **because** the weather is bad. (The word 'simply' is used to show the meaning of 就, which implies the insufficient reason.)

我们老师说，学生可以**因为**生病**而**不去上课，但是不应该**因为**天气不好**就**不去上课。

Wǒmen lǎoshī shuō, xuéshēng kěyǐ yīnwèi shēngbìng ér bú qù shàngkè, dànshì bù yīnggāi yīnwèi tiānqì bù hǎo jiù bú qù shàngkè.

Our teacher says that students can miss classes because they are sick, but they should not miss classes **simply because** the weather is bad.

(c) Making 因为……而/就 sentences negative

 Where to put the negative word in an 因为……而/就 sentence has been a confusing issue, even for advanced learners, since the English counterparts of the various possible sentences can be very similar. The following examples show how to use the negative word properly.

小李**因为**没有兄弟姐妹**而**觉得有一点寂寞。(= 小李**因为**没有兄弟姐妹，所以**觉得**有一点寂寞。)

Xiǎo Lǐ yīnwèi méiyǒu xiōngdì jiěmèi ér juéde yǒu yìdiǎn jìmò.

Xiao Li feels a little lonely because he does not have any siblings.

小王**从来不因为**没有兄弟姐妹**而**觉得寂寞。(This cannot be converted into 因为……所以…….)

Xiǎo Wáng cónglái bù yīnwèi méiyǒu xiōngdì jiěmèi ér juéde jìmò.

Xiao Wang never feels lonely (simply) because he does not have any siblings.

小张**因为**有很多兄弟姐妹**而**从来不觉得寂寞。(= 小张**因为**有很多兄弟姐妹，**所以**从来不觉得寂寞。)

Xiǎo Zhāng yīnwèi yǒu hěn duō xiōngdì jiěmèi ér cónglái bù juéde jìmò.

Xiao Zhang never feels lonely because he has many siblings.

他**从来不因为**担心会失败**而**不敢尝试。(This cannot be converted into 因为……所以…….)

Tā cónglái bù yīnwèi dānxīn huì shībài ér bù gǎn chángshì.

He is never afraid of trying anything because he is worried that he might fail.

他**因为**担心会失败而**从来不**敢尝试。(他因为担心会失败，**所以**从来不敢尝试。)

Tá yīnwèi dānxīn huì shībài er cónglái bù gǎn chángshì.

He never dares to try anything because he worries that he might fail.

29.3 The use of 虽然……，可是/但是……

但是 (*dànshì*) and 可是 (*kěshì*) are considered interchangeable. 但是 can be shortened into 但, but 可是 is only shortened into 可 in casual speech.

虽然今天天气很好，**可是**(or **但是**)我不能出去，我要在家准备明天的考试。(可是 or 但是 is not optional.)

Suīrán jīntiān tiānqì hěn hǎo, kěshì (or dànshì) wǒ bù néng chūqù, wǒ yào zài jiā zhǔnbèi míngtiān de kǎoshì.

Although today's weather is nice, I cannot go out. I must study at home for tomorrow's test.

(a) Placement of the subject

The subject in the 虽然 clause can appear before 虽然, whether or not it is the same subject in the 可是/但是 clause.

昨天的考试**虽然**很难，**可是**我考得很好，因为我准备得很充分。

Zuótiān de kǎoshì suīrán hěn nán, kěshì wǒ kǎo de hěn hǎo, yīnwèi wǒ zhǔnbèi de hěn chōngfèn.

Although yesterday's test was difficult, I did well because I was fully prepared.

小李**虽然**相当聪明，**但是**不够用功，所以考试成绩总是很差。

Xiǎo Lǐ suīrán xiāngdāng cōngmíng, dànshì bú gòu yònggōng, suǒyǐ kǎoshì chéngjī zǒngshì hěn chà.

Although Xiao Li is quite smart, he is not hardworking enough, so his test scores are always poor.

(b) Omitting 虽然

It is possible to have only 可是/但是 in a sentence without 虽然.

史密斯先生中文只学了半年多，**可是**已经认识几百个汉字了。

Shǐmìsī xiānsheng Zhōngwén zhǐ xué le bàn nián duō, kěshì yǐjīng rènshì jǐ bǎi ge Hànzì le.

Mr Smith has only studied Chinese for a little over half a year, but he already knows several hundred Chinese characters.

(c) Variations with 却 and 还是

The adverb 却 (*què*) can be used in a 可是/但是 sentence. When 却 is used, 可是/但是 becomes optional.

（虽然）医生开的药，他都吃了，（可是）病情**却**越来越严重。

(Suīrán) yīshēng kāi de yào, tā dōu chī le, (kěshì) bìngqíng què yuè lái yuè yánzhòng.

He has taken all the medicine that the doctor prescribed, but his condition is getting more and more serious.

- 却 and 可是/但是 can co-exist, but they do not replace each other since 可是/但是 (conjunction) should appear before the subject, whereas 却 (adverb) must appear after the subject

(Situation: The results of a beauty pageant have been announced.)

评审宣布，李小姐得了第三名。她**虽然**笑得很高兴，（但是）心里**却**相当难过。

Píngshěn xuānbù, Lǐ xiǎojiě dé le dì sān míng. Tā suīrán xiào de hěn gāoxìng, (dànshì) xīn lǐ què xiāngdāng nánguò.

The judges announced that Miss Li won third place. Although she smiled happily, she was, however, quite sad inside.

- 还是, meaning 'still', can be used in the 可是/但是 clause to indicate that there is no change or effect despite what was mentioned in the 虽然 clause. 还是 and 可是/但是 do not replace each other since 还是 is an adverb.

王先生**虽然**病了，可是**还是**天天都来上班。

Wáng xiānsheng suīrán bìng le, kěshì háishì tiān tiān dōu lái shàngbān.

Although Mr Wang is sick, he still comes to work every day.

<table>
<tr><td>Level</td></tr>
<tr><td>2</td></tr>
</table>

29.4 The use of 如果……，就……

如果 (*rúguǒ*) can be replaced by 要是 (*yàoshì*) to make the speech sound more casual; it can also be replaced by 倘若 (*tǎngruò*) to make it sound formal.

❧ Although 就 can be interpreted as meaning 'then', it is an adverb; therefore, it should not appear before the subject of the main clause.

王：明天是星期六，一起到郊外走走吧！

Wáng: Míngtiān shì xīngqī liù, yìqǐ dào jiāowài zǒu zǒu ba!

张：**要是**天气好，我**就**跟你去。（要是天气好，就我跟你去 is incorrect.）

Zhāng: Yàoshì tiānqì hǎo, wǒ jiù gēn nǐ qù.

Wang: Tomorrow is Saturday. How about if we go to the countryside for a walk?

Zhang: If the weather is nice, I will go with you.

(a) Variation with 那么

An optional word 那么 (*nàme*) can be used in the main clause. Although 那么 literally means 'then', 那么 and 就 do not replace each other since 那么 should appear before the subject of the sentence, whereas 就 should appear after it.

李：经理，明天的迎新会，在室内还是室外办？

Lǐ: Jīnglǐ, míngtiān de yíngxīn huì, zài shì nèi háishì shì wài bàn?

经理：**倘若**天晴，**那么**我们**就**在室外办；**倘若**下雨，**那么就**在室内。

Jīnglǐ: Tǎngruò tiān qíng, nàme wǒmen jiù zài shì wài bàn; tǎngruò xiàyǔ, nàme jiù zài shì nèi.

Li: Manager, will tomorrow's welcome party be held indoors or outdoors?

Manager: If it is clear (sunny), then we will hold it outdoors. If it rains, then it will be indoors.

(b) Forming questions or suggestions

When the main clause is not a simple statement, but a suggestion or a question, 就 usually is not used. However, 那么 can remain.

这个周末，你有没有事？**要是**没事，（那么，）想不想去郊外走走？ (There is no 就 because 想不想去郊外走走 is a question.)

Zhè ge zhōumò, nǐ yǒu méiyǒu shì? Yàoshì méi shì, (nàme) xiǎng bù xiǎng qù jiāowài zǒu zǒu?

Will you be busy this weekend? If you are not, would you like go to the countryside for a walk?

(c) When the main clause contains another adverb

When the main clause has another adverb, 就 can be optional and 那么 remains optional.

小王这么顽皮，如果我是他妈妈，（那么，）一定会被他气死。 (Because of the additional adverb 一定, 就 is optional.)

Xiǎo Wáng zhème wánpí, rúguǒ wǒ shì tā māma, yídìng huì bèi tā qì sǐ.

Xiao Wang is so naughty. If I were his mother, I would be terribly upset by him.

(d) Using the modal particle 了 to indicate a hypothetical situation

If 要是/如果/倘若 is used to indicate a hypothetical situation of a past event, the modal particle 了 is often used in the main clause to emphasize that the situation would have been different.

还好今天出门的时候带了钱。**要是**没带钱，这么好的东西，**就**没办法买**了**。

Háihǎo jīntiān chū mén de shíhòu dài le qián. Yàoshì méi dàiqián, zhème hǎo de dōngxi, jiù méi bànfǎ mǎi le.

Fortunately, I brought money with me when I left the house today. If I hadn't brought any money, I would have had no way to buy something this good.

(e) Casual speech: (要是/如果)……的话

In casual speech, 要是/如果 can be 要是/如果……的话 (*de huà*). When 的话 is used, 要是/如果 becomes optional.

张：明天你跟男朋友要去哪里约会？

Zhāng: Míngtiān nǐ gēn nán péngyǒu yào qù nǎlǐ yuēhuì?

李：天气好**的话**，就去公园照相；下雨**的话**，就去看电影。

Lǐ: Tiānqì hǎo de huà, jiù qù gōngyuán zhàoxiàng; xià yǔ de huà, jiù qù kàn diànyǐng.

Zhang: Where are you and your boyfriend going on a date tomorrow?

Li: If the weather is nice, we will go to the park to take pictures. If it rains, we will go to a movie.

Level
3

29.5 The use of 即使……，也……

即使 (*jíshǐ*) ……也 (*yě*) …… has two connotations: a hypothetical situation ('even if') or an extreme situation ('even').

即使 can be replaced by 就是 (*jiùshì*) or 就算 (*jiùsuàn*) to make the speech sound more casual.

(a) A hyphothetical situation: 'even if'

即使……也…… can imply a hypothetical situation that may or may not come true and 'even if' it were true or were to become true, it would result in the same effect.

王先生：小李人品不好，你不应该跟这种人结婚。

Wáng xiānsheng: Xiǎo Lǐ rénpǐn bù hǎo, nǐ bù yīnggāi gēn zhè zhǒng rén jiéhūn.

张小姐：你不是我爸爸，**就算**你是我爸爸，**也**没有权利反对我跟他结婚。

Zhāng xiǎojiě: Nǐ bú shì wǒ bàba, jiùsuàn nǐ shì wǒ bàba, yě méiyǒu quánlì fǎnduì wǒ gēn tā jiéhūn.

Mr Wang: Xiao Li's moral character is bad. You should not marry this kind of man.

Miss Zhang: You are not my father. **Even if** you were, you would have no right to oppose my marriage to him.

我没有钱。**就是**有，**也**不会借他。

Wǒ méiyǒu qián. Jiùshì yǒu, yě bú huì jiè tā.

I don't have any money. **Even if** I did, I would not loan him any.

我只对音乐有兴趣，所以我一定要念音乐。**即使**将来找不到工作，我**也**不在乎。

Wǒ zhǐ duì yīnyuè yǒu xìngqù, suǒyǐ wǒ yídìng yào niàn yīnyuè. Jíshǐ jiānglái zhǎo bú dào gōngzuò, wǒ yě bú zàihū.

I am only interested in music, so I insist on studying music. Even if I cannot find a job in the future, I don't care.

(b) An extreme situation: 'even'

即使……，也…… can also imply an extreme situation, and is translated into English as 'even'. The meaning is similar to 连 (*lián*) ……也……. In this case, an optional 是 (*shì*) usually follows 即使/就算. Again, the connotation is that 'even' an extreme case would result in the same effect.

张经理是一个工作狂，**就是**周末**也**去公司加班。

Zhāng jīnglǐ shì yí ge gōngzuò kuáng, jiùshì zhōumò yě qù gōngsī jiābān.

Manager Zhang is a workaholic. He even goes to work extra hours on the weekend.

老师：明天的数学考试非常容易。**即使是**数学最差的同学，**也**一定可以考得很好。

Lǎoshī: Míngtiān de shùxué kǎoshì fēicháng róngyì. Jíshǐ shì shùxué zuì chà de tóngxué, yě yídìng kěyǐ kǎo de hěn hǎo.

小李：我的数学这么差，**就算是**最容易的题目，我恐怕**也**答不出来。

Xiǎo Lǐ: Wǒde shùxué zhème chà, jiùsuàn shì zuì róngyì de tímù, wǒ kǒngpà yě dá bù chūlái.

Teacher: Tomorrow's mathematics test is very easy. Even those students who are poorest at mathematics can definitely do well.

Xiao Li: I'm so bad at mathematics. I probably won't be able to answer even the easiest questions.

29.6 The use of '无论 + question，都……'

无论 (*wúlùn*) can be replaced by 不管 (*bùguǎn*) to make the speech sound casual. Also, either 无论 or 不管 is optional. A sentence would have the same meaning without either word.

☞ See 33.14 for more on sentences without 无论 or 不管.

👁 When 无论 and 都 share the same subject, the subject must not be repeated. It can appear at the beginning of the sentence or before 都 (*dōu*).

张：这几天我很忙，明天下午的会，可不可以不来参加？
Zhāng: Zhè jǐ tiān wǒ hěn máng, míngtiān xiàwǔ de huì, kě bù kěyǐ bù lái cānjiā?
经理：明天的会非常重要，你**无论**多忙**都**得来参加。(你无论多忙你都得来 would be improper. But **无论**多忙**你都得来 is correct.)
Jīnglǐ: Míngtiān de huì fēicháng zhòngyào, nǐ wúlùn duō máng dōu děi lái cānjiā.
Zhang: I am busy these days. Can I skip tomorrow afternoon's meeting?
Manager: Tomorrow's meeting is very important. You must attend no matter how busy you are.

为了多运动，小王**无论**去**哪里都**骑自行车或者走路。
Wèile duō yùndòng, Xiǎo Wáng wúlùn qù nǎlǐ dōu qí zìxíngchē huòzhě zǒulù.
In order to get more exercise, Xiao Wang rides his bicycle or walks no matter where he is going.

《哈利波特》广受欢迎，**无论**大人**还是**小孩**都**喜欢看。
'Hālì Bōtè' guǎng shòu huānyíng, wúlùn dàrén háishì xiǎohái dōu xǐhuān kàn.
Harry Potter is widely popular. Everybody likes it, be it an adult or a child.

小兰决心要嫁给李先生，**无论**我**怎么**劝她，她**都**不听。
Xiǎolán juéxīn yào jià gěi Lǐ xiānsheng, wúlùn wǒ zěnme quàn tā, tā dōu bù tīng.
Xiaolan is determined to marry Mr Li. No matter how I urge her (not to), she will not listen.

29.7 The use of 不但……, 而且(也/还)……

不但 (*búdàn*) can be replaced by 不仅 (*bùjǐn*) or 不只 (*bùzhǐ*). When the 不但 and 而且 (*érqiě*) clauses share the same subject, it appears only once before 不但.

骑自行车不但方便，而且也是很好的运动，所以我每天都骑自行车去上班。
Qí zìxíngchē búdàn fāngbiàn, érqiě yě shì hěn hǎo de yùndòng, suǒyǐ wǒ měi tiān dōu qí zìxíngchē qù shàngbān.
Riding bicycles is not only convenient, but also a very good form of exercise, so I ride my bicycle to work every day.

- 不但 is optional as long as 而且 is used

王先生（**不但**）长得很帅，**而且**每个月赚不少钱，难怪喜欢他的女孩子很多。
Wáng xiānsheng (búdàn) zhǎng de hěn shuài, érqiě měi ge yuè zhuàn bù shǎo qián, nánguài xǐhuān tā de nǚ háizi hěn duō.
Not only is Mr Wang good-looking, but he also makes a lot of money every month. No wonder many girls like him.

- When 也 or 还 is used, 而且 becomes optional

  小李**不但**钢琴弹得好，（**而且**）小提琴**也**拉得不错。
  Xiǎo Lǐ búdàn gāngqín tán de hǎo, (érqiě) xiǎotíqín yě lā de búcuò.
  Not only does Xiao Li play the piano well, but he also plays the violin quite well.

- When the 不但 and 而且 clauses share the same subject, either 也 or 还 can be used

  小张**不但**会说日文，（**而且**）**还**（or **也**）会说法文。
  Xiǎo Zhāng búdàn huì shuō Rìwén, (érqiě) hái (or yě) huì shuō Fǎwén.
  Xiao Zhang can not only speak Japanese, but he can also speak French.

- Without 不但, 而且 can be used as a stand-alone word, meaning 'besides' or 'in addition'. The subject should always appear after 而且

  张：听说小王病了。
  Zhāng: Tīngshuō Xiǎo Wáng bìng le.
  李：唉！没错！**而且**他**还**失业了。
  Lǐ: Ài! Méi cuò. Érqiě tā hái shīyè le.
  Zhang: I heard that Xiao Wang is sick.
  Li: Alas! That's right! In addition, he has lost his job.

- When the 不但 clause and the 而且 clause do not have the same subject, 不但 should appear before the subject. 也 should be used in the 而且 clause; 还 cannot be used. The pattern is '不但 + subject A……, 而且 subject B 也……'

  《哈利波特》这套小说，广受欢迎，**不但**小孩子喜欢看，**而且**很多大人**也**被吸引住了。
  'Hālì Bōtè' zhè tào xiǎoshuō, guǎng shòu huānyíng, búdàn xiǎoháizi xǐhuān kàn, érqiě hěn duō dàrén yě bèi xīyǐn zhù le.
  The Harry Potter novels are widely popular. Not only do children enjoy reading them, but grown-ups are also riveted.

  数学考试以前，小王花了很多时间，帮助数学不好的同学。结果，**不但**他自己考得很好，**而且**他的朋友**也**都考得不错。
  Shùxué kǎoshì yǐqián, Xiǎo Wáng huā le hěn duō shíjiān, bāngzhù shùxué bù hǎo de tóngxué. Jiéguǒ, búdàn tā zìjǐ kǎo de hěn hǎo, érqiě tāde péngyǒu yě dōu kǎo de bú cuò.
  Before the mathematics exam, Xiao Wang spent a lot of time helping his classmates whose mathematics is not good. As a result, not only did he himself do well in the exam, but also all his friends did well.

29.8 The use of '不但 + negative (不/没有)……，反而(还)……'

(a) The connotation of 反而

With rare exceptions, the 不但 and 反而 (*fǎn'ér*) clauses should have the same subject, which must appear before 不但. The phrase in 反而 should be a positive sentence.

🕭 反而 is used to indicate that what happens does not stand to reason or is contrary to one's expectations; it does not have a direct counterpart in English.

第一次考试，我考得很差，所以我花了很多时间准备第二次考试；没想到，我**不但没有**进步，**反而**考得比第一次更差。
Dì yí cì kǎoshì, wǒ kǎo de hěn chà, suǒyǐ wǒ huā le hěn duō shíjiān zhǔnbèi dì èr cì kǎoshì; méi xiǎngdào, wǒ búdàn méiyǒu jìnbù, fǎn'ér kǎo de bǐ dì yī cì gèng chà.
I did poorly in the first test, so I spent a lot of time studying for the second test. I did not expect that not only did I not improve (my scores), I did even worse.

小王总说我随时可以请他帮忙。可是昨天我向他借钱，他**不但不**肯借我，**反而**(还)把我骂了一顿。

Xiǎo Wáng zǒng shuō wǒ suíshí kěyǐ qǐng tā bāngmáng. Kěshì zuótiān wǒ xiàng tā jiè qián, tā búdàn bù kěn jiè wǒ, fǎn'ér (hái) bǎ wǒ mà le yí dùn.

Xiao Wang always said that I could ask him for help anytime. But (when) I tried to borrow some money from him yesterday, not only would he not lend me any, he scolded me.

(b) 反而 as a stand-alone word

When there is a clear and self-explanatory context, the 不但 clause becomes optional and 反而 is used as a stand-alone word. In this case, 反而 must appear after the subject. (Keep in mind that 而且 must appear before the subject.)

👁 When the 不但 part is omitted, the meaning of 反而 depends completely on the context, and cannot be translated into an actual word in English.

老师骂了他以后，**他反而**笑了。

Lǎoshī mà le tā yǐhòu, tā fǎn'ér xiào le.

After the teacher scolded him, he smiled.

(The reasonable expectation was that he should have felt bad and cried; therefore, 他不但没哭 becomes redundant due to the clear context. Also, 反而 must appear after 他; therefore, 反而他笑了 is incorrect.)

小李真没良心，我帮了他这么多忙，**他反而**(还)在背后说我的坏话。

Xiǎo Lǐ zhēn méi liángxīn, wǒ bāng le tā zhème duō máng, ta fǎn'ér (hái) zài bèi hòu shuō wǒde huàihuà.

Xiao Li is really ungrateful. I have helped him so much, but (not only did he not thank me) he still says bad things about me behind my back.

(The context is that it stands to reason that he should have been grateful; therefore, 他不但不感谢我 is omitted.)

Exercises

I   Fill in the blanks with proper words (conjunctions).

vel
1

1   安娜 _____ 不会说中文，可是特别喜欢听中国歌曲。

2   因为今天天气不好，_____ 我不想出去，只想在家看看书。

3   王明的记性真差！十个生词，他已经记了一个多小时，可是 _____ 记不住。

4   男：这个星期六，你想做什么？
    女：_____ 天气好，就去野餐。
    男：天气不好呢？
    女：那 _____ 去看电影。

5   李先生 _____ 脾气好，而且很会赚钱，所以喜欢他的女孩子很多。

Level
2

6 小兰跟她男朋友吵架了，她妈妈不但不安慰她，_____ 还说一定是她不对。

7 经理把小张骂了一顿，小张心里虽然不高兴，脸上 _____ 没有表示出来。

8 王中是我们班最聪明的学生，可是 _____ 这个问题实在太难了，所以 _____ 王中也不会回答。

9 李小姐不但漂亮，_____ 脾气非常好。可惜我已经结婚了，_____ 我还没结婚 _____，我一定要追她。

10 我实在太喜欢这辆车了，所以 _____ 多贵，我都一定要买。

11 这样东西，一点用也没有，_____ 免费送我，我也不要。

12 真奇怪！老师在全班同学面前称赞李中，李中不但不开心，_____ 哭了。

13 在这个国家，上大学是免费的。所以 _____ 是穷人家的小孩，也可以上大学。

14 在这个国家，上大学是免费的。所以 _____ 是穷人家还是有钱人家的小孩，都可以上大学。

II Translate the following into Chinese using 因为……而/就. Do not use 所以 in any of the sentences.

Level
3

1 Wang Ming always feels happy because he has a pretty girlfriend.

2 Wang Ming frequently feels unhappy because he does not have a girlfriend.

3 Wang Ming never feels happy simply because he has a pretty girlfriend.

4 Wang Ming never feels unhappy simply because he does not have a girlfriend.

5 You cannot miss class simply because the weather is bad.

6 Yesterday Wang Ming could not go to classes because he had a high fever.

7 Wang Ming never misses classes simply because the weather is bad; but he will sometimes miss classes because he has to go out of town on business.

30 Conjunctions used in context

Context plays an important role in the use of the Chinese language. Certain conjunctions and conjunctive pairs are used in context only. In other words, these conjunctions and conjunctive pairs are used when the situation being discussed is already understood by people engaged in the dialogues or has just been mentioned by one of them. ☯ Their counterparts in English may not always show this grammatical feature; therefore, learners who are English speakers should pay attention to this unique feature in Chinese.

Level 2

30.1 The use of 既然......, (就)......

A comparison between the following two situations illustrates the significance of context.

(Situation: An excerpt from Xiao Wang's diary.)

> 今天早上起床以后，看到外面是个大晴天。我想，天气**既然**这么好，为什么不到公园走走呢？ (The sentence 外面是个大晴天 establishes the fact that 天气很好.)
> *Jīntiān zǎoshàng qǐchuáng yǐhòu, kàndào wàimiàn shì ge dà qíngtiān. Wǒ xiǎng, tiānqì jìrán zhème hǎo, wèishénme bú dào gōngyuán zǒu zǒu ne?*
> This morning when I got up, I saw that it was a bright sunny day outside. I thought to myself: since the weather was so nice, why not go to the park for a walk?

(Situation: An excerpt from Xiao Li's diary.)

> 今天早上起床以后，**因为**看到外面天气很好，**所以**决定到公园去走走。 (外面天气很好 is the first sentence about the weather; it is not in context. Therefore, 既然 should not be used.)
> *Jīntiān zǎoshàng qǐchuáng yǐhòu, yīnwèi kàndào wàimiàn tiānqì hěn hǎo, suǒyǐ juédìng dào gōngyuán qù zǒu zǒu.*
> Upon getting up this morning, because I saw that the weather outside was nice, I decided to go to the park for a walk.

When the main sentence is a simple statement, 就 should be used. When it is a question or a suggestion, 就 normally is not used. 既然 can appear before or after the subject.

The following examples show that what follows 既然 is a fact that has been established. If there is no need to repeat the fact, 这样 (*zhèyàng*) or 如此 (*rúcǐ*) must follow 既然.

> 王：你气色不太好，怎么回事？
> *Wáng: Nǐ qìsè bú tài hǎo, zěnme huí shì?*
> 张：最近常常觉得很累，吃不下，睡不好。
> *Zhāng: Zuìjìn chángcháng juéde hěn lèi, chī bú xià, shuì bù hǎo.*
> 王：**既然这样**(= **既然如此**)，你怎么还不快去看医生？ (or 你**就**应该快去看医生。)
> *Wáng: Jìrán zhèyàng (= Jìrán rúcǐ), nǐ zěnme hái bú kuài qù kàn yīshēng?*
> Wang: You don't look too well. What's the matter?

Zhang: Recently I often feel tired; I can't eat and I can't sleep well.
Wang: Since this is the case, how come you haven't hurried and gone to see a doctor? (*or* You should hurry and go see a doctor.)

李：小王真可恶！我帮过他很多忙，可是我昨天向他借五块钱，他竟然不肯借我。
Lǐ: Xiǎo Wáng zhēn kěwù! Wǒ bāng guò tā hěn duō máng, kěshì wǒ zuótiān xiàng tā jiè wǔ kuài qián, tā jìngrán bù kěn jiè wǒ.
丁：他**既然**不把你当朋友，你以后**就**别再帮他了。
Dīng: Tā jìrán bù bǎ nǐ dāng péngyǒu, nǐ yǐhòu jiù bié zài bāng tā le.
Li: Xiao Wang is really nasty. I have helped him a lot, but yesterday I asked to borrow $5 from him and surprisingly he would not lend it to me.
Ding: Since he did not treat you as a friend, don't help him anymore.

30.2 The use of 是因为

因为 (*yīnwèi*) is usually used to establish a cause or reason. When the cause or reason is already in context, 是因为 (*shì yīnwèi*) should be used; simply using 因为 would not be proper.

李：唉呀，我忘了带伞，你在这里等一下，我去那家便利商店买把伞。
Lǐ: Āiyā! Wǒ wàng le dài sǎn, nǐ zài zhèlǐ děng yíxià, wǒ qù nà jiā biànlì shāngdiàn mǎi bǎ sǎn.
张：天气预报说，今天不会下雨，你不用去买了。
Zhāng: Tiānqì yùbào shuō, jīntiān bú huì xiàyǔ, nǐ bú yòng qù mǎi le.
李：我要买伞**是因为**我不能晒太阳。（我要买伞，因为我不能晒太阳 is improper.）
Lǐ: Wǒ yào mǎi sǎn shì yīnwèi wǒ bù néng shài tàiyáng.
Li: Oh no! I forgot to bring an umbrella. You wait here for a moment. I'll go to that convenience store and buy an umbrella.
Zhang: The weather forecast said that it won't rain today. You don't have to buy an umbrella.
Li: (The reason) I have to buy an umbrella (is) because I cannot be exposed to the sun.
Compare: 太阳这么大！你在这里等一下，我得去买把伞，因为我不能晒太阳。
Tàiyáng zhème dà. Nǐ zài zhèlǐ děng yíxià, wǒ děi qù mǎi bǎ sǎn, yīnwèi wǒ bù néng shài tàiyáng.
The sun is so bright! Will you wait here for a moment? I have to go and buy an umbrella (parasol) because I cannot be exposed to the sun.

老师：王立，你今天怎么又没有交功课？又没写，对不对？
Lǎoshī: Wáng Lì, nǐ jīntiān zěnme yòu méiyǒu jiāo gōngkè? Yòu méi xiě, duì bú duì?
王立：昨天没交功课**是因为**没写，今天没交**是因为**忘了带来。
Wáng Lì: Zuótiān méi jiāo gōngkè shì yīnwèi méi xiě, jīntiān méi jiāo shì yīnwèi wàng le dài lái.
Teacher: Wang Li, how come you didn't turn in your homework again? You didn't do it again, right?
Wang Li: I didn't turn in my homework yesterday because I didn't do it, but I didn't turn it in today because I forgot to bring it.

30.3 The more formal use of (之) 所以……是因为……

In a more formal situation, the expression is (之) 所以 (*zhī suǒyǐ*)……是因为……. What follows (之) 所以 must be an established situation.

(Situation: Mr Zhang will not let his daughter continue to date a certain man.)

张太太：你为什么不喜欢咱们女儿的男朋友？
Zhāng tàitai: Nǐ wèishénme bù xǐhuān zánmen nǚ'ér de nán péngyǒu?
张先生：其实我并不讨厌他。我**之所以**反对他们交往**是因为**他太穷了。
Zhāng xiānsheng: Qíshí wǒ bìng bù tǎoyàn tā. Wǒ zhī suǒyǐ fǎnduì tāmen jiāowǎng shì yīnwèi tā tài qióng le.
Mrs Zhang: Why do you not like our daughter's boyfriend?
Mr Zhang: Actually, I do not dislike him. (The reason) I oppose their dating (is) because he is too poor.

30.4 The use of 'A 是 A, 可是/但是/不过......'

(a) General usage

The usage is similar to 虽然 (*suīrán*)......, 可是/但是/不过 (*kěshì/dànshì/búguò*) ....
However, what follows 虽然 may or may not be in context; but what is indicated by 'A' in the 'A 是 A' part must be explicitly mentioned. Also, what follows 是 can be negative.

(Situation: Anna spent a week in Shanghai, her friend Xiaolan asks her about it.)

小兰：听说你去了一趟上海，你对那里的印象怎么样？
Xiǎolán: Tīngshuō nǐ qù le yí tàng Shànghǎi, nǐ duì nàlǐ de yìnxiàng zěnmeyàng?
安娜：我觉得上海**虽然**是一个大都市，**可是**上海人不象一般大都市的居民那么冷漠。
Ānnà: Wǒ juéde Shànghǎi suīrán shì yí ge dà dūshì, kěshì Shànghǎi rén bú xiàng yìbān dà dūshì de jūmín nàme lěngmò.
小兰：上海的东西很**贵**，对不对？
Xiǎolán: Shànghǎi de dōngxi hěn guì, duì bú duì?
安娜：东西**贵是贵，可是**品质都相当好。 (The word 贵 has been mentioned; therefore, 贵是贵 can be used in place of 虽然贵.)
Ānnà: Dōngxi guì shì guì, kěshì pǐnzhì dōu xiāngdāng hǎo.
小兰：听说那里的交通很**乱**。
Xiǎolán: Tīngshuō nàlǐ de jiāotōng hěn luàn.
安娜：**乱是不乱，可是**车太多，所以停车是一个大问题。 (The word 乱 is in context; therefore, 乱是不乱 can be used to mean 虽然不乱.)
Ānnà: Luàn shì bú luàn, kěshì chē tài duō, suǒyǐ tíng chē shì yí ge dà wèntí.
Xiaolan: I heard that you made a trip to Shanghai. What is your impression of that place?
Anna: I feel that although Shanghai is a big city, the people there are not as cold as residents generally are in big cities.
Xiaolan: Things in Shanghai are expensive, right?
Anna: While things are expensive, their quality is quite good.
Xiaolan: I heard that traffic there is bad.
Anna: Although it's not bad, there are too many cars, so parking is a big problem.

(b) Variation with 倒

To contradict the other person's point, an optional word, 倒 (*dǎo*), can be used before 是.

房地产商：这个房子这么好，你为什么不想买？觉得**太贵**了吗？
Fángdìchǎn shāng: Zhè ge fángzi zhème hǎo, nǐ wèishénme bù xiǎng mǎi? Juéde tài guì le ma?
李先生：**贵(倒)是不贵，不过**厨房太小了。
Lǐ xiānsheng: Guì dǎo shì bú guì, búguò chúfáng tài xiǎo le.

Property salesperson: This house is so good. Why don't you want to buy it? Do you feel it is too expensive?

Mr Li: Although it is not expensive, its kitchen is too small.

(c) Variation with 就是

When a good quality is followed by a negative quality, 就是 (*jiùshì*) is frequently used in place of 可是/但是/不过.

> 房地产商：这个房子，您喜欢吗？
> *Fángdìchǎn shāng: Zhè ge fángzi, nín xǐhuān ma?*
> 王先生：喜欢**是**喜欢，**就是**价钱太贵了。
> *Wáng xiānsheng: Xǐhuān shì xǐhuān, jiùshì jiàqián tài guì le.*
> Property salesperson: Do you like this house?
> Mr Wang: Although I like it, it is too expensive.
> (喜欢 can be considered a good quality; 太贵 is considered a negative quality.)

Level 2

30.5 The use of 固然……, 但是/可是……

固然 (*gùrán*) ……, 但是/可是…… is also similar in meaning to 虽然……, 但是/可是……, but what follows 固然 is a condition that already exists in the context. Also, it is usually used to first acknowledge the value of the other person's opinion before bringing up the counter point. Unlike other conjunctives pairs, 固然 usually does not appear before the subject.

(Situation: Two managers are having a discussion about two job applicants before deciding which one they should offer the job to.)

> 张经理：她们工作经验差不多，可是李小姐的学历比较高，我认为我们应该请李小姐。
> *Zhāng jīnglǐ: Tāmen gōngzuò jīngyàn chàbùduō, kěshì Lǐ xiǎojiě de xuélì bǐjiào gāo, wǒ rènwéi wǒmen yīnggāi qǐng Lǐ xiǎojiě.*
> 王经理：李小姐的学历**固然**比较高，**可是**丁小姐会说日文跟法文。我认为我们需要象她这样的人。
> *Wáng jīnglǐ: Lǐ xiǎojiě de xuélì gùrán bǐjiào gāo, kěshì Dīng xiǎojiě huì shuō Rìwén gēn Fǎwén. Wǒ rènwéi wǒmen xūyào xiàng tā zhèyàng de rén.*
> Manager Zhang: Both of them have similar work experience, but Miss Li has a higher degree, so I think we should hire Miss Li.
> Manager Wang: Although Miss Li has a higher degree, Miss Ding can speak Japanese and French. I think we need someone like her.

Level 3

30.6 The use of 尽管……, (可是/但是) 还是……

尽管 (*jǐnguǎn*) is frequently translated as 'even though' in English. It is stronger in meaning and tone than 虽然 and what follows 尽管 is a fact that already exists in the context.

(a) General usage

尽管 indicates that in spite of a certain fact, it makes no difference to the situation; hence 还是 (*háishì*). 虽然 may or may not have this implication.

> 小兰：你一向不喜欢大都市，为什么去上海度假？ (This establishes the fact that Shanghai is a big city.)
> *Xiǎolán: Nǐ yíxiàng bù xǐhuān dà dūshì, wèishénme qù Shànghǎi dùjià?*
> 安娜：上海**尽管**是一个大都市，**可是还是**有不少幽静的地方。
> *Ānnà: Shànghǎi jǐnguǎn shì yí ge dà dūshì, kěshì háishì yǒu bùshǎo yōujìng de dìfang.*

Xiaolan: You have always disliked big cities. Why did you go to Shanghai on a holiday?

Anna: Even though Shanghai is a big city, there are still many secluded and quiet places.

(b) 尽管 vs. 即使

尽管 and 即使 share similarities in the sense that the situation remains the same. However, 尽管 is used to indicate a fact, whereas 即使 is used to indicate a hypothetical situation.

(Situation: Xiao Wang attempted to borrow money from Zhang, who refused.)

张：我不信任小王，所以，**尽管**我有钱，**但是还是**没有借他。(Zhang does have the money; therefore, he uses 尽管.)

Zhāng: Wǒ bú xìnrèn Xiǎo Wáng, suǒyǐ, jǐnguǎn wǒ yǒu qián, dànshì háishì méiyǒu jiè tā.

李：我也不信任他。**即使**我有钱，**也**不会借他。(Li does not have the money; therefore, he uses 即使.)

Lǐ: Wǒ yě bú xìnrèn tā. Jíshǐ wǒ yǒu qián, yě bú huì jiè tā.

Zhang: I don't trust Xiao Wang. Even though I had the money, I didn't lend it to him.

Li: I don't trust him, either. Even if I had the money, I would not lend it to him.

Exercises

Write sentences based on the situations provided. Each sentence must include conjunctive pairs used in context.

evel
2

1 Xiaolan confides to Anna that she does not really like Mr Wang even though she is dating him. Anna responds by saying that, given this fact, she should break up with him. What would Anna say?

2 Li Zhong is studying both Japanese and French. Someone asks him why he is studying these languages. Li Zhong says that he studies Japanese because his mother is Japanese; and French because he wants to study design in Paris in the future. What would Li Zhong say?

3 Mr and Mrs Wang are house hunting. They see a small house that is a reasonable price. They are debating whether they should buy it. Mrs Wang says that the house is too small. Mr Wang concedes this point but points out that it is inexpensive. What would Mr Wang say?

4 Mr Wang's best friend, Mr Li, has asked him for an emergency loan. Mrs Wang is opposed to this because they themselves are also short of money. Despite this, Mr Wang decides to loan the money to Mr Li. Write a sentence to describe what Mr Wang decides to do and under what circumstances.

5 Mr Ding's friends are surprised to see him at Anna's birthday party because everyone knows that Mr Ding has been busy with an important project. So they ask him if this means he is not as busy now. Mr Ding responds by saying that while he is still busy, he has to attend his best friend's birthday party. What would Mr Ding say?

6 Xiaoming's mother tells him to stop playing video games, but Xiaoming says he does not have anything to do. So his mother says that, since that is the case, she wants him to go clean up his room. What would his mother say?

Level
3

7 Miss Zhang tried on a pretty dress that she really liked, but decided against buying it. Her friend asked her if it was because the dress was too expensive. Miss Zhang responded by saying that although it was not expensive, it did not fit very well. What would Miss Zhang say?

8 Miss Zhang tried on a dress but decided not to buy it. The sales clerk asked her if it was because she did not like it. Miss Zhang responded by saying that although she liked it, the dress was too expensive. What would Miss Zhang have said?

9 A panel of judges is discussing who should be awarded first place in an essay competition. Judge Ding favours Wang Zhong because he thinks Wang Zhong has the most unique ideas. Judge Li agrees that Wang Zhong's ideas are unique, but he points out that his grammar is poor. How would Judge Li express these opinions?

10 Miss Li is beautiful and has many male admirers. Many are surprised when she decides to marry Wang Ming because he does not stand out among her admirers. Miss Li explains to her women friends that the reason she decided to marry Wang Ming is because he truly loves her. How would Miss Li say this?

31 The use of 才 and 就

才 (*cái*) and 就 (*jiù*) are among the most commonly used adverbs in Chinese. They are often opposite in meaning, but each can have its own meaning without the other one being the counterpart. ◑ 才 and 就 often cannot be directly translated into specific words in English. The proper usage of them depends heavily on the context.

31.1 Indicating the time an event takes/took place

才 and 就 are opposite in meaning when they are used to indicate the time when an action or event takes/took place.

(a) 才: later than usual or expected

才 implies that the event occurred/occurs later than usual or expected. It can also imply a delayed action. The modal particle 了 (*le*) is **not** used at the end of a 才 sentence, whether or not the event has taken place.

> 今天路上车特别多，我花了一个多小时才回到家。 (Implied: Normally it does not take me over an hour to get home.)
> *Jīntiān lù shàng chē tèbié duō, wǒ huā le yí ge duō xiǎoshí cái dào jiā.*
> There was particularly a lot of traffic today. It took me over an hour to (finally) get home.

> 老师：王明，你怎么现在才来？ (才 indicates that Wang Ming is later than expected.)
> *Lǎoshī: Wáng Míng, nǐ zěnme xiànzài cái lái?*
> 王明：对不起，闹钟坏了，所以今天早上八点才起床。 (才 indicates he got up later than usual.)
> *Wáng Míng: Duìbùqǐ, nàozhōng huài le, suǒyǐ jīntiān zǎoshàng bā diǎn cái qǐchuáng.*
> Teacher: Wang Ming, how come you only arrived now? (How come you are late?)
> Wang Ming: Sorry. My alarm clock was broken, so I didn't get up until eight o'clock.

(b) 就: earlier than usual or expected

就 implies that the event occurred/occurs sooner or earlier than usual or expected. The modal particle 了 can be used if the event has taken place or is habitual.

> 王先生因为身体不好，所以五十岁就退休了。 (就 implies that he retired early.)
> *Wáng xiānsheng yīnwèi shēntǐ bù hǎo, suǒyǐ wǔshí suì jiù tuìxiū le.*
> Because Mr Wang had health problems, he retired at 50.

> 今天交通特别顺畅，我花了一个半小时就回到家了。 (Implied: Normally it takes me longer.)
> *Jīntiān jiāotōng tèbié shùnchàng, wǒ huā le yí ge bàn xiǎoshí jiù huí dào jiā le.*
> Today's traffic was particularly smooth. It only took me one and a half hours to get home.

(c) 就: an immediate action

就 can also be used to imply an immediate action; that is, an action will be done without delay.

店员：这种数位相机在打折，您**现在就**买一个吧。
Diànyuán: Zhè zhǒng shùwèi xiàngjī zài dǎzhé, nín xiànzài jiù mǎi yí ge ba.
顾客：好，我回家去拿钱，**马上就**来。
Gùkè: Hǎo, wǒ huí jiā qù ná qián, mǎshàng jiù lái.
Store clerk: This type of digital camera is on sale. Why don't you buy one right now!
Customer: OK, I will go home to get some money. I will be right back.

经理：你可不可以下星期**就**开始来上班？
Jīnglǐ: Nǐ kě bù kěyǐ xià xīngqī jiù kāishǐ lái shàngbān?
王：不必等一星期，我明天**就**可以开始。
Wáng: Bú bì děng yì xīngqī, wǒ míngtiān jiù kěyǐ kāishǐ.
Manager: Can you start working (as early as) next week?
Wang: No need to wait until next week. I can start (as early as) tomorrow.

31.2 The use of 一……就……

Level 2

The 一……就…… structure indicates that the second action immediately follows/followed the first action. ☙ The subjects should appear before 一 and 就, but the same subject should not be repeated.

我每天一下班**就**回家给家人做晚饭。 (Do not say 我每天一下班我就回家给家人做晚饭.)
Wǒ měi tiān yí xiàbān jiù huí jiā gěi jiā rén zuò wǎnfàn.
Every day I go home to cook dinner for my family as soon as I get off work.

老师一走进教室，**学生就**站起来说："老师好。"(Do not say 一老师走进教室，就学生站起来说："老师好。")
Lǎoshī yì zǒu jìn jiàoshì, xuéshēng jiù zhàn qǐlái shuō: 'Lǎoshī hǎo.'
As soon as the teacher walked into the classroom, the students (immediately) stood up and greeted the teacher.

31.3 才 or 就: a subjective choice

Level 2

The choice of 才 or 就 is frequently subjective.

安娜：我打算二十五岁结婚。
Ānnà: Wǒ dǎsuàn èrshí wǔ suì jiéhūn.
小兰：什么？你打算二十五岁**才**结婚？
Xiǎolán: Shénme? Nǐ dǎsuàn èrshí wǔ suì cái jiéhūn?
小李：二十五岁**就**结婚？太早了吧！
Xiǎo Lǐ: Èrshí wǔ suì jiù jiéhūn? Tài zǎo le ba!
Anna: I plan to get married when I am 25.
Xiaolan: What? You plan to get married (as late as) 25?
Xiao Li: Getting married at 25? It's too early, isn't it?

31.4 Indicating how quickly or with how much effort a result is/was achieved

Level 2

才 and 就 are also used to indicate how soon or how easily the result of an effort is/was achieved. 就 implies the result was/can be achieved without much effort, whereas 才 implies a lot of effort.

小王记忆真好，一篇文章，他念两遍**就**记住了，我常常念十几遍**才**记住。
Xiǎo Wáng jìyì zhēn hǎo, yì piān wénzhāng, tā niàn liǎng biàn jiù jì zhù le, wǒ chángcháng niàn shí jǐ biàn cái jì zhù.

Xiao Wang has a really good memory. He reads an article (only) twice and he memorizes it. I often read it over ten times to (finally) memorize it. ('Only' is implied by 就, 'finally' is implied by 才.)

今天我在楼下叫了他**两次**他**就**下来**了**。 (就 implies I usually have to call him more than twice.)
Jīntiān wǒ zài lóu xià jiào le tā liǎng cì tā jiù xiàlái le.
Today I only called out to him twice from downstairs before he came down.

Compare: 这个问题，我问了他**两次**他**才**回答。 (才 implies that he delayed in giving a reply.)
Zhè ge wèntí, wǒ wèn le tā liǎng cì tā cái huídá.
I asked him the question twice before he (finally) replied.

evel
/3

31.5 只要……就…… vs. 只有……才……

Both the 只要 (*zhǐ yào*) ……就…… structure and the 只有 (*zhǐ yǒu*) ……才…… structure are used to indicate the condition (requirement) that is necessary for a certain result to take place. 只要……就…… implies that the results are easy to achieve, whereas 只有……才…… implies the opposite.

The subject for the 只要/只有 sentence can appear either before or after 只要/只有. If the 只要/只有 and 就/才 sentences share the same subject, it should not be repeated. If each of them has a different subject, the subject for the 就/才 sentence must appear before 就/才.

(a) 只要……就……: 'as long as'

只要……就…… can be translated as 'as long as' or 'only need to'. It implies that the result is easy to achieve.

张：这里的房子看起来都很不错，为什么价钱这么便宜？
Zhāng: Zhèlǐ de fángzi kàn qǐlái dōu hěn bú cuò, wèishénme jiàqián zhème piányí?
李：这个地方**只要**下雨**就**会淹水，所以愿意住这里的人不多。
Lǐ: Zhè ge dìfāng zhǐyào xià yǔ jiù huì yānshuǐ, suǒyǐ yuànyì zhù zhèlǐ de rén bù duō.
Zhang: Houses here all look nice. Why are the prices so cheap?
Li: It only needs to rain and there will be a flood here, so not many people are willing to live here.

儿子：对不起，这次考试考得这么差。
Érzi: Duìbùqǐ, zhè cì kǎoshì kǎo de zhème chà.
妈妈：没关系，**你只要**努力一点，下次**就**一定会进步。
Māma: Méi guānxi, nǐ zhǐyào nǔlì yìdiǎn, xià cì jiù yídìng huì jìnbù.
爸爸：**只要你**下次有进步，我**就**给你买一个新的电脑。
Bàba: Zhǐyào nǐ xià cì yǒu jìnbù, wǒ jiù gěi nǐ mǎi yí ge xīn de diànnǎo.
Son: I am sorry I did so poorly in this test.
Mother: It's OK. You only need to study a little harder and you will definitely improve next time.
Father: As long as you show improvement next time, I will buy you a new computer.

(b) 只有……才……: 'only if'

只有……才…… can be translated as 'only if' or 'only when'. It is used to imply that there is only one way to achieve the result.

只有你去劝他，他**才**会改变主意，因为别人的话，他都不相信。
Zhǐyǒu nǐ qù quàn tā, tā cái huì gǎibiàn zhǔyì, yīnwèi biérén de huà, tā dōu bù xiāngxìn.

Only if you go persuade him will he change his mind, because he does not believe in anybody else's words.

- 只有 can be followed by a noun

👁 有 is not optional although there is no counterpart for it in an equivalent English sentence.

小王说话喜欢夸张，**只有傻瓜才**会相信他的话。 (Do not say 只傻瓜才会相信他的话。)
Xiǎo Wáng shuōhuà xǐhuān kuāzhāng, zhǐyǒu shǎguā cái huì xiāngxìn tāde huà.
Xiao Wang likes to exaggerate when he talks. Only fools will believe his words.

(c) 只要……就…… or 只有……才……: a subjective choice

The choice of 只要……就…… or 只有……才…… can be subjective.

只要把王先生请来当顾问，问题**就**能解决。 (Implied: The solution is easy.)
Zhǐyào bǎ Wáng xiānsheng qǐng lái dāng gùwèn, wèntí jiù néng jiějué.
As long as we hire Mr Wang to be our consultant, the problem can be solved.

只有把王先生请来当顾问，问题**才**能解决。 (Implied: Only Mr Wang can solve our problem.)
Zhǐyǒu bǎ Wáng xiānsheng qǐng lái dāng gùwèn, wèntí cái néng jiějué.
Only by hiring Mr Wang to be our consultant can the problem be solved.

31.6 Some independent meanings of 就 and 才

Level 2/3

才 and 就 do not always serve as counterparts to one another. The following are some of their independent meanings.

(a) 就: 'immediacy'

就 conveys a sense of 'immediacy' both in terms of time (☞ see 31.1) and location.

姐姐：奇怪，我的字典怎么不见了？你帮我找找，好不好？
Jiějie: Qíguài, wǒde zìdiǎn zěnme bú jiàn le? Nǐ bāng wǒ zhǎo zhǎo, hǎo bù hǎo?
妹妹：不用找了，你看，你的字典**就在**你自己的桌子上。
Mèimei: Bú yòng zhǎo le, nǐ kàn, nǐde zìdiǎn jiù zài nǐ zìjǐ de zhuōzi shàng.
Older sister: Strange, how come my dictionary has disappeared? Will you help me look (for it)?
Younger sister: No need to look. Look! Your dictionary is right (there) on your desk.

(b) 就: 'exactness'

就 convey the sense of 'exactness' or 'none other than . . .'. Whatever is being referred to must be in context.

(Situation: A waiter has recommended several famous dishes to the customers.)

服务员：除了这几个名菜以外，菜单上还有很多不错的菜，您看看。
Fúwùyuán: Chúle zhè jǐ ge míngcài yǐwài, càidān shàng hái yǒu hěn duō bú cuò de cài, nín kàn kàn.
客人：不用看了，我们**就要**你介绍的那三道菜。
Kèrén: Bú yòng kàn le, wǒmen jiù yào nǐ jièshào de nà sān dào cài.
Waiter: In addition to these few famous dishes, there are many more on the menu. They are all quite good. Please take a look (at the menu).
Customer: No need to look any more. We want exactly the three dishes you recommended.

(Situation: Anna and her friend Xiaolan are looking at Anna's photo album.)

小兰：这个穿黑衬衫的是谁？

Xiǎolán: Zhè ge chuān hēi chènshān de shì shéi?

安娜：他**就是**我跟你提过的那位王先生。 (The use of 就 indicates that Mr Wang is someone that Xiaolan has heard of.)

Ānnà: Tā jiù shì wǒ gēn nǐ tí guo de nà wèi Wáng xiānsheng.

Xiaolan: Who is the person wearing a black shirt?

Anna: He **is** (exactly) the Mr Wang I have mentioned to you before.

(c) 就是: indicating an exception

就是 can be used to indicate an exception after making a sweeping statement. In this case, what follows 就是 should be a sentence or a verbal phrase. It cannot be simply a noun.

我家的人**都**喜欢吃辣的，**就是**我不喜欢。

Wǒ jiā de rén dōu xǐhuān chī là de, jiùshì wǒ bù xǐhuān.

Everybody in my family likes spicy food, except me.

王：下星期四晚上有空吗？我要请几个朋友来吃饭。

Wáng: Xià xīngqī sì wǎnshàng yǒu kòng ma? Wǒ yào qǐng jǐ ge péngyǒu lái chī fàn.

李：真可惜，下星期我天天**都**有空，**就是**星期四没空。

Lǐ: Zhēn kěxí, xià xīngqī wǒ tiān tiān dōu yǒu kòng, jiùshì xīngqí sì méi kòng.

Wang: Are you free next Thursday evening? I am inviting a few friends over for dinner.

Li: Too bad, I am free every day next week except Thursday.

(d) 才 + expression with a number: 'only'

才 can be used to mean 'only'. What follows 才 must be a number or an expression involving a number. 才 and 只 (*zhǐ*) are not interchangeable since 只 must be followed by a verb.

李：奇怪，小张怎么还没来？

Lǐ: Qíguài, Xiǎo Zhāng zěnme hái méi lái?

王：现在**才**四点，他六点**才**会来。

Wáng: Xiànzài cái sì diǎn, tā liù diǎn cái huì lái.

Li: Strange, how come Xiao Zhang is not here yet?

Wang: It's only 4 o'clock. He won't be here until 6 o'clock.

王：这本书**才**五块！怎么这么便宜？ (这本书**只要**五块 is correct as well.)

Wáng: Zhè běn shū cái wǔ kuài! Zěnme zhème piányí?

店员：我们这里的书都是二手的，所以特别便宜。

Diànyuán: Wǒmen zhèlǐ de shū dōu shì èrshǒu de, suǒyǐ tèbié piányí.

王：可惜今天我**只带**了三块，不然，一定要买。 (我**才带**了三块 is acceptable.)

Wáng: Kěxí jīntiān wǒ zhǐ dài le sān kuài, bùrán, yídìng yào mǎi.

Wang: This book is only $5! How come it's so cheap?

Clerk: All our books are second-hand, so they are particularly cheap.

Wang: Too bad I only brought $3; otherwise, I would definitely buy it.

(e) 才: 'just'

才 can be used to indicate that an action only took place a very short time ago. In this sense, 才 and 刚 (*gāng*) are similar in meaning. When a second action follows the action that has just taken place, 就, which implies 'too soon', normally goes with the second action.

客人：不早了，我该回家了。

Kèrén: Bù zǎo le, wǒ gāi huí jiā le.

主人：怎么**才**(= 刚)来**就**要走？

Zhǔrén: Zěnme cái (= gāng) lái jiù yào zǒu?

Guest: It's getting late. I should go home.

Host: You just arrived; how come you are leaving (already)?

真气人！昨天**才**买的电脑，今天**就**坏了。

Zhēn qìrén! Zuótiān cái mǎi de diànnǎo, jīntiān jiù huài le.

Really upsetting! The computer I just bought yesterday is already broken today.

(f) 才……(呢): a rebuttal

才 can be used in a rebuttal to indicate that a statement made by another person is wrong while establishing one's own point of view as being correct. The modal particle 呢 (*ne*) is used when it is a face-to-face exchange or in a less formal situation.

(Situation: Two people are having an unpleasant verbal fight.)

王：你是一只猪！

Wáng: Nǐ shì yì zhī zhū!

李：你**才**是一只猪**呢**！

Lǐ: Nǐ cái shì yì zhī zhū ne!

Wang: You are a pig!

Li: **You** are the one that's a pig (not me!)

(Situation: A couple are trying to adopt a cat.)

先生：这只灰色的很可爱，收养这只，好吗？

Xiānsheng: Zhè zhī huī sè de hěn kě'ài, shōuyǎng zhè zhī, hǎo ma?

太太：不要！这只虎斑的**才**可爱**呢**！ (Implied: 灰的不可爱。)

Tàitai: Bú yào! Zhè zhī hǔ bān de cái kě'ài ne!

Husband: This grey one is cute. Let's adopt this one, OK?

Wife: No! This one with tiger stripes is the cute one. (Implied: The grey one is not cute.)

很多人说，看中国电影是练习中文最好的办法，可是我认为，听中国流行歌曲**才**是最好的办法。 (才 implies that I consider the other people's opinion to be wrong and my own opinion is correct.)

Hěn duō rén shuō, kàn Zhōngguó diànyǐng shì liànxí Zhōngwén zuì hǎo de bànfǎ, kěshì wǒ rènwéi, tīng Zhōngguó liúxíng gēqǔ cái shì zuì hǎo de bànfǎ.

Many people say that watching Chinese movies is the best way to practise Chinese; but I think that listening to Chinese pop songs is the best way (and watching movies is not).

Exercises

Fill in each blank with 就 or 才 based on the context provided.

Level 2

1 太太：现在 ＿＿＿ 六点，今天怎么这么早 ＿＿＿ 下班了？

　　先生：今天没有提早下班，可是交通特别顺畅，只开了半小时 ＿＿＿ 到家了。

2 如果你想学好中文，没有别的办法，只有多听、多说、多读 ＿＿＿ 学得好。

3 李太太：你儿子 ＿＿＿ 十七岁，怎么 ＿＿＿ 已经搬到外面去住了？

　　张太太：你记错了，我儿子去年 ＿＿＿ 十八岁了。

4　王：这是什么地方？

　　李：这 _____ 是天安门广场。

　　王：哦，是吗？天安门在哪里？

　　李：你看，那个高高的建筑，那 _____ 是天安门。

5　小王真聪明，别人要花好几个小时 _____ 学得会的东西，他常常不到半小时 _____ 学会了。

6　老师：张明，请你说一说，这个成语是什么意思？

　　张明：老师，这个成语您还没有教我们呢！

　　老师：谁说的？这个成语我上星期 _____ 教你们了。

7　张：今天的功课实在太多了，我花了三个小时 _____ 写完。

　　李：什么？ _____ 三小时 _____ 写完了？我写了五个小时， _____ 写好一半。

8　丁：我认为，一个人如果想把中文学好，最好的办法 _____ 是多看中国电影、多听中文歌曲。

　　张：我不同意。我觉得，多跟中国人练习 _____ 是最好的办法。

9　妈妈：你怎么现在 _____ 回来？

　　儿子：现在 _____ 六点，还不算晚啊！

　　妈妈：你忘了吗？你出门的时候，说你五点 _____ 会回来的。

10　老师：这个成语是什么意思？

　　学生：我忘了。

　　老师：这个成语是昨天 _____ 学的，怎么你今天 _____ 忘了？

11　李：今天真倒霉，一出门 _____ 摔了一跤。

　　张：那不算什么！小王 _____ 倒霉呢！他一出门 _____ 被车撞了。

32 The use of adverbs in contracted sentences

The focus of this chapter will be on the type of contracted sentence that is defined as a complex sentence without the conjunctive in the subordinate clause (the first word in a conjunctive pair). The omission of the first word in a conjunctive pair often results in the appearance of one or two simple sentences.

👁 As a stand-alone word, the second word (often an adverb) in a conjunctive pair frequently does not convey a clear meaning to tell the relationship between the subordinate clause and the main clause. Therefore, it is important to recognize what the omitted first word is. This can be achieved by paying attention to the use of the second word in the conjunctive pair as well as the context.

☞ See Chapter 29 for detailed information on conjunctive pairs.

Level 2/3

32.1 The use of 就

(a) 'If'

如果/要是 (rúguǒ/yàoshì) can be omitted from 如果/要是……, 就 (jiù) ……, resulting in only 就 in the main clause.

> 张：下星期六晚上的派对，你去不去？
> *Zhāng: Xià xīngqī liù wǎnshàng de pàiduì, nǐ qù bú qù?*
> 王：不忙我**就**去。你呢？
> *Wáng: Bù máng wǒ jiù qù. Nǐ ne?*
> 张：你去我**就**去。
> *Zhāng: Nǐ qù wǒ jiù qù.*
> Zhang: Are you going to the dance next Saturday?
> Wang: I'll go **if** I am not busy. How about you?
> Zhang: I'll go **if** you go.

> 安娜：昨天的舞会，幸亏小兰没去；去了**就**糟糕了。
> *Ānnà: Zuótiān de wǔhuì, xìngkuī Xiǎolán méi qù; qù le jiù zāogāo le.*
> 小李：为什么呢？
> *Xiǎo Lǐ: Wèishénme ne?*
> 安娜：因为她男朋友带了另外一个女孩去。
> *Ānnà: Yīnwèi tā nán péngyǒu dài le lìngwài yí ge nǚhái qù.*
> Anna: Fortunately Xiaolan didn't go to yesterday's dance. **If** she had gone, it would have been bad.
> Xiao Li: Why?
> Anna: Because her boyfriend brought another girl to the dance.

(b) 'Since'

既然 (*jìrán*) can be omitted from 既然……, 就……, resulting in only 就 in the main clause.

(Situation: A student calls his teacher on the phone.)

学生：我今天发烧、肚子痛。
Xuéshēng: Wǒ jīntiān fāshāo, dùzi tòng.
老师：不舒服**就**不用来上课了。
Lǎoshī: Bù shūfú jiù bú yòng lái shàngkè le.
Student: Today I have a fever and a stomach-ache.
Teacher: **Since** you are not feeling well, you don't have to come to class.

客人：你真会做菜。这些菜都太好吃了！
Kèrén: Nǐ zhēn huì zuò cài. Zhè xiē cài dōu tài hǎochī le!
主人：喜欢**就**多吃点吧！
Zhǔrén: Xǐhuān jiù duō chī diǎn ba!
Guest: You are really good at cooking. All these dishes are delicious!
Host: **Since** you like them, have some more!

(c) 'As long as'

只要 (*zhǐyào*) in 只要……, 就…… can be omitted.

学外语，没有别的诀窍，多听，多说，多念**就**学得好。
Xué wàiyǔ, méiyǒu biéde juéqiào, duō tīng, duō shuō, duō niàn jiù xué de hǎo.
When it comes to studying a foreign language, there is no other secret. **As long as** you listen more, speak more and read more, you can master it.

王先生总以为，花钱给孩子请家教，孩子的成绩**就**会好，其实事情没有他想的那么简单。
Wáng xiānsheng zǒng yǐwéi, huā qián gěi háizi qǐng jiājiào, háizi de chéngjì jiù huì hǎo, qíshí shìqíng méiyǒu tā xiǎng de nàme jiǎndān.
Mr Wang always thinks that, **as long as** he spends money on hiring tutors for his child, the child's grades will be good. Actually, things are not as simple as he thinks.

(d) 'So'

Sometimes, 就 can imply 因为 (*yīnwèi*) ……, 所以 (*suǒyǐ*)…… without the presence of 因为 or 所以 at all. In this case, what follows 就 is usually an action that has been taken as a consequence of another event.

我在约好见面的地方等了他十几分钟，他没来，我**就**回家了。
Wǒ zài yuē hǎo jiànmiàn de dìfang děng le tā shí jǐ fēnzhōng, tā méi lái, wǒ jiù huíjiā le.
I waited for him at the place we had agreed to meet for more than ten minutes. He didn't show up, **so** I went home.

王先生听说李小姐住院了，**就**买了一束花去医院看她。
Wáng xiānsheng tīngshuō Lǐ xiǎojiě zhùyuàn le, jiù mǎi le yí shù huā qù yīyuàn kàn tā.
Mr Wang heard that Miss Li had been hospitalized, **so** he bought a bunch of flowers and went to the hospital to visit her.

32.2 The use of 也

Level 3

As a stand-alone word, 也 (*yě*) means 'also'. In a contracted sentence, its meaning of 'also' is not obvious. This may result in difficulty in comprehending the sentence.

(a) 'Even if'

即使/就算 (*jíshǐ/jiùsuàn*) can be omitted, resulting in only 也 in the sentence.

王：因为经费有限，所以我们没法付你太高的工资。
Wáng: Yīnwèi jīngfèi yǒuxiàn, suǒyǐ wǒmen méi fǎ fù nǐ tài gāo de gōngzī.
李：没关系，这么有意义的事，没钱我也愿意做。
Lǐ: Méi guānxi, zhème yǒu yìyì de shì, méi qián wǒ yě yuànyì zuò.
Wang: Because our budget is limited, we cannot pay you too high a wage.
Li: It's OK. Such meaningful work. **Even if** there were no pay, I would be willing to do it.

别忘了，老板说笑话的时候，不好笑咱们也得笑。
Bié wàng le, lǎobǎn shuō xiàohuà de shíhòu, bù hǎoxiào zánmen yě děi xiào.
Don't forget! When our boss tells a joke, **even if** it is not funny, we have to laugh.

(b) 'No matter'

无论/不管 (*wúlùn/bùguǎn*) can be omitted, resulting in only 也 or 都 (*dōu*). (也 tends to be used when the main clause is negative.) A question word must appear after 无论/不管.

☞ See 32.3 for more on (无论……,) 都…….

这件事，小兰已经下定决心，我怎么劝她，她也不肯改变主意。
Zhè jiàn shì, Xiǎolán yǐjīng xià dìng juéxīn. Wǒ zěnme quàn tā, tā yě bù kěn gǎibiàn zhǔyì.
Xiaolan has made up her mind about this matter. **No matter how** I urge her (to do otherwise), she will not change her mind.

品质这么差的东西，多便宜也不会有人要买。
Pǐnzhí zhème chà de dōngxi, duō piányí yě bú huì yǒu rén yào mǎi.
This thing is of such poor quality. **No matter how** inexpensive it was, no one would want to buy it.

来不及了，谁来帮忙，也没有用了。
Lái bù jí le, shéi lái bāngmáng, yě méiyǒu yòng le.
It's too late now. **No matter who** comes to help, it would be of no use.

(c) 'Even if' and 'no matter'

When the subordinate clause has 再 (*zài*) and the main clause has 也 or 都, the contracted sentence conveys a meaning similar to both 无论/不管……, 也/都…… and 即使……, 也…….

他是不会帮你的，你再求他也没用。
Tā shì bú huì bāng nǐ de, nǐ zài qiú tā yě méi yòng.
He is definitely not going to help you. **No matter how** you beg him (or **even if** you beg him more) it would be of no use.

王先生：我不要跟小张说话。
Wáng xiānsheng: Wǒ bú yào gēn Xiǎo Zhāng shuō huà.
王太太：他是咱们女儿的男朋友，你再不喜欢他也要对他客气点。
Wáng tàitai: Tā shì zánmen nǚ'ér de nán péngyǒu, nǐ zài bù xǐhuān tā yě yào duì tā kèqì diǎn.
Mr Wang: I don't want to talk to Xiao Zhang.
Mrs Wang: He is our daughter's boyfriend. **No matter how much** you **dislike** him, you have to be a little nicer to him.

(d) Conveying disapproval or annoyance

也 can be used to imply a mild disapproval or annoyance because someone did not do what he or she should have done after a certain event. Similarly, it can be used to imply that someone did something he or she should not have done. In this case, it is not clear what the omitted conjunctive word is.

(Situation: Xiao Zhang is the boyfriend of Mr and Mrs Wang's daughter.)

王先生：小张，吃了饭，怎么**也**不帮忙洗碗？
Wáng xiānsheng: Xiǎo Zhāng, chī le fàn, zěnme yě bù bāngmáng xǐ wǎn?
王太太：这种话，你怎么**也**说得出来？小张是来做客的。
Wáng tàitai: Zhè zhǒng huà, nǐ zěnme yě shuó de chūlái? Xiǎo Zhāng shì lái zuò kè de.
Mr Wang: Xiao Zhang, how come you don't help do the dishes after dinner?
Mrs. Wang: How could you have said something like this? Xiao Zhang is here as our guest.

(Situation: At the counter in a coffee shop.)

服务员：先生，请您等十分钟，您的咖啡就会好了。
Fúwùyuán: Xiānsheng, qǐng nín děng shí fēnzhōng, nínde kāfēi jiù huì hǎo le.
顾客：什么？买杯咖啡**也**要等十分钟？ (也 conveys a sense of annoyance. Without the phrase 买杯咖啡, 也 could not be used since a contracted sentence should have two parts.)
Gùkè: Shénme? Mǎi bēi kāfēi yě yào děng shí fēnzhōng?
Waiter: Sir, please wait ten minutes and your coffee will be ready.
Customer: What? I have to wait ten minutes for a cup of coffee?

Level 3

32.3 The use of 都

(a) 'Even'

都 in a contracted sentence can convey the sense that something is extreme. What has been omitted in the subordinate clause is 连 (*lián*), which means 'even'. The two verbs must be the same and the main clause must be negative.

王：你看过《哈利波特》没有？
Wáng: Nǐ kàn guò 'Hālì Bōtè' méiyǒu?
李：《哈利波特》？《哈利波特》是什么？我**听都没听**过，怎么可能会看过？
Lǐ: 'Hālì Bōtè?' 'Hālì Botè' shì shénme? Wǒ tīng dōu méi tīng guò, zěnme kěnéng huì kàn guò?
Wang: Have you read *Harry Potter*?
Li: *Harry Potter*? What is *Harry Potter*? I have not **even** heard of it; how could I have read it?

那个问题太容易了，我**想都不用想**就会回答。
Nà ge wèntí tài róngyì le, wǒ xiǎng dōu bú yòng xiǎng jiù huì huídá.
That question was too easy. I didn't **even** have to think to know how to answer it.

(b) 'No matter'

无论/不管 can be omitted, resulting in 也 or 都. 也 tends to be in a negative sentence, whereas 都 can be in either a positive or a negative sentence. ☞ See 32.2 for 也.

女儿：你说我该买德国车还是日本车？
Nǚ'ér: Nǐ shuō wǒ gāi mǎi Déguó chē háishì Rìběn chē?

爸爸：随便你。你买**哪**国车我**都**不付钱。

Bàba: Suíbiàn nǐ. Nǐ mǎi nǎ guó chē wǒ dōu bú fù qián.

Daughter: Do you think I should buy a German car or a Japanese car?

Father: Do whatever you want. **No matter which** car you buy, I won't pay for it.

女儿：下星期我的生日舞会，我可以请几个朋友来参加？

Nǚ'ér: Xià xīngqī wǒde shēngrì wǔhuì, wǒ kěyǐ qǐng jǐ ge péngyǒu lái cānjiā?

妈妈：咱们家够大，你请**几**个**都**可以。

Māma: Zánmen jiā gòu dà. Nǐ qǐng jǐ ge dōu kěyǐ.

Daughter: How many friends can I invite to my birthday party next week?

Mother: Our house is big enough. You can invite **however** many you want.

32.4 The use of 却, 倒 and 又

Level 3

The similarity in meaning shared by 却 (*què*), 倒 (*dǎo*) and 又 (*yòu*) lies in the fact the omitted words can be 虽然 (*suīrán*) or 尽管 (*jǐnguǎn*) and that a contradiction or an unexpected result exists between the subordinate clause and the main clause.

(a) 却

却 can be thought of as meaning 'however'.

小李有钱**却**从来不浪费。

Xiǎo Lǐ yǒu qián què cónglái bú làngfèi.

(Although) Xiao Li is rich, he is, **however**, never wasteful.

(b) 倒

倒 is usually used to imply that something is contrary to what people might expect.

真没想到，你年纪不大，知识**倒**挺丰富的。

Zhēn méi xiǎng dào, nǐ niánjì bú dà, zhīshí dǎo tǐng fēngfù de.

This is really unexpected. Although you are young, you have quite a lot of knowledge.

(c) 又

又 shows a direct contrast or contradiction between two actions.

你说了**会来又没来**，主人当然不高兴。（会来 and 没来 are in direct contradiction.）

Nǐ shuō le huì lái yòu méi lái, zhǔrén dāngrán bù gāoxìng.

You had said you would come but you didn't come. Of course the host was unhappy.

Exercises

Choose the proper word to fill the gap in each contracted sentence that follows.

Level 2

1 李：明天我要跟几个朋友去爬山，你要不要一起去？

    丁：天气好我 ＿＿＿ 跟你们去。

2 王：明天有一个重要的考试，你怎么还在看电视？快去准备考试吧。

    李：准备什么？这门课的东西，我完全不懂，再准备 ＿＿＿ 不会及格的。

3 张：你的英文说得真好，你是怎么学的？
　　李：其实学英文并不难，多听、多说、多读 ＿＿＿ 可以学得很好。

4 我儿子聪明 ＿＿＿ 不肯努力学习，所以考试总是考得很差。

5 安娜：你想，这件衣服，我穿了，会好看吗？
　　小兰：很难说。你去试试看吧！试了 ＿＿＿ 知道。

6 李：那本书早就卖完了，你去哪里 ＿＿＿ 买不到了。
　　王：我不相信。
　　李：不相信你 ＿＿＿ 去买买看吧！

Level

3

7 王先生：请你嫁给我吧！
　　李小姐：对不起，我还不想结婚呢！
　　王先生：你不想嫁给我，我们 ＿＿＿ 别再交往了吧！
　　李小姐：你的意思是，咱们朋友 ＿＿＿ 不能做了吗？
　　王先生：对，我就是这个意思。

8 王：那份工作，薪水不错，你为什么不做？
　　丁：那种工作太无聊，薪水多高我 ＿＿＿ 不愿意做。
　　李：是啊，你这么有钱，当然不愿意做这种工作。
　　王：有钱 ＿＿＿ 不能光待在家里不工作啊！

9 李：明天安娜家开派对，你去不去？
　　丁：不去。
　　李：是吗？你最好的朋友小兰说她要去呢！
　　丁：我最讨厌安娜。小兰去我 ＿＿＿ 不去。

10 王中真聪明，老师问的那个问题这么难，可是他想 ＿＿＿ 不用想就会回答。

33 The use of interrogative pronouns

Interrogative pronouns are similar to the *wh*-question words in English. In addition to being used to ask questions, interrogative pronouns can be used in making sweeping statements and can be used in negative statements as well.

The interrogative pronouns in Chinese are 谁 (*shéi*), 哪 (*nǎ*), 什么 (*shénme*), 哪里 (= 哪儿) (*nǎlǐ = nǎr*), 怎么 (*zěnme*), 怎么样 (*zěnmeyàng*), 多 (*duō*), 多少 (*duōshǎo*), 几 (*jǐ*), 为什么 (*wèishénme*) and 干嘛 (*gànmá*).

<table><tr><td>Level
1</td></tr></table>

33.1 Word order when using interrogative pronouns

Using interrogative pronouns to ask questions does not involve a change of word order in Chinese. Basically, an interrogative pronoun replaces the word that is being sought as the answer.

> 王：这是**什么**？ (Do not say 什么是这.)
> *Wáng: Zhè shì shénme?*
> 李：（这）是我爸爸送我的生日礼物。
> *Lǐ: (Zhè) shì wǒ bàba sòng wǒ de shēngrì lǐwù.*
> Wang: What is this?
> Li: It's the birthday present my father gave me.

> 客人：请问，你们家的洗手间在**哪里**？ (Do not say 哪里是你们家的洗手间？)
> *Kèrén: Qǐng wèn, nǐmen jiā de xǐshǒujiān zài nǎlǐ?*
> 主人：就在客厅旁边。
> *Zhǔrén: Jiù zài kètīng pángbiān.*
> Guest: Excuse me. Where is the bathroom in your house?
> Host: It's right next to the living room.

<table><tr><td>Level
1/2</td></tr></table>

33.2 哪 and 什么

哪 should be followed by a measure word. When 哪 is used, the choice of answer is usually limited. When 什么 is used, the answer is not limited.

> 小兰：晚上的舞会，你打算**穿什么**去？
> *Xiǎolán: Wǎnshàng de wǔhuì, nǐ dǎsuàn chuān shénme qù?*
> 安娜：我打算穿小礼服。你看，我有好几件，你说，我应该**穿哪件**？
> *Ānnà: Wǒ dǎsuàn chuān xiǎo lǐfú. Nǐ kàn, wǒ yǒu hǎo jǐ jiàn, nǐ shuō, wǒ yīnggāi chuān nǎ jiàn?*
> Xiaolan: What do you plan to wear to go to the party this evening?
> Anna: I plan to wear a cocktail dress. Look, I have several. Tell me: which one should I wear?

Sometimes, it is hard to decide whether the choices are limited or not. In this case, either 什么 or '哪 + measure word' can be used.

你喜欢**什么类型**的女孩？ = 你喜欢**哪种类型**的女孩？

Nǐ xǐhuān shénme lèixíng de nǚhái? = Nǐ xǐhuān nǎ zhǒng lèixíng de nǚhái?

What type of girl do you like? = Which type of girl do you like?

Level 2 | 33.3 怎么 #1

怎么 can mean 'how come?' or 'how' as in 'how is it done?'

丁：如果有人用英文跟我说"对不起"，我应该**怎么**回答？

Dīng: Rúguǒ yǒu rén yòng Yīngwén gēn wǒ shuō 'duìbùqǐ', wǒ yīnggāi zěnme huídá?

李：我已经教过你十几遍了，你**怎么**总是记不住呢？

Lǐ: Wǒ yǐjīng jiāo guò nǐ shí jǐ biàn le, nǐ zěnme zǒngshì jì bú zhù ne?

Ding: If someone says 'sorry' to me in English, **how** should I reply?

Li: I have already taught this to you more than ten times; **how come** you can never remember?

Level 2 | 33.4 怎么 #2

👁 Sometimes, an expression that would use 'what' in English would be an expression with 怎么 in Chinese. As a stand-alone word, 怎么 shows slight surprise or puzzlement.

(Situation: Anna found Xiaolan crying.)

安娜：小兰，你**怎么**了？

Ānnà: Xiǎolán, nǐ zěnme le?

小兰：我把小张借我的电脑弄坏了，现在我不知道该**怎么办**？

Xiǎolán: Wǒ bǎ Xiǎo Zhāng jiè wǒ de diànnǎo nòng huài le, xiànzài wǒ bù zhīdào gāi zěnme bàn?

安娜：**怎么**？你自己没有电脑吗？（怎么？ here shows a slight surprise.）

Ānnà: Zěnme? Nǐ zìjǐ méiyǒu diànnǎo ma?

Anna: Xiaolan, **what** happened to you (**what's** the matter)?

Xiaolan: I broke the computer Xiao Zhang lent me. Now I don't know **what to do**.

Anna: **What** was going on? You don't have your own computer?

Level 1/2 | 33.5 怎么样

怎么样 can be used in place of 怎么 to indicate how something is done. But only 怎么样 can be used to ask about one's opinion of something or what something is like.

张：下午一起去看《阿凡达》，**怎么样**？

Zhāng: Xiàwǔ yìqǐ qù kàn 'Ā Fán Dá', zěnmeyàng?

李：这个电影，我看过了。

Lǐ: Zhè ge diànyǐng, wǒ kàn guò le.

张：是吗？你觉得这个电影**怎么样**？

Zhāng: Shì ma? Nǐ juéde zhè ge diànyǐng zěnmeyàng?

Zhang: How about if we go see *Avatar* in the afternoon?

Li: I have seen this movie.

Zhang: Is that so? **What** do you think of the movie? (Literally: **How** do you feel about the movie?)

Level 2 | 33.6 多

多, when translated into English, also means 'how'; but it is always followed by an adjective. An optional verb, 有 (*yǒu*), can be used before 多 when the phrase is used to describe a noun.

张：你去过李老师家，对不对？他的房子**怎么样**？

Zhāng: Nǐ qù guo Lǐ lǎoshī jiā, duì bú duì? Tāde fángzi zěnmeyàng?

丁：对，我去过，他家非常大。

Dīng: Duì, wǒ qù guò, tā jiā fēicháng dà.

张：是吗？**(有)多大**？

Zhāng: Shì ma? (Yǒu) duō dà?

Zhang: You have been to Teacher Li's house, right? **How** is his house?

Ding: That's right. I have been there. His house is very big.

Zhang: Oh, is that so? **How big**?

王：你家离学校**(有)多远**？你每天**怎么**来学校？

Wáng: Nǐ jiā lí xuéxiào (yǒu) duō yuǎn? Nǐ měitiān zěnme lái xuéxiào?

李：不太远，我每天都走路来。

Lǐ: Bú tài yuǎn, wǒ měitiān dōu zǒulù lái.

王：要走**多长**时间呢？(or 要走**多久**呢？)

Wáng: Yào zǒu duō cháng shíjiān (duō jiǔ) ne?

Wang: **How far** is your house from school? **How** do you come to school every day?

Li: Not very far. I walk here every day.

Wang: **How long** (time) do you have to walk?

33.7 多少

Level 2

多少 can mean 'how much' or 'how many'. When it means 'how many', the expected answer tends to be a number bigger than ten. Otherwise, 几 is usually used. When 多少 means 'how many', a measure word is optional and is frequently not used.

爸爸：这个学校有**多少(个)**学生？**多少**是外国学生？每年学费**多少**钱？

Bàba: Zhè ge xuéxiào yǒu duōshǎo (ge) xuéshēng? Duōshǎo shì wàiguó xuéshēng? Měi nián xuéfèi duōshǎo qián?

儿子：这些我都不知道，我只知道外国学生的学费比较高。

Érzi: Zhè xiē wǒ dōu bù zhīdào, wǒ zhǐ zhīdào wàiguó xuéshēng de xuéfèi bǐjiào gāo.

爸爸：哦？高**多少**？

Bàba: Ò? Gāo duōshǎo?

Father: **How many** students are there at this school? **How many** are foreign students? **How much** is the tuition fee per year?

Son: I don't know any of these (answers). I only know that foreign students' tuition is higher.

Father: Oh? **How much** higher?

Besides being an interrogative pronoun, 多少 can be used as an adverb, meaning 'more or less'.

王先生：唉！钱又用完了，去向小李借吧！

Wáng xiānsheng: Ài! Qián yòu yòng wán le, qù xiàng Xiǎo Lǐ jiè ba!

王太太：小李也不是有钱人，他能借咱们**多少**？

Wáng tàitai: Xiǎo Lǐ yě bú shì yǒuqián rén, tā néng jiè zánmen duōshǎo?

王先生：小李是我最好的朋友，他**多少**会借咱们一些的。

Wáng xiānsheng: Xiǎo Lǐ shì wǒ zuì hǎo de péngyǒu, tā duōshǎo huì jiè zánmen yì xiē de.

Mr Wang: Oh no! Our money's run out again. Let's borrow some from Xiao Li.

Mrs Wang: Xiao Li is not a rich man, either. **How much** can he loan us?

Mr Wang: Xiao Li is my best friend. He **more or less** will loan us some.

健身房每个月的会费虽然不高，但**多少**是个负担，所以我没参加。

Jiànshēnfáng měi ge yuè de huìfèi suīrán bù gāo, dàn duōshǎo shì ge fùdān, suǒyǐ wǒ méi cānjiā.

Although the monthly membership for the gym is not high, it is **more or less** a burden, so I did not join (the membership).

33.8 几

几 must be followed by a measure word (except for a noun that doesn't take a measure word). When the expected answer is a number smaller than ten, 几, rather than 多少, is used. There can be exceptions to this general rule since one's expectation and the actual answer may not always match.

一年有**几**天？一天有**几个**小时？= 一年有**多少**天？一天有**多少(个)**小时？

Yì nián yǒu jǐ tiān? Yì tiān yǒu jǐ ge xiǎoshí? = Yì nián yǒu duōshǎo tiān? Yì tiān yǒu duōshǎo (ge) xiǎoshí?

How many days are there in a year? How many hours are there in one day?

你家有**多少**平方尺？**几**层楼？**几个**卧房？**几个**洗手间？

Nǐ jiā yǒu duōshǎo píngfāng chǐ? Jǐ céng lóu? Jǐ ge wòfáng? Jǐ ge xǐshǒujiān?

How many square feet is your house? **How many** storeys? **How many** bedrooms? **How many** bathrooms?

- 几 can be used in a statement to mean 'a few'. Although the context usually helps clarify the meaning, confusion can sometimes arise without the presence of punctuation

李：我今天想吃中国菜，咱们找家中国餐馆吃一顿吧！

Lǐ: Wǒ jīntiān xiǎng chī Zhōngguó cài, zánmen zhǎo jiā Zhōngguó cānguǎn chī yí dùn ba.

王：好啊！这附近有**几家**不错的中国餐馆。

Wáng: Hǎo a! Zhè fùjìn yǒu jǐ jiā búcuò de Zhōngguó cānguǎn.

Li: I feel like eating Chinese food today. Let's find a Chinese restaurant to have a meal at.

Wang: OK! There are **a few** decent Chinese restaurants in this area. (With a question mark, the same sentence could mean 'How many Chinese restaurants are there in this area?')

- When asking a question with the expectation of a number being the answer, such as a room number, use 几 or 多少, not 什么

王小姐住**几楼几号**？她的电话号码是**多少**？(or 她的电话是**多少号/几号**？)

Wáng xiǎojiě zhù jǐ lóu jǐ hào? Tāde diànhuà hàomǎ shì duōshǎo? (or Tāde diànhuà shì duōshǎo hào/jǐ hào?)

What is Miss Wang's floor **number** and room **number**? **What** is her telephone **number**?

老师：二十五的一半是**多少**？谁知道？

Lǎoshī: Èrshí wǔ de yí bàn shì duōshǎo? Shéi zhīdào?

学生：是十二点五。

Xuéshēng: Shì shíèr diǎn wǔ.

Teacher: **What** is half of 25? Who knows (the answer)?

Student: It's 12.5.

33.9 为什么

为什么 is literally the combination of 'for' and 'what'. It is usually used to ask about a reason or cause. It is similar in meaning to 怎么 ('how come'), but 怎么 sounds more casual. Normally, the subject of the sentence should appear before 为什么.

李：这里有把椅子，**你为什么**坐在地上？（为什么你坐在地上 sounds odd.）
Lǐ: Zhèlǐ yǒu bǎ yǐzi, nǐ wèishénme zuò zài dì shàng?
王：那把椅子的腿坏了。
Wáng: Nà bǎ yǐzi de tuǐ huài le.
Li: There is a chair here. Why are you sitting on the floor?
Wang: The legs of that chair are broken.

- When 为什么 is used to ask a question which implies a contrast between two subjects, the subject normally appears after 为什么

  老师：王明，**你**昨天**为什么**没来上课？
  Lǎoshī: Wáng Míng, nǐ zuótiān wèishénme méiyǒu lái shàng kè?
  王明：因为我头痛。
  Wáng Míng: Yīnwèi wǒ tóu tòng.
  老师：李中昨天也头痛，**为什么他**能来，**你**不能来呢？
  Lǎoshī: Lǐ Zhōng zuótiān yě tóu tòng, wèishénme tā néng lái, nǐ bù néng lái ne?
  Teacher: Wang Ming, why didn't you come to class yesterday?
  Wang Ming: Because I had a headache.
  Teacher: Li Zhong also had a headache yesterday. Why is it that he could come to class but you couldn't?

- When asking about someone's reason for doing something, particularly about the purpose of coming and going somewhere, 做什么 (*zuò shénme*) is a more proper way to ask this question. The word order involving 做什么 is different from a 为什么 expression

  安娜：昨天是你的生日，你男朋友**为什么**没来参加你的生日派对呢？你们分手了吗？
  Ānnà: Zuótiān shì nǐde shēngrì, nǐ nán péngyǒu wèishénme méi lái cānjiā nǐde shēngrì pàiduì ne? Nǐmen fēnshǒu le ma?
  小兰：没有，他没来是因为他去日本了？
  Xiǎolán: Méiyǒu, tā méi lái shì yīnwèi tā qù Rìběn le.
  安娜：哦，他**去日本做什么**？
  Ānnà: Ò, tā qù Rìběn zuò shénme?
  Anna: Yesterday was your birthday. **Why** didn't your boyfriend come to your birthday party? Have you broken up?
  Xiaolan: No. He didn't come because he has gone to Japan.
  Anna: Oh. **Why (for what purpose)** has he gone to Japan?

Level 2

33.10 干嘛

干嘛 is similar in meaning to 做什么 (*zuò shénme*) in the sense that both are used to ask about the purpose for doing something; however, 干嘛 sounds extremely casual.

  妈妈：半夜了，你**为什么**还要出门去？
  Māma: Bànyè le, nǐ wèishénme hái yào chūmén qù?
  儿子：刚才小兰打电话来叫我马上到她家去一趟。
  Érzi: Gāngcái Xiǎolán dǎ diànhuà lái jiào wǒ mǎshàng dào tā jiā qù yí tàng.
  妈妈：这么晚了，她还叫你去她家**干嘛**？
  Māma: Zhème wǎn le, tā hái jiào nǐ qù tā jiā gànmá?
  Mother: It's already midnight. **Why** are you going out?
  Son: Xiaolan called me just now and asked me to immediately go to her house.
  Mother: It's already so late. **Why (for what)** would she ask you to go to her house?

When 干嘛 is not used to ask about the purpose of coming or going somewhere, it appears after the subject (similar to 为什么), instead of at the end of the sentence.

干嘛 can be used to ask about purpose or reason, but not cause. In the following sentences, 干嘛 cannot be used in place of 为什么 since 干嘛 means 'what for' and is generally not used to ask about causes.

张：今天食堂里的菜很不错，**你为什么**(or **怎么**)没胃口？
Zhāng: Jīntiān shítáng lǐ de cài hěn búcuò, nǐ wèishénme (or zěnme) méi wèikǒu?
丁：因为我这两天感冒，不舒服，所以不想吃东西。
Dīng: Yīnwèi wǒ zhè liǎng tiān gǎnmào, bù shūfú, suǒyǐ bù xiǎng chī dōngxi.
张：最近天气这么好，我真不懂，**为什么**(or **怎么**)有这么多人感冒？
Zhāng: Zuìjìn tiānqì zhème hǎo, wǒ zhēn bù dǒng, wèishénme (or zěnme) yǒu zhème duō rén gǎnmào?
Zhang: Today the food at the cafeteria is not bad. Why didn't you have any appetite?
Ding: Because I've had a cold these last few days; I am not feeling well, so I don't feel like eating.
Zhang: The weather has been so nice recently. I really don't understand why so many people have caught colds.

太太：小李人品、家世都不错，咱们女儿要嫁他，你**干嘛**反对？
Tàitai: Xiǎo Lǐ rénpǐn, jiāshì dōu búcuò, zánmen nǚ'ér yào jià tā, nǐ gànmá fǎnduì?
先生：女儿才二十岁，**干嘛**这么早结婚？
Xiānsheng: Nǚ'ér cái èrshí suì, gànmá zhème zǎo jiéhūn?
Wife: Xiao Li's personal character and family background are both good. **Why** do you oppose our daughter marrying him?
Husband: Our daughter is only 20 years old. **Why** marry so early?

33.11 什么时候 and 几点

什么时候 (*shénme shíhòu*), literally 'what time', means 'when' in Chinese. 几点 (*jǐ diǎn*) means 'what time'.

李：张经理，您**什么时候**有空？我想跟您谈谈。
Lǐ: Zhāng jīnglǐ, nín shénme shíhòu yǒu kòng? Wǒ xiǎng gēn nín tán tán.
张：我今天下午有空，你想你可以**几点**到我的办公室来？
Zhāng: Wǒ jīntiān xiàwǔ yǒu kòng, nǐ xiǎng nǐ kěyǐ jǐ diǎn dào wǒde bàngōngshì lái?
Li: Manager Zhang, **when** will you have time? I would like to talk to you.
Zhang: I am free this afternoon. **What time** do you think you can come to my office?

33.12 The use of question marks with indirect questions

In Chinese, there is no distinction between a direct question or an indirect question in terms of word order. Therefore, it is not unusual to have a question mark after an indirect question.

(Situation: Xiao Zhang was not paying attention to what the teacher was saying.)

老师：现在我要请每位同学轮流说一说，你们今天是**怎么**来学校的？
Lǎoshī: Xiànzài wǒ yào qǐng měi wèi tóngxué lúnliú shuō yì shuō, nǐmen jīntiān shì zěnme lái xuéxiào de?
小张：小王，请告诉我，老师刚才**说什么**？
Xiǎo Zhāng: Xiǎo Wáng, qǐng gàosù wǒ, lǎoshī gāngcái shuō shénme?
Teacher: Now I am going to ask each of you to take turns stating how you got to school today.
Xiao Zhang: Xiao Wang, please tell me what the teacher just said.

33.13 Interrogative pronouns in negative statements

(a) 什么, 多少 and 几

什么, 多少 and 几 can be used in negative statements to mean 'not much' or 'not many'. The word 没(有) (*méiyǒu*) often appears in such statements.

Without 多少 or 什么, the following sentences would still be correct, but the meanings would be different.

> 李：昨天的派对，我请了很多朋友，可是**没有多少**人来(= **没有几个**人来)，我很失望。
> *Lǐ: Zuótiān de pàiduì, wǒ qǐng le hěn duō péngyǒu, kěshì méiyǒu duōshǎo rén lái*
> *(= méiyǒu jǐ ge rén lái), wǒ hěn shīwàng.*
> 王：那是因为你的派对总是**没有什么**好吃的东西。
> *Wáng: Nà shì yīnwèi nǐde pàiduì zǒngshì méiyǒu shénme hǎochī de dōngxi.*
> Li: I invited many friends to my party yesterday, but **not many** people came. I was disappointed.
> Wang: It's because there was **never much** good food at your parties.

> 他真聪明，最难的数学问题，他也**不用花什么**时间就能解答。
> *Tā zhēn cōngmíng, zuì nán de shùxué wèntí, tā yě bú yòng huā shénme shíjiān jiù néng jiědá.*
> He is truly smart. He **didn't** have to spend **much time** to solve even the hardest mathematics problem.

(b) '怎么 + adjective'

'怎么 + adjective' can be used in a negative statement with 不 (*bù*) to mean 'not very'. In addition, '怎么 + verb' in a negative sentence can mean 'not very much'.

> 房地产商：这个房子，您喜不喜欢？
> *Fángdìchǎn shāng: Zhè ge fángzi, nín xǐ bù xǐhuān?*
> 王先生：**不怎么**喜欢，因为我觉得地点**不怎么**好。
> *Wáng xiānsheng: Bù zěnme xǐhuān, yīnwèi wǒ juéde dìdiǎn bù zěnme hǎo.*
> Property salesperson: Do you like this house?
> Mr Wang: I **don't** like it **very much** because I feel that the location is **not very** good.

33.14 Using interrogative pronouns to make sweeping statements: 'anybody', 'anything', etc.

An interrogative pronoun can be used to make a sweeping statement. Essentially, it is a contracted sentence since 无论/不管 (*wúlùn/bùguǎn*) has been omitted.

☞ See 32.2 and 32.3 for more on contracted sentences with 也 (*yě*) and 都 (*dōu*).

Since interrogative pronouns are not used to ask questions in this particular pattern, each of them has a different meaning derived from their original one. For example, 谁 means 'anybody' or 'everybody'; 什么 means 'anything' or 'everything'; and so on. Sometimes, the expression 'no matter' is used to translate this structure.

The basic word order for this structure is: 'interrogative pronoun + 都/也 + verb'.

(a) Positive and negative sentences

也 tends to be used in a negative sentence, although, in some cases, it can appear in a positive sentence as well. 都 can appear in either a positive or a negative sentence. Without 也 or 都, the sentence would either be incomprehensible or become a question by mistake.

张：听说这个电影很不错，谁想去看？一起去吧！
Zhāng: Tīngshuō zhè ge diànyǐng hěn búcuò, shéi xiǎng qù kàn? Yìqǐ qù ba!
李：这么有名的电影，**谁都**想去看，可是还没上演呢！去哪里看？
Lǐ: Zhème yǒumíng de diànyǐng, shéi dōu xiǎng qù kàn, kěshì hái méi shàngyǎn ne! Qù nǎlǐ kàn?
Zhang: I heard that this movie was quite good. Who wants to go see it? Let's go together.
Li: It's such a famous movie; everybody wants to see it. But it has not premiered yet. Where are you going to see it?

(b) Placement of the interrogative pronoun

Even when the interrogative pronoun is the object of the verb, it must appear before the verb.

听说张先生的新房子非常漂亮，**谁都想**去参观一下，可是他**谁都**不**请**。(谁 is the subject of 想 but the object of 请.)
Tīngshuō Zhāng xiānsheng de xīn fángzi fēicháng piàoliàng, shéi dōu xiǎng qù cānguān yíxià, kěshì tā shéi dōu bù qǐng.
I've heard that Mr Zhang's new house is extremely pretty. **Everybody wants** to go visit, but he is not going to **invite anyone**.

(Situation: Xiao Wang has invited Miss Li to go to the park with him.)

李：你知道那个公园有**多远**吗？走不到的！我不去！
Lǐ: Nǐ zhīdào nà ge gōngyuán yǒu duō yuǎn ma? Zǒu bú dào de! Wǒ bú qù!
王：你放心，我买了一辆新车，**多远**的地方咱们**都**能去。
Wáng: Nǐ fàngxīn, wǒ mǎi le yí liàng xīn chē, duō yuǎn de dìfāng zánmen dōu néng qù.
Li: Do you have any idea **how far** that park is? It cannot be reached on foot. I am not going.
Wang: Don't worry. I've bought a new car. We can go anywhere **no matter how far** it is.

(c) Placement of the subject

When the interrogative pronoun is the object of the verb, the subject of the sentence can appear either before the interrogative pronoun or before 都/也.

这星期，**我哪里也**不去，**谁**的电话(**我**)**也**不接，多重要的事，我**也**不管。
(哪里, 电话 and 事 are the objects of 去, 接 and 管 respectively.)
Zhè xīngqī, wǒ nǎlǐ yě bú qù, shéide diànhuà (wǒ) yě bù jiē, duō zhòngyào de shì, wǒ yě bù guǎn.
This week, I won't go anywhere; I won't answer anybody's phone calls and I won't take care of any business (no matter how important it is).

李：你昨天去的那个派对好不好玩？
Lǐ: Nǐ zuótiān qù de nà ge pàiduì hǎo bù hǎowán?
王：不好玩，因为**我谁都**不认识(= **谁我都**不认识)。
Wáng: Bù hǎowán, yīnwèi wǒ shéi dōu bú rènshì.
Li: Was the party you went to fun?
Wang: It wasn't fun because I didn't know anybody.

(d) Word order when there are two verbs

When there are two verbs in the sentence, it is usually the second verb that appears after 都/也. The first verb may appear either before or after the interrogative pronoun, depending on the meaning of the sentence.

小兰已经打定主意了，所以我**说什么**，她**都**不听。（说 is before 什么.）
Xiǎolán yǐjīng dǎ dìng zhǔyì le, suǒyǐ wǒ shuō shénme, tā dōu bù tīng.
Xiaolan has made up her mind; therefore, whatever I say (no matter what I say), she won't listen.

Compare: 这件事情太复杂了，所以我**怎么解释**，她**都**不懂。（解释 is after 怎么.）
Zhè jiàn shìqíng tài fùzá le, suǒyǐ wǒ zěnme jiěshì, tā dōu bù dǒng.
This matter is too complicated; therefore, no matter how I explain, she doesn't understand.

小李个性外向，讨人喜欢，所以他**到哪里都**能很快就交到朋友。
Xiǎo Li gèxìng wàixiàng, tǎo rén xǐhuān, suǒyǐ tā dào nǎlǐ dōu néng hěn kuài jiù jiāo dào péngyǒu.
Xiao Li is outgoing and likable; therefore, wherever he goes, he can quickly make new friends.

(e) 怎么都 and 怎么也

It should be noted that the expression 'no matter what' in English is 怎么都 or 怎么也 in Chinese.

门卡住了，所以我**怎么都**打不开。
Mén kǎ zhù le, suǒyǐ wǒ zěnme dōu dǎ bù kāi.
The door is jammed, so I cannot open it **no matter what**.

(Situation: Anna was looking for a book that had been missing. Xiaolan told her to just go buy another copy.)

安娜：那本书是从图书馆借来的，所以我**怎么都**得把它找到。
Ānnà: Nà běn shū shì cóng túshūguǎn jiè lái de, suǒyǐ wǒ zěnme dōu děi bǎ tā zhǎodào.
Anna: That book was borrowed from the library. So I have to find it **no matter what**.

33.15 Using two identical interrogative pronouns: 'no matter'

Level 2

Two identical interrogative pronouns can appear in one statement to convey the meaning 'no matter'. 就 *(jiù)* normally appears between the two phrases.

借书的人：请问，我一次可以借几本？
Jiè shū de rén: Qǐng wèn, wǒ yí cì kěyǐ jiè jǐ běn?
图书馆工作人员：你想借**几本就**借**几本**。
Túshūguǎn gōngzuò rényuán: Nǐ xiǎng jiè jǐ běn jiù jiè jǐ běn.
Library patron: Excuse me, how many books can I borrow each time?
Library staff: You can borrow however many you want (to borrow).

王：你说，咱们今天该点些什么菜？
Wáng: Nǐ shuō, zánmen jīntiān gāi diǎn xiē shénme cài?
李：你想吃**什么**咱们**就**点**什么**。
Lǐ: Nǐ xiǎng chī shénme zánmen jiù diǎn shénme.
Wang: Tell me, what dish do you think we should order today?
Li: We will order whatever dishes you feel like eating.

以前我总以为，等我退休以后，想去**哪里就**可以去**哪里**。现在我退休了，却**哪里都**不想去了。
Yǐqián wǒ zǒng yǐwéi, děng wǒ tuìxiū yǐhòu, xiǎng qù nǎlǐ jiù kěyǐ qù nǎlǐ. Xiànzài wǒ tuìxiū le, què nǎlǐ dōu bù xiǎng qù le.
In the past I always thought that I would be able to go anywhere I wanted to go after I retired. Now I have retired, but I don't feel like going anywhere any more.

Exercises

Translate the following sentences into Chinese, taking into account any instructions given in parentheses.

evel
2

1 Male: The weather is so nice. How about if we go to the park to take a walk?

Female: Sure. How are we going to go? By bus or by car?

2 Mrs Wang: Do you have any idea how expensive this car is? How can we afford it?

Mr Wang: I truly like this car. No matter how expensive it is, I am going to buy it.

3 Wife: How come the dishes that were just washed are still dirty? What's going on?

Husband: What? (showing slight surprise or puzzlement, not 什么) Is the dishwasher broken again?

4 Anna: Xiao Wang! How come you are here? It's raining so hard. How did you get here?

Wang: I came to see you because there is something very important that I wanted to tell you. So no matter how hard it was raining, I had to come.

evel
3

5 I feel like having a cup of coffee. Do you know where I can find a coffee shop? (Literally: Where is there a coffee shop?)

6 Li: Whom should we ask to be our representative to answer the teacher's question?

Ding: What representative? Whoever is called on by the teacher will answer the questions. (Use two identical interrogative pronouns for the 'whoever' expression.)

7 Female: What time is it now? Why are you not in class? What are you doing here? (= Why did you come here?)

Male: Today the teacher dismissed the class at 2 o'clock. I don't have much to do this afternoon, so I came to invite you to go to a movie. The cinema is showing (having) four movies; which do you want to see?

Female: Great! We will go see whichever one you want to see. (Use two identical interrogative pronouns for the 'whichever' expression.)

8 Li: When do you usually do (physical) exercise?

Ding: There are not many people at the gym on Sunday mornings. (An interrogative pronoun must be used to express 'not many.') So I always exercise on Sunday mornings.

Li: What good exercise equipment does your gym have?

Ding: This gym is inexpensive, so there is not much good equipment. (An interrogative pronoun must be used to express 'not much'.)

34 Rhetorical questions

Rhetorical questions are not used to ask questions but to make statements using a question format. The reason for using a question to make a statement is to strengthen the effect of the statement. No answer or reply is expected when a rhetorical question is asked. The punctuation used at the end of a rhetorical question can be either a question mark or an exclamation mark.

Level 1/2

34.1 Basic rhetorical questions

Nearly all questions can be asked in a rhetorical way depending on the context in which the question is uttered.

> 张：哎呀！都几点了？小王怎么还不来？（都几点了 is a rhetorical question meaning 'it's late'.）
> *Zhāng: Āiyā! Dōu jǐ diǎn le? Xiǎo Wáng zěnme hái bù lái?*
> 李：谁知道！/你问我，我问谁？/我怎么知道？（All are rhetorical questions meaning 'I don't know'.）
> *Lǐ: Shéi zhīdào!/Nǐ wèn wǒ, wǒ wèn shéi?/Wǒ zěnme zhīdào?*
> Zhang: Oh no! What time is time already? How come Xiao Wang is not here yet?
> Li: Who knows!/You are asking me and whom should I ask?/How should I know?

Level 1/2

34.2 Making positive and negative statements with rhetorical questions

Rhetorically, a negative question is used to make a positive statement whereas a positive question is used to make a negative statement.

(Situation: Mr Wang wants to buy a fancy car and Mrs Wang points out that they cannot afford such a car.)

> 王太太：谁不想买这种车？可是，咱们有这个钱吗？
> *Wáng tàitai: Shéi bù xiǎng mǎi zhè zhǒng chē? Kěshì, zánmen yǒu zhè ge qián ma?*
> Mrs Wang: Who doesn't want to buy a car like this? But, do we have the money?

(Situation: Two brothers are fighting over some money left on the table. The younger one insists that the money belongs to him and the older one uses a rhetorical question to say he cannot prove it.)

> 哥哥：你说是你的，上面写着你的名字吗？
> *Gēge: Nǐ shuō shì nǐde, shàngmiàn xiě zhe nǐde míngzì ma?*
> Older brother: You said it's yours. Is your name written on it?

Level 1/2

34.3 Using affirmative–negative questions in a rhetorical way

An affirmative–negative question used in a rhetorical way means the speaker wants the listener to share the same feeling or opinion. Phrases such as 你说 (*nǐ shuō*) and 你想一想 (*nǐ xiǎng yì xiǎng*) are used.

王：你今天为什么看起来这么气？

Wáng: Nǐ jīntiān wèishénme kàn qǐlái zhème qì?

李：儿子考试又不及格，**你说**，**我气不气**？ ('我气吗?' does not convey the same meaning. '我会不气吗?' conveys a similar effect, however, since a negative question indicates a positive statement.)

Lǐ: Érzi kǎoshì yòu bù jígé, nǐ shuō, wǒ qì bú qì?

Wang: Why do you look so angry today?

Li: My son failed a test again. Tell me, should I be mad or not?

我侄子才三岁就认得几百个字了，**你说**，这个小孩**聪明不聪明**？

Wǒ zhízǐ cái sān suì jiù rènde jǐ bǎi ge zì le, nǐ shuō, zhè ge xiǎohái cōngmíng bù cōngmíng?

My nephew is only three years old, but he already recognizes several hundred characters. Tell me, is this child smart or not?

34.4 The use of 不是……吗?

This expression is used when what happens is not in keeping with what the speaker already knows. The speaker thus uses it to reaffirm what he or she knows. It is often followed or preceded by a real question using 为什么 (*wèishénme*) or 怎么 (*zěnme*).

(Situation: Mr Wang said that he would drop by at 5 o'clock, but by 6 o'clock he still has not shown up.)

王先生**不是**说五点会来**吗**？现在都六点了，他怎么还没来？

Wáng xiānsheng bú shì shuō wǔ diǎn huì lái ma? Xiànzài dōu liù diǎn le, tā zěnme hái méi lái?

Didn't Mr Wang say he would be here by five? It's already six. How come he is not here yet?

小丁：昨天我看到安娜跟王先生一起去看电影。

Xiǎo Dīng: Zuótiān wǒ kàn dào Ānnà gēn Wáng xiānsheng yìqǐ qù kàn diànyǐng.

小李：安娜**不是**已经有男朋友了**吗**？

Xiǎo Lǐ: Ānnà bú shì yǐjīng yǒu nán péngyǒu le ma?

Xiao Ding: Yesterday I saw Anna going to a movie with Mr Wang.

Xiao Li: Doesn't she already have a boyfriend?

不是……吗 can be followed by a suggestion. In this case, the speaker simply wants to strengthen the effect of a statement, which may not be inconsistent with an existing situation.

(Situation: Upon seeing an announcement for a singing contest, Zhang urges his friend Wang to enter the contest because Zhang believes that Wang is a good singer.)

张：你歌**不是**唱得很好**吗**？（=你歌唱得**不是**很好**吗**？）你去报名参加比赛吧！

Zhāng: Nǐ gē bú shì chàng de hěn hǎo ma? (= Nǐ gē chàng de bú shì hěn hǎo ma?) Nǐ qù bàomíng cānjiā bǐsài ba!

Zhang: Isn't is true that you sing well? (Meaning: Aren't you a good singer?) Why don't you sign up for the contest!

At least five variations can be derived from the basic 不是……吗 structure.

(a) When the verb is 是

When the verb in the rhetorical question happens to be 是，是 should be used only once.

(Situation: Upon learning that his fiancé will not invite her best friend Xiaolan to their wedding, Mr Zhang is surprised.)

张：为什么？你们两个**不是**最好的朋友**吗**？ (Meaning: 你们两个**是**最好的朋友.)
Zhāng: Wèishénme? Nǐmen liǎng ge bú shì zuì hǎo de péngyǒu ma?
Zhang: Why? Aren't the two of you best friends?

(b) Adding 也 or 都 when the verb is 是

If the adverb 也 (*yě*) or 都 (*dōu*) is necessary in the 不是……吗 structure and the verb happens to be 是, the expression is 不也是……吗/不都是……吗.

(Situation: Although both Xiao Wang and Xiao Zhang are Xiao Li's good friends, Xiao Li has told his parents that he will only invite Xiao Wang to his birthday dinner.)

妈妈：怎么不请小张呢？他**不也是**你的好朋友**吗**？ (Meaning: 他**也是**你的好朋友.)
Māma: Zěnme bù qǐng Xiǎo Zhāng ne? Tā bù yě shì nǐde hǎo péngyǒu ma?
爸爸：我也觉得奇怪，他们两个**不都是**你的好朋友**吗**？ (Meaning: 他们**都是**你的好朋友.)
Bàba: Wǒ yě juéde qíguài, tāmen liǎng ge bù dōu shì nǐde hǎo péngyǒu ma?
Mother: How come you are not inviting Xiao Zhang? Isn't he also your good friend?
Father: I also think it's curious. Aren't they both your good friends?

(c) Adding 也 or 都 when the verb is *not* 是

If the adverb 也 or 都 is necessary in the 不是……吗 structure and the verb is **not** 是, the expression is 不是也……吗/不是都……吗.

(Situation: Xiao Li's parents are under the impression that Xiao Li has invited both Xiao Wang and Xiao Zhang for dinner. But only Xiao Zhang shows up.)

妈妈：你**不是也**请了小王**吗**？ (Meaning: 你**也请**了小王.) 为什么只有小张来了呢？
Māma: Nǐ bú shì yě qǐng le Xiǎo Wáng ma? Wèishénme zhǐyǒu Xiǎo Zhāng lái le ne?
爸爸：我也觉得奇怪，他们两个你**不是都**请了**吗**？ (Meaning: 他们两个你**都请**了.)
Bàba: Wǒ yě juéde qíguài, tāmen liǎng ge nǐ bú shì dōu qǐng le ma?
Mother: Didn't you also invite Xiao Wang? Why is it that only Xiao Zhang came?
Father: I also think it's curious. Didn't you invite both of them?

(d) A rhetorical question or a negative question?

While it is important to make the distinction between 不也是……吗/不都是……吗 and 不是也……吗/不是都……, it is equally important to know that 也不是……吗/都不是……吗 is also a legitimate question, albeit not a rhetorical one, but a negative question.

(Situation: Anna is under the impression that the two books on the desk belong to Zhang. But when Zhang is about to leave, he only picks up the English book, not the Chinese book.)

安娜：这本中文书**不也是**你的**吗**？你怎么只带那本英文的，不带这本呢？
Ānnà: Zhè běn Zhōngwén shū bù yě shì nǐde ma? Nǐ zěnme zhǐ dài nà běn Yīngwén de, bú dài zhè běn ne?
Anna: Isn't this Chinese book also yours? How come you only took that English book with you, but not this Chinese one?

(Situation: Two coats are in Xiaolan's room. Anna knows that the green coat belongs to Xiaolan's sister, so she assumes that the blue one belongs to Xiaolan. But Xiaolan's sister comes to take both away.)

安娜：那件蓝色的大衣**也不是**你的**吗**？ (This is a negative question, not a rhetorical question.)
Ānnà: Nà jiàn lánsè de dàyī yě bú shì nǐde ma?
Anna: The blue coat isn't yours as well(, is it)?

(e) Adding 就 when the verb is 是

When the adverb is 就 (*jiù*) and the verb is 是; the expression is 不就是……吗.

(Situation: Mr Wang is looking for today's newspaper. His wife says it is in his hand.)

> 王太太：你手上拿的**不就是**今天的报纸**吗**？ (Meaning: 你手上拿的**就是**今天的报纸.)
>
> *Wáng tàitai: Nǐ shǒu shàng ná de bú jiù shì jīntiān de bàozhǐ ma?*
>
> Mrs Wang: Isn't what you are holding in your hand (exactly) today's newspaper?

(f) Adding 就 when the verb is *not* 是

When the adverb is 就 and the verb is **not** 是，the expression 不是就……吗 is frequently shortened to 不就……吗.

(Situation: Xiaolan has put off doing her homework until the very last minute. And she is anxious now. Her mother points out that she should have done it earlier.)

> 妈妈： 要是你昨天就把功课写完，现在**不就**轻松了**吗**？ (Meaning: 现在**就**轻松了.)
>
> *Māma: Yàoshì nǐ zuótiān jiù bǎ gōngkè xiě wán, xiànzài bú jiù qīngsōng le ma?*
>
> Mother: If you had done your homework yesterday, wouldn't you feel relaxed now?

34.5 可不是吗

Level 1

可不是吗 (*kě bú shì ma*) is a very casual expression used to agree with what someone else has said.

> 王： 这几天的天气真热得受不了。
>
> *Wáng: Zhè jǐtiān de tiānqì zhēn rè de shòu bù liǎo.*
>
> 李： **可不是吗**!
>
> *Lǐ: Kě bú shì ma!*
>
> Wang: The weather these days is really unbearably hot.
>
> Li: Isn't it true!

34.6 The use of 何必 and 何苦

Level 1/2

(a) 何必

何必 (*hébì*) literally means 'why must?' Therefore, it is used in a rhetorical question to mean 'no need to'. An optional modal particle 呢 (*ne*) is frequently used.

(Situation: Mrs Li is going to call a plumber to fix some plumbing problem. But Mr Li says it's not necessary.)

> 李先生：这种小问题，**何必**花钱请人修？ 我自己来修。
>
> *Lǐ xiānsheng: Zhè zhǒng xiǎo wèntí, hébì huā qián qǐng rén xiū? Wǒ zìjǐ lái xiū.*
>
> Mr Li: Why do we have to spend money to hire someone to fix such a small problem? I will fix it myself.

何必呢 can be an independent expression which follows a statement. 呢 in this case is not optional.

(Situation: Zhang realizes that he has been ripped off by a street vendor and he wants to go and argue and get his money back. Wang tries to tell him not to.)

> 王： 为了一点小钱去跟一个摊贩吵，**何必呢**？
>
> *Wáng: Wèile yìdiǎn xiǎo qián qù gēn yí ge tān fàn chǎo, hébì ne?*
>
> Why do you have to argue with a street vendor over such a small amount of money?

(b) 何苦

何苦 (*hékǔ*) and 何苦呢 have similar meanings and usage to 何必 and 何必呢, but they are only used to refer to unpleasant or trivial matters that are not worth the trouble.

(Situation: Mrs Ding is mad because her son has said something rude to her. Mr Ding tries to calm her.)

丁先生：他是小孩子，不懂事，**何苦**为了他生这么大的气呢？

Dīng xiānsheng: Tā shì xiǎo háizi, bù dǒngshì, hékǔ wèile tā shēng zhème dà de qì ne?

Mr Ding: He is a child and immature. Why get so mad because of him? (It's not worth getting mad.)

(Situation: Xiaolan is vexed over a pair of lost sunglasses. Anna tells her it's not worth it.)

安娜：掉了一付太阳眼镜就这么烦恼，**何苦呢**？

Ānnà: Diào le yí fù tàiyáng yǎnjìng jiù zhème fánnǎo, hékǔ ne?

Anna: Why so vexed simply because you have lost a pair of sunglasses? (It's not worth it!)

34.7 The use of 哪里

Level 3

While 哪里 (*nǎlǐ*) literally means 'where', it is used in a rhetorical question to make a negative statement. Therefore, 哪里 replaces either 不 (*bù*) or 没 (*méi*).

One of the proper responses to 谢谢 (*xièxie*: 'thank you') in Chinese is 哪里 because it is a rhetorical way to say 'not at all'.

张：昨天的电视上的天气预报不是说今天会下大雨吗？你怎么没带伞呢？

Zhāng: Zuótiān diànshì shàng de tiānqì yùbào bú shì shuō jīntiān huì xià dà yǔ ma? Nǐ zěnme méi dài sǎn ne?

王：我最近忙得要命，**哪里有**时间看电视？ (Meaning: **没有**时间看电视.)

Wáng: Wǒ zuìjìn máng de yàomìng, nǎlǐ yǒu shíjiān kàn diànshì?

Zhang: Didn't the weather forecast on TV yesterday say that it would rain hard today? How come you didn't bring an umbrella?

Wang: I have been busy to death lately. Where would I get the time (from my busy schedule) to watch TV?

妈妈：你要出门了吗？别忘了带雨伞。

Māma: Nǐ yào chū mén le ma? Bié wàng le dài yǔsǎn.

女儿：今天天气这么好，**哪里**需要带雨伞！ (Meaning: **不**需要带雨伞.)

Nǚ'ér: Jīntiān tiānqì zhème hǎo, nǎlǐ xūyào dài yǔsǎn!

Mother: Are you about to go out? Don't forget to take an umbrella with you.

Daughter: Today's weather is so nice. Why would I need to take an umbrella?

34.8 The use of 难道......(吗)

Level 2/3

This expression is used to interpret a situation in front of the speaker. The subject can appear either before or after 难道 (*nándào*), and 吗 (*ma*) is optional.

(Situation: Mrs Li is trying to read the newspaper, but her husband is standing behind her reading the headlines out loud.)

李太太：别再念了，行不行？**难道**我不认识字**吗**？

Lǐ tàitai: Bié zài niàn le, xíng bù xíng? Nándào wǒ bú rènshì zì ma?

Mrs Li: Can you stop doing that? **Do you mean to say that** I can't read?

(Situation: Anna tells her friend Xiaolan that Mr Wang has been sending her flowers and calling her ever since they met at a party last week.)

安娜： 他又给我送花，又给我打电话，**他难道**想追我吗？
Ānnà: Tā yòu gěi wǒ sòng huā, yòu gěi wǒ dǎ diànhuà, tā nándào xiǎng zhuī wǒ ma?
小兰： 这么明显的事，你还要问吗？**难道你**自己还看不出来？
Xiǎolán: Zhème míngxiǎn de shì, nǐ hái yào wèn ma? Nándào nǐ hái kàn bù chūlái?
Anna: He has been sending me flowers and also calling me. **Could it be that** he is trying to pursue me?
Xiaolan: Do you have to ask about such an obvious matter? **Are you saying that** you yourself could not tell (what his intention is)?

34.9 Using 怎么 in a rhetorical way

怎么 (*zěnme*) can be used in a rhetorical way to make a negative statement. In this case, it may not always have an exact counterpart in English.

(Situation: Wang says something to Zhang. Zhang is sceptical and Wang assures him it's true.)

张： 你说的都是真的吗？
Zhāng: Nǐ shuō de dōu shì zhēn de ma?
王： 我**怎么**会骗你呢？ (Meaning: 我不会骗你的.)
Wáng: Wǒ zěnme huì piàn nǐ ne?
Zhang: Is everything you said true?
Wang: Would I lie to you? (There is no direct translation between the English and Chinese for 怎么 in this expression.)

(Situation: Mrs Ding tries to tell her husband not to trust Li.)

丁先生： 放心吧！我们是好朋友，他**怎么**会骗我呢？
Dīng xiānsheng: Fàngxīn ba! Wǒmen shì hǎo péngyǒu, tā zěnme huì piàn wǒ ne?
丁太太： **怎么**不会？他又不是你的兄弟，连兄弟都可能骗你呢！
Dīng tàitai: Zěnme bú huì? Tā yòu bú shì nǐde xiōngdì, lián xiōngdì dōu kěnéng piàn nǐ ne!
Mr Ding: Don't worry! We are good friends. How is it possible that he would cheat me?
Mrs Ding: Why not? (怎么 has no exact counterpart in English.) He is not your brother. Even your brother can cheat you.

34.10 Using 什么 in a rhetorical way

When 什么 (*shénme*) is used in a rhetorical question, the tone is frequently a harsh one.

(a) 'Adjective + 什么': indicating disagreement

什么 can follow an adjective, which must have been mentioned already or exist in the context. It is used to indicate a disagreement. In a regular question, 什么 usually does not follow an adjective.

(Situation: Mrs Wang's daughter has married into a rich family. Mrs Li congratulates Mrs Wang, but Mrs Wang does not like her son-in-law.)

李太太： 王太太，恭喜你，女儿嫁了一个这么好的丈夫！
Lǐ tàitai: Wáng tàitai, gōngxǐ nǐ, nǚ'ér jià le yí ge zhème hǎo de zhàngfū!
王太太： **好什么**？连大学都没有毕业。
Wáng tàitai: Hǎo shénme? Lián dàxué dōu méiyǒu bìyè.
Mrs Li: Mrs Wang, congratulations! Your daughter has married such a nice man.
Mrs Wang: What's so nice about him? He didn't even graduate from university.

王：火车就要开了，小李怎么还不来？赶不上火车就麻烦了！
Wáng: Huǒchē jiù yào kāi le, Xiǎo Lǐ zěnme hái bù lái? Gǎn bú shàng huǒchē jiù máfán le!
丁：**紧张什么**？赶不上，就坐下班，反正咱们也没有急事。
Dīng: Jǐnzhāng shénme? Gǎn bú shàng, jiù zuò xià bān, fǎnzhèng zánmen yě méiyǒu jíshì.
Wang: The train will depart soon. How come Xiao Li is still not here? If we miss the train, we will be in trouble.
Ding: What are you anxious about? If we miss this one, then we'll get the next one. Anyway, we don't have any urgent business.

(b) 'Verb + 什么': 'no need to'

什么 can appear after a verb to mean 'no need to', or 'don't' (in an imperative sentence). The tone is harsh. 什么 does not have a direct counterpart in English in this context.

王：车站就在前面，咱们去坐公共汽车吧！
Wáng: Chēzhàn jiù zài qiánmiàn, zánmen qù zuò gōnggòng qìchē ba!
李：走路去五分钟就到了，坐**什么**公共汽车！ (Meaning: 不用坐公共汽车.)
Lǐ: Zǒulù qù wǔ fēnzhōng jiù dào le, zuò shénme gōnggòng qìchē!
Wang: The bus stop is right ahead. Let's take the bus!
Li: It takes only five minutes if we walk. Why take the bus?

(Situation: Anna is crying because she has done poorly in the test and is about to be punished by her mother.)

妈妈：你哭**什么**？哭也还是要罚。
Māma: Nǐ kū shénme? Kū yě háishì yào fá.
Mother: Don't cry! Even if you cry, you will still be punished.

Level 2

34.11 Frequently used rhetorical questions with 什么

The following are some frequently used rhetorical questions involving the use of 什么.

(a) 关你什么事？

This literally means 'what business is it of yours?' The negative statement it is making is 不关你的事 ('it is none of your business').

姐姐：别跟小李交往，他配不上你。
Jiějie: Bié gēn Xiǎo Lǐ jiāowǎng, tā pèi bú shàng nǐ.
妹妹：我跟谁交往，**关你什么事**？
Mèimei: Wǒ gēn shéi jiāowǎng, guān nǐ shénme shì?
Older sister: Don't date Xiao Li. He is not good enough for you.
Younger sister: **What business is it of yours** whom I date?

(b) 有什么好……的？

This means 'what is there to . . . ?' meaning 'there is no point . . .' The 好 (*hǎo*) in this expression is not optional since it implies 'worth'.

李太太：你儿子马上就要毕业了，你现在一定很高兴吧！
Lǐ tàitai: Nǐ érzi mǎshàng jiù yào bìyè le, nǐ xiànzài yídìng hěn gāoxìng ba!
丁太太：唉，**有什么好**高兴**的**！工作还没有找到呢！
Dīng tàitai: Ài, yǒu shénme hǎo gāoxìng de! Gōngzuò hái méiyǒu zhǎodào ne!
Mrs Li: Your son is about to graduate. You must be happy now.
Mrs Ding: Alas, what is there to be happy about? He has not found a job yet.

(Situation: Mr Wang is about to take a holiday with his whole family. A co-worker asks him if he is looking forward to it.)

王先生：**有什么好**期待**的**？我宁可待在家里休息休息。

Wáng xiānsheng: Yǒu shénme hǎo qídài de? Wǒ nìngkě dāi zài jiā lǐ xiūxi xiūxi.

Mr Wang: What is there to look forward to? I would rather stay home and rest.

(c) 又有什么关系呢？

This expression means 'what does it matter whether or not . . .', meaning 'it does not matter whether or not . . .'. It usually follows a statement of 'as long as . . .'. Also, it should be noted that neither 又 (*yòu*) nor 呢 (*ne*) is optional in this particular expression.

(Situation: Xiaoming is upset because he did poorly in a test even though he had studied hard for it. His mother tries to console him.)

妈妈：只要你努力了，成绩**好不好又有什么关系呢**？

Māma: Zhǐyào nǐ nǔlì le, chéngjī hǎo bù hǎo yòu yǒu shénme guānxi ne?

Mother: As long as you worked hard, what does it matter whether your grade is good or not?

Exercises

Interpret the meaning of each of the following situations and write rhetorical questions accordingly.

Example

It's been raining for several days. Li asks Wang if it is still going to rain the next day. Wang uses a rhetorical question to say no one knows. A good choice would be 谁知道! (*Shéi zhīdào!*), which means 'who knows?' Wang can also use a rhetorical question to say he does not know. A good choice would be 我怎么知道？ (*Wǒ zěnme zhīdào?*)

1 Mrs Wang has two daughters, Xiaolan and Xiaoying. It always seems to Miss Zhang that Mrs Wang is partial to Xiaolan. Miss Zhang and several other women are discussing this.

   (a) Miss Zhang uses a rhetorical question to state that they are both Mrs Wang's daughters. The rhetorical question is followed by a real question of why she is partial to Xiaolan.

   (b) Miss Li uses a rhetorical question to interpret the situation by thinking that Xiaoying is not Mrs Wang's birth daughter.

   (c) Miss Chen says that she does not believe it. She also uses a rhetorical question to say that it is not likely that Mrs Wang would be partial because she thinks Mrs Wang is a good mother.

   (d) Miss Ding uses a rhetorical question to say that she agrees with Miss Chen.

2 Anna has decided to marry Mr Wang. Her friend Miss Zhang is discussing this situation with a group of friends. Because Mr Wang makes too little money, Miss Zhang does not think Anna should marry him. She also worries that Anna will not be happy in the future.

(a) Miss Ding uses a rhetorical question to point out that it is not Miss Zhang's business whom Anna wants to marry.

(b) Miss Chen uses a rhetorical question to say that being poor does not matter because Mr Wang really loves Anna.

(c) Miss Li uses a rhetorical question to tell Miss Zhang there is nothing to worry about since Anna is not a child any more.

(d) Miss Wen uses a rhetorical question to bluntly tell Miss Zhang there is no need to worry because it is not as if Anna is her younger sister.

3 A nosy neighbour comments on the fact that Mr and Mrs Li's 35-year-old son does not have a girlfriend.

(a) The nosy neighbour asks if this means he (the son) does not plan to get married.

(b) Mrs Li replies with a rhetorical question that he (her son) does not have time to date because he is too busy with his work.

(c) Mr Li angrily tells the neighbour it is none of her business whether his son plans to marry or not.

(d) The neighbour tells Mr Li there is no need for him to get angry because she does not have any bad intentions.

(e) After the neighbour is gone, Mrs Li tells Mr Li it is not worth getting angry over such a small matter.

(f) Mr Li uses a rhetorical question to say that it is not a small matter.

4 Li Ming was diligent and did well in the test, but Anna did poorly. Two teachers are discussing them.

(a) Teacher Wang is puzzled because he thinks Anna is equally diligent. So he uses a rhetorical question to state his opinion about Anna. It is followed by a real question to express his puzzlement.

(b) Teacher Li uses a rhetorical question to say that Anna is not diligent and is, in fact, very lazy.

(c) Teacher Wang uses a rhetorical question to say that Anna stays at the library until midnight every day. He uses another rhetorical question to say that she cannot possibly be lazy.

Key to exercises

1 The basic formation of a Chinese sentence

1 王先生跟他女朋友都不喜欢看电影。
Wáng xiānsheng gēn tā nǚ péngyǒu dōu bù xǐhuān kàn diànyǐng.

2 丁先生也在中国教英文。
Dīng xiānsheng yě zài Zhōngguó jiāo Yīngwén.

3 我儿子现在都在中国学中文。/现在我儿子都在中国学中文。
Wǒ érzi xiànzài dōu zài Zhōngguó xué Zhōngwén./Xiànzài wǒ érzi dōu zài Zhōngguó xué Zhōngwén.

4 我常去花店为妈妈买花。
Wǒ cháng qù huādiàn wèi māma mǎi huā.

5 他三月去中国，六月从上海去北京。
Tā sānyuè qù Zhōngguó, liùyuè cóng Shànghǎi qù Běijīng.

6 王先生喜欢李小姐不是秘密。
Wáng xiānsheng xǐhuān Lǐ xiǎojiě bú shì mìmì.

7 天气不好的时候，我总是在家看电视。
Tiānqì bù hǎo de shíhòu, wǒ zǒngshì zài jiā kàn diànshì.

8 这个房子，厨房太小，价钱也太贵。
Zhè ge fángzi, chúfáng tài xiǎo, jiàqián yě tài guì.

9 我的朋友不都是中国人，我也有日本朋友。
Wǒde péngyǒu bù dōu shì Zhōngguó rén, wǒ yě yǒu Rìběn péngyǒu.

10 昨天小王借李小姐两本书，今天她只还小王一本。
Zuótiān Xiǎo Wáng jiè Lǐ xiǎojiě liǎng běn shū, jīntiān tā zhǐ huán Xiǎo Wáng yì běn.

2 The eleven types of question in Chinese

1 你有没有女朋友？ (Do you have a girlfriend?)
Nǐ yǒu méiyǒu nǚ péngyǒu?

2 今天会下雨吗？ (Is it going to rain today?)
Jīntiān huì xià yǔ ma?

3 今天你想吃中国菜还是法国菜？ (Do you feel like eating Chinese food or French food today?)
Jīntiān nǐ xiǎng chī Zhōngguó cài háishì Fǎguó cài?

4 你想不想喝一杯咖啡或者茶？ (Would you like a cup of coffee or tea?)
Nǐ xiǎng bù xiǎng hē yì bēi kāfēi huòzhě chá?

5 谁有问题？ (Who has questions?)
Shéi yǒu wèntí?

6 你知(道)不知道李老师的办公室在哪里？ (Do you know where Teacher Li's office is?)
Nǐ zhī(dào) bù zhīdào Lǐ lǎoshī de bàngōngshì zài nǎlǐ?

7 你妹妹呢？ (Where is your sister? *or* What has happened to your sister?)
Nǐ mèimei ne?

8 这本书是你的吧！ (This book must be yours, isn't it?)
Zhè běn shū shì nǐde ba!

9 **(a)** 你高(兴)不高兴?/你高兴吗? (Are you happy?)
   Nǐ gāo(xìng) bù gāoxìng?/Nǐ gāoxìng ma?
   (b) 你不高兴吗？ (Aren't you happy?)
   Nǐ bù gāoxìng ma?

10 你倒了？那这是什么？
Nǐ dǎo le? Nà zhè shì shénme?
(倒 is the verb for 'taking out the trash'. 那 in this situation means 'in this case'.)
(You took out the trash already? Then what is this?)

3 The use of 是, 在 and 有, and the definiteness of nouns

1 我家有五个人，这五个人是我爸妈、我哥哥、我妹妹跟我。
Wǒ jiā yǒu wǔ ge rén, zhè wǔ ge rén shì wǒ bàmā, wǒ gēge, wǒ mèimei gēn wǒ.

2 桌子上面有两本书，一本是我的，一本是我弟弟的。
Zhuōzi shàngmiàn yǒu liǎng běn shū, yì běn shì wǒde, yì běn shì wǒ dìdi de.

3 我男朋友是中国人，他现在在英国。
Wǒ nán péngyǒu shì Zhōngguó rén, tā xiànzài zài Yīngguó.

4 王：你的中文词典在哪里？我借一下，好吗？
Wáng: Nǐde Zhōngwén cídiǎn zài nǎlǐ? Wǒ jiè yíxià, hǎo ma?
张：我没有中文词典。
Zhāng: Wǒ méiyǒu Zhōngwén cídiǎn.

5 王：这辆日本车是你的吗?/这辆日本车是不是你的?
Wáng: Zhè liàng Rìběn chē shì nǐde ma?/Zhè liàng Rìběn chē shì bú shì nǐde?
李：我有两辆车，一辆是美国车，一辆是德国车。我没有日本车。
Lǐ: Wǒ yǒu liǎng liàng chē, yí liàng shì Měiguó chē, yí liàng shì Déguó chē, wǒ méiyǒu Rìběn chē.

6　李：树下有一辆车，是你的吗？
Lǐ: Shù xià yǒu yí liàng chē, shì nǐde ma?
　　张：不是，我的车在车库里。
Zhāng: Bú shì, wǒde chē zài chēkù lǐ.

7　丁：我的中文词典在哪里？王中，在你那里吗？
Dīng: Wǒde Zhōngwén cídiǎn zài nǎlǐ? Wáng Zhōng, zài nǐ nàlǐ ma?
　　王：不在(我这里)，在李明那里。
Wáng: Bú zài (wǒ zhèlǐ), zài Lǐ Míng nàlǐ.

8　王：这里有一台电脑，是谁的？是你的吗?/是不是你的？
Wáng: Zhèlǐ yǒu yì tái diànnǎo, shì shéi de? Shì nǐde ma?/Shì bú shì nǐde?
　　丁：不是，我的电脑在我宿舍里。李明，是不是你的？
Dīng: Bú shì, wǒde diànnǎo zài wǒ sùshè lǐ. Lǐ Míng, shì bú shì nǐde?
　　李：也不是我的，我没有电脑。
Lǐ: Yě bú shì wǒde, wǒ méiyǒu diànnǎo.

9　新学生：请问，厕所在哪里？
Xīn xuéshēng: Qǐng wèn, cèsuǒ zài nǎlǐ?
　　老师：在五楼，这楼没有。
Lǎoshī: Zài wǔ lóu, zhè lóu méiyǒu.
　　新学生：这不是五楼吗？
Xīn xuéshēng: Zhè bú shì wǔ lóu ma?
　　老师：不是，我们现在在四楼。
Lǎoshī: Bú shì, wǒmen xiànzài zài sì lóu.

10　王：这里有两本语法书，哪本是你的？
Wáng: Zhèlǐ yǒu liǎng běn yǔfǎ shū, nǎ běn shì nǐde?
　　李：都不是我的，我没有语法书。
Lǐ: Dōu bú shì wǒde, wǒ méiyǒu yǔfǎ shū.

4 The functions of 的, relative clauses and noun clauses

1　我有很多喜欢听古典音乐的朋友。（1）
Wǒ yǒu hěn duō xǐhuān tīng gǔdiǎn yīnyuè de péngyǒu.

2　这么可爱的小男孩，是你儿子吗？（1）
Zhème kě'ài de xiǎo nánhái, shì nǐ érzi ma?

3　你看，这就是我上星期买的新车。（1）
Nǐ kàn, zhè jiù shì wǒ shàng xīngqī mǎi de xīn chē.

4　这是谁的日本车？是新的还是二手的？（3）
Zhè shì shéide Rìběn chē? Shì xīn de háishì èrshǒu de?

5　今年爸爸送我的生日礼物是一辆新车。（1）
Jīnnián bàba sòng wǒ de shēngrì lǐwù shì yí liàng xīn chē.

6　我听说那家新开的书店有很多从日本来的杂志。（2）
Wǒ tīngshuō nà jiā xīn kāi de shūdiàn yǒu hěn duō cóng Rìběn lái de zázhì.

7　张：昨天我去看了一个很好看的中国电影。（1）
　　Zhāng: Zuótiān wǒ qù kàn le yí ge hěn hǎokàn de Zhōngguó diànyǐng.
　　李：是不是老师上星期给我们介绍的那个？（1）
　　Lǐ: Shì bú shì lǎoshī shàng xīngqī gěi wǒmen jièshào de nà ge?

8　王太太：昨天我儿子在家办了一个非常大的舞会。（1）
　　Wáng tàitai: Zuótiān wǒ érzi zài jiā bàn le yí ge fēicháng dà de wǔhuì.
　　李太太：哦，是吗？来的人多不多？（1）
　　Lǐ tàitai: Ó, shì ma? Lái de rén duō bù duō?
　　王太太：相当多。都是他在学校认识的年轻人。（1）
　　Wáng tàitai: Xiāngdāng duō, dōu shì tā zài xuéxiào rènshì de niánqīng rén.

9　丁：你看，我买了一本王老师写的语法书。（1）
　　Dīng: Nǐ kàn, wǒ mǎi le yì běn Wáng lǎoshī xiě de yǔfǎ shū.
　　李：我也买了一本王老师的书。可是，我买的是他写的一本小说。（3）
　　*Lǐ: Wǒ yě mǎi le yì běn Wáng lǎoshī de shū. Kěshì, wǒ mǎi de shì tā xiě de yì běn
　　xiǎoshuō.*

10　妹妹昨天买的那条裙子颜色不好看。（1）
　　Mèimei zuótiān mǎi de nà tiáo qúnzi yánsè bù hǎokàn.

11　二十一世纪的中国人已经没有"重男轻女"的观念了。（2）
　　Èrshí yī shìjì de Zhōngguó rén yǐjīng méiyǒu 'zhòng nán qīng nǚ' de guānniàn le.

5 Position words

1　咖啡馆跟花店中间有一家银行。
　　Kāfēiguǎn gēn huādiàn zhōngjiān yǒu yì jiā yínháng.

2　这条路上有三个房子，中间那个是我家。
　　Zhè tiáo lù shàng yǒu sān ge fángzi, zhōngjiān nà ge shì wǒ jiā.

3　学生宿舍在图书馆跟书店的中间。
　　Xuéshēng sùshè zài túshūguǎn gēn shūdiàn de zhōngjiān.

4　桌子上有两本书，上面那本是我的。
　　Zhuōzi shàng yǒu liǎng běn shū, shàngmiàn nà běn shì wǒde.

5　(a)　学生宿舍对面有两家咖啡馆。
　　　　Xuéshēng sùshè duìmiàn yǒu liǎng jiā kāfēiguǎn.
　　(b)　我在右边那家工作。
　　　　Wǒ zài yòubiān nà jiā gōngzuò.

6　(a)　我家有三个卧房，两个在二楼。
　　　　Wǒ jiā yǒu sān ge wòfáng, liǎng ge zài èr lóu.
　　(b)　在一楼的那个是我的。
　　　　Zài yī lóu de nà ge shì wǒde.
　　(c)　我的卧房旁边是一个小厨房，厨房中间有一张饭桌。
　　　　*Wǒde wòfáng pángbiān shì yí ge xiǎo chúfáng, chúfáng zhōngjiān yǒu yì zhāng
　　　　fànzhuō.*

7 我家左边是一家花店，右边是一家银行。
Wǒ jiā zuǒbiān shì yì jiā huādiàn, yòubiān shì yì jiā yínháng.

8 图书馆旁边的大楼是学生宿舍。
Túshūguǎn pángbiān de dà lóu shì xuéshēng sùshè.

9 对面那家书店里有一个咖啡馆。
Duìmiàn nà jiā shūdiàn lǐ yǒu yí ge kāfēiguǎn.

10 这家书店里面的咖啡馆也有茶。
Zhè jiā shūdiàn lǐmiàn de kāfēiguǎn yě yǒu chá.

6 Prepositional constructions

I

1 今天晚上我没空，我要在家给我爸妈写信。
Jīntiān wǎnshàng wǒ méi kòng, wǒ yào zài jiā gěi wǒ bàmā xiě xìn.
I am not free this evening. I have to write a letter to my parents at home.

2 从我家走路去图书馆要十五分钟。
Cóng wǒ jiā zǒulù qù túshūguǎn yào shíwǔ fēnzhōng.
Walking to the library from my house takes 15 minutes.

3 彼得常常跟他的中国朋友练习说中文。
Bǐdé chángcháng gēn tāde Zhōngguó péngyǒu liànxí shuō Zhōngwén.
Peter often practises speaking Chinese with his Chinese friends.

4 我男朋友现在在中国学中文，昨天他从北京寄来几张照片。
Wǒ nán péngyǒu xiànzài zài Zhōngguó xué Zhōngwén, zuótiān tā cóng Běijīng jì lái jǐ zhāng zhàopiàn.
My boyfriend is studying Chinese in China right now. Yesterday he sent (by mail) a few photos from Beijing.

5 那个人不是中国人吗？为什么我用中文跟他说话，他不懂呢？
Nà ge rén bú shì Zhōngguó rén ma? Wèishénme wǒ yòng Zhōngwén gēn tā shuō huà, tā bù dǒng ne?
Isn't that person Chinese? Why is it that he does not understand me when I speak with him in Chinese?

6 张：小王，你要去哪里？
Zhāng: Xiǎo Wáng, nǐ yào qù nǎlǐ?
王：去给我女朋友买生日礼物；明天是她的生日。
Wáng: Qù gěi wǒ nǚ péngyǒu mǎi shēngrì lǐwù; míngtiān shì tāde shēngrì.
Zhang: Xiao Wang, where are you going?
Wang: I am going to buy a birthday present for my girlfriend. Tomorrow is her birthday.

7 我来中国以后，每天都用筷子吃饭，现在我已经习惯了。
   Wǒ lái Zhōngguó yǐhòu, měi tiān dōu yòng kuàizi chī fàn, xiànzài wǒ yǐjīng xíguàn le.
   Since I came to China, I have been eating with chopsticks every day. Now I am already used to it.

8 我们从王老师那里学到很多有用的知识。
   Wǒmen cóng Wáng lǎoshī nàlǐ xuédào hěn duō yǒuyòng de zhīshì.
   We learned a great deal of useful knowledge from Teacher Wang.

9 小王上课的时候常常用手机给他的朋友发短信。
   Xiǎo Wáng shàng kè de shíhòu chángcháng yòng shǒujī gěi tāde péngyǒu fā duǎnxìn.
   Xiao Wang often sends text messages to his friends by mobile phone during class time.

10 上午我男朋友给我打电话，请我跟他去公园玩，可是我告诉他，今天天气不好，我想在家看电视。
   Shàngwǔ wǒ nán péngyǒu gěi wǒ dǎ diànhuà, qǐng wǒ gēn tā qù gōngyuán wán, kěshì wǒ gàosù tā, jīntiān tiānqì bù hǎo, wǒ xiǎng zài jiā kàn diànshì.
   My boyfriend called me in the morning and asked me go to the park with him, but I told him that since today's weather was not good, I wanted to watch TV at home.

11 我在法国学中文，所以没有中国人跟我练习说中文。昨天我的中文老师说，她下星期会给我介绍一个中国朋友，以后我可以常常用中文说话。
   Wǒ zài Fǎguó xué Zhōngwén, suǒyǐ méiyǒu Zhōngguó rén gēn wǒ liànxí shuō Zhōngwén. Zuótiān wǒde Zhōngwén lǎoshī shuō, tā xià xīngqī huì gěi wǒ jièshào yí ge Zhōngguó péngyǒu, yǐhòu wǒ kěyǐ chángcháng yòng Zhōngwén shuōhuà.
   I am studying Chinese in France, so there are no Chinese people to practise speaking Chinese with me. Yesterday my Chinese teacher said that she would introduce a Chinese friend to me; in the future, I can often speak in Chinese.

12 李明在咖啡馆工作。他每天下课以后，就从教室走路去咖啡馆工作。
   Lǐ Míng zài kāfēiguǎn gōngzuò. Tā měi tiān xià kè yǐhòu, jiù cóng jiàoshì zǒulù qù kāfēiguǎn gōngzuò.
   Li Ming works at a coffee shop. Every day after class, he walks from the classroom to the coffee shop to work.

II

1 外地人：请问火车站在哪里？
   Wàidì rén: Qǐng wèn, huǒchē zhàn zài nǎlǐ?
   本地人：你往前走，差不多五分钟就到了。
   Běndì rén: Nǐ wǎng qián zǒu, chàbùduō wǔ fēnzhōng jiù dào le.
   Visitor: Excuse me, where is the train station?
   Local person: Go straight ahead, and you will be there in about five minutes.

2 我对学习外语非常有兴趣，所以我会说日文跟法文。
   Wǒ duì xuéxí wàiyǔ fēicháng yǒu xìngqù, suǒyǐ wǒ huì shuō Rìwén gēn Fǎwén.
   I am extremely interested in studying foreign languages, so I can speak Japanese and French.

3 他靠亲戚朋友借他的钱念完了大学。

Tā kào qīnqī péngyǒu jiè tā de qián niàn wán le dàxué.

He relied on money his relatives and friends had loaned him to finish his college education.

4 我为他做了这么多事，他居然也没有说一声"谢谢"，真气人！

Wǒ wèi tā zuò le zhème duō shì, tā jūrán yě méiyǒu shuō yì shēng 'xièxie', zhēn qìrén.

I did so much for him, and, to my surprise, he didn't even say 'thank you'. This is really upsetting.

5 老王很不诚实，他对我说的话，我完全不相信。

Lǎo Wáng hěn bù chéngshí, tā duì wǒ shuō de huà, wǒ wánquán bù xiāngxìn.

Lao Wang is dishonest. I completely don't believe anything he says to me.

6 为了赚一些零用钱，我去一家中国餐馆当服务员。

Wèile zhuàn yìxiē língyòngqián, wǒ qù yì jiā Zhōngguó cānguǎn dāng fúwùyuán.

In order to earn some pocket money, I went to a Chinese restaurant to work as a waiter.

7 关于你上次开会提出的问题，我们已经想到了一个解决的办法。

Guānyú nǐ shàng cì kāi huì tíchū de wèntí, wǒmen yǐjīng xiǎngdào le yí ge jiějué de bànfǎ.

Regarding the problem you brought up at the last meeting, we have come up with a solution.

8 那位作家根据他自己亲身的经历写了一篇很有名的短篇小说。

Nà wèi zuòjiā gēnjù tā zìjǐ qīnshēn de jīnglì xiě le yì piān hěn yǒumíng de duǎnpiān xiǎoshuō.

That author wrote a famous short story based on his personal experiences.

7 Imperative sentences and the use of 别

1 这件事虽然不是秘密，但是请你别告诉任何人。

Zhè jiàn shì suīrán bú shì mìmì, dànshì qǐng nǐ bié gàosù rènhé rén.

2 王：我要告诉你一个秘密，但是请你别告诉小张。

Wáng: Wǒ yào gàosù nǐ yí ge mìmì, dànshì qǐng nǐ bié gàosù Xiǎo Zhāng.

李：好，我不告诉他，请快告诉我这个秘密。

Lǐ: Hǎo, wǒ bú gàosù tā, qǐng kuài gàosù wǒ zhè ge mìmì.

3 老师：彼得，这是中文课，不可以说英文。

Lǎoshī: Bǐdé, zhè shì Zhōngwén kè, bù kěyǐ shuō Yīngwén.

彼得：安娜，老师说什么？

Bǐdé: Ānnà, lǎoshī shuō shénme?

安娜：他叫你别说英文。

Ānnà: Tā jiào nǐ bié shuō Yīngwén.

4 妈妈：我叫你别跟小王交朋友，你为什么不听？
Māma: Wǒ jiào nǐ bié gēn Xiǎo Wáng jiāo péngyǒu, nǐ wèishénme bù tīng?
儿子：你别管我跟谁交朋友。
Érzi: Nǐ bié guǎn wǒ gēn shéi jiāo péngyǒu.
妈妈：我是你妈妈，我不管你，谁管你？
Māma: Wǒ shì nǐ māma, wǒ bù guǎn nǐ, shéi guǎn nǐ?

5 王先生：奇怪，汽车怎么发动不了了？别是坏了。
Wáng xiānsheng: Qíguài, qìchē zěnme fādòng bù liǎo le? Bié shì huài le.
王太太：我看不是坏了，是没油了。
Wáng tàitai: Wǒ kàn bú shì huài le, shì méi yóu le.

6 女儿：希望明天别下雨，如果下雨，我跟小王就不能去野餐了。
Nǚ'ér: Xīwàng míngtiān bié xià yǔ, rúguǒ xià yǔ, wǒ gēn Xiǎo Wáng jiù bù néng qù yěcān le.
妈妈：不管明天下不下雨，我都不希望你跟小王出去。
Māma: Bùguǎn míngtiān xià bú xià yǔ, wǒ dōu bù xīwàng nǐ gēn Xiǎo Wáng chū qù.
女儿：我已经不是小孩了，我希望你别管我的事。
Nǚ'ér: Wǒ yǐjīng bú shì xiǎohái le, wǒ xīwàng nǐ bié guǎn wǒde shì.

7 王：下班以后，我们一起去啤酒馆喝啤酒，好不好？
Wáng: Xià bān yǐhòu, wǒmen yìqǐ qù píjiǔguǎn hē píjiǔ, hǎo bù hǎo?
李：医生叫我别喝酒，我不去。
Lǐ: Yīshēng jiào wǒ bié hē jiǔ, wǒ bú qù.
丁：我太太不让我喝酒，我也不去。
Dīng: Wǒ tàitai bú ràng wǒ hē jiǔ, wǒ yě bú qù.
王：别告诉你太太，我也不告诉她。你跟我去，好吗？
Wáng: Bié gàosù nǐ tàitai, wǒ yě bú gàosù tā. Nǐ gēn wǒ qù, hǎo ma?

8 The progressive aspect and the continuous aspect

1 王：那些人在做什么？
Wáng: Nà xiē rén zài zuò shénme?
李：他们在等公共汽车(呢)。
Lǐ: Tāmen zài děng gōnggòng qìchē (ne).

2 李：王中，对不起这时候给你打电话，你在睡觉吗？
Lǐ: Wáng Zhōng, duìbùqǐ zhè shíhòu gěi nǐ dǎ diànhuà, nǐ zài shuìjiào ma?
王：没关系，我没有在睡觉，我在写功课呢。你也在写功课吗？
Wáng: Méi guānxi, wǒ méiyǒu zài shuìjiào, wǒ zài xiě gōngkè ne. Nǐ yě zài xiě gōngkè ma?
李：没有，我在看电视(呢)。
Lǐ: Méiyǒu, wǒ zài kàn diànshì (ne).

3 王：你(现在)在看电视吗？
Wáng: Nǐ (xiànzài) zài kàn diànshì ma?
李：没有，我在上网(呢)。
Lǐ: Méiyǒu, wǒ zài shàngwǎng (ne).
王：快开电视。王老师在唱歌呢。
Wáng: Kuài kāi diànshì. Wáng lǎoshī zài chàng gē ne.

4 我到家的时候，电视开着，可是家里的人都在睡觉，没有人在看电视。
Wǒ dào jiā de shíhòu, diànshì kāi zhe, kěshì jiā lǐ de rén dōu zài shuìjiào, méiyǒu rén zài kàn diànshì.

5 每天我回到家的时候，我妈妈总是在做晚饭。我爸爸有时候在看报，有时候在看电视。
Měi tiān wǒ huí dào jiā de shíhòu, wǒ māma zǒngshì zài zuò wǎnfàn. Wǒ bàba yǒu shíhòu zài kàn bào, yǒu shíhòu zài kàn diànshì.

6 张：那里为什么有这么多人？他们在做什么？
Zhāng: Nàlǐ wèishénme yǒu zhème duō rén? Tāmen zài zuò shénme?
李：他们都在等着买电影票(呢)。
Lǐ: Tāmen dōu zài děng zhe mǎi diànyǐng piào (ne).

7 老师指着墙上的照片说："现在请你们看着这些照片回答我的问题。"
Lǎoshī zhǐ zhe qiáng shàng de zhàopiàn shuō: 'Xiànzài qǐng nǐmen kàn zhe zhè xiē zhàopiàn huídá wǒde wèntí'.

8 王：你在看报吗？有什么大新闻？
Wáng: Nǐ zài kàn bào ma? Yǒu shénme dà xīnwén?
李：我不知道。我不是在看新闻，我在找工作(呢)。
Lǐ: Wǒ bù zhīdào. Wǒ bú shì zài kàn xīnwén, wǒ zài zhǎo gōngzuò (ne).
王：你在找工作吗？长城中国餐馆正在找服务员呢。
Wáng: Nǐ zài zhǎo gōngzuò ma? Chángchéng Zhōngguó cānguǎn zhèng zài zhǎo fúwùyuán ne.
李：我知道，可是他们在找有经验的人。
Lǐ: Wǒ zhīdào, kěshì tāmen zài zhǎo yǒu jīngyàn de rén.

9 经理：所有员工请来我的办公室。
Jīnglǐ: Suǒyǒu yuángōng qǐng lái wǒde bàngōngshì.
王先生：经理，有些人在开会(呢)。
Wáng xiānsheng: Jīnglǐ, yǒuxiē rén zài kāihuì (ne).
经理：没在开会的人，请立刻来我的办公室。
Jīnglǐ: Méi zài kāihuì de rén, qǐng lìkè lái wǒde bàngōngshì.

10 我正要进电梯的时候，看到电梯里的四个人都在打(or 讲)电话。所以我决定等下一班电梯。
Wǒ zhèng yào jìn diàntī de shíhòu, kàndào diàntī lǐ de sì ge rén dōu zài dǎ (or jiǎng) diànhuà. Suǒyǐ wǒ juédìng děng xià yì bān diàntī.

9 The use of 了 (the perfective aspect particle and modal particle)

1 **(a)** *Zuótiān Wáng xiānsheng qǐng wǒ chī fàn.*

2 **(c)** *Yǐqián wǒ cháng hē kāfēi, měi tiān dōu hē liǎng, sān bēi.*

3 **(a)** *Lǎoshī yào wǒmen kàn de nà xiē shū, nǐ kàn le ma?*

4 **(a)** *Zhè cì kǎoshì, nǐ wèishénme kǎo de zhème chà, nǐ zhǔnbèi méiyǒu?*

5 (b) *Zuótiān wǎnshàng wǒ méiyǒu shuìjiào, yīnwèi wǒ zhěng ge wǎnshàng dōu zài xiě gōngkè.*

6 (b) *Zhāng xiānsheng mǎi le chē jiù dài tā nǚ péngyǒu qù dōufēng le.*

7 (b) *Wǒmen míngtiān xià le kè yìqǐ qù kàn diànyǐng, hǎo bù hǎo?*

8 (c) *Ānnà měi tiān chī le wǔfàn jiù qù túshūguǎn xuéxí.*

9 (b) *Wǒ xià ge yuè jiù yào qù Běijīng xué Zhōngwén le.*

10 The use of 过 (the experiential aspect particle)

1 那本书我已经看过(or 了)两遍了，我不想再看了。
Nà běn shū wǒ yǐjīng kàn guo (or le) liǎng biàn le, wǒ bù xiǎng zài kàn le.

2 王：你以前用过筷子吗？
Wáng: Nǐ yǐqián yòng guo kuàizi ma?
李：我没用过。
Lǐ: Wǒ méi yòng guo.

3 老师：你用 ∅ 毛笔写过字吗？
Lǎoshī: Nǐ yòng máobǐ xiě guo zì ma?
学生：没有 ∅。
Xuéshēng: Méiyǒu.

4 他们来 ∅ 北京一个多星期了，参观过(or 了)很多地方。
Tāmen lái Běijīng yí ge duō xīngqī le, cānguān guo (or le) hěn duō dìfāng.

5 我十岁的时候，去过英国，在那里住过(or 了)三个月 ∅。
Wǒ shí suì de shíhòu, qù guo Yīngguó, zài nàlǐ zhù guo (or le) sān ge yuè.

6 昨天我去 ∅ 医院看医生的时候，医生说，我得了肺炎。他问我以前得过肺炎没有，我告诉 ∅ 他，我小时候也得过一次。
Zuótiān wǒ qù yīyuàn kàn yīshēng de shíhòu, yīshēng shuō, wǒ dé le fèiyán. Tā wèn wǒ yǐqián dé guo fèiyán méiyǒu, wǒ gàosù tā, wǒ xiǎo shíhòu yě dé guo yí cì.

7 妈妈：今天的功课，你写了没有？
Māma: Jīntiān de gōngkè, nǐ xiě le méiyǒu?
儿子：我写了，可是弟弟没有写 ∅。
Érzi: Wǒ xiě le, kěshì dìdi méiyǒu xiě.

8 昨天我在王先生家吃 ∅ 饭的时候，用了一下儿筷子。用 ∅ 筷子吃 ∅ 饭真有意思，我从来没有用 ∅ 筷子吃过饭。
Zuótiān wǒ zài Wáng xiānsheng jiā chī fàn de shíhòu, yòng le yí xiàr kuàizi. Yòng kuàizi chī fàn zhēn yǒu yìsi. Wǒ cónglái méiyǒu yòng kuàizi chī guo fàn.

9 我小时候身体不好，得过两次肺炎。上中学的时候，没有得过大病；可是上个月我
又得了一次肺炎，到现在还没有好 ∅。
*Wǒ xiǎo shíhòu shēntǐ bù hǎo, dé guo liǎng cì fèiyán. Shàng zhōngxué de shíhòu,
méiyǒu dé guo dà bìng; kěshì shàng ge yuè wǒ yòu dé le yí cì fèiyán, dào xiànzài
hái méiyǒu hǎo.*

10 客人：你爸爸去哪里了？
Kèrén: Nǐ bàba qù nǎlǐ le?
男孩：他去日本了。
Nánhái: Tā qù Rìběn le.
客人：他以前去过日本吗？
Kèrén: Tā yǐqián qù guo Rìběn ma?
男孩：没有 ∅。但是他去过很多别的国家。
Nánhái: Méiyǒu. Dànshì tā qù guo hěn duō biéde guójiā.

11 王：我没有来过你们学校，请你带我参观一下儿，好不好？
*Wáng: Wǒ méiyǒu lái guo nǐmen xuéxiào. Qǐng nǐ dài wǒ cānguān yíxiàr, hǎo bù
hǎo?*
张：我们等一下儿吧。李先生也没有来过，可是他现在还没来 ∅，他来了我就带
你们一起参观。
*Zhāng: Wǒmen děng yíxiàr ba. Lǐ xiānsheng yě méiyǒu lái guo, kěshì tā xiànzài hái
méi lái, tā lái le wǒ jiù dài nǐmen yìqǐ cānguān.*

11 Auxiliary verbs

1 丁：图书馆里不可以吸烟。
Dīng: Túshūguǎn lǐ bù kěyǐ xī yān.
张：好，我不吸烟。可(以)不可以喝水呢？
Zhāng: Hǎo, wǒ bù xī yān. Kě(yǐ) bù kěyǐ hē shuǐ ne?
丁：我想应该可以喝水。
Dīng: Wǒ xiǎng yīnggāi kěyǐ hē shuǐ.
Ding: Smoking is not allowed in the library.
Zhang: OK, I won't smoke. Is drinking water allowed?
Ding: I think you should be able to drink water.

2 张：今天下午，我和小李要去河边玩，你想不想一起去？
Zhāng: Jīntiān xiàwǔ, wǒ hé Xiǎo Lǐ yào qù hé biān wán, nǐ xiǎng bù xiǎng yìqǐ qù?
王：我很想去，可是我想我不能去，因为我妈妈说，我还不会游泳，所以不可以去
河边玩。
*Wáng: Wǒ hěn xiǎng qù, kěshì wǒ xiǎng wǒ bù néng qù, yīnwèi wǒ māma shuō,
wǒ hái bú huì yóuyǒng, suǒyǐ bù kěyǐ qù hébiān wán.*
Zhang: Xiǎo Lǐ and I are going to have some fun by the river this afternoon. Would
you like to go with us?
Wang: I would like to go very much, but I don't think I can go because my mother
says that I don't know how to swim yet, and therefore I am not allowed to go to the
riverside to have fun.

3 李: 小王，你妹妹真漂亮，你可(以)不可以给我们介绍一下？
Lǐ: Xiǎo Wáng, nǐ mèimei zhēn piàoliàng, nǐ kě(yǐ) bù kěyǐ gěi wǒmen jièshào yíxià?
王: 你想认识我妹妹吗？没问题，我给你们介绍。可是，我妹妹不会说中文，
你只能跟她说英文。
Wáng: Nǐ xiǎng rènshì wǒ mèimei ma? Méi wèntí, wǒ gěi nǐmen jièshào. Kěshì, wǒ mèimei bú huì shuō Zhōngwén, nǐ zhǐ néng gēn tā shuō Yīngwén.
Li: Xiao Wang, your younger sister is really pretty. Can you introduce us?
Wang: You would like to know my sister? No problem, I will introduce you. But my younger sister does not know how to speak Chinese. You can only speak English with her.

4 王: 老师今天问的那个问题，你会不会回答？
Wáng: Lǎoshī jīntiān wèn de nà ge wèntí, nǐ huì bú huì huídá?
李: 那个问题很容易，我会回答。
Lǐ: Nà ge wèntí hěn róngyì, wǒ huì huídá.
Wang: Did you know how to answer the question that the teacher asked today?
Li: That question was easy. I knew how to answer it.

5 张: 我家有咖啡，也有矿泉水，你想喝哪个？
Zhāng: Wǒ jiā yǒu kāfēi, yě yǒu kuàngquán shuǐ, nǐ xiǎng hē nǎ ge?
丁: 我想喝酒，有没有啤酒？
Dīng: Wǒ xiǎng hē jiǔ, yǒu méiyǒu píjiǔ?
张: 医生说，你身体不好，不该喝酒。你忘了吗？
Zhāng: Yīshēng shuō, nǐ shēntǐ bù hǎo, bù gāi hē jiǔ. Nǐ wàng le ma?
Zhang: There is coffee at my house, and there is also mineral water. Which would you like to drink?
Ding: I feel like drinking alcohol. Is there any beer?
Zhang: The doctor said you are not healthy and you should not drink alcohol. Have you forgotten?

6 丁: 桌上有咖啡，你要不要喝杯咖啡？
Dīng: Zhuō shàng yǒu kāfēi, nǐ yào bú yào hē bēi kāfēi?
王: 有没有牛奶？我不想喝没有牛奶的咖啡。
Wáng: Yǒu méiyǒu niúnǎi? Wǒ bù xiǎng hē méiyǒu niúnǎi de kāfēi.
丁: 应该有。你去厨房找一找。
Dīng: Yīnggāi yǒu. Nǐ qù chúfáng zhǎo yì zhǎo.
Ding: There is coffee on the table. Do you want to have a cup of coffee?
Wang: Is there milk? I don't feel like having coffee without milk.
Ding: There should be some. Go to the kitchen to look.

7 丁: 你知道不知道王老师在哪里？
Dīng: Nǐ zhīdào bù zhīdào Wáng lǎoshī zài nǎlǐ?
李: 现在两点半，我想他现在应该在教室里教书。
Lǐ: Xiànzài liǎng diǎn bàn, wǒ xiǎng tā xiànzài yīnggāi zài jiàoshì lǐ jiāoshū.
丁: 我想问他一个问题；你想，我可(以)不可以现在进教室问他？
Dīng: Wǒ xiǎng wèn tā yí ge wèntí; nǐ xiǎng, wǒ kě(yǐ) bù kěyǐ xiànzài jìn jiàoshì wèn tā?
李: 我想，别人正在上课的时候，我们不应当进他们的教室。
Lǐ: Wǒ xiǎng, biérén zhèng zài shàngkè de shíhòu, wǒmen bù yīngdāng jìn tāmen de jiàoshì.

Ding: Do you know where Teacher Wang is?

Li: It's 2:30 now. I think he should be teaching in the classroom now.

Ding: I would like to ask him a question. Do you think I can enter the classroom to ask him?

Li: I think that we should not enter other people's classroom when they are having a class.

8 张：朋友请我跟他们一起去游泳的时候，我总是<u>不能</u>去，因为我<u>不会</u>游泳。我真想学，你<u>可(以)不可以</u>教我？

   Zhāng: Péngyǒu qǐng wǒ gēn tāmen yìqǐ qù yóuyǒng de shíhòu, wǒ zǒngshì bù néng qù, yīnwèi wǒ bú huì yóuyǒng. Wǒ zhēn xiǎng xué, nǐ kě(yǐ) bù kěyǐ jiāo wǒ?

   王：对不起，我很愿意教你，可是我<u>不能</u>教你，因为我太忙了。小丁，你<u>能不能</u>教小张？

   Wáng: Duìbùqǐ, wǒ hěn yuànyì jiāo nǐ, kěshì wǒ bù néng jiāo nǐ, yīnwèi wǒ tài máng le. Xiǎo Dīng, nǐ néng bù néng jiāo Xiǎo Zhāng?

   丁：我也<u>不能</u>教他，因为我也<u>不会</u>游泳。

   Dīng: Wǒ yě bù néng jiāo tā, yīnwèi wǒ yě bú huì yóuyǒng.

   Zhang: When my friends ask me to go swimming with them, I never can go because I don't know how to swim. I really would like to learn. Can you teach me?

   Wang: Sorry, I am willing to teach you but I can't because I am too busy. Xiao Ding, can you teach Xiao Zhang?

   Ding: I can't teach him either, because I also don't know how to swim.

9 张：老王很<u>会</u>作菜，他作的法国菜特别好吃。

   Zhāng: Lǎo Wáng hěn huì zuò cài, tā zuò de Fǎguó cài tèbié hǎochī.

   李：那我<u>应该</u>请他教我作几道他的拿手菜，因为我正想学作菜呢。

   Lǐ: Nà wǒ yīnggāi qǐng tā jiāo wǒ zuò jǐ dào tāde náshǒu cài, yīnwèi wǒ zhèng xiǎng xué zuò cài ne.

   Zhang: Lao Wang is good at cooking. The French food he makes is particularly delicious.

   Li: Then I should ask him to teach me how to make some of his special dishes because I am just thinking about learning how to cook.

10 奇怪！车怎么<u>不能</u>动了？该不是坏了吧！

   Qíguài, chē zěnme bù néng dòng le, gāi bú shì huài le ba!

   Strange! How come the car can't move? Could it be that it's broken down?

12 The complement of state and the complement of degree

1 我昨天晚上睡得不好，所以今天早上起得很晚。

   Wǒ zuótiān wǎnshàng shuì de bù hǎo, suǒyǐ jīntiān zǎoshàng qǐ de hěn wǎn.

2 王中学习得很努力，所以，老师的问题，他总是回答得很对。

   Wáng Zhōng xuéxí de hěn nǔlì, suǒyǐ, lǎoshī de wèntí, tā zǒngshì huídá de hěn duì.

3 安娜跟王中跳舞都跳得不错，可是我跳得更好。

   Ānnà gēn Wáng Zhōng tiàowǔ dōu tiào de bú cuò, kěshì wǒ tiào de gèng hǎo.

4　李太太：听说你的两个孩子都在学作菜。谁的菜作得好？
Lǐ tàitai: Tīngshuō nǐde liǎng ge háizi dōu zài xué zuò cài, shéi de cài zuò de hǎo?
　　王太太：法国菜，儿子作得好；中国菜，女儿作得好。
Wáng tàitai: Fǎguó cài, érzi zuò de hǎo; Zhōngguó cài, nǚ'ér zuò de hǎo.

5　我弟弟跑得不快，可是他游泳游得很快。
Wǒ dìdi pǎo de bú kuài, kěshì tā yóuyǒng yóu de hěn kuài.

6　王：李明告诉我，你英文说得很流利。你教我说英文，好不好？
Wáng: Lǐ Míng gàosù wǒ, nǐ Yīngwén shuō de hěn liúlì. Nǐ jiāo wǒ shuō Yīngwén, hǎo bù hǎo?
　　丁：其实我的英文说得很差。你应该去请一个说得好的人教你。
Dīng: Qíshí wǒde Yīngwén shuō de hěn chà. Nǐ yīnggāi qù qǐng yí ge shuō de hǎo de rén jiāo nǐ.

7　李太太：我儿子中文学得怎么样？
Lǐ tàitai: Wǒ érzi Zhōngwén xué de zěnmeyàng?
　　老师：他学习得很认真，所以他的字写得很漂亮，他语法也学得很好，不过日常会话，他还说得不流利。
Lǎoshī: Tā xuéxí de hěn rènzhēn, suǒyǐ tāde zì xiě de hěn piàoliàng, tā yǔfǎ yě xué de hěn hǎo, búguò rìcháng huìhuà, tā hái shuō de bù liúlì.

8　妈妈：你吃得太多了，别吃了，爸爸还没有吃呢!
Māma: Nǐ chī de tài duō le, bié chī le, bàba hái méiyǒu chī ne!
　　儿子：我饿得要命(or 我饿死了)，你今天菜作得太少了。
Érzi: Wǒ è de yàomìng (or Wǒ è sǐ le), nǐ jīntiān cài zuò de tài shǎo le.

9　他开车总是开得太快，他妈妈叫他别开得太快，他很不高兴。
Tā kāichē zǒngshì kāi de tài kuài, tā māma jiào tā bié kāi de tài kuài, tā hěn bù gāoxìng.

10　今天的考试，他准备得很好，所以考得非常好。
Jīntiān de kǎoshì, tā zhǔnbèi de hěn hǎo, suǒyǐ kǎo de fēicháng hǎo.

13 The complement of duration

1　丁：你以前在北京住了(or 过)几个月？
Dīng: Nǐ yǐqián zài Běijīng zhù le (or guo) jǐ ge yuè?
　　李：我没有在北京住过。可是我在上海住了八个月了。
Lǐ: Wǒ méiyǒu zài Běijīng zhù guo. Kěshì wǒ zài Shànghǎi zhù le bā ge yuè le.

2　王：我上大学的时候，学过(or 了)四年半(的)中文。
Wáng: Wǒ shàng dàxué de shíhòu, xué guo (or le) sì nián bàn (de) Zhōngwén.
　　丁：真的吗？你上了几年大学？
Dīng: Zhēn de ma? Nǐ shàng le jǐ nián dàxué?
　　王：我一共上了五年。
Wáng: Wǒ yígòng shàng le wǔ nián.

3 王：这个问题，我想了五个小时了，还是不会回答。
Wáng: Zhè ge wèntí, wǒ xiǎng le wǔ ge xiǎoshí le, háishì bú huì huídá.
李：真的吗？我只想了五分钟就知道答案了。
Lǐ: Zhēn de ma? Wǒ zhǐ xiǎng le wǔ fēnzhōng jiù zhīdào dá'àn le.

4 妈妈：你看了快四小时(的)电视了，别看了。
Māma: Nǐ kàn le kuài sì xiǎoshí (de) diànshì le, bié kàn le.
儿子：我写了一下午(的)功课，请让我再看半小时。
Érzi: Wǒ xiě le yí xiàwǔ (de) gōngkè, qǐng ràng wǒ zài kàn bàn xiǎoshí.

5 中国人：你中国话说得真好。你来中国多长时间了？
Zhōngguó rén: Nǐ Zhōngguó huà shuō de zhēn hǎo. Nǐ lái Zhōngguó duō cháng shíjiān le?
外国人：哪里。我来中国五个月了。来中国以前，我学了(or 过)两年(的)中文。
Wàiguó rén: Nǎlǐ. Wǒ lái Zhōngguó wǔ ge yuè le. Lái Zhōngguó yǐqián, wǒ xué le (or guo) liǎng nián (de) Zhōngwén.

6 李：从这里去学校要坐多久(的)公共汽车？
Lǐ: Cóng zhèlǐ qù xuéxiào yào zuò duō jiǔ (de) gōnggòng qìchē?
王：我不知道，我总是骑自行车去学校，我每天都要骑二十分钟。
Wáng: Wǒ bù zhīdào, wǒ zǒngshì qí zìxíngchē qù xuéxiào. Wǒ měi tiān dōu yào qí èrshí fēnzhōng.

7 张：听说你学了很多年(的)外语，是真的吗？
Zhāng: Tīngshuō nǐ xué le hěn duō nián (de) wàiyǔ, shì zhēn de ma?
李：是真的。我学过法文、日文跟西班牙文。法文，我学了十年，日文我学了五年了，西班牙文，也学了三年了。
Lǐ: Shì zhēn de. Wǒ xué guo Fǎwén, Rìwén gēn Xībānyáwén. Fǎwén, wǒ xué le shí nián, Rìwén, wǒ xué le wǔ nián le, Xībānyáwén, yě xué le sān nián le.

8 小王跟他的女朋友认识三年了。最近他们常常吵架，他女朋友已经三个星期没有跟他说话了。
Xiǎo Wáng gēn tāde nǚ péngyǒu rènshì sān nián le. Zuìjìn tāmen chángcháng chǎojià, tā nǚ péngyǒu yǐjīng sān ge xīngqī méiyǒu gēn tā shuō huà le.

9 三个月没有下雨了，这星期居然开始下了。可是一下就下了三天。
Sān ge yuè méiyǒu xià yǔ le, zhè xīngqī jūrán kāishǐ xià le. Kěshì yí xià jiù xià le sān tiān.

14 The complement of quantity

1 王：你看过几遍《老人与海》？ (or《老人与海》你看过几遍?)
Wáng: Nǐ kàn guo jǐ biàn 'Lǎorén Yǔ Hǎi'?
李：英文的，我看过两遍；中文的，我也看过一遍。
Lǐ: Yīngwén de, wǒ kàn guo liǎng biàn; Zhōngwén de, wǒ yě kàn guo yí biàn.

2 丁：你看过《卧虎藏龙》吗？
Dīng: Nǐ kàn guo 'Wò Hǔ Cáng Lóng' ma?
李：在电视上看过两次，可是每次都没有看完。 (Do not say 在电视上看过两遍 in this case.)
Lǐ: Zài diànshì shàng kàn guo liǎng cì, kěshì měi cì dōu méiyǒu kàn wán.

3 昨天我去了他家两趟(or 我去了两趟他家)，可是每次他都不在。今天我要再去一趟。
Zuótiān wǒ qù le tā jiā liǎng tàng, kěshì měi cì tā dōu bú zài. Jīntiān wǒ yào zài qù yí tàng.

4 王明上课的时候在睡觉。老师叫了他两声，他都没听见。我踢了他两脚(or 两下)，他才醒过来。
Wáng Míng shàng kè de shíhòu zài shuìjiào, lǎoshī jiào le tā liǎng shēng, tā dōu méi tīngjiàn. Wǒ tī le tā liǎng jiǎo (or liǎng xià), tā cái xǐng guòlái.

5 昨天我不舒服，上了五、六次厕所。 (Do not say 我上了厕所五、六次.)
Zuótiān wǒ bù shūfú, shàng le wǔ, liù cì cèsuǒ.

6 上个月我病了两次，去医院看了五次医生。
Shàng ge yuè, wǒ bìng le liǎng cì, qù yīyuàn kàn le wǔ cì yīshēng.

7 我们请老师再唱一遍那首歌，他点了一下头，喝了两口水，就开始唱了。
Wǒmen qǐng lǎoshī zài chàng yí biàn nà shǒu gē, tā diǎn le yí xià tóu, hē le liǎng kǒu shuǐ, jiù kāishǐ chàng le.

8 我帮过张小姐很多次(忙)，可是她只谢过我一次。
Wǒ bāng guo Zhāng xiǎojiě hěn duō cì (máng), kěshì tā zhǐ xiè guo wǒ yí cì.

9 王先生跟王太太结婚才半年，可是已经吵过十次架。(Do not say 吵过架十次.)
Wāng xiānsheng gēn Wáng tàitai jiéhūn cái bàn nián, kěshì yǐjīng chǎo guo shí cì jià.

10 他骗过我几次，可是我决定再相信他一次。
Tā piàn guo wǒ jǐ cì, kěshì wǒ juédìng zài xiāngxìn tā yí cì.

11 那个小贩骗过好几次观光客，所以警察也抓过他好几次。
Nà ge xiǎofàn piàn guo hǎo jǐ cì guānguāngkè, suǒyǐ jǐngchá yě zhuā guo tā hǎo jǐ cì.

12 李先生离过两次婚，我不懂他为什么打算再结一次(婚)？ (Do not say 离过婚两次 or 再结婚一次.)
Lǐ xiānsheng lí guo liǎng cì hūn, wǒ bù dǒng tā wèishénme dǎsuàn zài jié yí cì (hūn)?

15 The complement of direction

I

1 安娜： 你的男朋友在对面叫你，你为什么不过去呢？
Ānnà: Nǐ de nán péngyǒu zài duìmiàn jiào nǐ, nǐ wèishénme bú guò qù ne?
小兰： 他是男的，应该他过来。
Xiǎolán: Tā shì nán de, yīnggāi tā guò lái.
安娜： 要是你不过去，他也不过来，你们就不能谈话了。
Ānnà: Yàoshì nǐ bú guò qù, tā yě bú guò lái, nǐmen jiù bù néng tánhuà le.
Anna: Your boyfriend is calling you from across the street. Why don't you go across the street?
Xiaolan: He is a man; he should come over.
Anna: If you don't go over and he doesn't come over, either, you two won't be able to talk.

2 你看，他们都在山上，我们也上去吧！
Nǐ kàn, tāmen dōu zài shān shàng, wǒmen yě shàng qù ba!
Look, they are all up on the mountain. Let's go up, too.

3 (妈妈给小明打电话。 *Māma gěi Xiǎomíng dǎ diànhuà.*)
妈妈：小明，大家都在家里等你一起吃饭，你为什么还不回来呢？
Māma: Xiǎomíng, dàjiā dōu zài jiā lǐ děng nǐ yìqǐ chī fàn, nǐ wèishénme hái bù huí lái ne?
(Xiaoming's mother calls him on the telephone.)
Mother: Xiaoming, everybody is waiting for you at home to eat dinner together. Why haven't you come back?

4 上星期我的好朋友李中从上海寄来了一封信，他在信上问我什么时候可以到那里去看他。
Shàng xīngqī wǒde hǎo péngyǒu Lǐ Zhōng cóng Shànghǎi jì lái le yì fēng xìn, tā zài xìn shàng wèn wǒ shénme shíhòu kěyǐ dào nàlǐ qù kàn ta.
Last week, my good friend Li Zhong sent me a letter from Shanghai. In the letter, he asked me when I could go there to visit him.

5 我听说你喜欢吃法国点心，所以我去店里给你买来了一些，都在厨房里，你去吃吧！
Wǒ tīngshuō nǐ xǐhuān chī Fǎguó diǎnxīn, suǒyǐ wǒ qù diàn lǐ gěi nǐ mǎi lái le yì xiē, dōu zài chúfáng lǐ, nǐ qù chī ba!
I heard that you like to eat French pastries, so I went to the bakery and bought (and brought) some for you. They are in the kitchen. Go have some!

6 上星期我给爸爸寄去了一封信，请他下个月来中国看我的时候，给我带一本汉英词典来。昨天爸爸打了一个电话来，告诉我他不能到中国来看我了，所以我要的词典，他会寄来。
Shàng xīngqī wǒ gěi bàba jì qù le yì fēng xìn, qǐng tā xià ge yuè lái Zhōngguó kàn wǒ de shíhòu, gěi wǒ dài yì běn Hàn Yīng cídiǎn lái. Zuótiān bàba dǎ le yí ge diànhuà lái, gàosù wǒ tā bù néng dào Zhōngguó lái kàn wǒ le, suǒyǐ wǒ yào de cídiǎn, tā huì jì lái.
Last week, I mailed a letter to my father, asking him to bring me a Chinese–English dictionary next month when he comes to visit me. Yesterday, my father called me and told me that he would not be able to come to China to see me anymore. Therefore, he would send the dictionary I want by mail.

7 今天我请几个朋友来我家开派对，每个朋友都带来了一个他们在家作的菜，但是小李去店里买了一瓶酒来。
Jīntiān wǒ qǐng jǐ ge péngyǒu lái wǒ jiā kāi pàiduì, měi ge péngyǒu dōu dài lái le yí ge tāmen zài jiā zuò de cài, dànshì Xiǎo Lǐ qù diàn lǐ mǎi le yì píng jiǔ lái.
Today I invited a few friends to my house for a party. Everyone brought a dish they made at home, but Xiao Li went to the store and bought (and brought) a bottle of wine.

II

1 你别站在那里了，快坐下来休息休息吧！(说话的人也站着。)
Nǐ bié zhàn zài nàlǐ le, kuài zuò xiàlái xiūxi xiūxi ba! (Shuōhuà de rén yě zhàn zhe.)
Don't stand there anymore. Sit down and take a break! (The speaker is also standing.)

2 这家小吃店人太多了，我不想在这里吃，我们<u>买</u>一些小吃<u>回</u>家<u>去</u>吃，好不好？
Zhè jiā xiǎochī diàn rén tài duō le, wǒ bù xiǎng zài zhèlǐ chī, wǒmen mǎi yìxiē xiǎochī huí jiā qù chī, hǎo bù hǎo?
This snack shop is too crowded. I don't want to eat here. Let's buy some snacks and go home to eat, OK?

3 这个人从十楼<u>跳下来</u>，所以他很快就死了。（说话的人在大楼外面。）
Zhè ge rén cóng shí lóu tiào xiàlái, suǒyǐ tā hěn kuài jiù sǐ le. (Shuōhuà de rén zài dà lóu wàimiàn.)
This man jumped down from the tenth floor, so he died quickly. (The speaker is outside the building.)

4 十点了，饭馆里还有很多客人在吃饭，从外面又<u>走进来</u>几个人，今天生意真好！
Shí diǎn le, fànguǎn lǐ hái yǒu hěn duō kèrén zài chī fàn, cóng wàimiàn yòu zǒu jìnlái jǐ ge rén, jīntiān shēngyì zhēn hǎo!
It's 10 o'clock already. There are still many customers eating in our restaurant, and a few more people have just walked in. Business is really good today!

5 我每天下午都<u>带</u>我的狗<u>出去</u>玩。
Wǒ měi tiān xiàwǔ dōu dài wǒde gǒu chūqù wán.
Every afternoon, I take my dog out to play.

6 在中国，老师一进教室，小学生就会从椅子上<u>站起来</u>说："老师好。"
Zài Zhōngguó, lǎoshī yí jìn jiàoshì, xiǎo xuéshēng jiù huì cóng yǐzi shàng zhàn qǐlái shuō: 'Lǎoshī hǎo.'
In China, as soon as the teacher enters the classroom, all the students stand up from their chairs and say, 'Hello, Teacher.'

7 你看，山上有一个漂亮的亭子，咱们<u>爬上</u>山<u>去</u>照几张相吧！
Nǐ kàn, shān shàng yǒu yí ge piàoliàng de tíngzi, zánmen pá shàng shān qù zhào jǐ zhāng xiàng ba!
Look, there is a pretty pavilion on the mountain. Let's climb up the mountain to take some pictures.

8 爸爸每次出国，都会给我<u>带</u>礼物<u>回来</u>。
Bàba měi cì chū guó, dōu huì gěi wǒ dài lǐwù huílái.
Every time my father goes overseas, he will bring gifts back for me.

9 河上有一条桥，我打算<u>游过去</u>，再从桥上<u>走回来</u>。
Hé shàng yǒu yì tiáo qiáo, wǒ dǎsuàn yóu guòqù, zài cóng qiáo shàng zǒu huílái.
There is a bridge on the river. I plan to swim across the river and then walk back here on the bridge.

16 The complement of result

1 王：墙上有一个牌子，你<u>看见</u>(or 到)了没有？
Wáng: Qiáng shàng yǒu yí ge páizi, nǐ kàn jiàn (or dào) le méiyǒu?
丁：我<u>看见</u>(or 到)了，可是上面写的字，我没有<u>看懂</u>。
Dīng: Wǒ kàn jiàn (or dào) le, kěshì shàngmiàn xiě de zì, wǒ méiyǒu kàn dǒng.

Wang: There was a sign on the wall. Did you see it?

Ding: I did, but I did not understand the words on the sign.

2 他学游泳只学了两个多小时就学会了。

Tā xué yóuyǒng zhǐ xué le liǎng ge duō xiǎoshí jiù xué huì le.

He had only spent a little over two hours before he learned how to swim.

3 我的车修好了，今天我们可以开车出去玩了。

Wǒde chē xiū hǎo le, jīntiān wǒmen kěyǐ kāichē chūqù wán le.

My car is fixed. Today we can drive my car and go out to have fun.

4 今天的功课太多了，我写了两个多小时，还没有写好(or 完)。

Jīntiān de gōngkè tài duō le, wǒ xiě le liǎng ge duō xiǎoshí, hái méiyǒu xiě hǎo (or wán).

There is too much homework today. I have been working on it for over two hours, and I still have not finished.

5 我告诉他我姓张，可是他听错了，所以他叫我常先生。

Wǒ gàosù tā wǒ xìng Zhāng, kěshì tā tīng cuò le, suǒyǐ tā jiào wǒ Cháng xiānsheng.

I told him that my last name is Zhang, but he heard it wrong, so he called me Mr Chang.

6 我的英文不好，所以那个英国人说的话，我没有听懂。

Wǒde Yīngwén bù hǎo, suǒyǐ nà ge Yīngguó rén shuō de huà, wǒ méiyǒu tīng dǒng.

My English is not good, so I did not understand what that Englishman said.

7 要买那本畅销书的人太多了，我去了两趟书店，都没有买到。

Yào mǎi nà běn chàngxiāo shū de rén tài duō le, wǒ qù le liǎng tàng shūdiàn, dōu méiyǒu mǎi dào.

There are too many people who want to buy that best-selling book. I made two trips to the bookshop, but I did not get the book.

8 站住，别走！我是老师，我还没说完话呢，你怎么可以走？

Zhàn zhù, bié zǒu! Wǒ shì lǎoshī, wǒ hái méi shuō wán huà ne, nǐ zěnme kěyǐ zǒu?

Hold it (Stand still)! Don't go. I am the teacher. I have not finished talking, how could you leave?

9 今天的比赛，德国队输了，因为有两个球，他们没有接住。

Jīntiān de bǐsài, Déguó duì shū le, yīnwèi yǒu liǎng ge qiú, tāmen méiyǒu jiē zhù.

The German team lost in today's game because there were two balls that they did not catch.

10 妈妈：这种巧克力糖很贵，你要慢慢地吃。

Māma: Zhè zhǒng qiǎokèlì táng hěn guì, nǐ yào màn màn de chī.

儿子：这么一小块，我一口就吃掉了。

Érzi: Zhème yì xiǎo kuài, wǒ yì kǒu jiù chī diào le.

Mother: This kind of chocolate is expensive. You must eat slowly.

Son: Such a little piece. I can eat it all in one bit.

11   大家都准备好了吗？咱们上飞机吧！自己的行李，一定要拿好！

Dàjiā dōu zhǔnbèi hǎo le ma? Zánmen shàng fēijī ba! Zìjǐ de xínglǐ, yídìng yào ná hǎo!

Is everybody ready? Let's board the airplane! You must carry your own luggage securely!

12   今天我收到一封王小姐去年寄给我的信，因为她把地址写错了，所以过了一年这封信才寄到我家。

Jīntiān wǒ shōu dào yì fēng Wáng xiǎojiě qùnián jì gěi wǒ de xìn, yīnwèi tā bǎ dìzhǐ xiě cuò le, suǒyǐ guò le yì nián, zhè fēng xìn cái jì dào wǒ jiā.

Today I received a letter which Miss Wang sent to me last year. Because she wrote my address wrong, it took a year for the letter to reach my house.

17 The complement of potential

1   这个教室只有二十把椅子，坐不下三十个人。

Zhè ge jiàoshì zhǐ yǒu èrshí bǎ yǐzi , zuò bú xià sānshí ge rén.

This classroom has only 20 chairs. It cannot seat 30 people.

2   这么重的桌子，你一个人搬得动吗？要不要我来帮你一下？

Zhème zhòng de zhuōzi, nǐ yí ge rén bān de dòng ma? Yào bú yào wǒ lái bāng nǐ yíxià?

Such a heavy table, can you (do you have the strength to) carry it by yourself? Do you want me to come and help you?

3   英文小说我看不懂，因为我的英文不好。

Yīngwén xiǎoshuō wǒ kàn bù dǒng, yīnwèi wǒde Yīngwén bù hǎo.

I cannot read (cannot understand) English novels because my English is not good.

4   听说那本书非常畅销，想买的人很多，你快去买吧，去晚了，就买不到了。

Tīngshuō nà běn shū fēicháng chàngxiāo, xiǎng mǎi de rén hěn duō, nǐ kuài qù mǎi ba, qù wǎn le, jiù mǎi bú dào le.

I heard that that book is extremely popular, and that many people want to buy it. Hurry and go buy it. If you go late, you won't be able to get it.

5   老师：坐在后面的同学，听得见(or 到)我说的话吗？

Lǎoshī: Zuò zài hòumiàn de tóngxué, tīng de jiàn (or dào) wǒ shuō de huà ma?

学生：听得见(or 到)，可是黑板上的字，我们看不见(or 到/清楚)。

Xuéshēng: Tīng de jiàn (or dào), kěshì hēibǎn shàng de zì, wǒmen kàn bú jiàn (or dào/qīngchǔ).

Teacher: Can those students who sit in the back (of the classroom) hear what I say?

Student: Yes, we can. But we cannot see (or we cannot see clearly) words on the blackboard.

6   主人：还有很多菜，再吃一点吧！

Zhǔrén: Hái yǒu hěn duō cài, zài chī yìdiǎn ba!

客人：不了，谢谢，我吃不下了。

Kèrén: Bù le, xièxie, wǒ chī bú xià le.

Host: There is still plenty of food. Why don't you have some more!

Guest: No, thanks. I cannot eat any more (I have no room any more).

7 那本书，我已经找了三天了，我想，可能找不到了。
Nà běn shū, wǒ yǐjīng zhǎo le sān tiān le, wǒ xiǎng, kěnéng zhǎo bú dào le.
I have been looking for that book for three days. I think I probably won't be able to find it any more.

8 汽车在路上坏了，飞机起飞以前我到不了机场了。
Qìchē zài lù shàng huài le, fēijī qǐfēi yǐqián, wǒ dào bù liǎo jīchǎng le.
My car broke down on the road. I will not be able to reach the airport before the flight takes off.

9 王：昨天我在街对面叫了你五、六次，你怎么不过来呢？
Wáng: Zuótiān wǒ zài jiē duìmiàn jiào le nǐ wǔ, liù cì, nǐ zěnme bú guòlái ne?
张：因为那时候街上车太多了，我过不去。
Zhāng: Yīnwèi nà shíhòu jiē shàng chē tài duō le, wǒ guò bú qù.
Wang: Yesterday I called to you from across the street five or six times. How come you didn't come over?
Zhang: Because there were too many cars on the street at that time, I could not cross over.

10 香港的房价太高了，所以我只买得起一个很小的房子。
Xiānggǎng de fáng jià tài gāo le, suǒyǐ wǒ zhǐ mǎi de qǐ yí ge hěn xiǎo de fángzi.
House prices in Hong Kong are too high, so I can only afford (to buy) a very small house.

11 我一个人只有两只手，你想我怎么拿得了这么多东西？你快过来帮我拿一些。
Wǒ yí ge rén zhǐ yǒu liǎng zhī shǒu, nǐ xiǎng wǒ zěnme ná de liǎo zhème duō dōngxi? Nǐ kuài guòlái bāng wǒ ná yixie.
I only have two hands. How do you think I can handle to carry so many things? Hurry and come over here to help me carry some.

12 我听说那本书很便宜，用不了两块钱就买得到。
Wǒ tīngshuō nà běn shū hěn piányí, yòng bù liǎo liǎng kuài qián jiù mǎi de dào.
I heard that that book is inexpensive. It is available for less than $2.

13 我们学校的宿舍住得下一千多个学生，可是宿舍的停车场只停得下五百辆车，所以我常常找不到停车的地方。
Wǒmen xuéxiào de sùshè zhù de xià yì qiān duō ge xuéshēng, kěshì sùshè de tíngchēchǎng zhǐ tíng de xià wǔ bǎi liàng chē, suǒyǐ wǒ chángcháng zhǎo bú dào tíng chē de dìfāng.
Our school's dormitory can accommodate over 1,000 students, but the parking lot for the dormitory can hold only 500 cars, so I frequently cannot find a place to park.

14 张先生：今天是你的生日，咱们叫一只龙虾吧！
Zhāng xiānsheng: Jīntiān shì nǐde shēngrì, zánmen jiào yì zhī lóngxiā ba!
张太太：龙虾？咱们怎么吃得起龙虾？
Zhāng tàitai: Lóngxiā? Zánmen zěnme chī de qǐ lóngxiā?
Mr Zhang: Today is your birthday. Let's order a lobster!
Mrs Zhang: Lobster? How can we afford to eat lobster?

18 The adverbial modifier with 地

1 王先生老了，所以他(走)路走得很慢。
   Wáng xiānsheng lǎo le, suǒyǐ tā (zǒu) lù zǒu de hěn màn.

2 今天早上我起得很早，所以现在我可以慢慢(地)走去学校。
   Jīntiān zǎoshàng wǒ qǐ de hěn zǎo, suǒyǐ xiànzài wǒ kěyǐ màn màn (de) zǒu qù xuéxiào.

3 王明学习得很认真，所以考试总是考得很好。
   Wáng Míng xuéxí de hěn rènzhēn, suǒyǐ kǎoshì zǒngshì kǎo de hěn hǎo.

4 我年轻的时候，跑得很快；现在每天只能慢慢(地)跑半小时，因为医生说我需要运动。
   Wǒ niánqīng de shíhòu, pǎo de hěn kuài; xiànzài měi tiān zhǐ néng màn màn (de) pǎo bàn xiǎoshí, yīnwèi yīshēng shuō wǒ xūyào yùndòng.

5 王先生送李小姐一个包得很漂亮的礼物，李小姐高兴地说："谢谢。"
   Wáng xiānsheng sòng Lǐ xiǎojiě yí ge bāo de hěn piàoliàng de lǐwù, Lǐ xiǎojiě gāoxìng de shuō: 'Xièxie.'

6 李太太觉得李先生开得太快了，所以她着急地说："别开得这么快。我们时间很多，你应该慢慢(地)开。"
   Lǐ tàitai juéde Lǐ xiānsheng kāi de tài kuài le, suǒyǐ tā zháojí de shuō: 'Bié kāi de zhème kuài. Wǒmen shíjiān hěn duō, nǐ yīnggāi màn màn (de) kāi.'

7 李先生听了，不高兴地说："你看，别人都开得比我更快。"
   Lǐ xiānsheng tīng le, bù gāoxìng de shuō: 'Nǐ kàn, biérén dōu kāi de bǐ wǒ gèng kuài.'

8 哥哥跟我回到家的时候，妈妈正在生气地骂弟弟。哥哥紧张地说："今天的考试，我也考得很差。妈妈一定会气得不让我看电视。"
   Gēge gēn wǒ huí dào jiā de shíhòu, māma zhèng zài shēngqì de mà dìdi. Gēge jǐnzhāng de shuō: 'Jīntiān de kǎoshì, wǒ yě kào de hěn chà. Māma yídìng huì qì de bú ràng wǒ kàn diànshì.'

9 北京的交通出名地坏。你开车的时候，一定要仔细(地)看(or 注意看/注意地看)路标。
   Běijīng de jiāotōng chūmíng de huài. Nǐ kāi chē de shíhòu, yídìng yào zǐxì (de) kàn (or zhùyì kàn/zhùyì de kàn) lùbiāo.

10 因为王太太菜作得很好，所以王先生结婚以后，就慢慢(地)胖起来了。
   Yīnwèi Wáng tàitai cài zuò de hěn hǎo, suǒyǐ Wáng xiānsheng jiéhūn yǐhòu, jiù màn màn (de) pàng qǐlái le.

19 The 是......的 structure

1 (b) *Wǒ shì cóng Běijīng lái de, bú shì Shànghǎi.*

2 (c) *Wǒ xiě le yì běn xiǎoshuō.*

3 (a) *Nǐde nán péngyǒu gàosù wǒ de.*

4 (a) *Ò, shìma? Tāmen shì jǐ diǎn zǒu de?*

5 (a) *Wǒ gēn wǒ xiānsheng shì zài Zhōngguó jié de hūn.*

6 (c) *Zhè běn shū shì wǒ māma xiě de.*

7 (b) *Nǐ bàba tuìxiū yǐqián, shì zuò shénme de?*

8 (a) *Shì shéi bǎ wǒde mìmì gàosù nǐ de?*

9 (b) *Yīnwèi nà jiàn dàyī tài guì le, wǒ mǎi bù qǐ.*

10 (c) *Wǒ shì yì jiǔ jiǔ liù nián zài Zhōngguó shēng de.*

11 (b) *Wáng xiānsheng shì zěnme sǐ de, méiyǒu rén zhīdào.*

12 (a) *Zhāng Míng, shì nǐ! Nǐ zěnme lái le?*

13 (c) *Wǒ shì zuò huǒchē lái de.*

14 (a) *Bàba gàosù wǒ de.*

20 Subjectless sentences and existential sentences

1 昨天只来了三个客人，不过这三个客人今天又来了。
Zuótiān zhǐ lái le sān ge kèrén, búguò zhè sān ge kèrén jīntiān yòu lái le.

2 这里的冬天，天天刮风，有时候还下雪。
Zhèlǐ de dōngtiān, tiān tiān guā fēng, yǒu shíhòu hái xià xuě.

3 春天了，虽然有时候下雨，可是很少刮风了。
Chūntiān le, suīrán yǒu shíhòu xià yǔ, kěshì hěn shǎo guā fēng le.

4 雨下得太大了。下大雨的时候，我不喜欢出去。
Yǔ xià de tài dà le. Xià dà yǔ de shíhòu, wǒ bù xǐhuān chūqù.

5 王先生：张先生的手机号码，你写在哪里？(or 你把张先生的手机号码写在哪里?)
Wáng xiānsheng: Zhāng xiānsheng de shǒujī hàomǎ, nǐ xiě zài nǎlǐ? (or Nǐ bǎ Zhāng xiānsheng de shǒujī hàomǎ xiě zài nǎlǐ?)
王太太：日历上写着两个号码，我不知道哪个是他的手机号码。
Wáng tàitai: Rìlì shàng xiě zhe liǎng ge hàomǎ, wǒ bù zhīdào nǎ ge shì tāde shǒujī hàomǎ.

6 妈，楼下来了两个我不认识的人。
Mā, lóu xià lái le liǎng ge wǒ bú rènshì de rén.

7 张太太：我的新车，你为什么又停在树下？ (or 你为什么又把我的新车停在树下？)
Zhāng tàitai: Wǒde xīn chē, nǐ wèishénme yòu tíng zài shù xià? (or Nǐ wèishénme yòu bǎ wǒde xīn chē tíng zài shù xià?)
儿子：我回家的时候，车库里放了 (or 放着) 几个大箱子，所以我不能把车停在车库里。
Érzi: Wǒ huí jiā de shíhòu, chēkù lǐ fàng le (or fàng zhe) jǐ ge dà xiāngzi, suǒyǐ wǒ bù néng bǎ chē tíng zài chēkù lǐ.

8 她走以前，在一张纸上写了几个字，然后把那张纸放在我的口袋里。我打开一看，上面写了 (or 写着) 她的名字跟电话号码。
Tā zǒu yǐqián, zài yì zhāng zhǐ shàng xiě le jǐ ge zì, ránhòu bǎ nà zhāng zhǐ fàng zài wǒde kǒudài lǐ. Wǒ dǎkāi yí kàn, shàngmiàn xiě le (or xiě zhe) tāde míngzì gēn diànhuà hàomǎ.

9 王明：外面停了 (or 停着) 一辆新车，是不是你的？（听说你买了一辆新车，现在停在外面的那辆，是不是你的？）
Wáng Míng: Wàimiàn tíng le (or tíng zhe) yí liàng xīn chē, shì bú shì nǐde? (Tīngshuō nǐ mǎi le yí liàng xīn chē, xiànzài tíng zài wàimiàn de nà liàng, shì bú shì nǐde?)
李中：不是，我的车停在车库里。我不会把新买的车停在街上的。（新买的车，我是不会停在街上的。）
Lǐ Zhōng: Bú shì, wǒde chē tíng zài chēkù lǐ. Wǒ bú huì bǎ xīn mǎi de chē tíng zài jiē shàng de. (Xīn mǎi de chē, wǒ shì bú huì tíng zài jiē shàng de.)

10 我住在一楼。最近认识了一个姓张的老先生，他跟他太太住在三楼。张先生告诉我，二楼住了两个美国人，这个大楼一共住了五家人。(住了 sounds better than 住着.)
Wǒ zhù zài yī lóu. Zuìjìn rènshì le yí ge xìng Zhāng de lǎo xiānsheng, tā gēn tā tàitai zhù zài sān lóu. Zhāng xiānsheng gàosù wǒ, èr lóu zhù le liǎng ge Měiguó rén, zhè ge dàlóu yígòng zhù le wǔ jiā rén.

21 The 把 structure

1 王：你把那封信给丁小姐了没有？
Wáng: Nǐ bǎ nà fēng xìn gěi Dīng xiǎojiě méiyǒu?
李：还没有呢，因为昨天我没有看到她。 (Not convertible)
Lǐ: Hái méiyǒu ne, yīnwèi zuótiān wǒ méiyǒu kàndào ta.

2 现在我要去图书馆借一本小说。 (Not convertible)
Xiànzài wǒ yào qù túshūguǎn jiè yì běn xiǎoshuō.

3 王：请把我说的话记住。
Wáng: Qǐng bǎ wǒ shuō de huà jì zhù.
李：请放心，我已经把那些话写在一个本子上了。
Lǐ: Qǐng fàngxīn, wǒ yǐjīng bǎ nà xiē huà xiě zǎi yí ge běnzi shàng le.

4 明天别忘了带一个照相机来。 (Not convertible)
Míngtiān bié wàng le dài yí ge zhàoxiàngjī lái.

5 丁：你不可以**把**我说的话告诉小王。
*Dīng: Nǐ bù kěyǐ **bǎ** wǒ shuō de huà gàosù Xiǎo Wáng.*
李：我根本不认识小王。 (Not convertible)
Lǐ: Wǒ gēnběn bú rènshì Xiǎo Wáng.

6 小明：你包了太多饺子了，我一个人吃不了一百个饺子。 (Not convertible)
Xiǎomíng: Nǐ bāo le tài duō jiǎozi le, wǒ yí ge rén chī bù liǎo yì bǎi ge jiǎozi.
妈妈：我们可以**把**你吃不完的留到明天吃。
*Māma: Wǒmen kěyǐ **bǎ** nǐ chī bù wán de liú dào míngtiān chī.*

7 我听说王老师住院了；我想去医院看他。 (Not convertible)
Wǒ tīngshuō Wáng lǎoshī zhùyuàn le; wǒ xiǎng qù yīyuàn kàn tā.

8 你说的话，我听不清楚。 (Not convertible) 你可不可以**把**那些话再说一遍？
*Nǐ shuō de huà, wǒ tīng bù qīngchǔ. Nǐ kě bù kěyǐ **bǎ** nà xiē huà zài shuō yí biàn?*

9 我**把**新秘书的名字忘了，所以我请李先生**把**她的名字再告诉我一次。
*Wǒ **bǎ** xīn mìshū de míngzì wàng le, suǒyǐ wǒ qǐng Lǐ xiānsheng **bǎ** tāde míngzì zài gàosù wǒ yí cì.*

10 王：你弟弟病了三天了，你怎么还不**把**他送去医院？
*Wáng: Nǐ dìdi bìng le sān tiān le, nǐ zěnme hái bù **bǎ** tā sòng qù yīyuàn?*
李：昨天送去了，可是医生说他只是感冒，所以叫我**把**他带回家来休息。
*Lǐ: Zuótiān sòng qù le, kěshì yīshēng shuō tā zhǐ shì gǎnmào, suǒyǐ jiào wǒ **bǎ** tā dài huí jiā lái xiūxí.*

11 他去那家新开的百货公司给他女朋友买了一个很贵的礼物。 (Not convertible)
Tā qù nà jiā xīn kāi de bǎihuò gōngsī gěi tā nǚ péngyǒu mǎi le yí ge hěn guì de lǐwù.

22 Passive structures

I

1 这篇文章写得很好，所以被老师放在我们班的博客(or 部落格)上了。
Zhè piān wénzhāng xiě de hěn hǎo, suǒyǐ bèi lǎoshī fàng zài wǒmen bān de bókè (or bùluògé) shàng le.

2 这本小说是一位有名的中国作家写的。
Zhè běn xiǎoshuō shì yí wèi yǒumíng de Zhōngguó zuòjiā xiě de.

3 她的电脑被偷了，所以她的生活受到很大的影响。
Tāde diànnǎo bèi tōu le, suǒyǐ tāde shēnghuó shòudào hěn dà de yǐngxiǎng.

4 李：自从我来到中国以后，被摊贩骗过(or 了)好几次。
Lǐ: Zìcóng wǒ lái dào Zhōngguó yǐhòu, bèi tānfàn piàn guo (or le) hǎo jǐ cì.
张：我也被骗过。
Zhāng: Wǒ yě bèi piàn guo.
王：我从来没有被骗过。
Wáng: Wǒ cónglái méiyǒu bèi piàn guo.

5　今天早上妈妈被我放的音乐吵醒了，所以我被她骂了(can be 我被骂了一顿)。
Jīntiān zǎoshàng māma bèi wǒ fàng de yīnyuè chǎo xǐng le, suǒyǐ wǒ bèi tā mà le (can be wǒ bèi mà le yí dùn).

6　我被他烦得一件事也不能做。
Wǒ bèi tā fán de yí jiàn shì yě bù néng zuò.

II

1　那几张纸叫风(给)吹走了。= 那几张纸让风(给)吹走了。= 那几张纸给风吹走了。
Nà jǐ zhāng zhǐ jiào fēng (gěi) chuī zǒu le. = Nà jǐ zhāng zhǐ ràng fēng (gěi) chuī zǒu le. = Nà jǐ zhāng zhǐ gěi fēng chuī zǒu le.

2　王立的爸爸是医生，王立受到(了)他的影响，决定以后也要当医生。
Wáng Lì de bàba shì yīshēng, Wáng Lì shòudào (le) tāde yǐngxiǎng, juédìng yǐhòu yě yào dāng yīshēng.

3　我上星期买的古董花瓶叫(or 让)我儿子(给)打破了。
Wǒ shàng xīngqī mǎi de gǔdǒng huāpíng jiào (or ràng) wǒ érzi (gěi) dǎ pò le.

4　王明被选作我们的班长。
Wáng Míng bèi xuǎn zuò wǒmen de bānzhǎng.

5　李中的建议受到(or 遭到)全班同学的反对。
Lǐ Zhōng de jiànyì shòudào (or zāodào) quán bān tóngxué de fǎnduì.

6　王先生是我们的代表；你的问题由他回答。
Wáng xiānsheng shì wǒmen de dàibiǎo; nǐde wèntí yóu tā huídá.

7　因为这条河的水受到(了)严重的污染，所以河里的鱼不能吃。
Yīnwèi zhè tiáo hé de shuǐ shòudào (le) yánzhòng de wūrǎn, suǒyǐ hé lǐ de yú bù néng chī.

8　最近王中常常获得(or 得到、受到)老师的夸奖。
Zuìjìn Wáng Zhōng chángcháng huòdé (or dédào, shòudào) lǎoshī de kuājiǎng.

23 Making comparisons (1)

1　昨天的考试，王中考得比我更好(or 还好)。
Zuótiān de kǎoshì, Wáng Zhōng kǎo de bǐ wǒ gèng hǎo (or hái hǎo).
Wang Zhong did even better than I did in yesterday's test.

2　我跑得不比王中慢。
Wǒ pǎo de bù bǐ Wáng Zhōng màn.
I don't run any slower than Wang Zhong.

3　我的房子没有李先生的大，可是比他的贵。
Wǒde fángzi méiyǒu Lǐ xiānsheng de dà, kěshì bǐ tāde guì.
My house is not as big as Mr Li's, but it is more expensive than his.

4 我们班的同学都没有李明(那么)聪明。
Wǒmen bān de tóngxué dōu méiyǒu Lǐ Míng (nàme) cōngmíng.
None of the students in our class is as smart as Li Ming.

5 我哥哥不比我高，(or 我不比我哥哥矮，)可是他比我胖很多(or 胖得多/胖多了)。
Wǒ gēge bù bǐ wǒ gāo, (or wǒ bù bǐ wǒ gēge ǎi,) kěshì tā bǐ wǒ pàng hěn duō (or pàng de duō/pàng duō le.)
My older brother is not taller than I am, (or I am not shorter than my older brother, but he is much heavier (fatter) than I am.

6 昨天没有今天(这么)冷。
Zuótiān méiyǒu jīntiān (zhème) lěng.
Yesterday was not as cold as today.

7 我工作的时间比张先生长，可是赚的钱没有他多。 (or 张先生工作的时间比我短，可是我赚的钱没有他多。)
Wǒ gōngzuò de shíjiān bǐ Zhāng xiānsheng cháng, kěshì zhuàn de qián méiyǒu tā duō. (or Zhāng xiānsheng gōngzuò de shíjiān bǐ wǒ duǎn, kěshì wǒ zhuàn de qián méiyǒu tā duō.)
My work hours are longer than Mr Zhang's, but my income (the money I make) is not as much as his.

8 李先生的房子，卧室没有我的多，厨房也没有我的大。
Lǐ xiānsheng de fángzi, wòshì méiyǒu wǒde duō, chúfáng yě méiyǒu wǒde dà.
Mr Li's house does not have as many bedrooms as my house does, and his kitchen is not as big as mine.

9 李中学习得比他的同学努力，所以他考试的成绩也比他们好。
Lǐ Zhōng xuéxí de bǐ tāde tóngxué nǔlì, suǒyǐ tā kǎoshì de chéngjī yě bǐ tāmen hǎo.
Li Zhong studies more diligently than his classmates, so his test grades are better than theirs.

10 李老师的学生不比王老师的少，可是王老师比李老师喜欢(or 爱)抱怨。
Lǐ lǎoshī de xuéshēng bù bǐ Wáng lǎoshī de shǎo, kěshì Wáng lǎoshī bǐ Lǐ lǎoshī xǐhuān (or ài) bàoyuàn.
Teacher Li does not have fewer students than Teacher Wang, but Teacher Wang likes to complain more than Teacher Li does.

24 Making comparisons (2)

1 张老师：我从来没有教过象王明这么聪明的学生。
Zhāng lǎoshī: Wǒ cónglái méiyǒu jiāo guo xiàng Wáng Míng zhème cōngmíng de xuéshēng.
李老师：我教过跟他一样聪明的学生，可是没有教过比他更聪明的。
Lǐ lǎoshī: Wǒ jiāo guo gēn tā yíyàng cōngmíng de xuéshēng, kěshì méiyǒu jiāo guo bǐ tā gèng cōngmíng de.

2 李中跟他弟弟一样高，可是没有他弟弟那么瘦(= 不象他弟弟那么瘦)。
Lǐ Zhōng gēn tā dìdi yíyàng gāo, kěshì méiyǒu tā dìdi nàme shòu (= bú xiàng tā dìdi nàme shòu).

3 这两件大衣颜色跟式样都一样，可是质料不一样，所以价钱差很多。
Zhè liǎng jiàn dàyī yánsè gēn shìyàng dōu yíyàng, kěshì zhíliào bù yíyàng, suǒyǐ jiàqián chà hěn duō.

4 李：张先生的女朋友真漂亮，王先生的女朋友没有她那么漂亮。
Lǐ: Zhāng xiānsheng de nǚ péngyǒu zhēn piàoliàng, Wáng xiānsheng de nǚ péngyǒu méiyǒu tā nàme piàoliàng.
丁：可是我知道她跟张先生的女朋友一样善良。
Dīng: Kěshì wǒ zhīdào tā gēn Zhāng xiānsheng de nǚ péngyǒu yíyàng shànliáng.
陈：如果我认识一个象(or 有)王先生的女朋友那么漂亮的女孩，我会非常高兴。
Chén: Rúguǒ wǒ rènshì yí ge xiàng (or yǒu) Wáng xiānsheng de nǚ péngyǒu nàme piàoliàng de nǚhái, wǒ huì fēicháng gāoxìng.

5 李：今天真冷，如果明天象今天这么冷(= 如果明天象今天一样冷)，我就要待在家里。
Lǐ: Jīntiān zhēn lěng, rúguǒ míngtiān xiàng jīntiān zhème lěng (= rúguǒ míngtiān xiàng jīntiān yíyàng lěng), wǒ jiù yào dāi zài jiā lǐ.
王：明天不会跟今天一样冷，会比今天更冷。
Wáng: Míngtiān bú huì gēn jīntiān yíyàng lěng, huì bǐ jīntiān gèng lěng.

6 女：你什么时候来看我？
Nǚ: Nǐ shénme shíhòu lái kàn wǒ?
男：明年吧！明年我不会象今年这么忙。
Nán: Míngnián ba! Míngnián wǒ bú huì xiàng jīnnián zhème máng.
女：好吧！不过别又象上次一样，上次你出发前一天取消了你的班机。
Nǚ: Hǎo ba! Búguò bié yòu xiàng shàng cì yíyàng, shàng cì nǐ chūfā qián yì tiān qǔxiāo le nǐde bānjī.

7 这里的风景像画一样美。
Zhèlǐ de fēngjǐng xiàng huà yíyàng měi.

8 王：如果我象他那么有钱，我会买一幢跟他一样大的房子。
Wáng: Rúguǒ wǒ xiàng tā nàme yǒuqián, wǒ huì mǎi yí zhuàng gēn tā yíyàng dà de fángzi.
丁：那个房子没有那么大。虽然我没有(or 不象)他那么有钱，可是我已经有了一幢比他更大的房子。
Dīng: Nà ge fángzi méiyǒu nàme dà. Suīrán wǒ méiyǒu (or bú xiàng) tā nàme yǒuqián, kěshì wǒ yǐjīng yǒu le yí zhuàng bǐ tā gèng dà de fángzi.

9 虽然安娜没有(or 不象)王中那么聪明，可是她也不象(or 没有)王中那么懒，所以他们的考试成绩总是差不多。
Suīrán Ānnà méiyǒu (or bú xiàng) Wáng Zhōng nàme cōngmíng, kěshì tā yě bú xiàng (or méiyǒu) Wáng Zhōng nàme lǎn, suǒyǐ tāmen de kǎoshì chéngjī zǒngshì chàbùduō.

25 Measure words

1 这个房子非常大，有五间卧房、三个半洗澡间。
Zhè ge fángzi fēicháng dà, yǒu wǔ jiān wòfáng, sān ge bàn xǐzǎojiān.
This house is extremely big; there are five bedrooms and three and half bathrooms.

2   一星期有**七天**，我天天都学习中文。
    Yì xīngqī yǒu qī tiān, wǒ tiān tiān dōu xuéxí Zhōngwén.
    There are seven days in a week. I study Chinese every day.

3   我每天都喝**三杯**咖啡。
    Wǒ měi tiān dōu hē sān bēi kāfēi.
    I drink three cups of coffee every day.

4   桌子上面**那本英文书**是谁的?
    Zhuōzi shàngmiàn nà běn Yīngwén shū shì shéide?
    Whom does the English book on the table belong to?

5   我们班每人都有**一个**中文名字。
    Wǒmen bān měi rén dōu yǒu yí ge Zhōngwén míngzì.
    Everyone in my class has a Chinese name.

6   这一群**小狗**真可爱。
    Zhè yì qún xiǎo gǒu zhēn kě'ài.
    This group of small dogs is really cute.

7   这件大衣不是我的，**我的新大衣**是黑色的。
    Zhè jiàn dàyī bú shì wǒde, wǒde xīn dàyī shì hēi sè de.
    This coat is not mine; my new coat is black.

8   王明不是个好人，你怎么会认识**这种人**(or **这样的人**)?
    Wáng Míng bú shì ge hǎo rén, nǐ zěnme huì rènshì zhè zhǒng rén (or zhèyàng de rén)?
    Wang Ming is not a nice person. How did you get to know this type of a person (or such a person)?

9   我在上海住过三星期，也在北京住过**半年**(or **一年半**)。
    Wǒ zài Shànghǎi zhù guo sān xīngqī, yě zài Běijīng zhù guo bàn nián (or yì nián bàn).
    I lived in Shanghai for three weeks; I also lived in Beijing for half a year (or one and a half years).

10 我喜欢蓝色，所以昨天买了**三条蓝裙子**。
    Wǒ xǐhuān lán sè, suǒyǐ zuótiān mǎi le sān tiáo lán qúnzi.
    I like the colour blue, so I bought three blue skirts yesterday.

11 桌上有**两个大杯子**，我跟弟弟口渴，所以一人喝了一大杯水。
    Zhuō shàng yǒu liǎng ge dà bēizi, wǒ gēn dìdi kǒu kě, suǒyǐ yì rén hē le yí dà bēi shuǐ.
    There were two big glasses on the table. My younger brother and I were thirsty, so each of us drank a big glass of water (Meaning: a full glass of water).

12 你说，你喝了**多少瓶**啤酒?
    Nǐ shuō, nǐ hē le duōshǎo píng píjiǔ?
    Tell me, how many bottles of beer did you drink?

13 你看过哪些有名的中国小说? (or 你看过哪本有名的中国小说?)
Nǐ kàn guo nǎ xiē yǒumíng de Zhōngguó xiǎoshuō? (or Nǐ kàn guo nǎ běn yǒumíng de Zhōngguó xiǎoshuō?)
Which famous Chinese novels have you read? (*or* Which famous Chinese novel have you read?)

26 Verb reduplication and adjective reduplication

1 (b) 妈妈: 小明，饭已经做好了，你先去洗洗手再来吃。
Māma: Xiǎomíng, fàn yǐjīng zuò hǎo le, nǐ xiān qù xǐ xǐ shǒu zài lái chī.

2 (c) 你可不可以在这里等等我? 我要去一下洗手间。
Nǐ kě bù kěyǐ zài zhèlǐ děng děng wǒ? Wǒ yào qù yíxià xǐshǒujiān.

3 (a) 我在车站等了等，车没来，我就决定走路去学校了。
Wǒ zài chēzhàn děng le děng, chē méi lái, wǒ jiù juédìng zǒulù qù xuéxiào le.

4 (c) 这个问题，我们应该好好地讨论讨论，不能现在就决定。
Zhè ge wèntí, wǒmen yīnggāi hǎo hǎo de tǎolùn tǎolùn, bù néng xiànzài jiù juédìng.

5 (a) 昨天我很累，吃完晚饭，看了看电视，就去睡觉了。
Zuótiān wǒ hěn lèi, chī wán wǎnfàn, kàn le kàn diànshì, jiù qù shuìjiào le.

6 (c) 李先生，你认识王小姐吗? 我来给你们介绍一下。
Lǐ xiānsheng, nǐ rènshì Wáng xiǎojiě ma? Wǒ lái gěi nǐmen jièshào yíxià.

7 (b) 店员: 这件大衣是最上等的质料，你摸摸看。
Diànyuán: Zhè jiàn dàyī shì zuì shàngděng de zhíliào, nǐ mō mō kàn.

8 (a) 小明一看到爸爸回家了，就高高兴兴地去给爸爸开门。
Xiǎomíng yí kàndào bàba huí jiā le, jiù gāo gāo xìng xìng de qù gěi bàba kāi mén.

9 (b) 你看，前面那个高高的建筑，就是我们学校的学生宿舍。
Nǐ kàn, qiánmiàn nà ge gāo gāo de jiànzhù, jiù shì wǒmen xuéxiào de xuéshēng sùshè.

27 The use of 以前, 以后 and 时候

1 昨天我很忙；上课以前在图书馆学习；下课以后去咖啡馆工作。晚上吃了晚饭以后，还得准备下星期的考试。
Zuótiān wǒ hěn máng; shàng kè yǐqián zài túshūguǎn xuéxí; xià kè yǐhòu qù kāfēiguǎn gōngzuò. Wǎnshàng chī le wǎnfàn yǐhòu, hái děi zhǔnbèi xià xīngqī de kǎoshì.

2 我十几岁的时候，就决定以后要当作家。
Wǒ shí jǐ suì de shíhòu, jiù juédìng yǐhòu yào dāng zuòjiā.

3 李：王太太，你什么时候有空？我想来你家看你。
Lǐ: Wáng tàitai, nǐ shénme shíhòu yǒu kòng? Wǒ xiǎng lái nǐ jiā kàn nǐ.
王：我每天吃了晚饭以后都有空。你明天晚上来吧！
Wáng: Wǒ měi tiān chī le wǎnfàn yǐhòu dōu yǒu kòng. Nǐ míngtiān wǎnshàng lái ba!
李：太好了！你要我几点来？
Lǐ: Tài hǎo le! Nǐ yào wǒ jǐ diǎn lái?
王：我女儿八点半睡觉。她睡觉以前，我要给她洗澡；所以请你七点半以前来。
Wáng: Wǒ nǚ'ér bā diǎn bàn shuìjiào. Tā shuìjiào yǐqián, wǒ yào gěi tā xǐzǎo; suǒyǐ qǐng nǐ qī diǎn bàn yǐqián lái.

4 王：你知道不知道张先生什么时候来上海？
Wáng: Nǐ zhīdào bù zhīdào Zhāng xiānsheng shénme shíhòu lái Shànghǎi?
李：他下个月在北京参加了一个国际会议以后就会来。
Lǐ: Tā xià ge yuè zài Běijīng cānjiā le yí ge guójì huìyì yǐhòu jiù huì lái.
王：他来的时候，谁去机场接他？
Wáng: Tā lái de shíhòu, shéi qù jīchǎng jiē tā?
李：到时候再说吧！
Lǐ: Dào shíhòu zài shuō ba!

5 十年以前有手机的人不多；十年以后，没有手机的人大概不会太多了。
Shí nián yǐqián yǒu shǒujī de rén bù duō; shí nián yǐhòu, méiyǒu shǒujī de rén dàgài bú huì tài duō le.

6 以前李明跟我是好朋友；那时候，我们差不多天天都互相打电话。可是后来我发现他骗了我几次，现在我们不说话了。以后我选择朋友的时候，会很小心。
Yǐqián Lǐ Míng gēn wǒ shì hǎo péngyǒu; nà shíhòu, wǒmen chàbùduō tiān tiān dōu hùxiāng dǎ diànhuà. Kěshì hòulái wǒ fāxiàn tā piàn le wǒ jǐ cì, xiànzài wǒmen bù shuōhuà le. Yǐhòu wǒ xuǎnzé péngyǒu de shíhòu, huì hěn xiǎoxīn.

7 以前我还吃肉的时候，每星期吃三次汉堡；后来，我变成了一个素食者。现在我跟我男朋友去汉堡店吃饭的时候，我只吃薯条。
Yǐqián wǒ hái chī ròu de shíhòu, měi xīngqī chī sān cì hànbǎo; hòulái, wǒ biànchéng le yí ge sùshízhě. Xiànzài wǒ gēn wǒ nán péngyǒu qù hànbǎo diàn chī fàn de shíhòu, wǒ zhǐ chī shǔtiáo.

8 我爸妈还没有离婚以前(or 我爸妈离婚以前/我爸妈还没有离婚的时候)，差不多天天吵架。那时候，我告诉自己，以后我结了婚，为了孩子，一定不跟丈夫吵架。
Wǒ bàmā hái méiyǒu líhūn yǐqián (or Wǒ bàmā líhūn yǐqián / Wǒ bàmā hái méiyǒu líhūn de shíhòu), chàbùduō tiān tiān chǎojià. Nà shíhòu, wǒ gàosù zìjǐ, yǐhòu wǒ jié le hūn, wèile háizi, yídìng bù gēn zhàngfū chǎojià.

28 Modal particles

1 妈妈：小明，你为什么又在吃点心？你已经这么胖了，别再吃了！
Māma: Xiǎomíng, nǐ wèishénme yòu zài chī diǎnxīn? Nǐ yǐjīng zhème pàng le, bié zài chī le.
爸爸：好了，让他吃吧，别唠叨了。
Bàba: Hǎo le, ràng tā chī ba, bié lāodāo le.

Mother: Xiaoming, why are you eating snacks again? You are already so overweight, stop eating.
Father: Enough! Why don't you just let him eat. Stop nagging.

2 这本词典上面写着你的名字，是你的吧！借我用一下，好吗？
Zhè běn cídiǎn shàngmiàn xiě zhe nǐde míngzì, shì nǐde ba! Jiè wǒ yòng yíxià, hǎo ma?
Your name is written in this dictionary; it must be yours, right? Can I borrow it for a while?

3 妈妈：爸爸呢？他回家了吗？
Māma: Bàba ne? Tā huí jiā le ma?
儿子：他在客厅里看电视呢。
Érzi: Tā zài kètīng lǐ kàn diànshì ne.
Mother: Where is your father? Has he come home?
Son: He is watching TV in the living room.

4 李：最近我快忙死了，天天都半夜以后才上床睡觉 ∅ 。
Lǐ: Zuìjìn wǒ kuài máng sǐ le, tiān tiān dōu bànyè yǐhòu cái shàngchuáng shuìjiào.
王：那明天晚上的舞会，你不能去了？
Wáng: Nà míngtiān wǎnshàng de wǔhuì, nǐ bù néng qù le?
李：我还没有决定呢！因为后天是星期天，所以星期六晚上，我想轻松一下。
Lǐ: Wǒ hái méiyǒu juédìng ne! Yīnwèi hòutián shì xīngqī tiān, suǒyǐ xīngqī liù wǎnshàng, wǒ xiǎng qīngsōng yíxià.
Li: Lately I have been almost busy to death. I go to bed after midnight every day.
Wang: This means you cannot go to the dance party tomorrow evening, right?
Li: I have not decided yet. Because the day after tomorrow is Sunday, I want to relax a little bit on Saturday evening.

5 妈妈：现在几点了？小明怎么还没回来呢？平常这个时候，他早就回来了。大家都在等他回来吃饭呢。
Māma: Xiànzài jǐ diǎn le? Xiǎomíng zěnme hái méi huí lái ne? Píngcháng zhè ge shíhòu, tā zǎo jiù huí lái le. Dàjiā dōu zài děng tā huí lái chī fàn ne.
爸爸：不用急，还不到八点呢！咱们再等十分钟吧！
Bàba: Bú yòng jí, hái bú dào bā diǎn ne! Zánmen zài děng shí fēnzhōng ba!
女儿：如果十分钟以后他还是没回来呢？我饿死了。
Nǚ'ér: Rúguǒ shí fēnzhōng yǐhòu tā háishì méi huí lái ne? Wǒ è sǐ le.
爸爸：那我们就不等了。
Bàba: Nà wǒmen jiù bù děng le.
Mother: What time is it already? How come Xiaoming is not home yet? Usually he would have been back long before this time. Everybody's waiting for him to be back to have dinner.
Father: No need to get anxious. It is not 8 o'clock yet. Let's wait another ten minutes.
Daughter: What if he is still not back after ten minutes? I am hungry to death.
Father: Then we won't wait for him any longer.

6 男：星期六晚上一起去吃饭，好吗？
Nán: Xīngqī liù wǎnshàng yìqǐ qù chī fàn, hǎo ma?

女：对不起，我不能去外面吃饭。
Nǚ: Duìbùqǐ, wǒ bù néng qù wàimiàn chī fàn.
男：哦？为什么呢？
Nán: Ò? Wèishénme ne?
女：你大概不知道吧，我最近正在减肥呢！
Nǚ: Nǐ dàgài bù zhīdào ba, wǒ zuìjìn zhèng zài jiǎnféi ne!
男：那我们星期六晚上做什么呢？
Nán: Nà wǒmen xīngqī liù wǎnshàng zuò shénme ne?
女：去看场电影吧！我好久没看电影了。
Nǚ: Qù kàn chǎng diànyǐng ba! Wǒ hǎojiǔ méi kàn diànyǐng le.
男：哦，那你还没看过《哈利波特》了？去看《哈利波特》吧！
Nán: Ò, nà nǐ hái méi kàn guo 'Hālì Bōtè' le? Qù kàn 'Hālì Bōtè' ba!
女：我对这个电影没有兴趣。
Nǚ: Wǒ duì zhè ge diànyǐng méiyǒu xìngqù.
男：那《阿凡达》呢？
Nán: Nà 'Ā Fán Dá' ne?
女：太好了！听说这个电影不错，咱们就去看《阿凡达》吧。
Nǚ: Tài hǎo le! Tīngshuō zhè ge diànyǐng bú cuò, zánmen jiù qù kàn 'Ā Fán Dá' ba.
Male: Shall we go out for dinner on Saturday evening?
Female: Sorry, I cannot go out to eat.
Male: Oh? Why?
Female: You must not know that I have been trying to lose weight.
Male: Then what shall we do on Saturday evening?
Female: Let's go to a movie. I haven't seen a movie in a long time.
Male: Oh, then that'll mean you have not seen *Harry Potter*, right? Let's go see *Harry Potter*.
Female: I am not interested in this movie.
Male: Then what about *Avatar*?
Female: Great! I heard that this movie is quite good. Let's go see *Avatar*.

7 老师：这是什么字？谁知道？王中，你知道吗？
Lǎoshī: Zhè shì shénme zì? Shéi zhīdào? Wáng Zhōng, nǐ zhīdào ma?
王中：老师，我们还没有学过那个字呢！
Wáng Zhōng: Lǎoshī, wǒmen hái méiyǒu xué guo nà ge zì ne!
老师：哦，是吗？好，那我问你另外一个。……这个呢？学过了吗？
Lǎoshī, Ò, shì ma? Hǎo, nà wǒ wèn nǐ lìngwài yí ge. ……Zhè ge ne? Xué guò le ma?
王中：学过了，可是我想不起来那个字的意思。
Wáng Zhōng: Xué guo le, kěshì wǒ xiǎng bù qǐlái nà ge zì de yìsi.
老师：王中不认识这个字，李明，你呢？
Lǎoshī: Wáng Zhōng bú rènshì zhè ge zì. Lǐ Míng, nǐ ne?
Teacher: What is this character? Who knows? Wang Zhong, do you know this character?
Wang Zhong: Sir, we have not yet learned that character!
Teacher: Oh, is that so? OK, then I will ask you another one. …What about this one? Have you learned it?
Wang Zhong: Yes, but I cannot recall the meaning of that character.
Teacher: Wang Zhong does not know this character. Li Ming, how about you?

8 女： 你到了中国以后，可能会很忙 ∅，可是一定要记得常常给我打电话 ∅。
*Nǚ: Nǐ dào le Zhōngguó yǐhòu, kěnéng huì hěn máng, kěshì yídìng yào jìde
chángcháng gěi wǒ dǎ diànhuà.*
男： 没问题，我一定会打<u>的</u>。
Nán: Méi wèntí, wǒ yídìng huì dǎ de.
Female: After you arrive in China, you probably will be busy, but you must
remember to call me often.
Male: No problem, I definitely will.

29 Conjunctive pairs

I

1 安娜<u>虽然</u>不会说中文，可是特别喜欢听中国歌曲。
Ānnà suīrán bú huì shuō Zhōngwén, kěshì tèbié xǐhuān tīng Zhōngguó gēqǔ.
Although Anna does not know how to speak Chinese, she likes to listen to Chinese
songs very much.

2 因为今天天气不好，<u>所以</u>我不想出去，只想在家看看书。
Yīnwèi jīntiān tiānqì bù hǎo, suǒyǐ wǒ bù xiǎng chū qù, zhǐ xiǎng zài jiā kàn kàn shū.
Because today's weather is not good, I don't feel like going out; I only want to stay
home and read.

3 王明的记性真差！十个生词，他已经记了一个多小时，可是<u>还是</u>记不住。
*Wáng Míng de jìxìng zhēn chà! Shí ge shēngcí, tā yǐjīng jì le yí ge duō xiǎoshí, kěshì
háishì jì bú zhù.*
Wang Ming has a really bad memory. There are only ten vocabulary words, and he
has been trying to memorize them for over an hour, but he still cannot memorize
them.

4 男： 这个星期六，你想做什么？
Nán: Zhè ge xīngqī liù, nǐ xiǎng zuò shénme?
女： <u>如果</u>天气好，<u>就</u>去野餐。
Nǚ: Rúguǒ tiānqì hǎo, jiù qù yěcān.
男： 天气不好呢？
Nán: Tiānqì bù hǎo ne?
女： 那<u>就</u>去看电影。
Nǚ: Nà jiù qù kàn diànyǐng.
Male: What would you like to do this Saturday?
Female: Let's go for a picnic if the weather is nice.
Male: What if the weather is bad?
Female: Then we will go to a movie.

5 李先生<u>不但</u>脾气好，<u>而且</u>很会赚钱，所以喜欢他的女孩子很多。
*Lǐ xiānsheng búdàn píqì hǎo, érqiě hěn huì zhuàn qián, suǒyǐ xǐhuān tā de nǚ háizi
hěn duō.*
Mr Li is not only nice-tempered, but is also good at making money; therefore, many
girls like him.

6 小兰跟她男朋友吵架了，她妈妈不但不安慰她，<u>反而</u>还说一定是她不对。
Xiǎolán gēn tā nán péngyǒu chǎojià le, tā māma búdàn bù ānwèi tā, fǎn'ér hái shuō yídìng shì tā bú duì.
Xiaolan had a fight with my boyfriend. Her mother not only would not console her; she would instead say that it must have been her fault.

7 经理把小张骂了一顿，小张心里虽然不高兴，脸上<u>却</u>没有表示出来。
Jīnglǐ bǎ Xiǎo Zhāng mà le yí dùn, Xiǎo Zhāng xīn lǐ suīrán bù gāoxìng, liǎn shàng què méiyǒu biǎoshì chūlái.
The manager scolded Xiao Zhang. Although Xiao Zhang was upset inside, he did not let it show in his face.

8 王中是我们班最聪明的学生，可是<u>因为</u>这个问题实在太难了，所以<u>就是</u>(or 连、即使是)王中也不会回答。
Wáng Zhōng shì wǒmen bān zuì cōngmíng de xuéshēng, kěshì yīnwèi zhè ge wèntí shízài tài nán le, suǒyǐ jiùshì (or lián, jíshǐ shì) Wáng Zhōng yě bú huì huídá.
Wang Zhong is the smartest student in our class, but because this question is truly too difficult, even Wang Zhong does not know how to answer it.

9 李小姐不但漂亮，<u>而且</u>脾气非常好。可惜我已经结婚了，<u>如果</u>我还没结婚的话，我一定要追她。
Lǐ xiǎojiě búdàn piàoliàng, érqiě píqì fēicháng hǎo. Kěxī wǒ yǐjīng jiéhūn le, rúguǒ wǒ hái méi jiéhūn de huà, wǒ yídìng yào zhuī tā.
Miss Li is not only pretty, but also has a nice temper. It is a pity that I am already married. If I weren't married, I would definitely pursue her.

10 我实在太喜欢这辆车了，<u>所以无论</u>(or 不管)多贵，我都一定要买。
Wǒ shízài tài xǐhuān zhè liàng chē le, suǒyǐ wúlùn (or bùguǎn) duō guì, wǒ dōu yídìng yào mǎi.
I really like this car; therefore, no matter how expensive it is, I will buy it.

11 这样东西，一点用也没有，<u>就算</u>(or 即使)免费送我，我也不要。
Zhè yàng dōngxi, yìdiǎn yòng yě méiyǒu, jiùsuàn (or jíshǐ) miǎnfèi sòng wǒ, wǒ yě bú yào.
This thing is completely useless. Even if it were given to me for free, I would not want it.

12 真奇怪！老师在全班同学面前称赞李中，李中不但不开心，<u>反而</u>哭了。
Zhēn qíguài! Lǎoshī zài quán bān tóngxué miànqián chēngzàn Lǐ Zhōng, Lǐ Zhōng búdàn bù kāixīn, fǎn'ér kū le.
How strange! The teacher praised Li Zhong in front of the entire class. Not only was Li Zhong not happy, instead, he cried.

13 在这个国家，上大学是免费的；所以<u>即使</u>(or 就算)是穷人家的小孩，也可以上大学。
Zài zhè ge guójiā, shàng dàxué shì miǎnfèi de; suǒyǐ jíshǐ (or jiùsuàn) shì qióng rén jiā de xiǎohái, yě kěyǐ shàng dàxué.
In this country, going to university is free; therefore, even children of poor families can go to university.

14 在这个国家，上大学是免费的；所以<u>无论</u>(or <u>不管</u>)是穷人家还是有钱人家的小孩，都可以上大学。

Zài zhè ge guójiā, shàng dàxué shì miǎnfèi de; suǒyǐ wúlùn (or bùguǎn) shì qióng rén jiā háishì yǒuqián rén jiā de xiǎohái, dōu kěyǐ shàng dàxué.

In this country, going to university is free; therefore, whether one is from a rich family or from a poor family, one can go to university.

II

1 王明因为有一个很漂亮的女朋友而总是觉得很快乐。

Wáng Míng yīnwèi yǒu yí ge hěn piàoliàng de nǚ péngyǒu ér zǒngshì juéde hěn kuàilè.

2 王明常常因为没有女朋友而觉得不快乐。 (or 王明因为没有女朋友而常常觉得不快乐。)

Wáng Míng chángcháng yīnwèi méiyǒu nǚ péngyǒu ér juéde bú kuàilè.

3 王明从来不因为有一个很漂亮的女朋友就觉得快乐。

Wáng Míng cónglái bù yīnwèi yǒu yí ge hěn piàoliàng de nǚ péngyǒu jiù juéde hěn kuàilè.

4 王明从来不因为没有女朋友就觉得不快乐。

Wáng Míng cónglái bù yīnwèi méiyǒu nǚ péngyǒu jiù juéde bú kuàilè.

5 你不能因为天气不好就不去上课。

Nǐ bù néng yīnwèi tiānqì bù hǎo jiù bú qù shàng kè.

6 昨天王明因为发高烧而不能去上课。

Zuótiān Wáng Míng yīnwèi fā gāo shāo ér bù néng qù shàng kè.

7 王明从来不因为天气不好就不去上课，可是他有时候会因为要出差而不去上课。

Wáng Míng cónglái bù yīnwèi tiānqì bù hǎo jiù bú qù shàng kè, kěshì tā yǒu shíhòu huì yīnwèi yào chūchāi ér bú qù shàng kè.

30 Conjunctions used in context

1 安娜：既然你不喜欢他，就应该跟他分手。

Ānnà: Jìrán nǐ bù xǐhuān tā, jiù yīnggāi gēn tā fēnshǒu.

2 李中：我学日文是因为我妈妈是日本人，学法文是因为我以后想去巴黎学设计。

Lǐ Zhōng: Wǒ xué Rìwén shì yīnwèi wǒ māma shì Rìběn rén, xué Fǎwén shì yīnwèi wǒ yǐhòu xiǎng qù Bālí xué shèjì.

3 王先生：这个房子小是小，可是不贵。

Wáng xiānsheng: Zhè ge fángzi xiǎo shì xiǎo, kěshì bú guì.

4 尽管王太太反对，王先生还是决定把钱借给李先生。

Jǐnguǎn Wáng tàitai fǎnduì, Wáng xiānsheng háishì juédìng bǎ qián jiè gěi Lǐ xiānsheng.

5 丁先生：我忙是忙，可是安娜是我最好的朋友，所以我一定要来参加她的生日舞会。
Dīng xiānsheng: Wǒ máng shì máng, kěshì Ānnà shì wǒ zuì hǎo de péngyǒu, suǒyǐ wǒ yídìng yào lái cānjiā tāde shēngrì wǔhuì.

6 妈妈：既然你没事做，就去把你的房间整理一下吧！
Māma: Jìrán nǐ méi shì zuò, jiù qù bǎ nǐde fángjiān zhěnglǐ yíxià ba!

7 张小姐：那件衣服贵(倒)是不贵，就是不太合身。
Zhāng xiǎojiě: Nà jiàn yīfú guì (dǎo) shì bú guì, jiùshì bú tài héshēn.

8 张小姐：我喜欢是喜欢，就是太贵了。
Zhāng xiǎojiě: Wǒ xǐhuān shì xǐhuān, jiùshì tài guì le.

9 李：王中的想法固然很特别，可是他的语法不好。
Lǐ: Wáng Zhōng de xiǎngfǎ gùrán hěn tèbié, kěshì tāde yǔfǎ bù hǎo.

10 李小姐：我(之)所以决定跟王明结婚是因为他实在很爱我。
Lǐ xiǎojiě: Wǒ (zhī) suǒyǐ juédìng gēn Wáng Míng jiéhūn shì yīnwèi tā shízài hěn ài wǒ.

31 The use of 才 and 就

1 太太：现在才六点，今天怎么这么早就下班了？
Tàitai: Xiànzài cái liù diǎn, jīntiān zěnme zhème zǎo jiù xià bān le?
先生：今天没有提早下班，可是交通特别顺畅，只开了半小时就到家了。
Xiānsheng: Jīntiān méiyǒu tízǎo xià bān, kěshì jiāotōng tèbié shùnchàng, zhǐ kāi le bàn xiǎoshí jiù dào jiā le.
Wife: It's only 6 o'clock. How come you got off work so early today?
Husband: I didn't get off work early today. But somehow the traffic was particularly smooth. I only drove for half an hour and I got back.

2 如果你想学好中文，没有别的办法，只有多听、多说、多读才学得好。
Rúguǒ nǐ xiǎng xué hǎo Zhōngwén, méiyǒu biéde bànfǎ, zhǐyǒu duō tīng, duō shuō, duō dú cái xué de hǎo.
If you want to learn Chinese well, there is no other way. Only by listening more, speaking more, and reading more can you master it.

3 李太太：你儿子才十七岁，怎么就已经搬到外面去住了？
Lǐ tàitai: Nǐ érzi cái shíqī suì, zěnme jiù yǐjīng bān dào wàimiàn qù zhù le?
张太太：你记错了，我儿子去年就十八岁了。
Zhāng tàitai: Nǐ jì cuò le, wǒ érzi qùnián jiù shíbā suì le.
Mrs Li: Your son is only 17 years old. How come he has already moved out?
Mrs Zhang: You've remembered it wrong. My son already turned 18 last year.

4 王：这是什么地方？
Wáng: Zhè shì shénme dìfāng?
李：这就是天安门广场。
Lǐ: Zhè jiù shì Tiān'ānmén guǎngchǎng.

王：哦，是吗？天安门在哪里？
Wáng: Ò, shì ma? Tiān'ānmén zài nǎlǐ?
李：你看，那个高高的建筑，那就是天安门。
Lǐ: Nǐ kàn, nà ge gāo gāo de jiànzhù, nà jiù shì Tiān'ānmén.
Wang: What's this place?
Li: This **is** (the famous) Tian'anmen Square.
Wang: Oh, is that so? Where is Tian'anmen?
Li: Look, that tall building, **That** is Tian'anmen.

5 小王真聪明，别人要花好几个小时才学得会的东西，他常常不到半小时就学会了。
Xiǎo Wáng zhēn cōngmíng, biérén yào huā hǎo jǐ ge xiǎoshí cái xué de huì de dōngxi, tā chángcháng bú dào bàn xiǎoshí jiù xué huì le.
Xiao Wang is really smart. He often needs only less than half an hour to learn things that other people need several hours to learn.

6 老师：张明，请你说一说，这个成语是什么意思？
Lǎoshī: Zhāng Míng, qǐng nǐ shuō yì shuō, zhè ge chéngyǔ shì shénme yìsi?
张明：老师，这个成语您还没有教我们呢！
Zhāng Míng: Lǎoshī, zhè ge chéngyǔ nín hái méiyǒu jiāo wǒmen ne!
老师：谁说的？这个成语我上星期就教你们了。
Lǎoshī: Shéi shuō de? Zhè ge chéngyǔ wǒ shàng xīngqī jiù jiāo nǐmen le.
Teacher: Zhang Ming, please tell us what this proverb means.
Zhang Ming: Sir, you have not taught us that proverb.
Teacher: Who says so? I already taught you this proverb last week.

7 张：今天的功课实在太多了，我花了三个小时才写完。
Zhāng: Jīntiān de gōngkè shízài tài duō le, wǒ huā le sān ge xiǎoshí cái xiě wán.
李：什么？才三小时就写完了？我写了五个小时，才写好一半。
Lǐ: Shénme? Cái sān xiǎoshí jiù xiě wán le? Wǒ xiě le wǔ ge xiǎoshí, cái xiě hǎo yí bàn.
Zhang: There really was too much homework today. It took me three hours to finally finish it.
Li: What? It took you only three hours to finish? I worked on it for five hours and I only finished half of it.

8 丁：我认为，一个人如果想把中文学好，最好的办法就是多看中国电影、多听中文歌曲。
Dīng: Wǒ rènwéi, yí ge rén rúguǒ xiǎng bǎ Zhōngwén xué hǎo, zuì hǎo de bànfǎ jiù shì duō kàn Zhōngguó diànyǐng, duō tīng Zhōngwén gēqǔ.
张：我不同意。我觉得，多跟中国人练习才是最好的办法。
Zhāng: Wǒ bù tóngyì. Wǒ juéde, duō gēn Zhōngguó rén liànxí cái shì zuì hǎo de bànfǎ.
Ding: I think that, if one wants to learn Chinese well, the best way is to watch more Chinese movies and to listen more to Chinese songs.
Zhang: I don't agree. I feel that to practise more often with Chinese people **is** the best way to learn.

9 妈妈：你怎么现在才回来？
Māma: Nǐ zěnme xiànzài cái huí lái?

儿子：现在<u>才</u>六点，还不算晚啊！

Érzi: Xiànzài cái liù diǎn, hái bú suàn wǎn a!

妈妈：你忘了吗？你出门的时候，说你五点<u>就</u>会回来的。

Māma: Nǐ wàng le ma? Nǐ chū mén de shíhòu, shuō nǐ wǔ diǎn jiù huì huí lái de.

Mother: How come you were late? (What took you so long?)

Son: It's only 6 o'clock. It is not late yet.

Mother: Did you forget that you said you would be home at 5 o'clock when you left the house?

10 老师：这个成语是什么意思？

Lǎoshī: Zhè ge chéngyǔ shì shénme yìsi?

学生：我忘了。

Xuéshēng: Wǒ wàng le.

老师：这个成语是昨天<u>才</u>学的，怎么你今天<u>就</u>忘了？

Lǎoshī: Zhè ge chéngyǔ shì zuótiān cái xué de, zěnme nǐ jīntiān jiù wàng le?

Teacher: What does this proverb mean?

Student: I've forgotten.

Teacher: You just learned this proverb yesterday; how come you've already forgotten?

11 李：今天真倒霉，一出门<u>就</u>摔了一跤。

Lǐ: Jīntiān zhēn dǎoméi, yì chū mén jiù shuāi le yì jiāo.

张：那不算什么！小王<u>才</u>倒霉呢！他一出门<u>就</u>被车撞了。

Zhāng: Nà bú suàn shénme! Xiǎo Wáng cái dǎoméi ne! Tā yì chū mén jiù bèi chē zhuàng le.

Li: Today I was really unlucky. The moment I left my house, I slipped and fell.

Zhang: That's nothing! Xiao Wang is the one who was unlucky. As soon as he left his house, he was hit by a car.

32 The use of adverbs in contracted sentences

1 李：明天我要跟几个朋友去爬山，你要不要一起去？

Lǐ: Míngtiān wǒ yào gēn jǐ ge péngyǒu qù pá shān, nǐ yào bú yào yìqǐ qù?

丁：天气好我<u>就</u>跟你们去。

Dīng: Tiānqì hǎo wǒ jiù gēn nǐmen qù.

Li: I am going hiking in the mountains with a few friends tomorrow. Do you want to go with us?

Ding: I will go with you if the weather is nice.

2 王：明天有一个重要的考试，你怎么还在看电视？快去准备考试吧。

Wáng: Míngtiān yǒu yí ge zhòngyào de kǎoshì, nǐ zěnme hái zài kàn diànshi? Kuài qù zhǔnbèi kǎoshì ba!

李：准备什么？这门课的东西，我完全不懂，再准备<u>也</u>不会及格的。

Lǐ: Zhǔnbèi shénme? Zhè mén kè de dōngxi, wǒ wánquán bù dǒng, zài zhǔnbèi yě bú huì jígé de.

Wang: There is an important test tomorrow. How come you are still watching TV? Go and prepare for the test now.

Li: What is there to prepare? I completely do not understand the materials for this class. No matter how much I prepare, I won't pass the test.

3 张：你的英文说得真好，你是怎么学的?

Zhāng: Nǐde Yīngwén shuō de zhēn hǎo, nǐ shì zěnme xué de?

李：其实学英文并不难，多听、多说、多读<u>就</u>可以学得很好。

Lǐ: Qíshí xué Yīngwén bìng bù nán, duō tīng, duō shuō, duō dú jiù kěyǐ xué de hěn hǎo.

Zhang: You speak English so well. How did you learn it?

Li: Actually English is not hard to learn. As long as you listen more, speak more and read more, you can learn it well.

4 我儿子聪明<u>却</u>不肯努力学习，所以考试总是考得很差。

Wǒ érzi cōngmíng què bù kěn nǔlì xuéxí, suǒyǐ kǎoshì zǒngshì kǎo de hěn chà.

My son is smart yet he is unwilling to study hard; so he always does poorly in tests.

5 安娜：你想，这件衣服，我穿了，会好看吗?

Ānnà: Nǐ xiǎng, zhè jiàn yīfú, wǒ chuān le, huì hǎokàn ma?

小兰：很难说。你去试试看吧！试了<u>就</u>知道。

Xiǎolán: Hěn nán shuō. Nǐ qù shì shì kàn ba! Shì le jiù zhīdào.

Anna: Do you think I would look good if I wear this dress?

Xiaolan: It's hard to say. Why don't you go try it on? Once you try it on, we will know.

6 李：那本书早就卖完了，你去哪里都买不到了。

Lǐ: Nà běn shū zǎo jiù mài wán le, nǐ qù nǎlǐ dōu mǎi bú dào le.

王：我不相信。

Wáng: Wǒ bù xiāngxìn.

李：不相信你<u>就</u>去买买看吧！

Lǐ: Bù xiāngxìn nǐ jiù qù mǎi mǎi kàn ba!

Li: All copies of that book have long been sold out. Wherever you go, you will not be able to get it now.

Wang: I don't believe it.

Li: If you don't believe it, you go try and buy it (and see what happens).

7 王先生：请你嫁给我吧！

Wáng xiānsheng: Qǐng nǐ jià gěi wǒ ba!

李小姐：对不起，我还不想结婚呢！

Lǐ xiǎojiě: Duìbùqǐ, wǒ hái bù xiǎng jiéhūn ne!

王先生：你不想嫁给我，我们<u>就</u>别再交往了吧！

Wáng xiānsheng: Nǐ bù xiǎng jià gěi wǒ, wǒmen jiù bié zài jiāowǎng le ba!

李小姐：你的意思是，咱们朋友<u>也</u>不能做了吗?

Lǐ xiǎojiě: Nǐde yìsi shì, zánmen péngyǒu yě bù néng zuò le ma?

王先生：对，我<u>就</u>是这个意思。

Wáng xiānsheng: Duì, wǒ jiù shì zhè ge yìsi.

Mr Wang: Will you marry me?

Miss Li: Sorry, but I don't want to get married yet.

Mr Wang: Since you don't want to marry me, let's not date any more.

Miss Li: Do you mean that we cannot even be friends?

Mr Wang: That's right. That is exactly what I mean.

8 王：那份工作，薪水不错，你为什么不做？
Wáng: Nà fèn gōngzuò, xīnshuǐ bú cuò, nǐ wèishénme bú zuò?
丁：那种工作太无聊，薪水多高我都不愿意做。
Dīng: Nà zhǒng gōngzuò tài wúliáo, xīnshuǐ duō gāo wǒ dōu bú yuànyì zuò.
李：是啊，你这么有钱，当然不愿意做这种工作。
Lǐ: Shì a, nǐ zhème yǒuqián, dāngrán bú yuànyì zuò zhè zhǒng gōngzuò.
王：有钱也不能光待在家里不工作啊！
Wáng: Yǒuqián yě bù néng guāng dāi zài jiā lǐ bù gōngzuò a!
Wang: The salary for that job is not bad. Why wouldn't you take the job?
Ding: That type of work is too boring. No matter how high the salary is, I am not willing to do it.
Li: Yeah! You are so wealthy; of course, you are not willing to do this type of work.
Wang: Even if you are wealthy, you can't just stay home and not go out to work.

9 李：明天安娜家开派对，你去不去？
Lǐ: Míngtiān Ānnà jiā kāi pàiduì, nǐ qù bú qù?
丁：不去。
Dīng: Bú qù.
李：是吗？你最好的朋友小兰说她要去呢！
Lǐ: Shì ma? Nǐ zuì hǎo de péngyǒu Xiǎolán shuō tā yào qù ne!
丁：我最讨厌安娜。小兰去我也不去。
Dīng: Wǒ zuì tǎoyàn Ānnà. Xiǎolán qù wǒ yě bú qù.
Li: There will be a party at Anna's house tomorrow. Are you going?
Ding: I am not going.
Li: Is that so? Your best friend Xiaolan said that she would go.
Ding: I hate Anna. Even if Xiaolan goes, I won't go.

10 王中真聪明，老师问的那个问题这么难，可是他想都不用想就会回答。
Wáng Zhōng zhēn cōngmíng, lǎoshī wèn de nà ge wèntí zhènme nán, kěshì tā xiǎng dōu bú yòng xiǎng jiù huì huídá.
Wang Zhong is really smart. The question our teacher asked was so difficult, but he didn't even have to think and he knew how to answer it.

33 The use of interrogative pronouns

1 男：天气这么好，去公园走走，怎么样？
Nán: Tiānqì zhème hǎo, qù gōngyuán zǒu zǒu, zěnmeyàng?
女：好啊！怎么去？坐公共汽车还是开车？
Nǚ: Hǎo a! Zěnme qù? Zuò gōnggòng qìchē háishì kāi chē?

2 王太太：你知道这辆车有多贵吗？我们怎么买得起？
Wáng tàitai: Nǐ zhīdào zhè liàng chē yǒu duō guì ma? Wǒmen zěnme mǎi de qǐ?
王先生：我实在太喜欢这辆车了，多贵我都要买。
Wáng xiānsheng: Wǒ shízài tài xǐhuān zhè liàng chē le, duō guì wǒ dōu yào mǎi.

3 太太：刚洗好的碗怎么还是脏的？这是怎么回事？
Tàitai: Gāng xǐ hǎo de wǎn zěnme háishì zāng de? Zhè shì zěnme huí shì?
先生：怎么？洗碗机又坏了吗？
Xiānsheng: Zěnme? Xǐwǎn jī yòu huài le ma?

4 安娜： 小王! 你怎么来了？ 雨下得这么大，你是怎么来的?
Ānnà: Xiǎo Wáng? Nǐ zěnme lái le? Yǔ xià de zhème dà, nǐ shì zěnme lái de?
王： 我来找你是因为有一件很重要的事我要告诉你。所以雨多大我也要来。
Wáng: Wǒ lái zhǎo nǐ shì yīnwèi yǒu yí jiàn hěn zhòngyào de shì wǒ yào gàosù nǐ. Suǒyǐ yǔ duō dà wǒ yě yào lái.

5 我想喝杯咖啡，你知不知道哪里有咖啡馆?
Wǒ xiǎng hē bēi kāfēi, nǐ zhī bù zhīdào nǎlǐ yǒu kāfēiguǎn?

6 李： 我们应该请谁当代表来回答老师的问题?
Lǐ: Wǒmen yīnggāi qǐng shéi dāng dàibiǎo lái huídá lǎoshī de wèntí?
丁： 什么代表？ 谁被老师叫到谁就回答。
Dīng: Shénme dàibiǎo? Shéi bèi lǎoshī jiào dào shéi jiù huídá.

7 女： 现在几点？ 你为什么不在教室里上课？ 你来做什么？ (or 你来干嘛?)
Nǚ: Xiànzài jǐ diǎn? Nǐ wèishénme bú zài jiàoshì lǐ shàng kè? Nǐ lái zuò shénme? (or Nǐ lái gànmá?)
男： 今天老师两点就让我们下课了，下午我没有什么事，所以我想请你去看电影。电影院有四个电影，你想看哪个?
Nán: Jīntiān lǎoshī liǎng diǎn jiù ràng wǒmen xià kè le. Xiàwǔ wǒ méiyǒu shénme shì, suǒyǐ wǒ xiǎng qǐng nǐ qù kàn diànyǐng. Diànyǐngyuàn yǒu sì ge diànyǐng, nǐ xiǎng kàn nǎ ge?
女： 太好了! 你想看哪个我们就看哪个。
Nǚ: Tài hǎo le! Nǐ xiǎng kàn nǎ ge wǒmen jiù kàn nǎ ge.

8 李： 你平常什么时候运动?
Lǐ: Nǐ píngcháng shénme shíhòu yùndòng?
丁： 星期天早上健身房没有什么人(or 没有多少人)，所以我总是星期天早上运动。
Dīng: Xīngqī tiān zǎoshàng jiànshēnfáng méiyǒu shénme rén (or méiyǒu duōshǎo rén), suǒyǐ wǒ zǒngshì xīngqī tiān zǎoshàng yùndòng.
李： 你的健身房有什么(or 有哪些)好的运动设备?
Lǐ: Nǐde jiànshēnfáng yǒu shénme (or yǒu nǎ xiē) hǎo de yùndòng shèbèi?
丁： 这个健身房很便宜，所以没有什么好的设备。
Dīng: Zhè ge jiànshēnfáng hěn piányí, suǒyǐ méiyǒu shénme hǎo de shèbèi.

34 Rhetorical questions

1 张： 小兰跟小英不都是王太太的女儿吗？ 为什么王太太好像比较喜欢小兰呢?
Zhāng: Xiǎolán gēn Xiǎoyīng bù dōu shì Wáng tàitai de nǚ'ér ma? Wèishénme Wáng tàitai hǎoxiàng bǐjiào xǐhuān Xiǎolán ne?
李： 难道小英不是王太太亲生的女儿吗?
Lǐ: Nándào Xiǎoyīng bú shì Wáng tàitai qīnshēng de nǚ'ér ma?
陈： 我不相信王太太会偏心，她是一个这么好的妈妈，怎么会偏心?
Chén: Wǒ bù xiāngxìn Wáng tàitai huì piānxīn, tā shì yí ge zhème hǎo de māma, zěnme huì piānxīn?
丁： 可不是吗!
Dīng: Kě bú shì ma!

2 丁：安娜要跟谁结婚，关你什么事？
Dīng: Ānnà yào gēn shéi jiéhūn, guān nǐ shénme shì?
陈：王先生这么爱安娜，他穷一点又有什么关系呢？
Chén: Wáng xiānsheng zhème ài Ānnà, tā qióng yìdiǎn yòu yǒu shénme guānxi ne?
李：安娜不是小孩子了，何必为她担心？
Lǐ: Ānnà bú shì xiǎo háizi le, hébì wèi tā dānxīn?
文：安娜又不是你妹妹，你担什么心？
Wén: Ānnà yòu bú shì nǐ mèimei, nǐ dān shénme xīn?

3 邻居：难道你儿子不打算结婚吗？
Línjū: Nándào nǐ érzi bù dǎsuàn jiéhūn ma?
李太太：我儿子工作忙得要命，他哪里有时间交女朋友？
Lǐ tàitai: Wǒ érzi gōngzuò máng de yàomìng, tā nǎlǐ yǒu shíjiān jiāo nǚ péngyǒu?
李先生：我儿子结婚不结婚，关你什么事？
Lǐ xiānsheng: Wǒ érzi jiéhūn bù jiéhūn, guān nǐ shénme shì?
邻居：我没有恶意，你何必发脾气？
Línjū: Wǒ méiyǒu èyì, nǐ hébì fā píqì?
李太太：你何苦为这种小事发脾气？
Lǐ tàitai: Nǐ hékǔ wèi zhè zhǒng xiǎo shì fā píqì?
李先生：这怎么是小事？
Lǐ xiānsheng: Zhè zěnme shì xiǎo shì?

4 王：安娜不是也很用功吗？为什么考得这么差呢？
Wáng: Ānnà bú shì yě hěn yònggōng ma? Wèishénme kǎo de zhème chà ne?
李：安娜哪里用功？她懒得要命。
Lǐ: Ānnà nǎlǐ yònggōng? Tā lǎn de yàomìng.
王：她不是每天晚上都在图书馆待到半夜吗？怎么会懒呢？
Wáng: Tā bú shì měi tiān wǎnshàng dōu zài túshūguǎn dāi dào bànyè ma? Zěnme huì lǎn ne?

Index